THE HISTORY OF MANAGEMENT THOUGHT

Fifth Edition

DANIEL A. WREN

The University of Oklahoma

JOHN WILEY & SONS, INC.

Publisher   *Susan Elbe*
Associate Publisher   *Judith Joseph*
Production Manager   *Pam Kennedy*
Senior Acquisitions Editor   *Jayme Heffler*
Marketing Manager   *Heather King*
Production Editors   *Kelly Tavares, Sarah Wolfman-Robichaud*
Managing Editor   *Kevin Dodds*
Illustration Editor   *Wendy Stokes Hodge*
Cover Design   *Benjamin Reece*
Cover Images   *© Art Wolfe/Getty Images*

This book was set in Minion by Leyh Publishing, LLC and printed and bound by Courier Westford. The cover was printed by Phoenix Color Corp.

This book is printed on acid free paper. ∞

ISBN 0-471-66922-9

Printed in the United States of America

Dedication

To Leon, Maude, and Karen

my links with the past;

To Jonathan, Laura, and Lynda;

and to another generation,

Karen Nicole, Tanner Ray, and Ethan Daniel

my links with the future.

Brief Contents

Contents

About the Author

Daniel A. Wren, Ph.D., University of Illinois, is the David Ross Boyd Professor of Management Emeritus and Curator of the Harry W. Bass Business History Collection at the University of Oklahoma. He has served as President of the Southern Management Association, as Chairman of the Management History Division of the Academy of Management, is a Fellow of the Southern Management Association, and a Fellow of the Academy of Management. He has been honored with the Merrick Foundation Award for teaching excellence and received the Distinguished Educator Award from the national Academy of Management for his contributions "as the foremost management historian of his generation." His research has appeared in numerous scholarly journals and he is the author of *White Collar Hobo: The Travels of Whiting Williams* (Iowa State University Press) and, with Ronald Greenwood, coauthor of *Management Innovators: The People and Ideas that have Shaped Modern Business* (Oxford University Press).

Preface

Our knowledge about the history of management thought increases constantly and developments in the past ten years beg for a historical perspective. The purpose of this fifth edition is to update the material as we have learned more about the history of our discipline and to extend our knowledge in light of more recent events to bring our understanding closer to the present. Readers of previous editions will find the same basic chronological framework in the present one. The most noticeable change will be the sections adding technological parallels in each part to accompany the economic, social, and political framework. Readers will also find more archival data and previously unpublished materials that further illuminate our understanding. New sections on industrial relations and corporate governance have been placed in the historical framework and developments in organization theory, business policy/strategic management, international business, and other historically evergreen topics such as leadership and motivation have been revised to provide currency and yield a more substantial theoretical foundation for today's students and scholars. My continuing hope is that readers will find in these pages the reward of knowing the past as a foundation for understanding the present and preparing for the future.

I have tried to make the book an unfolding story about the lives and the times of those who are our intellectual predecessors. These individuals have left us a heritage that we often take for granted, frequently do not acknowledge, and sometimes reject because we do not think yesterday's solutions have any practical value for today's problems. But these men and women were very much as we are: they were attempting to cope with the manifold problems of managing mass assemblages of human and physical resources; they were trying to develop philosophies and theories about human behavior; they were agents for change; and they were struggling with the age-old problems of allocating scarce resources to meet the goals and desires of organizations and people. Our problems today are basically the same, only the proposed solutions have changed as we have learned more, as we have sharpened our diagnostic tools, and as cultural values have changed.

This book did not reach a fifth edition without the continuing interest of scholars who care about the history of management thought and the students who find value in these pages. My colleagues in the Management History Division of the Academy of Management contributed in many ways and this group provides a forum for exchanging ideas and improving our understanding of management history. More specifically, let me thank Art Bedeian and Pete Petersen for vetting this manuscript and my appreciation also to Al Bolton, Jack Duncan, David Van Fleet, and Bill Wolf for their continuing interest and encouragement. Thanks also to Ron Greenwood and Dick Hodgetts, both now deceased, whose enthusiasm for management history will never be forgotten. Credit for photographs appear in the text but special thanks goes to Kerry Magruder for the electronic magic that brought these images to print. For supplementary materials to bring the electronic age to the classroom, I express my appreciation to Regina Greenwood and Julia Teahen. If I have neglected to mention someone who deserves credit, let us attribute that to a 'senior moment.' Now, onward to the task of exploring the history of management thought.

Daniel A. Wren
Norman, Oklahoma
September, 2004

Early Management Thought

Part I covers a wide span of time and traces developments in management thought up to the scientific management era in the United States. After a brief introduction to the role of management in organizations, this part examines examples of very early management thought and then demonstrates how changes in the economic, social, and political environments set the stage for the Industrial Revolution. This revolution created certain management problems in the embryonic factory system and led to the need for a formal study of management. The genesis of modern management thought is found in the work of early pioneers who sought to solve the problems created by the factory system. Part I concludes by tracing this genesis of management thought to the United States and examining early experiences with the factory, some early management writers, and the cultural environment of the United States before the scientific management era.

CHAPTER 1

A Prologue to the Past

The practice of management is ancient, but formal study of the body of management knowledge is relatively new. Management is essential to organized endeavors. For a broad working definition let us view management as an activity that performs certain functions to obtain the effective acquisition, allocation, and utilization of human efforts and physical resources to accomplish some goal. Management thought, then, is the existing body of knowledge about the activity of management, its functions, purpose, and scope.

The purpose of this study is to trace the significant periods in the evolution of management thought from its earliest informal days to the present. The study of management, like the study of people and their cultures, is an unfolding story of changing ideas about the nature of work, the nature of human beings, and the functioning of organizations. The methodology of this study of management will be analytic, synthetic, and interdisciplinary. It will be analytic in examining people who made significant contributions, their backgrounds, their ideas, and their influence. It will be synthetic in examining trends, movements, and environmental forces that furnish a conceptual framework for understanding individuals and their approaches to the solution of management problems. It will be interdisciplinary in the sense that it includes—but moves beyond—traditional management writings to draw upon economic history, sociology, psychology, social history, political science, and cultural anthropology in order to place management thought in a cultural and historical perspective. The objective is to place management thought in the context of its cultural environment and thereby to understand not only what management thought was and is, but also to explain why it developed as it did.

We should study the past to illuminate the present, but management history as a separate area of study is generally neglected in most schools of business administration. A smattering of history is taught at various levels, but the area generally lacks depth, direction, and unity. Henry Wadsworth Longfellow said, "Let the dead past bury its dead," but there is much to be said for resurrection. We live and study in an age represented by a diversity of approaches to management. Students are presented with quantitative, behavioral, functional, and other approaches in their various courses. Although such a variety of intellectual inputs may be stimulating, it typically leaves students with a fragmented picture of management and assumes that they have the ability to integrate these various ideas for themselves.

In many cases, this burden is far too great. A study of evolving management thought can present the origins of ideas and approaches, trace their development, grant some perspective in terms of the cultural environment, and thus provide a conceptual framework that will enhance the process of integration. A study of the past contributes to a more logical, coherent picture of the present. Without a knowledge of history, individuals have only their own limited experiences as a basis for thought and action. As one scholar commented, "[History] is the universal experience—definitely longer, wider, and more varied than any individual's experience."[1] History should therefore equip perceptive people with additional alternatives and answers to build into their decision-making models. Lawrence distinguishes between historical research (inquiry into past persons and events) and historical perspective (using history as raw material for understanding the present). The object of historical perspective is to "sharpen one's vision of the present, not the past.... It pushes thinking about alternative explanations for phenomena, helps identify more or less stable concepts, and expands research horizons by suggesting new ways of studying old questions."[2] Carson and Carson noted that "management history [is] a unique and valuable form of knowledge."[3] Present pedagogy can be improved, knowledge expanded, and insights gained by examining the lives and labors of management's intellectual progenitors. Theory, a legitimate goal in any discipline, is based on the warp and woof of individuals' ideas in the fabric of management. By tracing the origin and development of modern management concepts, we can better understand the analytical and conceptual tools of our trade. In understanding the growth and development of large-scale enterprise, the dynamics of technology, the ebb and flow of cultural values, and the changing assumptions about the nature and nurture of people, we can better equip young men and women with the skills and attitudes they need to prepare themselves for future positions of responsibility.

Today is not like yesterday, nor will tomorrow be like today; yet today is a synergism of all our yesterdays, and tomorrow will be the same. Mark Twain said that history may not repeat itself "but sometimes it rhymes."[4] There are many

---

1. B. H. Liddell Hart, Why Don't We Learn From History? (London: George Allen and Unwin, 1972), p. 15.

2. Barbara S. Lawrence, "Historical Perspective: Using the Past to Study the Present," Academy of Management Review 9 (April 1984), pp. 307, 311.

3. Paula Phillips Carson and Kerry D. Carson, "Theoretically Grounding Management History as a Form of Knowledge," Journal of Management History 4 (1998), p. 29.

4. Mark Twain, quoted by Thomas K. McGraw, "Why History Matters to Managers," Harvard Business Review 64 (January–February 1986), p. 83.

lessons in history for management scholars; the important one is the study of the past as prologue.

A CULTURAL FRAMEWORK

How have our concepts of managing organizations evolved throughout history? To understand this evolution, this dynamic process of change and growth, we need to establish a cultural framework of analysis for the evolution of management thought. Management is not a closed-end activity, since managers operate organizations and make decisions within a given set of cultural values and institutions. Thus management has open-system characteristics in that managers affect their environment and in turn are affected by it.

Culture is our total community heritage of nonbiological, humanly transmitted traits and includes the economic, social, and political forms of behavior associated with the human race. Culture is a very broad subject, so this study is limited to those specific economic, social, political, and technological ideas that influence the job of managing an organization. Human behavior is a product of past and present cultural forces, and the discipline of management is also a product of the economic, social, political, and technological forces of the past and present. As Bedeian has observed "past arrangements—institutions, roles, cultural forms—are not simply superseded, but transformed and recombined to produce the present. In this sense, the past repeatedly informs and reinforms the present such that the search for understanding is never finished."[5] Modern individuals examine present organizations and read contemporary authors, yet they have little appreciation of the background of our technology, political bodies, or arrangements for the allocation of resources. Management thought did not develop in a cultural vacuum; managers have always found their jobs affected by the existing culture.

In the study of modern management, the past must be examined to see how our communal heritage was established. The elements of our culture were previously described as economic, social, political and technological. In practice, these elements are closely interrelated and interact to form the total culture; they are separated here and throughout the following pages only for ease of presentation. Here our attention shall be confined to the portions of our culture that apply most directly to management, omitting other cultural phenomena, such as art, music, and so on.

THE ECONOMIC FACET

The economic facet of culture is the relationship of people to resources. Resources may be created by humans or nature; the term denotes as well both tangible objects

---

5. Arthur G. Bedeian, "Exploring the Past," *Journal of Management History* 4 (1998), p. 4. See also Arthur G. Bedeian, "The Gift of Professional Maturity," *Academy of Management Learning and Education* 3 (2004), pp. 92–98.

and intangible efforts that can be utilized to achieve some stated end. Physical resources include land, buildings, raw materials, semifinished products, tools, and equipment or other tangible objects used by people and organizations. Technology, our understanding of the art and applied science of making and using tools and equipment, advances at different rates and influences how resources are used at any given time in history.

Human thought and effort are also resources because they design, assemble, shape, and perform other activities that result in the production of some product or service. Every society has the economic problem of a scarcity of resources and a multiplicity of economic ends. The mobilization of these scarce resources to produce and distribute products, services, and satisfaction has taken a variety of forms throughout history. Heilbroner characterized these methods of allocating resources as by tradition, by command, and by the market.[6] The traditional method operates on past societal precepts; technology is essentially static, occupations are passed down from one generation to the next, agriculture predominates over industry, and the social and economic systems remain essentially closed to change. The command method is the imposition of the will of some central person or agency on the rest of the economy to determine how resources are allocated and utilized. The economic commander-in-chief may be the monarch, the fascist dictator, or the collectivist central planning agency. What is to be produced, what prices and wages will be, and how economic goods and services are to be distributed are decisions made by some central source. The market method, which Heilbroner noted as a relatively recent phenomenon, relies on an impersonal network of forces and decisions to allocate resources. Prices, wages, and interest rates are set by a bargaining process between those who have the product or service and those who want it; all resources flow to their best reward and no central agency nor prior precepts need to intervene. In actual practice, modern societies display a mixture of the elements of tradition, command, and the market. Much of our total cultural heritage has been influenced by tradition and command as the predominant economic philosophies. However, we will see later that the market philosophy created the need for the formal, systematic development of a body of management thought. In brief, the state of technology and the source of decisions about the societal allocation of resources have a large bearing on how managers go about their jobs. A tradition-directed economy circumscribes the role of the manager with prior precepts; the command orientation makes the manager an executor of central decisions; but the market system opens the way to the innovative utilization of resources to meet a multiplicity of ends.

THE SOCIAL FACET

The social facet refers to the relationship of people to other people in a given culture. Humans do not live alone but find advantages in forming groups for mutual

---

6. Robert L. Heilbroner, *The Making of Economic Society* (Englewood Cliffs, N.J.: Prentice-Hall, 1962), pp. 10–16.

survival or for furthering personal goals. In forming groups, the initial input is a variety of people of differing needs, abilities, and values. Out of this heterogeneity, some homogeneity must evolve or the group will not survive. Thus all participants form a "contract," which encompasses some common rules and agreements about how to behave to preserve the group. The unwritten but nevertheless binding contract defines assumptions about the behavior of others and expectations about the reciprocal treatment of the individual. It includes some agreement about how best to combine and coordinate efforts to accomplish a given task, be it the making of an economic product or achieving the satisfaction of social fellowship.

Values, or cultural standards of conduct defining the propriety of a given type of behavior, are another part of social interactions. Thus ethics in interpersonal relations is an age-old problem. Economic transactions, deeply imbedded in social trust, are an integral part of a societal contract. Values shift from one time period to another and from one culture to another. Managerial efforts are affected by the relationships between individuals and the group and by the social values prevailing in the culture.

THE POLITICAL FACET

The political part of culture is the relation of the individual to the state and includes the legal and political arrangements for the establishment of social order and for the protection of life and property. The absence of state and order is anarchy; unless there is some provision for protection of rational beings from irrational ones, the result is total economic, social, and political chaos. Where order begins, anarchy ends. Political institutions that bring order and stability take a variety of forms, ranging from representative government to a monarchy or dictatorship. Political assumptions about the nature of humankind range from one end of the continuum, self-governing people, to the other extreme position, direction from one person or a ruling body at the top, which imposes its will on others based on the assumption that people cannot, or will not, govern themselves. Provisions for property, contracts, and justice are also key concepts in the political aspect of cultures. In a democracy, people typically have the right of private property, the freedom to enter or not to enter into contracts, and an appeal system for justice. Under a dictatorship or monarchy, the right to hold and use private property is severely restricted, the right to contract is limited, and the system of justice depends on the whims of those in power. The cultural role of management is affected by the form of government, by the power to hold or not hold property, by the ability to engage in contracts for the production and distribution of goods, and by the appeal mechanism available to redress grievances.

THE TECHNOLOGICAL FACET

Technology is the art and applied science of making tools and equipment. Historians refer to past eons such as the Stone Age, the Iron Age, and the Bronze Age when humans made tools of these materials to use for various purposes. Since this primitive past, technology has been advancing for thousands of years, sometimes rapidly, sometimes more slowly, and proceeding at a different pace in various cultures.

Technology is a means to an end, which can produce beneficial as well as detrimental results. Landes has warned

> That the wrestling and exploitation of knowledge are perilous acts, but man must and will know, and once knowing, will not forget ... the marriage of science and technology are the climax of millennia of intellectual advance. They have also been an enormous force of good and evil, and there have been moments when the evil has far outweighed the good. Still, the march of knowledge and technique continues....[7]

It is this progress that has moved us from labor intensive to capital intensive to knowledge intensive possibilities for industry and trade.

Technology often does not advance in tradition-bound or closed societies because it threatens status quo. Kieser has written of medieval guilds, which kept

> Production and selling conditions for all members to be as equal as possible. No [guild] master should be able to gain and advantage at the expense of his co-masters...the master was only allowed to employ a restricted number of journeymen...and he was not allowed to choose these men himself....Wages and working hours were uniformly regulated. The pursuit of customers was strictly forbidden.... Innovations were suppressed.[8]

Clinging to past precepts provides no incentive to seek new knowledge, to explore, nor to experiment. Science and technology cannot advance without education, the freedom of inquiry, and the encouragement of risk taking.

Culture makes a difference, and we will see examples of how technology affects the economic, social, and political facets of human existence. By applying science in an artful manner, we have the potential of influencing all facets of our culture. In his inaugural address in 1790, America's first president, George Washington, said, "Knowledge is in every country the surest basis of public happiness." This quest for knowledge is never ending, impelling us to learn, to do better, to live better.

Interacting to form any culture, the economic, social, political, and technological facets are useful tools of analysis for examining the evolution of management thought. Managers are affected by their cultural environment, and the ways in which

---

7. David S. Landes, *The Unbound Prometheus* (Cambridge: The University Press, 1969), p. 555. For a global perspective, see David S. Landes, *The Wealth and Poverty of Nations: Why Some Are So Rich and Some So Poor* (New York: W.W. Norton), 1998.

8. Alfred Kieser, "Organizational, Institutional, and Societal Evolution: Medieval Craft Guilds and the Genesis of Formal Organizations," *Administrative Science Quarterly* 34 (1989), p. 553.

they allocate and utilize resources have evolved within the changing views about economic, social, and political institutions and values and technological know-how.

PEOPLE, MANAGEMENT, AND ORGANIZATIONS

From this introduction to the cultural environment of management, let us turn more specifically to the basic elements of our study. Even before people began to record their activities, they encountered the necessity of managing their efforts in cooperative endeavors. As an overview, Figure 1-1 begins with the state of nature and traces the quest for needs satisfaction through organizations. Management, an activity essential to organized endeavors, facilitates the operation of organizations in order to satisfy the needs of people.

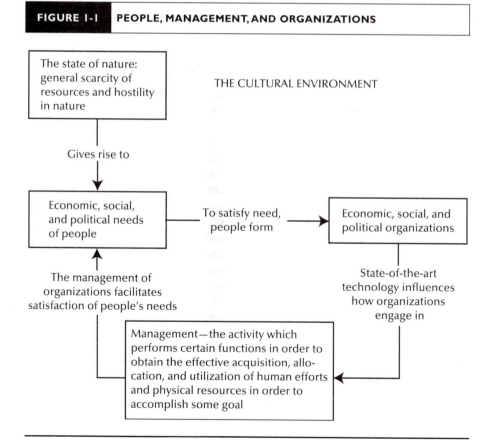

FIGURE 1-1   PEOPLE, MANAGEMENT, AND ORGANIZATIONS

The state of nature: general scarcity of resources and hostility in nature

THE CULTURAL ENVIRONMENT

Gives rise to

Economic, social, and political needs of people

To satisfy need, people form

Economic, social, and political organizations

The management of organizations facilitates satisfaction of people's needs

State-of-the-art technology influences how organizations engage in

Management—the activity which performs certain functions in order to obtain the effective acquisition, allocation, and utilization of human efforts and physical resources in order to accomplish some goal

THE HUMAN BEING

The human being is the fundamental unit of analysis in the study of humankind, the study of organizations, and the study of management. Humans have always faced a relatively hostile environment characterized by scarce food supplies, inadequate shelter, and, in general, a paucity of other resources with which to satisfy their manifold needs. Humans are not biologically stronger than many other species that exist or have existed on earth. To explain their survival we must look beyond the physical powers of human beings for other characteristics that have enabled humans to progress to the point of controlling and manipulating their environment within certain natural physical boundaries. Even these boundaries are constantly challenged as we explore outer space and expand our technology.

The solution to the question of why humans have survived is found in their ability to reason. In the long evolutionary process, it was not always the most physically fit who survived, for humans were still physically inferior to many other predators, but it was the most cognitively capable who fashioned tools and weapons, mastered the use of fire, developed the ability to think conceptually, advanced their powers of communication, and engaged in group activities that required a marked degree of planning, cooperation, and coordination. These were the people who fashioned equalizing clubs and spears for defense, who formed implements for tilling the soil, and who developed organizational means that gave humans a differential advantage over their natural enemies.

Paleoanthropologists have constantly pushed our knowledge of humankind further and further into the past.[9] They found *Homo habilis,* "handy man," who fashioned tools; *Homo erectus,* who characterized bipedalism; and *Homo sapiens,* the thinker. Humans are thinkers, doers, and makers; they are active, creative, and ever changing in their quest to better themselves and their species. Their most basic needs are economic ones, those necessary to physical survival in a harsh world in which food, drink, shelter, and other fundamental needs of life must be obtained. With cultural advancement, these economic needs become more complex, but they still form a base of human existence. Beyond these basic needs, which are essential to existence itself, are social needs. These needs for affiliation most probably arose out of physiological drives in the sex act and the selection of a mate. The family became the most elementary unit of human group relationships, an organization that provided both satisfaction as well as duties. Survival of the family became a goal, and humans found that they could better protect and enhance their welfare by forming groups or tribes for mutual advantage in food gathering, defense, and family care activities. As Bronowski concluded: "We are joined in families, the families are joined in kinship groups, the kinship groups in clans, the clans in tribes, and the tribes in nations. This is the most primitive revelation of a hierarchy of organization, layer upon layer, that links the present to the past of man's existence."[10]

---

9. For example, see Donald Johanson and Maitland A. Edey, *Lucy: The Beginnings of Humankind* (New York: Simon and Schuster, 1981).

10. Jacob Bronowski, *The Ascent of Man* (Boston: Little, Brown, and Company, 1973), pp. 95–96.

Early humans found that the knowledge and skills of one generation must be transmitted to the next if the species were to survive. Such were the elementary beginnings of education and the transmission of knowledge. In forming groups and living with their fellow humans to minister to both economic and social needs, they required rules and a means to ensure the viability of the organization. They formed elementary political units with agreed-upon codes governing economic, social, political, and often religious behavior. Out of these common economic, social, and political needs, organized human activity began. People found advantages in participating and cooperating with others to achieve their own goals.

ORGANIZATIONS AND MANAGEMENT

As humans have evolved, so have organizations. People found that they could magnify their own abilities by working with others and could thereby better satisfy their own needs. The inputs of various skills and abilities into the group led to the recognition that some were better at some tasks than others. Group tasks were differentiated, that is, there was a division of labor to take advantage of these varying skills. Once labor was divided, some agreement had to be reached about how to structure and interrelate these various work assignments in order to accomplish group objectives. Quite logically, the group also stratified tasks and developed a hierarchy of authority or power. Perhaps the assignment of work to others was made by the strongest, the eldest, or the most articulate of the group, who became the earliest leader. In any case, the group had to achieve some unity of agreement about what was to be done, how, and who would be responsible for accomplishment.

This most elementary appearance of the first organization is reflected in essentially the same common elements of organizations throughout history. First, there had to be a goal, a purpose, an objective, or something to be accomplished. Perhaps it was the annual berry picking, the hunt, the sowing of a crop, or the defense of the group from marauding nomads. Second, people had to be attracted to the purpose or the common will in order to participate. They had to perceive that it was in their best interest to work toward the group goal. The first bonds of organization were in people's attraction to the group as a means of satisfying their own needs. Third, the organizational members needed something with which to work or fight. These were the resources or means to the end and comprised the people themselves, the weapons, the tilling implements, or whatever. Fourth, various activities of the participants had to be structured so that their actions would interact and be interrelated in achieving the common goal. If each proceeded without timing and coordination of effort, the result would be chaos. Finally, the group discovered that results could be better achieved if someone had the assigned task of keeping the whole group on its course toward the goal. Someone had to resolve differences of opinion, decide on strategy and timing, and maintain the structure of activities and relationships toward the objective. This emergence of an activity of managing apart from the activities of doing was to become an essential aspect of all types of cooperative endeavors. Management as an activity has always existed to make people's desires manifest through organized effort. Management facilitates the efforts of people in organized groups and arises when people seek to cooperate to achieve goals.

People have always participated in organizations, and organizations have always existed to serve the ends of people. These ends are manifold and are reflected in organizational arrangements for the satisfaction of economic needs and wants, for the provision for individual and social desires, for the transmission of knowledge from one generation to the next, and for the protection of life and property from internal and external threats. As their conceptual ability has been refined through evolution, people have refined their understanding of the art of arranging physical and human resources toward purposeful ends. We call this art "management," and its evolution is the focal point of our study.

Summary

Our ideas about people, management, and organizations have evolved within the context of various cultural values and institutions throughout history. The development of a body of knowledge about how to manage has also evolved within a framework of the economic, social, political, and technological facets of various cultures. Management thought is both a process in and a product of its cultural environment and must be examined within this cultural framework. People have natural economic, social, and political needs that they seek to satisfy through organized efforts. Management arises as individuals seek to satisfy these needs through group action, and it facilitates the accomplishment of goals for the individual and the group. Various organizations, such as the family, the tribe, the state, and the church, have appeared throughout history as means to people's ends. People create organizations to enlarge on their own specialized talents, to protect themselves, to enrich their lives, and to satisfy a variety of other needs. To reach these ends, organizations are formed of people who have a common purpose and who are attracted to the group in order to satisfy their needs. These organizations must be managed, and our study will focus on how our ideas about management have evolved over time.

CHAPTER 2

Management before Industrialization

Historically, industrialization is a relatively recent phenomenon. Humankind existed for eons before the great advances in power, transportation, communications, and technology that came to be known as the Industrial Revolution. Before industrialization, organizations were primarily the household, tribe, church, military, and government. Some people engaged in economic undertakings, but not on a scale to compare with what would emerge as a result of the Industrial Revolution. Nevertheless, there was still a need for management in the conduct of military campaigns, in household affairs, in the administration of government, and in the operation of the church. This chapter examines these first attempts at management in early civilizations and discusses the changing cultural values that would lead to the Industrial Revolution.

MANAGEMENT IN EARLY CIVILIZATIONS

THE NEAR EAST

As group affiliations evolved from the family to the nation, the question of organizational authority became a problem. In the family, authority rested in the patriarch or the matriarch, but in the nation, there was often a conflict between chiefs and priests, the former claiming secular power, the latter, heavenly dominion. From this struggle, this division of authority, came the idea of the priest-ruler or divine king. A king was not a King until ordained by priests, a tradition that long endured.

One such divine king was the Babylonian Hammurabi (ca. 2123–2071 B.C.E.), who received his right to rule and his code of laws from the sun god. Babylon, near modern Baghdad, rested between the Tigris and the Euphrates rivers in what was once called the cradle of civilization. Hammurabi issued a code of 282 laws, which governed business dealings, personal behavior, interpersonal relations, punishments, and a host of other societal matters. Law 104, for example, was the first historical mention of accounting. It dealt with the handling of receipts and established an agency relationship and accountability between the merchant and the agent. His Code also regulated wages and fees, such as fixing surgeon's fees and wages for "builders, brickmakers, tailors, stonemasons, boatmen, herdsmen, and laborers."[1] In 604 B.C., when Nebuchadnezzar was King of Babylonia, weavers of cloth were paid in food, the quantity granted depending upon the spinner or weaver's output. This was before, and possibly influenced, the later biblical notion "If anyone will not work, let him not eat" (2 Thess. 3:10), or, in the words of the prophet Mohammed, "He who neither worketh for himself, nor for others, will not receive the reward of God."[2] In the case of the weavers the motive was clear; in Hammurabi's Code, however, there was no incentive to do more than required since wages were regulated. Here were early examples of authority, and differing ideas about wage payments.

THE FAR EAST

The ancient Chinese civilization has opened its doors occasionally to let westerners peek in. The oldest known military treatise is the product of the Chinese general Sun Tzu (ca. 600 B.C.E.). He wrote of marshaling the army into subdivisions, of establishing gradations of rank among the officers, and of using gongs, flags, and signal fires for communications. He advocated lengthy deliberations and sound plans before going into battle: "Thus do many calculations [plans] lead to victory, and few calculations to defeat." It is possible that General Sun Tzu held a staff officer's position: "The General that hearkens to my counsel and acts upon it, will conquer.... The General that hearkens not to my counsel nor acts upon it, will suffer defeat." It appears that the problems of line and staff relationships are at least 2,500 years old. Sun Tzu also provided strategic decision rules for the leaders:

> This is the art of offensive strategy: when our forces are ten to the enemy's one, to surround him; when five to one, to attack him; if double his strength, to divide him ... if equally matched, you may engage him; if weaker numerically, be capable of withdrawing; if quite unequal in every way, be capable of eluding him.[3]

If the marketplace is a surrogate for war, "competitive strengths" can be compared to "forces," and "competitor" to "enemy," and we can see the historical foundations of modern management strategy.

---

1. Robert F. Harper, ed., *The Code of Hammurabi: King of Babylon* (Chicago: University of Chicago Press, 1904), p. 281.

2. Cited in MOW International Research Team, *The Meaning of Working* (New York: Academic Press, 1987), p. 4.

3. Sun Tzu, *The Art of War,* trans. Samuel B. Griffith (Oxford: Oxford University Press, 1963), pp. 79–80.

Confucius (ca. 552–479 B.C.E.) left his mark on the ages through his moral teachings and only incidentally through his advocacy of a merit system. In his time, the highest respectable goal was service in the government: merchants ranked only slightly above convicts in social esteem. The competition for governmental posts was severe, and Confucius advocated that offices should go to individuals of proven merit and ability. Merit exams, based on Confucian advice, began during the Han dynasty (206 B.C.E.–A.D. 220). Merit as a basis for selection would in time lead to merit rating (performance appraisal) for promotions. Although the record is spotty, the Sung dynasty started a merit rating system around A.D. 962. Research indicates that the Chinese had problems with bureaucracy, much as we do today. Selection of officials on the basis of classical scholarship qualities did not always bring the best administrators to office. Corruption and manipulation by officials and lesser functionaries were common, leading to numerous attempts to reform the system.[4]

The Chinese bureaucracy was fully developed into a hierarchy of officials perhaps as early as 1000 B.C.E., long before Confucius. Indeed, the Confucian philosophy was in contradiction to the legalists of that time. The legalists sought to use rewards and punishments through a system of laws to ensure performance, whereas Confucius advocated cultivating and improving the moral nature of people to secure cooperation. How ancient this struggle between the formalists and the humanists, the system and the individual! There is also evidence that the Chinese were familiar with the division of labor and the departmental form of organization as early as A.D. 1. An inscription on a rice bowl indicates that it was made in a government workshop in which there was a high degree of specialization of labor among the various artisans. The workshop was divided into three departments: accounting, security, and production.[5] Such artifacts enable us to understand the age-old practice of management.

Chanakya Kautilya (ca. 332–298 B.C.E.) was a noted and feared minister to Chandragupta Maurya, the greatest statesman of Hindu India. Kautilya's *Arthasastra* founded Indian public administration and contained advice on how to establish and maintain economic, social, and political order. Kautilya cautioned that it was difficult to find competent officials because humans "are naturally fickle-minded, and like horses at work, exhibit constant change in their temper." Further, "it is impossible for a government servant not to eat up, at least, a bit of the King's revenue." To keep order, he advised close controls, severe punishment, a network of spies within the government to watch other employees, and techniques to tempt employees to test their loyalty. Kautilya's assumptions about human nature are as modern as they are ancient, as are the prescriptions he provided on maintaining order. Although he was largely unknown in the Western world, we find his ideas again in the words of others. Kautilya also wrote on the desired traits in administrators ("of high ancestry ... blessed with wisdom ... eloquent ... intelligent, enthusiastic ... sociable") and how

---

4. Richard L. A. Sterba, "Clandestine Management in the Imperial Chinese Bureaucracy," *Academy of Management Review* 3, no. 1 (January 1978), pp. 69–78.

5. Rodger D. Collons, "Factory Production—1 A.D.," *Academy of Management Journal* 14, no. 2 (June 1971), pp. 270–273.

to select personnel through interviews and checking references. He wrote of the use of staff advisers ("Never listen to just one or two"), established departments with directors, and prepared detailed job descriptions for various offices.[6] Although he worked in public administration, his writings reinforce the idea of how ancient many of our management concepts and assumptions are.

EGYPT

The Egyptians developed extensive irrigation projects as an adjunct to the annual inundation by the Nile, and the engineering feats of the pyramids and canals were marvels superior to anything the Greeks and Romans later developed. Mining and most engineering projects were state monopolies and required the development of an extensive bureaucracy to administer state affairs. The labor supply consisted of both freemen and slaves. Strong cultural traditions bound freemen to occupations, and chains took care of other labor problems.

There is evidence that the Egyptians were aware of limits to the number of people one manager could supervise. In the earliest dynasties, it was the custom to kill and bury workers and servants with the departed pharaoh. With more civilization came the progressive idea of burying carvings or of making engravings to represent or symbolize the presence of servants rather than killing them. Whether this was due to a moral advancement or to a scarcity of labor cannot be determined historically. The interesting thing learned from the excavated engravings of servants (*ushabtis,* or "answerers") was that there was a ratio of about ten servants to each supervisor. Excavations also revealed distinctive dress for managers and workers. The supervisors wore kilts or robes, while the ushabtis were dressed so as to represent their trade or occupation.[7] The "rule of ten" in the span of control was an Egyptian practice that can be found in numerous civilizations, as we shall see shortly.

One of the most ancient terms used to describe a professional managerial role is *vizier;* from this we derive the word "supervisor." The existence of this office was recorded as early as 1750 B.C.E., although it is probably more ancient than that. One of the best known viziers was the Hebrew Joseph, who had been sold into bondage by his brothers. Because of Joseph's ability to forecast, the pharaoh made him vizier. This was delegation, leaving spiritual matters in the hands of the pharaoh and temporal matters in the hands of Joseph. The office of vizier was an ancient office of director, organizer, coordinator, and decision maker. Under the vizier, an elaborate bureaucracy was developed to measure the rise of the Nile River, on which every part of the economy depended, to forecast the grain crop and revenues, to allocate these revenues to the various governmental units, and to supervise all industry and trade. Here were some rather sophisticated (for the times) methods of managing

---

6. T. N. Ramaswamy, ed., *Essentials of Indian Statecraft: Kautilya's Arthasastra* (London: Asia Publishing House, 1962).

7. W. M. Flinders Petrie, *Social Life in Ancient Egypt* (London: Constable & Co. Ltd., 1924), pp. 21–22.

through forecasting, planning work, dividing the work among the various people and departments, and establishing a "professional" full-time administrator to coordinate and control the state enterprise.

THE HEBREWS

The Old Testament is a story of the leadership of a people in quest of a land. The great leaders of the Hebrew people combined spiritual and secular powers; examples include Abraham (ca. 1900 B.C.E.), Joseph (ca. 1750 B.C.E.), Moses (ca. 1300 B.C.E.), and David (ca. 1000 B.C.E.). After the great leaders had passed away, tribal leadership became the task of judges who led by virtue of their possession of spiritual power, or what has come down to us as "charisma." The Book of Judges tells how twelve judges, in successive reigns amounting to 410 years, held sway over Israel.

It is very likely, however, that it was the Egyptians who provided the seeds for the managerial concepts we see reported in the Bible. Joseph was sold into slavery, rose to be the vizier, and gained valuable administrative experience. Moses, while in captivity in Egypt, observed the Egyptian "rule of ten." The Bible tells us that it was on the advice of his father-in-law, Jethro (thus making Jethro the first known management consultant), that Moses "chose able men from all over Israel and made them judges over the people—thousands, hundreds, fifties, and tens. They were constantly available to administer justice. They brought the hard cases to Moses but judged the smaller matters themselves" (Living Bible, Exod. 18:25–26). Thus Moses was able to employ an exception principle in managing, as well as to establish a more orderly organizational structure for tribal management. Other managerial advice can be found in the Bible: "Without deliberation, plans come to nothing; where counselors are many, plans succeed" (Prov. 15:22). This bears a marked resemblance to the advice of Sun Tzu, who was a continent and many years away. For controlling, we are told: "Where there are many hands, lock things up" (Ecclus. 42:6).[8] Leadership, delegation, span of management, planning, organizing, and controlling were managerial practices found among ancient peoples.

GREECE

Will Durant captured the essence of the rise and fall of many civilizations in writing "a nation is born stoic, and dies epicurean."[9] In the stoic phase of the cycle, adversity breeds cohesion and deprivation fosters initiative. Self-control, thrift, hard work, and an orderly life bring prosperity. As affluence reigns, self-control becomes self-indulgence, thrift becomes a vice, industry and perseverance yield to opportunism, and social order breaks down. Epicureans take no thought for the morrow

---

8. For other examples, see Robert L. Hagerman, "Accounting in the Bible," *Accounting Historians Journal* 7 (Fall 1980), pp. 71–76.

9. Will Durant, *The Story of Civilization, Part I: Our Oriental Heritage* (New York: Simon and Schuster, 1935), p. 259.

and decline begins; the fall comes not from without, but from internal decay. The cycle was true for Greece and for Rome. America was founded by stoics, the Puritans; does the past foretell the future?

The institutions, art, language, drama, and literature of ancient Greece form a significant part of our own culture. However, Greek economic philosophy was antibusiness, and trade and commerce were considered beneath the dignity of the Greek ideal. Work, considered ignoble by the aristocratic or philosophical Greek, was to be carried out by slaves and less than respectable citizens. Manual workers and merchants were excluded from citizenship in the Greek democracy because of the low esteem given to manual and trade occupations. Government administration was based solely on election and participation by all citizens, and the prevailing philosophy discouraged professional experts as administrators.

Socrates (469–399 B.C.E.) observed that managerial skills were transferable: "[the] management of private concerns differs from that of public concerns only in magnitude ... neither can be carried on without men ... and those who understand how to employ [others] are successful directors of private and public concerns, and those who do not understand, will err in the management of both."[10] Plato (ca. 428–348 B.C.E.), a pupil of Socrates, remarked on human diversity and how this led to the division of labor:

> I am myself reminded that we are not all alike: there are diversities of natures among us which are adapted to different occupations.... And, if so, we must infer that all things are produced more plentifully and easily and of a better quality when one man does one thing which is natural to him and does it at the right time, and leaves other things [duties].[11]

This notion that a division of labor would optimize productivity would persist for nearly 2,000 years, forming the basis for organizing work and determining how to best utilize the diverse abilities of people.

Aristotle (384–322 B.C.E.), a student of Plato, provided numerous insights into management and organization in his *Politics*. Some examples include

1. On the specialization of labor: "Every work is better done which receives the sole, and not the divided attention of the worker"
2. On departmentation: "Every office should have a special function [and one question is] should offices be divided according to the subjects with which they deal, or according to the persons with which they deal?"

---

10. Xenophon, [Socrates'] *Memorabilia and Oeconomicus*, trans. E. C. Marchant (Cambridge, Mass.: Harvard University Press, 1968), p. 189.

11. Plato, *Republic*, trans. Benjamin Jowett), Great Books of the Western World, vol. 7, bk 2 (Chicago: Encyclopedia Britannica, Inc., 1952), p. 317.

3. On centralization, decentralization, and delegation of authority: "We should also know over which matters several local tribunals are to have jurisdiction, and [those] in which authority should be centralized; for example, should one person keep order in the market and another in some other place, or should the same person be responsible everywhere?"

4. On synergy: "The whole is naturally superior to the part."

5. On leadership: "He who has never learned to obey cannot be a good commander."[12]

In his *Metaphysics,* Aristotle developed the thesis that reality is knowable through the senses and through reason. By rejecting mysticism, Aristotle became the father of the scientific method and established the intellectual foundation for the Renaissance and the Age of Reason. Eventually this spirit of scientific inquiry would form a basis for scientific management.

Another Greek, Xenophon, described the advantages of the division of labor (ca. 370 B.C.E.):

> There are places [workshops] even where one man earns a living by only stitching shoes, another cutting them out, another by sewing the uppers together, while there is another who performs none of these operations but only assembles the parts. It follows ... that he who devotes himself to a very highly specialized line of work is bound to do it in the best possible manner.[13]

Greece fell to the Romans, a hardy stock of people from the banks of the Tiber. It destroyed itself by depleting its forests and natural resources, by internal moral decay, by political disorder, and by decimating its leadership through revolts and counterrevolts. Stoicism, like its later Christian counterparts Calvinism and Puritanism, produced the strongest characters of that time. Despite its antitrade philosophy, the age of Greece illustrates the first seeds of democracy, the advent of decentralized participatory government, the first attempts to establish individual liberty, the beginnings of the scientific method for problem solving, and some early insights into the division of labor, departmentation, delegation, and leadership.

ROME

Rome was born stoic and conquered the decaying Hellenic civilization. The Romans developed a quasi-factory system to manufacture armaments for the legions, for the pottery makers who produced for a world market, and later for textiles that were

---

12. Aristotle, *Politics,* trans. Benjamin Jowett, Great Books of the Western World, vol. 9 (Chicago: Encyclopaedia Britannica, Inc., 1952), pp. 474, 487, 500.

13. Cited by Friedrick Klemm, *A History of Western Technology* (New York: Charles Scribner's Sons, 1959), p. 28.

sold for export. The famous Roman road system was built to speed the distribution of goods, as well as to speed the movement of troops to dissident colonies. The Romans inherited the Greek disdain for trade and left business activities in the hands of Greek and Asian freemen. A growing external trade required commercial standardization, and the state developed a guaranteed system of measures, weights, and coins. The first resemblance to a corporate organization appeared in the form of joint-stock companies, which sold stocks to the public in order to carry out government contracts to supply the war effort. There was a highly specialized labor force that, with few exceptions, worked in small shops as independent artisans selling for the market rather than for individual customers. Free workers formed guilds (*collegia*) but these were for social aims and mutual benefits, such as defraying the cost of funerals, rather than for establishing wages, hours, or conditions of employment. The state regulated all aspects of Roman economic life: it levied tariffs on trade, set fines on monopolists, regulated the guilds, and used its revenues to fight a multitude of wars. Large-scale organizations could not exist, since the government prohibited joint-stock companies for any purpose other than the execution of government contracts.

The Roman army followed the "rule of ten," although its application varied from time to time. The cavalry had *decuriones,* units of ten horse soldiers, with three decuriones constituting a *turma* and ten turmae (three hundred cavalry) supporting a legion. Centurions led one hundred soldiers (even though actual troop size rarely reached that level), and these centuries were organized into cohorts, with ten cohorts making up a legion. Thus the Roman genius for order and discipline established units to perform certain tasks as well as a hierarchy of authority to ensure performance. Other contributions of Rome to our heritage came chiefly from law and government, which were manifestations of this concern for order. Roman law became a model for later civilizations, and the Roman separation of legislative and executive powers provided a model system of checks and balances for later constitutional governments.

THE CATHOLIC CHURCH

From its seedbed in the Middle East, Christianity faced theological as well as organizational problems. As the faith spread, novel sects grew, and the first blush of a youthful theology threatened to become an adolescence of diversity. Early congregations operated independently, each defining its own doctrine and conditions for membership. Bishops became heads of various local churches, and the roles of presbyters and deacons began to emerge as assistants for the bishop. By the third century A.D., an ordered hierarchy was more apparent with the addition of subdeacons and acolytes, who performed personal and secretarial duties, and exorcists and readers, who performed liturgical duties. All these ranks were enumerated by Bishop Cornelius in a message to Fabius of Antioch (A.D. 251). At the Council of Arles (A.D. 314) some bishops were made more equal than others, giving rise to a chief bishop, the bishop of Rome. At the Council of Nicaea (A.D. 325), the bishop of Rome was named to the office of pope.

The outcome was centralized doctrine and authority in Rome and the papacy. However, the conflict between centralized and decentralized authority has reappeared throughout history, not only in the Catholic church but in other organizations. In modern organizational terms, the Catholic church leaders perceived a need to institutionalize the organization, that is, to specify policies, procedures, doctrine, and authority. The problem is a recurring one even today: the need for unanimity of purpose, yet discretion for local problems and conditions.

FEUDALISM AND THE MIDDLE AGES

Renaissance writers coined the phrase "Middle Ages" to refer to what occurred from the decline of Rome to the Renaissance period. Slavery became uneconomical in the late Roman period: the upkeep of slaves was costly and they showed no particular enthusiasm for their work. The abolition of slavery came not with moral progress but with economic change. Development of free people as tenant farmers proved to be more economical. The growth of large estates and the political disorder following the fall of Rome led to economic, social, and political chaos, ripe for the emergence of the feudal system. Feudalism as a cultural system prevailed from about 600 to about 1500. At the base of the feudal system were the serfs, who tilled plots of land owned by the manorial lords, much like modern sharecroppers, and were given military protection in exchange for a portion of the products of their labor. The feudal system tied people to the land, fixed rigid class distinctions, established an age of landed aristocracy that was to endure to the Industrial Revolution, forced education to a standstill, made poverty and ignorance the hallmark of the masses, and completely stifled human progress until the Age of Reformation. It is no wonder that some historians prefer to call this period the Dark Ages.

Although some writers romanticize the Middle Ages for chivalry, the Crusades, the healthy agrarian life, and the dignity of the artisan, the period was really rather bleak. Many of the problems typically associated with the Industrial Revolution actually began during this period. People razed the forests for fire and cooking wood, ignoring any reforestation needs, and overgrazed or tilled carelessly the open lands. As the forests diminished, coal became a more important source of fuel, thus creating air pollution. Eleanor, queen of England, was forced from her castle at Nottingham in 1257 by the coal smoke and fumes from a nearby village. Water pollution resulted from human and animal waste flowing from open sewers into the streams. The situation grew worse until the British parliament passed the first known antipollution legislation in 1388, almost four centuries before the Industrial Revolution.[14] These were nasty, brutish times, but developing events would lead to better days.

---

14. Jean Gimpel, *The Medieval Machine* (New York: Holt, Rinehart, and Winston, 1976), pp. 75–85.

THE REVIVAL OF COMMERCE

Feudalism gave birth to the Crusades and, in turn, died as a result of them. Two centuries of religious fervor had left Jerusalem in the hands of the Muslims, and Europe was seething with the potential for change. The Crusades also stimulated commerce by opening new trade routes and exposing parochial, feudal Europe to the wealth of the Middle East. The Crusades weakened Christian belief. Embarking on their journeys with invincible religious conviction, the Crusaders returned with the realization that Middle Eastern culture was superior in manners, morals, trade, industry, and warfare.

Another eye-opener was the return of a Venetian trader, Marco Polo (1254–1324), from the Far Eastern lands of China, Tibet, Burma, and India in 1295. In addition to his fantastic tales of a previously unseen part of the world, he told how the Tartar (actually, Tatar) tribes of Mongolia and Manchuria organized their armies for battle: "[The Chief] puts himself at the head of an army of a hundred thousand horses ... and appoints an officer to the command of ten men, and others to command a hundred, a thousand, and ten thousand men respectively ... by this arrangement each officer has only to attend to the management of ten men or ten bodies of men."[15] How did these Far Eastern lands, having never before visited or been visited by the West, arrive at this "rule of ten"? For that matter, how did the Incas, a civilization that flourished from about 1200 to 1532 in what is roughly modern Peru and Chile, have "a decimal system of controls, with overseers of ten, a hundred, a thousand, and up to ten thousand people"?[16] History often reveals more than it resolves.

The results of the cultural confrontations of the Crusades led to a more secular life in Europe through weakening religious bonds. Interest arose in exploration, and a new spirit of trade and commerce filled the land of feudalism. New markets, new ideas, the rise of towns, the first seeds of a new middle class, freer circulation of money and credit instruments, and the resurgence of political order created the base for the Renaissance and the Reformation.

Before the Industrial Revolution, how were goods produced? Many products were made or grown in the home for a family's use. Other products, however, came from two basic methods of industrial organization: the guilds and the domestic system. Guilds, as far as we know, existed primarily between 1100 and 1500 and consisted of two types: merchant guilds, which were the buyers and sellers of goods; and craft guilds, which were the makers of the goods. Within the craft guilds there was a hierarchy of authority of masters, journeymen, and apprentices. The master owned the tools and raw materials and the finished product; journeymen were paid workers who had finished their apprenticeship but had not yet established their own

---

15. Marco Polo, *The Travels of Marco Polo* (New York: The Modern Library, 1954), p. 92. Written in 1298.

16. John Hemming, "The Lost Cities of the Incas," in J. J. Thorndike, ed., *Discovery of Lost Worlds* (New York: American Heritage, 1979), p. 263.

shop; and apprentices were those who were learning the trade. Each town or village typically regulated the number of masters to be permitted for any craft, the number of apprentices a master could have, and the *maximum* wages an apprentice could earn. If an apprentice ran away, wanted posters appeared and law enforcement authorities were sent for the culprit. Each guild was protected from competition by the local officials who forbade the entry of products from outside the village and, in turn, taxed or licensed the guilds as the price of their protection. As we saw in Chapter 1, the craft guilds also suppressed innovations.

Guilds were regulated as to quality of work and acted to control certain types of work: for example, craft guild rules prohibited shoemakers from tanning hides, which was the job of the tanners, and weavers from dyeing cloth, which was the job of the dyers. Conversely, tanners and dyers had to stick to their own work also. Thus craft guilds used the division of labor to gain greater job control. The modern union practices of controlling job access, defining the jurisdiction of each craft, and restricting encroachment by others is a legacy of the medieval age.

Merchant guilds were numerous and resembled modern trade associations. Merchants of earlier times were intermediaries in trade, buying raw materials to sell to producers or taking finished products for resale. Merchants were thus the corner-stone of what was called the domestic, or "putting out," system of production. A mer-chant procured raw material and contracted the work out to individual workers or families who, using their own equipment, would complete the product in their homes and then return it to the merchant for a wage. The faults of the domestic sys-tem lay in the simple tools and technology, with little incentive to improve them, and in the inefficiencies of small-scale production with a limited division of labor. As the volume of trade grew the domestic system proved inefficient, and the need for more capital, the benefits of specializing labor, and the economies of scale of a centralized workplace led to the factory system.

In the domestic system, however, we find an early example of what moderns term "transaction cost economics," the idea that, in some instances, a managerial hierarchy may allocate resources more effectively than the market. The domestic sys-tem relied on the negotiation of contracts with those who would do the work in their homes, and the price that would be paid for that work would be the ongoing market price. In their homes, workers could work at their own pace, making the completion of the product unpredictable from the point of view of the merchant. There was no monitoring of performance, possibly leading to an uneven quality of the finished product. Payment for performance provided an incentive, however, for the worker to finish the work as contracted with the merchant. At any point in time, the merchant could have numerous contracts in operation, making monitoring of work more difficult. With the emergence of steam power and the factory system, we will see how a central workplace and a managerial hierarchy facilitated monitoring of performance, reduced risk and uncertainty, and gave the firm an advantage over the domestic means of production.

Growing trade also required a rationalization of the methods of keeping accounts. Although traders and bankers such as Francesco Datini of Prato and

Genoa and the Medicis of Florence were using the essentials of double-entry book-keeping as early as 1340,[17] a Franciscan monk, Luca Pacioli, first described it in print in his *Summa de Arithmetica, geometrica, proportioni, et proportionalita* in 1494. Pacioli's system was the first information system for management: it provided the entrepreneur with information on cash and inventory position and enabled a check on cash flow. The system did not keep track of costs, however. It was not until the twentieth century that any advancements were made on Pacioli's system.

As trade expanded, the emerging economic order placed more souls in jeopardy with respect to the prevailing church doctrine against charging interest and the profit motive. Saint Thomas Aquinas, a thirteenth-century theologian, had addressed the issue of justice in trade matters with the idea of a "just price," which was the market, or prevailing, price. In 1468, Friar Johannes Nider extended this notion by developing certain trade rules (we might call them a code of ethical conduct), which, if followed, would assure merchants that their transactions were just. For example, the rules declared that the goods should be "lawful, honorable, and useful"; that the price should be just; that the seller should beware (*caveat venditor*) and not engage in "trickery" nor "intimidation" nor sell to "simpletons" who would not be informed buyers; and that those who buy "looking for nothing but a rise in prices [i.e., speculation] sin gravely."[18] Nider's book, written during the Renaissance, was the first to focus on business ethics, and it indicates that an ancient concern for ethical trade practices is woven into our social fabric. As one author summarized Nider's message for today:

> Nider's thoughts are surprisingly modern.... Through his eyes we see the moral dilemmas of the past and of the present; the moral choices that must be made in everyday life in business and our personal conduct; and the need for guidelines that provide the ropes to keep us from falling. Nider addressed evergreen issues that ethicists faced in the past and encounter in the present—that laws alone cannot deflect human frailties nor chicanery; that ultimate responsibility for one's actions cannot be avoided; and that virtuous conduct is necessary in exchange relationships.[19]

Feudalism was dead, interred by the expansion of trade, the growth of urbanization, the creation of a merchant class, and the development of strong central governments. But the age of industrialization had not yet arrived. New wine was

---

17. Morgen Witzel, *Builders and Dreamers: The Making and Meaning of Management* (London: Prentice-Hall, 2002).

18. Johannes Nider, *On The Contracts of Merchants*, trans. Charles H. Reeves, ed. Ronald B. Shuman (Norman, Okla.: University of Oklahoma Press, 1966), pp. 38–45. Originally published in Cologne in 1468 as *De Contractibus Mercatorum*.

19. Daniel A. Wren, "Medieval or Modern? A Scholastic's View of Business Ethics, circa 1430," *Journal of Business Ethics* 28 (2000), p. 117.

fermenting, straining the old societal containers. What was needed now was a new spirit, a new sanction for human efforts.

THE CULTURAL REBIRTH

The new wine that was straining the cultural containers was a trinity of forces that would eventually lead to the Industrial Revolution and a new culture for humankind. These forces established the cultural foundations of a new industrial age that brought people from subservience to newfound freedoms in economic arrangements for the allocation of resources, in social relations, and in political institutions. The rediscovery of the classics and renewed interest in reason and science epitomized the Renaissance and broke the ancient hold of theology on people through the Protestant Reformation and the subsequent Protestant ethic. The liberty ethic established new concepts in relations between people and the state through constitutional government. The market ethic brought forth the notion of a market-directed economy. These three ethics, or standards for cultural conduct, interacted in practice to change cultural values toward people, work, and profits. The outcome of this cultural rebirth was the creation of a new environment that would lead to the need for the formal study of management.

THE PROTESTANT ETHIC

During the Middle Ages the Catholic church dominated life and provided the hope of an afterlife as the only consolation for this one. With the church as superstate, the admonitions of doctrine against lending for interest, against desiring anything from this world other than subsistence, and against materialistic trade and profits perpetuated the opinion of business as an evil necessity. The complete domination of life by the church led people to think not of this world, but of the other; not of gain, but of salvation. According to the church, the self-interest of trade diverted people's thoughts from God to gain, from obedience to initiative, and from humility to activity.

The loosening of religious bonds by the Crusades and the spread of general prosperity through the revival of commerce was bound sooner or later to lead to a revolt against the church. Although earlier individuals had protested the practices of the Roman Catholic Church, Martin Luther is generally considered the architect of the Protestant Reformation. He agreed with the church, however, in condemning interest, considered commerce a "nasty business," and spoke out vehemently against the Fuggers, the leading commercial family in Germany.

John Calvin was inspired by the reformation attempts of Luther and, like Luther, he followed the Augustinian creed of predestination and brought to the Reformation a somber view of the smallness and weakness of humans. His view of a combination of church and state as ideal led to his theocracy of Geneva and clearly repudiated the philosophy of the Renaissance. Calvin's concept of the elect, those predestined to be saved, gave a new spirit to his followers. Since everything was pre-determined, all people should believe that they were of the elect and, based on this divine election, would have the courage to face the tribulations of any harsh world. Did the stern Protestantism of Luther and Calvin provide the religious sanctions for rational capitalism?

Max Weber would answer in the affirmative by stating the case for Protestantism having created the spirit of capitalism. Weber made a clear distinction between the irrational, unlimited greed for gain and the rational capitalism of the Protestant ethic:

> The impulse to acquisition, pursuit of gain, of money, of the greatest possible amount of money, has in itself nothing to do with capitalism. This impulse [to acquisition] has been common to all sorts and conditions of men at all times and in all countries of the earth, wherever the objective possibility of it is or has been given. It should be taught in the kindergarten of cultural history that this naïve idea of capitalism must be given up once and for all. Unlimited greed for gain is not in the least identical with capitalism, and is still less its spirit. Capitalism *may* even be identical with the restraint, or at least a rational tempering, of this irrational impulse. But capitalism is identical with the pursuit of profit, and forever *renewed* profit, by means of continuous, rational, capitalistic enterprise. For it must be so: in a wholly capitalistic order of society, an individual capitalistic enterprise which did not take advantage of its opportunities for profit-making would be doomed to extinction.[20]

Weber began his search for an explanation of the capitalistic spirit by noting the overwhelming number of Protestants among business leaders, entrepreneurs, and highly skilled laborers, and more highly technically and commercially trained personnel. In Weber's view, Luther developed the idea of a calling in the sense of a task set by God, a life task. This was a new idea brought about during the Reformation, and became a central dogma of Protestant denominations. It discarded Catholic notions of subsistence living and monastic asceticism by urging individuals to fulfill the obligations imposed on them in this world, that is, their calling (German *Beruf*). It placed worldly affairs as the highest form of moral activity for the individual and gave the performance of earthly duties a religious significance and sanction. Every person's occupation was a calling, and all were legitimate in the sight of God. Weber did not say that Luther intended capitalism to follow from his concept of the calling; on the contrary, later connotations led to refinement of this idea into a success-oriented spirit of capitalism. The calling did place a new interpretation on the purpose of life: instead of waiting for the Judgment Day, a person should choose and pursue an

---

20. Max Weber, *The Protestant Ethic and the Spirit of Capitalism*, trans. Talcott Parsons (New York: Charles Scribner's Sons, 1958), p. 17. Originally published in Germany in 1905 and revised in 1920 to include answers to various critics.

occupation, not for the purpose of material gain beyond needs, but because it was divine will. The result of this Protestant dogma was a worldly asceticism that asked people to renounce earthly sensuality to labor in this world for the glorification of God. All people had to consider themselves members of the elect, and if they did not, their lack of confidence was interpreted as a lack of faith. To attain self-confidence, people had to engage in intense worldly activity, for that and that alone could dispel religious doubts and give certainty of grace. In practice, this came to mean that God helps those who help themselves.

Catholic laypersons, in contrast, fulfilled their required religious duties conscientiously. Beyond that minimum their good works did not need to form a rationalized system of life. They could use their good works to atone for particular sins, to better their chances for salvation, or as a sort of insurance premium for later years. To make a sharper distinction, Weber described the demands of Calvinism:

> The God of Calvinism demanded of his believers not single good works, but a life of good works combined into a unified system. There was no place for the very human Catholic cycle of sin, repentance, atonement, release, followed by a renewed sin. Nor was there any balance of merit for a life as a whole which could be adjusted by temporal punishments or the Churches' [*sic*] means of grace.[21]

The Calvinist was therefore required to live a life of good works, not an inconsistent series of wrongs balanced by repentant rights. Weber saw this as a keystone in developing a spirit of effort and gain; people were no longer able to give free rein to irrational impulses but were required by dogma to exercise self-control over their every action. They proved their faith by worldly activity, acting with zeal and self-discipline.

This new Protestant asceticism, which Weber also characterized as Puritanism, did not condone the pursuit of wealth for its own sake, for wealth would lead to pleasure and to all the temptations of the flesh. Instead, activity became the goal of the good life. Numerous corollaries developed in practice: (1) wasting time was the deadliest of sins, since every hour wasted was negating the opportunity to labor for the glory of God; (2) willingness to work was essential: "He who will not work shall not eat"; (3) the division and specialization of labor was a result of divine will, since it led to the development of a higher degree of skill and improvement in the quality and quantity of production and hence served the good of all; and (4) consumption beyond basic needs was wasteful and therefore sinful: "Waste not, want not."[22] According to Weber, each of these ideas had a significant impact on the motivations of people, leading to a spirit of enterprise.

Intense activity moved people from a contemplative life to one of continuous physical and mental labor. Willingness to work placed the motivational burden on

---

21. *Ibid.*, pp. 117.
22. *Ibid.*, pp. 157–173.

individuals, and their self-directed, self-controlled lives gave them an internal gyro-scope. The specialization of labor placed each person in a calling and required a person's best, and the nonspecialized worker demonstrated a lack of grace. The Protestant ethic postulated that God desired profitability, that this was a sign of grace, and that to waste anything and reduce profits or to forgo what might be a profitable venture worked against God's will. By not seeking luxury, people created a surplus or profit from their labors. The created wealth could not be consumed beyond a person's basic needs, and thus the surplus was to be reinvested in other ventures or in the improvement of present ones.

Protestantism resulted in specific guidelines for the creation of a capitalistic spirit. According to Weber, people had a duty to work, a duty to use their wealth wisely, and a duty to live self-denying lives. An unequal distribution of goods in the world was divine providence at work, since each person had unequal talents and therefore reaped unequal rewards. Wealth was no assurance of heaven, and the poor did not need to worry as long as they performed their calling properly. For Weber, the spirit of capitalism was created by the Protestant ethic, which equated spiritual worth and temporal success. With no room for self-indulgence and with the tenets of self-control and self- direction, a new age of individualism had been born.

A CRITICISM OF THE WEBERIAN THESIS

Every thesis generates its antithesis and Weber's Protestant ethic is no exception. R. H. Tawney reversed Weber's thesis and argued that capitalism was the cause and justification of Protestantism, not the effect. Tawney noted that Catholic cities were chief commercial centers, that Catholics were leading bankers, and that the capitalistic spirit was present in many places far in advance of the sixteenth- and seventeenth-century influences that Weber discussed. According to Tawney, "Is it not a little artificial to suggest that capitalist enterprise had to wait, as Weber appears to imply, till religious changes had produced a capitalist spirit? Would it not be equally plausible, and equally one-sided, to argue that the religious changes were themselves merely the result of economic movements?"[23]

In Tawney's view, the rise of capitalism was action and reaction, molding and in turn being molded by other significant cultural forces. The Renaissance brought a new focus on reason, discovery, exploration, and science; all were challenges to the monolithic authority of the church. The Renaissance contributed the humanist's views that made life on earth more important and brought the promise of a new social order in which there would be mobility for people; it signaled the mastery of people over their environment rather than the reverse case of the Middle Ages.[24] Growing economic life posed new problems for church doctrine; and

---

23. R. H. Tawney, Foreword to Weber's *Protestant Ethic,* p. 8. While Weber and earlier writers addressed traditional Catholicism, Michael Novak has noted changes in Catholicism that challenge the exclusivity of a "Protestant Ethic." See Novak's *The Catholic Ethic and the Spirit of Capitalism* (New York: Free Press, 1993) and *Business as a Calling* (New York: Free Press, 1996).

24. R. H. Tawney, *Religion and the Rise of Capitalism* (London: John Murray, 1926), pp. 61–63.

merchants and artisans engaged in profit-making activities regardless of dogma. Perhaps, then, the Reformation was an attempt to create materialistic loopholes for the emerging merchant class.

With two sets of assumptions, two different conclusions could be reached: (1) Weber's notion that the church changed and then the spirit of capitalism abounded; or (2) Tawney's view that economic motivation was steam pushing on the lid of church authority until the safety valve of a change in dogma (i.e., the Reformation and its later proliferation into various sects) could sanction economic efforts.

MODERN SUPPORT FOR WEBER

Despite the criticisms of Weber's thesis, there is modern evidence that Protestants hold different values toward work. In *The Achieving Society,* McClelland began a search for the psychological factors that were generally important for economic development. The factor he isolated was the need for achievement, or the shorthand version, "n achievement." McClelland's study was both historical and cross-cultural and his findings support Weber's thesis. First, McClelland found that high n achievement was essential to engaging in entrepreneurial activities; second, that high n achievement in a society was significantly correlated to rapid economic development; and third, that certain ethnic, religious, and minority groups showed marked differences in n achievement. He found that children of Protestants had higher n achievement than children of Catholics, and children of Jews had still higher n achievement. McClelland concluded that individualistic religions, for example, the Protestant ones, tended to be associated with a high need for achievement, while authoritarian religions, such as traditional Catholicism, tended to have a lower need for achievement. He did concede, however, that there are wide variations among various modern Catholic communities.

What was involved in the need for achievement was not so much the need to reach certain goals, such as wealth, status, respect, and so on, but the need to enjoy the satisfactions of success. Wealth was a way of keeping score, not the goal. The entrepreneurial personality was characterized by special attitudes toward risk taking, willingness to expend energy, willingness to innovate, and a readiness to make decisions and accept responsibility. Historically the concern for achievement appeared in a culture some fifty or so years before a rapid rate of economic growth and prosperity. McClelland found this to be true in ancient Greece (before its golden age), in Spain in the Middle Ages (before the age of exploration), and in England during two different periods. The first period was from 1500 to 1625 when Protestantism and Puritanism were growing in strength concurrently with a need for achievement. The second period came in the eighteenth century just prior to the Industrial Revolution. The reasoning that McClelland used to support Weber was basically thus: (1) the Protestant Reformation emphasized self-reliance rather than reliance on others in all facets of life; (2) Protestant parents changed child-rearing practices to teach self-reliance and independence; (3) McClelland and his associates demonstrated empirically that these practices led to a higher need for achievement in sons; and (4) a higher need for achievement led to spurts of economic activity such as that characterized by Weber as the spirit of capitalism.[25] Therefore, McClelland was able to draw a relationship empirically between the influence of Protestantism and Weber's spirit of modern capitalism.

Lenski summarized the criticisms of Weber, evaluated them, and presented the evidence both for and against Weber. On balance, he found the evidence more in favor of Weber than against him. Lenski examined vertical mobility and concomitant characteristics of aspirations, ambition, and attitudes toward work in an attempt to define the relationship between religious affiliation and the ability of people to move upward in the job world. The findings resulted in a ranking of first (most mobile), Jews; second, Protestants; and third (least mobile), Catholics. Lenski's explanation resided in the differences among these three groups with respect to achievement motivation and their attitudes toward work. Jews and Protestants showed a positive attitude toward work and derived satisfaction from work. Catholics held neutral attitudes toward work and indicated that it was done for some purpose other than the satisfaction that came from work itself. In Lenski's view, "Catholics continued to regard work primarily as a necessary evil; a consequence of Adam's fall and a penalty for sin. By contrast, Protestants came to view it as an opportunity for serving God, or, in the Deist version, for building character."[26]

The implications of McClelland's and Lenski's findings can be far-reaching for contemporary people. Not only did they find empirical support for Weber, but their work suggests that achievement values can be taught and instilled in various societies. In underdeveloped nations the problem may be underachievement; if so, an inculcation of achievement values would provide means for self-help programs to speed the progress of or the adjustment to industrialization.

THE LIBERTY ETHIC

Given the postulates of a need for achievement and the sanctions of individual rewards for worldly efforts, the political system must be conducive to individual liberty. The divine right of kings, the aristocracy of the manor lord, the exercise of secular authority by the church, and serfdom as a birthright were not favorable conditions for developing an industrialized society. In the Age of Enlightenment, political philosophers began to stimulate the thoughts of people with such new ideas as equality, justice, the rights of citizens, a rule of reason, and notions of a republic governed by the consent of the governed. These were radical ideas in those times, ideas that threatened the existing order with a profound revolution in the views of the relationship between citizen and state.

---

25. David C. McClelland, *The Achieving Society* (New York: Van Nostrand Rinehold Co., 1961), pp. 47–53. See also John W. Atkinson, *A Theory of Achievement Motivation* (New York: D. Van Nostrand Co., 1966).

26. Gerhard Lenski, *The Religious Factor: A Sociological Study of Religious Impact on Politics, Economics, and Family Life* (Garden City, NY: Doubleday and Co., 1961), p. 83.

Before this facet of the cultural rebirth, political theory called for the domination of the many by the few and found its best proponents in Nicolo Machiavelli and Thomas Hobbes. Machiavelli, an out-of-office administrator and diplomat in the city-state of Florence, wrote *The Prince* in 1513.[27] He was an experienced observer of the intrigues of state and papacy and set forth a how-to book for a ruler or aspiring ruler. *The Prince*, dedicated to Lorenzo di Piero de Medici, was an exposition on how to rule; not how to be good or wise, but how to rule successfully. Machiavelli identified three ways to the top: "fortune," "ability," and "villainy." Those who rose through their good fortune had little trouble in getting to the top spot, but had difficulty maintaining it because they must depend on the good will of others and were indebted entirely to those who elevated them. Those who gained the crest by ability endured a thousand difficulties getting there, but would be able to maintain their position more easily. Villainy, an oft-chosen path in Machiavelli's Florence, used methods that would gain power, but not glory; afterwards their crown would always rest uneasily as they awaited the next villain or revolt.[28]

Machiavelli's basic assumption about the nature of people was indicative of his rationale for the type of leadership he advocated: "Whoever desires to found a state and give it laws, must start with the assumption that all men are bad and ever ready to display their vicious nature, whenever they may find occasion for it."[29] To cope with these brutes, rulers were justified in pursuing any leadership style that suited their purpose. They should be concerned with having a good reputation, but not with being virtuous; should they have to choose between being feared and being loved, it would be better to be feared; and, above all, rulers must be both like a lion and like a fox, employing force and deceit. Machiavelli wrote of the ruler, but not of the ruled; of power, but not of rights; and of ends, but not of means. Machiavelli fed the ideas of Lord Acton about power corrupting, and absolute power corrupting absolutely. Machiavellian has come to connote those unscrupulous, crafty, and cunning in policy. For his time, and perhaps for ours, Machiavelli personified the command philosophy of governing people.

Thomas Hobbes's *Leviathan* (1651) was a later argument for a strong central leadership. He began his analysis with humankind in a state of nature, without civil government, and proceeded to the conclusion that some greater power, the Leviathan, must exist to bring order from chaos.[30] This person or body became sovereign; since it was given all rights by the governed, its powers could not be revoked, and it became an absolute sovereign. It made no difference to Hobbes whether the

---

27. Nicolo Machiavelli, *The Prince,* trans. Luigi Ricci (New York: New American Library, 1952). Written in 1513, but not published until 1532 because of its controversial nature.

28. Daniel A. Wren and Ronald G. Greenwood, *Management Innovators: The People and Ideas That Have Shaped Modern Business* (New York: Oxford University Press, 1998), pp. 191–194.

29. Nicolo Machiavelli, *Discourses on Livy,* trans. Alan H. Gilbert, reprinted in *Machiavelli: The Chief Works and Others,* vol. 1 (Durham, N.C.: Duke University Press, 1956), p. 203.

30. Thomas Hobbes, *Leviathan, or the Matter, Forme, and Power of a Common-Wealth Ecclesiastical and Civill,* (London: printed for Andrew Ckooke, at the Green Dragon in St. Paul's Churchyard, 1651).

Adam Smith (statue by Hans Gasser). ©Hunterian Art Gallery, University of Glasgow.

sovereign was civil or ecclesiastical, as long as the central power regulated all overt conduct and expression, both civil and religious. The sovereign ruled all, and the individual was subordinate to those who ruled.

In the history of human liberty, John Locke's essay *Concerning Civil Government* (1690) must stand as a great contribution to political theory and an effective instigator of political action. It served to state the principles of the English bloodless revolution of 1688, which brought about fundamental changes in the English constitution. It also set the stage for the American Revolution of 1776 by inspiring the authors of the Declaration of Independence, and furnished inspiration to Jean Jacques Rousseau's *Social Contract* and the ensuing French Revolution. Perhaps no other one person has had such a profound effect on political theory and action. Locke attacked the divine right of kings, whose proponents traced it to Adam's God-given right to rule his children, and set forth some new concepts of authority: "who shall be judge whether the prince or legislative body act contrary to their trust? ... To this I reply, the people shall be judge."[31]

This notion found more explicit support in America's Declaration of Independence:

> We hold these truths to be self-evident, that all men are created equal; that they are endowed by their creator with certain inalienable rights; that among these are life, liberty, and the pursuit of happiness. That to secure these rights, governments are instituted among men deriving their just powers from the consent of the governed.

Locke's work is so broad that it is possible here only to sample his main contributions: first, that people are governed by a natural law of reason and not by the arbitrary rules of tradition nor the whims of a central authoritarian figure; and second, that civil society is built on private property. The law of nature and reason commands one not to harm another's possessions and individuals enter into a civil society in order to preserve more perfectly their liberty and property, which are then protected by both natural law and civil law. Since people have a natural right to property, the state cannot take it away, but must protect their right to it.

---

31. John Locke, *Second Essay Concerning Civil Government*, Great Books of the Western World, vol. 35 (Chicago: Encyclopaedia Britannica, 1952), p. 81. Originally published in 1690.

Locke was a Puritan in the England of Cromwell. His writing must have affected that of Adam Smith and most certainly established the basis for Rousseau's writings. In the emergence of the philosophical Age of Enlightenment, Locke put forth a new civil order: (1) a law based on reason, not arbitrary dictates; (2) a government deriving its powers from the governed; (3) liberty to pursue individual goals as a natural right; and (4) private property and its use in the pursuit of happiness as a natural and legally protected right. These four ideas interwove in practice to form a solid political foundation for industrial growth. It provided a sanction for laissez-faire economics and the pursuit of individual rewards, guaranteed the rights of property, gave protection to contracts, and provided for a system of justice among people.

THE MARKET ETHIC

Economic thinking was basically sterile during the Middle Ages, since localized, subsistence-level economies needed no economic theory to explain their workings. Early people perceived the main factors of production as land and labor, and even the latter did not pose much of a problem. Capital as an input factor was scorned and its return damned. Any idea that management was a resource input to the organization was completely lacking in early economic thought.

In the sixteenth and seventeenth centuries, the reemergence of strong national entities began to reshape economic thought. As new lands were discovered through exploration, new trade routes and new products created an international market. This revolution in trade resulted in the economic philosophy of mercantilism and injected the government into a central role of financing and protecting trade in order to build strong national economies. This economic chauvinism meant that the state intervened in all economic affairs, engaged in state economic planning, and regulated private economic activity to a large degree.[32] Mercantilism eventually fell of its own weight. Much of its planning went awry because it tried to keep alive uneconomic enterprises, curbed private initiative, built elaborate bureaucratic, red-tape controls, and fostered wars and trade rivalries that destroyed the very markets it was trying to create. The mercantilists were a philosophical contradiction to the emerging eighteenth-century Age of Enlightenment. The mercantilists thought only of the state, whereas the philosophy of the enlightenment championed individual rights and viewed all human institutions in terms of the contribution they could make to the happiness of each individual.

In the eighteenth century, the Physiocratic school of economic thought emerged to challenge mercantilism. Francois Quesnay, its founder, maintained that wealth did not lie in gold and silver but sprang from agricultural production. He advocated laissez-faire capitalism, meaning that the government should leave alone the mechanisms of the market; for him, economics had a natural order and harmony and government intervention interfered with the natural course of events.

---

32. John Fred Bell, *A History of Economic Thought,* 2nd ed. (New York: Ronald Press, 1967), p. 53.

Adam Smith (1723–1790), a Scottish political economist, was not a Physiocrat per se but was influenced by that school's view of a natural harmony in economics. In *Wealth of Nations,* Smith established the classical school and became the founder of liberal economics. Smith thought that the tariff policies of mercantilism were destructive and that, rather than protecting industry, these policies penalized efficiency by a state fiat and consequently misallocated the nation's resources. Smith proposed that only the market and competition be the regulators of economic activity. The "invisible hand" of the market would ensure that resources flowed to their best consumption and their most efficient reward, and the economic self-interest of each person and nation, acting in a fully competitive market, would bring about the greatest prosperity of all. As Smith stated it:

> As every individual, therefore, endeavors as much as he can both to employ his capital in the support of domestick industry, and so to direct that industry that its produce may be of the greatest value; every individual necessarily labours to render the annual revenue of the society as great as he can. He generally, indeed, neither intends to promote the publick interest, nor knows how much he is promoting it. By preferring the support of domestik to that of foreign industry, he intends only his own security; and by directing that industry in such a manner as its produce may be of the greatest value, he intends only his own gain, and he is in this, as in many other cases, led by an invisible hand to promote an end which was no part of his intention. Nor is it always the worse for the society that it was no part of it. By pursuing his own interest he frequently promotes that of the society more effectually than when he really intends to promote it. I have never known much good done by those who affected to trade for the publick good.[33]

For Adam Smith, the concept of specialization of labor was a pillar of this market mechanism. He cited the example of the pin makers: when each performed a limited operation, they could produce 48,000 pins a day, whereas one unspecialized worker could produce no more than twenty pins per day. He admitted that this was a trifling example, but he found the same principles of division of labor operating successfully in many industries:

> This great increase of the quantity of work which, in consequence of the division of labour, the same number of people are capable of performing, is owing to three different circumstances: first, to the increase of dexterity in every particular workman; secondly, to the saving of the time which is commonly lost in passing from one species of work to another; and lastly, to the invention of a great number of machines

---

33. Adam Smith, *An Inquiry Into the Nature and Causes of the Wealth of Nations,* (London: W. Strahan and T. Cadell in the Strand, 1776), vol. 2, bk. IV, ch. 2, p. 350. This solitary mention of the "invisible hand" was also used in an economic context in Smith's *The Theory of Moral Sentiments* (London: W. Strahan and T. Cadell, 1759), pt. IV, ch. 1, p. 466.

which facilitate and abridge labour, and enable one man to do the work of many.[34]

Although Smith saw the benefits of specialized labor, he also foresaw its dysfunctional consequences:

> The man whose whole life is spent in performing a few simple operations ... naturally loses, therefore, the habit of [mental] exertion, and generally becomes stupid and ignorant as it is possible for a human creature to become.... His dexterity at his own particular trade seems ... to be acquired at the expense of his intellectual, social, and martial virtues.[35]

Smith argued that it was the province of government, through public education, to overcome the debilitating effects of the division of labor. In his view, the manager, in order to gain productivity, must rely on the division of labor. The concept of division of labor benefited all society and provided an economic rationale for the factory system. When markets were limited, a household or domestic production arrangement could meet market needs. As the population grew and as new trade territories became feasible, a greater division of labor was possible and the factory system as a productive device began to gain momentum.

The first edition of *The Wealth of Nations* was published in March 1776 and was sold out in six months; the second edition (1778) contained minor changes; but the third edition (1784) contained substantial revision, among them Smith's concern for joint-stock, that is, limited liability firms. In Britain, the joint-stock form of organization had been established previously by royal charter or by an act of Parliament, such as the East India Company, and the Hudson Bay Company. Apparently, individuals were forming other joint-stock companies in preference over "private copartnery," or partnerships, and Smith had doubts about this arrangement:

> The directors of such [joint-stock] companies, however, being the managers rather of other people's money than of their own, it cannot well be expected, that they should watch over it with the same anxious vigilance with which the partners in a private copartnery frequently watch over their own. Like the stewards of a rich man, they are apt to consider attention to small matters as not for their master's honour, and very easily give themselves a dispensation from having it. Negligence and profusion, therefore, must always prevail, more or less, in the management of the affairs of such a company.[36]

During Smith's time, the largest employers were textile firms, and these were not capital intensive. Yet Smith anticipated that the separation of shareholder ownership

---

34. Smith, *Wealth of Nations,* vol. 1, bk. I, ch. 1, pp. 9–11.

35. *Ibid.,* vol. 2, bk. V, ch. 1, pp. 366–367.

36. *Ibid.,* 3rd ed. (1784), vol. 2, bk. 5, ch. 1, pp. 123–124. Compare this with the New Testament parable of the hired shepherd who flees when the flock is endangered. John 10:11–13.

and management by nonowners had a potential downside. Those who managed "other people's money" incurred less personal risk (except, perhaps, the loss of their jobs) and would be less vigilant and prudent in their duties.

When his writing appeared in the early stages of the Industrial Revolution, Smith found a large number of vocal supporters and fertile soil for his liberal economics. He was in tune with the philosophy of the Enlightenment and the newly emerging group of entrepreneurs who wished to sweep away the restrictions of mercantilism and the controlling power of the landed aristocracy. Great Britain found in the market ethic an economic sanction for private initiative rather than mercantilism, competition rather than protection, innovation rather than economic stagnancy, and self-interest rather than state interest as the motivating force. The market ethic was another element in this trinity of forces that created the cultural environment for the flowering of the industrial system.

SUMMARY

Early management thought was dominated by cultural values that were antibusiness, antiachievement, and largely antihuman. Industrialization could not emerge when people were bound to their stations in life, when monarchs ruled by central dictates, and when people were urged to take no thought of individual fulfillment in this world but to wait for a better one. Before the Industrial Revolution, economies and societies were essentially static, and political values involved unilateral decision making by some central authority. Although some early ideas of management appeared, they were largely localized. Organizations could be run on the divine right of the king, on the appeal of dogma to the faithful, and on the rigorous discipline of the military. There was little or no need to develop a formal body of management thought under these nonindustrialized circumstances.

Three forces were interacting and combining to provide for a new age of industrialization. Characterized as ethics, or standards governing human conduct, they illustrate how economic, social, and political attitudes were changing during the cultural rebirth. The ethics discussed were in reality a struggle between the old traditional and the newly emerging society. The Protestant ethic was a challenge to the central authority of the church and a response to the needs of people for achievement in this world; the liberty ethic reflected the ancient struggle between monolithic and representative forms of government and sought to protect individual rights; and the market ethic was a gauntlet flung before the landed aristocracy who preferred mercantilism. The struggle represented here is an old one: the state versus the individual, human rights and due process versus whimsical autocracy, and centralization versus decentralization. The struggle goes on.

This cultural rebirth would establish the preconditions for industrialization and subsequently the need for a rational, formalized, systematic body of knowledge about how to manage. The emergence and refinement of the market economy required managers to become more creative and to be better informed about how best to manage an organization. Faced with a competitive, changing environment, the manager had to develop a body of knowledge about how best to utilize resources. People began thinking of individual gain and had to be accommodated in some rational managerial framework. The emergence of modern management had to be based on rational ways of making decisions; no longer could the organization be operated on the whims of a few. This change did not come suddenly but evolved over a long period of time as the culture changed. How these changes came about and how they affected the evolution of management thought is the subject of this book. It is an intriguing story.

3 The Industrial Revolution: Problems and Perspective

The Industrial Revolution heralded a new age for civilization. The cultural rebirth had created new social, economic, and political conditions ripe for advances in science and technology. Subsequent improvements in technology made possible large combinations of physical and human resources and ushered in the factory system to replace the domestic system of production. This chapter will examine the salient characteristics of the Industrial Revolution and the managerial problems it created, as well as attempt to achieve some perspective on the consequences of this cultural revolution.

THE INDUSTRIAL REVOLUTION IN GREAT BRITAIN

Industrial progress is always closely tied to advancements in science and technology. In the fifteenth century, Johannes Gutenberg (1400–1468) developed the first metallic movable type for a printing press and opened the door to an information revolution that continues today. While medieval scientists attempted to deduce physical laws from the writings of Plato, Aristotle, Saint Augustine, and the Bible, a new age of scientific inquiry began in the sixteenth and seventeenth centuries as church bonds loosened. This Age of Reason, this revolution in scientific thought, was the product of such individuals as Francis Bacon, Nicolaus Copernicus, Galileo, William Gilbert, William Harvey, Isaac Newton, and others. The scientific revolution emphasized the spirit of observation and inquiry and established the foundation for the technological revolution that was to follow.

Ever since humankind began to improve methods of tilling the soil, making weapons, and weaving cloth, there have been advancements in technology or the art and applied science of making and using tools and equipment. Technology has been evolving and advancing for thousands of years, but a revolution came in late-eighteenth-century

England that marked the beginning of an advance in technology more rapid than ever before. The essence of this revolution was the substitution of machine power for human, animal, wind, water, and other natural sources of power. Deane, in pinpointing the emergence of the Industrial Revolution, illustrated the difference between preindustrialized and industrialized societies. Preindustrial societies are characterized by low per capita income, economic stagnation, dependence on agriculture, a low degree of specialization of labor, and very little geographical integration of markets. Industrial societies are characterized by rising or high per capita income, economic growth, low dependence on agriculture, a high degree of specialization of labor, and a widespread geographical integration of markets.[1] Using these factors as indicators, Deane concluded that the shift in Great Britain from a preindustrial to an industrial nation became most evident in 1750 and accelerated thereafter.

THE STEAM ENGINE

In Chapter 2 we saw the two primary methods of production, the domestic system and the craft guilds. In both, the scale of production was small, the market limited, and the work was labor, rather than capital, intensive. Merchants put out materials to homes, where families spun, bleached, dyed, or performed whatever functions were necessary. Thus we find the ancient sources of family names for weavers, dyers, tailors, fullers, and so on. In craft shops, work was passed from one stage to another as, for example, tanners did their work, passed it along to curriers, and in turn came the shoemakers and the saddlers who turned the prepared leather into finished products. Labor was specialized, capital investment low, and the power source resided in humans, animals, and the forces of nature.

Great Britain's largest industry of this time was textiles. From the colonies came the cotton, wool, and other fibers to be cleaned, combed, spun, and so on into cloth. Mechanical improvements in the textile industry preceded the Industrial Revolution. John Kay began the mechanization of weaving with his flying shuttle in 1733; in 1765, James Hargreaves changed the position of the spinning wheel from vertical to horizontal, stacked the wheels on top of one another, and wove eight threads at once by turning them all with one pulley and belt. He called his gadget the spinning jenny (after his wife) and added more wheels and power until he could weave eighty threads at once. In 1769, Richard Arkwright developed a water frame that stretched the cotton fibers into a tighter, harder yarn. His factories grew with this innovation until by 1776 he employed five thousand workers.

Despite these mechanical improvements, the heart of the Industrial Revolution was really the steam engine. The steam engine was not new: Hero of Alexandria (ca. A.D. 200) had developed one for the sake of amusement; others had built models but had had mechanical problems. Thomas Newcomen had developed a steam-propelled engine to pump water out of coal mines that were flooding as deeper and deeper

---

1. Phyllis Deane, *The First Industrial Revolution* (London: Cambridge University Press, 1965), pp. 5–19.

shafts went down. It was the task of James Watt, trained as a maker of scientific instruments, to perfect the earlier work of others. Watt developed his first workable steam engine in 1765, but financing and moving from the prototype to an industrial installation took eleven years. During this time he formed a partnership with Matthew Boulton, a leading British ironmaster, to make steam engines. In 1776, Watt's first engine was sold to John Wilkinson for use in his ironworks. To set a price, an agreement was made that the steam engine would be rated at the equivalent of how many horses could do the same amount of work; hence the derivation of the word *horse-power* for mechanical engines.

James Watt. Courtesy of the History of Science Collections, University of Oklahoma Libraries.

Until 1782, however, Watt's engines were used only to pump water and blow air for blast furnaces to smelt metals. In 1781, Watt made his greatest technological break-through when he was able to transform the up-and-down motion of the drive beam into the rotary motion of an engine. This led to a host of new uses for steam power; for example, lifting coal and ore from mines, supplying power for breweries and oil mills, and eventually powering railway locomotives and steamships. In 1788, Watt patented a fly-ball governor, which adjusted the flow of steam to promote the uniform speed of the engine. This first cybernetic control device operated on a centrifugal principle: as the engine sped up, arms on a rotating shaft rose and the steam intake vents closed, reducing power intake; as the engine slowed, the arms dropped, allowing more power.

The historian Arnold Toynbee noted that two men, Adam Smith and James Watt, were the most responsible for destroying the old Britain, building a new one, and launching the world toward industrialization. Smith brought about the revolution in economic thought; Watt, the revolution in the use of steam power.[2] Harnessed to the wheels of a hundred industries, the steam engine provided more efficient and cheaper power, power for ships, trains, and factories, revolutionizing British commerce and industry. Steam power lowered production costs, lowered prices, and expanded markets. A spirit of innovation led to inventions, inventions led to factories, and factories led to a need for direction and organization. The expanded market called for more workers, more machines, and a larger production scale on a regular basis. Capital was needed to finance these larger undertakings, and the individuals who could command the capital began to bring together workers and machines under one common authority. Instead of being in their homes, for example, weavers were in a workplace with a steam engine to power their looms;

---

2. Arnold Toynbee, *The Industrial Revolution* (Boston: Beacon Press, 1956), p. 89. Originally published in 1884.

similarly, combers, bleachers, dyers, and so on found their efforts shifting from the home to the factory. As these workers came into the central workplace, there was a greater need for monitoring and coordinating their efforts. The factory system proceeded irregularly in various industries, but the new age of industrialization was evident. A new power source was perfected, a greater capital intensity was required, the need for directing and coordinating efforts was paramount, and the fledgling factory system toddled forth to create an abundance such as the world had never seen.

MANAGEMENT: THE FOURTH FACTOR OF PRODUCTION

Before the Industrial Revolution, economic theory focused on two factors of production, land and labor, and recognized capital as an input factor only as church bonds loosened. In addition to these, another began to evolve, the entrepreneur. Richard Cantillon, an Irishman who moved to Paris and made a fortune in currency speculation, appears to have been the first to use the word entrepreneur in an economic sense. His pre–Industrial Revolution *Essay on the Nature of Commerce,* published some years after his death, used the word "entrepreneur" very loosely.[3] "Entrepreneur" applied to anyone who bought or made a product at a certain cost to sell at an uncertain price. In Cantillon's description, it described the work of any self-employed persons such as farmers, water-carriers, brewers, hatmakers, chimney-sweeps, and so forth. As one authority has observed, Cantillon's entrepreneur

> May be a merchant or landowner but he equally may be a capitalist employing labour; in all cases, however, the entrepreneurial role remains distinctly that of someone making decisions under uncertainty.[4]

Cantillon's *Essay* influenced the idea of Francois Quesnay, leader of the Physiocrats, who recognized a farmer-entrepreneur, but held that manufacturing and commerce were sterile and unable to produce a surplus. Adam Smith recognized the entrepreneur as a factor, but treated the return or the surplus created as a return to capital. Writing after Adam Smith, Jean Baptiste Say (1767–1832) provided a more definitive explanation of the entrepreneurial role. According to Say, entrepreneurship

> Requires a combination of moral qualities that are not often found together. Judgment, perseverance, and a knowledge of the world as well as of business. [The entrepreneur] is called upon to estimate with tolerable accuracy the importance of the specific product, the probable amount of the demand, and the means of its production: at

---

3. Richard Cantillon, *Essai sur la Nature du Commerce au General,* ed. and trans. Henry Higgs (London: Macmillan & Co., 1931). Cantillon wrote this between 1730 and 1734; he died in 1734; and his book was published in 1755. In translation, Higgs took Cantillon's *entrepreneur* literally, that is, "undertaker."

4. Mark Blaug, *Great Economists before Keynes* (Cambridge: Cambridge University Press, 1986), p. 38.

one time he must employ a great number of hands; at another, buy or order the raw material, collect laborers, find consumers, and give at all times a rigid attention to order and economy; in a word, he must possess the art of superintendence and administration.[5]

Say noted that some entrepreneurs owned the undertaking but more frequently than not they owned only a share, having borrowed from others or having formed a partnership. The entrepreneur thus became a manager for others and assumed an additional risk in combining the factors of land, labor, and capital. For assuming the added risk in combining the traditional three factors of production, the entrepreneur became a fourth factor of production and received a separate reward for managing in addition to a return on the personal capital invested. (A point that Adam Smith failed to see.) As the organization grew, the entrepreneur alone could not direct and control all activities, and it became necessary to delegate some activities to a level of submanagers. These submanagers were the first nonowning, salaried managers who had the responsibility of making decisions within a broader framework of policies established by the entrepreneur. As the entrepreneur expanded the organization and took on an increasing number of lower-level managers, many problems were to arise in the process of delegation.

MANAGEMENT PROBLEMS IN THE EARLY FACTORY

The emerging factory system posed management problems different from those ever encountered before. The church could organize and manage its properties because of dogma and the devotion of the faithful; the military could control large numbers of personnel through a rigid hierarchy of discipline and authority; and governmental bureaucracies could operate without having to meet competition or show a profit. The managers in the new factory system could not resort to any of these devices to ensure the proper utilization of resources.

The Industrial Revolution spawned a number of industries, and the early 1800s were characterized by the growth of these firms in an increasingly competitive environment. For the firm, the pressure for growth came from the need for economies of scale to compete more effectively. Some advocated resisting the pressures for growth; for example, a report of the Committee on Woollen Manufacturers of 1806 stated that the development of large factories would not lead to many advantages for the entrepreneur. By continuing the domestic system, the entrepreneur could save much capital investment and would not need to "submit to the constant trouble and

---

5. Jean Baptiste Say, *A Treatise on Political Economy,* 2 vols., trans. C.R. Princep (Boston: Wells and Lilly, 1821), vol. 2, p. 72. Originally published as *Traite d'Economie Politique,* 2 vols. (Paris: chez Deterville, 1803). Princep translated *entrepreneur* as "master-agent" or "adventurer"; as neither is very descriptive, the French term has been Anglicized.

solicitude of watching over a numerous body of workmen."[6] Competition still demanded growth, but the retarding factor was the lack of a pool of trained managers who could cope with large-scale factory problems. Hence the size of the early firm was often limited by the number of people the entrepreneur could supervise personally. The result was a dual line of advance for the factory system: on the one hand, technology and capital made a larger scale of production possible and forces of competition made a larger size imperative; on the other hand, the enlargement of operations created a myriad of managerial problems.

THE LABOR PROBLEM

Once an entrepreneur decided to embark on a venture, capital had to be raised to buy the power source, machinery, buildings, tools, and so forth. None of this could become a reality until workers were employed to operate the machinery and perform the necessary duties. Developing a workforce, however, was not an easy task. Broadly conceived, the labor problem had three aspects: recruitment, training, and motivation. The existing labor force consisted largely of unskilled agrarian workers, and the shift from a small workshop, a farm, or a family-operated operation was a drastic one for these people. They had to pull up roots from a long-familiar milieu and go to the brawling, bustling city for employment. Andrew Ure and others complained that factory work was uncongenial to the typical workers, who were accustomed to the domestic or agrarian life and did not look kindly on the monotony of factory jobs, the year-round regularization of hours, and the constant demands of attention to their work. Workers tended to be restless, shiftless, and deviant. The firm of Roebuck and Garrett, for example, moved their factory from Birmingham, England, to Scotland because they found the Scots were more reliable and obedient.[7] A contemporary observer described early textile weavers as fiercely independent and generally insubordinate. For the most part, they were Puritans and were as opposed to factory regimen and the managerial hierarchy of authority as they were to the Church of England.[8]

The transition from the farm to the factory was eased for some workers, however, by the prospects of a steadier job and wage incentives. Agrarian workers were accustomed to a subsistence living derived from the vagaries of the soil and the seasons. Studies of labor mobility in Great Britain during the period of industrial growth showed that workers were moving toward the north and west where the factories were primarily located. This demonstrated a "sensitivity of labor to wage incentives," as the workers now had the opportunity to improve their standard of

---

6. Sidney Pollard, *The Genesis of Modern Management: A Study of the Industrial Revolution in Great Britain* (Cambridge, Mass: Harvard University Press, 1965), p. 11.

7. *Ibid.*, p. 161.

8. Richard Guest, *A Compendious History of the Cotton Manufacture* (Manchester, England: Joseph Pratt, 1823), pp. 40–43.

life.[9] Of course, not all workers responded to the cash stimulus, preferring their agrarian or craft pursuits.

Particularly vexing to employers, however, was the shortage of skilled labor. Some skilled labor did exist in small, scattered guilds and workshops, but these workers were more resistant to factory life. The Woolcombers Guild, for example, resisted mechanization and factory work, preferring their guild tradition. In the midlands of England, the center of the textile industry, wool combers were in such short supply that this advertisement appeared: "To Woolcombers. Wm. Toplis and Co. have opened a free shop, at Mansfield ... for Combers from any part of the Kingdom. The prices given are equal to any society [i.e. guild] and good steady workmen may make very handsome wages."[10] Employers also had to offer all sorts of inducements to skilled workers and had to make major concessions to keep them on the job. The loss of key workers could shut down an entire factory. James Watt had pressing problems with finding workers who could cut and fit the valves and cylinders to the proper tolerances; indeed, many of his early failures were of execution, not design. Arkwright kept his skilled people working extra hours because they were so scarce. Many iron mills kept their furnaces going even in slack times in order to keep from losing their labor force. Employers used every possible medium to advertise for workers, and one authority reported that children and paupers were employed only after other sources of labor were absorbed.[11] In brief, it was difficult to recruit a workforce that had the necessary skills. Labor mobility was enhanced by wage incentives, but traditions bound some to their trades and others to their agrarian life.

Training

The second major problem was that of training. Once the personnel were recruited, they had to be taught the new skills of an industrial life. Literacy was uncommon, and basic educational skills were lacking; drawings, instruction sheets, and procedures for machine operation demanded some ability to read, to figure, and to respond with predictable results. Training was conducted largely by oral instruction, demonstration, and trial and error. The new employee learned from someone else, usually a coworker, how to operate a machine or process a piece of material. Standardized methods were unheard of, and workers blithely followed the precepts of someone else who knew little more than they. The shortage of skilled workers, such as machinists, millwrights, and instrument makers, was a serious problem. An even more serious problem, however, came in the form of the new skills needed in the factory, because no previous jobs had required exactly these same skills.

---

9. R. M. Hartwell, "Business Management in England during the Period of Early Industrialization: Inducements and Obstacles," in C. J. Kennedy, ed., *Papers of the Sixteenth Business History Conference* (Lincoln, Nebr.: 1969), p. 66.

10. Cited in Stanley D. Chapman, *The Early Factory Masters: The Transition to the Factory System in the Midlands Textile Industry* (New York: Augustus M. Kelley, 1967), p. 192.

11. *Ibid.,* p. 168.

Transferring the workers' existing skills to new situations meant problems of training as well as resistance to the new methods. The traditional prejudices against anything new added to management's discomfort. Finally, workers were not accustomed to abiding by the accuracy and tolerances demanded by the technique of interchangeable parts on which many factories were based. Even the relatively crude measuring tools required instruction for use. The workers, accustomed to individualizing their work, resisted the standardization of parts, methods, and tools required by the interchangeable-parts method of production.

The haphazard acquisition of knowledge from coworkers or inept supervisors, the lack of standard methods of work, and worker resistance to new methods posed serious problems for efficient factory operation. Employers resorted to developing their own schools to teach elementary arithmetic and geometry and other skills needed in the factory and not available in the populace. Jobs were specialized because of the ease of teaching them to the workers. The goal was not only efficiency, but also solving the practical problems of finding and training personnel. In short, industrialization required an educated workforce, something sorely lacking in the early days of the Industrial Revolution. Jobs were limited in scope to ease the training problems, and employers sought to provide opportunities to develop employees' skills.

Discipline and Motivation

The third problem, and by no means the least considerable, was that of discipline and motivation. Accustomed to the craft traditions of independence and the agrarian mores of self-sufficiency, workers had to develop habits of industry, such as punctuality, regular attendance, the acceptance of a new regime of supervision, and the mechanical pacing of work effort. Instead of supervising by the traditional aspects of artisanry and the hallowed master-servant relationship, the factory substituted a different discipline: it demanded regularity rather than spurts of work, and accuracy and standardization rather than individuality in design and methods. Apparently the new habits did not come easily: worker attendance was irregular; feast days, which were common traditions in the domestic system, caused large-scale absenteeism for factory operators; and workers tended to work in spurts by laboring long hours, collecting their money, and then disappearing for countless days of dissipation. As one observer commented, "If a person can get sufficient [income] in four days to support himself for seven days, he will keep holiday the other three; that is, he will live in riot and debauchery."[12] Some workers took a weekly holiday they called Saint Monday, which meant either not working or working very slowly at the beginning of the week. To combat the problem of feast days, some early employers resorted to using the traditional holidays for company-sponsored outings and feasts to build company loyalty, break the monotony of the work year, and cement personal relations. For example, Arkwright held a feast for

---

12. J. Powell, *A View of Real Grievances* (1772), quoted in Asa Briggs, ed., *How They Lived*, vol. 3 (Oxford: Basil Blackwell, 1969), p. 184.

five hundred employees at his Cromford mill in 1776, and Matthew Boulton hosted seven hundred at his Soho plant.

Machine smashing, although sporadic, was another disciplinary problem. However, much of this behavior antedated the perfection of the steam engine and the growth of large factories. In 1753, John Kay's flying shuttle and other inventions were smashed and his home destroyed by workers protesting the introduction of this laborsaving machinery. James Hargreaves suffered a similar fate at his Blackburn mill in 1768. Operators of the old hand spinners were convinced that the new jenny would put them out of work, so they raided Hargreaves's house and smashed his machines. The machine-breaking era peaked in 1811–1812, and the movement gained a label for the machine smashers, the Luddites, which originated because a youth in Ludlam had smashed his knitting frame when his father had been too harsh with him.

The Luddite movement never had a unified purpose nor a single leader. Scattered groups did the smashing, each proclaiming they were following orders from their fictitious general, "Ned Ludd." The name "Luddite" was first used in 1811, when a rash of machine breaking occurred, primarily in the hosiery-knitting trade around Nottingham. However, these protests appeared to be based on grounds other than fear of unemployment resulting from technological advancement. In Nottingham wages were falling, unemployment was rampant, and food prices were rising owing to the government's policy on food imports. Machine smashing was a convenient way to demonstrate dissatisfaction, although it was other latent forces, not technology, that caused the problem.[13] Disciplinary efforts against the Luddites were rather draconian. One Luddite, named Mellor, assassinated a mill owner, and he and his followers were hanged in York (1812). Public fears of further violence led to more hangings of Luddites (Nottinghamshire, Lancaster, and Chester), and the movement soon died for lack of leadership.

Efforts to motivate people fell into three categories and, on close inspection, appear to have changed only in application, not theory, up to the present day. Positive inducements (the carrot), negative sanctions (the stick), and efforts to build a new factory ethos became the methods for providing motivation and discipline. The carrot was the opportunity to earn more money through wage incentives; thus the employee's pay was based on output or performance. This notion of wage incentives represented a major break with tradition. Economists of the seventeenth and eighteenth centuries of the mercantilist school of economics believed that income and the supply of labor offered were negatively related, that is, as wages rose, workers would choose to go spend their money, returning only after it had been spent and more was needed. This viewpoint may be illustrated in the conclusion of a wool merchant who worked under the domestic system:

---

13. Malcolm I. Thomis, *The Luddites: Machine Breaking in Regency England* (Hamden, Conn.: Archer Books, 1970).

> It is a fact well known ... that scarcity, to a certain degree, promotes industry ... a reduction of wages in the woolen manufacture would be a national blessing and advantage, and no real injury to the poor. By this means we might keep our trade, uphold our rents, and reform the people in the bargain.[14]

This pre–Industrial Revolution point of view that the hungriest worker was the best worker justified keeping wages low to ensure an abundant, motivated workforce. In contrast were the writings of Adam Smith:

> The wages of labour are the encouragement of industry, which, like every other human quality, improves in proportion to the encouragement it receives.... When wages are high, accordingly, we shall always find the workmen more active, diligent, and expeditious than where they are low.... Some workmen, indeed when they can earn in four days what will maintain them through the week, will be idle the other three. This, however, is by no means the case with the greater part. Workmen, on the contrary, when they are liberally paid by the piece, are very apt to over-work themselves, and to ruin their health and constitution in a few years.... If masters [employers] would always listen to the dictates of reason and humanity, they have frequent occasion rather to moderate, than to animate the [work] of many of their workmen.[15]

With an appeal to moderation in application, the classical economics of Adam Smith disagreed with the tradition that the worker must be kept at the subsistence level and that the best worker was the hungriest one. Rather, Adam Smith held that monetary incentives brought out the best in people and that they would work harder to get more. Often called the "economic man" assumption, this break with mercantilistic theory brought the opportunity for individual rewards based on initiative.

The factory system continued the domestic system practice of payment based on output. Wage incentives were used more widely in operations that were labor intensive, that is, where the cost of labor was a large part of total cost and where payment could be tied to individual performance. For example, almost one-half the British cotton-mill workers were on piece rates, as were workers in Boulton and Watt's engine works, but in coal mining, which emphasized teamwork, group piecework plans were tried but were generally ineffective.[16] Performance standards, however, were based on the historically average times for the jobs rather than on a careful study of the jobs themselves and the time that task completion should take.

14. J. Smith, *Memoirs of Wool* (1747), quoted in Briggs, p. 213.

15. Adam Smith, *The Wealth of Nations* (1776), vol. 1, bk. I, ch. 8, p. 100.

16. E. Brian Peach and Daniel A. Wren, "Pay for Performance from Antiquity to the 1950's," *Journal of Organizational Behavior Management* 12, no. 1 (1992), p. 12.

The stick, negative sanctions, was a practice for which the early industrial system is frequently criticized. Corporal punishment, especially of children, was used, though authors disagree on its frequency and severity. The prevailing attitude toward children, even in respectable homes, was that they should be seen and not heard and that to spare the rod was to spoil the child. In the context of the period, employers treated children as they were accustomed to being treated at home,[17] although that does not condone the treatment.

Graduated fines were more common methods of discipline: one plant fined workers thirty cents for being absent Monday morning and seventy cents for singing, swearing, or being drunk.[18] Since wages often amounted to two or three dollars a week, this was a fairly large portion of a worker's pay. Samuel Oldknow, considered one of the most progressive employers of the period, posted the following rule:

> That when any person, either Man, Woman or Child, is heard to CURSE or SWEAR, the same shall forfeit One Shilling—And when any Hand is absent from Work (unless unavoidably detained by sickness, or Leave being first obtained), the same shall forfeit as many Hours of Work as have been lost; and if by the Job or Piece, after the Rate of 2 [shillings] 6 [pence] per Day—Such Forfeitures to be put into a Box, and distributed to the Sick and Necessitous, at the discretion of their Employer.[19]

The third method of motivation was a general concept oriented toward creating a new factory ethos. The goal was to use religious morals and values to create the proper attitudes toward work. The encouragement of moral education, even on company time and in early company towns, reading of the Good Book, regular attendance at church, and exhortations to avoid the deadly sins of laziness, sloth, and avarice were methods of inculcating in the working population the right habits of industry. A coalition of employers and ministers exhorted the populace to guard against the moral depravities, which were not only sinful, but led to a lackadaisical, dissipated workforce. The Quaker Lead Company, for example, punished workers for "tippling [drinking], fighting, and night rambling."[20] Doubtless this moral suasion emanated from more than a concern for the soul of the worker. Pollard presented a succinct statement of these attempts to create a new ethos: "The drive to raise the level of respectability and morality among the working classes was not undertaken for their own sake, but primarily ... as an aspect of building up a new factory discipline."[21]

---

17. Chapman, *Early Factory Masters,* p. 203.

18. Pollard, *Genesis of Modern Management,* p. 187.

19. The rule was posted December 1, 1797, and is reprinted in B. W. Clapp, ed., *Documents in English Economic History,* vol. 1 (London: G. Bell and Sons, Ltd., 1976), p. 387. Capitalization is from the original.

20. Pollard, *Genesis of Modern Management,* p. 193.

21. *Ibid.,* p. 197.

THE SEARCH FOR MANAGERIAL TALENT

In addition to the problems of finding, training, and motivating workers, there was also a problem finding qualified managers. As organizations grew, the ability of an owner-manager to supervise the employees was diminished, and an intermediate level of supervision appeared. Judging from early literature, the salaried managers, that is, those in the layer of management below entrepreneur, were usually illiterate workers promoted from the ranks because they evidenced a greater degree of technical skills or had the ability to keep discipline. Typically they were paid only a little more than the other workers and more often than not were attracted to the managerial position because it gave them the power to hire their spouses and children to work in the factory. Untrained in the intricacies of managing, the managers were left on their own to develop a leadership style. Problems were met and solved on an ad hoc basis, and only a few managers could learn from the experiences of others in solving factory problems or handling people. The general view of leadership was that success or failure to produce results depended on the character of the leader, on personal traits and idiosyncrasies, and not on any generalized concepts of leadership. Other sources of management talent provided little enlightenment. Entrepreneurs frequently used relatives in managerial positions, presumably based on the assumption that they were more trustworthy or would act to preserve their potential inheritance. This practice also provided training that would help secure ownership and keep control in the family for the next generation. Another source of talent was the countinghouse; entrepreneurs recruited likely-looking bank clerks and tellers, thinking they probably had both business and financial acumen. On-the-job experience was relied on to furnish recruits with the necessary knowledge for managing.

The transformation of Great Britain from an agrarian to an industrial society meant that there was no managerial class, or, in modern terms, no group of professional managers. First, there was no common body of knowledge about how to manage. The training of managers supplemented experience on the job with instruction in techniques of production, sources and characteristics of materials, operations of machines, trade practices, and the legal obligations of the firm. This training was oriented toward a specific industry, cotton, woolen, mining, or whatever, and did not lend itself readily to generalization. A manager, trained in one industry, was bound to that industry; to move to another the manager would need to learn new skills. Second, there was no common code of management behavior, no universal set of expectations about how a manager should act. Codes were developed for specific industries and gave advice about the manager's responsibility for safety, the security of the plant and equipment, design standards for engineering, and procedures to follow in safeguarding the owner's interests.

James Montgomery of Glasgow, Scotland, prepared what were most probably the first management texts.[22] Montgomery's managerial advice was largely technical

---

22. James Montgomery, *The Carding and Spinning Masters' Assistant; or the Theory and Practice of Cotton Spinning* (Glasgow: J. Niven, Jr., 1832); idem, *The Cotton Spinner's Manual* (Glasgow: J. Niven, Jr., 1835). Montgomery's contributions are discussed and portions of the 1832 work are reproduced in James P. Baughman, ed., "James Montgomery on Factory Management, 1832," *Business History Review* 42, no. 2 (Summer 1968), pp. 219–226.

in nature; he advised how to discern quality and quantity of work, how to adjust and repair machinery, how to keep costs down, and how to "avoid unnecessary severity" in disciplining subordinates. He noted that a manager must be "just and impartial—firm and decisive—always on the alert to prevent rather than check faults after they have taken place...."[23] This latter comment on controlling was perceptive, and indicated an early understanding that the control function is essentially looking forward rather than backward. However, Montgomery's advice was for the cotton industry and, like most other early writers, he did not seek to develop any generalized principles of management.

Montgomery was so highly regarded as a manager that he was brought to the United States in 1836 to become superintendent of the York Mills in Saco, Maine. This gave Montgomery the opportunity to conduct what was probably the first comparative study of management through the analysis of different economies. He found that the United States had higher costs of production, paid higher wages (including wages for women), but had lower costs of materials. British firms had lower costs, paid lower wages, but paid more for raw materials. The relative competitive efficiency resided in Great Britain, in Montgomery's opinion, because the British firms were better managed.[24] Montgomery's study was of cotton mills only, but it gives some idea of the differing states of managerial knowledge in the United States and Great Britain in 1840.

Early managerial salaries left much to be desired. The first-line supervisors, or overlookers, were paid little more than the workers. Often the white-collar salaried managers were paid on the basis of their social class rather than on the extent of their responsibility. By 1800, however, Pollard noted that the shortage of talent had forced payment based on the job and not the person.[25] By 1830, the salaries of nonowner managers had risen rapidly and compressed the differential between their pay and that of the owner managers. By the mid-nineteenth century, John Stuart Mill observed that those who managed others had to possess a higher "intelligence factor," that is, "something acquired through education, both formal and informal and on the job learning."[26] Those who were superintendents of others faced many nonroutine obligations dealing with complex problems, justifying their higher salaries. Mill disagreed with Adam Smith's concern about the separation of ownership and management. The "zeal" of hired managers could be stimulated by connecting "their pecuniary interest with the interest of their employers, by giving them part of their remuneration in the form of a percentage of the profits."[27] In history we find the seeds of incentives for nonowning salaried managers to tie their efforts more closely to the performance of the firm.

---

23. Baughman, quoting Montgomery, in "James Montgomery on Factory Management, 1832," p. 226.

24. James Montgomery, *The Cotton Manufacture of the United States of America Contrasted and Compared with That of Great Britain* (London: John N. Van, 1840), p. 138.

25. Pollard, *Genesis of Modern Management*, p. 139.

26. P. Bruce Buchan, "John Stuart Mill—Contributions to the Principles of Management: The Intelligence Factor," *British Journal of Management* 4 (1993), p. 71.

27. John Stuart Mill, quoted in Buchan, p. 73.

In Great Britain, but not in France or Italy, the status of the entrepreneur was rising, inducing many young people to seek their fortunes in commerce, or at least to become a junior partner in a large firm. The second- and third-generation offspring of the founder-entrepreneur changed their style to give more status to the salaried managers. They tended to delegate more to and depended more on the salaried managers. Perhaps their affluence, built by the success of preceding generations, made them less desirous of becoming personally involved in daily activities; or perhaps the firms had grown to such a size and the fund of managerial talent had reached such a point that finding reliable subordinates was easier than it had been for their predecessors. In the early factory, the problems of finding and developing managerial talent were acute. There were no business schools for recruiting and no systematic programs for developing people into managers, and managerial skill was judged a localized, idiosyncratic matter.

MANAGEMENT FUNCTIONS IN THE EARLY FACTORY

In addition to the difficulties of staffing the factory, the task of acquiring competent submanagers, and the avoidance of the Luddites, early managers faced planning, organizing, and controlling problems similar to those faced by managers today. In planning operations, the early factory required more farsightedness than the domestic system. As the factory system developed, the new industrialist became more rational, more pragmatically interested in laying a foundation for long-term growth rather than short-term speculative gains. Early mines required long-range planning to develop the veins, and early factories required costly equipment. As capital was sunk, business managers had to be more rational and more aware of the long-term implications of their decisions. Examples of planning in industry are few, and those that do exist are largely technically oriented rather than comprehensive in company scope and application. Robert Owen and Richard Arkwright led the way in preplanning factory layout. Their requirements, or principles, emphasized the orderliness of the work flow and factory cleanliness.

Factory technology demanded the planning of power sources and connections, the arrangement of machinery and space for a smooth flow-through of work, and the reduction of confusion through bins and well-placed stores of materials. The firm of Boulton and Watt also stressed factory layout and developed detailed systems for controlling stocks of materials and parts. They engaged in rudimentary work study for production planning, work flow, and assembly methods at their Soho factory (the engine works).[28] The use of standardized, interchangeable parts made planning necessary, both in design and execution of the assembly. James Watt, Jr., saw

---

28. Erich Roll, *An Early Experiment in Industrial Organization: Being a History of the Firm of Boulton and Watt*, 1775–1805 (London: Longmans, Green and Co., 1930). The development of relatively advanced managerial techniques at Boulton and Watt is credited to the founders' sons, Matthew Robinson Boulton and James Watt, Jr. (p. xv).

at an early stage that standard parts would lessen the tasks of controlling work and that detailed planning and proper initial execution would ensure that the final product would meet specifications. Standard parts also eased repairs for the customer and reduced both the company's and the customer's inventory of spare parts, thus simplifying the stock control system.

In organizing, managers were limited to a large extent by the caliber of the subordinate managers. Early departmentation, or the grouping of activities, was often based on the number of partners or relatives. With a gesture toward egalitarianism, each one became a department head with one or two salaried managers below to supervise the workers. It has been estimated that in 1820 in the cotton industry there was an average of one first-line supervisor for every twenty-eight workers.[29] Similar ratios were apparent in mining, construction, and other textile firms, suggesting that the organizations were relatively flat, with few levels of management. These small firms were typically family owned and managed, staff personnel were little more than clerks, and the firms were rarely fully integrated; for example, a cotton mill spun cloth, but relied on other firms or agents to finish the process and sell the merchandise.

There is evidence in the textile industry that technology played an important role in how activities and relationships were structured in the emerging factory system.[30] In the beginning, most workshops followed a batch processing technology; that is, there were relatively short runs of manufacturing a quantity of like products at the same time, followed by another batch of slightly different products, and so on. This description seems to characterize the textile industry until the early 1800s.

As new applications of steam power were made, another technology emerged as more efficient. The new strategy was to arrange the power-driven machines in a line sequence to flow toward completion of the product. This flow technology resembled more the mass production assembly line, with an output of large quantities of standardized products made at a lower per unit cost and intended for a mass market. With this increase in production quantity, it became more economical to specialize labor even further, adding each person's efforts to the flow of work. It was not a moving assembly line as we know it today, but the product was moved from one stage of production to another by carts, workers, chutes, and so on. Departments were established for the various operations necessary to the product flow. With more departments came the need for another level of management to coordinate the work as it flowed from one stage to another. The consequence was scalar organizational growth, creating a taller hierarchy of management and more elaborate procedures and systems so efforts could be integrated. It appears that early textile firms discovered long ago that technology affects the organizational structure. Early batch production methods allowed more informality; however, the application of steam-driven power led to a new factory technology, which required more formality in organizational design.

---

29. Pollard, *Genesis of Modern Management*, p. 135.

30. Stanley D. Chapman, "The Textile Factory before Arkwright: A Typology of Factory Development," *Business History Review* 48, no. 4 (Winter 1974), pp. 468–473.

In controlling performance, entrepreneurs faced numerous problems. Needing to delegate authority to cope with larger enterprises since they could no longer personally oversee all operations, they found that the shortage of trained and trusted submanagers posed problems of accountability. As Adam Smith had observed, it was a rare salaried manager who would exercise the same vigilance over other people's money as over his or her own. Accounting knowledge had not advanced since Pacioli, and its use as an aid to managers was an almost unheard-of phenomenon. Books were kept to account for earnings, wages, material, and sales, but few managers used these accounts as an aid to decision making. Josiah Wedgwood, manufacturer of various pottery products, was one of those few, and he refined his accounts until he was able to use them in setting prices, fixing worker piece rates, determining the percentage of selling expenses to sales, and tracing the embezzlement of certain funds by his head clerk.[31] Unfortunately, it would be more than a century later before better costing techniques were developed.

Through trial-and-error experience, early entrepreneurs attempted to cope with the problems of managing a factory and a workforce. The emphasis on technical rather than managerial problems was probably due to the crude state of the technological art and the pressure to keep abreast of competition and to make the new gadgets work. Management was deemed a localized matter, not subject to generalization, and success was thought to depend on the personal qualities of the managers, not on their grasp of broader principles of management. Management was a personal art, not a discipline; pragmatic, not theoretical; and parochial, not universal.

Some individuals were attempting to fill this void in management knowledge, and their efforts are the subject of Chapter 4. Before turning to them, let us try to gain some perspective on the cultural impact of the Industrial Revolution.

CULTURAL CONSEQUENCES OF THE INDUSTRIAL REVOLUTION

The revolution was not only technological but cultural. The new machines, the new factories, and the new cities shook people's tradition-based roots and demanded participation in a new era. In the hearts of many there is an idealization of the agrarian life before industrialization. Critics have charged that capitalism, together with its offspring—the market and factory systems—robbed people of a golden age of equality and freedom. More specifically, the criticisms have been that people were enslaved to the owners of capital, that they became little more than a commodity in the marketplace of life, that capitalists exploited child and female labor, and that industrialization created poverty, urbanization, pollution, and a host of other societal ills. Let us examine some of these criticisms and attempt to gain a perspective on the cultural consequences of this new age of industrialization and capitalism.

---

31. Neil McKendrick, "Josiah Wedgwood and Cost Accounting in the Industrial Revolution," *Economic History Review*, 2nd ser., 23 (April 1970), pp. 45–67.

THE CONDITION OF THE WORKER

Economics earned its sobriquet, the dismal science, during the early nineteenth century. Thomas Malthus set out to disprove the optimism of Adam Smith and liberal economics with his famous population argument. Malthus postulated that population increases in geometric proportion while the food supply at best increases only arithmetically. The population is limited by the means of subsistence and the masses tend to reproduce beyond these means, preventing any improvement in their condition. Government relief of the poor only encourages a population increase, food prices go up, and the poor are no better off. The only answer for Malthus (he was not very optimistic about the outcome) was to restrict the supply of labor and to encourage self-restraint in the reproduction of the masses. His was a hopeless view of people as no more than commodities in the marketplace of life, basically powerless to overcome their disadvantage.

David Ricardo did not appear much more optimistic; his "iron law of wages" said that in the long run real wages would tend to stabilize at some minimum level that would provide the worker with just enough means to subsist. The Utopian socialists, such as Robert Owen, saw people as powerless in their environment and wanted to replace the individualism of the market with a communal life. The Utopians did not write of the necessity of revolt but felt they could achieve change through their writings and by example. An opposite view was developed by Karl Marx and Friedrich Engels, who advocated the need for force as the midwife of history. Because people were powerless in their view, and because they were kept at the subsistence level by the exploitation of the factory masters, they had to unite to break their chains. Although the writings of Marx and Engels were more political essays than economic analyses, they did reflect the economists' dismal view of the world at that time.

Were people powerless and exploited to the poverty level by capitalism? The subsistence level for the masses was not new; they had spent the previous thousand or more years in essentially the same status but as agrarian peasants tied to a feudal landlord. Under mercantilism, the British government regulated wages to keep them low in order to maintain a favorable balance of trade, and, as we saw earlier, it was a common belief that low wages provided an incentive to work. The Industrial Revolution did not create poverty; it inherited it. With Adam Smith came the new market-based philosophy that high wages made people more diligent. The rise of capitalism was creating the means for releasing people from drudgery through laborsaving machines, making people more productive and better paid for less exertion of effort.[32] Furthermore, it is difficult to agree with Marx and Engels that the workers were exploited by the factory owners for basically two reasons: first, the severe shortage of labor would have diminished the managers' power to do as they liked with their labor; and second, workers' real wages were steadily rising from 1790

---

32. Friedrich A. Hayek, "History and Politics," in F. A. Hayek, ed., *Capitalism and the Historians* (Chicago: University of Chicago Press, 1954), pp. 15–16.

to 1830 and the workers' lot was improving "well above the level of mere subsistence."[33] For those who were willing to enter the factory and learn its new skills, the new machines and methods made them more productive and raised wages; in turn, added industrial efficiency reduced the prices of goods and raised real wages. The increasing use of incentive payment plans held out a promise of economic betterment for people; no longer tied to remitting a tithe to the feudal lord, workers could, through effort, enhance their own well-being.

Working conditions and the need for time thrift have also been cited by critics as examples of how the agrarian golden life was lost. Hopkins, however, studied a heavily industrialized region of England and concluded "that there was no marked deterioration of working conditions ... [and to suggest that] the majority of workers ... were forced to become the slaves of a new time discipline is really a very doubtful proposition, and its unthinking repetition can serve only to perpetuate a historical myth."[34] Any claims of worker exploitation should be considered as being of doubtful validity; through incentives, rising real wages, steady employment, and regular hours, workers were improving their lot when compared with their previous subsistence levels.

CHILD AND FEMALE LABOR

Child and female labor were not inventions of the Industrial Revolution. The domestic system and agricultural life required the participation of all and were built on the family as the basic economic unit. One authority noted that child labor was at its worst in the domestic system long before the factory system.[35] Child and female workers were found primarily in the textile industry, where the technology was simple, and rarely in other industries. Employers would have preferred a mature, stable, adult workforce, but these individuals were scarce and hard to attract. Concern in Great Britain over child labor practices led to two famous parliamentary investigations: the first in 1819 at the behest of Robert Owen, and chaired by Sir Robert Peel, himself an extensive employer of children in his factories, and the second by the Sadler Committee of 1832. Extensive and detailed evidence was given before these committees.[36] Children often began working a twelve-hour day (including meals) at age five, and occasionally spent a fourteen-hour day at the factory. This practice was widespread, being found in the cotton, wool, flax, and silk mills, and existing legislation concerning child labor provided

---

33. T. S. Ashton, "The Standard of Life of the Workers in England: 1790–1830," in Hayek, *Capitalism*, p. 158.

34. Eric Hopkins, "Working Hours and Conditions during the Industrial Revolution: A Re-Appraisal," *Economic History Review* 35 (February 1982), pp. 63, 66.

35. R. Whatley Cooke Taylor, *Introduction to a History of the Factory System* (London: Richard Bentley & Sons, 1886), p. 402.

36. For some excerpts, see E. Royston Pike, "Hard Times," *Human Documents of the Industrial Revolution* (New York: Praeger Publishers, 1966), especially pp. 100–218.

no enforcement mechanism. In their testimony, witnesses described the hours (long), wages (low), working conditions (often extremely poor), and the methods of discipline (often harsh). Overall, however, there is evidence that "the Industrial Revolution [did] not increase exploitation [but] gradually improved the situation of children.... Industrialization, far from being the source of the enslavement of children, was the source of their liberation."[37] Industrialization created more jobs and better jobs; as workers' wages and their real wages rose, child labor declined.

Female workers were attracted to the factory for the wages to build a dowry, for the opportunity of finding a husband, or to supplement the family income. One observer, Mantoux, felt that the entrepreneurs were "tyrannical, hard, sometimes cruel, their passions and greeds were those of upstarts. They had the reputation of being heavy drinkers and of having little regard for the honour of their female employees."[38] Mantoux was guilty of overgeneralization; ample examples can be given, such as Josiah Wedgwood, Matthew Boulton, James Watt, John Wilkinson, Robert Owen, and a host of others, for whom there is no evidence of loose and fancy-free behavior toward their female employees.[39] Only one specific case was cited in parliamentary testimony, and the tenor of the critics' position was that of the "temptations and opportunities" presented by the presence of both males and females in the same workshop.[40] Evidently, if the workers had been segregated by gender, no testimony would have appeared at all. In contrast with the traditional norm of paying what was "suitable" for women's work, Burnette found that, during the Industrial Revolution, "Women seem to have been paid market wages, and the assertion that women were paid customary [i.e., traditional] wages needs to be revised."[41] There was also great concern that unemployed females would be forced by circumstances to prostitution, but a Doctor Hawkins presented evidence for Manchester that of the fifty prostitutes who had been apprehended in the previous four years (1829–1833), only eight came from the factories, while twenty-nine came from the ranks of former household servants.[42]

Evidence concerning child and female labor is contradictory; most testimony hints at the moral degradation of factory life, but the hard statistics are lacking. It appears that emotional and religious overtones were given more credence, isolated

---

37. Clark Nardinelli, "Were Children Exploited during the Industrial Revolution?" in P. J. Uselding, ed., *Research in Economic History,* vol. 11 (1988), p. 268.

38. Paul J. Mantoux, *The Industrial Revolution in the Eighteenth Century,* trans. Marjorie Vernon (New York: Macmillan Co., 1928), p. 397.

39. See W. O. Henderson, *J. C. Fischer and His Diary of Industrial England 1814–1851* (New York: Augustus M. Kelley, 1966), p. 57. Undoubtedly some of these individuals existed, as they do in all ages, but Fischer maintained that they were not representative of the era.

40. Pike, "Hard Times," p. 285, with the lurid title of "Seduction in the Mills."

41. Joyce Burnette, "An Investigation of the Female-Male Wage Gap during the Industrial Revolution in Britain," *Economic History Review* 50 (1997) p. 278.

42. Pike, "Hard Times," p. 297.

instances were ballooned, and no thorough studies compared the past with the conditions at that time. As textile technology advanced and as income rose, child labor decreased dramatically before the passage of legislation regarding the employment of children.[43] What the critics have overlooked is the fact that capitalism was slowly but surely allowing the release of children from the workforce. As better machines were developed to perform the simple jobs, it became uneconomical to employ children. It was an economic force—broadening capitalism—not legislative fiat nor a moral rebirth that freed children from the looms.[44] As for legislation and governmental bodies, it was the Poor Law Authorities, a government office, that sent the paupers into the factories! The paupers were poor or deserted children legally in the care of the state; to relieve the state of the burdens of maintenance, they were sent to whomever would accept their care and feeding.

To understand the critics of the factory system, it is necessary to consider the Victorian value system that was in operation. The Victorian period began before Queen Victoria ascended the throne in 1837.[45] The Victorian values of a profound social conscience about employing women and children and a formal adherence to strict standards of personal and social morality began forming around 1800. Economic and social conditions had been worse before the Industrial Revolution, but the Victorian value sets of people like Charles Dickens established the rationale for criticizing the emerging factory system.

There is evidence that the factory system led to a general rise in the standard of living (something lacking in the previous thousand years), to falling urban death rates and decreasing infant mortality. These factors led to a population explosion in Great Britain: its inhabitants increased from six million in 1750 to nine million in 1800 and to twelve million in 1820. Further, infant mortality before the age of five fell from 74.5 percent in 1730–1749 to 31.8 percent in 1810–1829. The absence of significant medical advances during the period suggests the conclusion that people were better able to feed, clothe, and care for themselves.[46] Heilbroner pointed out that factory life, even with urban poverty, represented an improvement over life in an agrarian and domestic system. Poverty was not new; it had just been collected in one place, the city, and made more easily visible to the legislators, intellectuals, and others. Isolated and scattered, agrarian poverty did not shock the sensibilities, but next door and down the street, it became a problem. Heilbroner further answered

---

43. Clark Nardinelli, "Child Labor and the Factory Acts," *Journal of Economic History* 40 (December 1980), pp. 739–755.

44. W. H. Hutt, "The Factory System of the Early Nineteenth Century," in Hayek, *Capitalism*, p. 184.

45. John W. Osbourne, *The Silent Revolution: The Industrial Revolution in England as a Source of Cultural Change* (New York: Charles Scribner's Sons, 1970), pp. ix–xi.

46. Margaret C. Buer, *Health, Wealth and Population in the Early Days of the Industrial Revolution, 1760–1815* (London: George E. Routledge & Sons, 1926), p. 30. Cited by Robert Hessen, "The Effects of the Industrial Revolution on Women and Children," in Ayn Rand, *Capitalism: The Unknown Ideal* (New York: American Library, 1966), p. 104.

the critics of the Industrial Revolution in saying that the criticism was based on political and not economic unrest. Great Britain of that period was characterized by a surging interest in rights and justice and in political reform; the populace had "a critical temper of mind before which any economic system would have suffered censure."[47] This criticism was directed at the entrepreneurs, not because they were to blame, but because they were a convenient symbol of change.

One cannot tax capitalism with the unsavory conditions and practices of the Industrial Revolution. The factory system inherited child and female labor, poverty, and long working hours from the past, it did not create them; the new age of industrial capitalism was creating through the factory a method for people to gain leverage for a better life.

SUMMARY

The Industrial Revolution created a new cultural environment and a revised set of problems for management. People's needs were becoming more complex as they sought to adjust to life in the city and to factory life. Organizations were being reshaped by the demands for heavy infusions of capital, by the division of labor, and by the need for economical, predictable performance. Organizations needed to innovate and compete in a market economy; this created pressures for growth and the economies to be obtained from large-scale production and distribution. Economic theory recognized that the entrepreneur-manager performed a distinct role in combining the traditional three factors of production in the ever-growing factory system. With size came the need for managers, the need for a capable, disciplined, trained, motivated workforce, and the need for rationalizing the planning, organizing, and controlling of operations in the early enterprise. The next chapter examines some early management pioneers who proposed solutions for coping with the growing factory system.

---

47. Robert L. Heilbroner, *The Making of Economic Society* (Englewood Cliffs, N.J.: Prentice-Hall, 1962), pp. 85–86.

4 Management Pioneers in the Early Factory

A prevailing theme so far has been the relationship of management thought to its cultural environment. The factory system posed new problems for owners, managers, and society at large. This chapter focuses on four individuals who pioneered in proposing solutions to the manifold pressures of coping with the earliest industrial organizations. History leaves a notoriously scanty scent. Records and memorabilia are lost or destroyed, notable ideas may never be committed to writing, and judgments must be made on perhaps a small part of what actually occurred. Of the early management pioneers, history has provided us with the best records for four men: Robert Owen, Charles Babbage, Andrew Ure, and Charles Dupin.

ROBERT OWEN: THE SEARCH FOR A NEW HARMONY

Robert Owen (1771–1858) was a paradox in the turbulent era of the Industrial Revolution. A successful entrepreneur himself, he attempted to halt the surge of industrialism and the evils he saw in it as he called for a new moral order based on a social reorganization. He had a vision of a new industrial society that was to be a combination of agricultural and industrial commune and harkened back to the lost days of more primitive people. Philosophically, he viewed people as powerless, held in the grips of revolutionary forces of the new age of machinery, which destroyed moral purpose and social solidarity. His struggle was a long and frustrating one, and he appears in history as a King Canute ordering the waves of progress to recede.

EARLY MANAGERIAL EXPERIENCES

A self-made man imbued with the self-confidence that typified the early entrepreneurs, Owen, at the age of eighteen, founded his first factory in Manchester, England, during an

Robert Owen, portrait by Mary Ann Knight. Courtesy of the Picture Library, National Galleries of Scotland.

age of war prosperity when many were getting rich. There was a great impetus in cotton trade, and the new water frame, the weaving machines of Arkwright and Crompton, and the power sources of Watt made large factories feasible. Owen described his introduction to managing: "I looked very wisely at the men in their different departments, although I really knew nothing. But by intensely observing everything, I maintained order and regularity throughout the establishment, which proceeded under the circumstances far better than I had anticipated."[1] Owen's firm was profitable, but he decided to become a salaried manager and sold his equipment to a Mr. Drinkwater and became employed by him. Still with a modicum of experience, he applied himself to the new position:

> I looked grave, inspected everything very minutely ... I was in with the first [workers] in the morning, and I locked up the premises at night. I continued this silent inspection and superintendence day by day for six weeks, saying merely yes or no to the questions ... I did not give one direct order about anything. But at the end of that time I felt myself so much master of my position as to be ready to give directions in every department.[2]

Owen, left on his own by Drinkwater, made a success of the mill. He rearranged the equipment, bettered the conditions of the workers, and achieved a great deal of influence over his subordinates. He later attributed his success with the workers to his "habits of exactness" and his knowledge of human nature. He left Drinkwater in 1794 or 1795 to establish a new partnership, the New Lanark, Scotland, venture. At New Lanark, he encountered the ubiquitous problem of scarcity of labor and noted, "It was most difficult to induce any sober, well-doing family to leave their home to go into cotton mills as then conducted."[3] Perhaps this difficulty in attracting labor influenced his personnel policies and he began forming his visions of a new society. At New Lanark, he employed between four hundred and five hundred parish apprentices, the pauper children furnished by the Poor Law Authorities to whomever would take them. The children worked thirteen hours per day including an hour and a quarter off for meals. Owen continued to employ children but tried to improve their living and working conditions even though he could not persuade his

---

1. Robert Owen, *The Life of Robert Owen* (London: Effingham Wilson, 1857; reissued by Augustus M. Kelley, 1967), pp. 31–32.

2. *Ibid.*, p. 39.

3. *Ibid.*, p. 79.

partners to accept all his reforms. His reform efforts aimed to reshape the whole village of New Lanark, including the streets, houses, sanitation, and educational system.

At New Lanark, Owen began to form some new ideas about the welfare of society. Industrial progress, he felt, was not adequate to support the growing population. He prepared a report to the citizens of Lanark County that began with "manual labor, properly directed, is the source of all wealth and national prosperity." The economic and social problem was to develop agriculture to use more intensive methods of cultivation to feed more people. He therefore prepared a plan:

1. To cultivate the soil with a spade instead of the plough.
2. To make such changes as the spade cultivation requires, to render it easy and profitable to individuals, and beneficial to the country.
3. To adopt a standard of value, by means of which, the exchange of the products of labour may proceed without check or limit, until wealth shall become abundant, that any further increase to it will be useless, and will not be desired.[4]

Owen's spade husbandry plan of 1821 would create jobs, enabling more people to be employed, thereby increasing their ability to consume the products of industry. This plan of creating more arduous, menial jobs flew in the face of the mechanical progress that was being made at that time. It was a preface, however, to his plans that would lead to his formula for a communal society.

At New Lanark, Owen faced the same disciplinary problems faced by other manufacturers. Like others who had attempted to create a new factory ethos, he tried to use moral suasion rather than corporal punishment. He developed one particularly unique device, the silent monitor, to aid discipline. Under this system, Owen awarded four types of marks to his superintendents, and they in turn rated their subordinates. These marks were translated into color codes of black, blue, yellow, and white in ascending order of merit. A block of wood was mounted on each machine and the four sides painted according to the code. At the end of each day, the marks were recorded, translated, and the appropriate color side of the block turned to face the aisle. Owen reported that he "passed daily through all the rooms and the workers observed me always to look at these telegraphs—when black I merely looked at the person and then at the colour."[5] This wooden albatross motivated laggards to overcome their deficiency and supposedly induced the white block good guys to maintain theirs. It was most certainly a precursor of modern management's public posting of sales and production data to instill departmental pride or to encourage competition.

---

4. Robert Owen, Report to the County of Lanark of a Plan for Relieving Public Distress (Glasgow: Wardlaw and Cunninghame, 1821), p. 131.

5. Owen, *The Life of Robert Owen,* p.80. The electric telegraph of Samuel Morse had not been invented; Owen used "telegraph" to mean viewing a record of performance from a distance.

THE CALL FOR REFORM

Predating Mayo, Roethlisberger, Likert, and others who have urged concern for the human resource asset of the firm, Owen set forth his rationale for a new philosophy:

> You will find that from the commencement of my management I viewed the population [the labor force] … as a system composed of many parts, and which it was my duty and interest so to combine, as that every hand, as well as every spring, lever, and wheel, should effectually cooperate to produce the greatest pecuniary gain to the proprietors. … Experience has also shown you the difference of the results between a mechanism which is neat, clean, well-arranged, and always in a high state of repair; and that which is allowed to be dirty, in disorder, without the means of preventing unnecessary friction, and which therefore becomes, and works, much out of repair … If, then, due care as to the state of your inanimate machines can produce such beneficial results, what may not be expected if you devote equal attention to your vital machines [the human resource], which are far more wonderfully constructed?[6]

Owen chided his fellow manufacturers for not understanding the human element. He charged that they would spend thousands on the best machines, yet buy the cheapest labor. They would spend time improving machines, specializing labor, and cutting costs, yet make no investment in the human resource. He appealed to their pecuniary instincts, claiming that money spent on improving labor "would return you, not five, ten, or fifteen per cent for your capital so expended, but often fifty, and in many cases a hundred per cent."[7] He claimed a 50 percent return at New Lanark, and said it would shortly reach 100 percent. He claimed that it was more profitable to show such concern for people and that it also served to relieve the "accumulation of human misery."

Accounting records from the New Lanark venture indicate that Owen's estimates of return on investment and profits were only slightly exaggerated. At New Lanark, the partners each took 5 percent of their investment as a return to capital, and then prorated the share of each partners' profits based on their investment. During Owen's involvement at New Lanark (1799–1828), his approximate share of gross profits was £128,500 (British pounds sterling) plus 5 percent of his £130,000 capital (£6,500 per year). His annual return on investment typically exceeded 15 percent, and, from 1811 to 1814, some 46 percent.[8]

---

6. *Ibid.*, app. B, p. 260.

7. *Ibid.*, p. 261.

8. John Butt, "Robert Owen as a Businessman," in *Robert Owen, Prince of Cotton Spinners*, ed. John Butt (Bristol: David & Charles, 1971), pp. 199–201, 211–13.

Owen's venture at New Lanark was profitable, but at least one person doubted whether this was due to his personnel policies. One biographer noted that profits in the cotton-spinning industry at that time were so large, averaging 20 percent or more on capital invested, that any personnel policy could have been profitable. "In fact the margin of profit was so wide that we need scarcely look for any other explanation of Owen's success as a manufacturer."[9] Whatever the reasons for his own success, Owen deplored the commercialism of life. He declared an intellectual war on capitalism and also attacked the church because it condoned the evils of the new industrial age. These views branded him as a radical and made it more difficult for him to persuade others of the need for reform. Owen felt that the crucial error of all established religions was the preaching of the doctrine of human responsibility. He held that humans were creatures of their environment, relatively incapable of escaping it without a moral rearmament through education. Contrary to the church view that good character was promoted by the promise of rewards and punishment, especially in the hereafter, Owen felt that character developed solely if the material and moral environment was proper. To these ends, he became more active politically in about 1813 and proposed a factory bill to prohibit the employment of any child under the age of ten and to limit work to ten hours per day with no night work for children. His proposal was too radical for other manufacturers and politicians of that time. After many political intrigues, the bill became law in 1819, but instead of applying to all factories, it applied only to cotton mills and set the age limit at nine and not ten.

A biographer suggested that, frustrated in his attempts to reform society, Owen became slightly mad in 1817.[10] Failing to achieve his goals in Great Britain, he read an ad in the *London Times* that offered for sale some thirty thousand acres in Posey County, Indiana, in the United States of America. The sellers were a religious society, the Harmonians, followers of George Rapp; the asking price was £30,000 and the land was situated along the Wabash River. In the decade or so that the Harmonians had been there, some two thousand acres had been cleared for vineyards, orchards, and gardens; a sawmill, machine shops, and cotton and woolen mills had been erected; and numerous brick and log dwellings had been completed.

Owen acquired the property, renamed it New Harmony, and set out to achieve his social reforms. The primary goal of Owen's new moral society was to provide for the happiness of its members. A new currency would be created based on the labor credits, there would be no division of labor, everyone would receive a general education, and while people would be trained for jobs, they would be able to work in other jobs as they wished. Freedom of speech was guaranteed, and women were guaranteed the same rights and privileges as men. Owen promised to give the property to the community.

News of New Harmony spread quickly, and by the time it opened, 800 people were ready to move onto the property formerly occupied by 700 Harmonians.

---

9. Frank Podmore, *Robert Owen, a Biography* (New York: Appleton, 1924), p. 642.

10. G. D. H. Cole, *The Life of Robert Owen*, 3rd ed. (Hamden, Conn.: Archon Books, 1966), p. 197.

While the quantity of people that came to live in New Harmony was a problem, the greatest difficulty arose from the quality of the settlers. There were a few dedicated people who were aware of Owen's beliefs and took them as their own, but there were also those who had heard that New Harmony was a place where you could work a little, or not at all, and the society would still feed, clothe, and house you. For a few months the excitement of the new adventure kept everyone's morale high, but steadily the excitement and newness began to wear off. For lack of brewers, the brewery was idle. Because there were no millers, the grain mill was not in use. With only a few dozen farmers, the task of feeding a population swollen to nearly one thousand was a difficult one. While the communal society was by no means ready to collapse, its problems seriously lowered the general morale. Owen assumed the position of governor, and many felt that in reassuming his previous position of complete authority, he was abandoning his promise to turn all property over to the community. Owen tried to reorganize the society, but gave up, leaving in 1827.[11]

After New Harmony, Owen found himself both financially and emotionally broken. Owen had thought that what he had learned and applied in his cotton mills could be applied to the whole society, but he was unable to persuade others that his new moral order was realistic and not Utopian. As a reformer, Owen devised laws for relief of the poor and proposed solutions to unemployment problems. He proposed Villages of Cooperation, like New Harmony, which would have a communal sharing of surplus and be based on agriculture. He fought against the Malthusian doctrine of overpopulation, saying that if all shared, none would hunger. He deplored the evils of the division of labor; in his ideal system, each person would do a number of different jobs, switching easily from one to another. For him, it was the evils of the wage system and capitalism that maintained life at a subsistence level. In 1834, Owen led the British Trade Union movement, a working-class movement based on the idea of collective action to control the means of production. He failed. Nevertheless, Robert Owen, a Utopian socialist, sowed the first seeds of concern for the human element in industry.

CHARLES BABBAGE: THE IRASCIBLE GENIUS

To call Charles Babbage (1792–1871) an irascible genius is to pay him the greatest compliment, for he fitted both qualities and emerged as a significant figure in management thought well before Frederick W. Taylor. Largely technique oriented like his contemporaries, Babbage, through his application of technological aids to human effort, earned a place in history as the patron saint of operations research and management science. He theorized and applied a scientific approach to management long before the scientific management era began in the United States. Born in Devonshire,

---

11. More detailed accounts of the New Harmony experiment may be found in Podmore, *Robert Owen*, ch. 13; and George B. Lockwood, *The New Harmony Movement* (New York: Appleton, 1905), pp. 59–68.

England, the son of a wealthy banker, Babbage used his inheritance in a lifelong quest "into the causes of all those little things and events which astonish the childish mind."[12] He remarked that his first question after receiving a new toy was invariably, "Mamma, what is inside of it?" and he also invariably broke open the toy if the answer did not appear satisfactory. The value of his work was recognized by few of his contemporaries, and he was generally considered a crackpot by his neighbors. His personal traits were not endearing to those who disturbed his cogitations. In retaliation against the ubiquitous English organ-grinders, he blew bugles and created a commotion outside his house to scare them away. One contemporary, perhaps a neighbor, wrote, "He spoke as if he hated mankind in general, Englishmen in particular, and the English Government and organ grinders most of all."[13]

THE FIRST COMPUTER

Babbage's scientific output was phenomenal. He demonstrated the world's first practical mechanical calculator, his difference engine, in 1822. Ninety-one years later its basic principles were being employed in Burroughs's accounting machines. Babbage had governmental support in his work on the difference engine, but his irascibility cost him the support of government bureaucrats for his analytical engine, a versatile computer that would follow instructions automatically. As early as 1833, he conceived his analytical engine that could, in effect, scan a stream of instructions and put them into operation. Touring textile mills in France, he saw looms weaving very complicated patterns from instructions cut into cards. A silk weaver, Joseph Marie Jacquard, had developed punched cards strung together to make a chain and to fall at the appropriate time with a hole signaling the loom to lift a thread and become part of the design, or a blank that stopped a thread. The Jacquard loom anticipated the binary zero/one, off/on system of George Boole's algebra that formed the principle for modern computer operations. Babbage borrowed Jacquard's concept, but demonstrated foresight in his use of punch cards for the storage of information as well as the guidance of machine operations. Half a century later, Herman Hollerith invented the earliest practical punched-card tabulating machine, probably building on the ideas of Jacquard and Babbage.

In concept, Babbage's computer had all the basic elements of a more modern version. It had a store (or memory device), a mill (or arithmetic unit), a punch-card input system, external memory storage, and conditional transfer.[14] In retrospect, "Babbage's genius was not in the calculating power of his engine but in the

---

12. Charles Babbage, *Passages from the Life of a Philosopher* (London: Longman Green, 1864), p. 7.

13. "The Cranky Grandfather of the Computer," *Fortune,* March 1964, pp. 112–113. See also an excellent biography by Maboth Moseley, *Irascible Genius: A Life of Charles Babbage, Inventor* (London: Hutchinson & Co. Publishers, 1964).

14. In computer terminology, conditional transfer refers to the "if" statement: that is, instructing the computer "if such and such occurs, follow this path; if not, proceed in the normal sequence of control."

mechanization of the organizing and logical control of the arithmetic function."[15] Babbage also conceived an "apparatus for printing on paper, one, or if required, two copies of the results" of the output—a Victorian version of a modern printer.[16] Babbage was so fascinated with designing his Analytical Engine that he never built one. One design would suggest an improvement, then another, and another because he could never stop short of perfection. Shortly before his death in 1871 he wrote: "If I survive some few years longer, the Analytical Engine will exist, and its works will afterwards be spread over the world."[17] For more than a century his work would lie dormant, awaiting other times and other people to advance his seminal ideas.

One of the few bright spots in Babbage's life was his friendship with Augusta Ada (1816–1852), countess of Lovelace and daughter of the poet Lord Byron. The countess had a gift for mathematics and engineering and was one of the few who really understood Babbage's work. She wrote treatises on his work, expressed his ideas better than he could, and wrote programs for the computer. She warned people against becoming dependent on the computer, which "has no pretentions [sic] whatever to originate anything … [and would] do whatever we know how to order it to perform."[18] Together with Babbage, she developed a surefire system for betting on horses; unfortunately, the horses did not follow the system and the countess had to pawn her jewels. Undaunted by the countess's loss of the family jewels (though the count of Lovelace was upset), Babbage continued his work and developed for his computer gaming programs that were a forerunner of modern business gaming techniques. He limited his research to developing a computer program to play tick-tacktoe and chess, but he saw that the machine (he called it an automaton) could be programmed to make the best possible combinations of positions and moves, including anticipation as far as three moves in advance. Development of this automaton to play chess and ticktacktoe certainly must have brought him to the fringe of probability theory in programming for player positions and decision alternatives.

ANALYZING INDUSTRIAL OPERATIONS

Inevitably, Babbage's inquisitive mind and wide interests led him to write of management. His most successful book was *On the Economy of Machinery and Manufactures,* published in 1832. Babbage became interested in manufacturing and management as a result of his problems supervising construction of his own engine, and he visited a wide variety of British and French factories. He described in great detail the tools and machines, discussed the "economical principles of manufacturing," and,

---

15. Daniel A. Wren, "A Calculating Genius," *Knowledge Management* 2 (May 1999), p. 104.

16. Details of Babbage's printing apparatus are provided in Harry W. Buxton, *Memoir of the Life and Labours of the Late Charles Babbage, Esq. F.R.S.,* ed. Anthony Hyman (Cambridge, Mass: The MIT Press, 1988), p. 182.

17. Babbage, *Passages from the Life of a Philosopher,* p. 449.

18. Margot Strickland, *The Byron Women* (London: Peter Owen Ltd., 1974), pp. 206–207.

in the true spirit of inquiry for an operations researcher, analyzed operations, the kinds of skills involved, and the expense of each process and suggested directions for improving the then-current practices.[19]

As a management scientist, Babbage was interested in machinery, tools, the efficient use of power, developing counting machines to check quantity of work, and economy in the use of raw materials; these he called the mechanical principles of manufacturing. He developed a "method of observing manufactories," which was closely akin to a scientific, systematic approach to the study of operations. The observer prepared a list of questions about the materials used, normal waste, expenses, tools, prices, the final market, workers, their wages, skill required, length of work cycle, and so on. In essence it was the same procedure that an operations analyst or a consultant would use in approaching an assignment. Babbage emphasized the difference between "making" products (which could be done in small workshops) and "manufacturing," operating on a larger scale which necessitated the careful arrangement of the "whole system of [the] factory" to reduce the cost of production. In this early concept of economies of scale, Babbage also recognized that a competitive market called for "ingenuity," innovation and improvement, if a firm was to remain viable.

On the human side, he recalled the Luddite movement and pleaded with workers to recognize that the factory system worked for their betterment: "It is of great importance that the more intelligent amongst the class of workmen should examine the correctness of these views; because ... the whole class may ... be led by designing persons to pursue a course, which ... is in reality at variance with their own best interests."[20]

His attempts to show the mutuality of interests between the worker and the factory owner were somewhat similar to what Frederick Taylor said seventy-five years later. According to Babbage:

> the prosperity and success of the master manufacturer is essential to the welfare of the workman ... whilst it is perfectly true that workmen, as a class, derive advantage from the prosperity of their employers, I do not think that each individual partakes of that advantage exactly in proportion to the extent to which he contributes to it ... it would be of great importance, if ... the mode of payment could be so arranged, that every person employed should derive advantage from the success of the whole; and that the profits of each individual should advance, as the factory itself produced profit, without the necessity of making any change in wages.[21]

---

19. Charles Babbage, *On the Economy of Machinery and Manufactures* (London: Charles Knight, 1832), pp. 94–96. It should be noted that Babbage's discussion of expenses has the appearance of an early form of cost accounting. However, it differed from modern cost accounting in that it described costs rather than providing for an analysis of what costs ought to be, as under a standard cost system.

20. *Ibid.,* p. 192.

21. Babbage, *On the Economy of Machinery and Manufactures,* 3rd ed. (1833), p. 253.

Babbage's profit-sharing scheme had two facets: that a portion of wages would depend on factory profits; and that the worker "should derive more advantage from applying any improvement he might discover," that is, a bonus for suggestions. Workers would receive a fixed salary based on the nature of their task plus a share in the profits, and the suggestion system would use a committee to determine the proper bonus for production savings. Babbage saw a number of advantages in his proposal: (1) each worker would have a direct interest in the firm's prosperity; (2) each would be stimulated to prevent waste and mismanagement; (3) every department would be improved; and (4) "it would be the common interest of all to admit [hire] only the most respectable and skillful [workers]." In effect, the work group, operating under a profit-sharing plan, would act to screen out undesirables who would reduce its share. Finally, Babbage saw his scheme as removing the necessity for combinations of workers, since their interests would be the same as those of the employers. With this mutuality of interests between worker and manager, neither would oppress the other and all would prosper.

Beyond his significant scientific contributions, Charles Babbage made significant advancements in understanding the problems of the emerging factory system. His analytic, scientific approach to the study of manufacturing, his recognition of the need for new incentives to enlist the cooperation of the worker, and his search for new harmonies between manager and worker placed him as a person of vision in management.

ANDREW URE: PIONEERING IN MANAGEMENT EDUCATION

It was the task of Andrew Ure (1778–1857) to provide academic training for fledgling managers in the early factory system. Ure studied at Edinburgh and Glasgow universities, receiving his M.D. from the latter in 1801. In 1804, Ure became professor of chemistry and natural philosophy at Anderson's College in Glasgow, where he was to remain until 1839. Dr. John Anderson, the founder of the college, had lectured on science and through his will founded an institution to educate adult workers in science.[22] Educational pressures for technically trained white-collar workers and managers soon shifted the composition of Ure's classes from workers to clerks, warehouse workers, artisans, and shopkeepers; from these classes managers for the ever-growing factory system were to be recruited. Ure knew the French engineer and

---

22. We know relatively little about Dr. John Anderson. At the University of Glasgow, Anderson gave James Watt a model of Thomas Newcomen's engine to repair. Watt recognized the deficiencies and began to work on the ideas that led to his engine. Anderson also had Andrew Ure as a student at the University of Glasgow, and hired him to teach when Anderson started his college for working people, which was the beginning of Britain's mechanics institutes.

management writer Charles Dupin, and when Dupin visited Great Britain in 1816–1818, Ure escorted him around the Glasgow factories. Dupin commented that many of the managers of these factories were Ure's own students. This fact was acknowledged by Ure, who said that his students were "spread over the [United] Kingdom as proprietors and managers of factories."[23] Dupin's work was influenced by Ure, and, in turn, as suggested later, influenced Henri Fayol, another pioneer whose ideas helped lead to modern management theory.

PRINCIPLES OF MANUFACTURING

Ure, deeply concerned with industrial education, set out to prepare for publication a systematic account of the principles and processes of manufacturing. The essential principle of the factory system was the substitution of "mechanical science for hand skill … [and to provide] for the graduation of labor among artisans."[24] Although Ure devoted a large portion of his book to the technical problems of manufacturing in the silk, cotton, woolen, and flax industries, he eventually dealt with the problems of managing. Obviously pro-management in his analysis, Ure sought an automatic plan to prevent individual intractable workers from stopping work as they pleased and thereby throwing a whole factory into disorder. According to Ure, workers had to recognize the benefits of mechanization and not resist its introduction. To establish this automatic plan, management had to "arrange and connect" manufactures to achieve a harmony of the whole. In every establishment there were "three principles of action, or three organic systems: the mechanical, the moral and the commercial."[25]

Although these formed no clear-cut notions of organizing work, Ure did seek to place them in the harmony of a "self-governing agency." "Mechanical" referred to the techniques and processes of production; "moral" to the condition of personnel; and "commercial" to sustaining the organization through selling and financing. The mechanical part of manufactures was treated extensively by the scientist Ure; the moral aspect brought out the pro-management side of the educator. The factory system of Ure's day was under attack from a number of sources, and Ure set out to defend industrial practices. He argued that factory operatives were better treated "as to personal comforts" than artisans or other workers in nonindustrial establishments. They ate better, enjoyed more leisurely labor because of the machines provided by the factory owner, and were better paid. Instead of appreciating this largess, factory workers engaged in strikes, sabotaged equipment, and caused capital losses for their employers, thus working against their own continued employment. Rebutting the investigations into child labor, Ure noted that most of the witnesses

---

23. Andrew Ure, *The Philosophy of Manufactures: Or an Exposition of the Scientific, Moral and Commercial Economy of the Factory System of Great Britain* (London: Charles Knight, 1835), p. viii.

24. *Ibid.,* p. 20.

25. *Ibid.,* p. 55.

had never visited the factories; he also engaged in some character assassination, charging that one witness was an atheist, one a tavern keeper, and one an assaulter of women. For positive evidence, Ure noted that children lived in well-kept cottages, received both practical and religious education, and were better fed and enjoyed better health than children in the general community. Children employed in agriculture were paid half the factory wages and kept in ignorance. Citing medical investigations sponsored by the Factory Commission, Ure concluded that the incidence of disease, the dietary habits, and the general state of health of all factory workers were better than in the general population.

To illustrate worker nonappreciation of employers' concern for their health, Ure cited an instance in which large ventilating fans had been installed in one factory to reduce the foulness of the air. Instead of thanking the employer, the workers complained that the fresh air had increased their appetites and therefore they were entitled to a corresponding wage increase! The factory owner reached a compromise with his workers by running the fan only half the day, thereafter hearing no more complaints about foul air or appetites. In terms of the evidence presented in Chapter 3, Ure was probably more right than wrong concerning the condition of labor. He was a defender of the factory system, seeing more benefits accruing to society than disadvantages.

Ure based his conclusions on an 1833 survey of cotton mills in England, primarily those in the Lancashire district, the heart of the textile industry.[26] The survey covered 1,070 mills owned by 157 firms of all sizes, ranging from nineteen to 1,692 employees. Of these one thousand plus mills, 332 were still using water to power their looms, some fifty plus years after the Industrial Revolution was triggered by the steam engine. The estimated amount of capital needed for 12,000 throstles and 24,000 mule spinning machines, plus building, land and other equipment was £47,134. Capital intensity was increasing due to the cost of steam power and the mule spinner of Samuel Crompton. Female employees exceeded the number of males (51.6 to 49.4 percent); adults, those age eighteen and above, comprised 59 percent of the work force, with those under age eighteen forming 41 percent.

Ure drew some comparisons of the cotton industry with the year 1804, and found that the average work week had declined from seventy-four to sixty-nine hours; the average annual wage had increased from sixty to sixty-five shillings in 1833; and the purchasing power (real wages) of the sixty-five shillings was greater in 1833 than the sixty in 1804. For example, in 1804 sixty shillings would buy 117 pounds of flour and 62.5 pounds of meat; in 1833 sixty-five shillings would buy 267 pounds of flour and 85 pounds of meat. From these data, Ure formed his conclusions about the progress in the cotton industry compared with agricultural workers who were still laboring at subsistence income levels. Child and female labor were widely used in the cotton mills, but no more than previously in the domestic system or in agriculture. Rising

---

26. Andrew Ure, *The Cotton Manufactures of Great Britain*, 2 vols. (London: Charles Knight, 1836), vol. 1, pp. 334–42. For a map of the Lancashire Cotton District, see Michael Huberman, *Escape from the Market: Negotiating Work in Lancashire* (Cambridge: Cambridge University Press, 1996), p. 4.

real wages, a trend toward shorter and more regular hours, and advancing mechanization were the hallmarks of Ure's cotton industry study. Ure's focus on the cotton industry precluded any generalization about management, but saw progress in the advance of mechanization and the condition of labor.

CHARLES DUPIN: INDUSTRIAL EDUCATION IN FRANCE

A second individual who pioneered in industrial education was the French engineer Baron Charles Dupin (1784–1873). As noted earlier, Dupin had visited Great Britain (1816–1818) and observed the results Andrew Ure was obtaining in preparing individuals for factory management. In 1819, Dupin was named professor of mathematics and economics at the Conservatory of Arts and Professions in Paris.[27] He must have immediately initiated his own curriculum, for in 1831 he wrote, "For twelve years I have had the honor of teaching geometry and mechanics applied to the arts, in favor of the industrial class ... on the most important questions to the well-being, education, and morality of the workers, to the progress of national industry, to the development of all means of prosperity that work can produce for the splendor and happiness of our country."[28] One of Dupin's colleagues at the conservatory was Jean Baptiste Say, a professor of industrial economy. Say was the person who brought Adam Smith's ideas to France and added to them by identifying management as a fourth factor of production. Since Say and Dupin taught the evening classes "beginning at 8:30 P.M. to artisans and working mechanics [who] have completed the labours of the day," it is reasonable to assume that both Say and Ure influenced Dupin's view of management.[29] Dupin's contribution lay in the influence he had on the course of industrial education and perhaps, though there is no direct historical support, on the later work of Henri Fayol. Fayol is generally credited with being the first to distinguish between technical and managerial skills and the possibility and necessity of teaching management. Yet examine this passage from Dupin, eight decades or so earlier:

> It is to the director of workshops and factories that it is suitable to make, by means of geometry and applied mechanics, *a special study* of all the ways to economize the efforts of workers. ... For a man to be a director of others, manual work has only a secondary importance; it is his intellectual ability (*force intellectuelle*) that must put him in the top position,

---

27. *La Grande Encyclopaedie*, vol. 15, p. 81.

28. Charles Dupin, *Discours sur le Sort des Ouvriers* [*Discourse on the Condition of the Workers*] (Paris: Bachelier Librairie, 1831), p. 1.

29. "The Conservatory of Arts," *American Mechanics Magazine* 1 (July 2, 1825) p. 343.

and it is in instruction such as that of the Conservatory of the Arts and Professions, that he must develop it.[30]

The special study would be the classes Say, Dupin, and Ure were teaching, and Dupin clearly distinguished this type of program from manual or technical instruction. Fayol, himself educated as an engineer in France, could possibly have read Dupin and gleaned his own notions of teaching management.

Hoaglund reported that by 1826, Dupin's materials on management had been presented in ninety-eight French cities to five thousand or more workers and supervisors.[31] Since his *Discours* was not published until 1831, the number of people he influenced must be greatly expanded. Dupin also demonstrated a rudimentary grasp of the concept of time study and the need to balance work loads after labor was divided: "When [the] division of work is put into operation the most scrupulous attention must be exercised to calculate the duration of each type of operation, in order to proportion the work to the particular number of workers that are assigned to it."[32] He wrote of the need for clear, concise instructions to workers, for producing the desired level of work with the least expenditure of worker energy, and for studying each type of industry in order to find and publish the best results of industrial practice.

The *Discours* was not so much an examination of management as it was an exhortation to remove industrial strife. Dupin also recognized worker uneasiness over the introduction of mechanization into French industry, discussed the work of James Watt, and encouraged workers and managers to recognize the benefits of mechanization to them and to society. Regarding the dangers of technological displacement, he noted that before Watt's engine, British industry employed fewer than one million workers; by 1830, over three million were employed in industry and combined with machinery were equivalent to the power of seven million workers. For Dupin this was ample proof that mechanization created jobs rather than destroyed them. Evidently the French had their Luddites and Dupin indicated that such resistance to mechanization was futile. As a solution, he called for widespread industrial training to permit the agrarian and unskilled worker to share in the prosperity of industrialization: "He who perfects the machines tends to give them the advantage over the worker; he who perfects the worker, gives him the same fighting chance, and makes the machine serve his well-being, instead of having to suffer from their competition. Let us concern ourselves with man involved with the difficulties of the work and of the industry."[33] These were insights applicable not only to early

---

30. *Ibid.,* pp. 12–13. Emphasis added. (Author's translation.)

31. John H. Hoaglund, "Management before Frederick Taylor," *Proceedings of the Academy of Management,* ed. Billy Goetz, December 1955, pp. 15–24.

32. Charles Dupin, *Geometrie et Mechanique des Arts et Metiers et des Beaux Arts* (Paris: Bachelier, 1826). Cited and translated by Hoaglund, "Frederick Taylor," p. 30.

33. Dupin, *Discours,* p. 9.

nineteenth-century France but also to the world of the twentieth and the twenty-first centuries.

THE PIONEERS: A FINAL NOTE

The four pioneers discussed here were formulating the seeds of a management discipline. But, at their best, these were sparse and rudimentary. What prevented the formalization of a body of management thought during this early stage rather than some three-quarters of a century later? Why did Frederick Taylor, and not Charles Babbage, receive credit for founding scientific management? In retrospect, the reasons are manifold. First, early writings emphasized the techniques and not managing per se. In an age of expanding technology, it was difficult for early writers to separate the managerial function from the technical and commercial aspects of running a firm. Management was more concerned with finance, production processes, selling, and acquiring labor, all of which were indeed critical at the time, rather than with developing principles or generalizations about management. An analogy might be that of young children learning to walk: the motor urge is so great and consumes so much of their energy and attention that the development of speech is retarded. As the skill of walking is perfected, speech develops. The early entrepreneurs were just learning to walk in the new factory system; the technical and human problems consumed so much of their time that they had little left over for articulating generalizations about management.

Second, the period was dominated by the technical genius, the inventor-pioneer, and the owner-founder. Success or failure was more likely to be attributed to their individual characteristics rather than to any generalized ideas about what skills managers needed. Each industry and its problems were considered unique, and hence the principles derived by one entrepreneur were not considered applicable to different situations. Finally, the state of the art of disseminating knowledge must be considered. Few were literate, books were expensive, and schools were either classically oriented toward developing scholars or technique oriented toward the artisan. Scholars read the books of other scholars; it is not likely that Babbage, Dupin, and Ure were widely read by the practicing manager. The classes of Say, Ure, and Dupin undoubtedly reached into some factories, but this was probably only a minor fraction of the total management market.

SUMMARY

In Great Britain, and France to a lesser extent, can be found the genesis of modern management thought. Robert Owen appealed to the heart as well as to the pocketbook in his search for a New Harmony between the human factor and the age of machines. Charles Babbage appealed to the mind, became the grandfather of scientific management, and applied a scientific approach to management before Taylor.

Andrew Ure taught his experiences and observations and developed managers for the new factories. Dupin learned from Ure and worked with Say to start management classes in France. With the genesis of management thought in Great Britain, the exodus of our story will be the study of management in the United States before the scientific management era.

5 The Industrial Revolution in the United States

The nineteenth century in the United States was an age of dynamic growth and expansion of the factory system. A colony of mighty Great Britain twenty-four years before the beginning of this age and torn by half a decade of internecine strife in mid-century, the United States was to become the world's leading political and industrial force by the close of the century. This chapter focuses on the Industrial Revolution in the United States, the industries it spawned, and the work of some pre–Civil War management pioneers.

ANTEBELLUM INDUSTRY AND MANAGEMENT

America was a colony for almost as many years as it has been a nation. For its settlers, the lure was manifold: social betterment, economic opportunity, religious freedom, and political separation. No element explains the whole, for the nation that was to emerge was a conglomerate of parts defying a separate identification and explanation. The newcomers to these alien, and often, hostile shores were aristocrats as well as felons, tramps, and petty criminals as well as budding tycoons. Efforts to develop colonial manufactures were frowned on by Great Britain, for they posed the possibility of dangerous competition for Great Britain's early factories. Two documents of 1776 tolled the death of mercantilism: the Declaration of Independence and Adam Smith's *Wealth of Nations*. America's economic heritage was largely mercantile, but the pressures for an escape from the policies of Great Britain were strong. Coincident with the Declaration of Independence in America, Smith's book appeared in Great Britain. It was a declaration of economic independence.

In the years between 1776 and 1787 the ideas of Adam Smith were widely read and discussed by U.S. business and political leaders. Smith's writings fitted into the philosophical concept of the new nation held by those who protested the strong role of government in economic matters. Smith's laissez-faire inclinations were acceptable to the framers of the Constitution. Article I, Section 8, gave Congress the power to impose and collect taxes, borrow money, coin money, fix standards of weights and measures, punish counterfeiters, issue patents, and "regulate commerce with foreign nations and among the several states." Except for those powers, government was to have a relatively hands-off approach to economic affairs and to act primarily to maintain uniformity and order among the states. In addition to a favorable political climate, economic and social conditions were ripe. The United States was a land rich in natural resources, with a growing labor supply. Many colonial merchants had made their fortunes in trade. These funds, aided by the dicta of thrift of early Puritanism, made increasing amounts of capital available for manufacturing. Three of these prosperous merchants, William Almy, Smith Brown, and Moses Brown, of Providence, Rhode Island, provided the capital that opened the industrial age of the United States.

EARLY INDUSTRIAL DEVELOPMENT

Great Britain sought to prevent industrial development by prohibiting the sale of manufacturing equipment and the emigration of skilled labor to the United States. Samuel Slater (1768–1835), an experienced builder and mechanic for the machinery of Richard Arkwright, the British textile pioneer, called himself a farmer on his emigration papers and gained passage to the United States. At this time, cloth was made in the home for home use, put out by various merchants under the domestic system, and occasionally made in small manufactories with hand looms. The firm of Almy and Brown had a small textile operation, but Moses Brown foresaw tremendous possibilities in the more advanced Arkwright machinery. Dangling the lure of a partnership, Brown induced Samuel Slater to bring his technical knowledge to their operations. The result was the country's first technologically advanced textile mill of seventy-two spindles at Pawtucket, Rhode Island, in 1790. Although the Almy, Brown, and Slater partnership did not last, this became known as the Rhode Island System, and it followed closely the managerial practices found in Great Britain. The Rhode Island System relied on a sole proprietorship or a partnership as the form of ownership; spun fine yarn in the mill, but put out weaving to be done by families in the homes. Slater exercised supervision of operations, assisted by his sons, his brother, and other relatives.

By 1808, the United States could boast of fifteen mills, over half of them connected with Slater and his assorted associates. Another conflict with Great Britain, the War of 1812, was to lead to another surge in U.S. textiles. Francis Cabot Lowell, a prominent merchant, had visited Great Britain and observed textile manufacturing by a new power loom driven by waterwheels, rather than by hand-driven looms. Lowell copied these designs and founded the Boston Manufacturing Company of Waltham, Massachusetts. Rather than emulating Slater's management methods, the Waltham System used joint-stock companies and the corporate form of ownership; did not put out work but integrated spinning and weaving to manufacture goods in large quantities; hired nonfamily supervisors and managers for their mills; and relied on adult female labor.

By 1816 the Waltham System became the dominant method of textile manufacturing. Slow to change, Slater and his colleagues waited almost a decade before they changed their strategy.[1] In 1827, Slater became one of the few to use steam-driven power looms at his Steam Cotton Manufacturing Company in Providence, Rhode Island. Whereas other manufacturers depended on the level of water flowing in rivers and streams, Slater was able to regularize production and employment. Slater also began to integrate the manufacturing operations to spin, weave, and finish cloth, ending the putting-out activities. As Slater's mills became more successful, numbering some fifteen separate locations by 1835, he ran out of relatives and began to hire professional managers to whom he delegated the authority and responsibility of running the various mills. Slater also pioneered the use of a factory ledger to accumulate data in order to determine the cost of producing a yard of cloth. Finally, Slater moved to vertically integrate his operations: moving forward to establish a sales operation in New York and backward by employing individuals to go to sources and purchase the raw materials needed. In brief, the Slater story provides an excellent example of the dynamics of early U.S. enterprise and its strategic response to technological as well as foreign and domestic competitive pressures.

The textile mills also provide some early ideas on organization and management as well as personnel policies. Although the firms were relatively small, a managerial hierarchy did develop when those who owned gradually had to relinquish personal supervision because of the growth of the firm. Thus Slater, Lowell, and others employed salaried managers and created an intermediate level of management. There is also evidence that some rudimentary staff duties were evolving. A mill manager was often "assisted by a superintendent, a technically trained man, and there were overseers with technical responsibilities that cut across the operations of the mill: overseers of repairs … or of belting."[2] Thus machinists, woodworkers, and other technically competent persons were hired to oversee the repairs, for example, while still other supervisors were responsible for managing the work force as well as the technical overseers. Supervisors did not need both technical and managerial ability (remember Charles Dupin?) but could rely on specialists. In these early mills, we may have found the antecedents of Frederick Taylor's "functional foremen."

Personnel policies, like managerial strategies, also differed between Slater's Rhode Island System and the Waltham System of Lowell and his associates. The early work force was largely unskilled, since Great Britain attempted to prevent skilled workers from emigrating to the United States.[3] To attract workers, Slater's Rhode

---

1. Barbara M. Tucker, *Samuel Slater and the Origins of the American Textile Industry, 1790–1860* (Ithaca, N.Y.: Cornell University Press, 1984), especially pp. 99–124.

2. Steven Lubar, "Managerial Structure and Technological Style: The Lowell Mills, 1821–1880," in Jeremy Atack, ed., *Business and Economic History* 12 (March 1984), p. 21.

3. Theodore Marburg, "Aspects of Labor Administration in the Early Nineteenth Century," *Business History Review* 15, no. 1 (February 1941), pp. 1–10.

Island System was patterned after the British practice of employing the whole family if possible, and it therefore resulted in more child labor. In contrast, the Waltham System was designed to attract female labor to the factory by establishing company boarding houses. Workers in the Waltham System textile factories were mainly young Yankee females, and they were brought to the factories from neighboring farms by agents who toured the countryside and emphasized the moral and educational advantages of factory work.[4] The females had to be in at 10:00 P.M., and their moral conduct was carefully watched by a housemother.

Even that vocal critic of the British factory system, Charles Dickens, praised the Waltham System factories for their treatment of labor. He reported that the female factory workers were clean, healthy, and of sound moral deportment. He felt the British could learn a great deal by the U.S. example.[5] However, it appears that the Waltham plan was less successful in keeping a labor force; Ware estimated that the females working in New England cotton mills stayed, on the average, one year.[6] The introduction of steam-powered looms, however, had a dramatic effect on the employment of child labor: "with the mechanization of picking and weaving in the early 1820s, Pawtucket's factory system had reached maturity and as a consequence had come to rely increasingly on adult factory labor."[7] Consequently, the U.S. factory did not demonstrate evils in the same depth as did the British factory. Employers were paying high wages to attract and hold their labor, child labor was not as prevalent, and abuses were less frequent and less severe.[8]

The U.S. worker was less resistant to the introduction of machinery, and the Luddites found few followers, except in Pittsburgh, where some hand-loom weavers rioted and destroyed their machines. Americans also took a different stance with respect to organized labor. A legacy from laws concerning guilds in Great Britain was the view that combinations of workers were conspiracies in restraint of trade and therefore illegal. Local craft unions made some headway in the United States but often ran into court-ordered injunctions when they sought to strike. In a landmark case in 1842 (*Commonwealth v. Hunt*), the Supreme Court of Massachusetts held that a combination of workers was not illegal per se, though if the object of the combination were criminal, then it could be prohibited. The court held that seeking a closed shop (workers must be union members) and striking were not illegal goals and that worker alliances for those purposes were proper. Although the decision applied only

---

4. Thomas C. Cochran and William Miller, *The Age of Enterprise* (New York: Harper and Row, 1961), p. 19.

5. Charles Dickens, *American Notes for General Circulation*, vol. 1 (London: Chapman and Hall, 1842), pp. 156, 163–164. Corroborating evidence for Dickens's observations may be found in William Scoresby, *American Factories and Their Female Operatives* (Boston: W. D. Ticknor Co., 1845).

6. Norman Ware, *The Industrial Worker: 1840–1860* (Gloucester, Mass.: Peter Smith Co., 1959), p. 149.

7. Gary B. Kulik, "The Beginnings of the Industrial Revolution in America: Pawtucket, Rhode Island, 1672–1829," Ph.D. dissertation, Brown University, 1980, p. 341.

8. Ross M. Robertson, *History of the American Economy* (New York: Harcourt Brace Jovanovich, 1955), p. 184. Based on his own research, Ware also found fewer evils in the U.S. factory system.

to Massachusetts, it discouraged attempts in other states to prosecute worker organizations on conspiracy grounds. In brief, early U.S. industrial development was fostered by the economic, social, and political conditions that encouraged work, thrift, innovation, and competition. The U.S. Industrial Revolution began in textiles but would soon evolve into more far-reaching effects.

THE AMERICAN SYSTEM OF MANUFACTURES

In 1851, the Great Exhibition of the Industry of All Nations was staged in London in the Crystal Palace. What amazed the visitors most was the U.S. exhibit of the unpickable locks of Alfred Hobbs, the sewing machine of Isaac Singer, the repeating pistol of Samuel Colt, and the mechanical reaper of Cyrus McCormick. Not only were these products superior to those of other nations, they were all made in a unique fashion—the parts were built to such exacting standards that they were interchangeable, so a person could pick up the parts at random and assemble a complete product. This emergent production technique became known as the American System of Manufactures.

To conclude that manufacture by interchangeable parts was solely the work of the U.S. industry would be inaccurate. As early as 1436, the Arsenal of Venice (Italy) was manufacturing warships by means of standard parts. For example, all bows were built to fit any arrow; all stern posts fit all rudders; and the deck furnishings and riggings were all uniform.[9] Weapons makers in Switzerland, France, and other countries had followed this principle in their work; however, no one had moved the principle of interchangeable parts from weaponry to industry until the Americans did so. What could have happened in the United States to lead to this advance?

In the United States, as elsewhere, it began in the manufacture of arms. Early private contractors, such as Eli Whitney and Simeon North, had made small batches of arms using interchangeable parts, but with limited success.[10] The Springfield (Massachusetts) Armory was established in 1795 as a central workshop to bring weapons makers together to produce armaments, but it really did not begin to develop improved management techniques until Colonel Roswell Lee became superintendent in 1815. Under Lee, a reorganization centralized authority and established definite areas of responsibilities. An early piece-rate accounting system was developed for wage payments and later used to control the time spent by workers and the materials used. The specialization of labor also increased: in 1815, there were thirty-six different occupational specialties; in 1820, eighty-six; and by 1825,

---

9. Claude George, *The History of Management Thought*, 2nd ed. (Englewood Cliffs, N.J.: Prentice-Hall, 1972), p. 39.

10. More information about Eli Whitney and the American system of manufactures can be found in Robert S. Woodbury, "The Legend of Eli Whitney and Interchangeable Parts," *Technology and Culture*, vol. 1 (1960), pp. 235–253; see also David A. Hounshell, *From the American System to Mass Production, 1800–1932* (Baltimore: The Johns Hopkins University Press, 1984).

one hundred.[11] Arms were made by specialists rather than by craft workers in metals and wood. New developments in metalworking machines and tools and improved gauges to measure the accuracy of parts came into use. Thus, the parts could be manufactured to closer tolerances, which increased their interchangeability. Colonel Lee also tightened discipline with a new policy in 1816 that prohibited "scuffling or playing in the shops, wanton destruction of government property, noise, gambling ... [and] the grazing of cattle or swine on public property."[12] The Springfield Armory was not a profit-making organization, but it provides us with a better prototype for the development of a modern factory than the early textile mills. The division of labor, the clearly defined organization, the use of accounting techniques for wage payments and control of time and material costs, the uniform standards, the measurement techniques for inspection and control, and the advanced methods of metalworking were all crucial to what came to be called the American System of Manufactures.

The developments at the Springfield Armory were not typical of what was happening in the private sector. In 1832, a report was submitted to the secretary of the treasury, Louis McLane, that provided a partial census of U.S. manufactures of that time. In the ten states surveyed, there were 106 manufacturing establishments with $100,000 or more in assets; eighty-eight of these were in textiles, twelve in iron making, and a scattering of others in the production of nails, axes, glass, and so on. Only thirty-six of the companies in the ten states employed 250 or more workers; thirty-one of these were textile firms, three were in iron, and the others were in nails and axes.[13] In 1832, the Springfield Armory employed 246 workers, so it must be ranked among the largest organizations of this period. Other than the textile companies and a few iron makers, most organizations were relatively small, employing an average of ten to twelve persons. The McLane report also indicated that most firms were family owned and managed as sole proprietorships or partnerships and that corporations were few. Finally, steam power was rarely used, as the firms relied primarily on water power. Recalling Andrew Ure's study of the Lancashire cotton mills during this same period, there are remarkable similarities in the size of the firms, and how they were managed, but the British were ahead on the use of steam power.

In short, U.S. manufacturing before 1835 was characterized by small, family-run, water-powered organizations. In the 1840s and 1850s, however, U.S. entrepreneurs unleashed a host of products and implements that would revolutionize industry. The principles of manufacturing pioneered at the Springfield Armory and elsewhere provided the basis for the later manufacture of axes, shovels, sewing machines, clocks, locks, watches, steam engines, reapers, and other products. What

---

11. Alfred D. Chandler, Jr., *The Visible Hand: The Managerial Revolution in American Business* (Cambridge, Mass.: Harvard University Press, 1977), p. 73.

12. Russell I. Fries, "Springfield Armory, 1794–1820: An Early Industrial Organization," unpublished paper, Orono, Maine, 1967, p. 29.

13. Chandler, *Visible Hand*, pp. 60–62.

visitors admired at the Crystal Palace exhibit of 1851 was the product of a long chain of developments—beginning with early experimentation and transferring to private industry. Mass production had not yet been perfected, but its antecedents were present.

THE RAILROADS: PIONEERING IN U.S. MANAGEMENT

Although textiles represented the largest private enterprises of this period in the United States, a transportation and communication revolution was on the horizon. Development of the iron rail, flanged wheel, and puffing locomotive began around 1830. Opposed initially by the canal supporters, who were fearful of its competition, the rail industry by 1850 had brought a new dimension to U.S. life. It started with Colonel John Stevens of Hoboken, New Jersey, who obtained from the New Jersey legislature the country's first railroad charter in 1815.[14] Deemed eccentric, he could not obtain financial backing until 1830 when he built the twenty-three-mile-long Camden and Amboy Railroad. Stevens made numerous other technical contributions and earned the title Father of American Engineering. After the Camden and Amboy other lines, such as the Chesapeake and Ohio and the Baltimore and Ohio, were built and expanded, until by 1850, 9,000 miles of track extended all the way into Ohio. The railroad would provide a revolution in transportation, and, as we shall see, an emphasis on managing in a systematic fashion. First, however, let us examine a concurrent revolution in communication, the telegraph.

THE COMMUNICATION REVOLUTION

Tom Standage reminds us that humans are chronocentric; that is, we have

> the egotism that one's own generation is poised on the cusp of history. Today, we are repeatedly told that we are in the midst of a communication revolution. But the electric telegraph was in many ways, far more disconcerting for the inhabitants of that time [the 1800s] than today's advances are for us ... Heavier than air flying machines were, after all, thought by the Victorians to be totally impossible. But for the Internet—well, they [the Victorians] had one of their own.[15]

---

14. An interesting account of John Stevens's various activities, including his anticipation by three years of Fulton's steamboat, may be found in Dorothy Gregg, "John Stevens: General Entrepreneur," in William Miller, ed., *Men in Business* (New York: Harper & Row, 1957), pp. 120–152.

15. Tom Standage, *The Victorian Internet: The Remarkable Story of the Telegraph and the Nineteenth Century's On-Line Pioneers* (New York: Walker and Company, 1998), p. 213. Standage cites instances of romance blossoming and marriages made via the telegraph, as well as a familiar contemporary problem, a concern for privacy.

This "Victorian Internet" that Standage refers to was the telegraph, the invention of Samuel F. B. Morse, who built on a long line of scientific discoveries about electricity and magnetism. The possibilities of "distance signaling" through metal wires were developed by Morse in 1832, but not patented until 1837, the same year that William Cooke and Charles Wheatstone obtained a British patent and installed thirteen miles of wires on poles along Britain's Great Western Railroad. Morse gained a competitive advantage by developing a code, consisting of dots and dashes, which became the standard format for transmitting messages.

The telegraph provided the beginnings of a nationwide communication system. An experimental line was completed between New York and Washington, D.C., in 1844, and by 1860 about fifty thousand miles of wires and poles crisscrossed the eastern half of the country. Usually built along railroad rights of way, the telegraph facilitated the transportation system as well as handling commercial and personal messages. The impact on business communication was dramatic—where it might take days, weeks, or months for messages to be sent and received, the telegraph shrank the world of words. News items could be sent by telegraph, enabling daily newspapers to keep their readers informed; stock prices were sent from trade exchanges via ticker tape for investors; money could be sent by wire; a submarine cable under the Atlantic Ocean connected America to Great Britain and the European continent; and credit for the first electronic commerce belongs to Richard Sears, who used his skills at telegraphy to sell a shipment of gold-filled watches through other station agents along the Minneapolis and Saint Louis Railroad.

These technological revolutions, the railroad and the telegraph, in transportation and communication would sweep away local trade barriers, open new lands for settlement, extend markets and reshape distribution strategies, and provide an inexpensive, rapid, year-round means for travel and commerce.

THE AGE OF RAILS

The railroads were truly the United States' first big business. The textile industry, though growing and dominating the Northeast, never developed into companies of the size and scope of the railroads. Textile firms remained relatively small, the Springfield Armory rarely employed more than 250 people, and capital investment in industry was relatively low. The railroads, however, grew to such a size and complexity that means had to be developed of coping with massive financial requirements, developing integrated systems of trackage and station agents, spreading large fixed costs, and handling a labor force dispersed over a wide geographical area. These factors required managers to develop ways of managing the first U.S. industry of larger than local scope. Unlike textile and other plants, railroad operations were spread out and could not be controlled by personal inspection of the hundreds of stations and thousands of miles of track, thus making communications a significant problem. The investments in track and rolling stock were immense, and extensive long-range planning was required to prevent large fixed capital outlays from being placed in the wrong market area. Passenger safety and the prevention of damage to or loss of cargo were critical to successful operations. Scheduling service required planning and coordination, and standing rules and policies had to be developed to guide the decisions of lower organizational elements.[16]

The twenty-three-mile track of John Stevens's Camden and Amboy line required little in the way of organization and management. Other lines, however, grew in scope and distance. In 1841, after a series of accidents, the Western Railroad of Massachusetts established certain areas of responsibility and a clear hierarchy of authority to ensure performance. Another large line, the Baltimore and Ohio (B&O), was reorganized in 1847 by Benjamin Latrobe to separate operations from finance and to establish departments for functions, such as machine shops, road maintenance departments, and so on. Although the Western and the B&O responded to growth with more definitive organizational structures, it was the New York and Erie Railroad that pioneered systematic management in the first big business in the United States.

DANIEL MCCALLUM: SYSTEM AND ORGANIZATION

Daniel Craig McCallum (1815–1878) was born in Scotland but came to the United States in 1822.[17] He received some elementary schooling in Rochester, New York, but decided not to enter his father's occupation of tailor. He left home and school, became an accomplished carpenter and architect, and designed and built numerous buildings. He left this field to join the New York and Erie Railroad Company in 1848. He showed a talent for management as well as engineering and became superintendent of the Susquehanna Division, where he developed an early set of procedures to govern that division's operations. Faced with growing problems of rail integration and a high accident rate, the Erie management made McCallum general superintendent of the Erie line in May 1854. In June of 1854, the workers went on strike for ten days; not for shorter hours nor more pay, but in defiance of McCallum's institution of his system.

To McCallum, good management was based on good discipline, specific and detailed job descriptions, frequent and accurate reporting of performance, pay and promotion based on merit, a clearly defined hierarchy of authority of superiors over subordinates, and the enforcement of personal responsibility and accountability throughout the organization. He stated his principles of management as:

1. A proper division of responsibilities;

---

16. Alfred D. Chandler, Jr., ed., *The Railroads: The Nation's First Big Business, Sources and Readings* (New York: Harcourt Brace Jovanovich, 1965), pp. 9–10.

17. Personal data on McCallum are from W. Jerome Arnold, "Big Business Takes the Management Track," *Business Week,* April 30, 1966, pp. 104–106, and Dumas Malone, ed., *Dictionary of American Biography,* vol. 6 (New York: Charles Scribners' Sons, 1965), p. 565.

Daniel C. McCallum, circa 1865.

2. Sufficient authority conferred to enable such responsibilities to be fully carried out;

3. The means of knowing whether such responsibilities are faithfully executed;

4. Great promptness in the report of all derelictions of duty, so that evils may be corrected quickly;

5. Such information to be obtained through a system of daily reports and checks that will not embarrass principal officers nor lessen their influence with their subordinates; and

6. The adoption of a system, as a whole, that will not only enable the general superintendent to detect errors immediately, but will also point out the delinquent.[18]

McCallum developed a high degree of organizational specificity to carry out these principles. First, he separated and identified each grade of worker as to task and required all workers to wear a prescribed uniform with the insignia of their grade. Second, he developed comprehensive rules to limit the ability of individuals to do their tasks as they pleased. Rule 6, for example, mandated that the engineer was responsible if the train ran off a switch, even if the switch operator had not done a proper job. Engineers were expected to slow down at all switches, whether they were stopping or not, to check the switches personally.[19]

Finally, McCallum developed a formal organizational chart (which his advocate Henry Varnum Poor had lithographed and put on sale to the general public for a price of $1). The chart took the form of a tree and depicted the lines of authority and responsibility, the division of labor among operating units, and the communication lines for reporting and control. The roots of the tree represented the board of directors and the president; the branches were the five operating divisions plus the staff service departments of engine repairs, car, bridge, telegraph, painting, treasurer's, and secretary's offices; the leaves were the various local freight and ticket forwarding offices, subordinate supervisors, crews, and so on to the lowest element. Adherence to the formal lines of authority was to be absolute:

> The enforcement of a rigid system of discipline ... is indispensable to success. All subordinates should be accountable to, and be directed by their immediate superiors only; as obedience cannot be enforced where

---

18. Daniel C. McCallum, "Superintendents' Report," in *American Railroad Journal*, ed. H.V. Poor, vol. 29 (April 12, 1856), pp. 225–226. Reprinted in Daniel A. Wren, ed., *Early Management Thought* (Brookfield, Vt.: Dartmouth Publishing Company, 1997), p. 9.

19. Walter Licht, *Working for the Railroad* (Princeton, N.J.: Princeton University Press, 1983), pp. 246–247.

the foreman in immediate charge is interfered with by a superior officer giving orders directly to his subordinates.[20]

McCallum saw no exceptions to this unity of command principle; to do otherwise would break down his control system, which was based on personal accountability.

McCallum also developed information management to probably the highest state of the art for the times. He used the telegraph to make operations safer as well as to facilitate administration by requiring hourly reports to show the position of every train in the system, daily reports on passengers and cargo, and monthly reports to give management statistical accounts for planning, rate making, and control. He designed a clever cross-check control system by requiring both freight and passenger conductors to report on train movements, loadings, damaged freight, and so on; by comparing the reports, he could readily spot discrepancies and dishonesty.

McCallum's system was successful from management's point of view, but trouble was brewing over Rule 6. The engineers had never forgiven McCallum; twenty-nine engineers had been dismissed for breaking Rule 6 and for avoiding various other safety rules McCallum had devised. A six-month strike ensued, and McCallum was unable to replace the striking engineers. He resigned, along with the company president, in 1857. However, McCallum had earned the highest praise of Henry Varnum Poor, the eminent editor of the *American Railroad Journal* and spokesperson for the industry. Poor later had some doubts about the system, but thought that it was a step in the right direction.

McCallum's managerial days were not over, however. While on the Erie, he had invented and patented (1851) an inflexible arched truss bridge. In 1857 he established the McCallum Bridge Company and built bridges throughout the country, earning an income of $75,000 per year. In 1862 he was asked by Secretary of War Stanton to manage the nation's railways, with the power to seize and operate any railroad necessary to the Union's war effort. By the end of the war he was a major general and his main feat was supplying General Sherman's 200-day Atlanta campaign.[21] After the war, McCallum served as a consultant for the Atlantic and Great Western Railroad and the Union Pacific. Failing health prompted an early retirement to Brooklyn, where he did not get into the bridge business but wrote poetry. His best-known poem was "The Water-Mill," which concluded:

Possessions, Power, and blooming health,
must all be lost at last,
The mill will never grind with water
that is past

---

20. McCallum, in Chandler, *Railroads*, p. 104.

21. An extensive account of McCallum's managerial feats in running the Northern railroads during the Civil War may be found throughout Thomas Weber, *The Northern Railroads in the Civil War* (New York: Columbia University Press, 1952).

McCallum's approach to management was not lost, despite his setbacks at the Erie. Henry Poor publicized his work widely, and numerous others followed McCallum's style in systematizing the country's first big business. Albert Fink developed a cost accounting system that used information flows, classification of costs, and statistical control devices and became a model for modern corporate control.[22] Auditing as a separate staff function from accounting also began on the railroads. As early as 1847, the B&O used an internal auditor to check on the handling of receipts and disbursements. External auditing by independent public accounting firms also began as early as 1854, as stockholders, separate from management, wanted to verify management's reports.[23]

Organizational growth, geographical separation of activities, and the separation of ownership and management were the driving forces for systematizing railroad management. The most faithful adoption of McCallum's system, however, came on the Pennsylvania Railroad. J. Edgar Thomson and Thomas A. Scott applied McCallum's ideas for geographical departmentation, formal lines of authority and responsibility, communications, line and staff duties, measuring performance, and cost accounting. The Pennsylvania tree bore the fruit of systematic management, not the Erie. On the Pennsylvania was a young manager who learned McCallum's system from Thomson and Scott; his name was Andrew Carnegie, and he will enter our story again shortly.

HENRY V. POOR: A BROADER VIEW OF MANAGEMENT

Henry Varnum Poor (1812–1905), through his position as editor of the *American Railroad Journal,* essayed to become the conscience of the first large business. Whereas McCallum spoke of internal operating problems, Poor looked for broader principles of railroad operations, including financing, regulation, and the role of the railroad in U.S. life. Poor was well educated and came from a more select background than McCallum; his biographer tells us that Poor was thoroughly imbued with the romance and optimism of the nineteenth-century United States.[24] As editor of the *Journal* in the pre–Civil War years, Poor made it the leading business periodical of the day and a reliable source of information for the railroad investor as well as the manager. His editorials discussed railroad developments, problems, and needed reforms in operating practices and presented detailed financial and operating data. After the war, his *Manual of Railroads in the United States* continued his efforts to further the dissemination of

---

22. Albert Fink, "Classification of Operating Expenses," in *Annual Report of the Louisville and Nashville Railroad Company* (1874), in Chandler, *Railroads,* pp. 108–117.

23. James L. Boockholdt, "A Historical Perspective on the Auditor's Role: The Early Experiences of the American Railroads," *The Accounting Historians Journal* 10 (Spring 1983), pp. 69–86.

24. Alfred D. Chandler, Jr., *Henry Varnum Poor: Business Editor, Analyst, and Reformer* (Cambridge, Mass.: Harvard University Press, 1956). An interesting sidelight is that Chandler is the great-grandson of Henry Varnum Poor.

financial and operating information.[25] His life was marked throughout by the critical age of railroads coming from infancy to maturity and by their amazing impact on opening the West and tying the United States together with a web of steel.

In its early years, the Erie was one of Poor's favorite targets, for it was poorly managed and financed. The advent of McCallum's reforms soon made Poor the biggest booster of the Erie as an example of proper management. Poor saw a need for managerial reform through development of a group of professional managers rather than speculators and promoters to build the nation's transportation system. Poor looked for a science, or system, of management, and from McCallum's work Poor gleaned three fundamental principles: organization, communication, and information.[26] Organization was basic to all management: there had to be a careful division of labor from the president down to the common laborer, each with specific duties and responsibilities. Workers should be directly accountable to their immediate superiors; Poor repeatedly used the terms "responsibility" and "accountability" in his editorials. Communication meant devising a method of reporting throughout the organization to give top management a continuous and accurate accounting of operations. Finally, information was "recorded communication"; Poor saw the need for a set of operating reports to be compiled for costs, revenues, and rate making. This third principle was an early appearance of a database concept in management literature in the sense that management would build up a fund of data on operations to analyze the present system and to provide a basis for changes to improve service. The influence of McCallum on Poor's writing is readily apparent, and the development of the third principle can be traced to Albert Fink's efforts to install statistical control systems in the corporate structure.

Just as McCallum's work was becoming widely known, in large part owing to Poor's editorials, Poor began having doubts about whether organization, communication, and information were adequate principles to encompass the task of management. Poor visited Great Britain in 1858 to view its railway system, and on his return he wrote about "the grave difficulties of adapting human capabilities and current business practices and institutions to the severe requirements demanded by the efficient operation of such large administrative units." Both in Great Britain and on the Erie, Poor saw worker resistance developing to the discipline required by systematic management. The tighter control required to bring order from chaos, the limiting of individual discretion in the performance of tasks, and the rigid hierarchical specifications of a formal organization were all leading to worker protests against the system. This protest was not new in the annals of management history, nor has the issue ever been fully resolved. Poor, however, thought these protests were too extreme and defended the need for systematization: "We can see no other way in which such a

---

25. Henry V. Poor established *Poor's Publishing* in 1860 to provide financial information about other industries; in 1941, a merger with *Standard Statistics* created the *Standard and Poor's* of today.

26. Chandler, *Poor*, pp. 146–147. Chandler's work is based on Poor's editorials and will be cited here without referring to specific dates and issues of the *Journal*.

vast machine can be safely and successfully conducted," that is, except through order, system, and discipline.

Accordingly, Poor began to look for some broader principles to overcome the dangers of "regarding man as a mere machine, out of which all the qualities necessary to be a good servant can be enforced by the mere payment of wages. But duties cannot always be prescribed and the most valuable are often voluntary ones."[27] Close prescription of duties and the bureaucratization of management reduced incentives and would inevitably lead the railroads, in Poor's view, to the problems inherent in the rigid managerial structures such as those of the military and the government. Poor's solution was a leadership that would overcome dullness and routine by infusing the organization with an esprit de corps. Top management should become "the soul of the enterprise, reaching and infusing life, intelligence and obedience into every portion of it. This soul must not be a fragmentary or disjointed one giving one direction to the head, another to the hands, and another to the feet. Wherever there is lack of unity there will be a lack of energy—of intelligence—of life—of accountability and subordination."[28]

In anticipating Fayol's unity of direction principle by sixty years, Poor regarded the problems of top management as those of assuming and of getting subordinates to assume a total systems view of the organization. Leaders not only had to know all aspects of railroad operation and administration but also needed to be able to handle people, to know the total system, and to prevent interdepartmental conflicts that could destroy unity of purpose. The breakdown in leadership came from two sources: selection on some basis other than ability or training, and lack of an information system to pinpoint weak managers. Poor's pleas for professional managers to manage well the property of others were not dissimilar to the problems Adam Smith had pointed out nearly a century before.

EMERGING GOVERNANCE ISSUES

Early textile mills were largely owned and managed by partnerships and sole proprietorships. The money was "all in the family," and requirements for accounting and financial reporting were reduced. Adam Smith cautioned of the dangers of joint-stock, limited liability firms where ownership and management were typically separated and rarely did anyone watch over other people's money as they would exercise vigilance over their own. Smith was deceased, however, by the time of the earliest incident of this problem appeared when the British railroad system was developing. The railroads required capital, both debt and equity financing, on a scale unknown to any previous business ventures.

George Hudson, a friend of the British railway pioneer and innovator George Stephenson, envisioned a network of rails for the whole of England, Scotland, and

---

27. *Ibid.*, p. 155.
28. *Ibid.*, p. 157.

Wales. In 1844, Hudson began promoting assorted ventures to raise capital for new lines and to acquire existing ones. Under British law, each joint-stock company was authorized by a separate Act of Parliament, leading to different charters and requirements for each. At this time, there were no general rules for accounting and financial reporting, and corporate law was in its infancy. The railways held a romantic fascination for investors, leading to waves of rampant speculation in railway shares, or, in more modern terms, "irrational exuberance." It has been estimated that, by 1845, £71 million British pounds sterling had been invested in railroads, and another 620 new railway schemes amounted to £563 million pounds sterling, equivalent to over two-thirds of the national debt of Great Britain.[29]

Hudson took advantage of these speculative impulses, and by 1849, nearly one-third of Great Britain's five thousand miles of lines were under his management or control. In addition, he had raised money to buy land, build docks, and form canal ventures. He was, as all Britain knew, the "Railway King."[30] His operations extended from Brighton and Southampton in the southeast of that island nation, to Edinburgh in the northeast.

An early, if not the earliest, example of top management malfeasance exists in the deeds of George Hudson. He paid dividends out of capital, both existing and borrowed; altered accounts of railway traffic and revenue to indicate more profitability than existed; published false statements to investors; and, in one instance, bought iron rails from one of his lines for £9 each and sold them to another of his interests for £11, pocketing a £6,000 profit.

Parliament passed a Companies Clauses Consolidation Act in 1845 to bring some uniformity to corporate charters, to require "full and true" accounts to be maintained, and to mandate that three directors and the chief executive sign and verify the firm's balance sheet. It was not legislation, however, that stopped Hudson's chicanery; his actions led to shareholder investigations and lawsuits. His estimated ill-gotten gains amounted to £598,785.[31] Hudson went into exile, and his creditors were never fully satisfied.

How does the brief account of George Hudson fit into America's economic development and the efforts of Henry Varnum Poor? Poor kept abreast of railroad developments abroad and addressed governance issues in his editorials. For example, he complained that railroads did not separate construction from operating costs, thus screening the cost of operations from the investor. It was not an uncommon practice to put operating expenses in the construction account, thus showing higher profits from operations. This practice enabled the declaration of higher dividends that otherwise would have been unwarranted. (Does history provide explanations for why we have rules for accounting practice?)

---

29. J.J. Glynn, "The Development of British Railway Accounting, 1800–1911," in R.H. Parker and B.S. Yamey, eds, *Accounting History: Some British Contributions* (Oxford: Clarendon Press, 1994), pp. 327–342.

30. Richard S. Lambert, *The Railway King, 1800–1871* (London: George Allen and Unwin, 1934).

31. *Ibid.*, p. 273.

What was the path to reform? According to Poor:

> Now the germ of all improvement is *knowledge* … the only way to introduce honesty into the management of railroads is to expose every thing in or about it, to the public gaze. Concealment in either case is certain to breed disease. Instances are very rare in which integrity is preserved unless strict accountability is exacted. Such accountability to the public should be exacted from directors of railroads. … For the dishonesty and incapacity in the management of railroads the holders of their securities have in a great measure to thank themselves. They put them in charge of a body of men, responsible to no authority, who soon come to practice concealment, either to escape the consequences of mistake or dishonesty. The perpetuation of their power is an easy matter, so long as they can sustain themselves by the various modes resorted to for borrowing.[32]

Poor lashed out against the promoters and speculators and reflected the laissez-faire spirit by calling for unrestricted competition. Rates should not be regulated by government and the only legislation necessary was that to protect "honest rational men" from the dishonest promoters. He insisted that the rapid development of the U.S. railroad system was "proof that reliance on the self-interest of individuals operating under conditions of unrestricted competition resulted in the greatest good for the greatest number."[33] Through publicity to inform stockholders and the public, through professionalization of management, and through protection of the rational from the irrational, the railroads could achieve their proper role in the economy.

Henry Varnum Poor articulated issues that face management today and will be present tomorrow. His position that the role of government was to protect, not to control, illustrates a recurring problem of management vis-à-vis government. His search for order out of chaos without destroying individual incentive and dignity also is a recurring problem. He was one of our most outstanding early contributors to management thought.

Summary

In 1790, the largest city in the United States of America was New York, with a population of 33,131; next came Philadelphia, with a population of 28,522; and then Boston, with 18,300 persons. Even the largest city was smaller than the student body

---

32. Henry V. Poor, "How to Improve the Management of Railroads," *American Railroad Journal* 30 (June 20, 1857), p. 392. For a concise history of the law and American railroads before the Civil War, see Charles W. Wootton and Christie L. Roszkowski, "Legal Aspects of Corporate Governance in Early American Railroads," *Business and Economic History* 28 (Winter 1999), pp. 325–336.

33. Chandler, *Poor*, p. 260.

at some of today's state universities. In 1790, an estimated 90 percent of the estimated total population of 3,231,533 was engaged in agriculture. From the time of gaining independence from Great Britain up to 1860, the United States made marvelous progress. Textile factories provided inexpensive clothing to a national market, replacing the domestic system of production; railroads spread westward, opening new lands and opportunities; the telegraph sent messages tapping across vast distances; and mechanical devices such as the sewing machine and the reaper caused others to praise the American System of manufacturing.

When we think of modern enterprise, it is essential that we think of this period as critical. The domestic system of putting out work into homes was disappearing, to be replaced by family and partner owned and managed small-scale firms in a central work place powered by the steam engine. Capital requirements increased with the railroads, the telegraph enabled the growth of the firm for economies of scale and scope, and this growth created the need for a hierarchy of nonowning managers. If one views the enterprise as an input-throughput-output system, the inputs come from external markets in the form of human, capital, technology, and other resources. Through a hierarchy of managers, the firm became a means of transforming these inputs and coordinating and monitoring their use. For the outputs of the firm, the market came into play through consumer demand. In this way, we can see how events in the early nineteenth century helped shape the nature of the business firm.

If you were a male and born in Massachusetts in 1789, you could expect to live 34.5 years, and if you were a female, 36.5 years. By 1855, these expectancies had risen to 38.7 and 40.9 years, respectively. Not only were people living longer, but they were living better: real wages (purchasing power) rose from an index number of forty-one in 1820 to fifty-seven in 1860 (1913 = 100).[34] By 1860, there were an estimated 1,385,000 people employed in manufacturing; 20 percent of these were females, and child labor in factories had all but disappeared. Times were better, and this was only the beginning of the Industrial Revolution in the United States.

----

34. Edgar W. Martin, *The Standard of Living in 1860* (Chicago: University of Chicago Press, 1942), pp. 220, 415.

6 Industrial Growth and Systematic Management

Threpe years of internecine strife from 1861 to 1865 were a tragic pause in the move of the United States toward world industrial leadership. When the Industrial Revolution reached the United States, it spawned the textile industry, opened new vistas in manufacturing techniques at the Springfield Armory, and created our first big business on the railroads. This chapter will describe how the revolution resumed in the growth of enterprise, discuss the renaissance of systematic management, and examine the economic, social, political, and technological situations in the United States on the eve of the scientific management era.

THE GROWTH OF U.S. ENTERPRISE

The Industrial Revolution in the United States began in textiles, but textile firms made relatively few advancements over earlier British management methods. The Waltham System and Samuel Slater, in his later years, exemplified integrated firms, employed professional managers, and adopted steam power. Most firms in the United States prior to the Civil War, however, were family owned and managed, small, and technologically underdeveloped. The Springfield Armory used more advanced management techniques, but systematic management really began on the railroads. The railroads, powered by steam, led a transportation revolution; the telegraph and the transatlantic cable created a communication revolution. Together, these forces combined to create the growth of large-scale organizations.

THE ACCUMULATION OF RESOURCES

No student of U.S. business history has a keener eye for the growth of large organizations than Alfred D. Chandler,

Jr.[1] In some early work, Chandler traced the history of various firms and delineated four phases in the history of the large U.S. enterprise: (1) "the initial expansion and accumulation of resources"; (2) "the rationalization of the use of resources"; (3) "the expansion into new markets and lines to help assure the continuing full use of resources"; and (4) "the development of a new structure" that rationalized the renewal of growth. For different companies, the phases started and ended at different times, depending on the state of technology and the firm's ability to react to and capitalize on market opportunities. During the latter part of the nineteenth century, many major industries were forming and would fit into Chandler's phase 1 or resource accumulation stage.

Chandler further noted two facets of industrial growth and their time periods: (1) horizontal growth from 1879 to 1893 and (2) vertical growth from 1898 to 1904. Horizontal growth occurred when producers in similar fields combined through mergers, pools, or trusts to gain economies of scale in manufacturing. Examples include firms in oil, beef, sugar, tobacco, rubber, liquors, and so on. Mergers into larger units enabled the firm or firms to control their market, gain financial leverage, and cut production costs. Vertical growth occurred when firms moved backward or forward in terms of the production process. Moving backward meant the acquisition of raw material sources or suppliers; moving forward meant establishing marketing outlets for the firm's own products. For example, a petroleum-refining company would move backward to explore, acquire oil leases, drill, and build pipelines to its refinery; it would move forward to acquire wholesale agents and perhaps its own retail stations.

Chandler found a close connection between advancements in transportation and communication and the accumulation of resources that led to industrial growth. When transport was crude and slow, markets for products were largely localized, so there was little or no need to enlarge the volume of goods manufactured. Thus the domestic system was entirely appropriate to its time because it served limited markets with little capital investment. When the Industrial Revolution provided steam power for locomotives and steamboats, markets were extended and a larger scale of production with more advanced mechanization became desirable. Communication techniques, such as the telegraph, provided a network to connect suppliers, producers, distributors, and consumers over a larger geographical area. With improved transportation and communication, it became possible to produce and market in volume; thus production could be done in large batches or in continuous processing, and firms could seek volume distribution in a mass market. A greater capital intensity was required for this enlarged scale of output and distribution. As the capital investment rose, for example, with large blast furnaces for steel production, costs could be

---

1. The subsequent discussion relies heavily on Alfred D. Chandler, Jr., *Strategy and Structure: Chapters in the History of the Industrial Enterprise* (Cambridge, Mass.: MIT Press, 1962); idem, *The Visible Hand: The Managerial Revolution in American Business* (Cambridge, Mass.: Harvard University Press, 1977); idem, *Scale and Scope: The Dynamics of Industrial Capitalism* (Cambridge, Mass.: Harvard University Press, 1990).

reduced only if these expensive pieces of equipment could be used at some optimal output level. In Chandler's terms, these capital-intensive industries had to operate at a "minimum efficient scale" (i.e., at the level that resulted in the lowest unit costs) in order to attain a cost advantage. With a cost advantage, prices could be lowered and markets extended, and eventually the whole cycle of mechanization, greater output, increased distribution volume, and so on, would be repeated.

There are limits, of course, to the cost advantages of large-scale production and volume marketing. In Chandler's thesis, however, this explanation of mass production illustrates the growth of enterprise and the need for a managerial hierarchy. The key to organizational success is not in capacity (the potential to produce or sell) but in how well the throughput is managed. There must be a smooth flow of inputs in terms of employees, materials, supplies, and so on into the factory where the production is done (throughput). Then a well-coordinated system is needed for the outputs (finished products) to flow through the distribution channels to the customers. Chandler's analysis of organizational growth and the need for a managerial hierarchy to coordinate organizational work is of far-reaching importance. As we view the latter half of the nineteenth century in the United States, we can see how advances such as new production processes for making steel, refining sugar and corn products, milling grains, canning, and packaging led to the growth of enterprise, as Chandler's thesis would predict. One of the best examples of organizational growth and the throughput notion is found in the story of Andrew Carnegie.

CARNEGIE AND THE GROWTH OF ENTERPRISE

The name of Andrew Carnegie (1835–1919) conjures a portrait of an entrepreneur who built an empire in steel and left a fortune in the millions. But where did Carnegie learn his management skills? Carnegie, an immigrant like so many other entrepreneurs of this age, early learned the trade of a telegrapher. Thomas A. Scott, superintendent of the Western Division of the Pennsylvania Railroad, hired Carnegie as his personal telegrapher for dispatching trains over the mountainous divisional lines. Carnegie learned fast, and made his mark one day when he untangled a traffic tie-up after a derailment. Scott was absent at the time, and Carnegie sent out orders using Scott's initials. He was rewarded for this usurpation of authority, and his initiative led to a change in the organization by providing for a delegation of dispatching authority (formerly, only the superintendent had the authority). Carnegie learned of railroad management from Scott and J. Edgar Thomson, who, as mentioned earlier, had applied McCallum's ideas to the Pennsylvania Railroad. It was McCallum's system of organization, reporting, accounting, and control that Carnegie learned at the railroad. At age twenty-four, Carnegie became superintendent of the Western Division, which at the time was the largest division of the nation's largest railroad. Under his supervision, divisional traffic quadrupled, track mileage doubled, and the division had the lowest ton-per-mile costs of any railroad in the United States. Carnegie was offered the post of general superintendent in 1865, but declined because he wanted to become an entrepreneur rather than a salaried manager.

Andrew Carnegie, circa 1878.

To understand Carnegie and his influence, it is necessary to examine the development of the steel industry. Steel is the sinew of any industrial economy. Iron, because of its impurities, caused many problems for early machine designers and factory owners. The race to improve iron production proceeded, as is often the history of invention, on separate concurrent paths in Great Britain and the United States. William Kelly of Kentucky began his experiments in 1847 and perfected a system of refining iron by subjecting it to a blast of hot air in a specially built furnace. Unfortunately, Kelly did not apply for a patent until 1857, two years after Sir Henry Bessemer had obtained his patent in Great Britain. The Bessemer process, based on the same idea, was quite an improvement over the very slow process of puddling iron (the removing of carbon and other impurities by passing heated gases over the molten iron).

In 1865, the steel industry in the United States was not integrated. Some firms owned the furnaces that smelted the ore into pig iron; others had the rolling mills and forges that converted the pig iron into bars or slabs; and still others took the bars or slabs and rolled them into rails, sheets, nails, wire, or whatever. Between each of these independent operations, an intermediary took the output of one and sold it to the next producer, also taking a profit for providing this service. After Carnegie saw the Bessemer process in operation, he had a vision of how this improved technology could be used. In 1872, he decided to concentrate on steel because "Every dollar of capital or credit, every business thought, should be concentrated upon the one business upon which a man has embarked. He should never scatter his shot. ... Put all your eggs in one basket, and then watch that basket, is the true doctrine—the most valuable rule of all."[2]

Using the Bessemer converters, Carnegie began to integrate operations, cutting out the intermediaries' profits, speeding up the volume of throughput, and selling aggressively to extend the market for steel products. He used cost accounting to assist in setting prices to undersell his competitors who did not know their costs. He integrated vertically into iron and coal mines and other steel-related operations in order to ensure a flow of materials into the furnaces to use their capacity more fully. By coordinating the flow of materials, the furnaces, forges, rolling mills, and so forth, he could move the process faster from its beginning, as ore, into finished steel products. By combining the Bessemer technology with the management methods of Daniel McCallum, Carnegie became a success.

---

2. Andrew Carnegie, *The Empire of Business* (New York: Doubleday, Doran, 1933), p. 100.

It was on the Pennsylvania Railroad that Carnegie learned how to measure performance, control costs, and assign authority and responsibility; it was in the steel industry that he applied these lessons.[3] Until 1908 and the perfection of the open hearth method of making steel, the Bessemer process was the basis for the world's steel industry. When Carnegie started, iron rails cost $100 per ton; when he sold his steel interests in 1900, one ton of steel rails cost $12. Perhaps that was Carnegie's greatest philanthropy, or, as Jonathan Swift expressed it in *Gulliver's Travels:* "Whoever could make two ears of corn or two blades of grass to grow upon a spot of ground where only one grew before, would deserve better of mankind and do more essential service to his country than the whole race of politicians put together."[4] To unscramble the metaphor, Carnegie found a way to combine technology and management to create more jobs, reduce prices, expand markets, and advance industrial development. In 1868, the United States produced 8,500 tons of steel and Great Britain, 110,000; in 1879, the countries' outputs were nearly equal; but by 1902, the United States produced 9,138,000 tons and Great Britain produced 1,826,000. U.S. industry was showing its mettle.

THE RENAISSANCE OF SYSTEMATIC MANAGEMENT

The steel industry has provided an illustration of the growth of business after the Civil War. Steel was not the only industry, however, to thrust the United States into the world limelight and reinforce British and European beliefs in the superiority of the American System of Manufactures. As technology advanced in transportation, communication, machine making, and power sources, old industries were revitalized and new ones emerged to grow into large-scale enterprises. Chandler saw this phase as the accumulation of resources and noted the relationship between velocity of throughput in capital-intensive industries and the growth of a managerial hierarchy to coordinate the activities necessary to achieve the minimally efficient scale of production. In summary, management was the key to the efficient use of an organization's resources.

Daniel McCallum brought systematic management to some of the railroads, and Andrew Carnegie learned his lessons well and created a steel colossus. As other firms and other industries began to grow, they, too, faced the problems of managing large-scale organizations. They needed to plan for the acquisition of people, materials, equipment, and capital; to organize these resources by dividing labor, delegating authority, assigning responsibility, and grouping activities into departments; to lead

---

3. Numerous parallels between McCallum and Carnegie may be found in Harold C. Livesay, *Andrew Carnegie and the Rise of Big Business* (Boston: Little, Brown, 1975).

4. Jonathan Swift, *Gulliver's Travels,* Great Books of the Western World, vol. 36 (Chicago: Encyclopaedia Britannica, Inc., 1952), p. 78. Originally published in 1726.

and coordinate human efforts by providing incentives, handling interpersonal relations, and providing a means of communication within the organization; and to control by measuring performance, comparing actual to planned performance, and taking corrective action when necessary. With growth there came the need to formalize communications for purposes of coordination and control, especially in written memos and reports (with coordinating copies to all concerned).[5] At this time, however, there was very little understanding of the job of the manager; a great deal of emphasis was placed on technical or financial ability but very little on management itself. Faced with the accumulation of resources in large-scale enterprises, how could managers learn to manage better?

ENGINEERS AND ECONOMISTS

Engineers played a large role in building canals and railroads and in designing and installing industrial equipment. Thus, they frequently became the managers of enterprises; examples include Samuel Slater, Daniel McCallum, and others. The professionalization of engineering began with the formation of the American Society of Civil Engineers in 1852, followed by the American Institute of Mining Engineers in 1871. Neither of the groups, however, was interested in the problems of the factory, power sources, machine belting, or the operations of a machine shop or other type of factory. The first forum for those interested in factory problems appears to have been the *American Machinist,* an "illustrated journal of practical mechanics and engineering" that began in 1877. In 1878, James Waring See, writing under the name of Chordal, began a series of letters to the editor of the *American Machinist.* See was a veteran of working in and supervising machine shops.[6] He established a successful practice as a consulting engineer and used his letters to the editor to describe machine shop practices and management. He advocated systems of work that resulted from two principles: "a place for everything and everything in its place" and "specific lines of duty for each man."[7] See noted that good workers rarely made good supervisors and that good supervisors should not bully their workers but should be tactful and understanding. Soldiering, or a worker's deliberate slowing of output, existed and could be handled best if the supervisor had an "understanding with [the worker] that he is to work for you five days a week for pay, and soldier one day at his own expense … one week-day idle in a man's life will make him feel glad to get into the shop for five days of occupation."[8] See also advocated paying high wages to

---

5. Jo Anne Yates, *Control Through Communication: The Rise of System in American Management* (Baltimore: Johns Hopkins University Press, 1989).

6. William F. Muhs, Charles Wrege, and Arthur Murtuza, "Extracts from Chordal's Letters: Pre-Taylor Shop Management," in K. H. Chung, ed., *Proceedings of the Academy of Management* (San Diego, 1981), pp. 96–100.

7. James W. See, *Extracts from Chordal's Letters* (New York: American Machinist Publishing, 1880), p. 242.

8. *Ibid.,* p. 139.

attract better workers, the standardization of tools, and other techniques for better shop management. Except to readers of the *American Machinist,* See's writings remained relatively obscure for a century. It would appear, however, that his experiences and advice may have influenced later writers even though his work was not cited explicitly.

The *American Machinist* also had a hand in another signal event of this period, the formation of the American Society of Mechanical Engineers (ASME) in 1880. The ASME first met at the Stevens Institute of Technology, Hoboken, New Jersey, and its purpose was to address those issues of factory operation and management neglected by the other engineering groups. A landmark meeting of the ASME was held in Chicago in May 1886. Henry R. Towne (1844–1924), an engineer, co-founder of the Yale Lock Company, and president of the Yale and Towne Manufacturing Company, presented a paper entitled "The Engineer as an Economist." Towne observed that

> There are many good mechanical engineers; there are also many good "businessmen"; but the two are rarely combined in one person. But this combination of qualities ... is essential to the management of industrial works, and has its highest effectiveness if united in one person ... the matter of shop management is of equal importance with that of engineering ... and the *management of works* has become a matter of such great and far-reaching importance as perhaps to justify its classification also as one of the modern arts.[9]

Since no group appeared to be concerned with management, Towne proposed that the ASME create an economic section to act as a clearinghouse and forum for shop management and shop accounting. Shop management would deal with the subjects of organization, responsibility, reports, and all that pertained to the executive management of works, mills, and factories. Shop accounting would treat the questions of time and wage systems, determination and allocation of costs, methods of bookkeeping, and all matters that pertained to manufacturing accounts.

A second significant paper at the 1886 ASME meeting was presented by Captain Henry Metcalfe, an intellectual heir of the pioneering work of Roswell Lee of the Springfield Armory. In 1881, at the Frankford Arsenal (near Philadelphia) and the Watervliet Arsenal (Troy, New York), Metcalfe had a shop-order system of accounts that used cards to facilitate the coordination and control of various batches of work as they flowed through the shop.[10] These cards accompanied the work and the amount of labor spent, and materials used were recorded on the cards. When the order was finished, management could determine direct costs (such as labor and

---

9. Henry R. Towne, "The Engineer as an Economist," *Transactions, ASME* 7 (1886), pp. 428–429. Italics are Towne's.

10. Henry Metcalfe, "The Shop-Order System of Accounts," *Transactions, ASME* 7 (1886), pp. 440–468. This paper was a summary of Metcalfe's pioneering book in cost accounting, *The Cost of Manufactures and the Administration of Workshops, Public and Private* (New York: John Wiley and Sons, 1885).

materials) as well as indirect costs (administrative overhead). In the discussion that followed, Frederick W. Taylor of Midvale Steel said they had been using a similar system for the past ten years, except that Midvale used a central office and clerks, rather than the supervisors, to handle much of the paperwork. Taylor had joined the ASME in 1886. We shall learn more about Taylor later.

Almost all the discussion of the Towne and Metcalfe papers focused on the shop-order system of accounts, and the creation of an economic section of the ASME received scant notice. Despite evidence that business leaders were coming from technical schools, such as the Stevens Institute of Technology, and that their duties were managerial rather than technical,[11] only four other papers on management subjects were presented at the ASME meetings from 1887 to 1895.[12] This lack of attention was probably due to a lack of clarity about the skills and abilities a manager needed. A manager, at that time, was part engineer, part business leader, and part accountant. The emphasis was on the shop, that is, manufacturing, and not on the whole organization. Shop management focused on the machine shops, where the trend had been to move from small batch production to a larger scale of output based on the American System of Manufactures. The problem was how to handle the increased throughput volume.

One early writer noted that large-scale manufacture required the "utmost system … necessary in every detail [for] the economy and uniformity of production."[13] Thus *system* referred to the development of rules, standards, and procedures to handle the increased volume of activity in the production shop. Included in systematic management would be topics such as setting standards for tools, quality and quantity of work, coordination of work flow through routing and scheduling, wage incentives, accounting for costs, assigning responsibility, and handling labor problems such as soldiering.[14]

In other circles there was a resurgence of interest by economists in management as a factor of production. Jean Baptiste Say had made this observation earlier, and it was reborn in the 1880s and 1890s. An economist of this period, Edward Atkinson,

---

11. The Stevens Institute of Technology had 600 graduates between 1872 and 1896; of these, 230 (38 percent) were in executive positions by 1900. William D. Ennis, "The Engineering Management of Industrial Works," *Engineering Magazine* 22 (November 1901), pp. 241–246.

12. Hirose noted, however, that some mechanical engineers favored scientific management; only in 1920 did the majority of ASME members agree to a separate division of management. Mikiyoshi Hirose, "The Attitude of the American Society of Mechanical Engineers toward Management: Suggestions for a Revised Interpretation," *Kansai University Review of Economics and Business* 25 (September 1996), pp. 125–148.

13. Oberlin Smith, "System in Machine Shops," *American Machinist* 8 (October 31, 1885), p. 1.

14. Joseph A. Litterer, "The Emergence of Systematic Management as Shown by the Literature of Management from 1870 to 1900," Ph.D. dissertation, University of Illinois, Urbana, 1959. From this came two excellent articles: Joseph A. Litterer, "Systematic Management: The Search for Order and Integration," *Business History Review* 35 (Winter 1961), pp. 461–476; and idem, "Systematic Management: Design for Organizational Recoupling in American Manufacturing Firms," *Business History Review* 37 (Winter 1963), pp. 369–391.

noted that a "difference in management will alter results, in the same place, at the same time, in the use of similar machinery."[15] Alfred Marshall (1842–1924) and his wife, Mary Paley Marshall, wrote of the economics of industry, noting earnings of management as separate from the profit returned to shareholders, a clear distinction between shareowners and employed managers. The manager of large capital

> Always requires rarer natural abilities and a more expensive training than the management of small capital requires ... [those] who conduct a large business must look far ahead, and wide around him; and he must be continually on the look out for improved methods of carrying on his business ... [and] devotes all his energies to planning and organizing, to forecasting the future and preparing for it.[16]

As the Marshalls noted, management required special, rarer abilities, and performed certain actions to manage the business firm, such as forecasting, planning, and organizing. These functions of management were not discussed in detail, but the Marshalls noted the work of management long before it would be recognized in the writings of Henri Fayol. The Marshalls also noted the division of labor in the firm, but this did not lead to monotonous jobs "when the work is light, and the hours of work not excessive." They noted the economies of scale for large firms, and the internal economies that could be attained by more efficient management. In this latter sense, the Marshallian view of the firm would make it superior to the market in allocating resources.

The writing of the Marshalls about the economics of industry was a prelude to Alfred Marshall's fame as the founder of the Cambridge (England) or neoclassical school of economic thought. His long-enduring principles of economic texts provided a basis for business management with the inclusion of "organization" as an "agent" of production, following the style of Jean Baptiste Say. Marshall indicated the differential advantage that management could provide:

> A manufacturer of exceptional ability and energy will apply better methods, and perhaps better machinery than his rivals: he will organize better the manufacturing and the marketing sides of his business; and he will bring them into better relation to one another. By these means he will extend his business; and therefore he will be able to take greater advantage from the specialization both of labour and of plant. Thus he will obtain increasing return and also increasing profit.[17]

---

15. Edward Atkinson, *The Distribution of Products* (New York: G. P. Putnam's Sons, 1885), p. 62.

16. Alfred Marshall and Mary Paley Marshall, *The Economics of Industry* (London: Macmillan, 1884), p. 139.

17. Alfred Marshall, *Principles of Economics,* 8th ed. (New York: Macmillan, 1920), p. 614.

Economists, such as the Marshalls, had less impact than the mechanical engineers at this stage in developing management thought. The perceived problem resided in factory management, not the firm as an enterprise. Thus, methods and systems were deemed critical on achieving internal economies of scale. Another, much broader, issue concerned the relations between labor and capital and was referred to as the labor question or the labor problem.

THE LABOR QUESTION

Earlier we reviewed criticisms of the factory system in Great Britain and the Victorian sense of conscience with respect to the employment of women and children and other issues and determined that, although problems did exist, the factory system was not the cause. Women and children had worked before, under the domestic system, and, if anything, the Industrial Revolution enabled a social and economic uplift. Reformers, however, tend to have short memories and a small regard for hard facts. Speaking from their heart and conscience, U.S. reformers also attacked the factory system as the cause of numerous problems. One of the most outspoken critics was Washington Gladden, a Columbus, Ohio, minister, who articulated the major problems of the times as labor unrest, intemperance, poverty, slums, and child and female labor.[18] According to Gladden, solutions for labor unrest resided largely in organizing workers into strong unions to resist employers, providing profit sharing for workers, and requiring arbitration of labor-management disputes. Temperance was essential: the greatest evil for workers was alcohol, because of its contribution to poverty and an ever-widening circle of effects such as slums, family disintegration, and other social evils. As Richard T. Ely, one of the early proponents of the Social Gospel, put it, "drink [is] the poor man's curse so often, and so often the rich man's shame."[19] Some social problems, such as child and female labor, could be dealt with only through legislation. Above all, society must be Christianized and the Golden Rule applied by both labor and management. Similar appeals were made by others for profit sharing, the right to organize trade unions, arbitration of industrial disputes, cooperative stores for workers, and national legislation to govern the hiring and firing of employees, the employment of women and children, and sanitation in workplaces.[20]

Whereas reformers defined the labor question as a broad one, engineers and economists saw the answers as residing in a more limited sphere. Methods and

---

18. Washington Gladden, *Working People and Their Employers* (New York: Arno Press, 1969). Originally published in 1876. See also Jacob H. Dorn, *Washington Gladden: Prophet of the Social Gospel* (Columbus: Ohio State University Press, 1966).

19. Richard T. Ely, *The Labor Movement in America* (New York: T Y. Crowell, 1886), p. ix.

20. For an example, see William E. Barns, ed., *The Labor Problem* (New York: Harper and Brothers, 1886); for a contrary view, see Simon Newcomb, *A Plain Man's Talk on the Labor Question* (New York: Harper and Brothers, 1886).

systems would improve factory operations, but there had to be some incentive provided to obtain worker cooperation and stimulate their response to the need to improve output. Many managers of that period, such as James W. See, noted the common problem of low productivity, which was due to soldiering, or the deliberate restriction of output. Workers tended to work in spurts, take it easy when the supervisor was not present, and do less than their abilities would allow. The one thing that engineers and economists felt they could do to solve this problem was create some payment system based on performance, that is, wage incentives or piecework payments.

In Chapter 3 we noted that Adam Smith broke with the mercantilist position that the hungriest worker was the best. Smith advocated high wages to make workers more "active, diligent, and expeditious," but noted that some employees would overwork themselves if employers did not moderate those impulses. Smith's writing also suggested a backward bending supply curve of labor, that is, workers would work in spurts, then be absent from work once their income reached the desired level to engage in leisure activities, or perhaps rest.

Another English economist, David Schloss, reported that workers disliked piecework because "the difficulty of fixing a piece wage [rate] is very great" and often depended upon the employers' idea of how quickly the work should be done.[21] Employers also were prone to "nibble" at the rate, that is, gradually increase the amount of work expected for the same wage payment. Schloss also reported a "lump of labor" phenomenon, that is, in the worker's mind there was a fixed amount of work to be done and, by working more slowly, this amount of work could be spread more thinly over the work force. Schloss attributed the fallacy of lump of labor perception to how work standards were set at that time, that is, 1894.[22] Essentially, an individual's day's work was determined by an uneasy balance between what the supervisor expected and the pressures from co-workers. If the worker did too little, the ire of the supervisor was incurred, with possible dismissal from the job. If the worker did too much, group pressures to hold back production would increase, based on the assumption of a lump of labor. Thus, a day's work was an informally bargained compromise between contending forces.

Although there were doubts about the efficacy of payment for results rather than time-work, there appeared to be a connection between higher pay, lower per unit costs, and greater productivity. A U.S. economist, Edward Atkinson, observed that "the cheapest labor is the best-paid labor; it is the best-paid labor applied to machinery that assures the largest product in ratio to the capital invested."[23] If an employer paid low wages, the output would also be low; but if workers were paid well and combined with machinery, the output would be high. Schoenhof, for

———
21. David F. Schloss, "Why Working-Men Dislike Piece Work," *Economic Review* 1 (1891), pp. 313, 320. Reprinted in Wren, *Early Management Thought*, pp. 229–244.

22. David F. Schloss, *Methods of Industrial Remuneration* (London: Williams and Norgate, 1894).

23. Atkinson, *Distribution of Products*, p. 63.

example, compared various countries and found that those that paid the highest wages had the lowest costs.[24] Thus, nail makers in Pittsburgh were paid ten times as much as those in Great Britain, yet their nails cost one-half as much. This paradox of high wages and low costs resurfaces in the scientific management movement, which is presented in the next section.

If high wages led to increased productivity and to lower costs per unit, then the solution resided in linking pay with performance. One set of proposals involved profit sharing, which was recognized as early as 1775 by the French economist A. R. J. Turgot, practiced by the Parisian housepainting firm of *Maison Leclaire,* and advocated by Charles Babbage. Profit sharing would encourage workers to produce more at less cost because they would share in the benefits. By 1887, over thirty U.S. firms had adopted some form of profit sharing, including John Wanamaker Dry Goods, Pillsbury Flour, Procter & Gamble, and Yale and Towne.[25] Yale and Towne, however, dropped profit sharing after a brief period when its chief executive, Henry R. Towne, contended that profit sharing was not an appropriate solution to the problem of greater worker productivity. In profit sharing, savings from worker efforts in one department could be offset by a lack of diligence in others. Instead, Towne proposed to determine costs and productivity for each work unit or department and to return to them the gains according to their own performance. Towne's plan guaranteed a wage rate to each employee, plus a fifty–fifty split of the gain in the worker's department.[26]

Another proposal was Frederick A. Halsey's "Premium Plan of Paying for Labor," in which he attacked the evils of both profit sharing and individual piece-work systems.[27] He saw a lack of motivation in profit sharing and abuses in the piece-rate system. Halsey proposed that incentives be based on past production records, plus a guaranteed minimum wage, plus a premium for doing more work. The premium would amount to about one-third more than the daily or hourly rate and leave two-thirds of the added value to accrue to the employer, who would be therefore less inclined to cut the rate.

In 1895, Frederick W. Taylor proposed a method or rate-setting and a piece-rate system as a "step toward partial solution of the labor problem." From that point forward, the systematic management movement was in firmer hands and had a more coherent direction. But the foundations had been prepared: organizations had grown, resources accumulated, the labor question debated, and the need for resource rationalization became apparent. Systematic management was a prelude and a cohort of what came to be known as scientific management. We will return to this story later.

---

24. J. Schoenhof, *The Economy of High Wages* (1893), cited in Litterer, "Systematic Management: The Search for Order and Integration," p. 463. Litterer notes other studies that yielded similar findings.

25. Nicholas P Gilman, *Profit Sharing between Employer and Employee* (Boston: Houghton Mifflin, 1889); and Mary W. Calkins, *Sharing the Profits* (Boston: Ginn, 1888).

26. Henry R. Towne, "Gain Sharing," *Transactions, ASME* 10 (1889), pp. 600–625.

27. *Transactions, ASME* 12 (1891), pp. 755–764.

BIG BUSINESS AND ITS CHANGING ENVIRONMENT

No nation can undergo a transformation as the United States did in the last half of the nineteenth century without substantial repercussions. An examination of the U.S. response to industrialization is necessary to understand the forces that would shape the twentieth century. We have seen the accumulation of resources and systematic management as an emerging response to the growth of large-scale organization. Let us look beyond these developments to examine evolving notions of business and society, the beginnings of a national labor movement, the new technologies that transformed how people lived, and the changing relationship between government and business.

BUSINESS AND SOCIETY: BARONS OR BENEFACTORS?

Virtuous conduct seldom makes news. Historians and journalists are awed by the extraordinary and, more frequently than not, overemphasize it to the detriment of those quiet, sturdy, responsible people who, unheralded, are the true productive builders. Criticism of business leaders and their practices began to appear primarily in the latter third of the nineteenth century. Although the origins are obscure, one early reference described Cornelius Vanderbilt as a medieval baron, drawing an analogy to the feudal lords who built castles along the Rhine River in order to exact tolls from those who passed by. The phrase *robber barons* appeared later, and Matthew Josephson popularized this phrase to such a point that the public often equated any business leader with this value system. It would be impossible to examine all those deemed to be robber barons, but some thumbnail sketches will reveal why Josephson felt that some business leaders were behaving in socially irresponsible ways.

Commodore Cornelius Vanderbilt gained control of the New York and Harlem railroad line by bribing the New York state legislature and manipulating stock. Daniel Drew had the dubious honor of being the first to engage in the practice that came to be called watering stock. He had purchased a herd of cattle with an enlistment bonus from his Civil War army days. In transporting the herd to market, he fed them salt to make them thirsty, then offered them all the water they could drink and sold at a very large profit some temporarily overweight cattle. Together with Jay Gould and Jim Fisk, Drew turned to railroading and soon gave the Erie line its reputation for mismanagement in the days following Daniel McCallum. The Western railroaders, led by Collis P. Huntington and aided by Leland Stanford, Sr., purchased the favors of legislators who could grant them free government land, award franchises, and pass enabling legislation. One year Huntington paid $200,000 to get a bill through Congress; he later complained that Congress was costing up to a half million dollars a session and moaned, "I am afraid this damnation Congress will kill us."[28]

---

28. Matthew Josephson, *The Robber Barons* (New York: Harcourt Brace Jovanovich, 1934), p. 357.

Not all of the barons were railroad men. John D. Rockefeller combined audacity and cunning in building his South Improvement Company and the Standard Oil colossus. By conspiring with the railroads, he was able to extract rebates on his freight and receive rebates on oil shipped by his rivals. Andrew Carnegie at one point owned or controlled two-thirds of the nation's young steel industry. The Homestead strike earned Carnegie poor press when union efforts were met with a force of Pinkerton detectives (hired to protect the plant) who were brutally stoned and beaten by the striking workers. State troops moved in and secured the plant for a wholly nonunion crew; in the process fourteen were killed and 163 wounded. These men represented, at least for Josephson, the most unsavory practices in U.S. business leadership.

What motivated the robber barons? For some social historians, it was the publication in 1859 of Charles Darwin's book *On the Origin of Species by Means of Natural Selection, or the Preservation of Favored Races in the Struggle for Life*. This book set forth his theories concerning evolution and natural selection through the struggle for existence. Social scientists seized Darwin's theories in an attempt to apply them to human society and the result was "social Darwinism."[29] The most striking phrases of Darwinism, "struggle for existence" and "survival of the fittest," suggested that nature would provide that the most fit in a competitive situation would win. Thus, through unrestricted competition, the most fit would survive and move up the social ladder of success and the unfit would occupy the lower class structures and eventually be eliminated through evolution.

Are these allegations true? One historian claimed that businesspeople were pragmatic doers who worked out the rules as they met them; they read or heard little of Darwin or Adam Smith and cared little for abstract social and economic theories.[30] Another agreed: "It is not true that this commitment [to competition] was grounded on Darwinian premises." Few businesspeople knew enough of Darwin "to turn biology to the uses of self-justification."[31] What can be concluded about the effect of social Darwinism on the thought and practices of those in business? The economics of the period led to mergers rather than to cutthroat competition as social Darwinism would predict. For example, Chandler saw Rockefeller's efforts as attempts to gain economies of scale rather than as an effort to monopolize the industry. Under Rockefeller, the cost of a gallon of kerosene went from 1.5 cents before the Standard Oil trust to less than one-half of 1 cent by 1885.[32] Before the

---

29. Richard Hofstadter, *Social Darwinism in American Thought* (Boston: Beacon Press, 1945), p. 4.

30. Edward C. Kirkland, *Dream and Thought in the Business Community, 1860–1900* (Ithaca, N.Y.: Cornell University Press, 1956), p. 14. Another who shares this pragmatic view is Peter D. A. Jones, ed., *The Robber Barons Revisited* (Boston: D. C. Heath, 1968), pp. v–xi.

31. Raymond J. Wilson, ed., *Darwinism and the American Intellectual: A Book of Readings* (Homewood, Ill.: Dorsey Press, 1967), p. 93.

32. Alfred D. Chandler, Jr., "The Emergence of Managerial Capitalism," *Business History Review* 5 (Winter 1984), pp. 473–503.

discovery and refining of oil, animal fat was used for lubricating wheels and gears, and before kerosene, whale oil was used for lighting. Perhaps saving the whales was not Rockefeller's intention, but kerosene kept them from extinction. Earlier we saw that Carnegie drove the price of steel downward constantly, which may have been his greatest philanthropy. Business leaders gave bribes when politicians forced them to do so; for example, when Ezra Cornell sought a charter from the New York State legislature to found a college at Ithaca, he had to strike a "bargain" with the "friends of Geneseo College," who, in return for a $25,000 gift to that college, would assure him the needed votes. As Cornell noted in his "cipher" book, "Such is the influence of corrupt legislation."[33]

It is highly doubtful that business leaders found much in social Darwinism. Rather, it appears that the period was one of change, and business leaders were highly visible targets for the critics.

> The creation of the Robber Baron stereotype seems to have been the product of an impulsive popular attempt to explain the shift in the structure of American society ... most critics appeared to slip into the easy vulgarizations of the "devil-view" of history which ingenuously assumes that all misfortunes can be traced to the machinations of an easily located set of villains—in this case, the big businessmen of America.[34]

Rising in counterpoint to social Darwinism was another set of ideas that came closer to grasping the policies and practices of the nineteenth-century business leader. This new consciousness was described earlier as the Social Gospel, and it was seen as Christianity in action by people such as Washington Gladden. We will return to the Social Gospel and how it led to improved personnel practices and to an interest in the problems of industry.

Another set of developments also suggests that business leaders were far more generous than typically assumed. Were there any benefactions by business to society during this period? The philanthropy of business people is as ancient as business itself, including patrons of arts and letters, providers of funds for community projects, donors to churches, and endowers of educational institutions. No one questioned the right of successful persons to give away some or all of their fortunes; after all, it was their money to do with as they pleased. But what of this new phenomenon, the corporation? Could its managers and directors give away a portion of its profits to non-business-related endeavors?

Two legal principles, the notion of limited charter powers and that of management as trustee of the stockholders' property, combined to form the nineteenth-century legal basis regarding corporate philanthropy. A case precedent in 1881

---

33. Carl L. Becker, *Cornell University: Founders and Founding* (Ithaca, N.Y.: Cornell University Press, 1943), pp. 103–107, 154.

34. John Tipple, "The Anatomy of Prejudice: Origins of the Robber Baron Legend," *Business History Review* 33 (Winter 1959), p. 521.

involved the Old Colony Railway Company of Massachusetts, which had subscribed to underwrite the financial loss suffered by a "world's peace jubilee and international music festival." Despite the fact that the railroad had increased passenger traffic because of the jubilee, the court ruled in favor of the shareholders that this subscription was *ultra vires* (i.e., outside its chartered powers).[35] In Great Britain in 1883, the West Cork Railroad Company attempted to compensate its employees for the loss of their jobs occasioned by the dissolution of the corporation. In ruling against the company, Lord Justice Bowden stated the guiding rule: "Charity has no business sitting at the board of directors qua charity ... [the board of directors] can only spend money which is not their's [*sic*], but the company's, if they are spending it for purposes which are reasonably incidental to the carrying on of the business of the company."[36] What might or might not be reasonably incidental would receive some clarification in the Steinway case. The court allowed piano manufacturers Steinway and Sons to buy an adjoining tract of land to be used for a church, library, and school for their employees. The court's reasoning was that the employees would benefit, so there was a definite quid pro quo accruing to the corporation's benefit in better employee relations.[37] In short, the law was fairly clear in the position that corporations were chartered to do specific things, that managers and directors were trustees of the property of the shareholders, and that directors could give away assets only if it was of measurable benefit to the corporation. Each of the legal points sorely constrained corporate philanthropy, and it would be almost three-quarters of a century before corporations could engage in philanthropic endeavors of general benefit.

Although corporate philanthropy might be questioned, it would be unlikely that the hand of individual charity would be nipped. Individual philanthropy would be the vehicle for expressing the social conscience of the nineteenth-century entrepreneur. Only a few of the great philanthropist-business leaders can be mentioned here.[38] Ezra Cornell pioneered in telegraphy, made a fortune from the Western Union Company, and provided the money to found a college (in Ithaca, New York), which would naturally be named for him; William Colgate helped people get closer to godliness with the manufacture of soap, and he and his heirs gave so much to a college that it changed its name to his; Moses Brown, Samuel Slater's partner, founded Rhode Island College in Providence (1770), which became Brown University in 1804; Johns Hopkins, founder of the Baltimore and Ohio Railroad, also founded the eminent university in Baltimore that bears his name; and Cornelius Vanderbilt made a large bequest in 1873 that converted a small Methodist seminary in Nashville into a well-known university that received its name from him.

---

35. *Davis v. Old Colony Railway Company,* 131 Mass. 258 (1881).

36. *Hutton v. West Cork Railroad Company,* 23 Chancery Division Reports 654 (1883).

37. *Steinway v. Steinway and Sons,* 40 N.Y.S. 718 (1896).

38. For an extensive list, see Daniel A. Wren, "American Business Philanthropy and Higher Education in the Nineteenth Century," *Business History Review* 57 (Autumn 1983), pp. 321–346. See also Mark Sharfman, "Changing Institutional Rules: The Evolution of Corporate Philanthropy, 1883–1953," *Business and Society* 33 (December 1994), pp. 236–269.

There were more: Joseph Wharton, whose $100,000 grant enabled the nation's first school of business, at the University of Pennsylvania; Edward Tuck, who honored his father with a gift of $300,000 to Dartmouth College to start the Amos Tuck School of Administration and Finance (1899); Leland Stanford, who honored his son with a university (1891); John Stevens, who provided for an institute of technology (1870); and James B. Duke, who established the trust fund to create Trinity College (later renamed for the Duke family). Good fortune did not smile on all colleges who hoped for a philanthropist. Daniel Drew gave a $250,000 promissory note to endow a Methodist theological seminary in Madison, New Jersey. The seminary started its work, but Daniel Drew went bankrupt and was never able to deliver the promised money. Nonetheless, the seminary was named Drew University.

Other philanthropists are better known. Rockefeller endowed the University of Chicago in 1896, gave millions through a general education fund to educate southern African-Americans, and by the time of his death in 1937 had given away half a billion dollars as well as provided for the future of the foundation that bears the family name. Carnegie had given away $350 million by the time of his death (1919), and his libraries, university, and foundation are enduring monuments to his expressed stewardship of wealth philosophy. Despite such generosity, both Rockefeller and Carnegie were denounced by the Congressional Committee on Industrial Relations in 1915 as "menaces to society."[39] Their efforts were seen as intrusions into the province of government and reflected the fear that business charity had the potential of increasing the control of the business community over society.

Times have changed: income and inheritance taxes make it difficult to accumulate as much wealth as did the entrepreneurs of the nineteenth century, the legal question of corporate philanthropy has been clarified (as we shall see later), and public expectations about the role of business in society have changed. But we are the recipients today of the benefactions of the nineteenth-century builders of the United States.

BUSINESS AND LABOR: THE CONDITION OF THE WORKER

Earlier we saw that the *Commonwealth v. Hunt* decision (1842) removed combinations of workers from the conspiracy doctrine that had prevailed in Great Britain. In the United States, labor organizations were found among craft workers, such as in the building trades, and among so-called brotherhoods of railway employees. Attempts of other workers to form unions were generally less successful. The National Labor Union, headed by William H. Sylvis, sought to supplant the wage system with cooperative production in which the workers would pool their resources, supply their own labor, and manage the factories. The Noble Order of the Knights of Labor,

---

39. Cited by Clarence C. Walton, *Corporate Social Responsibilities* (Belmont, Calif.: Wadsworth, 1967), pp. 41–42.

organized in 1867, sought an eight-hour day, the establishment of a bureau of labor statistics, protection of child labor, a graduated income tax, government ownership of railroads and telegraph lines, the abolition of national banks, and a system of cooperation to take the place of wages. Neither of these organizations survived.

Labor violence in the 1880s and 1890s fueled public fears of unions. The Molly Maguires terrorized the populace with murders and other atrocities in the Pennsylvania coalfields. The Haymarket Affair (1886), in which the Knights of Labor tried to enforce a general strike in Chicago, led to several deaths. The Homestead strike (1892) and the Pullman strike (1894) were other examples of violence brought about by confrontations between labor and management. Public fear of radicals and anarchists, who were often equated with legitimate union organizers, kept the union movement at a relative standstill in terms of growth as a percentage of the labor force. Total union membership grew from 300,000 members in 1870 to 868,000 in 1900; however, in 1870, only 5 percent of the total labor force was organized; this percentage declined in the 1880s and 1890s, but recovered and rose to 4.8 by 1900.

One successful union was the American Federation of Labor, organized in 1886 as a federation of craft unions that concentrated on the pursuit of immediate economic gains for the worker on the job rather than on distant political reforms. Under the leadership of Samuel Gompers, membership increased from fewer than 200,000 in 1886 to more than 2,865,000 at the time of Gompers' death in 1924. [40] Industrial workers, however, had to await other times and a changing public opinion to legitimize their attempts at organization.

Immigration provided a growing work force for this period of rapid industrial growth: Chinese were brought in to build the railroads, and Irish, Germans, and Swedes populated the coalfields and steel mills of the United States. After 1880, another flow of Slavs, Poles, and Italians added to the swelling work force. The increased supply of labor did not result in lower wages for the U.S. worker. Daily wages and annual earnings in manufacturing increased 50 percent between 1860 and 1890, and real wages (the purchasing power of the workers' incomes) increased 60 percent from 1860 to 1890 (1.6 percent compounded annually).[41] In summary, the U.S. worker benefited from the growth of industry in terms of employment and real income.

INVENTIVE AND INNOVATIVE IMPULSES

Earlier we saw the influence of the railroads in creating a national market, probing the interior of lands where nature had furnished no natural pathways. When the Union Pacific and the Central Pacific railroads met at Promontory, Utah in 1869, a golden spike commemorated the spanning of the nation, connecting east and west,

---

40. Philip A. Taft, *The A.F.L. in the Time of Gompers* (New York: Harper and Row, 1957), ch. 3.

41. Ross M. Robertson, *History of the American Economy,* 3rd ed. (New York: Harcourt Brace Jovanovich, 1973), pp. 379–380.

the beginning of a network of rails that would increase from 35,000 miles in 1865 to 193,000 by 1900. Technological advancements made rail travel more pleasurable: steel rails replaced iron ones; George Pullman introduced the sleeping car in 1865; and George Westinghouse developed the air brake in 1868, making rail travel safer. The railroads fostered a retailing revolution, as we shall see, by creating greater time and place utility through mass distribution. With the railroads, interstate commerce was facilitated, but also made more complicated because there were no standard times from one area to the next. It could be noon in Chicago, 12:30 P.M. in Pittsburgh, and 11:45 A.M. in St. Louis, a most confusing situation for the shipper or the traveler. The solution was four time zones, based on the 75th, 90th, 105th, and 120th meridians. Standard times became effective on the railways in 1883, but the U.S. Congress did not accept this until 1918.

The railroads were only one technological advancement in America's last half of the nineteenth century. The remarkable spirit of inventive and innovative impulses that shaped America's technological advances were due to a number of prime movers, individuals whose ideas created the wealth of the nation. As Locke expressed it, "for wealth to be created, individuals must create it … *prime movers* … moved society forward by the force of their own creative imagination, their own energy, and their own productive capacity."[42] We find these individuals during this time pushing forward the nation's capacity to produce more, to create jobs, and to devise means of making, moving and packaging a cornucopia of consumer products that had few, if any, precedents.

The telegraph was the companion of railroads in this revolution in commerce. Chandler expressed these revolutions of communication and transportation and the growth of enterprise in terms of scale and scope: *scale* referred to the increased size of a single operating unit making a single product, and *scope* was used to describe the processes within a single operating unit to distribute more than one product.[43] Carnegie's vertical integration in the steel industry indicated the economies of scale; and using his facilities for different types of steel products would illustrate economies of scope. As scale and scope expanded, the need for a team of managers to plan, coordinate and monitor the functions of the firm increased. With the rail system, the telegraph, and Alexander Graham Bell's telephone, it became possible to produce, transport, and sell in national and international markets.

The business firm of the last half of the nineteenth century was an entirely different creation from the localized, family owned and managed, and labor intensive firms of the pre–Civil War period. To mention all of the prime movers in the creation of the emerging capital intensive, large-scale, professionally managed firms is beyond our present task. Some, such as Thomas Edison and George Westinghouse, enabled the natural force of electricity to be transformed, transmitted, and controlled by humans. John D. Rockefeller's domination of the kerosene market for

---

42. Edwin A. Locke, *Prime Movers: Traits of the Great Wealth Creators* (New York: American Management Association, 2000), p. 7.

43. Chandler, *Scale and Scope,* pp. 17–28.

lighting would be replaced with electricity. Bell's telephone did not need to follow the railroad tracks and marked the beginning of the American Telephone and Telegraph Company. Elisha Gray invented the first fax machine, his "telautograph" for facsimile writing and drawing for transmission over the telegraph.

With improvements in communication and transportation came the mass marketers, the chain-retailers, mail order houses, and food merchants such as the Great Atlantic and Pacific Tea Company. Refrigerated rail cars transformed the meat packing industry, and brought numerous perishable products to distant markets. The American System of Manufactures enabled mass production of Isaac Singer's sewing machines and Cyrus McCormick's grain harvester. Christopher Sholes licensed his typewriter to Eliphalet Remington for production by the Remington Arms Company. Andrew Carnegie's stronger, lighter, structural steel enabled high-rise buildings, but Elisha Otis's elevator made travel to the top less taxing. These were a few of those prime movers whose ideas were the basis of emerging large-scale enterprise in manufacturing, communications, marketing, distilling, refining, transporting, and food processing.

Corporate research and development did not begin until the twentieth century with Bell Labs, General Electric, Du Pont, and others who followed. The latter part of America's nineteenth century was the age of the individualistic inventors and innovators, the wealth creators of a new material abundance in the history of humankind.

BUSINESS AND GOVERNMENT: THE SEEDS OF REFORM

U.S. government of the nineteenth century was not noted for its progressiveness. The spoils system prevailed (that is, to the winner belong the spoils), and various attempts at reform had failed. Finally, shortly after the assassination of President James Garfield by a disappointed office seeker, the Civil Service Act of 1883 (better known as the Pendleton Act after its senatorial sponsor) was passed. The intent of the civil service reform was to bring qualified employees, rather than political favorites, to government and to provide some stability in the governmental infrastructure. Thus, the seeds of systematic management and rationalization appear to have been operational in the public as well as the private sector.

Credit for attempting to bring system to governmental service must be given to Woodrow Wilson, then a young professor at Bryn Mawr College. In 1887, Wilson recognized that civil service reform must extend beyond personnel matters into the organization and methods of governmental offices. To accomplish this, Wilson recommended "administrative study to discover, first, what government can properly and successfully do, and secondly, how it can do these proper things with the utmost possible efficiency and the least possible cost either of money or energy." The study of government, according to Wilson, had focused too long on politics and not enough on how to manage the public's business. After all, "the field of administration is a field of business … removed from the hurry and strife of politics.… The object of administrative study is to rescue executive methods from the confusion and costliness of empirical experience and set them on foundations laid deep in stable principle."[44] Wilson would move on to higher office, but his thinking was clear in terms of bringing improved systems and methods to government.

In terms of national policy there were few effective efforts at the regulation of business, as government held true to a narrowly construed commerce clause. The first attempts to reform business practices came very logically with the railroads. In 1869, Massachusetts passed the first statutes regulating railroads; the Granger laws of the seventies brought regulation to others, and the Interstate Commerce Act of 1887, though it proved generally ineffective in practice, became the first national regulation. Beyond the railroads, the Sherman Antitrust Act of 1890 sought to check corporate trusts and monopoly practices "in restraint of trade." Poorly defined and narrowly construed, it was generally ineffectual. To illustrate further the hands-off policy, even taxpayers benefited. The first peacetime federal income tax was imposed by the Wilson-Gorman Tax Act of 1894. It levied a 2 percent personal tax on all incomes above $4,000 and a 2 percent tax on all corporate net income. In 1895, the Supreme Court declared the act unconstitutional. Taxpayers could rest easy for a few more years. In brief, the nineteenth-century political environment remained relatively laissez-faire, true to the precepts of Adam Smith; the twentieth century would bring a host of changes in this philosophy.

SUMMARY OF PART I

Part I of this study has been an examination of management thought prior to the scientific management era in the United States and may be visually conceptualized as Figure 6-1. People, a fundamental focus of our study, have manifold needs and wants, which they seek to satisfy through organized endeavors. In organizations, management is an activity that performs certain functions in order to obtain the effective acquisition, allocation, and utilization of human efforts and physical resources to meet the organization's objectives and yield positive benefits to organizational members. The cultural environment, characterized as having economic, social, technological and political facets, shapes values and forms institutional arrangements that have a significant bearing on people, organizations, and management as an activity.

Early civilizations reflected some attempts to relate individuals to organizations, but generally placed a low value on economic activity and held a parochial view of the management function. The cultural rebirth brought new views of people, economic activity, social values, and political arrangements and established the preconditions for the Industrial Revolution. This technological and cultural revolution created the factory system to replace the domestic system and posed managerial problems on a scale never before encountered. Broadly viewed, these problems

---

44. Woodrow Wilson, "The Study of Administration," *Political Science Quarterly* 2 (June 1887), pp. 197, 210.

FIGURE 6-1   **SYNOPSIS OF EARLY MANAGEMENT THOUGHT**

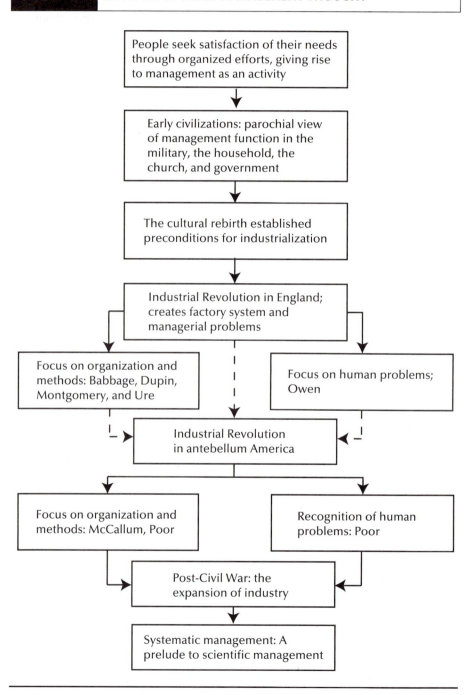

may be grouped in three categories: (1) the organizational and methods problems of melding technology, materials, organizational functions, and productive processes in an efficient manner; (2) the human problems of acquiring, developing, stimulating, and controlling human behavior toward preconceived ends; and (3) the managerial problem of fusing both these facets in order to accomplish objectives.

Throughout this study of management thought, we will see that various writers shift their relative emphasis on the importance of the organization and methods facets vis-à-vis the human facet. This does not mean that these two facets are mutually exclusive, but that it is a matter of relative focus, and this focus to a large degree is influenced by the cultural environment. For example, Charles Babbage was concerned with the human problems of the factory, but his primary interest was the analysis of production techniques. Robert Owen, on the other hand, was more concerned with the impact of industrialization on people. Likewise, Henry Varnum Poor was concerned with the systematization of the railroads but recognized the interaction of the organization and methods facets with the human facet.

Figure 6-1 illustrates in summary form management thought before scientific management. It shows early ideas about management activity, depicts the relative emphases of management pioneers, and provides the basis for the beginnings of the scientific management era in the United States.

The Scientific
Management Era

Part II begins with the work of Frederick W. Taylor and examines management thought in Europe, the United States, and elsewhere up to the early 1930s. Taylor provided the major thrust for an era characterized by a search for efficiency and systematization in management thought. Around Taylor others, such as Carl Barth, H. L. Gantt, Frank and Lillian Gilbreth, Morris Cooke, and Harrington Emerson, were spreading the gospel of efficiency in the United States. Though the work of Taylor and his followers dominated this era, some early behavioral contributions are also reviewed as a prelude to the emergence of human relations in industry. Part II next examines the work of Henri Fayol and Max Weber, who wrote during the scientific management era but whose contributions to the development of management thought were recognized much later. Finally, this part concludes with a conceptual view of the economic, social, and political conditions that constituted the cultural environment of scientific management.

CHAPTER 7

The Advent of
Scientific Management

E arlier chapters reviewed the transformation of American industry in the post–Civil War period. Although the United States entered the Industrial Revolution with textiles, its first big business was the railroads. Daniel McCallum introduced systematic management on the Erie, and his ideas moved onward to influence other railroads and Carnegie in steel. Railroads opened new markets, and the telegraph connected the nation for financial, production, marketing, and other transactions.

Another stage of the Industrial Revolution began in the latter half of the nineteenth century. It was a complex, uneven, and interacting outcome of technological advances, changing power sources, evolving labor-management relations, and a desperate need to bring all these factors into some concordance by systematizing managerial practices. As engineers were vital to developing and installing advances in technology and power, it was natural that they became a prime source of information about management practices. Henry Towne, for example, called for engineers to look beyond the technical side of manufacturing and become involved in the economizing of efforts within the factory. One of the young engineers who responded to the Towne paper was Frederick W. Taylor, and he is the focal point of this chapter.

FREDERICK WINSLOW TAYLOR: THE EARLY YEARS

Frederick Winslow Taylor (1856–1915) was born in Germantown, Pennsylvania. His father was a fairly prosperous lawyer of Quaker stock and his mother traced her Puritan roots to a Plymouth, Massachusetts, ancestor who arrived in America in 1629.[1] Taylor's early education was

1. The life of Taylor is a popular subject for biographies. A much cited source is Frank Barkley Copley, *Frederick W. Taylor: Father of Scientific Management*, 2 vols. (New York: Harper and Row, 1923). Other useful sources are Charles D. Wrege and Ronald G. Greenwood, *Frederick W. Taylor, the Father of Scientific Management: Myth and Reality* (Homewood, Ill.: Business One Irwin, 1991); Daniel Nelson, *Frederick W. Taylor and the Rise of Scientific Management* (Madison: University of Wisconsin Press, 1980); and Robert Kanigel, *The One Best Way: Frederick Winslow Taylor and The Enigma of Efficiency* (New York: Viking, 1997).

liberally sprinkled with the classics, the study of French and German, and occasional trips to Europe. His parents intended that he should follow his father's profession of law and duly enrolled him at Phillips Exeter Academy to prepare for Harvard. The competition was stiff, and Taylor's zeal and restless energy led to late nights and long hours, eventually impairing his eyesight and causing headaches. Although he passed the Harvard entrance exams with honors, and eyeglasses solved the vision and headache problems, Taylor decided to turn away from law school and into an apprenticeship as a patternmaker and machinist with the Enterprise Hydraulic Works of Philadelphia. He started his four-year apprenticeship at no wage (since his father was a man of means) and was making the grand sum of $3 a week when he finished his apprenticeship in 1878. At Enterprise, Taylor developed an empathy for the workers' point of view; he could swear with the best of them and admired their sense of pride in their skill. However, he saw about him what he called "bad industrial conditions," worker restriction of output, poor management, and lack of harmony between workers and managers.

TAYLOR AT MIDVALE

Taylor moved to Midvale Steel, Philadelphia, in 1878 as a common laborer. The economic consequences of the financial panic of 1873 lingered, and jobs were scarce. Midvale, under the presidency of William Sellers, was one of the leading steel firms of the era. There, Taylor rose from common laborer to clerk, to machinist, to gang boss of the machinists, to supervisor of the machine shop, to master mechanic in charge of repairs and maintenance throughout the plant, and to chief engineer—all in six years. His twelve years at Midvale (1878–1890) were years of experimentation that provided the basis for Taylor's ideas about shop management. Realizing that he lacked a scientific education, he enrolled in a home study course from Stevens Institute of Technology, in Hoboken, New Jersey. Taylor never attended classes except to take examinations, and he graduated with a degree in mechanical engineering in 1883.[2] He studied for a total of two and a half years, all the while fulfilling his full-time duties at Midvale.

Taylor had no training in management and relied solely on his own investigations as to what should be done. The company had established a differential piecework incentive system that Taylor knew to be ineffective from his working days. Midvale management felt that the workers would control their own behavior and would be properly motivated once given the piece-rate incentive. When Taylor became gang boss, he learned otherwise. He estimated that worker output was only one-third of what was possible.

The restriction of output at Midvale was classified by Taylor as "natural soldiering" and "systematic soldiering." Natural soldiering proceeded from "the natural

---

2. Jane G. Hartye, quoted in *The Stute*, vol. 91, no. 13 (December 6, 1991). Hartye was the long-time curator of the Taylor Collection at the Stevens Institute of Technology.

instinct and tendency of men to take it easy"; systematic soldiering came from the workers' "more intricate second thought and reasoning caused by their relations with other men."[3] Natural soldiering could be overcome by a manager able to inspire or force workers to come up to the mark. Systematic soldiering posed a different problem, and managers for years had been attempting to cope with the tendency of individuals to conform to group output norms. Why did workers soldier? Taylor answered as follows: first, they believed that to work faster would throw large numbers of workers out of work; second, the defective management systems then in use forced workers to work slowly to protect their own interests; and third, they adhered to rule-of-thumb work methods handed down from generation to generation.[4]

Frederick W. Taylor from his Midvale days, circa 1886. Courtesy Frederick Winslow Taylor Collection, Stevens Institute of Technology, Hoboken, New Jersey.

Taylor placed the blame on management, not on the workers, for he thought that it was management's job to design the jobs properly and to offer the proper incentives to overcome worker soldiering.

In no small part, systematic soldiering arose out of a "lump of labor" theory, which postulated that there was a limited amount of work in the world and that to do more today left less to be done tomorrow; that is, you could work yourself or your fellow employees out of a job if you worked too fast. A daily or hourly wage system encouraged soldiering, because pay was based on attendance and position, not effort. Working harder brought no reward, and thus workers were actually encouraged to be lazy. Piece-rate systems, old long before Taylor's time, sought to encourage individual incentive and initiative by paying workers on the basis of their output, but such systems had generally been failures; standards were often poorly set, employers cut the rates when workers earned too much, and workers hid their shortcut methods and improvements from management to protect themselves. With ample experience of cuts when they exceeded a certain amount of income, workers developed a consensus about how much each should produce and earn, not only to protect themselves but undoubtedly also to avoid the ridicule of the less capable. The workers perceived that management envisioned some maximum sum of pay and any earnings beyond that would lead to rate cuts. Taylor did not blame the

---

3. Frederick W. Taylor, *Shop Management* (New York: Harper and Row, 1903), p. 30.

4. Frederick W. Taylor, *The Principles of Scientific Management* (New York: Harper and Row, 1911), pp. 15–16.

workers; in fact, he sympathized with them because he felt that it was the wage system, not the workers, that was at fault.

Taylor's initial experiences as a machine-shop supervisor resulted in a bitter encounter with the workers. He told them that he knew they could do more and that he was going to see that they did. Taylor started by showing them how to use the lathes to get more output with very little more effort. He failed in retraining the machinists because they refused to follow his instructions; he then turned to training common laborers who, after learning the method, joined the group and resisted increased production. Taylor admitted, "I was up against a stone wall. I did not blame these laborers in my heart; my sympathy was with them all the time."[5] Taylor cut the rate to make the men work harder to earn the same pay. The men retaliated by breaking and jamming the machines. Taylor countered by a system of fines (the proceeds going to a worker benefit fund) for equipment damage. Eventually Taylor not only won the battle with the machinists but learned a valuable lesson as well. Never again would he use the system of fines, and he later established strict rules against rate cutting. More importantly, the young Taylor realized that a new industrial scheme was essential to prevent such bitter labor-management encounters. It was at this time at Midvale Steel that Taylor started to search for improved industrial practices.

THE SEARCH FOR SCIENCE IN MANAGEMENT

Taylor thought he could overcome soldiering by a careful investigation of work that could then be used in setting performance standards: once the workers saw that the rate was properly set, they would know that it was based on facts and not whims and their motivation to soldier would be reduced. The problem was in defining a full and fair day's standard for each task. Taylor set out to determine what the workers *ought* to be able to do with their equipment and materials, and this became the beginning of what was to be named scientific management, that is, the use of a scientific fact-finding method to determine empirically the right ways to perform tasks. Initially, Taylor probably did not envision that this step was the beginning of further applications to many jobs and industries. He did it because he felt that it would be a way to overcome the worker antagonism and resistance he had encountered earlier. He had the workers' interests in mind when he determined that management should have the responsibility for setting standards, planning work, and devising incentive schemes. He abhorred the previous methods of setting a rate based on past performance, leaving it up to the worker to be motivated to meet that rate, and cutting the rate if the worker earned too much.

Time study became the foundation of the Taylor system, and some questioned Taylor's claim to originality. Charles Babbage had earlier demonstrated the use of a watch in recording the labor operations and times necessary in the manufacture of

---

5. Copley, *Taylor,* vol. 1, p. 162.

pins. In 1912, a subcommittee of the American Society of Mechanical Engineers issued a report on time study that made no mention of Taylor's work but referenced Adam Smith and Charles Babbage. Taylor contributed to a discussion of this report in an effort to clarify his concept of time study and answer the doubters of his originality.

> Time study was begun in the machine shop of the Midvale Steel Company in 1881.... It is true that the form of Tables 1 and 2 [the Babbage contribution to the ASME report] is similar to that of the blanks recording time study, but here the resemblance ceases. Each line in Table 2, for instance, gives statistics regarding the average of the entire work of an operative who works day in and day out, in running a machine engaged in the manufacture of pins. This table involves no study whatever of the movements of the man, nor of the time in which the movements should have been made. Mere Statistics as to the time which a man takes to do a given piece of work do not constitute "time study": "time study," as its name implies, involves a careful study of the time in which work ought to be done ... [rather than] the time in which the work actually was done.[6]

Taylor's distinction supported his claim to originality since he was using time study for analytical rather than descriptive purposes; that is, future versus past uses of data. Taylor's time study had two phases: analytical and constructive. In analysis, each job was broken into as many simple elementary movements as possible, useless movements were discarded, the quickest and best methods for each elementary movement were selected by observing the most skilled worker at each, and the movement was timed and recorded. To the recorded time, percentages were added to allow for unavoidable delays and interruptions, to cover the newness of workers to a job, and for rest periods. The constructive phase involved building a file of elementary movements and times to be used wherever possible on other jobs or classes of work. Further, this phase led to consideration of improvements in tools, machines, materials, methods, and the ultimate standardization of all elements surrounding and accompanying the job.[7]

Whereas Babbage was content with gross times of actual performance, Taylor's method broke the job into component parts, tested them, and reconstructed the job as it *should* be done. Taylor thought that such scientific study on the job would form a proof to the worker to overcome resistance. In a later defense before his critics, Taylor denied that he sought exactness. "All we hope to do through time study is to get a vastly closer approximation as to time than we ever had before."[8]

———

6. *Ibid.*, pp. 225–226.

7. Taylor, *Shop Management*, pp. 149–176.

8. Copley, *Taylor*, vol. 1, pp. 234–235.

THE QUEST FOR IMPROVED INCENTIVES

The search for effective incentive plans is probably as old as humankind. Payment based on performance was the basis of the domestic system of production, and piece-rate incentives were used before and during the Industrial Revolution. As American industry developed after the Civil War, numerous schemes were proposed for paying labor, such as Henry Towne's gain sharing and Frederick Halsey's premium plan. Taylor's first paper presented to the ASME proposed a plan for paying labor and also attacked both the Towne and the Halsey plans.[9] The weakness in both, in Taylor's view, was that they assumed the workers' current output was the production standard, and they sought to induce workers to produce more by sharing the gain from their extra efforts with management. Taylor proposed a new system consisting of three parts: (1) observation and analysis through time study to set the rate, or standard; (2) a differential rate system of piecework that Charles Brinley had developed at Midvale Steel; and (3) "paying men and not positions."

In Taylor's opinion, profit sharing failed because it discouraged personal ambition by allowing all to share in profits regardless of their contribution and because of the "remoteness of the reward." This latter criticism of profit sharing was an early insight into the psychological principle of temporal contiguity, that is, the timing of the reinforcement with regard to the behavior, and reflected Taylor's view that a share of the profits at the end of the year gave little incentive for improved daily performance.

In his 1895 paper, Taylor had clearly put the onus on management to take charge, accept its responsibilities, and move away from the old system of leaving the work up to the worker. In the discussion following his presentation Taylor said he was "much surprised and disappointed that elementary rate-fixing has not received more attention during the discussion."[10] The participants discussed different payment plans but evidently did not realize that proper performance standards had to be established first. Under Taylor's plan, a rate-setting department planned the work and set a rate or standard for each task. Based on thorough study, this rate moved the measurement of job performance from guesswork and tradition to a more rational basis.

Once the standard was set, the incentive payment rate worked two ways: those who did not meet the standard received an ordinary rate of pay, and those who did attain the standard received extraordinary pay. The incentive became that of following the proper methods and making the standard in order to be rewarded. The notion of paying workers and not positions was designed partially to overcome soldiering but mainly to individualize workers by paying for their efforts and not for

---

9. Frederick W. Taylor, "A Piece-Rate System, Being a Step Toward Partial Solution of the Labor Problem," *Transactions, ASME* 16 (1895), pp. 856–883. This paper is reprinted in Sasaki Tsuneo and Daniel A. Wren (editors), *Intellectual Legacy of Management Theory*, ser. 2, pt 1, vol. 2 (London: Pickering and Chatto, 2002). pp. 59–108.

10. Taylor, "Piece-Rate System," p. 903.

their class of work. Taylor also recognized noneconomic incentives, such as hope of rapid promotion or advancement; shorter hours of work; better surroundings and working conditions; and "[the supervisor's] personal consideration for, and friendly contact with, workmen which comes only from a genuine and kindly interest in the welfare of those under him."[11]

Taylor's 1895 paper also outlined his view on unions:

> The writer is far from taking the view held by many manufacturers that labor unions are an almost unmitigated detriment to those who join them, as well as to employers and the general public. The labor unions ... have rendered a great service not only to their members, but to the world, in shortening the hours of labor and in modifying the hardships and improving the conditions of wage workers.... When employers herd their men together in classes, pay all of each class the same wages ... the only remedy for the men lies in combination; and frequently the only possible answer to encroachment on the part of their employers is a strike.... This state of affairs is far from satisfactory and the writer believes the system of regulating wages and conditions of employment of whole classes of men by conference and agreement between the leaders, unions and manufacturers to be vastly inferior ... to the plan of stimulating each workman's ambition by paying him according to his individual worth, and without limiting him to the rate of work or pay of the average of his class.[12]

Taylor saw no necessity for unions under his system of incentive management. Unions, to maintain their group solidarity, insisted on a common rule and a standardization of wages and conditions for all. Individualized treatment was a threat to the group. For Taylor, this view prevented workers from fulfilling their personal desires because they were to be treated as part of the masses. People should be inspired to better themselves à la the Protestant ethic, and not lumped into one class and treated like everyone else.

This early paper on performance standards, incentives, and the proper relation between worker and manager anticipated Taylor's philosophy of mutual interests between those parties. Countering a more-less assumption that if the workers got more, the employer naturally got less, Taylor saw a mutuality of interests rather than natural conflict between labor and management. This was his statement of the "paradox of high wages and low costs," which on the surface appear to be diametrically opposed concepts. Instead of the employers' practice of buying the cheapest labor and paying the lowest wages possible and the workers' desire to gain all they could get for the least they could give, Taylor advocated paying first-class workers a high

---

11. Taylor, *Principles of Scientific Management*, pp. 33–34.

12. Taylor, "Piece-Rate System," p. 882; also in Taylor, *Shop Management*, pp.185–186, 859–860.

wage, thereby inducing them to produce more under standard, efficient conditions with no greater expenditure of effort than formerly. The result would be more productivity and hence lower per unit labor costs to the employer and higher wages to the worker, thus satisfying both parties. To summarize, Taylor said the aim of each establishment should be:

1. That each workman should be given as far as possible the highest grade of work for which his ability and physique fit him.
2. That each workman should be called upon to turn out the maximum amount of work which a first-rate man of his class can do and thrive.
3. That each workman, when he works at the best pace of a first-class man, should be paid from 30 percent to 100 percent according to the nature of the work which he does, beyond the average of his class.[13]

This notion of a "first-class man" indicated that Taylor was aware of the need to match people's abilities to the requirements of the job. Although he never practiced fully what he preached, the phrase "first-class man" caused him much grief when trying to explain it to others. In testimony before a special congressional committee, Taylor defined his "first-class man":

> I believe the only man who does not come under "first-class" as I have defined it, is the man who can work and will not work. I have tried to make it clear that for each type of workman some job can be found at which he is first class, with the exception of those men who are perfectly well able to do the job but won't do it.[14]

Under these terms, non-first-class workers would be those who were physically or mentally unsuited for the work assigned (in which case they should be retrained or transferred to another job for which they were suited) or who were unwilling to give their best. In setting rates for each job, Taylor set the standard at the pace a first-class worker "can keep up for a long term of years without injury to his health. It is a pace under which men become happier and thrive."[15] The first-class pace was not based on spurts of activity nor on strain, but on the normal pace that a worker could sustain. Basically, Taylor was laying the foundations for sound personnel management, that is, the match of workers' abilities to the job.

It was management's task to find the work for which employees were best suited, to assist them in becoming first-class workers, and to provide them with an incentive to give their best. Taylor's views on the first-class worker were closely intertwined with his personal philosophy of "the will to get there," the success drive that was the basis

---

13. Taylor, *Shop Management*, pp. 28–29.

14. *Hearings before Special Committee of the House of Representatives to Investigate the Taylor and Other Systems of Shop Management under Authority of House Resolution 90* (Washington, D.C.: U.S. Government Printing Office, 1912), p. 1451.

15. Taylor, *Shop Management*, p. 25.

of his own life. It was his observation that the major difference between individuals was not in brains, but in will, the drive to achieve.[16] First-class workers were people with ambition who were suited to their work, not superhumans, as the term came to connote to many people.

THE TASK MANAGEMENT SYSTEM

At Midvale, Taylor was laying the foundations of what he preferred to call task management. An essential ingredient was time study and the development of performance standards; a second ingredient was the selection of workers who could meet those standards when motivated by the differential piece rate. But the system was still incomplete, and Taylor began to build further. Taylor defined management as "knowing exactly what you want men to do, and then seeing that they do it in the best and cheapest way." Taylor added that no concise definition could fully describe the art of management but that "the relations between employers and men form without question the most important part of this art."[17] He saw unevenness in the quality of management in the shop and challenged the assumption that if the right person was hired the methods would take care of themselves. Management had the explicit responsibility to design the job or task so that the greatest productivity was possible rather than rely on the offering of incentives to induce people to produce more.

Task management depended on careful planning. Each worker each day was given a definite task with detailed written instructions and an exact time allowance for each element of the work based on time study, and methods, tools, and materials were standardized. The worker who performed the task in the time allotted received extraordinarily high wages, whereas ordinary wages went to those who took more time than allotted. An immediate problem under task management was the pressure placed on the manager to plan, organize, and guide the work toward completion. To cope with this increasing complexity in managing, Taylor developed a unique form of supervision called "functional foremen." Taylor specified the qualities that he felt made up a well-rounded foreman: "brains; education; special or technical knowledge; manual dexterity or strength; tact; energy; grit; honesty; judgment or common sense; and good health."[18]

Taylor thought that it was almost impossible to find a person with all these traits, but that by specializing the job, physical and mental demands on the incumbent could be reduced.[19] Initially, Taylor employed assistants to prepare instruction

---

16. Copley, *Taylor,* vol. 1, p. 183.

17. Taylor, *Shop Management,* p. 21.

18. *Ibid.,* p. 96.

19. Richard Whiting found that Taylor's concept of functional foremen was also used as early as 1884 by John Richards, owner and manager of the San Francisco Tool Company. Richards, apparently also having difficulty in finding well-rounded foremen, created five separate functional areas in the shop with one person in charge of each. Richard J. Whiting, "John Richards—California Pioneer of Management Thought," *California Management Review* 6, no. 2 (Winter 1963), p. 37.

cards and perform other detailed tasks for Taylor when he was foreman. As his idea evolved, he gave more and more responsibility to these individuals by further segregating and delegating the functions. The typical manager of that day was not much of a planner; workplace layout largely dictated planning and no one else had developed task planning to the degree that Taylor had. Taylor's new style began with a distinction between the planning of work and its performance, a notable advance for the times.

In the planning department, the "order of work route clerk" determined the flow of the work and the exact order of work by each class of workers and machines; the "instruction card clerk" furnished written information on tools, materials, the piece rate and premium, and other operating instructions; the "time and cost clerk" sent the time ticket for recording times taken and costs incurred and ensured the return of this data; and the "shop disciplinarian" kept a record of each worker's "virtues and defects," served as a "peacemaker," and performed the function of selecting and discharging employees. In the performance segment of supervisory responsibilities, the "gang boss" had charge of all work up to the time that the piece was placed in the machine; the "speed boss" took over when the material was in the machine and determined the tools, the cut, and machine speed; the "inspector" was responsible for quality of work; and the "repair boss" was in charge of care and maintenance of the machinery.

The functional foreman concept (Figure 7-1) was an expediency; it provided a shop with supervision in a relatively short time versus the long-range search for and development of well-rounded managers. Taylor saw no conflict in his system with the unity-of-command idea of the military. To him, *knowledge* must prevail; orders were given to workers on the basis of the specialized knowledge of the clerk or boss and not on the basis of the authority inherent in the position. Hence there was no conflict, since each worker had only one boss on any one particular aspect of the job, such as speed of machine, repairs, and so on. With Taylor's general objectives of harmony and mutuality of interests between workers and management, he foresaw that the spirit of cooperation would obviate any inherent conflicts under the functional arrangement.

Taylor had little difficulty in selling his functional principle to the workers; the supervisors, however, resisted the system because it contracted their authority and range of activities.[20] Taylor did not specify that a separate person had to be in charge of each function; in smaller units, one person might perform all the planning tasks or some other grouping of duties. Taylor's purpose was to focus specialized management knowledge on the work. As his concept has evolved to the present, this is now done by *functional authority* over a task, not over the worker, and without circumventing the supervisor. Taylor's concept never became widespread in practice. Its failures did not arise from confusion of workers or a violation of unity of command but from the recognition that it failed to develop well-rounded managers who could cope

---

20. Copley, *Taylor,* vol. 1, p. 292 .

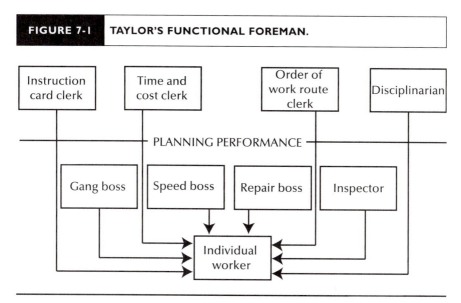

FIGURE 7-1   **TAYLOR'S FUNCTIONAL FOREMAN.**

Adapted from Frank B. and Lillian M. Gilbreth, *Applied Motion Study* (New York: Sturgis & Walton Co., 1917).

with a variety of shop problems through the use of staff assistants. In essence, functionalization was an attempt at decentralization, intending to strip authority from the general manager to place it in the hands of specialized, lower-level managers.

This early attempt at decentralization of authority was designed to bring about a shift in the duties of the general manager, who was to avoid the minutiae of shop management, leaving that to specialists, and was to be concerned only with exceptions. The "exception principle" was one of Taylor's more important contributions:

> Under it the manager should receive only condensed, summarized, and invariably comparative reports, covering ... all of the exceptions to past averages or to the standards ... both the especially good and especially bad exceptions ... leaving him free to consider broader lines of policy and to study the character and fitness of the important men under him.[21]

For Taylor all authority was based on knowledge, not position, and the exception principle enabled a check on who was and who was not meeting the delegated responsibility.

---

21. Taylor, *Shop Management*, p. 126

TAYLOR: THE MANAGER AND THE CONSULTANT

The years at Midvale had been full ones: full-time duties and numerous promotions; teaming with his brother-in-law, Clarence M. Clark, to win the first U.S. Lawn Tennis Association's amateur double tennis championship in 1881; the mechanical engineering degree from the Stevens Institute in 1883; marriage to Louise Spooner in 1884; scientific studies of the art of cutting metals and machine belting; and development of the essentials of task management all yielded a busy twelve years for Taylor. In 1890, he left Midvale to become general manager of the Manufacturing Investment Company (MIC), a converter of wood products into paper fiber. His experiences at MIC were not wholly rewarding. Taylor felt that the fault was with the new papermaking process the company was using, while the owners felt that Taylor lacked the broad executive experience necessary to make the company operate properly. In 1893, Taylor resigned with a contempt for financiers who were interested only in "making money quickly" and had "absolutely no pride of manufacture."[22] Taylor's experience at MIC would not be his last encounter with executives who, in Taylor's opinion, were resistant to change and to the improvements engineers could provide.

Although Taylor developed a contempt for financiers, he did realize his shortcomings in accounting. At MIC, R. D. Hayes, a former railroad manager, revamped the company's bookkeeping system and hired William D. Basley, an experienced railroad accountant, to keep the system operating. Basley had worked for the Newark and Hudson Railroad, which was controlled by the Erie Railroad, where Daniel McCallum had developed accounting and reporting systems in the 1850s.[23] Taylor was impressed by the Hayes-Basley system of accounts, which would later form the basis of his own accounting system, so the years at MIC had not been a total loss. With his newly acquired knowledge of accounting and his engineering background, Taylor decided to become a consulting engineer for management.

One of Taylor's first clients was the Simonds Rolling Machine Company, where he conducted his experiments in the manufacture of bicycle ball bearings. In the finishing room, 120 women inspected the final product for flaws, a most tedious job for ten and a half hours per day. Over a period of time, Taylor shortened the work day gradually to eight and a half hours, introduced morning and afternoon rest periods, identified those who were better inspectors, and put the workers on piecework. The interaction of the variables in the situation was complex, and it would be difficult to fix causes and results. However, the outcome was that thirty-five women did the work of 120, accuracy improved by two-thirds, productivity increased from 5 million to 17 million bearings per month, wages were averaging 80–100 percent more than formerly, and "each girl was made to feel that she was the object of especial care

---

22. Taylor, quoted in Nelson, *Taylor*, p. 53.

23. Charles D. Wrege, "Nineteenth Century Origins of 'Bookkeeping under the Taylor System,'" in K. H. Chung, ed., *Proceedings of the Academy of Management* (Dallas: Academy of Management, 1983), pp. 106–110; see also Nelson, *Taylor*, pp. 54–55.

and interest on the part of management."[24] At Simonds, Taylor also introduced his newly learned accounting system to set up expense classifications, distribute overhead expenses, and improve materials handling and control systems in addition to his work with the ball-bearing inspectors.

Another of Taylor's clients was the Steel Motor Company (Johnstown, Pennsylvania), a division of the Johnson Company. For the Steel Motor Company, Taylor developed a system of cost accounts for material purchases, inventories, and issuance of stores. Taylor also devised a routing, or assembly, chart showing how all the parts were brought together to form the electrical motor.[25] The people who hired Taylor were Tom L. Johnson, the firm's founder; A. J. Moxham, who later became an executive with the Du Pont Company; and Coleman du Pont. When Pierre du Pont wanted a cost-accounting system for the Du Pont Powder Company, Moxham brought Taylor's system to that organization.[26]

Taylor's most challenging and controversial consulting assignment was the Bethlehem Steel Company of South Bethlehem, Pennsylvania. Taylor came to Bethlehem Steel largely at the request of Joseph Wharton, founder of America's first school of business at the University of Pennsylvania, who owned one-fourth of Bethlehem Steel. At that time, Bethlehem's management was under investigation by the federal government for overcharging and price colluding on certain defense contracts. Desiring to decrease costs and improve business practices, the company hired Taylor in 1898. From the beginning, Taylor and some of Bethlehem's managers were in disagreement. Taylor was assertive in his dealings with the executives and chastised them for encouraging a lack of cooperation among the managers. He was finally able to convince top management to reorganize the plant, but thereby made some enemies who sought every opportunity to subvert his efforts.

Taylor installed a system of functional foremen, established a planning department, organized the toolroom and storeroom, and implemented his accounting system. To help him, Taylor brought in at various times Sanford E. Thompson, who probably did more time studies than Taylor ever dreamed of doing; Henry L. Gantt, who had worked with Taylor at Midvale; Carl Barth, a whiz at mathematics; Dwight V. Merrick, who became a leading authority on time study; James Gillespie, who had been involved with time studies at the Simonds Rolling Machine Company; and Maunsell White, who had helped Taylor with his metal-cutting experiments.

In 1899, the price of pig iron rose sharply, and Bethlehem promptly sold its 10,000 tons in inventory. In loading the pigs (which weighed ninety-two pounds on average) for shipment, Taylor saw an opportunity to study worker fatigue, a subject

---

24. Taylor, *Principles of Scientific Management*, pp. 95–96. Nyland used Taylor's work at Simonds to illustrate the contribution of Taylor to reducing hours of work in industry. See Chris Nyland, "Taylorism and Hours of Work," *Journal of Management History* 1, no. 2 (1995), pp. 8–25.

25. Michael Massouh, "Technological and Managerial Innovation: The Johnson Company, 1883–1889," *Business History Review* 50, no. 1 (Spring 1976), pp. 66–67.

26. H. Thomas Johnson, "Management Accounting in an Early Integrated Industrial: E. I. Du Pont de Nemours Powder Company, 1903–1912," *Business History Review* 49, no. 2 (Summer 1975), p. 194.

that had fascinated him since Midvale. He assigned James Gillespie and Hartley C. Wolle the task of studying the loading of pig iron. Taylor convinced management that the workers should be placed on piecework, and Gillespie and Wolle were to study, improve, and oversee the operation. Gillespie and Wolle selected ten of the "very best men" and ordered them to work at "maximum speed." During the first day, the workers loaded seventy-five tons each, filling one car. Since the average tons per day had previously been about twelve and a half tons per worker, the workers were exhausted. Gillespie and Wolle then deducted 40 percent for time to be allotted to rest and delays, establishing the new standard at forty-five tons per worker per day.

Taylor then set the piece rate at $0.0375 per ton, which meant that the worker who met the standard would get $1.69 for that day. Since the average rate for common labor was $1.15 per day, the incentive would exceed 60 percent of the base pay.

Taylor used the pig-iron-handling story in his writings after 1899 and in his later talks to those who gathered at his home, Boxly, in Chestnut Hill, Pennsylvania. One June 4, 1907, a stenographer was hired to record Taylor's "Boxly" talk, a relatively standardized presentation that included the story of "Schmidt." Taylor stated that "I picked out a Pennsylvania Dutchman" as a first-class worker who would load the forty-five tons of pig iron for the increased payment.[27] Schmidt, whose real name was Henry Noll (Knolle), became the focal point of Taylor's example of how to stimulate higher performance through incentive payments. Noll was chosen because James Gillespie and Hartley Wolle's report said "Henry Knolle, who only weighs 135 pounds, is one of the best men."[28] The story of Schmidt found its way into the literature of management, past and present, as an example of scientific management, often to the neglect of Taylor's other contributions.

While Taylor's tale of Schmidt is a charming one, Wrege and Perroni examined the various versions of Taylor's pig-iron-handling story, and the report by Gillespie and Wolle, and reported numerous inconsistencies. Among these discrepancies were the reasons for shipping the pig iron, the amount to be loaded, the method of loading, the number of those in the pig-iron gang, and so on, to the conclusion that Schmidt was Taylor's "pig-tale," an embellishment of what happened.[29]

Working from a film that portrays Frank Gilbreth studying pig-iron handling, Hough and White concluded that Taylor's figures were basically accurate. They maintained that the tale of Schmidt was more important as an "object lesson" for Taylor's audiences:

---

27. Charles D. Wrege, "F. W. Taylor's Lecture on Management, 4 June 1907, an Introduction," *Journal of Management History* 1 (1995), pp. 4–7; the stenographer's transcript follows on pp. 8–32.

28. James Gillespie and H. C. Wolle, "Report on the Establishment of Piecework in Connection with the Loading of Pig Iron, at the Works of the Bethlehem Iron Co., South Bethlehem, PA," June 17, 1899, Taylor Collection, Stevens Institute of Technology, Hoboken, N.J., Files 32A and 32J. I am indebted to Jill Hough for the photocopy.

29. Originally, Wrege and Perroni stated that Taylor had embellished the pig-iron report. See Charles D. Wrege and Amadeo G. Perroni, "Taylor's Pig-Tale: A Historical Analysis of Frederick W. Taylor's Pig-Iron Experiment," *Academy of Management Journal* 17 (March 1974), pp. 6–26. Later, Wrege and Greenwood, in *Taylor*, p. 102, wrote that the "pig-tale" was "prepared by Taylor's assistant, Morris L. Cooke." The mystery remains: the penmanship was Cooke's, but were the words Cooke's or Taylor's?

The story was not intended as a precise, scientific account of the pig-iron loading experiments. Rather, Taylor used the tale in an effort to persuade listeners that systematic management could be applied to even the most basic work processes and still yield substantial improvement.[30]

Support for the position that the pig-tale was an object lesson comes from an unpublished document that was not available to Hough and White. In a 1915 speech to the Cleveland Advertising Club, a stenographer recorded Taylor's words:

Most people think scientific management is chiefly handling pig-iron. I do not know why (laughter). I do not know how they have gotten that impression, but a large part of the community has that impression. The reason I chose pig-iron for the first illustration is that, if you can prove to any one that the strength, the effort of these four principles [Taylor's] when applied to such rudimentary work as that, the presumption is that it can be applied to something better. The only way to prove it is to start at the bottom and show these four principles all along the line.[31]

Taylor's intent was to illustrate, but he was inconsistent in his story. The anecdote of Schmidt was an interesting one for his audience but omitted other facts that enable us to understand these studies more fully. For the record, the Gillespie and Wolle report reveals three first-class workers, not one. Henry Noll (Schmidt) was joined in this elite group by Joseph Auer and Simon Conrad. In June 1899, for example, Conrad loaded an average of 55.1 tons of pig-iron and earned an average $2.07 per day for thirteen days on incentive pay; Auer averaged 49.9 tons and $1.87 for eleven days; and Noll (Schmidt) averaged 45.9 tons and $1.72 for eleven days. Taylor's choice of Schmidt (Noll) to illustrate his first-class worker oversimplified the situation.

Further, for those who think these workers were exploited, working day in, day out to achieve the incentive rate, the fact is that they never worked more than three days without going off the incentive rate and back to day work. The workers could choose not to work on the incentive plan; besides, they were fatigued and needed the rest. For the time span of the pig-iron study, March 30 to May 31, 1899, Noll and Conrad worked a total of thirty-six days on incentive and forty-one on day work;

30. Jill Hough and Margaret A. White, "Using Stories to Create Change: The Object Lesson of Frederick Taylor's 'pig-tale,'" *Journal of Management* 27 (2001), pp. 585–601. In *The Quest of the Best Way: Original Films of Frank B. Gilbreth* (Harry W. Bass Business History Collection, University of Oklahoma), one of the narrators, James S. Perkins, states, "Gilbreth agreed with Taylor's findings" with respect to the pig-iron study. Gilbreth's replication, however, raises numerous questions about how closely it paralleled the Gillespie and Wolle study.

31. Frederick W. Taylor, "The Principles of Scientific Management," address before the Cleveland Advertising Club, 3 March 1915. Manuscript from the Taylor Collection, Stevens Institute of Technology, reprinted in Sasaki Tsuneo and Daniel A. Wren, *Intellectual Legacy of Management Theory,* ser. 2, pt. 2, vol. 2 (London; Pickering and Chatto, 2002), pp. 387–441.

that is, less than one-half of their time was on the incentive rate. For all workers who worked at loading pig iron, Wrege and Hodgetts conclude that only 27 percent of their time was on the incentive rate.[32]

Although Taylor referred frequently to the pig-iron experiments at Bethlehem as a success, in fact they were less then ideal. Gillespie and Wolle were not careful in their time study (arbitrarily allowing 40 percent of the time for rests and delays); Taylor did not use Brinley's differential piece rate but set the rate of payment arbitrarily; and the workers were not scientifically selected. Even so, the results were impressive: yard labor costs fell from $0.072 per ton under day-work wages to $.033 per ton under piece rates; and the workers averaged 60 percent more in wages than they had before.

Another part of Taylor's work at Bethlehem earned him the continued animosity of management. Taylor introduced a cost-accounting system and referred to it as "in general the modern railroad system of accounting adapted and modified to suit the manufacturing business."[33] This was the Hayes-Basley accounting system that Taylor had learned at MIC and applied in various companies. Taylor's accounting system called for a rigorous classification of costs, and the reporting procedures clearly reflected his exception principle. Taylor abhorred the futility of post-mortem accounting that gave the manager annual, semiannual, or monthly reports, considering these too late for managerial action. He moved the cost-accounting function to his planning department and thereby generated cost reports coincident with daily operations reports. Costs then became an integral part of daily planning and control, not a subject for analysis after a long period of time had passed. The system was effective, in fact so effective that management tried to throw the system out. Apparently Bethlehem's management did not like such an accurate appraisal of their performance. Taylor eventually lost the struggle with Bethlehem's management and left the company in 1901, despite entreaties from Joseph Wharton to stay.

TAYLOR: THE PERIPATETIC PHILOSOPHER

Frederick and Louise Taylor were unable to have children of their own. In 1901, seventeen years after their marriage, and when Frederick Taylor was forty-five years old, a tragedy left four children of the Aiken family without parents. The Aikens were relatives of Mrs. Taylor's, and she and Fred adopted three of the children: Kempton, Robert, and Elizabeth. A fourth child, Conrad, was older and did not join the Taylor family—instead he became a Pulitzer Prize–winning poet and a literary

32. Charles D. Wrege and Richard M. Hodgetts, "Frederick W. Taylor's 1899 Pig Iron Observations: Examining Fact, Fiction and Lessons for the New Millennium," *Academy of Management Journal* 43 (2000), p. 1287.

33. Copley, *Taylor*, vol. 1, p. 364.

critic.[34] The Taylors and their new family moved from Bethlehem, Pennsylvania, to Philadelphia, where another stage in Taylor's career would begin.

At Midvale and Bethlehem, Taylor demonstrated his talents as an inventor and mechanical engineer. He invented and patented a steel hammer (for forging steel plates), numerous machine tools such as grinders, boring and turning mills (lathes), and, with Maunsell White, a process for cutting metal with high speed, "self-hardening" steel cutting tools. The Taylor-White process was patented in 1900, and Taylor's share of the royalties amounted to some $50,000 before the patent was nullified in 1909.[35]

About him Taylor witnessed various adoptions of his system, among the more notable the work of James Mapes Dodge at the Link-Belt Company and that of Wilfred Lewis at the Tabor Company, a manufacturer of molding machines. In his spare time, Taylor landscaped and renovated Boxly, the new family home near Philadelphia; developed new mixtures for soils to improve golf greens and thoroughly investigated the best grasses for them; and set out to design some new concepts in golf clubs. He developed a putter with a Y shaft, experimented with lengths and thicknesses of shafts, and spent a great deal of time in practice on the links, or, more euphemistically, in experimentation. He had taken up golf at the age of forty (i.e., in 1896), and his skills developed rapidly; he carried a handicap of eight when he won the handicap championships at the Philadelphia Country Club in 1902, 1903, and 1905. A plaque, bearing evidence of these victories, still hangs in the Philadelphia Country Club.[36]

In 1906, Taylor became president of the prestigious American Society of Mechanical Engineers. His fame was growing and those who were to spread Taylor's message were gathering. Henri Le Chatelier, Horace K. Hathaway, Morris L. Cooke, Sanford E. Thompson, Frank Gilbreth, and others were joining the earlier apostles, Gantt and Barth.

Asked to teach a course at Harvard in the area that was to become the Graduate School of Business Administration (1908), Taylor refused, saying that his system could be learned only in the shop. Professor Edwin Gay, soon to be dean of the school, told Taylor that the course on scientific management would be taught with or without him, period. Taylor succumbed, although he was never entirely happy about teaching his system in a classroom. Taylor was not against business education

34. John A. Bromer, J. Myron Johnson, and Richard P. Widdicombe, "A Conversation with Robert P. A. Taylor" (October 14 and 15, 1976), ch. 2, pp. 1–3, Taylor Collection. *Business Week* (May 15, 1995, p. 34) reported that Frederick W. Taylor was "micromanaging from the grave" with a gift of $10 million to the Stevens Institute of Technology. The article is a total fabrication. The gift came from Robert P. A. Taylor, and was given in the name of his foster father.

35. Thomas J. Misa, *A Nation of Steel* (Baltimore: John Hopkins University Press, 1995), pp. 197–198, 204–205. For White's typically unsung contribution to the Taylor-White process, see Christopher P. Neck and Arthur G. Bedeian, "Frederick W. Taylor, J. Maunsell White III, and the Matthew Effect: The Rest of the Story," *Journal of Management History* 2 (1996), pp. 20–25.

36. Personal communication from Rodger D. Collons, March 25, 1992.

but felt that experience was the only way to learn his particular system. Taylor's Harvard lectures began in 1909 and were given each winter through 1914.[37] For all his lectures, Taylor never accepted a penny of reimbursement, not even for traveling expenses. Likewise, he refused payment for the years of consulting he did in the navy shipyards at Brooklyn and in the army's Ordnance Department.

THE EASTERN RATE CASE

Taylor also found his system getting some extraordinary free publicity. The Boston lawyer Louis D. Brandeis was becoming known in the early twentieth century as the people's lawyer. In 1910, when a group of Eastern railroads asked the Interstate Commerce Commission for an increase in freight rates, Brandeis took up the cause of the shippers and brought about an unusual series of hearings that thrust Taylor's task management into the public eye. At a loss for a name to apply to the Taylor system, Brandeis, Gilbreth, Gantt, and several other engineers met in the Great Northern Hotel in New York City to discuss the matter.[38] Brandeis noted that Taylor frequently used the word "scientific" in his work; the others agreed with Brandeis and "scientific management" was the outcome. Brandeis's argument before the Interstate Commerce Commission was based on the inefficiency of railroad management, and his proposition was that no rate increase would be necessary if the railroads applied scientific management. To prove his case, a parade of witnesses testified about the efficiencies to be gained; James M. Dodge, H. K. Hathaway, Henry R. Towne, and Harrington Emerson were some of the proponents of adopting more efficient management methods based on the Taylor principles.

Hathaway testified about how scientific management had increased workers' wages at the Tabor Manufacturing Company; Dodge gave evidence of progress at the Link-Belt Company; and Gilbreth said that scientific management could be used in a union shop. It was Emerson's testimony, however, that sensationalized the hearings. Emerson had developed "standard unit costs" for the Atchison, Topeka and Santa Fe Railroad as a consultant; comparing the costs of other railroads with these standards, he estimated that $240 million could be saved in labor costs and $60 million in materials and maintenance.[39] His calculations were complex, overlooked differences among various railroads, never examined the question of the applicability of shop manufacturing practices to the transportation industry, and may have been presented for effect rather than for accuracy. Regardless of these potential limitations,

37. Frederick W. Taylor, "An Outline of the Organization of a Manufacturing Establishment under Modern Scientific or Task Management," one of Taylor's lectures at Harvard. The typescript from the Taylor Collection is reprinted in Sasaki and Wren, *Intellectual Legacy of Management Theory*, ser. 2, pt. 2, vol. 2, pp. 259–303.

38. Henry Van Riper Scheel, "Some Recollections of Henry Laurence Gantt," *Journal of Industrial Engineering* 12 (May–June, 1961), p. 221.

39. *Evidence Taken by the Interstate Commerce Commission in the Matter of Proposal Advances in Freight Rates by Carriers,* Senate Document 725, 61st Cong., 3rd sess. (Washington: U.S. Government Printing Office, 1911), pp. 3540–3551 and 3563–3564.

Emerson's testimony was sensational news. When Taylor was asked about Emerson's $300 million per year savings, Taylor replied:

> I believe we can save a million dollars a day, just as he said we can, but the reports of these hearings in Washington were not quite fair enough to say that it can't be done all at once. It would take four or five years.[40]

Taylor accepted the Brandeis-coined phrase "scientific management," but with reluctance, however, fearing that it sounded too academic. The phrase caught on with the press, however, and Taylor gained a place in the public spotlight. The hearings, with the decision going against the railroads, concluded that it was too early to judge the merits of the new management system; nevertheless, the publicity furnished an impetus to Taylor's ideas that had both desirable and undesirable characteristics. Harrington Emerson's testimony that the railroads could save a million dollars a day by applying scientific management had great appeal to cost-conscious manufacturers and to the public. On the other hand, organized labor, especially the machinists and the entrenched railway brotherhoods, were rising up to protest the introduction of these methods. For management to admit to using scientific management was to invite labor trouble.

WATERTOWN AND THE CONGRESSIONAL INVESTIGATION

The railroad hearings brought publicity but had some unusual repercussions. As noted, Taylor was striving to bring his system to improve the efficiency of governmental units, especially the Brooklyn navy yards and the army Ordnance Department. Taylor had failed in bringing more efficiency to the navy yards and received a few verbal bruises from the naval bureaucracy as his reward.[41] At the head of the army Ordnance Department was General William Crozier, who had read Taylor's work and saw its applicability to army arsenals. Crozier chose as test plants the arsenals at Watertown, Massachusetts, and Rock Island, Illinois. At Rock Island, a representative of the International Association of Machinists (IAM) arrived to agitate the workers against time studies. The IAM officers took up the fight against Taylor's methods in all government offices and sought to resist its introduction in other enterprises. As early as 1911, organized labor began to wage an all-out war on Taylor's system. At this time, public interest in scientific management was at its height because of the hearings on railroad rates.

Taylor wrote to Crozier to install the system at Watertown despite the resistance at Rock Island but to do so carefully, step by step, including sounding out the

---

40. Frederick W. Taylor, "The Conservation of Human Effort," address to the Philadelphia Club, January 14, 1911. Taylor Collection. Reprinted in Sasaki and Wren, ser. 2, pt. 2, vol. 2, pp. 256–257.

41. Peter B. Petersen, "Fighting for a Better Navy: An Attempt at Scientific Management (1905–1912)," *Journal of Management* 16 (March 1990), pp. 151–166.

sentiments of the workers in each department before beginning the time study. Dwight Merrick was doing the study and attempted to begin an analysis of the molders at Watertown. One of the molders refused, citing "the organization" (the union) as the reason for his refusal. Lt. Colonel Charles B. Wheeler, the commanding officer at the Watertown Arsenal, explained to the worker why the study was necessary. The worker again refused and was discharged for "refusal to obey orders."[42] The other molders followed, and in August of 1911 the first strike under Taylor's system occurred at the Watertown Arsenal. Taylor attributed the whole problem to a mistake in tactics: the sentiments of the molders had not been examined nor had they been briefed on the purposes of the time study. Taylor did not blame the union, but blamed a premature attempt to make the study without following his recommended technique of consulting the workers first.[43] The strike lasted one week, and the workers returned and offered no further resistance.

Union leaders, however, asked the congressional representatives from the Watertown and Rock Island districts to investigate. It was represented to Congress that the Watertown strike was due to an unsatisfactory treatment of labor resulting from the introduction of the Taylor system. As a consequence, the House appointed a special committee to investigate. The committee consisted of William B. Wilson, a former official of the United Mine Workers, then chair of the House Labor Committee and later secretary of labor under President Woodrow Wilson; William C. Redfield, a manufacturer who later became secretary of commerce under Wilson; and John Q. Tilson, the only Republican member, as an umpire.

The hearings began in October 1911 and ended in February 1912. Taylor spent twelve hours scattered over four days in the witness chair. As Copley stated, "terrorism was in the air" as the unions set out to harass Taylor. The testimony illustrates the hostility and sharpness in the questions and answers. For example, the following clash ensued over "the first-class man" with the Honorable Mr. Wilson presiding. (Previous to this testimony, there were some questions and discussion on the effect of scientific management on worker displacement.)

> The Chairman [Mr. Wilson]. Is it not true that a man who is not a good workman and who may not be responsible for the fact that he is not a good workman has to live as well as the man who is a good workman?

> Mr. Taylor. Not as well as the other workman; otherwise, that would imply that all those in the world were entitled to live equally well whether they worked or whether they were idle, and that certainly is not the case. Not as well.

---

42. Copley, *Taylor*, vol. 2, p. 344.

43. *Ibid.*, p. 344.

The Chairman. Under scientific management, then, you propose that because a man is not in the first class as a workman that there is no place in the world for him—if he is not in the first class in some particular line that this must be destroyed and removed?

Mr. Taylor. Mr. Chairman, would it not be well for me to describe what I mean by a "first-class" workman. I have written a good deal about "first-class" workmen in my books, and I find there is quite a general misapprehension as to the use of that term "first-class."

The Chairman. Before you come to a definition of what you consider a "first-class" workman I would like to have your concept of how you are going to take care, under your scientific management, of a man who is not a "first-class" workman in some particular line?

Mr. Taylor. I cannot answer that question until I define what I mean by "first-class." You and I may have a totally different idea as to the meaning of these words, and therefore I suggest that you allow me to state what I mean.

The Chairman. The very fact that you specify "first-class" would indicate that in your mind you would have some other class than "first-class."

Mr. Taylor. If you will allow me to define it I think I can make it clear.

The Chairman. You said a "first-class" workman can be taken care of under normal conditions. That is what you have already said. Now, the other class that is in your mind, other than "first-class," how does your system propose to take care of them?

Mr. Taylor. Mr. Chairman, I cannot answer that question. I cannot answer any question relating to "first-class" workmen until you know my definition of that term, because I have used these words technically throughout my paper, and I am not willing to answer a question you put about "first-class" workmen with the assumption that my answer applies to all I have said in my book.

The Chairman. You yourself injected the term "first-class" by saying that you did not know of a condition in normal times when a "first-class" workman could not find employment.

Mr. Taylor. I do not think I used that term "first-class."

Mr. Redfield. Mr. Chairman, the witness has now four times, I think, said that until he is allowed to define what he means by "first-class" no answer can be given, because he means one thing by the words "first-class" and he thinks that you mean another thing.

The Chairman. My question has nothing whatever to do with the definition of the words "first-class." It has to do with the other class than "first-class" not with "first-class." A definition of "first-class" will in no manner contribute to a proper reply to my question, because I am not asking about "first-class," but the other than "first-class" workmen.

Mr. Taylor. I cannot describe the others until I have described what I mean by "first-class."

Mr. Redfield. As I was saying when I was interrupted, the witness had stated that he cannot answer the question for the reason that the language that the chairman uses, namely, the words "first-class" do not mean the same thing in the Chairman's mind that they mean in the witness's mind, and he asks the privilege of defining what they do mean, so that the language shall be mutually intelligible. Now, it seems to me, and I think it is good law and entirely proper, that the witness ought to be permitted to define his meaning and then if, after his definition is made, there is any misunderstanding, we can proceed.[44]

Then the chair, Redfield, and Tilson engaged in spirited discussion of whether or not Taylor should be allowed to define his terms; Redfield and Tilson prevailed, and Taylor proceeded to his ideas of a first-class worker and concluded:

… among every class of workmen we have some balky workmen—I do not mean men who are unable to work, but men who, physically well able to work, are simply lazy, and who through no amount of teaching and instructing and through no amount of kindly treatment, can be brought into the "first-class." That is the man whom I call "second-class." They have the physical possibility of being "first-class," but they obstinately refuse to do so.

Now, Mr. Chairman, I am ready to answer your question, having clearly in mind that I have these two types of "second-class" men in view; the one which is physically able to do the work, but who refused to do it—and the other who is not physically or mentally fitted to do that particular job. These are the two types of "second-class" men.

The Chairman. Then, how does scientific management propose to take care of men who are not "first-class" men in any particular line of work?

Mr. Taylor. I give it up.

The Chairman. Scientific management has no place for such men?

Mr. Taylor. Scientific management has no use for a bird that can sing and won't sing.

---

44. *Hearings to Investigate the Taylor System*, pp. 1452–1453.

The Chairman. I am not speaking about birds at all.

Mr. Taylor. No man who can work and won't work has any place under scientific management.

The Chairman. It is not a question of a man "who can work and won't work;" it is a question of a man who is not a "first-class" man in any one particular line, according to your own definition.

Mr. Taylor. I do not know of any such line of work. For each man some line [of work] can be found in which he is first-class.[45]

In another instance, Taylor was being questioned by John R. O'Leary (third vice-president of the International Molder's Unions of North America) on the fines he had levied on workers at Midvale Steel:

Mr. O'Leary. Did I understand you to say that you had the permission and cooperation of the men in putting in that system?

Mr. Taylor. Yes … they ran it, invested the funds, took care of the sick; they furnished the doctor and nurse….

Mr. O'Leary. What did they charge the men who were injured, for the Doctor?

Mr. Taylor. Not a cent. The services were all free.

Mr. O'Leary. Are you aware that there have been many suits instituted against the Midvale Steel Co. to recover those fines, and that they were recovered?

Mr. Taylor. No; I am not aware of it.

Mr. O'Leary. Are you aware that men are fined a dollar for going to the urinal?

Mr. Taylor. I have not the slightest idea that is true. Who ever said that told an untruth. Nothing of that kind was done while I was there.[46]

No support for O'Leary's charges ever appeared in any other testimony. As Ida M. Tarbell, the muckraker of the Standard Oil days, declared:

One of the most sportsmanlike exhibits the country ever saw was Mr. Taylor's willingness to subject himself to the heckling and the badgering of labor leaders, congressmen, and investigators of all degrees of misunderstanding, suspicion and ill will. To a man of his temperament and

---

45. *Ibid.*, pp. 1455–1456.
46. *Ibid.*, pp. 745–746.

highly trained intellect, who had given a quarter of a century of the hardest kind of toil to develop useful truths, the kind of questioning to which he was sometimes subjected must have been maddening.[47]

From Tarbell, this was quite a compliment. Baited, insulted, and made to appear a beast, Taylor staggered from the stand at the close of his testimony. Taylor's pride was sorely wounded, his lifework reviled before a congressional committee. There was no victory for anyone in the final report of the committee. Phrased in good political double-talk, the report said that it was too early "to determine with accuracy their [Taylor's and other scientific management systems'] effect on the health and pay of employees and their effect on wages and labor cost."[48] The committee found no evidence to support abuses of workers nor any need for remedial legislation. It did refer to possible abuses, perhaps as a bone for opponents, but presented no evidence that they had occurred.

Despite the recommendation that no legislation was needed, the congressional representatives from the Watertown and Rock Island districts introduced a resolution to prevent the use of time-measuring devices and of incentive payments in any military agency of the government.[49] The resolution passed, and in considering appropriation bills for the army and navy in 1914–1915 a heated debate occurred in the Senate. Among the anti-Taylor, prorider advocates was Henry Cabot Lodge, descendant of the early Massachusetts textile tycoons, who spoke of ending "the days of slavery" brought about by men such as Taylor who thought it "profitable to work the slaves to the last possible point and let them die."[50] Such demagoguery clearly indicated his ignorance of what Taylor was attempting. The rider failed in the Senate, but was restored in conference between the two houses. After that, Congress after Congress continued to attach such riders to army and navy appropriation bills.[51] Taylor's system and the attempt to bring efficiency to government agencies was clearly crippled.

---

47. Tarbell, *New Ideals in Business,* p. 315, cited by Copley, *Taylor,* vol. 2, p. 347.

48. *Hearings to Investigate the Taylor System,* p. 1930.

49. U.S. House of Representatives, Labor Committee, *Hearings on House Resolution 8662, A Bill to Prevent the Use of Stop Watch or Other Time-Measuring Devices on Government Work and the Payment of Premiums or Bonuses to Government Employees* (Washington, D.C.: Government Printing Office, 1914).

50. Copley, *Taylor,* vol. 2, p. 351. Mary Barnett Gilson, an early employment counselor and later lecturer at the University of Chicago, called Senator Lodge an "exhibitionist" who tilted at windmills. M. B. Gilson, *What's Past Is Prologue* (New York: Harper and Row, 1940), p. 55.

51. Such antiscientific management legislation persisted until 1949, when time-study and incentive-bonus restrictions were removed from the statutes through the efforts of Senator Taft (Ohio) and Senator Flanders (Vermont). Milton J. Nadworny, *Scientific Management and the Unions: 1900–1923* (Cambridge, Mass.: Harvard University Press, 1955), p. 103.

THE MENTAL REVOLUTION

In the first decade of the twentieth century, great national concern was voiced by President Theodore Roosevelt and others over the depletion of America's resources. The national impetus exceeded a mere concern for natural resources to a much larger need for what the president called national efficiency. Taylor, who for almost three decades had fought against the misuse of both physical and human resources, gained a wide audience as a result of the railroad hearings. Taylor wrote about the need for national efficiency in *Principles of Scientific Management,* where he stated his objectives as:

> First. To point out, through a series of simple illustrations, the great loss which the whole country is suffering through inefficiency in almost all of our daily acts.
>
> Second. To try to convince the reader that the remedy for this inefficiency lies in systematic management, rather than in searching for some unusual or extraordinary man.
>
> Third. To prove that the best management is a true science, resting upon clearly defined laws, rules, and principles as a foundation. And further to show that the fundamental principles of scientific management are applicable to all kinds of human activities, from our simplest individual acts to the work of our great corporations, which call for the most elaborate cooperation.[52]

"The principal object of management," said Taylor, "should be to secure the maximum prosperity for the employer, coupled with the maximum prosperity for each employee."[53] Taylor's mutuality of interests emphasized a long-term growth of both parties to ensure prosperity for each. Taylor recognized that the efficiency experts were giving scientific management a black eye. He warned that "the mechanism of management must not be mistaken for its essence, or underlying philosophy."[54] This philosophy was based on a mutuality of interests and had four basic principles: "First. The development of a true science. Second. The scientific selection of the workman. Third. His scientific education and development. Fourth. Intimate friendly cooperation between the management and the men."[55] But neither these principles, nor any single part of Taylor's system, could be isolated as a major factor:

> It is no single element, but rather this whole combination, that constitutes scientific management, which may be summarized:

---

52. Taylor, *Principles of Scientific Management,* p. 7.

53. *Ibid.,* p. 9.

54. *Ibid.,* p. 128.

55. *Ibid.,* p. 130.

Science, not rule of thumb.

Harmony, not discord.

Cooperation, not individualism.

Maximum output, in place of restricted output.

The development of each man to his greatest efficiency and prosperity.[56]

A good many efficiency experts suddenly appeared in 1911 promising great cost reductions and improvements to those employers who would hire them. Taylor deplored these experts, fearing, and properly so, that they promised quick panaceas without grasping the fundamental attitudes that had to be changed and the necessity of gaining acceptance and of the step-by-step study, restudy, and installation of his methods. Taylor made a marked distinction between true scientific management and the efficiency craze. The difference was in a "mental revolution" on the part of the employer and the employee, which came about from mutual respect over a period of time and not from the adoption of the mechanics of the system. At the hearings, Taylor tried to clarify first what scientific management was not, and then what it was:

> Scientific management is not any efficiency device, not a device of any kind for securing efficiency; nor is it any bunch or group of efficiency devices. It is not a new system of figuring costs; it is not a new scheme of paying men; it is not a piecework system; it is not a bonus system; it is not a premium system; it is no scheme for paying men; it is not holding a stop watch on a man and writing things down about him; it is not time study; it is not motion study nor an analysis of the movements of men; it is not the printing and ruling and unloading of a ton of blanks on a set of men and saying, "Here's your system; go use it." It is not divided foremanship or functional foremanship; it is not any of the devices which the average man calls to mind when scientific management is spoken of. The average man thinks of one or more of these things when he hears the words "scientific management" mentioned, but scientific management is not any of these devices. I am not sneering at costkeeping systems, at time study, at functional foremanship, nor at any new and improved scheme of paying men, nor at any efficiency devices, if they are really devices that make for efficiency. I believe in them; but what I am emphasizing is that these devices in whole or in part are not scientific management, they are useful adjuncts to scientific management, so are they also useful adjuncts of other systems of management.

---

56. *Ibid.,* p. 140.

Now, in its essence, scientific management involves a complete mental revolution on the part of the workingman engaged in any particular establishment or industry—a complete mental revolution on the part of these men as to their duties toward their work, toward their fellow men, and toward their employers. And it involves the equally complete mental revolution on the part of those on the management's side—the foreman, the superintendent, the owner of the business, the board of directors—a complete mental revolution on their part as to their duties toward their fellow workers in the management, toward their workmen, and toward all of their daily problems. And without this complete mental revolution on both sides scientific management does not exist.

That is the essence of scientific management, this great mental revolution.[57]

What was the result of this mental revolution?

The great revolution that takes place in the mental attitude of the two parties under scientific management is that both sides take their eyes off of the division of the surplus as the all-important matter, and together turn their attention toward increasing the size of the surplus until this surplus becomes so large that it is unnecessary to quarrel over how it shall be divided. They come to see that when they stop pulling against one another, and instead both turn and push shoulder to shoulder in the same direction, the size of the surplus created by their joint efforts is truly astounding. They both realize that when they substitute friendly cooperation and mutual helpfulness for antagonism and strife they are together able to make this surplus so enormously greater than it was in the past that there is ample room for a large increase in wages for the workmen and an equally great increase in profits for the manufacturer. This, gentlemen, is the beginning of the great mental revolution which constitutes the first step toward scientific management.[58]

Taylor knew that his prime antagonists were the leaders of labor, not the laborers themselves, and was convinced of a conspiracy among union leaders to oppose his system. In a discussion between Taylor and Nels P. Alifas, representing the Metal Trades Department of the American Federation of Labor, Taylor presented the case for time study, improved work methods, and rewarding workers based on output. Alifas stated the position of the Metal Trades workers:

---

57. *Hearings to Investigate the Taylor System,* p. 1387.

58. *Ibid.,* pp. 1388–1389.

> Some people may wonder why we should object to a time study.... The objection is that in the past one of the means by which an employee has been able to keep his head above water and prevent being oppressed by the employer has been that the employer didn't know just exactly what the employee could do. The only way that the workman has been able to retain time enough in which to do the work with the speed with which he thinks he ought to do it, has been to keep the employer somewhat in ignorance of exactly the time needed. The people of the United States have a right to say we want to work only so fast. We don't want to work as fast as we are able to. We want to work as fast as we think it's comfortable for us to work. We are trying to regulate our work so as to make it an auxiliary to our lives and be benefited thereby.[59]

Taylor made repeated offers to Samuel Gompers, president of the American Federation of Labor, to come and see plants using scientific management and to get the facts for himself; Gompers refused.[60] In Taylor's view, union philosophy and that of scientific management were directly antagonistic in that unions built and encouraged antagonisms setting the worker apart from management, while scientific management encouraged a mutuality of interests. To Gompers, "more, more, more" meant labor's gains came from the employer's pocket; for Taylor, "more" came to both through improved productivity.

TAYLOR AND THE HUMAN FACTOR

In answer to charges of the coldness and impersonality of scientific management and in rebuttal to the alleged omission of the human factor from his management equation, Taylor wrote about systems and people: "No system can do away with the need of real men. Both system and good men are needed, and after introducing the best system, success will be in proportion to the ability, consistency, and respected authority of the management."[61] Taylor's view of human relations was more expansive:

59. "Scientific Shop Management," from a publication of the Milwaukee Federation of Labor, 1914, reprinted in John R. Commons, ed., *Trade Unionism and Labor Problems,* 2nd ser. (Boston: Ginn, 1921), pp. 148–149.

60. Copley, *Taylor,* vol. 2, pp. 403–404. In his testimony before the committee, Gompers categorically denied the existence of soldiering and labor resistance. *Hearings to Investigate the Taylor System,* p. 27. Gompers' biographer, Philip Taft, has suggested that Gompers himself was not unalterably opposed to scientific management. According to Taft, Gompers yielded to the influence of the socialist president of the International Association of Machinists, William H. Johnson, because the machinists were the largest and most powerful affiliate in the American Federation of Labor. Philip Taft, *The A. F. of L. in the Time of Gompers* (New York: Harper and Row, 1957), pp. 299–300.

61. Taylor, *Shop Management,* p. 148.

No system of management, however good, should be applied in a wooden way. The proper personal relations should always be maintained between the employers and men; and even the prejudices of the workmen should be considered in dealing with them.

The employer who goes through his works with kid gloves on, and is never known to dirty his hands or clothes, and who either talks to his men in a condescending or patronizing way, or else not at all, has no chance whatever of ascertaining their real thoughts or feelings.

Above all it is desirable that men should be talked to on their own level by those who are over them. Each man should be encouraged to discuss any trouble which he may have, either in the works or outside, with those over him. Men would far rather even be blamed by their bosses, especially if the "tearing out" has a touch of human nature and feeling in it, than to be passed by day after day without a word, and with no more notice than if they were part of the machinery.

The opportunity which each man should have of airing his mind freely, and having it out with his employers, is a safety-valve; and if the superintendents are reasonable men, and listen to and treat with respect what their men have to say, there is absolutely no reason for labor unions and strikes.

It is not the large charities (however generous they may be) that are needed or appreciated by workmen so much as small acts of personal kindness and sympathy, which establish a bond of friendly feeling between them and their employers.

The moral effect of this system on the men is marked. The feeling that substantial justice is being done them renders them on the whole much more manly, straightforward, and truthful. They work more cheerfully, and are more obliging to one another and their employers. They are not soured, as under the old system, by brooding over the injustice done them; and their spare minutes are not spent to the same extent in criticising [sic] their employers.[62]

On resistance to change:

Through generations of bitter experiences working men as a class have learned to look upon all change as antagonistic to their best interests. They do not ask the object of the change, but oppose it simply as change. The first changes, therefore, should be such as to allay the suspicions of the men and convince them by actual contact that the

---

62. *Ibid.,* pp. 184–185.

reforms are after all rather harmless and are only such as will ultimately be of benefit to all concerned.[63]

Taylor stated that it took two to five years to install his system fully; therefore, his reaction to Emerson's testimony promising quick savings. Scientific management was not an overnight panacea and required diligence and understanding when installations were attempted. Even then, there was never only one best way:

> Scientific management fundamentally consists of certain broad principles, a certain philosophy, which can be applied in many ways…. It is not here claimed that any single panacea exists for all of the troubles of the working people or of employers…. No system of management, no single expedient within the control of any man or any set of men can insure continuous prosperity to either workmen or employers.[64]

Then, three weeks before his death, he spoke to the Cleveland Advertising Club:

> Scientific management at every step has been an evolution, not a theory. In all cases the practice has preceded the theory … all the men that I know of who are connected with scientific management are ready to abandon any scheme, any theory, in favor of anything else that can be found which is better. There is nothing in scientific management that is fixed.[65]

In his twilight years Taylor realized that there was never only one best way, but that management should continually strive to find better ways through systematic investigation. Worried by the declining health of his wife, bedeviled by the antagonism of organized labor, and frustrated by the efficiency experts who borrowed the techniques and forgot the philosophy, Taylor's last days were nigh. In a drafty drawing room of a railcar while returning from one of his speaking trips, he caught pneumonia. He died in the hospital one day after his fifty-ninth birthday. His grave site at the West Laurel Hill Cemetery, Philadelphia, bears this epitaph: "Frederick W. Taylor, 1856–1915, Father of Scientific Management."

---

63. *Ibid.,* p. 137.

64. *Ibid.,* pp. 28–29. Taylor made a similar statement in his presentation at the first conference on scientific management: Frederick W. Taylor, "The Principles of Scientific Management," in *Scientific Management: First Conference at the Amos Tuck School, Dartmouth College* (Hanover, N.H.: Plimpton Press, 1912), p. 54.

65. Copley, *Taylor,* vol. 2, p. 348.

SUMMARY

Frederick W. Taylor was a central figure in the development of management thought. Entering the American industrial scene at a time of transition from entrepreneurial, manager-owner firms to large-scale, fully integrated corporations, Taylor gave a push and provided credibility to the idea of management. The engineers, having opened the door to economizing resource utilization, turned to technical subjects and left the way open for Taylor and others to promote systematic management with its popularized label of scientific management. Characterized by advancing technology, market growth, labor unrest, and a lack of knowledge about management, industry in the United States was ripe for methods, systems, and better ways to produce and market products. To meet this need, Taylor provided a voice, a spirit that captured the imagination of the public, business leaders, and academics.

Although Taylor died almost ninety years ago, he is still considered by management and business historians as number one on a list of the most influential contributors in the twentieth century.[66] Locke concluded that "Taylor's track record is remarkable ... *most of his insights are still valid today.*"[67] Nelson commented that social scientists have set up Taylor as a "straw man," forgetting that his "commitment [was] to knowledge, reason and continuous attention to detail that was equally antithetical to old-fashioned empiricism and to new-fashioned panaceas."[68] Today we say "work smarter, not harder," use ergonomics, and discover Taylor's influence in the study of work methods. Finally, Taylor's book *Shop Management* provided the first text for the teaching of industrial management to a growing body of college students who sought positions in industry.

Taylor had his failings as well as his virtues. Wrege and Greenwood observed:

> Taylor offered the world a better way to live through improved productivity, but he presented his ideas to the industrial world as a medicine instead of a candy—he may not have been the best salesperson for the philosophy. He was often arrogant, somewhat caustic, and inflexible in how his system should be implemented. A more reserved approach may have brought better results. It may have been style not substance which held back the Taylor Philosophy.[69]

---

66. Arthur G. Bedeian and Daniel A. Wren, "Most Influential Management Books of the 20th Century," *Organizational Dynamics* 29 (2001), pp. 221–225. See also Daniel A. Wren and Robert D. Hay, "Management Historians and Business Historians: Differing Perceptions of Pioneering Contributions," *Academy of Management Journal* 20 (1977), pp. 470–475.

67. Edwin A. Locke, "The Ideas of Frederick W. Taylor: An Evaluation," *Academy of Management Review* 7 (1982), pp. 22–23. Italics are Locke's.

68. Daniel Nelson, ed., *A Mental Revolution: Scientific Management Since Taylor* (Columbus: Ohio State University Press, 1992), p. 239.

69. Wrege and Greenwood, *Taylor,* p. 259.

Taylor's *Principles of Scientific Management* contained more advocacy than fact, and was more reform minded than scientific. He spoke of a "true science of management," yet in practice violated many of his own precepts. At Bethlehem Steel, for example, the time study was not carefully done nor was the rate rationally developed. He used Gantt's task and bonus scheme rather than Brinley's differential piece rate because it worked better. Thus he was willing to try a better way if it could be found—he never concluded that there was only one best way. In some cases Taylor was not original: for example, he adapted the railroad accounting system for use in manufacturing. In other instances he made positive breakthroughs, such as the establishment of a planning department to focus on that crucial activity; the use of staff specialists to bring expertise to the workplace; prescriptive time study to set standards for production planning and control; the exception principle; machine layout and design; and standardization of tools and methods. Some of his ideas, such as the functional foremen, never gained widespread use. The call for a mental revolution was a worthy ideal for then, now, and the future, yet it rarely has been attained.

On balance, Taylor left an indelible mark on his age and ours. He was not alone, but was joined by numerous others who would apply, adapt, refine, and spread the idea of scientific management. Taylor provided the polestar to a significant era in the evolution of management thought.

8

Spreading the Gospel of Efficiency

Space and time rarely allow the full measure of a person and that person's work. This is true of Frederick W. Taylor and also applies to those who worked with and followed Taylor in propagating the scientific management movement. This chapter focuses on six individuals who rallied around Taylor and were prominent in the embryonic days of scientific management: Carl G. Barth, Henry L. Gantt, Frank and Lillian Gilbreth, Harrington Emerson, and Morris L. Cooke. These people were in the vanguard in spreading the gospel of efficiency.

THE MOST ORTHODOX: CARL BARTH

Of all the disciples in the vanguard of the scientific management movement, Carl G. Barth (1860–1939) was the most orthodox. Barth was born in Norway and educated at the Horten Technical School before beginning his apprenticeship as a machinist in the Horten Navy Yard. Earning three cents per hour, he decided in 1881 to emigrate to America and the hope for better wages. His first job was with the William Sellers Company of Philadelphia, a leading machine tool manufacturer, where he began earning three dollars per day. He rose to the position of chief machine designer and the grand salary of twenty dollars a week in the fourteen years of work for the Sellers Company. The financial panic of 1893 led to Barth's loss of his position at Sellers, and he earned his livelihood by teaching mathematics and manual trades.[1]

He was an instructor at the Ethical Culture Day School in New York City when a colleague suggested that Frederick W. Taylor was searching for someone to handle the complex mathematical problems in his metal-cutting experiments.

---

1. Kenneth Bjork, *Saga in Steel and Concrete: Norwegian Engineers in America* (Northfield, Minn.: Norwegian American Historical Association, 1947), pp. 287–306.

Barth joined Taylor at Bethlehem and his first assignment was to help Henry L. Gantt with the feed and speed problems that had plagued Taylor since Midvale. Barth's solution was "a combination of a crude or embryonic logarithmic slide rule and a set of tables" of formulas that allowed the instantaneous solution of any machine feed and speed problem. Taylor credited Barth's mathematical genius for solving the variables and complexities of metal cutting.

When Taylor left Bethlehem at the urging of top management, Barth went with him and assisted in the first installations of scientific management at the Tabor Manufacturing Company, the Link-Belt Company, Fairbanks Scale, Yale and Towne, and later at the Watertown Arsenal. He also assisted George Babcock in installing scientific management in the Franklin Motor Car Company (1908–1912) and thus was a pioneer in the rationalization of that infant industry. In the days before the moving assembly line, the parts were brought to stationary work areas for assembly. Franklin made three models of cars—touring, runabout, and sedan—and relied on a sales forecast to determine which models to produce, when, and in what quantities. The models were then produced in lots, or batches. Franklin manufactured one hundred cars per month by this method, but it was not profitable because it incurred high costs and had rampant labor turnover (425 percent). After Barth finished installing scientific management, Franklin Motor Car was producing forty-five cars per day, wages were up 90 percent, labor turnover was less than 50 percent, and the company was profitable.[2] Later, Henry Ford and his colleagues would devise the moving assembly line method of automobile production, which would replace the small batch assembly methods of the past.

Barth lectured on scientific management at the University of Chicago (1914–1916) and at Harvard (1911–1916 and 1919–1922) and was "exceedingly proud of being accused of being Mr. Taylor's most orthodox disciple."[3] He resisted any tampering with Taylor's precepts and later maintained that only those who had worked directly with Taylor, such as himself, were the direct disciples who fully understood the task management system. Carl Barth's contribution to management thought was confined to his faithful execution of Taylor's precepts; his slide rule was unique and helpful, but was limited to a narrow aspect of the whole philosophy of scientific management. It was the work of others that would lead to more unique derivations in the gospel of efficiency.

THE MOST UNORTHODOX: H. L. GANTT

Henry Laurence Gantt (1861–1919) was born into a prosperous Maryland farm family. When the Civil War left the family destitute, Gantt learned at an early age the demands of hard work, frugal living, and the self-discipline required to make one's

---

2. George D. Babcock, *The Taylor System in Franklin Management: Application and Results* (New York: Engineering Magazine, 1917).

3. Carl G. Barth, "Discussion" *Transactions of the ASME* 34 (1912), p. 1204.

way in the world.[4] Graduating with distinction from Johns Hopkins University in 1880, he became a teacher of natural science and mechanics at his secondary school, McDonagh (1880–1883). He returned to college at the Stevens Institute of Technology, gained his degree as a mechanical engineer in 1884, became a drafter for an engineering firm, returned to his teaching post at McDonagh in 1886–1887, and then joined the Midvale Steel Company in 1887 as an assistant in the engineering department. Here the twenty-six-year-old Gantt met and began to work with a man who would have a significant influence on his future career, F. W. Taylor.

Henry L. Gantt as a student at the Johns Hopkins University, circa 1880. Courtesy of Peter B. Petersen.

Taylor and Gantt were an unusual team: they had a common interest in their quest for science in management and developed a deep mutual admiration for each other's work. Gantt grasped the essence of Taylor's work and, though they clashed at times, became a prime disciple of Taylor. He worked closely with Taylor at Midvale, followed him to the Simonds Rolling Machine Company to become superintendent, and joined him again at Bethlehem Steel; thus Gantt's early years and work were closely related to Taylor's. After 1901, however, Gantt became a consulting industrial engineer on his own, and, although he espoused the views of scientific management, a different Gantt developed in later years. During his lifetime he published over 150 titles, including three major books; made numerous presentations before the ASME (becoming vice president of that group in 1914); patented more than a dozen inventions; lectured at Stevens, Columbia, Harvard, and Yale; and became one of the first successful management consultants.

THE TASK AND BONUS SYSTEM

Gantt's ideas were largely influenced by Taylor, and the same elements appear in his early writings. The stress on the mutuality of interests between labor and management, the scientific selection of workers, the incentive rate to stimulate performance, detailed instructions on work, and the other familiar concepts are reflected in Gantt's work. Gantt also sought the efficient utilization of labor through scientific investigation and "harmonious cooperation" between labor and management. In his words, "the only healthy industrial condition is that in which the employer has the best men

---

4. Biographical data is from Leon P. Alford, *Henry L. Gantt: Leader in Industry,* prepared originally as a memorial volume for the ASME and later published by Harper and Row, New York, 1934. See also Alex W. Rathe, *Gantt on Management* (New York: American Management Association, 1961); and Peter B. Petersen, "A Further Insight into the Life of Henry L. Gantt: The Papers of Duncan Lyle," *Proceedings of the Southern Management Association,* New Orleans, 1984.

obtainable for his work, and the workman feels that his labor is being sold at the highest market price."[5]

On this road to high wages and low costs, Gantt saw some different possibilities for incentive systems. His view on unions paralleled that of Taylor, but he was more persuasive and philosophical in stating the issue:

> If the amount of wealth in the world were fixed, the struggle for the possession of that wealth would necessarily cause antagonism; but, [since] … the amount of wealth is not fixed, but constantly increasing, the fact that one man has become wealthy does not necessarily mean that someone else has become poorer, but may mean quite the reverse, especially if the first is a producer of wealth…. As long … as one party—no matter which—tries to get all it can of the new wealth, regardless of the rights of the other, conflicts will continue.[6]

The "more, more, more" of organized labor hence became an antagonistic force unless it cooperated in producing more for the benefit of the other party to the transaction—management—and vice versa. Gantt was not convinced that the differential piece rate was adequate to the task of bringing this desired cooperation to the operative workers. Instead, Gantt devised the "task work with a bonus" system, which paid workers a bonus of fifty cents per day if they completed all the work assigned for the day. Gantt later discovered that this plan offered little incentive beyond meeting the standard. To overcome this defect, he modified the plan to pay the workers for the time allowed plus a percentage of that time if they completed the job in the allowed time or less. For example, a worker could receive four hours' pay for doing a three-hour job in three hours or less.[7]

Further, Gantt adapted the idea of a colleague, E. P. Earle, to give a first-line supervisor a bonus for each worker who made the standard, plus an extra bonus if all the workers made it. Thus, if nine of ten workers made the standard, the first-line supervisor would receive ten cents per worker, or $0.90; if all ten made the standard, the first-line supervisor would receive fifteen cents per worker, or $1.50. To Gantt, this extra bonus for the first-line supervisor was for "bringing the inferior workmen up to the standard [and] made him devote his energies to those men who most needed them."[8] This was the first recorded attempt to make it in the financial interest of the first-line supervisor to teach the worker the right way. Gantt knew the importance of teaching from his own experience, and he felt that the bonus system would shift the first-line supervisor from a driver to a teacher and helper of subordinates. In this shift from concern for production to concern for the worker through

5. Henry L. Gantt, *Work, Wages, and Profits,* 2nd ed. (New York: Engineering Magazine, 1916), p. 33.

6. *Ibid.,* p. 55.

7. *Ibid.,* p. 165. For a detailed explanation and the computations necessary to Gantt's task and bonus plan, see Charles W. Lytle, *Wage Incentive Methods* (New York: Ronald Press, 1942), pp. 185–200.

8. Gantt, *Work, Wages, and Profits,* p. 115.

instruction and subsequently improved production, Gantt's work stands as an early landmark in the beginning of human behavioral thought. In Gantt's words, "Whatever we do must be in accord with human nature. We cannot drive people; we must direct their development."[9] Like Taylor, Gantt encountered more resistance from the first-line supervisor than from the workers. The main managerial obstacle was their reluctance to precisely define and carefully allocate tasks and to perform the higher caliber of work required of management to make the system succeed. Like the Taylor system, Gantt's plan called for the scientific investigation of the task, analysis and study of movements and times, standardization of conditions, and winning worker cooperation. Gantt's addition was providing management a direct financial interest.

THE HABITS OF INDUSTRY

In 1901, Gantt became a consulting industrial engineer and would serve some fifty clients before his death eighteen years later. The early opportunities were hand-offs from Taylor, who recommended Gantt and other faithfuls to take the jobs that Taylor no longer had time for. At the American Locomotive Company, Robins Conveying Belt Company, Brighton Mills, and other firms, Gantt installed the ideas and methods of Frederick Taylor. At Sayles Bleacheries (a job received per Taylor's referral system), Gantt encountered resistance from the minor executives and supervisors. Gantt struggled onward without the support of management, invented and patented three different machines to help reduce waste and inefficiency, but was frustrated when a strike by the workers in the folding room of one of the plants occurred. The workers in that shop folded 155 pieces of cloth each day for a weekly wage of ten dollars. These workers objected to Gantt's improvements in work methods, asked for a 10 percent increase in wages, and stopped work when the raise was refused. The strike spread and Gantt had to hire other workers and train them in the new methods. This experience at Sayles Bleacheries forced Gantt to rethink the methods of training workers; from then on, Gantt would require intensive training and development of employees as part of his consulting work.

In teaching the worker, Gantt felt the supervisor should do more than increase the worker's skill and knowledge; he added an ingredient to industrial education called the "habits of industry." These habits were industriousness and cooperation, which would facilitate the acquisition of all other knowledge. This idea, too, called for a break with the past, and Taylor's influence is seen once more: "the general policy of the past has been to drive; but the era of force must give way to that of knowledge, and the policy of the future will be to teach and lead, to the advantage of all concerned."[10]

---

9. *Ibid.*, p. 124.

10. *Ibid.*, p. 148.

The habits that had to be taught to the worker were those of "doing promptly and to the best of his ability the work set before him."[11] Stress should be placed on the pride that comes from quality as well as quantity of work. Gantt cited an example of a group of women who, working under the task and bonus system, formed a society of bonus producers with group membership available only to those who consistently earned the premium. To Gantt, this was the proper condition for all workers, since he was also concerned with worker morale. However, this situation could come about only after management had created the proper atmosphere of cooperation with and confidence in the employees. The results of his inculcation of habits would be higher wages, increased skill, and greater pleasure and pride for the worker, coupled with lower costs and greater productivity for the employer. Beyond these tangible manifestations of efficiency, the harmonious cooperation between labor and management would create that intangible élan, or morale, so vital to successful cooperative endeavors.

GRAPHIC AIDS TO MANAGEMENT

As a former schoolteacher, Gantt was oriented toward the dramatization of data through graphic means. One of his early subjects for graphing was the "fixing of habits of industry" through horizontal bars illustrating the progress of workers toward meeting the task standard. For each worker, a daily record was kept of whether he made the standard and received a bonus, recorded in black, or did not, recorded in red. The graph aided management and the worker since progress as well as reasons for not making the bonus was recorded, enabling management to pinpoint deficiencies and providing feedback to the worker. The progress in converting shops or departments from day work to task work could be seen by everyone as the chart contained progressively more and more solid black lines. As this method of charting succeeded in getting better performance, Gantt expanded his visual aids to include charts on the daily production balance, cost control, quantity of work per machine, quantity of work per worker in comparison with the original estimates, and the expense of idle machinery, among others.[12] However, his major breakthrough in charting came when he was serving as a dollar-a-year consultant to the Department of the Army during World War I.

The conversion of U.S. industry to wartime production did not come quickly and smoothly. The United States had the productive capacity, but the coordination of private industrial efforts with the governmental agencies was haphazard. Plants were scattered all over the nation, shipments were late, warehouses crowded or disorganized, and the Ordnance Department and the navy utilized their resources poorly. Gantt had had some contact with governmental work before the war. In 1911, with

---

11. *Ibid.*, p. 154.

12. Peter B. Petersen, "The Evolution of the Gantt Chart and Its Relevance Today," *Journal of Managerial Issues* 3 (Summer 1991), pp. 131–155.

Charles Day and Harrington Emerson, he was commissioned to study the organization and management of navy shipyards. Their efforts went for naught when the secretary of the navy announced that he would never allow scientific management in the shipyards.[13] As mentioned earlier, this was the period of the congressional hearings and general ill will against the efficiency movement. Gantt had also served as a consultant to General William Crozier at the Frankford Arsenal just prior to the war.[14] Crozier, influenced by Gantt's graphic displays, developed a series of progress and performance charts to aid in managing the ordnance arsenals. However, Crozier was removed from his position in 1917 and his successors allowed the system to lapse. When Gantt gave up his lucrative consulting work to aid the war effort, he puzzled over the problem of keeping track of the vast work of the various departments. Scheduling was especially crucial, and management lacked the necessary information to control and coordinate private contractors' efforts with those of the government agencies. Gantt spent three months trying to unravel the mess before realizing that "We have all been wrong in scheduling on a basis of quantities; the essential element in the situation is time, and this should be the basis in laying out any program."[15]

Gantt's solution was a bar chart for planning and controlling work. Although numerous variations were developed, the essence of the Gantt chart concept was to show how work was routed and scheduled through various operations to its completion. For example, a manager could see from the data in Figure 8-1 that this particular project or product was behind schedule. Corrective action would then be

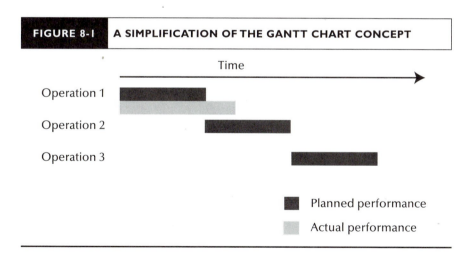

| **FIGURE 8-1** | **A SIMPLIFICATION OF THE GANTT CHART CONCEPT** |

Time

Operation 1

Operation 2

Operation 3

■ Planned performance

Actual performance

13. Peter B. Petersen, "Fighting for a Better Navy: An Attempt at Scientific Management (1805–1912)," *Journal of Management* 16 (March 1990), pp. 151–166.

14. Peter B. Petersen, "The Pioneering Efforts of Major General William Crozier (1855–1942) in the Field of Management," *Journal of Management* 15 (September 1989), pp. 503–516.

15. Alford, *Gantt*, p. 207.

taken to get the project back on schedule or to notify the customer of a late shipment or of an expected completion date.

Gantt's graphic aids to management planning and controlling were revolutionary for this period in management thought. In a ready graphic form, management
could see how plans were progressing and take whatever action necessary to keep
projects on time or within budget authorizations. Gantt never patented the concept,
nor profited from it, but his achievement did earn him the Distinguished Service
Medal from the government. A member of Gantt's consulting firm, Wallace Clark,
popularized the idea of the Gantt chart in a book that was translated into eight lan-
guages, formed the basis for the Soviet central planners to control their five-year
plans, and provided the world with a graphic means of planning and controlling
work.[16] All subsequent production control boards and charts drew their inspiration
from Gantt's original work; the modern variation became the Program Evaluation
and Review Technique (PERT), a computerized, more intricate scheme, founded on
the principles of planning and controlling times and costs. In Washington, D.C., the
war effort took a measurable turn as the result of Gantt's contributions. Materials
flowed more smoothly, shipbuilding blossomed, and the productive might of the
United States was brought to its greatest outpouring of goods. Surely this must have
provided some consolation for the man whose efforts to systematize governmental
operations had been spurned so few years before.

GANTT: THE LATER YEARS

After the death of Taylor, Gantt began developing some very different ideas regarding the role of the industrial engineer and the business firm as an institution. In
1916, he deplored the failure of U.S. industrial leadership, which, in his opinion, was
caused by the rise of leaders to power based on their influence and not their merit.
Gantt's new leadership would be based on fact, not opinion, and on ability, not
favoritism. The industrial engineer, not the financier nor the labor leader, would be
the new leader, because only the engineer could cope with the U.S. problem of production as the creation of wealth. The engineers would be an educated elite to lead
the United States, not with a concern for profits, but by stressing productive efficiency. Gantt's own notions regarding these changes were partially due to his reading of Thorstein Veblen, but mostly attributable to Charles Ferguson.[17]

In 1916, Gantt formed an organization called the New Machine, whose membership comprised engineers and other sympathetic reformers seeking to acquire political as well as economic power. Charles Ferguson, Gantt's inspiration, was a minister
who had served as a pundit for Colonel Edward M. House, President Wilson's adviser.
Ferguson was a "joyous mystic" who preached a "religion of democracy" that would

---

16. Wallace Clark, *The Gantt Chart: A Working Tool of Management* (New York: Ronald Press, 1922). For
further information on Wallace Clark, see Harold Smiddy, "Wallace Clark's Contribution to International
Management," *Advanced Management* 23 (March 1958), pp. 17–26.

17. Alford, *Gantt*, p. 264.

summon forth "an aristocracy of the capable to put down the rule of the mob and destroy privilege."[18] Gantt's New Machine operated on the premise that the engineer would form this "aristocracy of the capable." In a letter to President Wilson, the leaders of the New Machine called on the president to transfer "control of the huge and delicate apparatus [i.e., industry] into the hands of those who understand its operation," to establish employment bureaus for better placement of employees, and to set up "public service banks" to extend credit on the basis of ability and personality rather than property.[19]

Once the New Machine was rolling, Gantt lost his concern for mere factory matters and sought broader areas for reform. He attacked the profit system, and on this point he appears to have been largely influenced by the swirl of world events. In 1917, the czar was overthrown and collectivism came via violent bloodshed in Russia. The United States endured the great Red scare in 1919, and anarchists were seen lurking everywhere. The Socialist Eugene Debs was something of a folk hero; there had been Communist uprisings in Bavaria and Hungary; the Wobblies (the Industrial Workers of the World) were provoking labor unrest; and most people in the United States were firmly convinced that the Bolsheviks were about to overturn society. In the preface to his last book, written in 1919, Gantt said:

> The attempt which extreme radicals all over the world are making to get control of both the political and business systems on the theory that they would make the industrial and business serve the community, is a real danger so long as our present system does not accomplish that end.... [I]n order to resume our advance toward the development of an unconquerable democratic civilization, we must purge our economic system of all autocratic practices of whatever kind, and return to the democratic principle of rendering service, which was the basis of its wonderful growth.[20]

Gantt said that business leaders had emphasized profits, sought monopolies, and forgotten to give service to the community. He said, "The business system must accept its social responsibility and devote itself primarily to service, or the community will ultimately make the attempt to take it over in order to operate it in its own interest."[21] Further, "the engineer, who is a man of few opinions and many facts and many deeds, should be accorded the economic leadership which is his proper place in our economic system."[22] In November 1919, Gantt was stricken with a "digestive disturbance" and died at the age of fifty-eight. After Gantt's death, the New Machine dissolved. Henry Laurence Gantt, the most unorthodox of Taylor's followers, did not

---

18. Samuel Haber, *Efficiency and Uplift* (Chicago: University of Chicago Press, 1964), p. 45.

19. Alford, *Gantt*, pp. 269–277.

20. H. L. Gantt, *Organizing for Work* (New York: Harcourt Brace Jovanovich, 1919), pp. iv–v.

21. *Ibid.*, p. 15.

22. *New York Sunday World*, October 12, 1919, cited by Alford, *Gantt*, p. 298.

live to see the turn that management thought would take in the 1920s and afterward. Rather than the engineers providing the leadership advocated by the New Machine, U.S. management would turn to improved personnel management, union-management cooperation, employee representation plans, and, overall, a better understanding of the human factor in industry. Gantt would have liked that outcome as well.

PARTNERS FOR LIFE: THE GILBRETHS

Frank Bunker Gilbreth (1868–1924) and Lillian Moller Gilbreth (1878–1972) formed a husband-and-wife team that brought not only liveliness but significance to the early management movement. Frank was the son of a Maine hardware merchant, and he learned early the virtues of frugality and thrift characteristic of New England Puritanism.[23] When he was three years old, his father died, and the family moved to Boston. He was educated at Phillips Academy, Andover, and the Rice Grammar School. He prepped for the Massachusetts Institute of Technology, passed the qualifying exams, but decided instead to become an apprentice bricklayer at the tender age of seventeen. He rose to become chief superintendent of the Whidden Company. In 1895, he launched his own career as an independent contractor, and this work formed the basis for his first investigations and publications. Though working independently of Taylor, Gilbreth's early efforts paralleled what Taylor was doing. In his later years, he formed his own management consulting company and, for a while, was closely associated with the scientific management movement.

It was to the good fortune of modern management that Frank married Lillian Moller, for they formed a complementary team whose combined intellectual interests and assets brought a new dimension to the inchoate field of management. Lillian was the daughter of a German-born sugar refiner and spent her early years in Oakland, California. She was an exceptionally bright student, receiving her bachelor's and master's degrees in English from the University of California at Berkeley. She interrupted her work on her doctor's degree for a trip east; on that trip she met Frank, and their marriage in 1904 brought together two people who lived a most significant partnership. After the marriage, Lillian changed the focus of her academic interests to psychology, for she thought that this field would best complement the work her husband was doing. Combining marriage and the ever-growing family (there were eventually twelve children) with her assistance to Frank's work, Lillian continued to do her research on her thesis, "The Psychology of Management," and submitted it in 1912. The University of California informed her that the thesis was

---

23. Biographical information on the Gilbreths is from Edna Yost, *Frank and Lillian Gilbreth: Partners for Life* (New Brunswick, N.J.: Rutgers University Press, 1949). A treasure from the Gilbreth archives at Purdue University is Lillian M. Gilbreth, *As I Remember,* an autobiography written in 1941 but not published until 1998 (Norcross, Ga.: Engineering and Management Press). Popularized versions of their lives may be found in Frank B. Gilbreth, Jr., and Ernestine Gilbreth Carey, *Cheaper by the Dozen* (New York: Thomas Y. Crowell, 1948); and idem, *Belles on Their Toes* (New York: Thomas Y. Crowell, 1950).

The Gilbreth family at their summer home in Nantucket, 1923. Left to right—Frank (Sr.), Frank (Jr.), Bill, Fred, Dan, Jack, Bob, Jane, Lil, Martha, Ernestine, Anne, and Lillian Gilbreth. (Not pictured is Mary Elizabeth, who died at the age of six.) Courtesy of Ernestine Gilbreth Carey and the Gilbreth Family.

acceptable but that she would have to return to campus for a year of residency before the degree could be granted. Lillian had been led to believe that this requirement would be waived in her case, but the university officials were steadfast. Frank was furious and began looking for a publisher. The *Industrial Engineering Magazine* published the thesis in serial form (May 1912–May 1913), and it was eventually published in book form by the firm of Sturgis and Walton with the proviso that the author be listed as L. M. Gilbreth with no mention that the author was a woman.[24] *The Psychology of Management* stands in the literature as one of the earliest contributions to understanding the human factor in industry. Eventually the university authorities agreed that Lillian could spend her residency in any college that granted advanced degrees in industrial psychology or management. Such institutions were scarce at that time, but Frank discovered that Brown University was planning to offer a Ph.D. degree in applied management. At Brown, Lillian wrote a new dissertation, "Some Aspects of Eliminating Waste in Teaching," finally completing her Ph.D. degree requirements in 1915.[25] This was not the culmination but the beginning of many years of hard work. Frank's work became more famous, and Lillian's work on fatigue and psychology was a valuable supplement.

---

24. Yost, *Frank and Lillian Gilbreth*, p. 213.

25. Ronald G. Greenwood, Charles D. Wrege, and Regina A. Greenwood, "Newly Discovered Gilbreth Manuscript," in K. H. Chung, ed., *Academy of Management Proceedings* (Dallas, August 1983), p. 111.

This fruitful partnership was to end on June 14, 1924, when Frank died of a heart attack. What does a woman with a Ph.D. do at age forty-six when her husband has just died, she has a household full of children ranging in age from two to nineteen, and she has felt the rebuffs of being a woman in the "man's world" of the early twentieth century? The situation demanded courage, and the First Lady of Management was never found wanting in that characteristic. She went to Europe and took Frank's place at the International Management Conference in Prague; she continued the motion-study seminars for managers; and she relied on friends, such as Wallace Clark, to provide entrees to consulting jobs. The firsts that can be ascribed to Lillian Gilbreth are astounding: she became the first female member of The Society of Industrial Engineers in 1921; the first female member of the American Society of Mechanical Engineers; the first woman to receive the degree Honorary Master of Engineering (from the University of Michigan); the first female professor of management at an engineering school (at Purdue University in 1935); and the first female professor of management at Newark College of Engineering. The Gilbreth Medal, named for both Frank and Lillian, was awarded to Lillian in 1931—the only female recipient to date; she was also the only woman to receive the coveted Gantt Gold Medal and the only woman to be awarded the most prestigious CIOS Gold Medal. Is there any doubt about why she has been called the First Lady of Management?[26] In Frank's biography she wrote, "The Quest goes on."[27] She was to continue what she and Frank had started, and the following pages are but a summary of their quest.

SYSTEMATIZING THE CONSTRUCTION INDUSTRY

Although Frank Gilbreth was a contemporary of the founders of the scientific management movement, his own early work was done apart from any knowledge of what was happening at Midvale Steel. One of the first things he noted as a bricklayer's apprentice was the diversity in methods and speeds used by the workers. One set of motions was used for working fast, another for the slow pace, and yet another for teaching others how to lay bricks. Although bricklaying was an ancient occupation with long-established methods, Gilbreth set out to develop in writing the best ways of laying bricks, handling materials, rigging scaffolding, training apprentices, and, in general, improving methods while lowering costs and paying higher wages. The essence of the system of work he was developing as a superintendent, as a contractor, and later as a consultant was published as the *Field System,* the *Concrete System,* and the *Bricklaying System.*[28]

---

26. Ronald G. Greenwood, Regina A. Greenwood, and Jay A. Severance, "Lillian M. Gilbreth, First Lady of Management," in Jeffrey C. Susbauer, ed., *Academy of Management Proceedings* (San Francisco, 1978), p. 2.

27. Lillian Moller Gilbreth, *The Quest of the One Best Way: A Sketch of the Life of Frank Bunker Gilbreth* (Easton, Pa.: Hive, 1973), p. 64.

28. Portions of these are reprinted in William R. Spriegel and Clark E. Meyers, eds., *The Writings of the Gilbreths* (Homewood, Ill.: Richard D. Irwin, 1953), pp. 3–65.

The Field System was an accounting system without a set of books. It was designed to aid the construction contractor by showing costs, costs related to estimates, and the total cost of the job each Saturday up to the previous Thursday. No bookkeepers were needed, since the original memorandum or receipt was filed and there was no general ledger. Gilbreth developed other facets of the system and provided detailed instructions for its use, even including a rule about no smoking on the job and the admonition that whistle blasts at starting and quitting time should not be over four seconds long. He established a suggestion system, including a $10 first prize each month for the best idea on how to improve work, give better service to customers, or secure additional construction jobs. Included in the field system were provisions for photographing working conditions at the time of any accident for use in lawsuits or other claims. Another part of the system was a white-list card. This was an early appraisal form for workers, which the supervisor filled out on both desirables and undesirables. In an intermittent, transient trade such as construction, the Gilbreth white list became a valuable source of information for employers. Though his advice was quite detailed and applicable to construction, it was indicative of Gilbreth's desire to rationalize the workplace and is illustrative of what the whole scientific management movement was attempting.

The Concrete System contained detailed advice to concrete contractors. Gilbreth wrote here too of directing the workers, including the necessity of athletic contests between work groups to give them a spirit of competition in completing the job. The total job was divided into equal groups of workers who competed to finish a wall or build concrete pillars. *The Bricklaying System* was also technical but brought forth a facet of study new to the young Gilbreth. The original concern was with the training of young apprentices, and Gilbreth saw the wastes of hand-me-down instruction from experienced workers. He proposed the remedial step of finding the best way of laying bricks through motion study, followed by instruction, and insisted that the emphasis be placed on learning the right way before maximum output was expected of the new worker. This early work was but a prelude to his later in-depth analysis of motions and fatigue.

One characteristic of Gilbreth's lifelong quest was that he asked the workers to help improve methods and achieve motion economy for *their own sake* as well as for management's. He not only taught the workers how to handle bricks, but why that way was best. He thought that pride was an essential part of learning a trade and that this came only if workers knew their trade well. He stressed economy of effort, not speed, and sought to show how to improve productivity with no greater physical exertion. The result of his extensive analysis of bricklaying showed that the number of motions could be reduced from eighteen to four and that workers could increase their output from 1,000 to 2,700 bricks laid per day without increasing their effort. Like Taylor, Gilbreth found that the conditions of work greatly affected output; accordingly, he developed different types of scaffolding to suit the job, precise instructions on mortar consistency and trowel usage, and a "packet system" for proper conveyance and placement of bricks for the worker. Being a trained bricklayer himself undoubtedly helped Gilbreth win worker cooperation; however, he demonstrated early the need for worker involvement in making improvements, including incentives to do so, an emphasis on training, and, finally, the need to systematize without accelerating the worker's pace.

EXTENDING MOTION AND FATIGUE STUDY

In 1907, after he had developed the rudiments of his construction systems, Gilbreth met Frederick Taylor. They had a great deal in common, and Gilbreth soon became one of Taylor's most fervent advocates. In return, Taylor devoted eight pages of *Principles of Scientific Management* to Gilbreth's motion studies of bricklayers. Taylor also selected Gilbreth to represent him and the Taylor system at the New York Civic Forum and again in 1913, at the Western Economic Society. In 1911, Taylor asked Gilbreth to write the response to all the letters he received after the publication of *The Principles of Scientific Management,* which was serialized in the *American Magazine.*

When Frank Gilbreth was consulting with the New England Butt Company, a manufacturer of braiding machines, he wrote Taylor:

> I have just perfected a mechanical device for taking time study by photographing the time of day in hours, minutes, tenths of minutes, and hundredths of tenths of minutes....
>
> I do not believe that this method will ever wholly do away with the present stop watch method, but it will have a tremendous use in teaching certain elements of processes by the exhibition of these educational films.
>
> You will see that this process not only enables me to take the time study to the thousandth of a minute, eliminating all error due to the human element or to differences in mental time reactions, but that it also permits measuring the motions in three dimensions simultaneously...
>
> It would seem to me that this process and combination of clocks and motion picture machine should really go with your great invention of time study, and consequently if you will accept ownership of it as a present from me, or if you will undertake its control for the best interests of the great cause, I will be most happy to present it to you.[29]

Taylor declined Gilbreth's offer:

> It seems to me that in your photographic scheme you will ultimately be able to develop a very fine system of time study, and this will undoubtedly apply to a class of observations which it would be impossible to

---

29. F. B. Gilbreth to F. W. Taylor, April 18, 1912 and July 29, 1912. Correspondence files, Taylor Collection, Stevens Institute of Technology.

take in any other way. It is indeed difficult to foresee the full possibilities of our new system [i.e., scientific management]....

Thank you very much indeed for your kind offer to turn over these inventions to me. I, however, know nothing about photography, and am therefore entirely the wrong man to follow them up properly. They should be in the hands of someone who knows at least the first elements of photography, and I do not believe there is a better man for this purpose than you. Let me assure you, however, that I most cordially appreciate your kind thought.[30]

Gilbreth and Taylor's interests were essentially parallel, although they differed in terminology. Taylor called his work "time study," and Gilbreth called his "motion study." In practice they were measuring the same thing, with similar objectives of eliminating motions to reduce fatigue and improve productivity. Gilbreth maintained that the stopwatch was not an essential ingredient to his system, but, in one of the many amusing anecdotes about the Gilbreths in *Cheaper by the Dozen,* the children wrote that Frank was fascinated with time and always the efficiency expert at home and on the job. He buttoned his vest from the bottom up, instead of top down, because the former took only three seconds and the latter took seven. He used two shaving brushes to lather his face and found that he could reduce shaving time by seventeen seconds. He tried shaving with two razors, found that he could reduce the total shaving time by forty-four seconds, but abandoned this scheme because it took two minutes per bandage applied to the cuts. His children suggested that it was the two lost minutes that bothered him and not the cuts.[31]

At Providence, while Lillian was working on her doctorate, Frank turned his attention away from construction and extended motion study to the general field of manufacturing. Fatigue became a major focus, and he received help from Lillian in studying its causes and effects. The prevailing theory of the period was that fatigue was caused by a toxin generated by physical exertion and released in the blood. Every motion caused fatigue; hence any elimination of motions reduced fatigue. Gilbreth's analysis proceeded to isolating worker variables, such as anatomy, habits, mode of living, and so on, and variables in worker surroundings, such as clothes, color of walls, lighting, heating, tools, and so on. He finally isolated fifteen worker variables, fourteen variables in the surroundings, and thirteen variables of motion such as acceleration, length and path. As he developed his study, he found that it was difficult to follow motions with the unaided eye and that the study of gross movements was inadequate for the preciseness he needed.

Gilbreth developed two techniques to overcome this deficiency: a list of the most elementary motions and the use of motion-picture cameras and lights. Gross

30. F. W. Taylor to F. B. Gilbreth, August 24, 1912, Correspondence files, Taylor Collection.

31. Gilbreth and Carey, *Cheaper by the Dozen,* p. 3.

analysis of movements, such as "reach for tool," told Gilbreth little about the elements of that move. Accordingly, he created a list of seventeen basic motions, each called a *therblig* (Gilbreth spelled backwards with the "th" transposed), such as search, select, transport loaded, position, hold, and so on. These fundamental motions, which could not be further subdivided, gave Gilbreth a more precise way of analyzing the exact elements of any worker movement. The second technique used the then-infant technology of the motion-picture camera.[32] Gilbreth placed a large-faced clock, calibrated in fractions of minutes, in the field of vision of the camera as it filmed the worker under study. The pictures enabled Gilbreth to time the smallest motion of the worker. This was the beginning of what Gilbreth called micromotion study.

He also developed the "cyclegraphic" technique of attaching a small electric light bulb to the hand, finger, or arm of the worker, which allowed photographs to show a path of light through space as the worker moved. His "chronocyclegraph" used a flashing bulb, which showed acceleration and deceleration of movements by appearing in the film as a series of pear-shaped dots. Gilbreth found these laborious, meticulous methods necessary to improve methods, demonstrate correct motions, and train new operators. The Gilbreths also devised process charts as a technique for charting the flow of work as it moved through the shop. The technique, and the symbols used to depict the various stages in the process, remains essentially unchanged in modern systems analysis.

One should not confuse the techniques with what the Gilbreths were trying to build. Their search for efficiency and economy included flowcharts of products and work, a three-position plan of promotion, and a notion of the impact of motion study on the worker. All their techniques were focused on eliminating waste in industry. The promotion plan was designed to prepare workers for advancement and as a morale and incentive booster. According to the plan, each worker held three positions in the organization: first, the position last occupied and for which the worker was now serving as a teacher to the successor; second, the present position; and third, preparing for the next higher position. The system required charting promotion paths and records for appraising performance and kept the worker from getting lodged in blind-alley jobs. The psychology of motion study was to impress on the worker the benefits of reducing fatigue and improving pay through motion study. According to the Gilbreths, monotony came not from performing the job the same way each time, but from the lack of interest of management in the worker. Motion and fatigue study displayed management's interest and facilitated the elimination of monotony.

---

32. Earlier photographic studies of human and animal motions were by Etienne-Jules Marey and Eadweard Muybridge. See Sonya F. Premeaux, "The Flying Horse: Eadweard Muybridge's Contribution to Motion Study," *Journal of Applied Management and Entrepreneurship* 8 (October 2003), pp. 36–51

SUPPORT FOR THE SCIENTIFIC MANAGEMENT MOVEMENT

In 1911, several ASME members were finding it difficult to obtain the organization's recognition for papers on management. A rump faction, led by Frank Gilbreth, formed a separate organization, first called the Society to Promote the Science of Management, then, after Taylor's death, the Taylor Society.[33] Gilbreth was a vocal supporter of Taylor in the Eastern rate hearings and participated in coining the phrase "scientific management." Gilbreth's *Primer of Scientific Management* was designed to answer questions about this new phenomenon made famous by the rate hearings and the congressional investigation. In the foreword, Louis Brandeis said, "the Primer will prove of greatest value in helping to remove from the minds of workingmen misapprehensions which have led some well-meaning labor leaders to oppose a movement from which labor has most to gain."[34] Gilbreth proceeded in the *Primer* to pose common questions about scientific management and to provide answers in very basic terminology about the philosophy and practice of scientific management. No new information was provided, but the expository device of questions and answers reflected an excellent approach to win over adherents to the cause. The following are merely examples:

Q. Does it [scientific management] not make machines out of men?

A. ... Is a good boxer, or fencer, or golf player a machine? He certainly approaches closely the 100% mark of perfection from the standpoint of the experts in motion study. It is not nearly so important to decide whether or not he is a machine as to decide whether or not it is desirable to have a man trained as near perfection as possible....

Q. Does not the monotony of the highly specialized subdivision of work cause the men to become insane?

A. ... No, he will not become insane, for if his brain is of such an order that his work does not stimulate it to its highest degree, then he will be promoted, for under Scientific Management each man is specially trained to occupy that place that is the highest that he is capable....

Q. Does not the "speed boss" speed up the men to a point that is injurious to their health?

A. "Speed boss," like "task," is an unfortunate name ... the speed boss does not tell the men how fast they shall make their motions ... [but he does] tell the men at what speeds their machines shall run....

---

33. In 1936, the Taylor Society and the Society of Industrial Engineers merged to form the Society for Advancement of Management.

34. F. B. Gilbreth, *Primer of Scientific Management* (New York: Van Nostrand Reinhold, 1912), p. vii.

Q. If Scientific Management is a good thing for the workers, why do the labor leaders all oppose it?

A. They do not all oppose it. Some oppose it for the simple reason that they do not understand it; the others have visions that Scientific Management is something that will reduce the value of their jobs—and all are afraid, because of the bad treatment that workmen as a whole have had in the past, that Scientific Management is simply a new "confidence game," presented in a more attractive manner than ever before … they simply cannot imagine Dr. Taylor or any other practical man working for their interests unless there is a "comeback" somewhere….[35]

Gilbreth also observed that Taylor's ideas and scientific management should not be confused with what Henry Ford was doing with assembly line production. He toured a Ford assembly plant and was totally out of sympathy with how those jobs were designed:

At the Ford plant he [Gilbreth] saw men at benches too low for them, men stretching farther than their normal reach, men in uncomfortable positions as they put on rear wheels, and much other evidence of making workers adjust to the line rather than making the line conform to the best needs of human beings. Management claimed that people adjusted to these things and did not mind, just as contractors kept saying that bricklayers did not mind stooping for bricks.[36]

When Gilbreth left the construction business to start his consulting firm, there is evidence that this created a rift between Gilbreth and Taylor.[37] The trigger for this split appears to have started when Gilbreth was consulting with Herrman, Aukam & Company, a handkerchief manufacturer. Milton Herrman visited Taylor, complaining that Gilbreth had overcharged, and had taken his top assistant to work on another job in Germany. Taylor wrote Gilbreth of these complaints, ending his letter with "Is there anything that you wish me to do in this matter?"[38] Subsequently, Taylor dined with the Gilbreths at their home, received an autographed copy of Lillian Gilbreth's *Psychology of Management,* and the Herrmann, Aukam matter was discussed further. We do not know the course of that evening, but Horace K. Hathaway was sent at the request of Milton Herrman to pick up Gilbreth's work.

Gilbreth, working the other job with Auer Gesellschaft in Germany, did not write Taylor after Hathaway took the Herrmann, Aukam job, but wrote Lillian:

35. *Ibid.,* pp. 49–50, 53–54, 65, 887–888.

36. Yost, *Frank and Lillian Gilbreth,* p. 246.

37. See Milton Nadworny, "Frederick Taylor and Frank Gilbreth—Competition in Scientific Management," *Business History Review* 21, no. 1 (Spring 1957), pp. 23–34; and Daniel Nelson, *Frederick W. Taylor and the Rise of Scientific Management* (Madison: University of Wisconsin Press, 1980), pp. 131–136.

38. F. W. Taylor to F. B. Gilbreth, March 11, 1914. Taylor Collection, file 59A.

I think we are justified in not mentioning his [Taylor's] name in any books in the future, or at least just enough to clear ourselves of criticism. Perhaps that will bring him around ... We must have our own organization and we must have our own writings so made that the worker thinks we are the good exception.[39]

Ironically, Taylor later wrote Frank wishing him success in his work with Auer.[40]

What began as a Taylor-Gilbreth mutual admiration relationship grew cold and colder. As we will see, it would take the deft diplomacy of Lillian Gilbreth to bring the ideas of these two titans into a rapprochement.

THE PSYCHOLOGY OF MANAGEMENT

Lillian Gilbreth played an important role in her husband's work and earned as well a substantial reputation on her own.[41] She was not the originator of industrial psychology, but she brought a human element into scientific management through her training, insight, and understanding. She began by defining the psychology of management as "the effect of the mind that is directing work upon that work which is directed, and the effect of this undirected and directed work upon the mind of the worker."[42] Heretofore, management had been considered an area in which no one could hope to succeed who had not inherited the "knack"; with scientific management, it became possible to base management on laws and study it in the classroom. Successful management "lies on the man, not on the work," and scientific management provided a means to make the most of people's efforts. Gilbreth characterized three historical styles of management: traditional, transitory, and scientific. Traditional management was the driver, or Marquis of Queensbury, style that followed the unitary line of command and was typified by centralized authority. Gilbreth adapted the prizefighting term "Marquis of Queensbury" because she felt that it typified the physical and mental contest waged between worker and manager "according to the rules of the game." Transitory management referred to all forms in the interim stage between the traditional and the installation of scientific management. Scientific management, or the Taylor plan of management, described the goal toward which all firms should strive.

---

39. F. B. Gilbreth to L. M. Gilbreth, May 9, 1914. Gilbreth Collection, NF 112/0816-6.

40. F. W. Taylor to F. B. Gilbreth, May 22, 1914. Gilbreth Collection, NF 118/0816-64.

41. For instance, Lillian Gilbreth made significant contributions to the field of home economics by applying the principles and techniques of scientific management to the home. See Lillian M. Gilbreth, *The Home-Maker and Her Job* (New York: Appleton-Century-Crofts, 1927); and idem, *Management in the Home: Happier Living through Saving Time and Energy* (New York: Dodd, Mead, 1955).

42. L. M. Gilbreth, *The Psychology of Management: The Function of the Mind in Determining, Teaching and Installing Methods of Least Waste* (New York: Sturgis and Walton, 1914; reissued by Macmillan, 1921), p. 1.

Gilbreth compared and contrasted these three styles of management according to how they affected individuality, functionalization, measurement, analysis and synthesis, standardization, records and programs, teaching, incentives, and welfare. On individuality, she noted that psychologists up to that time had been largely concerned with the psychology of the crowd. Comparatively little work had been done on the psychology of the individual. Under traditional management, individuality was stifled by the power of the central figure; under scientific management, it became a fundamental principle in selection, incentives, and overall consideration of worker welfare, that is, "general well-being, mental, physical, moral and financial."[43] The object of scientific management was to develop each person to the fullest potential by strengthening personal traits, special abilities, and skills. The focus was on how management could develop the individual for their mutual benefit, not on the worker's use and exploitation, as under the Marquis of Queensbury type of management.

Functionalization promoted worker welfare by improving skills through specialization, enabling greater pride in output and higher wages; measurement ensured that individuals received the product of their labors; standardization improved morale and prevented the worker from becoming a machine; and teaching overcame fear and instilled pride and confidence in the worker. Traditional management relied solely on rewards and punishment, whereas scientific management attempted to enlist worker cooperation. The rewards under scientific management differed because they were predetermined (ensuring against fear of rate cutting), prompt (rather than delayed under profit sharing), and personal (in the sense that workers were rewarded for their efforts and not by their class of work). Under scientific management, the worker gained "mental poise and security" rather than the anxiety created by traditional management. Concerning welfare, scientific management promoted regular work, encouraged good personal habits, and fostered the physical, mental, moral, and financial development of the worker.

A strong psychological thread ran through all of Lillian Gilbreth's writings and she made contributions in several areas such as: the application of management and motion study techniques to the home, rehabilitation of the handicapped,[44] elimination of fatigue, and the use of leisure time to create "happiness minutes." As a result of Frank's service as an Army Major during World War I, he and Lillian became interested in how to use motion study to design jobs to retrain soldiers, especially amputees, so they could resume a productive life after the war. They developed devices to assist the disabled, such as a typewriter for a one-armed person, and Lillian worked with the General Electric Company to redesign home appliances for disabled homemakers. The Gilbreths were among those who lobbied Congress to pass the War Risk Insurance Act for disabled soldiers. Later, this act

---

43. *Ibid.*, p. 30.

44. See J. Michael Gotcher, "Assisting the Handicapped: The Pioneering Efforts of Frank and Lillian Gilbreth," *Journal of Management* 18 (1992), pp. 5–13.

served to pioneer legislation for those who were not war casualties but needed vocational rehabilitation.[45]

Lillian also contributed to healing the rift between Frank's motion study and Taylor's time study. In 1921, years after Taylor's death, the Gilbreths used the *Bulletin of the Taylor Society* to issue an "indictment" of time study. They attacked Taylor's followers (Carl Barth, Dwight Merrick, and Sanford Thompson) for continuing to promote stopwatch study because of their interest in selling time devices, forms, and books about time study. Further, time study was less precise, therefore less scientific, while motion study provided absolutely accurate times and the "one best way."[46] The attack was probably unnecessary. After Taylor's death, his followers began to recognize that in order to overcome, or reduce, union resistance they needed to remedy criticism regarding time study as synonymous with speeding up the workers. A shift in focus to using time and motion study in job analysis was apparent, and reflected Taylor's words:

> The enormous saving of time and therefore increase in the output which it is possible to effect through eliminating unnecessary motions and substituting fast for slow and inefficient motions for the men working in any of our trades can be fully realized only after one has personally seen the improvement which results from a thorough motion and time study....[47]

This statement, in addition to his frequent use of Frank Gilbreth's bricklaying studies as an example of scientific management at work, indicate there was no fundamental differences in their goals, but in the means employed.

The Gilbreths' indictment of time study, however, led to a divisiveness between them and followers of Taylor.[48] After Frank's death, Lillian wrote for Taylor Society readers that time and motion study were fundamentally complementary, that the stopwatch was used by Gilbreth followers when it was appropriate, but filmed studies were more accurate and useful.[49] With Lillian's joining of time and motion study, the circle to Taylor's earlier comments was complete, and history rhymed once more.

The contribution of the Gilbreths endured beyond their time. When we think of ergonomics or working smarter instead of harder, we should remember them. Lillian's first book was more management than psychology, but indicated how

---

45. Wren and Greenwood, *Management Innovators*, p. 146.

46. Frank B. and Lillian M. Gilbreth, "An Indictment of Stop-Watch Time Study," *Bulletin of the Taylor Society* 6 (June 1921), pp. 99–108.

47. Taylor, *Principles of Scientific Management*, p. 24.

48. See the comments that followed the Gilbreth paper in the *Bulletin of the Taylor Society*, cited above, pp. 109–135.

49. Lillian M. Gilbreth, "The Relations of Time and Motion Study," *Bulletin of the Taylor Society* 13 (June 1928), pp. 126–128.

scientific management fostered individual efforts. From Lillian's teaming with Frank, and carrying the quest onward after his death, we can see their many gifts to our management heritage. Although the admiration of Taylor turned to rivalry, and rivalry to reconciliation, the Gilbreths extended our understanding of work and the worker.

EFFICIENCY THROUGH ORGANIZATION: HARRINGTON EMERSON

Harrington Emerson (1853–1931) was a Presbyterian minister's son who believed in the Protestant virtues of thrift and the economical use of resources. Educated at numerous schools in Europe, he was symbolic of the new breed of efficiency engineers who were bringing new methods of time and cost savings to the burgeoning U.S. industry. Emerson began as a troubleshooter for the general manager of the Burlington Railroad and went on from there to become a consultant to the Atchison, Topeka, and Santa Fe Railroad. Beginning in 1904, Emerson installed better methods and equipment, centralized the manufacture of material and tools, and installed an individual reward system. After two years, output was up 57 percent, costs were down 36 percent, and the average pay of the workers was up 14.5 percent. Although there was a conflict with unionized shop workers (who lost the struggle), Emerson's methods were praised as an example of what scientific management could do for the railroads.[50] At this point in his career, Emerson perceived the need for applications of his efficiency concepts in areas other than the railroads. His work was largely independent of the Taylor movement, although he had corresponded with Taylor from 1903 onward.

Waste and inefficiency were the evils that Emerson saw pervading the entire U.S. industrial system. His experience had shown that railroad repair shops averaged 50 percent efficiency and that preventable labor and material wastes were costing the railroad industry $300 million annually (hence his well-publicized testimony of savings of $1 million a day).[51] Inefficiency was not confined to the railroads, according to Emerson, but could be found in manufacturing, agriculture, and education. National productivity was not a function of abundance or lack of natural resources in different countries, but the cause of prosperity was "ambition, the desire for success and wealth."[52] The United States had the wealth of resources and the stimulus of individual ambition for gain, which had led its rise as a world industrial power, yet it was losing its advantage as a result of inefficiency and wasted resources. To Emerson,

—

50. Carl Graves, "Applying Scientific Management Principles to Railroad Repair Shops—The Santa Fe Experience, 1904–1918," in Jeremy Atack, ed., *Business and Economic History,* 2nd ser., vol. 10 (1981), pp. 124–136.

51. In Chapter 7 it was suggested that Emerson had perhaps overstated his case for estimated savings, but it became sensational news. Taylor agreed that it might be possible, but not in less than four to five years.

52. Harrington Emerson, *Efficiency as a Basis for Operations and Wages* (New York: Engineering Magazine, 1911), p. 37.

one of the greatest problems was the lack of organization. Only through proper organization could machines, materials, and human efforts be directed to improve efficiency and reduce waste.

LINE AND STAFF ORGANIZATION

Taylor's idea of the "functional foreman" did not appeal to Emerson. He agreed with Taylor that the specialized knowledge of staff personnel was necessary, but differed in how to bring this about. Influenced by his European education, Emerson admired the organizational efforts of General Von Moltke, who had developed the general staff concept and made the Prussian army the tremendously efficient machine it was in the mid-nineteenth century.[53] The theory of the general staff concept was that each subject vital to military efforts was studied to perfection by a separate staff specialist, and these specialists formed a supreme general staff to advise the commander.

Standing alone and unaided, the line organization had serious deficiencies. Emerson sought to apply these staff principles to industrial practice to bring about "complete parallelism between line and staff, so that every member of the line can at any time have the benefit of staff knowledge and staff assistance."[54] Each firm was to have a chief of staff serving over four major subgroupings: one for personnel to plan, direct, and advise on everything pertaining to the well-being of employees; a second to advise on structures, machines, tools, and other equipment; a third for materials to include their purchase, custody, issue, and handling; and the fourth for methods and conditions to include standards, records, and accounting. Staff advice was available to all organizational levels and focused on planning: "It is the business of staff, not to accomplish work, but to set up standards and ideals, so that the line may work more efficiently."[55] The distinction between Emerson and Taylor is thus apparent: instead of making one person responsible for and with authority over each particular shop function, Emerson left supervision and authority to the line, which operated on the basis of planning and advice by the staff. This shift maintained the advantages of specialized knowledge and facilitated coordination without the disadvantages of splitting the chain of command.

PRINCIPLES OF EFFICIENCY

Emerson made other contributions in cost accounting, in using Hollerith punch-card tabulating machines for accounting records, and in setting standards for judging worker and shop efficiency. In cost accounting, for example, Emerson made a

---

53. *Ibid.,* pp. 64–66. Karl von Clausewitz noted the use of the general staff concept in the Prussian Army as early as 1793. Karl von Clausewitz, *On War* (New York: Random House, 1943), p. 489. Originally published in 1832.

54. Emerson, *Efficiency as a Basis for Operations and Wages,* p. 69.

55. *Ibid.,* p. 112.

clear distinction between historical cost accounting (descriptive) and "the new cost accounting," which estimated what costs should be before the work started. Although others had written of accounting for costs, Emerson appears to have been the first to apply the engineering notion of developing standards to reduce or remove variances from the standard to determine the progress toward efficiency (defined by Emerson as the "ratio of standard divided by actual" costs).[56] Emerson also devised an incentive system, which paid workers a 20 percent bonus for 100 percent efficiency (the standard time); above the 100 percent efficiency level workers also received their wages for the time saved plus the 20 percent bonus. For example, at 100 percent efficiency, the bonus was twenty cents per one dollar of wages; at 120 percent efficiency, forty cents per one dollar of wages; and at 140 percent, sixty cents.[57]

Emerson's efficiency work was somewhat overshadowed by the Taylor system, in part because of the railroad rate hearings. Emerson was one of the witnesses, and his studies of railroad efficiency were used by Louis Brandeis to show that the railroads did not need a rate increase if they applied the methods of the newly named scientific management. Subsequent to the hearings, Emerson published *Twelve Principles of Efficiency,* which became another landmark in the history of management thought. A chapter was devoted to each of the twelve principles; broadly conceived, the first five concerned relations with people and the remainder concerned methods, institutions, and systems. The principles were not isolated, but were interdependent and coordinated to form a structure for building a management system. In the preface, Emerson stated his basic premise: "It is not labor, not capital, not land, which has created modern wealth or is creating it today. It is ideas that create wealth, and what is wanted is more ideas—more uncovering of natural reservoirs, and less labor and capital and land per unit of production."[58]

No modern author could state the challenges facing today's global organizations more cogently. For Emerson, ideas were the dominant force that must be focused on eliminating waste and creating a more efficient industrial system. Principles were the instruments to reach this goal, and the basis of all principles was the line-staff form of organization, because Emerson felt that "the industrial hookworm disease is defective organization."[59] The first principle was "clearly defined ideals." This principle made explicit the need for agreement among all organizational participants on ideals and to

---

56. *Ibid.,* p. 102; and Harrington Emerson, "Standardization and Labor Efficiency in Railroad Shops," *Engineering Magazine* 42 (1911), pp. 10–16. See also Paul Sutcliffe, "The Role of Labor Variances in Harrington Emerson's 'New Gospel of Efficiency' (1908)," *Accounting and Business Research* 12 (Spring 1982), pp. 115–123; and Nathan Kranoski, "The Historical Development of Standard Costing Systems until 1920," in E. N. Coffman, ed., *The Academy of Accounting Historians Working Paper Series* 2 (1979), pp. 206–218.

57. Emerson, *Efficiency as a Basis for Operations and Wages,* pp. 193–196. At 120 percent, for example, 40 cents = 20 cents for bonus and 20 cents for working 20 percent more efficiently.

58. Harrington Emerson, *The Twelve Principles of Efficiency* (New York: Engineering Magazine, 1913), p. x.

59. *Ibid.,* p. 29.

pull in a "straight line." Emerson did not use the term "objectives" as contemporary authors do, but used "ideals" in essentially the same way. He hoped to reduce intraorganizational conflict, vagueness, uncertainty, and the aimlessness that arose when people did not understand or share a common purpose. The second principle, common sense, exhorted managers to take a larger view of problems and their relationships and to seek special knowledge and advice wherever it could be found. For example, any employee who had something of value to contribute could participate in decision making.[60] The third principle, competent counsel, was related to the second principle in that it pertained to building a competent staff. Discipline became the fourth principle and provided for obedience and adherence to organizational rules. It was a foundation for the other eleven principles and made the organization a system rather than anarchy. The fifth and final principle pertaining to people was that of the fair deal. The fair deal depended on the ability of the manager to establish a system of justice and fairness in all dealings with the worker. It was not a patronizing or altruistic relationship, but one of mutual advantage.

The seven principles pertaining to methods were more mechanistic and largely self-explanatory: "reliable, immediate, accurate, and permanent records" (information and accounting systems); "dispatching" (planning and routing of work); "standards and schedules" (methods and time for tasks); "standardized conditions"; "standardized operations"; "written standard practice instructions"; and "efficiency reward" (the incentive plan). Each principle was liberally sprinkled with examples of Emerson's consulting experience and formed a thorough, though often redundant, statement of his system.

Harrington Emerson achieved renown in his own time and his consulting firm was a seedbed for others who became distinguished consultants and executives, such as Earl K. Wennerlund, later a vice president of production at General Motors; Charles E. Knoeppel, who would form his own consulting firm and develop the "profitgraph," a forerunner to the breakeven chart; and Herbert N. Casson, who would take efficiency methods and scientific management to Great Britain.[61] Originally called Emerson Engineers, even though none of the members of the association were engineers, the firm later took the name Emerson Consultants, and it endures to the present.

Emerson testified before the House committee on Taylor's system and other efficiency systems; served as one of the experts on the Hoover Committee, which published *Elimination of Waste in Industry*; helped found the Efficiency Society (1912); and through his associates tried to bring more ethical practices to the field

---

60. William F. Muhs, "Worker Participation in the Progressive Era: An Assessment by Harrington Emerson," *Academy of Management Review* 7 (January 1982), pp. 99–102.

61. William F. Muhs, "The Emerson Engineers: A Look at One of the First Management Consulting Firms in the U.S.," in John A. Pearce II and Richard B. Robinson, Jr., eds., *Academy of Management Proceedings* 46 (1986), pp. 123–127. For extensive insights into the life and work of Herbert N. Casson, see Morgan Witzel, ed., *The Biographical Dictionary of Management* (Bristol, England: Thoemmes Press, 2001), pp. 137–144.

of management consulting by forming the Association of Consulting Management Engineers. Formed in 1932, a year after Emerson's death, the association was created because

> during the 1920's some of the well-established and competent management consultants became concerned at the number of incompetent and unscrupulous people offering professional counsel, and decided that an association in which only qualified and reputable practitioners could obtain membership would help in raising the standards of practice.[62]

Emerson's firm was one of the founders, and subsequently others, such as Robert W. Kent, of Bigelow, Kent, Willard and Company; C. E. Knoeppel of Knoeppel Industrial Counsel; Harry Hopf; Edwin G. Booz (later, Booz, Allen & Hamilton); James A. McKinsey (later McKinsey and Company); Wallace Clark; and A. T. Kearney, would join the association.

Emerson has been called the "high priest of efficiency" for his efforts to eliminate waste in industry.[63] His contributions were unique in terms of his advocacy of the line-staff organization and the development of standard cost accounting. His testimony at the Eastern Rate Case hearings brought the Brandeis-coined "scientific management" phrase to the attention of the press and the public, but was perhaps too dramatic and over generalized in its conclusions. An early management consultant, he recognized the danger of "experts" who climbed on the scientific management bandwagon, but without the appropriate qualifications, and the need for ethical standards of practice. Harrington Emerson was an important figure in spreading the good news of efficiency.

THE GOSPEL IN NONINDUSTRIAL ORGANIZATIONS: MORRIS COOKE

While Taylor, Barth, the Gilbreths, Gantt, and Emerson were searching for efficiency in industrial enterprises, Morris Llewellyn Cooke (1872–1960) was extending the gospel of efficiency to educational and municipal organizations. After receiving a B.S. in mechanical engineering from Lehigh University (1895), Cooke went to work in industry and was soon applying a "questioning method" to the wastes of industry long before he met or heard of F. W. Taylor. As Taylor began to publish and be known more widely, Cooke became an avid reader and defender of what Taylor was espousing. He

---

62. Philip W. Shay to author, March 5, 1971; from the files of the Association of Consulting Management Engineers, 347 Madison Ave., New York, NY.

63. [W. Jerome Arnold] "Famous Firsts: High Priest of Efficiency," *Business Week,* June 22, 1963, pp. 100, 104.

eventually met Taylor and evidently impressed him, since Taylor asked Cooke to become a member of a committee studying the administrative effectiveness of the ASME. Taylor personally financed the study and paid Cooke's salary; during the year-and-a-half study their friendship grew and Cooke became one of the insiders in the scientific management movement.

Distrustful of the so-called new breed of efficiency engineers, Taylor designated only four men as his disciples: Barth, Gantt, H. K. Hathaway, and Cooke. Once, on one of his assignments, Cooke saw a sign over the workers' entrance to a factory reading, "Hands Entrance"; he asked the owner, "Where do the heads and hearts enter?"—the sign was promptly removed.[64] Perhaps he was being flippant, but he made his point—scientific management called for more than hands.

In 1909, the president of the Carnegie Foundation for the Advancement of Teaching wrote Taylor asking for help in an economic study of administration in educational organizations. Taylor sent Cooke, and the resulting study was a bomb-shell in the academic world.[65] Although only physics departments were studied, since they were believed representative of the existing level of teaching and research, Cooke included nothing in his final report that he did not feel applied to other departments as well. The report was quite lengthy and detailed, and Cooke attempted something that few were then, or are today, eager to do, that is, measure the cost of input efforts and the resulting output in teaching and research.

His findings were quite upsetting: inbreeding (hiring the institution's own grad-uates) was widespread; management practices in education were even worse than the acknowledged poor state of industrial practice; committee management was a curse; departments enjoyed excessive autonomy, which worked against sound uni-versity coordination; professional pay should be based on merit and not longevity; and life tenure for professors should be scrapped and unfit teachers retired. Cooke recommended a "student hour" (one hour in class or laboratory per single student) as a standard to gauge the efficiency of professional effort. Professors should spend more time in teaching and research, leaving administration to specialists and not to committees. Assistants should be used more widely, allowing the higher-priced tal-ent to take more complex jobs. Salary increases should be based on merit or effi-ciency, and the costs of teaching and research should be more closely controlled by the central administration.

Initial reactions to the report were predictable: the president of the Massachusetts Institute of Technology said it read "as if the author received his training in a soap factory."[66] Nevertheless, some changes did come about, and, though there are still inefficiencies and abuses, educational administration has made some progress, except, perhaps, in the realm of committees.

---

64. Kenneth E. Trombley, *The Life and Times of a Happy Liberal: Morris Llewellyn Cooke* (New York: Harper and Row, 1954), p. 10.

65. M. L. Cooke, *Academic and Industrial Efficiency* (New York: Carnegie Foundation for the Advancement of Teaching Bulletin no. 5, 1910).

66. Trombley, *Cooke*, p. 11.

Taylor was giving his "Boxly talks" in his home and a stenographer was hired to transcribe his presentation of June 4, 1907, for Morris Cooke to "analyze and improve the lecture." A second purpose of the transcription was to provide a source for Cooke to write a book about the Taylor system. From the opening of his talk, Taylor indicated his assurance that task management (his preferred term before the popularized label of scientific management) was superior to previous ideas:

> I ought to say at the start that what I am going to say will sound extremely conceited. It will sound as though we were very much stuck on ourselves, but we are not so much stuck on ourselves as we are on the idea. I am very much stuck on the idea and not particularly on ourselves, although the general impression will be that we have a wonderfully high opinion of ourselves and of everything we are doing.

> I want to try to convince you that the task idea, because that is what is back of everything we do, is overwhelmingly better than the other idea in its practical results.[67]

The two-hour lecture, plus a question and answer period, was strongly worded and included the pig-iron handling and shoveling anecdotes among other ideas about Taylor's task management. When Taylor read the stenographic transcription, his biographer reported his reaction as "Did I say that?"[68] According to his biographer, Taylor was more careful after that in what he said and how he spoke about task management.

After Cooke acquired a copy of the Boxly talk, he told Taylor that he intended to write a book, tentatively entitled *Industrial Management,* to enable people to understand the Taylor system of management. In the course of events, Cooke's intended book was not published but, according to Wrege and Stotka, became Taylor's *Principles of Scientific Management.* Taylor "attached his name to someone else's work," and it was Cooke who "created a classic."[69] Was the "Father of Scientific Management" a plagiarist? Or, was this a mutual agreement between Taylor and Cooke to promote Taylor's ideas? The story is a convoluted one, but merits telling to examine the evidentiary trail.

The basis for Cooke's *Industrial Management* was Taylor's Boxly talks, which Cooke was to improve. In 1907, Cooke wrote Taylor that he intended "to edit 'Industrial Management' ... because I think to write a popular exposition of the Taylor System will be a thing worthwhile."[70] At one point, Taylor and Cooke would be co-authors as Cooke was "boiling down the Boxly talks." Cooke edited the Boxly

---

67. "Report of a Lecture by and Questions put to Mr. F. W. Taylor: A Transcript," *Journal of Management History* 1 (1995), pp. 8–32. The introduction is by Charles D. Wrege, pp. 4–7.

68. Copley, *Taylor,* vol. 2, p. 284.

69. Charles D. Wrege and Anne Marie Stotka, "Cooke Creates a Classic: The Story Behind F. W. Taylor's *Principles of Scientific Management,*" *Academy of Management Review* 3 (October, 1978), pp. 736–749.

70. *Ibid.,* p. 738.

talks manuscript, added forty-three pages from other sources, and rewrote thirty-one pages of Taylor's sixty-two page Boxly talk. Cooke's manuscript was not published, but sixty-nine pages of *Industrial Management* (which began with the stenographer's notes of Taylor's talk) were incorporated into Taylor's *Principles of Scientific Management*.[71] On this basis, Wrege and Stotka conclude that Cooke "created the classic" and that "Taylor's use of Cooke's manuscript is merely an example of his [Taylor's] tendency to publish, under his own name, material written by others."[72]

Is there another side to this story? In a draft of the *Industrial Management* manuscript, Cooke printed this comment:

> ... this chapter [Chapter 2] is very largely a recital of Mr. Taylor's personal experiences in the development of scientific management, and as such has been written by himself in the first person.[73]

Cooke told Taylor that he would forgo any profits from *Industrial Management,* but Taylor responded that he would assign all royalties from the *Principles of Scientific Management* to Cooke. The archives of Harper and Brothers, the publisher, indicate that $3,207.05 was paid to Cooke from June 1911 (the date of publication) until the last quarter of 1913.[74] According to Dean:

> ... the royalty money was likely a minor matter to both Taylor and Cooke. Neither of them needed the royalty money, as suggested by the fact that Cooke was making nearly $50,000 a year through Taylor [from consulting referrals]—a considerable sum considering the time. The royalty payment to Cooke was likely a mere gesture on Taylor's part for Cooke's contribution to Taylor's "principles."[75]

A reasonable conclusion is that Cooke contributed to, but did not create, the classic *Principles of Scientific Management.* He edited and enriched Taylor's talks at his home, Boxly, and received royalties for his efforts. It was an arrangement agreed upon and fulfilled, indicating the solid relationship between Taylor and Cooke.

In addition to working closely with Taylor and consulting with various business firms, Cooke also became involved in public administration. In 1911, a newly elected Reform mayor of Philadelphia asked Taylor to help out with municipal administration. Once more, Taylor sent Cooke into the breach. Cooke had been itching for reform ever since, as a poll watcher for the Reform party, he had been bullied by a

---

71. Wrege and Greenwood, *Taylor,* p. 182.

72. Wrege and Stotka, p. 749.

73. *Ibid.,* pp. 746–747.

74. *Archives of Harper and Brothers (1817–1914).* Reels 31 and 32 of microfilm published by permission of Harper and Row and the Butler Library, Columbia University. Index compiled by Christopher Feeney, University Press, Cambridge, 1982. I am indebted to Carol Carlson (Dean) Gunn for a photocopy.

75. Carol Carlson Dean, "The Principles of Scientific Management by Fred Taylor: Exposures in Print beyond the Private Printing," *Journal of Management History* 3 (1997), pp. 11–12.

machine politician. In the new administration, Cooke became the director of public works and brought scientific management to the governance of Philadelphia. In four years he saved the city over $1 million in garbage-collection costs, achieved a $1.25 million reduction in utility rates, fired 1,000 inefficient workers, established pension and benefit funds, opened channels of communication for workers and managers, and moved municipal administration from smoke-filled rooms into the sunshine. His book, *Our Cities Awake,* put forth his case for better-managed municipalities through application of the principles of scientific management. He successfully established a functional management organization patterned after Taylor's ideas, revamped budgeting procedures, hired numerous experts to replace political favorites, espoused management of the city by a professional city manager, and sought to replace committees by individuals who had responsibility and authority. He called for cooperation by offering an early idea of participation in management decision making:

> Here then is a work in which we can all have a hand, a work which will always be ineffectually done if it is confined to well-educated and highly trained men at the top … administrative leadership will in the future more and more consist in getting the largest possible number "into the play" in having the great body of employees increasingly critical in their judgments about both their own work and the work which is going on around them.[76]

Cooke saw that it was not the system, but the confidence of the people in the system that made scientific management effective.

After his work in Philadelphia and the pleas for municipal reform, Cooke opened his own consulting firm in 1916. Like the other pioneers, he contributed his knowledge to the War Department during World War I. Always concerned with gaining the cooperation of labor, he became increasingly interested in the growing national labor movement. He became a close friend of and adviser to Samuel Gompers, president of the American Federation of Labor. Cooke saw his task as that of bringing the labor and management factions together in a time when they were becoming more antagonistic. His advice was that labor was just as responsible for production as management; increased production improved the lot of both and it would form an effective barrier against both unemployment and low wages. This thesis was repeated in Cooke's last book, coauthored with Philip Murray, in which management was advised to "tap labor's brains" to get the ideas of those who were the closest to the work being done.[77]

During the administration of Franklin D. Roosevelt, Cooke held numerous positions, chief among them administrator of the Rural Electrification Administration

---

76. M. L. Cooke, *Our Cities Awake* (New York: Doubleday, 1918), p. 98.

77. M. L. Cooke and Philip Murray, *Organized Labor and Production* (New York: Harper and Row, 1940). Murray was president of the Congress of Industrial Organizations (CIO) and the United Steel Workers of America.

and of the New York State Power Authority. He also served as a troubleshooter for President Harry S. Truman; and when Cooke was asked by his biographer to list his lifetime accomplishments, he replied, "Rural electrification, inexpensive electricity in our homes, progress in labor-management relations, conservation of our land and water, and scientific management in industry."[78] To scientific management Morris Cooke had brought new ideas to develop harmonious cooperation between labor and management. He wanted more participation by workers, but most of all he sought to enlist the aid of the leaders of organized labor. If scientific management was to make any headway in the twentieth century, it required someone like Cooke to open new vistas in nonindustrial organizations and gain the support of the U.S. labor movement.

SUMMARY

The adolescence of a movement is analogous to life's teenage years in growth, rebellion, and the search for the mellowing of adulthood. From Taylor's notion of science in management at Midvale and Bethlehem to the maturity of the movement in the 1920s, scientific management had its adolescence of diversity in the individuals examined in this chapter. Carl Barth was the true believer who became a faithful executioner of Taylor's orthodoxy. Henry Gantt began under Taylor's guidance, contributed significantly, and then developed some different notions in his later years. The Gilbreths added motion study as a refinement to Taylor's time study, enlarged the study of fatigue, and emphasized the psychology of scientific management. Harrington Emerson polished Taylor's notions of efficiency, rejected his concepts of the "functional foreman" and of wage incentives, and brought national recognition to the movement at the Eastern rate hearings. Morris Cooke, nurtured by Taylor, brought the system to academic and municipal undertakings and sought a rapprochement between scientific management and organized labor. The gospel of efficiency had its doctrine, but changing times would bring new emphases.

---

78. Trombley, *Cooke*, p. 249.

CHAPTER 9

The Human Factor: Preparing the Way

Scientific management was born and nurtured in an era that stressed science as a way of life and living. It is not surprising, therefore, that the credo of scientific investigation spread to many areas, causing a shift from traditional, intuitive, pseudoscientific bases to more empirical, rational ones. This chapter examines how scientific management influenced the emerging field of personnel management and provided the ethic for industrial psychology. Other, more broadly inspired social forces were at work, and these are examined as they affected personnel management, industrial sociology, and industrial relations. Together, these ideas prepared the way for later developments in labor-management relations, human relations, and, eventually, organizational behavior.

PERSONNEL MANAGEMENT: A DUAL HERITAGE

The field of personnel management has a dual heritage and a beginning during this period of our study. The dual heritage comes from (1) the notion of personnel work as "welfare" or "industrial betterment" and (2) scientific management.

PERSONNEL AS WELFARE WORK

Paternalism, whether by the state, the church, or business, is as old as civilization. The feudal system was based on paternalistic ideals, and many early factory owners, such as Robert Owen, sought to provide various benefits, such as recreation, dancing lessons, meals, housing, education, sanitation, and so on. The New England Waltham Plan, discussed in Chapter 5, had paternalistic overtones as management looked after the education, housing, and morals of its employees. The McLane Report of 1832 depicted the typical firm as family owned and with relatively few employees. At this stage of organizational growth, that is, when firms were smaller, those who owned the firms managed them as well. The growth of the U.S. economy in the latter third of the nineteenth century, however, created unprecedented accumulations of human and physical resources in transportation and manufacturing organizations. This rapid growth moved the means of production from small workshops and homes to factories where it was possible to manufacture products on a grand scale. This growth was accompanied by some costs—one of them changing relations between managers and workers. The Social Gospel emerged as a counterpoint to social Darwinism. Rather than waiting for gradual improvement, those of the Social Gospel persuasion had a duty to reform social and economic conditions. One place where this reform could begin was labor-management relations. The industrial response was not surprising, but built on the familial traditions of the past in the form of industrial betterment or welfare work.

The first recorded attempt to establish an office for welfare work was at the National Cash Register Company in 1897. The company's founder and president, John H. Patterson, appointed Lena H. Tracy as the firm's first welfare director.[1] Joseph Bancroft and Sons had a welfare secretary in 1899, the H. J. Heinz Company employed a social secretary in 1902, the Colorado Fuel and Iron Company had a social secretary in 1901, and the International Harvester Company followed in 1903. Other cases include Filene's Department Stores, the Natural Food Company, Plymouth Cordage, John B. Stetson Company, Westinghouse Electric, and more.

The job of the social or welfare secretary was to improve the lives of workers, both off and on the job, hence the terms "welfare" and "industrial betterment." The social secretary listened to and handled grievances, ran the sick room of the workshop, provided for recreation and education, arranged transfers for dissatisfied workers, administered the dining facilities, prepared nutritious menus, and looked after the moral behavior of unmarried female factory employees.[2] The role was, more often than not, filled by women who had backgrounds in vocational guidance or social work. In addition to Lena H. Tracy at National Cash Register, other women in these positions included Gertrude B. Beeks at International Harvester, Elizabeth Briscoe at Bancroft and Sons, Florence Hughes at New Jersey Zinc, Laura Ray at Greenhut-Siegel, Aggie Dunn at H. J. Heinz, Lucy Bannister at Westinghouse, and Diana Hirschler at Filene's.[3] These social or welfare secretaries typically reported

1. See Lena Harvey Tracy, *How My Heart Sang: The Story of Pioneer Industrial Welfare Work* (New York: R. R. Smith Publisher, 1950); and John H. Patterson, "Altruism and Sympathy as Factors in Works Administration," *Engineering Magazine* 20 (1900) pp. 577–602; reprinted with photographs of NCR's activities in Wren, *Early Management Thought* (Aldershot, England; Dartmouth, 1997), pp. 403–428. Company bands and singing groups were also popular for morale building. See Kenneth S. Clark, *Music in Industry* (New York: National Bureau for the Advancement of Music, 1929).

2. For other companies and other duties of the social secretary, see William H. Tolman, *Social Engineering* (New York: McGraw, 1909), pp. 48–59. See also Stuart D. Brandes, *American Welfare Capitalism: 1880–1940* (Chicago: University of Chicago Press, 1976); and Nick Mandell, *The Corporation as Family: The Gendering of Corporate Welfare, 1890–1930* (Chapel Hill: University of North Carolina Press, 2002).

3. Lee Anne G. Kryder, "Transforming Industrial Welfare Work into Modern Personnel Management: The Contributions of Gertrude B. Beeks," unpublished paper presented at the Academy of Management meetings, Dallas, August 16, 1983; and Charles D. Wrege and Bernice M. Lattanzio, "Pioneers in Personnel Management: A Historical Study of the Neglected Accomplishment of Women in Personnel Management," working paper, Academy of Management, New Brunswick, N.J., 1977.

directly to the president or chief executive officer of the company, affording the first known opportunities for women to attain managerial status and to be in a position to influence corporate policy. In brief, one branch of thought regarding personnel relations grew out of the Social Gospel and was founded in the idea that concern for worker welfare would improve industrial conditions.

SCIENTIFIC MANAGEMENT AND PERSONNEL

The second branch of the dual heritage of personnel management began with scientific management. The typical factory at the turn of the century placed responsibility for the selection, training, and retention of employees in the hands of the line manager, usually the first-line supervisor. In describing his functional foremen, Frederick Taylor listed the duties of the shop disciplinarian as selecting and discharging employees, keeping performance records, handling disciplinary problems, administering wage payments, and serving as a peacemaker. Although Taylor described many of the tasks of an employment department, he did little to advance personnel practice, leaving that to his followers. In recognizing the need for an employment specialist, Taylor did prepare the way for the emergence of personnel as a staff rather than line task, as had been the previous practice.

Although the time period is not precise, it appears that the phrase "welfare work" began to decline about 1910 and was replaced with the phrase "employment management." According to Meyer Bloomfield, who was instrumental in forming an early employment managers association, "employment management" was better than "welfare work" because "Welfare work ... often lacked analysis, self criticism and human insight. Moreover, the good which [welfare] work could do was often vitiated by sentimentality, if not self-deception."[4] Mary B. Gilson, also a pioneer in the personnel field at the Clothcraft Shops of Joseph and Feiss in Cleveland, Ohio, recalled that those who went into welfare work had "faith in its power to ameliorate industrial unrest ... [but] the foundations of democracy can be strengthened by more fundamental measures than we then envisioned. I came to this conclusion through my observation of the installation of scientific management [at Clothcraft]."[5] With but few exceptions, welfare work waned and employment management became more systematic and professional early in the twentieth century.

In 1910, one of the model installations of the Taylor system, Plimpton Press, created an employment department and named Jane C. Williams as the first employment manager. The purpose of the department was to determine the suitability of applicants through job analysis, train and orient workers, maintain performance records, interview each worker once a month, review efficiency ratings every six months for pay

---

4. Meyer Bloomfield, "Man Management: A New Profession in the Making," in Daniel Bloomfield, ed., *Problems in Personnel Management* (New York: H. W. Wilson, 1923), p. 13.

5. Mary B. Gilson, *What's Past Is Prologue* (New York: Harper and Brothers, 1940), pp. ix–x; see also Charles D. Wrege and Ronald G. Greenwood, "Mary B. Gilson—A Historical Study of the Neglected Accomplishments of a Woman Who Pioneered in Personnel Management," in Jeremy Atack, ed., *Business and Economic History,* 2nd ser., vol. 11 (Urbana, Ill.: College of Commerce, University of Illinois, April 1982), pp. 35–42.

increases, hear grievances, provide a nurse in case of accident or illness, maintain a library of popular and technical magazines and books, help families with financial counseling, provide a lunchroom, and other tasks in undoubtedly the most advanced personnel department of that time.[6]

The path toward systematic personnel work was not smooth, however, and the experience of Henry L. Gantt at Bancroft Mills provides an illustration. Bancroft's first welfare secretary was Elizabeth Briscoe, who was appointed in 1902. In 1903, Bancroft ran into some severe productivity problems and employed Gantt as a consultant. Gantt's recommendations soon ran counter to the welfare orientation when he tried to improve personnel selection, to transfer or dismiss inefficient employees, and to demand regular attendance. Briscoe insisted that all workers, even inefficient ones, should be retained. Gantt argued that poor personnel relations and assignments were a contributing factor to the productivity problem that he had been hired to solve. Gantt was able to improve work methods, upgrade training, and install a bonus system in one department. He was able to show gains in productivity, but he was unable to implement fully his ideas because of the opposition of top management, especially that of John Bancroft. The younger, junior managers backed Gantt, but the older, senior managers backed Briscoe. When Gantt left in 1909, it appeared that welfare work had won out over scientific management.[7] In later years (1911–1927), however, Bancroft melded welfarism and scientific management, using welfarism to fit its management's Quaker beliefs about how people should be treated and using scientific management to keep productivity high so the firm could continue to exist. Gantt may have lost initially, but in the long run it was seen that welfare work and scientific management could lead the way to human betterment as well as to improved industrial practices.

The growing concern for standardizing and improving personnel practices led to the first professional associations for personnel staff specialists. The first national organization to deal with personnel matters was the National Association of Corporation Schools (NACS), founded in 1913 to advance the training and education of industrial employees. By 1917, the NACS had expanded its domain to human relations, meaning, employee relations. The second national organization, the National Association of Employment Managers (NAEM), grew out of a local Employment Managers Association started in Boston in 1912 by Meyer Bloomfield.

---

6. Jane C. Williams, "The Reduction of Labor Turnover in the Plimpton Press," *The Annals of the American Academy* 71 (May 1917), pp. 71–81.

7. Daniel Nelson and Stuart Campbell, "Taylorism versus Welfare Work in American Industry: H. L. Gantt and the Bancrofts," *Business History Review* 46, no. 1 (Spring 1972), pp. 1–16. Nelson and Campbell concluded that Gantt lost this battle at Bancroft; however, there is other evidence that Gantt introduced Bancroft's senior management to options they would pursue later. For this latter viewpoint, see Peter B. Petersen, "Henry Gantt's Work at Bancroft: The Option of Scientific Management," in John A. Pearce II and Richard B. Robinson, eds., *Academy of Management Proceedings* (San Diego, 1985), pp. 134–138. For more on Briscoe's contributions, see Peter B. Petersen, "A Pioneer in Personnel," *Personnel Administrator* 33 (June 1988), pp. 60–64.

By 1918 this idea had spread from the local to the regional to the national level to focus on employment practices. In 1922, these two groups (the NACS and the NAEM) merged to form the National Personnel Association.

Harlow Person introduced the first opportunity for college training of employment managers at Dartmouth's Amos Tuck School of Administration and Finance as early as 1915. Those at Tuck who wished to become employment managers had the opportunity to take a "special course in employment management and [prepare] a thesis which is the solution of a specific problem of management in a specific plant."[8] Through his role in the Society for the Promotion of the Science of Management (SPSM), later renamed the Taylor Society, Person was able to promote the study of employment management from a systematic point of view.

Despite rising professionalism, personnel practices of the 1910s continued to reflect a mixture of welfarism and efficiency in this time of transition. For example, Henry Ford, faced with a tight labor market and a worker turnover rate of 10 percent, formed an early employment department in 1914 called the Sociological Department. In that same year, Ford cut the length of the work day from nine to eight hours and raised the minimum wage from $2.50 to $5.00 per day. Ford saw this as "neither charity nor wages, but profit sharing and efficiency engineering."[9] Ford feared that the easy money of $5 per day would lead the workers astray, so he employed one hundred investigators—"advisers"—who visited the workers' homes to ensure that their homes were neat and clean, that they did not drink too much, that their sex life was without tarnish, and that they used their leisure time profitably. This sociological experiment lasted but three years and ended when Ford told Samuel S. Marquis, head of the department: "There is too much of this snooping around in private affairs. We'll change this from a Sociology Department to an Education Department."[10] Thereafter, the home visits by the advisers stopped, and the Ford Company turned its attention to advising and educating the employees. The employment staff was reduced to fifty, but the number of Ford employees grew from fourteen thousand in 1914 to fifty-three thousand in 1919.

Ford was one example of how employment departments began to be established in industry. One authority estimated that as many employment departments were created during 1919–1920 as had been created in all years previously.[11] Employers could see the success of Henry Ford and others and conclude that this added concern for their personnel led to a greater prosperity for all, labor and management. One study of the period 1913–1919, commissioned by the U.S. Bureau of

---

8. Harlow S. Person, "University Schools of Business and the Training of Employment Executives," *Annals of the American Academy* 65 (May 1916), p. 126.

9. Henry Ford, quoted in Loren Baritz, *The Servants of Power* (New York: John Wiley and Sons, 1960), p. 33.

10. John R. Commons, "Henry Ford, Miracle Maker," *The Independent* 102 (May 1, 1920), p. 160.

11. Robert F. Lovett, "Present Tendencies in Personnel Practice," *Industrial Management* 65 (June 1923), pp. 327–333.

Labor Statistics, determined that modern employment practices reduced labor turnover, thus reducing training and other costs while also providing employees with more stable employment, especially in larger firms. The larger the firm, the lower the turnover rate, because larger firms could pay better wages, provide better conditions, stabilize employment, and have a central department to look after employee welfare. Although most turnover was voluntary (i.e., few employees were discharged), the greatest turnover was found among the unskilled, and turnover for female employees was generally lower than for male employees.[12] Interest in advanced employment practices was not confined to the United States. In Great Britain, for example, Benjamin Seebohm Rowntree (1871–1954) brought to his York Cocoa Works an interest in human welfare that stopped slightly short of paternalism. Rowntree employed a sociologist in a psychological department who supervised company education, health, canteens, housing, and recreation.[13] Mary Follett (who will be discussed later) chose Rowntree's firm as a prime example of how a business should develop a social philosophy.

Interest in the human side of enterprise and in the potential of personnel management led to significant changes in assumptions about people in organizations. For instance, Ordway Tead partially recovered from an "instinct" explanation of human behavior to coauthor an early personnel text with Henry C. Metcalf.[14] They concluded that instincts and inborn tendencies still had a great deal to do with human conduct but that advances in personnel research were opening new vistas that enabled more scientific selection, placement, and training. Executives should adopt a personnel point of view, which assumed that there was a cause-and-effect relationship in behavior that could be studied for purposes of guiding human conduct.[15] Proper work habits could be formed and emotions controlled, and creative leadership could lead to reduced conflict and improved morale.

The typical personnel management text of this era examined such subjects as job analysis, job descriptions and specifications, psychological tests, methods of interviewing and selecting employees, merit ratings, promotion policies, analysis of labor turnover, training, and problems such as tardiness and absences. Training of supervisors was also included, but relatively little attention was paid to developing higher-level management.

In brief, the origins of personnel management were to lead to a common meeting ground by the 1920s. Although the welfare movement stressed the value of people to an organization, it lacked the rigor and professionalism necessary for the

---

12. Paul F. Brissenden and Emil Frankel, *Labor Turnover in Industry* (New York: Macmillan, 1922), especially pp. 54–79.

13. Morgen L. Witzel, "Benjamin Seebohm Rowntree," in M. L. Witzel, ed., *The Biographical Dictionary of Management* (Bristol, England: Thoemmes Press, 2001), vol. 2, pp. 863–865

14. Ordway Tead and Henry C. Metcalf, *Personnel Administration: Its Principles and Practice* (New York: McGraw-Hill, 1920).

15. Ordway Tead, *Human Nature and Management: The Applications of Psychology to Executive Leadership* (New York: McGraw-Hill, 1929), p. 9.

growth of modern organizations. Scientific management provided some of this rigor by being coupled with industrial psychology (which will be discussed soon), by actuating national interest in professional associations, and by inspiring the first college-level preparation for personnel specialists. Welfarism was not dead, but would continue in a less emphatic fashion in subsequent years. Scientific management, on the other hand, would find its goals and methods reshaped by the behavioral and social sciences. Together, welfarism and scientific management prepared the way for modern personnel management.

PSYCHOLOGY AND THE INDIVIDUAL

In Greek mythology, Plutus was the god of wealth; from this foundation came plutology, a branch of economic theory that dealt with how humans tried to satisfy their wants. Near the middle of the nineteenth century, Professor Hearn of Melbourne, Australia, put forth a theory that resembles more modern ideas:

> Food, drink, air and warmth are the most urgent of [our] necessities [which] … man shares with all other animals…. The satisfaction, therefore, of his primary appetites is imperative upon man … first in the degree of their intensity … and the first which he attempts to satisfy…. Man is able not merely to satisfy his primary wants, but to devise means for their better and more complete gratification…. Thus the comparative range of human wants is rapidly increased … as the attempt to satisfy the primary appetites thus gives rise to new desires … [and] when they have acquired such comforts they are pained at their loss, but their acquisition does not prevent them from continuing to desire a further increase.[16]

This anticipation (by some four score years) of a hierarchy of human needs and the premise that once one need is satisfied further needs are pursued was achieved not by empirical design but by observation and logical deduction. Before the advent of scientific management, psychology was based on such introspective, armchair, or deductive bases. Pseudosciences, such as astrology, physiognomy, phrenology, and graphology, were abundant as managers sought to select personnel on the bases of the movement and position of the stars, physical characteristics, bumps on the skull, and handwriting analysis.[17] Even in such reputable consulting firms as that of Harrington Emerson, Katherine H. M. Blackford, a physician, emphasized the study

---

16. William E. Hearn, *Plutology, or the Theory of the Efforts to Satisfy Human Wants* (Melbourne, Australia: G. Robertson, 1863), pp. 12–15.

17. For beginners, Mary H. Booth, *How to Read Character in Handwriting* (Philadelphia: John C. Winston, 1910); Katherine H. M. Blackford and Arthur Newcomb, *Analyzing Character: The New Science of Judging Men; Misfits in Business, the Home and Social Life* (New York: Blackford, 1916); and Gerald E. Fosbroke, *Character Reading Through Analysis of the Features* (New York: G. P. Putnam's Sons, 1914).

of physiognomy and graphology as an aid to selection. She advocated the study of facial and hair coloring, the shape of noses, facial expressions, and head proportions, such as "convex and concave faces," and other "psychophysical" variations in selecting employees. She found nine such psychophysical variables and also concluded that handwriting, like a person's voice, was an expression of the person's character and should be taken into account.[18]

TOWARD SCIENTIFIC PSYCHOLOGY

Elsewhere, psychology was escaping its introspective, pseudoscience beginnings. When Wilhelm Wundt opened his Leipzig laboratory in 1879, the scientific method first appeared in psychology. Wundt did not entirely abandon introspection but began to examine behavior through controlled experiments. As the founder of experimental psychology, he opened the way for applied and, eventually, industrial psychology. Wundt was searching for "psychological man" through studying the individual for universal mainsprings of human conduct. Observation of human behavior, combined with the emergence of the psychoanalytical theories of Freud, soon led to a widespread search for instincts to explain behavior and thought. People were not rational, but controlled by instincts, and, by understanding these instincts, the secrets of the hitherto unexplored mind could be opened for examination. Thorstein Veblen laid great stress on the instinct for manual skill; William James thought there were twenty-eight separate instincts; and Ordway Tead named ten.[19]

The disparities and disagreements among the lists of instincts soon proved that this approach was futile, and instinct theory was dismissed as an oversimplified view of behavior. However, the human variabilities noted in the attempts to develop instinct theory led to the recognition of individual differences. The study of human behavior had to study the individual, and here the psychologists found their alliance with scientific management.

THE BIRTH OF INDUSTRIAL PSYCHOLOGY

Scientific management gave industrial psychology its ethic, scope, and direction for research. The earliest objective of industrial psychology was

> The maximum efficiency of the individual in industry and his optimum adjustment … in the belief that, in the final analysis, the maximum efficiency of that individual in the industrial situation can

---

18. Katherine H. M. Blackford and Arthur Newcomb, *The Job, The Man, The Boss* (New York: Doubleday, 1916), ch. 7, pp. 176, 184.

19. Ordway Tead, *Instincts in Industry: A Study of Working Class Psychology* (Boston: Houghton Mifflin, 1918). Tead's list consisted of the parental, sex, workmanship, possession, self-assertion, submissiveness, herd, pugnacity, play, and curiosity instincts.

only be achieved by insuring his most satisfactory adjustment in that situation.[20]

While the engineer studied mechanical efficiency, the industrial psychologist studied human efficiency with the same goal in mind of improved overall greater productivity. Acceptance by industry of the heretofore ivory-tower psychologist was facilitated by the psychologist's interest in efficiency.

Hugo Münsterberg (1863–1916) was the creator of industrial psychology. Born in Danzig and educated in Wundt's Leipzig laboratory, he was soon enticed to the United States by William James, the great Harvard psychologist. In 1892, Münsterberg established his psychological laboratory at Harvard, which was to become the foundation stone in the industrial psychology movement. His interests were far-ranging, including the application of psychological principles to crime detection, education, morality, and philosophy. In industry, Münsterberg considered Taylor the "brilliant originator" of scientific management, but felt that the movement needed a broader foundation to prove of lasting value. To lay this foundation, Münsterberg visited with President Wilson, Secretary of Commerce Redfield, and Secretary of Labor W. B. Wilson in Washington to encourage them to create a government bureau dedicated to scientific research in the application of psychology to the problems of industry. National interest in scientific management was high, and Münsterberg sought to put science in the study of human behavior at the same level of national concern. According to Münsterberg, "While today the greatest care is devoted to the problems of material and equipment, all questions of the mind … like fatigue, monotony, interest, learning … joy in work … reward … and many similar mental states are dealt with by laymen without any scientific understanding."[21]

Even though the government bureau never materialized, Münsterberg's research efforts sought to answer certain perplexing industrial questions:

> We ask how we can find the men whose mental qualities make them best fitted for the work which they have to do; secondly, under what psychological conditions we can secure the greatest and most satisfactory output from every man; and finally how we can produce most completely the influences on human minds which are desired in the interests of business. In other words, we ask how to find the best possible work, and how to secure the best possible effects.[22]

Münsterberg's *Psychology and Industrial Efficiency* was directly related to Taylor's proposals and contained three broad parts: (1) "The Best Possible Man";

20. Morris S. Viteles, *Industrial Psychology* (New York: W. W. Norton, 1932), p. 4.

21. Margaret Münsterberg, *Hugo Münsterberg: His Life and Work* (New York: Appleton-Century-Crofts, 1922), p. 250. See also Frank J. Landy, "Hugo Münsterberg: Victim or Visionary?" *Journal of Applied Psychology* 77 (1992), pp. 787–802; and Jutta Spillman and Lothar Spillman, "The Rise and Fall of Hugo Münsterberg," *Journal of the History of the Behavioral Sciences* 29 (1993), pp. 322–338.

22. Hugo Münsterberg, *Psychology and Industrial Efficiency* (Boston: Houghton Mifflin, 1913), pp. 23–24.

(2) "The Best Possible Work"; and (3) "The Best Possible Effect." Part one was a study of the demands jobs made on people and the necessity of identifying those people whose mental qualities made them best fitted for the work they had to do. Part two sought to determine psychological conditions under which the greatest and most satisfactory output could be obtained from every person. Part three examined the necessity of producing the influences on human needs that were desirable for the interests of the business. For each of these objectives, Münsterberg outlined definite proposals for the use of tests in worker selection, for the application of research on learning in training industrial personnel, and for the study of psychological techniques to increase workers' motives and reduce fatigue. In character with experimental psychology, Münsterberg illustrated his proposals with his own evidence gathered from the study of trolley drivers, telephone operators, and ship's officers.

Taylor and others, such as Harlow Person, had envisioned contributions from psychologists to research into the human factor. Münsterberg fitted into this scheme, and the ethic of scientific management was readily apparent in the focus on the individual, the emphasis on efficiency, and the social benefits to be derived from application of the scientific method. As Taylor had called for a mental revolution and the recognition of the mutuality of interests between employees and employers, Münsterberg noted:

> We must not forget that the increase of industrial efficiency by future psychological adaptation and by improvement of the psychophysical conditions is not only in the interest of the employers, but still more of the employees; their working time can be reduced, their wages increased, their level of life raised.[23]

Concern for the human factor was increasing, and it began within the ethics and objectives of scientific management. After Münsterberg, there were others: Charles S. Myers, who pioneered industrial psychology in Great Britain; Walter D. Scott, who devised personnel classification tests for the U.S. Army during World War I; Cecil A. Mace, who performed the first experiments in goal setting as a motivational technique; Walter Van Dyke Bingham, whose Division of Applied Psychology at the Carnegie Institute of Technology led to the creation of the Bureau of Personnel Research; Morris S. Viteles, whose text became the "bible of industrial psychology;"[24] and more. It was Münsterberg, though, who paved the

---

23. *Ibid.*, pp. 308–309.

24. See C. S. Myers, *Industrial Psychology* (New York: People's Institute, 1925); Edmund C. Lynch, "Walter Dill Scott: Pioneer Industrial Psychologist," *Business History Review* 42, no. 2 (Summer 1968), pp. 147–170; Paula L. Phillips, "Cecil Alec Mace: The Life and Times of the Original Goal-Setting Experimenter," in J. L. Wall and L. R. Jauch, eds., *Academy of Management Best Papers Proceedings* (Miami Beach: Academy of Management, August 1991), pp. 142–146; Michelle P. Kraus, *Walter Van Dyke Bingham and the Bureau of Personnel Research* (New York: Garland, 1986). Morris S. Viteles, "Morris S. Viteles," in E. G. Boring and Gardner Lindzey, eds., *The History of Psychology in Autobiography*, vol. 5 (New York: Appleton-Century-Crofts, 1967), pp. 417–449.

way by establishing the roots and justification of the industrial psychology movement in scientific management.

During this era people became an organization's most vital asset, not out of sentimentality or moral uplift, but based on the view that concern for employee welfare would increase worker efficiency. Personnel departments proliferated, and worker welfare schemes were designed with the hope that happy, satisfied workers would be productive workers. Psychological testing, however, had not yet demonstrated its adequacy for the task of personnel selection, since research had failed to show any correlation between tests and job success.[25] An early employment manager noted that tests were unscientific, were administered by amateurs, were used as a substitute for judgment, and

Whiting Williams, working on the railroad, 1922. The Western Reserve Historical Society, Cleveland, Ohio.

were little better than fortune-telling for predicting human success.[26] Quacks abounded, throwing reputable psychologists into disrepute, as firms sought quick and simple solutions to human problems. After 1925, the testing fad declined and managers had less faith in measuring traits that would predict greater efficiency. Eventually this breach would be filled by the ethic of human relations as the road to greater productivity.

FOUNDATIONS OF THE SOCIAL PERSON: THEORY, RESEARCH, AND PRACTICE

Scientific management shaped its times and in turn was shaped by them. It provided the rationale for improved personnel management and for industrial psychology. The course of history is such that one idea typically leads to a better idea, and such was the fate of scientific management. Another set of forces, related to scientific management only in terms of time, would enlarge the view of industry by seeing it as a social institution. From this beginning, the road was paved for the era of the social human being.

THE ANTECEDENTS OF INDUSTRIAL SOCIOLOGY

As described earlier, the Social Gospel emerged as a counterpoint to social Darwinism. The Social Gospel was a liberal, socially conscious Protestantism that

---

25. For example, Henry C. Link suggested that more effort should be devoted to testing tests rather than people. H. C. Link, *Employment Psychology* (New York: Macmillan, 1921).

26. Gilson, *What's Past Is Prologue*, p. 64.

asked people to act to improve social conditions, including industry. One product of this Social Gospel was Whiting Williams (1878–1975), who was born into a relatively prosperous family, was well educated, and had tried his hand at various jobs before becoming vice president and director of personnel for the Hydraulic Pressed Steel Company of Cleveland, Ohio. Williams decided to apply the Social Gospel idea of direct involvement, so he shed his white collar and headed out disguised as a worker to study industrial conditions firsthand.[27] He felt the only way to discover the human problems of industry would be to become a participant-observer because "men's actions spring from their feelings rather than their thoughts, and people cannot be interviewed for their feelings."[28] His first job was in a steel mill cleaning out the open-hearth furnaces so they could be rebricked and refired. It was hot, dirty work; the shifts were twelve hours long; and the pay was forty-five cents per hour with time-and-a-half for hours over eight. This was Whiting Williams's introduction to the world of the worker, and, over a period of seven months, he worked in coal mines, a railroad roundhouse, a shipyard, and an oil refinery, as well as various steel mills.

According to Williams, the workers' prayer was, "Give us this day our daily job," because a job meant 'bread,' sustenance for the workers and their families. All persons—including managers—measured their individual worth and their value to society in terms of their jobs. Jobs influenced people's social standing, and how they earned their living influenced where and how they and their families lived. Without jobs, people were isolated not only economically, but also from the community and society: "[the worker's] vision of himself, his friends, his employer, and the whole of this world to come is circumscribed by his job."[29] This view made jobs central to people's lifestyles, friends, where they lived, how they spent their leisure time, and how they felt about themselves. "This vital connection between job status and social status means that the problem of effective relations with the worker inside the factory cannot be successfully separated from the whole problem of general social relations outside [the factory]."[30] This concept of the place of work as part of a broader social system marked Williams as being in advance of other theorists about human behavior and the importance of work.

Within the factory, Williams also observed the operations of a job hierarchy that had little or nothing to do with pay but rather emphasized the nature of the job. While working in the steel mill, he was promoted to millwright's helper. His pay was two cents per hour more, but his former fellow shovelers envied him not because of the pay increase, but because the nature of his job had changed from the dirty, hot

27. Daniel A. Wren, *White Collar Hobo: The Travels of Whiting Williams* (Ames: Iowa State University Press, 1987).

28. Whiting Williams, *What's on the Worker's Mind? By One Who Put on Overalls to Find Out* (New York: Charles Scribner's Sons, 1920), p. vi.

29. *Ibid.*, p. 299.

30. Whiting Williams, "Theory of Industrial Conduct and Leadership," *Harvard Business Review* 1 (April 1923), p. 326.

work of a shoveler to the cleaner, more pleasant work of an assistant to a skilled worker. Williams was also skeptical about the efficacy of the idea that people would work harder if they were given more money:

> We give the dollar altogether too great an importance when we con-
> sider it the cause of men's industry.... The dollar is merely an espe-
> cially convenient and simple means for facilitating the measurement of
> a man's distance from the cipher of insignificance among his fel-
> lows.... Beyond a certain point, the increase of wages is quite likely to
> lessen as to increase effort.[31]

Williams's view was unique in that he established earnings as a means of social comparison—that is, the pay a worker received was considered not in absolute terms, but relative to what others received. A person's "distance from the cipher of insignificance" among others was facilitated by using the dollar as a unit of account for measurement. This did not mean that money was not important, but that it was a carrier of social value that might enhance or deflate how people viewed themselves relative to others. Hence incentive plans were less than effective as motivators. The mainspring of workers was the "wish to enjoy the feeling of our worth as persons among other persons."[32] Togetherness in thinking, feeling, and working in groups was important to workers. From their peers the workers drew their social suste-nance, security, and concept of self-worth. Workers chose to get along with their coworkers because they could always find another job but could not always move from the community. From the employer, and especially the supervisor, they expected recognition and treatment conducive to preserving self-worth. It was not the paternalistic clubs, cafeterias, and recreation activities that won worker loyalty, but successful relations with the supervisor as a representative of management. Williams recommended an eleventh commandment, "Thou Shalt Not Take Thy Neighbor For Granted," and urged management to change from appeals to fear to appeals to "hope and surety of reward." Latent in Williams's study of the worker was Charles H. Cooley's "looking glass self" and the group as the primary social unit.

Other findings from Williams's shirtsleeve empiricism included (1) workers restricted output ("stringing out the job") because they perceived scarce job oppor-tunities, and employers tended to hire and lay off indiscriminately; (2) unions arose out of workers' desire for job security, and the unions would not have made much progress if employers had evidenced concern for this worker need; (3) long factory hours (e.g., twelve-hour shifts in steel mills) made both workers and supervisors grouchy and tired, causing interpersonal conflict; and (4) workers listened to radi-cal agitators because employers failed to speak "of the plans and purposes, the aims and ideals—the character of the company." Williams made a career of lecturing, con-sulting, and writing of his experiences as a worker. From time to time, he resumed

---

31. Williams, *What's on the Worker's Mind*, p. 323.

32. Whiting Williams, *Mainsprings of Men* (New York: Charles Scribner's Sons, 1925), p. 147.

his worker's disguise to study strikers and strikebreakers, unemployment, and labor-management relations in Great Britain and continental Europe.[33]

Despite his pioneering work in the field that today is called industrial sociology, Williams's efforts were generally not recognized. The roots of industrial sociology are traditionally traced to the Hawthorne studies, discussed in Chapter 13. Why? One explanation appears to be the academic distaste and disregard for any theory founded by nonacademicians. According to Keller, the personal and institutional academic prestige of those who propose a theory contributes to the influence and acceptance of that theory.[34] Williams was never affiliated with an academic institution; in contrast, the Hawthorne studies bore the seal of approval from the prestigious institutions of Harvard and MIT. These scholarly halos made academicians relatively oblivious to the findings of a nonacademician. Further, Williams's works were rarely reviewed in the scholarly sociology journals of that period. Finally, the relatively young field of sociology sought to become scientific and rigorous, and the Harvard and MIT people who were involved in the Hawthorne research had clearly established their credentials. The prestige of these established scholars from leading schools provided a legitimate cornerstone for a discipline. However, the real roots of industrial sociology appear to have been in the development of the U.S. Social Gospel in the late nineteenth century, rather than in the Hawthorne experiments at the Western Electric plant in the 1920s and 1930s.[35]

SOCIOLOGICAL THEORY AND HUMAN RELATIONS

The study of sociology began in the late nineteenth century as an outgrowth of its parent discipline, philosophy, rather than as an applied study. Max Weber, Emile Durkheim, and Vilfredo Pareto formed an intellectual triad of sociological theorists of the nineteenth century. Max Weber, who is discussed in Chapter 10, gave us a theory of bureaucracy as well as the notion of the Protestant ethic. Emile Durkheim (1858–1917) divided societies into two primary types: mechanical, or those dominated by a collective consciousness, and organic, or those characterized by specialization and division of labor and societal interdependence. Mechanical societies were bound together by friendliness, neighborliness, and kinship; however, the lack of such solidarity in organic societies led to anomie, or a state of confusion, insecurity, and "normlessness." According to Durkheim, restoration of social solidarity in organic societies had to come through a new "collective consciousness," which created values and norms and imposed them on the individual. In organic societies people must

---

33. Williams's study of Great Britain is found in *Full Up and Fed Up* (New York: Charles Scribner's Sons, 1921); his experiences in France, Germany, Italy, and Spain are reported in *Horny Hands and Hampered Elbows* (New York: Charles Scribner's Sons, 1922).

34. Robert T. Keller, "The Harvard 'Pareto Circle' and the Historical Development of Organization Theory," *Journal of Management* 10 (Summer 1984), p. 193.

35. Daniel A. Wren, "Industrial Sociology: A Revised View of Its Antecedents," *Journal of the History of the Behavioral Sciences* 21 (October 1985), pp. 311–320.

cooperate, love one another, and be willing to sacrifice the self to the group in order to promote solidarity.[36] Thus arose the antithesis of Adam Smith's self-interest as the basis for exchange. Durkheim substituted the group as the source of values and norms and as the new collective consciousness. It was in Durkheim's anomie that Elton Mayo found a new prescription for industrial solidarity.

Vilfredo Pareto (1848–1923) was the originator of the notion of the "social system." By social system, Pareto meant the state of society both at a specified moment and in the successive transformations that it underwent within a period of time. Characterized by mutually interdependent but variable units, society sought to maintain an equilibrium among its parts. If a disturbance occurred, the system lost its balance but would work back again toward equilibrium. Pareto's work might have remained just so much gibberish had it not been for Lawrence J. Henderson, a Harvard physiologist. Henderson formed a Pareto Circle and, through a series of seminars, influenced a number of scholars, such as Talcott Parsons and George Homans, both of whom saw organizations as interacting social systems. According to Heyl's research, "Mayo was never a full-fledged Paretian" even though he attended Henderson's seminars.[37] However, Mayo frequently cited Pareto and Henderson in discussing the nature of the social order and the need to balance the logic of efficiency and the logic of sentiments. Roethlisberger and Dickson, who wrote the definitive work on the Hawthorne studies, *Management and the Worker,* went even further in using Paretian notions of the factory as a social system and of social equilibrium.[38] Chester Barnard developed his idea of the organization as a cooperative system as well as his idea of equilibrating effectiveness and efficiency from Pareto. Part III presents more of the Paretian notions that formed a basis for human relations and organization theory.

Aside from the pioneering work of Pareto and Durkheim, a major school of sociological theory called social behaviorism was formed during the scientific management era. This school introduced the idea of the social person as the object of study and established social psychology as a fundamental branch of sociology. Charles Horton Cooley contributed the "looking glass self," or the idea that the social self arises reflectively in terms of a person's reactions to the opinions of others. Through group experiences a person forms the first notions of both self and social unity. George Herbert Mead began social psychology by suggesting that a person learns her or his own self through a process of taking the role of others in interactive situations. Society enters every person through the process of interaction, and the self is constantly being reshaped through these encounters.

---

36. Emile Durkheim, *The Division of Labor in Society,* trans. George Simpson (New York: Free Press, 1947).

37. Barbara S. Heyl, "The Harvard 'Pareto Circle,'" *Journal of the History of the Behavioral Sciences* 4 (October 1968), p. 322.

38. F. J. Roethlisberger and William J. Dickson, *Management and the Worker* (Cambridge, Mass.: Harvard University Press, 1939), especially pp. 551–568.

The notion of Gestalt psychology was coming into prominence owing to the work of the Austrian Christian von Ehrenfels (1890) and the German Max Wertheimer (1912). Prior to the Gestalt idea, Martindale characterized psychological theories as mechanistic in that they tended to emphasize fundamental units of study, for example, an element, a particle, or an individual. Gestalt psychology, on the other hand, represented an "organismic" approach, which emphasized not the parts or units but the patterns, wholes, configurations, and so on that made the whole appear to be more than the sum of its parts.[39] From these beginnings, Gestalt theory would pervade the ideas of social systems, group dynamics, and other behavioral research right up to the modern-day notions of general systems theory and sociotechnical systems.

SOME EARLY EMPIRICAL INVESTIGATIONS

The group and social facets of human behavior were gaining recognition in sociological theory and in the Gestalt idea of configurations. Empirical investigations into the human facet of industrial life were sparse, except for the work of Whiting Williams noted earlier. In addition, Richard Whiting uncovered the work of Paul Goehre, a German theological student, who took a job in a factory to investigate working conditions in 1891.[40] Goehre observed that the workers took more pride in producing a complete unit of work rather than an unidentifiable fragment, that higher productivity occurred when supervisors instilled a feeling of group interdependence and teamwork, and that there were informal group pressures for adherence to norms. Lower morale and lower efficiency were the result when people were isolated and felt a lack of "community of labour."

Henri DeMan anticipated by more than three decades Frederick Herzberg's methods of probing worker motivation. DeMan asked both wage earners and salaried workers in various parts of Germany to make a statement "concerning their own feelings about their daily work."[41] DeMan concluded that there was a natural instinct in people to find "joy in work." In this drive, positive motives were instincts for activity, self-assertion, constructiveness, and a longing for "mastery" (power). The negative factors that inhibited this natural impulse for joy in work were found in the job itself in elements such as detailed work, monotony, reduction of worker initiative, fatigue, and poor working conditions; and in "social hindrances," such as the dependent position of the worker, unjust wage systems, speedups, insecurity of livelihood, and lack of social solidarity. DeMan's sample (seventy-eight subjects) was

---

39. Don Martindale, *The Nature and Types of Sociological Theory* (Boston: Houghton Mifflin, 1960), pp. 285–435, 451–453.

40. Richard J. Whiting, "Historical Search in Human Relations," *Academy of Management Journal* 7 (March 1964), pp. 45–53. Goehre's work was translated into English as *Three Months in a Workshop* (London: Swan Sonnenschein, 1895).

41. Henri DeMan, *Joy in Work,* trans. Eden Paul (New York: Holt, Rinehart and Winston, 1929), p. 9.

limited, but his findings bear a remarkable similarity to Herzberg's later "motivation-hygiene" theory in many respects. DeMan felt that work itself was a motivator and that management's job was to remove the "hindrances" that prevented the worker from finding joy in work. While theory and research on the social side of industrial life were advancing, the practice of management also moved toward greater employee involvement in decision making.

EMPLOYEE PARTICIPATION IN DECISION MAKING

Founded upon John Locke's notion of a representative government of the people, for the people, and by the people, American workers would have a different future than their counterparts who had remained in their native lands. We have seen how *Commonwealth vs. Hunt* removed the conspiracy doctrine from combinations of workers, and how the American labor movement assumed less radical forms than in other lands. With this theme we will explore the democratization of the workplace along three paths that were present during the scientific management era: the trade union movement and the beginnings of industrial relations; union management cooperation; and employee representation plans.

THE TRADE UNION MOVEMENT AND INDUSTRIAL RELATIONS

The year 1886 was a momentous one. While Henry Towne was encouraging engineers to think in economic terms, the American Federation of Labor (AFL) was being formed with the leadership of Samuel Gompers. The AFL was a federation of craft unions that would succeed where the Knights of Labor and the National Labor Union had failed (see Chapter 6).

A third development of that eventful year was the publication of Richard Ely's *The Labor Movement in America*, which was a clarion call "designed to protect and advance the interest of the great mass of working classes" by uniting in associations to bargain collectively with employers.[42]

Richard T. Ely (1854–1943) was an ardent Christian Socialist, but his idea took a different turn from the industrial welfare advocates by emphasizing independent worker associations and proposing public ownership of the nation's railways and the gas, electric, telephone, and telegraph industries. He would later reverse his views regarding public ownership of these industries, but continued to see capitalist employers as a social class separate from the workers.[43] He insisted, however, that

---

42. Richard T. Ely, *The Labor Movement in America* (New York: T. Y. Crowell, 1886), p. 92.

43. Richard T. Ely, *Social Aspects of Christianity, and Other Essays* (New York: T. Y. Crowell, 1889), pp. 72–78; and idem, *Ground Under Our Feet: An Autobiography* (New York: Macmillan, 1938), pp. 251–252.

202 PART II THE SCIENTIFIC MANAGEMENT ERA

neither socialism nor communism could advance the cause of labor better than voluntary associations of workers uniting to negotiate with employers.

Preceding the publicity given scientific management in the Eastern Rate Case, organized labor had paid scant attention to Taylor and his followers. After the House of Representatives investigation into the Taylor and other systems of shop management, a U.S. Commission on Industrial Relations was created by an act of Congress in 1912 to "inquire into the general condition of labor in the principal industries of the United States" and other facets of industrial work and worker welfare.[44] One member of the commission was John Rogers Commons (1862–1945) who was hired for the University of Wisconsin faculty by Ely in 1904. Commons had taken an early position that the "clever devices of compensation," formulated by Taylor, Gantt, Emerson, and others, divided workers and forced individual bargaining.[45] Workers needed to organize to offset employers' bargaining strength.

As a member of the Industrial Relations Commission, Commons had the opportunity to visit with Taylor and "came to realize that improved methods of management and personnel administration were yet another valuable approach to solving labor problems and improving industrial relations."[46] Visits to Taylor system shops indicated to Commons that scientific management could work with unions, or not. At Plimpton Press, one of the most advanced scientifically managed shops, Commons saw that it was unionized and succeeding. Similarly, Clothcraft, another model Taylor shop, did not have a union, but was managed so well that a union was not necessary. Such companies were rare, he felt, and some 75 to 90 percent of the companies were so "inefficient or greedy ... that only the big stick of a union or government" could bring them up to the level of better managed firms.[47]

In his book *Industrial Goodwill*, Commons wrote of the need for workers to have a "voice," workplace participation through a union, and employers should consider workers as a "human resource" in whom parents, taxpayers, and the nation had made a significant investment, which should not be squandered.[48] (In this case, Commons' "human resource" was a factor of production to be valued for its contribution.) Commons admired Taylor:

> Mr. Taylor's great contribution to the subject [of incentive payments] was that of accurately *measuring the task* in advance, instead of leaving it to the hit-or-miss, cut-and-dry, methodology the old style of piecework incentives.[49]

---

44. *Final Report of the Commission on Industrial Relations,* Senate Document no. 415, 64th Cong., 1st sess. (Washington, D.C.: U.S. Government Printing Office, 1916), vol. 1, p.6.

45. John R. Commons, "Organized Labor's Attitude Toward Industrial Efficiency," *American Economic Review* 1 (September 1911), pp. 463–472.

46. Bruce E. Kaufman, "The Role of Economics and Industrial Relations in the Development of the Field of Personnel/Human Resource Management," *Management Decision* 40 (2002), p. 970.

47. John R. Commons, *Industrial Government* (New York: Macmillan, 1921), p. 263.

48. John R. Commons, *Industrial Goodwill* (New York: McGraw-Hill, 1919), pp. 129–130.

49. *Ibid.,* p. 13.

Despite Taylor's improvements, Commons felt that scientific management cut across "the solidarity of labor," placed job knowledge in the hands of the employer rather than the worker through time and motion study, and had the "defects of autocracy."[50] In recalling his life, Commons stated "I was trying to save capitalism by making it good ... as good as the best instead of negligent ... I wanted also to make trade unions as good as the best of them that I knew."[51] From his work on the Commission on Industrial Relations, his contact with Taylor, and observation of scientific management shops, Commons took a broader view of labor-management relations. He was concerned with institutions (we will treat his institutional economics later), the balance of power in the workplace and the relative disadvantage of individual workers, and the need to mend these factors either by industrial goodwill, sound managerial practices, or by union and/or governmental agencies.

Prior to World War I, the industrial welfare movement and scientific management's spur to industrial psychology provided the foundations of personnel management. Kaufman has clearly established the role of academic economists in expanding personnel management to include industrial relations after the war. Foremost among these individuals was John R. Commons, but others such as Paul Douglas (University of Chicago before becoming a U.S. senator), and Sumner Slichter (of Cornell and later Harvard University) were early writers on personnel subjects such as morale, turnover, absenteeism, profit sharing, bonus plans, job analysis, and so forth. Commons, for his leadership role, would be considered the "Father of Industrial Relations."[52] With few self-standing schools of business, and few, if any, doctorates in business administration, the economists took the lead in academia with "applied economics" meaning industrial relations/personnel management. Most faculty members held doctorates in economics, regardless of what subject they taught, sales, finance, personnel, and so on.[53]

Practitioners and consultants were also influential in reshaping industrial relations in the post World War I period. The existing philosophy of the American Federation of Labor, as represented by Samuel Gompers, was to bargain for more wages and to achieve gains for labor through power and not productivity.[54] Organized labor's position was that scientific management was autocratic, because it forced employees to depend on the employer's conception of fairness. Employees had no voice

———
50. *Ibid.,* pp. 13–16, 18–19.

51. John R. Commons, *Myself* (New York: Macmillan, 1934), p. 143.

52. Bruce E. Kaufman, *The Origins and Evolution of the Field of Industrial Relations in the United States* (Ithaca, N.Y.: ILR Press, 1993): idem, "John R. Commons: His Contributions to the Founding and Early Development of the Field of Personnel/HRM," *Proceedings of the 50th Annual Meeting of the Industrial Relations Research Association* (Madison, WI: IRRA, 1998), pp. 328–341.

53. Bruce E. Kaufman, "Personnel/Human Resource Management: Its Roots in Applied Economics," *History of Political Economy* 32 (2000), pp. 229–256; idem, "Human Resources and Industrial Relations: Commonalities and Differences," *Human Resource Management Review* 11 (2001), pp. 339–374.

54. Jean Trepp McKelvey, *AFL Attitudes toward Production: 1900–1932* (Ithaca, N.Y.: Cornell Studies in Industrial and Labor Relations, vol. 2, 1952), pp. 6–11.

in setting standards, determining rates, or deciding other work-related issues. When asked what organized labor wanted, Samuel Gompers, AFL president, said: "more, more, and then more."[55] "More" for labor was not in tune with Taylor's mental revolution, which called for more for everyone.

After Taylor's death, a number of people were instrumental in reformulating the official viewpoint of scientific management toward labor unions. Robert G. Valentine was one early revisionist who attempted a rapprochement between unions and scientific management as represented by the Taylor Society. Viewed with suspicion by the Taylorites, but praised by union leadership, he argued that the labor-management relationship was properly one of "consent." Consent was based on worker participation, and especially union participation, in reaching all decisions affecting labor.[56] Ordway Tead, a former partner in Valentine's consulting firm, urged the formation of company unions in order to get worker participation.[57] Although Tead and Valentine pushed for worker and union participation in management, the major intellectual break over Taylor's union position was made by Morris L. Cooke. Cooke became friendly with labor leaders, especially Gompers, and was the most influential in opening up a new era for labor-management relations. Cooke proposed to democratize management by advocating collective bargaining over rates, standards, and all matters affecting worker welfare. One avenue for employee participation, then, became that of belonging to a union.

THE ERA OF UNION-MANAGEMENT COOPERATION

To understand the era of union-management cooperation, it is necessary to reach back to the Social Gospel movement, which espoused industrial betterment and sought to resolve industrial unrest through organizations such as the National Civic Federation (NCF), formed in 1900.[58] The NCF sought to mediate disputes, educate the public about labor-management relations, improve industrial relations, and demonstrate that labor and management had mutual interests. The U.S. progressive movement succeeded the Social Gospel, and the progressives' view of labor-management relations found its foremost articulation in the ideas of President Woodrow Wilson, who promised labor that "there must be a genuine democratization of industry based upon a full recognition of the right of those who work ... to participate in some organized way in every decision which directly

---

55. Samuel Gompers, quoted by Florence Thorne, *Samuel Gompers: American Statesman* (New York: Greenwood, 1969), p. 41.

56. R. G. Valentine, "The Progressive Relation between Efficiency and Consent," *Bulletin of the Society to Promote the Science of Management* 2 (January 1916), pp. 28–29.

57. Ordway Tead, *Instincts in Industry: A Study of Working Class Psychology* (Boston: Houghton Mifflin, 1918), pp. 56–58, 218–220.

58. Marguerite Green, *The National Civic Federation and the American Labor Movement, 1900–1925* (Washington, D.C.: Catholic University Press, 1956).

affects their [the workers'] welfare."[59] During World War I, President Wilson's National War Labor Board also furthered many goals of organized labor: for example, it prohibited employers from engaging in antiunion activities, required time-and-one-half pay for work over eight hours per day, established the principle of shop committees elected by employees to confer with management regarding grievances, proposed the principle of a "living wage" for all workers (in practice, this became an early minimum wage), acknowledged the right of women to receive equal pay for equal work, and provided mediation and conciliation services to settle unresolved disputes.[60]

Under the Wilson administration almost one and a half million workers were added to union rolls, and union membership had almost doubled by 1920. After this glow of unionism, however, the economic, social, and political tides began to shift. A short, steep depression in 1921 weakened unions; further, companies were becoming increasingly benevolent, management was waging intense drives for the open shop, and government and the courts were becoming increasingly hostile to unionism. People in the United States saw radicals and Bolsheviks in every picket line and reacted against any concerted effort to change the status quo. Accordingly, union membership suffered, declining from around five million in 1920 to three and a half million in 1921. In this relatively hostile environment, labor leadership adopted the protective coloration characterized by a decade of union-management cooperation.

Under the leadership of Daniel Willard, president of the Baltimore and Ohio Railroad, and Bert M. Jewell, president of the Railway Employees Department of the AFL, a model plan of cooperation was developed following a nationwide railroad shop craft strike of 1922. Some firms, however, formed company unions, thus ousting the AFL. The leaders of organized labor saw that the momentum of a pro union government of the Wilson years was now gone. The response of organized labor was to cooperate with management with the proviso that the workers could elect representatives and bargain collectively. Management could install more efficient methods to improve productivity provided that labor would be recognized and involved.

Successful union-management cooperation could be found in the clothing trades and the railroads. The clothing unions, under the capable leadership of Sidney Hillman, were among the first segments of organized labor to agree to cooperation and implementation of scientific management techniques. The railroads also developed extensive plans for cooperation, first on the Baltimore and Ohio and then later on the Chesapeake and Ohio, the Chicago and North Western, the Canadian National Railway, and others. In each instance, the union implicitly

---

59. Quoted in Ray Stannard Baker, *The New Industrial Unrest: Reasons and Remedies* (Garden City, N.Y.: Doubleday, Page, 1920), p. 52. Woodrow Wilson was a student of Richard Ely's. See Ely, *Ground Under Our Feet*, pp. 108–119.

60. Valerie Jean Conner, *The National War Labor Board* (Chapel Hill: University of North Carolina Press, 1983). The seeds planted by the National War Labor Board would bear fruit for more than half a century through legislation such as the National Labor Relations Act, the Fair Labor Standards Act (FLSA), and the Equal Pay Amendment to the FLSA.

accepted the principles of scientific management and participated through joint union-management shop committees in improving work routing and scheduling, hiring practices, and job analysis.[61] As in the garment industry, scientific management had gained greater acceptance than was previously possible under resistant leadership. When William Green succeeded Gompers as AFL president in 1925, he increased the emphasis on cooperation. The AFL hired its own management consultant and in a 1930 statement, "Labor's Principles of Scientific Management," urged complete acceptance of scientific management. Using management research departments within the union, labor leadership emphasized that the worker actually needed the management engineer.[62] This new unionism completed a cycle in organized labor-scientific management relations. Except for worker participation through unions and recognition of the union's right to bargain, Frederick Taylor's *Principles of Scientific Management* were now accepted as valid by the labor world.

EMPLOYEE REPRESENTATION PLANS

While union-management cooperation plans involved organized labor, the idea of employee representation and participation through shop councils and committees emerged as another approach for achieving industrial cooperation. The roots of the employee representation movement were in part a continuation of the industrial betterment movement, in part a hope for a restoration of the prewar open-shop days, when unions had little influence, and in part an outgrowth of the old Social Gospel theme that labor and management could coexist peacefully if they recognized their common purpose. In the waning days of his term of office, President Wilson had appointed two industrial commissions to investigate the conflict-laden year 1919. One, vice-chaired by Herbert Hoover, concluded with an endorsement by the employers of the idea of workers being represented through employee-elected shop councils. These councils would give workers a choice to be represented without having to join a union and pay dues. Hoover disagreed with the unionists who felt that shop councils were antiunion. He felt that shop councils provided an alternative for workers who wished a voice and a choice in the economic system.[63]

The noted labor scholar John R. Commons undertook a study of thirty of these various plans for "industrial government" or industrial democracy. He studied the Nunn, Bush, and Weldon Shoe Company of Milwaukee, the Packard Piano Company, Filene's Department Store, Henry Dennison's plan, the Ford Motor Company, White Motor of Cleveland, and the Clothcraft Shop of Joseph and Feiss

61. Otto S. Beyer, "Experiences with Cooperation between Labor and Management in the Railway Industry," *Wertheim Lectures on Industrial Relations* (Cambridge, Mass., 1929).

62. Milton J. Nadworny, *Scientific Management and the Unions: 1900–1932* (Cambridge, Mass.: Harvard University Press, 1955), pp. 138–139.

63. Robert H. Zieger, "Herbert Hoover, The Wage Earner and the 'New Economic System,' 1919–1929," in Ellis W. Hawley, ed., *Herbert Hoover as Secretary of Commerce* (Iowa City: University of Iowa Press, 1981), pp. 84–85, 96–98.

Company. Commons praised Clothcraft as "the greatest experimental laboratory of industrial psychology that we have found in America."[64] Commons also noted that the White Motor Company required all supervisors and executives to spend one hour each day exercising in the company gymnasium to keep them "in splendid physique [and] … from indigestion and getting cross and sour with their work-men."[65] The results of this experiment in managerial exercise to improve labor-management relations were not recorded.

More characteristic of employee representation plans was that of the firm of Henry Dennison of Framingham, Massachusetts. In 1916, Dennison established the country's first company-sponsored unemployment compensation fund, which stabilized employment and provided worker security. He formed a works committee (1919) for employee representation and participation in management. Workers shared in company profits through a stock-dividend plan, and Dennison has been hailed as an innovator because of his ideas on employee relations.[66]

The Russell Sage Foundation sponsored numerous studies of employee representation plans, which typically reported lower worker turnover, a mutual prosperity of employee and employer, better channels for handling grievances, and a voice for workers. One danger noted, however, involved an employer with unrepentant antiunion tendencies who tried to dominate the shop council.[67] By 1924, there were some 814 employee representation plans in existence covering some one and a half million workers.[68] Despite union opposition to these so-called company unions, these plans prepared the way for the idea that workers could have a voice and be involved productively on the job.[69] Although these plans varied in means and ends, they characterized a growing feeling among employers that employees had something to contribute and should be given that opportunity. Some plans were perversions of that aim and were used to forestall unionization. For the most part, however, these plans represented mature and progressive directions in the evolution of labor-management relations.

SUMMARY

When the noted labor economist, Sumner Slichter, did a retrospective examination of labor policies in the 1920s, he wondered why employers did not take advantage

64. John R. Commons, "Lizzie Likes Her Job," *The Independent* 104 (November 6, 1920), p. 204.

65. John R. Commons, "What's Wrong with Labor?" *The Independent* 102 (April 3, 1920), p. 30.

66. W. Jack Duncan and C. Ray Gullett, "Henry Sturgis Dennison: The Manager and the Social Critic," *Journal of Business Research* 2, no. 2 (April 1974), pp. 133–143.

67. See the study of the Dutchess Bleachery, Wappingers Fall, New York, in Ben M. Selekman, *Sharing Management with the Worker* (New York: Russell Sage Foundation, 1924).

68. H. B. Butler, *Industrial Relations in the U.S.* (Geneva: International Labor Office, 1927), pp. 84–105.

69. Daniel Nelson, "The Company Union Movement, 1900–1937: A Reexamination," *Business History Review* 56 (Autumn 1982), pp. 335–357.

of the surplus of labor after World War I. The depression of 1920–21 had created a buyers market for labor, that is, employers had a surplus of workers from whom to choose, yet the 1920s created a number of progressive steps in benefits for workers. Employee turnover was low, employment stabilization policies had increased job security, real wages rose 11 percent, 300 companies had some form of employee stock ownership plan, 370 companies provided industrial pension plans, and more progress had been made in non-union than in union shops. Union membership was down 30 percent, yet employers did not take advantage of this by exploiting the workers. Instead, Slichter noted, employers had created "industrial goodwill" with group insurance plans, loans for and encouragement of home ownership, and giving vacations with pay.[70] The 1920s was a prosperity decade for employee and employer alike.

The scientific management era focused not only on efficiency but on the human factor as well. Before scientific management gained its momentum, the Social Gospel spawned the industrial betterment/welfare movement. From scientific management, however, came the inspiration for social scientists and psychologists to become involved in a more systematic study of employee selection and guidance. Industrial sociology came from different roots, but nevertheless made its way into thinking about how to improve our understanding of the worker and of labor-management relations. Finally, the 1920s witnessed a unique period in evolving management thought: academic economists contributed industrial relations as a means of addressing human factor issues; scientific management revisionists encouraged unions and promoted union-management cooperation; and worker participation in decision making through various employee representation plans occurred in non-union shops. The path was made ready for further developments in our understanding of people at work.

---

70. Sumner H. Slichter, "The Current Labor Policies of American Industries," *The Quarterly Journal of Economics* 3 (May 1929), pp. 393–435. See also Robert F. Foerster and Else H. Dietel, *Employee Stock Ownership in the United States* (Princeton, N.J.: Princeton University Press, 1926).

10

The Emergence of Management and Organization Theory

H istory rarely measures the full contribution of persons during their own lifetimes. Epitaphs are often prematurely written and other times bring added appreciation to individuals such as the two presented in this chapter. Both subjects lived during the later nineteenth and the early twentieth centuries; both wrote during the era of scientific management in the United States; both were Europeans; and both made lasting contributions to the evolution of management thought. One was a practicing manager and one an academician; one was trained in the physical sciences, the other in the social sciences; and neither was accorded the full measure of his contribution until some decades after his death. Henri Fayol, the French manager-engineer, created the first theory of management through his principles and elements of management. Max Weber, the German economist-sociologist, originated a theory of organizations through his conception of bureaucracy as the ideal of technical efficiency. Both sought to generalize theory and practice; yet it was the task of others to bring full appreciation to the impact of their thinking on modern management.

HENRI FAYOL: THE MAN AND HIS CAREER

Jules Henri Fayol (1841–1925) was born in Constantinople (now Istanbul), where his father was fulfilling his military service obligation by supervising construction projects under an agreement between France and Turkey.[1] Henri's parents, André and Eugénie Cantin Fayol, returned to France after André completed his military service. The family lived in La Voulte, where Henri received his elementary education in a missionary school. André worked as a superintendent at

---

1. Tsuneo Sasaki, "Henri Fayol's Family Relationships," *Journal of Management History* 1 (1995), pp. 14–15.

Henri Fayol, circa 1872.
Source: La Societe de Commentry-Fourchambault et Decazeville, 1854–1954, Paris: Brodard et Taupin, 1954, p. 160.

iron foundries in Le Pouzin and Le Teil, near La Voulte, and could afford to send Henri to a polytechnic school in the city of Valence, where he graduated from the *Lycée Impérial* in 1858. André Fayol was an engineer and Henri followed in his footsteps, entering the National School of Mines at Saint Étienne at the age of seventeen, graduating as a mining engineer at age nineteen in 1860, and was hired into the coal mine at Commentry. The Commentry mine was owned by the Société Boigues, Rambourg and Company, a limited partnership (*société en commandité*) that also owned the mills of Fourchambault and Torteron, a forge at d'Imphy, a foundry at Montlucon, and an iron mine at Berry. Following the death of several partners, the limited partnership of Boigues, Rambourg and Company was reorganized in 1874 as Commentry-Fourchambault (Comambault), a joint-stock company (*société ànonyme*).[2]

From 1860 until 1866 Fayol worked as an engineer and made notable advances in the technique of fighting the underground coal fires that plagued the company. His work was rewarded with a promotion to manager of the Commentry pits at age twenty-five; six years later, he was promoted to manager of a group of mines.[3] In 1888, Comambault was in dire financial straits: no dividends had been paid since 1885, the foundries at Fourchambault and Montlucon were losing money, and the coal deposits at Commentry and Montvicq were nearing depletion. Fayol was named managing director (chief executive officer) in 1888 and began to revitalize the company. He closed the foundry at Fourchambault and centralized production at Montlucon to gain economies of scale. He acquired new coal deposits at Brassac and Decazeville, and iron reserves at Joudreville. The firm was fully integrated backward to mine coal and iron ore, and forward to smelt the iron into steel and to sell both coal and steel. One of Fayol's top managers was Joseph Carlioz, who was in charge of Comambault's commercial department, which was responsible for both the procurement of raw materials and the sales of the finished product.[4] Fayol established research facilities to advance the firm's technological capacity; built alliances

———
2. Tsuneo Sasaki, "The Comambault Company Revisited," *Journal of Economics* (College of Economics, Nihon University, Tokyo, Japan) 68 (January 1999), pp. 113–128. Reprinted in Sasaki and Wren, *Henri Fayol and the Process School,* series 3 of the *Intellectual Legacy of Management Theory* (London: Pickering and Chatto, 2004).

3. John D. Breeze, "Harvest from the Archives: The Search for Fayol and Carlioz," *Journal of Management* 11 (Spring 1985), pp. 43–47. See also John D. Breeze and Arthur G. Bedeian, *The Administrative Writings of Henri Fayol: A Bibliographic Investigation,* 2nd ed. (Monticello, Ill.: Vance, 1988).

4. John D. Breeze, "Administration and Organization of the Commercial Function by J. Carlioz," in K. H. Chung, ed., *Proceedings of the Academy of Management* (New York, 1982), pp. 112–116.

with other firms; acquired other firms or resources as needed; proposed new mills to expand the geographical base of the company; utilized the abilities of staff specialists in research, manufacturing, and selling; and repositioned the firm into specialty steels to gain a competitive advantage.

Fayol, though trained and experienced as an engineer, had the perspective of a general manager of a multiunit, large-scale enterprise of ten thousand employees after the acquisition of Decazeville. For him, management was not so much that of devising systems and methods for increasing the velocity of throughput (as it had been for scientific management) as it was the orderly arrangement and integration of the production, sales, financial, and accounting functions of the organization. Fayol's "management function" was a way of identifying management as something apart from technical activities but essential to getting economy from their integration.

From his experiences, Fayol began to develop his ideas about management.[5] As a mining engineer in the Commentry mine, Fayol began keeping notes on events that occurred in the mines that affected output. For example, as early as 1861, he observed that all work had to be stopped because a horse working in the St. Edmund pits fell and broke its leg. A replacement could not be obtained due to the absence of the mine manager, and the keeper of the stable refused a replacement because he had no authority to do so.[6] Fayol's conclusion about the problem was not a result of his technical training but a managerial insight that authority to get things done must be present at all times, or delays and disorder would follow. In later years when he formulated the principle that authority and responsibility are inseparable, he may have recalled that early incident. As a supervisor, few of the problems he encountered called for his engineering skills but many for managerial ones. He grouped the workers in teams according to their preferences and reduced turnover because the workers stayed together for a long time in their groups; the groups became more cohesive by refusing to take in inferior or undesirable workers; and they worked harder as group members than otherwise. Fayol also reversed the division of labor by giving the work groups responsibility for timbering the mine rather than leaving this to specialists, and stopped using subcontractors, giving the supervisors more control over the timing and quality of work.[7]

In 1900, in a paper presented to the International Mining and Metallurgical Congress, he said: "All employees in an enterprise participate to a greater or lesser degree in the administrative function ... [and] have occasion to exercise their administrative faculties and be noticed for them. [Those] who are particularly talented can climb from the lowest rung to the highest levels of the hierarchy of an

5. Daniel A. Wren, "Henri Fayol: Learning from Experience," *Journal of Management History* 1 (1995), pp. 5–12.

6. Henri Fayol, diary entry of 29 July 1898. In Frédéric Blancpain, ed., "Les Cahiers Inédits d'Henri Fayol," *Bulletin de l'Institute International d'Administration Publique* 28 (1973), p. 23.

7. Donald Reid, "Fayol: From Experience to Theory," *Journal of Management History* 1 (1995), pp. 21–36.

organization."[8] Here Fayol was beginning to separate managerial ability from technical knowledge. In 1908, Fayol prepared a paper for the jubilee of the Society of the Mineral Industry in which further advancements in his thinking were apparent. First, Fayol noted that the effect of management on business activities was not fully understood and that technical expertise "can be completely destroyed by defective administrative procedures." Second, "a leader who is a good administrator but technically mediocre is generally much more useful to the enterprise than if he were a brilliant technician but a mediocre administrator." Thus, according to Fayol, organizational success depended more on the managerial abilities of its leaders than on their technical abilities. In the 1908 paper Fayol also developed an early list of principles of management: unity of command, hierarchical chain of command, separation of powers (which consisted of establishing departments, authority, subordination, responsibility, and control), centralization (degree of delegation), and order. In addition to his principles, Fayol spoke of *prévoyance* ("foresight"), the act of anticipating the future, planning, and preparing budgets. He also talked of the need for organizational charts, meetings, and reports, and an accounting system to keep managers informed.[9] In brief, Fayol's 1908 paper was a step forward in his thinking, but it lacked the depth, clarity, organization, and conceptual qualities that marked his magnum opus, *Administration industrielle et générale,* published in 1916, first in a technical journal, and then as a book in 1917. Translations followed slowly, and it was almost four decades before the United States began to appreciate Fayol's ideas.[10]

Ignorance of Fayol's work was not limited to the United States; even in France his work was largely overshadowed by that of Taylor because of the efforts of Henry Le Chatelier and Charles de Fréminville. From Fayol's retirement in 1918 to his death in 1925, he founded and presided over the meetings of the Center for Administrative Studies, a group formed to promote the advancement of Fayolisme. Shortly before his death, this group merged with the Le Chatelier-de Fréminville, or Taylorisme group, to form the Comité National de l'Organisation Française.[11] This merger was significant in that it brought together the two main French schools of management. Early interpretations of Fayol had placed his work in competition or

---

8. Daniel A. Wren, Arthur G. Bedeian, and John D. Breeze, "The Foundations of Henri Fayol's Administrative Theory," *Management Decision* 40 (2002), p. 908

9. *Ibid.,* p. 910, pp. 912–916.

10. See Henri Fayol, *Industrial and General Administration,* trans. J. A. Coubrough (Geneva: International Management Institute, 1930); Henri Fayol, "The Administrative Theory of the State," trans. Sarah Greer, in Luther Gulick and Lyndall Urwick, eds., *Papers on the Science of Administration* (New York: Institute of Public Administration, Columbia University, 1937), pp. 99–114; and Henri Fayol, *General and Industrial Management,* trans. Constance Storrs (London: Sir Isaac Pitman and Sons, 1949). Charles de Fréminvillé's "Henri Fayol: A Great Engineer, A Great Scientist, and A Great Management Leader," was published in the *Bulletin of the Taylor Society* 12 (February 1927), pp. 303–306, but had little, if any, impact on the early management writers.

11. John D. Breeze, "Henri Fayol's Centre for Administrative Studies," *Journal of Management History* 1 (1995), pp. 37–62.

contrast with Taylor's. Fayol insisted that this was not so and that the two were complementary in the sense that both sought to improve management through different avenues of analysis. In comparing the lives of these two men, one can see the reasons for their different perspectives.

These two fountainheads of management thought were quite dissimilar in many respects, though both were educated as engineers. Taylor started as a worker, gained promotions to supervisory positions, and spent most of his managerial and consulting career in situations that concerned production and, to some extent, accounting systems. He was interested in methods and systems as they pertained to the production part of an organization. Fayol, on the other hand, began as a member of the engineering group, moved into management, and gradually achieved the top management post in a large-scale, fully integrated enterprise. Thus Fayol saw management from the executive viewpoint of coordinating and integrating the functions of the whole firm. Taylor died relatively young amid much turmoil and controversy. Fayol lived a long life, did not publish his major work until he was seventy-five years old, and avoided the boiling waters of controversy. Taylor's star shone brightly while Fayol's was eclipsed, waiting other times and other persons who could write his proper epitaph.

THE NEED FOR MANAGEMENT THEORY

In earlier writings Fayol noted the importance of managerial ability to organizational performance. If management was important, then why did schools and universities neglect management to focus on teaching technical skills? The answer, according to Fayol, was the absence of management theory. Fayol defined theory as "a collection of principles, rules, methods, and procedures tried and checked by general experience."[12] Writing from long experience, he noted that a lot of managers theorized, but that in practice there existed many contradictions and little systematic reflection. This state of confusion made it more difficult to teach and practice management because managers' experiences were localized and not easily generalized to other managers or students of management.

Every organization required management: "Be it a case of commerce, industry, politics, religion, war, or philanthropy, in every concern there is a management function to be performed."[13] Thus, like Charles Dupin, Fayol felt that management was a special study, apart from technical matters, that could be taught in schools and universities as theory was developed and codified.

Managers, according to Fayol, needed certain qualities, knowledge, and experience:

1. Physical qualities: health, vigor, address (literally, manner of behaving)

---

12. Fayol, *General and Industrial Management*, trans. Storrs, p. 15. Except where specifically noted, the Storrs translation will be used since it is more readily available.

13. *Ibid.*, p. 41.

2. Mental qualities: ability to understand and learn, judgment, mental vigor, and adaptability

3. Moral qualities: energy, firmness, willingness to accept responsibility, initiative, loyalty, tact, dignity

4. General education: general acquaintance with matters not belonging exclusively to the function performed

5. Special knowledge: that peculiar to the function, be it technical, commercial, financial, managerial, and so on

6. Experience: knowledge arising from the work proper; the recollection of lessons a person has derived from things[14]

Fayol then graphed the relative importance of these requisites for personnel, depending on their location in the hierarchy. At the worker level, technical ability was most important; but as a person moved up the scalar chain, the relative importance of managerial ability increased while the need for technical ability decreased. The higher the level of authority, the more dominant became the need for managerial ability. Ability in commercial, financial, security, and accounting matters also diminished in importance farther up the scalar chain. In terms of differences in the size of the enterprise, the manager of a small firm needed relatively more technical ability, whereas in larger concerns, the upper levels needed managerial rather than technical ability.

The distinction between the relative importance of abilities was crucial to Fayol's development of the notion of *teaching* management. Regarding the proliferation of large firms and other organizations, he noted that future leadership should receive managerial training rather than cling to the past precepts of education for technical, commercial, and other abilities. Schools did not teach management, and it was assumed by industrial leaders that practice and experience were the only pathways to a managerial position. The reason for the absence of management teaching was the absence of theory. Fayol felt that theory was needed because (1) management was an activity found in all types of organizations; (2) managerial ability became more important as a person moved up the hierarchy; and (3) management could be taught. From these premises, Fayol used his experiences and observations to propose a body of knowledge that included principles as guides to thinking and practice and elements of management as a description of the functions managers performed.

THE PRINCIPLES OF MANAGEMENT

The notion of principles of management is often misunderstood and subject to controversy. Fayol's conception of a principle was not as rigidly based as the concept of a rule or law in the physical sciences. He used the term "principles" very reluctantly:

---

14. *Ibid.*, p. 7.

For preference I shall adopt the term principles whilst dissociating it from any suggestion of rigidity, for there is nothing rigid or absolute in management affairs, it is all a question of proportion. Seldom do we have to apply the same principle twice in identical conditions; allowance must be made for different and changing circumstances....

Therefore principles are flexible and capable of adaptation to every need; it is a matter of knowing how to make use of them, which is a difficult art requiring intelligence, experience, decision and proportion. Compounded of tact and experience, proportion is one of the foremost attributes of the manager. There is no limit to the number of principles of management, every rule or managerial procedure which strengthens the body corporate or facilitates its functioning has a place among the principles so long, at least, as experience confirms its worthiness. A change in the state of affairs can be responsible for change of rules which had been engendered by that state.[15]

Fayol's principles were derived from those that he used most frequently in his own experience. They were not immutable, but served as "lighthouses" to show the way to theory. Fayol's principles were:

1. Division of work
2. Authority
3. Discipline
4. Unity of command
5. Unity of direction
6. Subordination of individual interests to the general interest
7. Remuneration
8. Centralization
9. Scalar chain (line of authority)
10. Order
11. Equity
12. Stability of tenure of personnel
13. Initiative
14. Esprit de corps

Division of work was the well-known idea of specialization of labor and the advantages that accrued in reducing waste, increasing output, and easing the task of job training. Fayol thought that division of labor was not limited to technical work but could apply also to a "specialization of functions and separation of powers," that is, to managerial effort also. Fayol also recognized that some tasks could be enlarged

---

15. *Ibid.*, p. 19.

to act as a stimulus to the employees' efforts. For example, we saw earlier that when he was managing the Commentry mine he returned the responsibility for timbering the mine to the work crews, reversing the practice of using specialized personnel for this task.

Authority was defined as "the right to give orders and the power to exact obedience." Fayol distinguished between the formal authority held by the manager by virtue of office or rank and personal authority, which was "compounded of intelligence, experience, moral worth, ability to lead, past services, etc."[16] A good manager would complement his official authority with personal authority. Further, authority and responsibility were corollaries in the sense that wherever authority was exercised, responsibility arose. Fayol stated the classic case for authority being commensurate with responsibility, and this principle has appeared throughout management literature to become as inseparable as Mary and her little lamb.

Discipline was in essence based on obedience and respect between the firm and its employees. It was essential to success and grounded in respect rather than fear. Poor discipline was inevitably the result of poor leadership, and good discipline came from good leaders, clear agreements between management and labor regarding rules, and the judicious use of sanctions (penalties).

Unity of command, Fayol's fourth principle, was in opposition to Taylor's functional foremen. The principle that "for any action whatsoever an employee should receive orders from one superior only" was fundamental to Fayol's concept of an organization. Just as no person can serve two masters, dual command was a threat to authority, discipline, and stability.

Unity of direction meant "one head and one plan for a group of activities having the same objective." Unity of direction came from a sound organization structure and was essential to "unity of action, coordination of strength, and focusing of effort."

The principle of *subordination of individual interests to the general interest* was a plea to abolish "ignorance, ambition, selfishness, laziness, weakness and all human passions," which caused conflict when the individual or a group tried to prevail over the organization. In this early concept of agency theory, Fayol recognized that individuals who served only themselves were harmful to the interests of their fellow employees and others whose interests were affected by the successful performance of the firm.

Remuneration of personnel dealt with day wages, piece rates, bonuses, and profit sharing. Fayol concluded that the mode of payment depended on many factors and that the objective was to "make the personnel more valuable ... and also to inspire keenness."[17] His discussion fell short of suggesting an in-depth notion of motivation but indicated his awareness of the need to provide compensation and incentives.

---

16. Fayol, *General and Industrial Management,* pp. 19–21.

17. *Ibid.,* p. 32.

The principle of *centralization* was more lucid and showed some brilliant insights into organization:

> Centralization is not a system of management good or bad of itself, capable of being adopted or discarded at the whim of managers or of circumstances; it is always present to a greater or less extent. The question of centralization or decentralization is a simple question of proportion, it is a matter of finding the optimum degree for the particular concern. In small firms, where the manager's orders go directly to subordinates, there is absolute centralization; in large concerns, where a long scalar chain is interposed between manager and lower grades, orders and counterinformation, too, have to go through a series of intermediaries. Each employee, intentionally or unintentionally, puts something of himself into the transmission and execution of orders and of information received, too. He does not operate merely as a cog in a machine. What appropriate share of initiative may be left to intermediaries depends on the personal character of the manager, on his moral worth, on the reliability of his subordinates, and also on the condition of the business. The degree of centralization must vary according to different cases. The objective to pursue is the optimum utilization of all faculties of the personnel.[18]

The continuum of possibilities for centralization and decentralization, the possible communication distortions in the scalar chain, and the variables affecting the degree of decentralization were pillars for evolving theory. Fayol's notion of the centralization-decentralization continuum was explicit: "everything which goes to increase the importance of the subordinate's role is decentralization, everything which goes to reduce it is centralization."

The *scalar chain* was "the chain of superiors ranging from the ultimate authority to the lowest ranks." It showed the routing of the line of authority and the channels for the transmission of communications. To counter possible communication delays caused by the unity-of-command principle, Fayol developed his gangplank, which allowed communications to cross lines of authority but only if agreed to by all parties and if superiors were kept informed at all times. Thus Foreman F, desiring to communicate with Foreman P, could do so directly without reporting upward (F through E to A) and having that message in turn transmitted downward to P. The gangplank (see Figure 10-1) permitted swift, sure lateral communications without overloading circuits and preserved the principle of unity of command.

Order, the tenth principle, ensured a place for everything and everything in its place. It applied to materials, shop cleanliness, and personnel. For people, it meant each to a task and that task set neatly into a structure of activities. *Equity* resulted from kindliness and justice and provided a principle for employee relations. The

---

18. *Ibid.*, p. 37.

| **FIGURE 10-1** | **FAYOL'S GANGPLANK** |

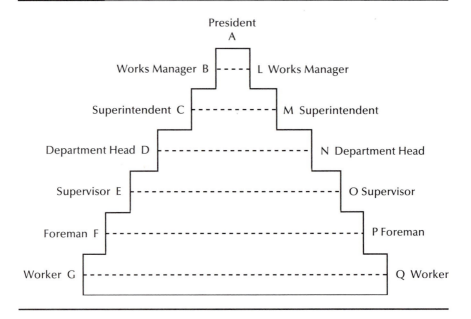

twelfth principle, *stability of tenure of personnel,* sought to provide for orderly personnel planning and provisions to replace human resources. *Initiative* as a principle exhorted individuals to display zeal and energy in all efforts. Finally, *esprit de corps* stressed building harmony and unity within the firm. "Dividing enemy forces to weaken them is clever, but dividing one's own team is a grave sin against the business."[19] In building esprit de corps, Fayol felt that managers abused written communications and should use verbal contacts whenever possible to promote speed and clarity. Formal, written communications "increased work and complications and delays harmful to business" and should be avoided.

Fayol's principles were intended as guides to theory and practice and were not exhaustive in scope, nor were they meant to be interpreted as rigid in application. The early factory system reflected many of these principles in practice, but it was Fayol's contribution to codify them into a conceptual schema. So much of the present-day management literature has been built on Fayol's ideas and terminology that it is difficult to see the uniqueness of his insights. For his time and in the context of the paucity of management literature, his ideas were fresh, illuminating, and milestones on the path of the evolving discipline of management. As Fayol concluded, "Without principles, we are working in the dark and in chaos; without experience and without judgment we are still working under great difficulties, even with

---

19. *Ibid.,* p. 40.

the best of principles. The principle is the lighthouse, which enables us to get our bearings, but it can only help those who know the way into port."[20]

THE ELEMENTS OF MANAGEMENT

Planning

Finding "the way into port" was also a matter of understanding what managers did. Fayol called this part of his theory the elements of management. The first element Fayol presented was planning, although at various times he used the French *prévoyance* (anticipation or foresight) instead of *préparer* (to plan). To Fayol, "managing means looking ahead" and foresight was an essential element of management. Any plan of action rested on (1) the firm's resources, that is, the buildings, tools, materials, personnel, sales outlets, public relations, and so on; (2) the nature of present work in process; and (3) future trends in all activities of the firm whose occurrence could not be predetermined. In modern terms, Fayol was describing a rudimentary strategic audit that assesses present capabilities and strengths and scans the environment to anticipate future trends. Fayol also provided an early notion of what modern authorities call contingency planning. "The best of plans cannot anticipate all unexpected occurrences which may arise, but it does include a place for these events and prepares the weapons which may be needed at the moment of being surprised."[21] On another occasion he observed:

> One cannot anticipate with precision everything which will happen over a longer period but one can minimize uncertainty and carry out one's program as a result … any long-term program should be susceptible to being changed according to the variety, complexity and instability of events. Like any living object the industrial enterprise undergoes continuing transformations: the personnel, the tooling, the methods, even the goals of the association change; the program must without ceasing be kept, as far as possible, in harmony with the environment.[22]

In developing the plan of action, Fayol put forth an early concept of participation: "The study of resources, future possibilities, and means to be used for attaining the objective call for contributions from all departmental heads within the framework of their mandate, each one brings to this study the contribution of his experience together with recognition of the responsibility which will fall upon him in executing the plan."[23] Such participation ensured that no resource was neglected

20. *Ibid.*, p. 42.

21. *Ibid.*, p. 49.

22. Henri Fayol, "L'Exposé des Principes Généraux d'Administration," in Wren, Bedeian, and Breeze, "The Foundations of Henri Fayol's Administrative Theory," p. 915.

23. Fayol, *General and Industrial Management* (Storrs), p. 48.

and promoted managerial interest in the plan. More attention would be given to planning by lower-echelon managers, since they had to execute what they themselves had planned. A good plan of action had the characteristics of unity (one overall plan followed by specific plans for each activity); continuity (both short-range and long-range plans); flexibility (the ability to adjust to unexpected events); and precision (eliminating as much guesswork as possible). Based on these characteristics, Fayol advised a series of separate plans that would together constitute one entire plan for the firm. Daily, weekly, monthly, annual, five-year, and ten-year forecasts (or plans) were prepared and redrafted as time passed or as conditions changed.

Fayol's stress on long-range planning was a unique contribution to management thought, and his ideas are as important today as they were for his own time. He also displayed some innovative insights into national planning for France. The French government planned and budgeted on an annual basis with little or no regard for long-term development; the result was hand-to-mouth operations and a lack of exercise of fiscal responsibility by the chiefs of state. Fayol attributed the blame to instability of tenure for the prime minister, and evidently this failing has been a continuing one for the French government. This first element of management, a combined function of planning and forecasting, was to be a fundamental building block for all organizations.

Organizing

Fayol's second element of management, organizing, included provisions for the structuring of activities and relationships as well as the procurement, evaluation, and training of personnel. Later writers split Fayol's organizing element into two elements: organizing and staffing (personnel or human resource management). For Fayol, to organize a business meant "to provide it with everything useful to its functioning: raw materials, tools, capital, personnel," and it was the duty of management to "see that the human and material organization is consistent with the objectives, resources, and requirements of the concern."[24] The organizational structure had to be so arranged as to provide unity of direction toward the objectives of the firm. The proper structure defined duties clearly, encouraged initiative and responsibility, harmonized activities and coordinated efforts, and ensured control without an "excess of regulation, red tape, and paper control." The organizational structure, however, was not an end in itself but had to be adapted to meet organizational needs: "to create a useful organization it is not enough to group people [into departments] and distribute duties; there must be knowledge of how to adapt the organic whole to requirements, how to find essential personnel and put each where he can be of most service. Of two organizations similar in appearance, one may be excellent, the other bad, depending on the personal qualities of those who compose them."[25] He

---

24. *Ibid.*, p. 53.

25. *Ibid.*, p. 57.

realized it was people, not structure, that made the difference. The organizational structure, then, had to be "consistent" (Fayol's word) with the "objectives, resources, and requirements" of the business. In retrospect, Fayol anticipated modern contingency and fit theory in organizational design.

In organization theory, the organizational pyramid is a product of functional and scalar growth. Functional growth is horizontal in that more people are added to functions as the organizational work load expands; scalar growth is vertical and caused by the need to add layers of supervision to direct and coordinate lower echelons. Each addition of workers in functional growth brings fresh supervisors, and in turn, these added supervisors require the addition of higher levels of management, resulting in continued scalar growth. Fayol built his functional and scalar growth processes on the basis of fifteen workers to a first-line supervisor and four supervisors to a higher-level supervisor or manager. For example, sixty workers required four supervisors, and in turn these four supervisors required one common manager. Fayol advocated a relatively narrow span of management throughout the organization. Whatever the level of authority, one manager was to have direct command over a small number of subordinates, "less than six, normally" according to Fayol. Only the first-line supervisor would have more, up to twenty or thirty employees, provided that the work was simple.

On the subject of staff, Fayol visualized a group of individuals who had the "strength, knowledge, and time" to assist a manager by acting as a "sort of extension of the manager's personality." The staff took orders only from the general manager, and Fayol compared it with the military concept of the general staff. The functions of the staff were to help carry out the manager's personal duties, such as correspondence, interviews, conferences, and so on, to provide liaisons and control, to gather information and assist in formulating future plans and to "search for improvements." The latter staff function was unique to Fayol's concept; he postulated that operating managers had neither the time nor the energy to devote to long-term research because they were too absorbed in the current and weighty problems of running the business. The staff, freed of daily cares, could search for better work methods, perceive changes in business conditions, and consider long-range matters.

Fayol's concept of staff was in direct opposition to Taylor's functional foremen. Fayol agreed with Taylor's goal, the necessity for specialized assistance, but disagreed with the means. Functional foremen negated the unity-of-command principle, and to Fayol this was treading on dangerous ground. Order must be maintained, and this was possible only if one person was clearly responsible to one other person: "So ... let us treasure the old type of organization in which unity of command is honored. It can, after all, be easily reconciled ... with the assistance [i.e., staff] given to super-intendents and foremen."[26] Organizational charts were a *sine qua non* of every enterprise. The preparation of a formal organizational chart enabled visualization of the organization as a whole, specified lines of authority, provided channels of communication, prevented the overlapping or encroachment of departments, avoided

---

26. *Ibid.*, p. 70.

dual-command situations, and clearly assigned duties and responsibilities. The chart itself was a managerial instrument for analyzing relationships between departments, specifying individuals and their tasks, and making modifications in the organization. Fayol did not completely develop his ideas or methods of departmentalizing operations, since this part of his work was never published during his lifetime.[27]

Turning from the organizational framework, Fayol developed the rudiments of a personnel or staffing function, which consisted of selection, evaluation, and training. Selection was examined only briefly and was viewed as a function of finding the qualities and knowledge in people to fill all levels of the organization. The consequence of poor selection was "commensurate with the rank of the employee;" Fayol advised that the length of time spent on selection should be increased as the level of position being filled rose. Evaluation of both managers and workers was based on "health and physical fitness," "intelligence and mental vigor," "moral qualities," and knowledge of the duties and responsibilities of the position. Fayol did not examine the problems of evaluating performance, nor did he recommend methods and procedures for its conduct. Like Taylor's, his view of the personnel function was limited; this is not a criticism, however, as personnel practices of the day were rudimentary in all cases. Training was dealt with at length primarily because Fayol had an ax to grind. He advocated a diminution of technical training and an increased teaching of managerial knowledge. Contemporary education was based on the premise that the value of engineers and industrial leaders bore "a direct relationship to the number of years devoted to the subject of mathematics." Fayol deplored the emphasis on mathematics: "Long personal experience has taught me that the use of higher mathematics counts for nothing in managing businesses…."[28] Basic mathematics helped train the mind, but further study should be devoted to management rather than more mathematics. Fayol sought balance and advised young engineers to study people, "their behavior, character, abilities, work, and even their personal interests."[29] Fayol thought that everyone should study management, for it was necessary in the home as well as in industrial and nonindustrial undertakings.

Command, Coordination, and Control

Almost 90 percent of Fayol's major work was devoted to planning and organizing (including staffing). This reflected the primacy of these elements in terms of preparation for the plans to be implemented through the organizational structure and the people in the various areas of responsibility. To set all of this into motion Fayol used

---

27. Part 3 of Fayol's intended work is published in Jean-Louis Peaucelle, *Henri Fayol, Inventeur des Outils des Gestion: Textes Originaux et Recherches Actuelles* (Paris: Economica, 2003). Peaucelle also provides further commentary on Fayol's ideas and other authors discuss Fayol's influence in Britain, Spain, and Japan.

28. Fayol, *General and Industrial Management* (Storrs), p. 84. Later, he referred to higher mathematics as special studies, such as calculus.

29. *Ibid.*, p. 91.

the word *commander* (to command) as well as *diriger* (to direct) as his third element. Since "command" has a more specific meaning in English, the best translation would be to direct or to supervise. Fayol felt this was an art and certain qualities, knowledge, and experience were necessary:

1. Have a thorough knowledge of personnel.
2. Eliminate the incompetent.
3. Be well versed in the agreements binding the business and its employees.
4. Set a good example.
5. Conduct periodic audits of the organization and use summarized charts to further the audits.
6. Bring together the chief assistants by means of conferences that provide for unity of direction and focusing of effort.
7. Not become engrossed in detail.
8. Aim at making unity, energy, initiative, and loyalty prevail among the personnel.[30]

In his diary, a July 29, 1898, entry read: "In business administration, the question of [managing] people represents more than one-half of the problem."[31] As a young manager, Fayol had built effective work teams in the mines, stopped paternalistic practices such as monitoring employee church attendance, closed company-owned stores in areas where local merchants were available, and demonstrated other people-management skills that led to his promotions. With people comprising one-half of the problems managers faced, communication skills were crucial. Fayol deemed conferences a very useful device for ensuring unity of direction and stressed that the manager must be constantly aware of all business activities. His caveat to avoid being engrossed in detail was not antithetical to keeping informed. The manager should be aware of everything, but not neglect large problems while lavishing attention on small ones. Through use of staff, proper definition of the organization, and use of oral and written reports, the manager could maintain direction and control of the main business issues. To encourage initiative, the manager should allow subordinates "the maximum share of activity consistent with their position and capability, even at the cost of some mistakes."[32] Authority should be delegated to develop employees' abilities and to avoid "drying up initiative and loyalty." Fayol's element of command set the organization in motion, provided for personal supervision through audits and meetings, and inspired unity, energy, and initiative.

Coordination, viewed by Fayol as a separate element of management, meant "to harmonize all the activities of a concern so as to facilitate its working, and its success." Later writers have stressed the role of coordination in all elements rather than

---

30. *Ibid.,* pp. 97–98.

31. Henri Fayol, in Blancpain, "Les Cahiers Inédits d'Henri Fayol," p. 24.

32. *Ibid.,* p. 103.

treating it as separate. To Fayol, coordination was a balancing act of keeping expenses equivalent to revenues, of maintaining equipment to meet production goals, and of ensuring that sales and production were consonant. Organization and planning facilitated coordination by specifying duties, establishing schedules, and focusing responsibilities on the objective. Command instilled initiative, and the conferences between manager and subordinates provided a clearinghouse for airing problems, progress, and plans. The conference was a quick, simple way of keeping informed and of ensuring organizational cohesion. Liaison officers, typically staff personnel, should be used to enhance coordination in the interim between conferences and in the care of establishments located far from the main office. The liaison position supplemented coordination, but did not replace the direct responsibility of the chief.

Control, Fayol's fifth element of management, consisted of "verifying whether everything occurs in conformity with the plan adopted, the instructions issued, and the principles established." The objective of control was to identify errors in order to correct them and prevent recurrence. Control was to be applied to people, objects, and activities. Effective control was based on prompt action, followed by sanctions if necessary. Control was impartial, and Fayol advised separation of the inspector from those being inspected to ensure independence of the control element. Control permeated all elements of the undertaking, including personnel, execution of plans, quality of work, financial activities, security, and information. Control also had an integrative effect on the other four elements, because it stimulated better planning, simplified and strengthened the organization, increased the efficiency of command, and facilitated coordination. In effect, control completed a cycle of managerial activities that could then be improved as the cycle (or the process) of management continued.

A FINAL NOTE

Henri Fayol had the orientation of top management. In his writing he distinguished between management as an overall task of guiding an enterprise toward its objectives and administration as a part of the manager's job that "only affects the personnel." In 1925, Henri Verney, one of Fayol's followers, dropped this distinction and synthesized management and administration. Whether or not this reflected Fayol's views shortly before his death is not known definitely.[33] Today, people tend to use the words "management" and "administration" interchangeably, so the distinction does not interfere with Fayol's contribution to management thought.

Placing Fayol's actions into the framework of his firm enhances an understanding of his view of administrative theory. He stated:

---

33. John D. Breeze and Frederick C. Miner, "Henri Fayol: A New Definition of Administration," *Proceedings of the Academy of Management,* R. C. Huseman, ed. (Detroit: 1980), pp. 110–113.

The responsibility of general management is to conduct the enterprise toward its objective by making optimum use of available resources. It is the executive authority, it draws up the plan of action, selects personnel, determines performance, ensures and controls the execution of all activities."[34]

Since Fayol was the managing director, the CEO, his perspective was of the overall success of the firm to include the formulation of goals, strategies, and plans and to work through others to insure that these activities were implemented. In brief, Fayol's actions were those illustrative of strategic decisions made by top management to position Comambault for a renewal of its viability. The long-term goals were profitability and survival for the firm, the welfare of its employees, and regained confidence of its shareholders. The courses of action and the decisions made were strategic in the sense that they were directed toward revitalizing the essential resource base, the coal and iron raw materials; upgrading the firm's capabilities through research, selecting capable subordinates, and acquiring capital for development and expansion; relocating the firm geographically to compete in a unified market; and repositioning the firm in specialty steels.[35] Fayol's actions were of general management utilizing the firm's physical and human resources in the most productive manner possible. He was a strategist before that term became popular and before he developed his experiences into a theory of management.

It is easy to underestimate the work of Fayol. His ideas and terminology are so commonplace to present management literature that they are taken for granted. Yet his notion of a theory of management that could be studied, taught, and practiced was an important milestone in the history of management. As Pollard commented, "At his time his attempt, the only one of its kind, to build a basic theory of management was invaluable. It was incomplete … but there was a great deal of value in it … which we would do well to remember today."[36] We know about management today, but Fayol's basic thoughts have been found to stand the test of time, enduring in their contribution to our knowledge.[37]

Fayol's elements of management provided the modern conceptualization of a management process; his principles were lighthouses to managerial action. The manager who operated solely on the principles and who was armed only with knowledge of the elements would not be effective. In essence, the manager needed

---

34. Fayol, *General and Industrial Management,* pp. 61–62.

35. Daniel A. Wren, "Henri Fayol as Strategist: A Nineteenth Century Corporate Turnaround," *Management Decision* 39 (2001), pp. 475–487.

36. Harold R. Pollard, *Developments in Management Thought* (New York: Crane, Russak, 1974), p. 99. See also Daniel A. Wren, "The Nature of Managerial Work: A Comparison of Real Managers and Traditional Management," *Journal of Managerial Issues* 4 (Spring 1992), pp. 17–30.

37. Michael J. Fells, "Fayol Stands the Test of Time," *Journal of Management History* 6 (2000), pp. 345–360; see also David Lamond, "Henry Mintzberg vs. Henri Fayol: Of Lighthouses, Cubists, and the Emperor's New Clothes," *The Journal of Applied Management and Entrepreneurship* 8 (October 2003), pp. 5–23.

to know more than how to plan, organize, command, coordinate, and control. Managers had to have some knowledge of the business activities (technical, commercial, etc.) that were being managed. The elements did not operate in a vacuum, but were applied to something, which for Fayol were the essential activities and resources of the firm.

BUREAUCRACY: MAX WEBER

The life and work of Max Weber (1864–1920) ran chronologically parallel to those of Henri Fayol and Frederick Taylor. Born in Germany to a life of affluence in a family of considerable social and political connections, Weber was an intellectual of the first degree with far-ranging interests in sociology, religion, economics, and political science. While in the final stages of preparing his classic book, *The Protestant Ethic and the Spirit of Capitalism,* Weber had an opportunity to visit the United States, which he considered the most capitalistic of all nations. In 1904, Weber was invited to St. Louis to a conference on the sociology of religion. His honorarium covered his travel expenses, so he combined his conference with a tour to see firsthand how the spirit of capitalism abounded in the United States.

The economic developments he observed in the United States were somewhat different from those in Germany. U.S. manufacturing and marketing had grown to large-scale enterprise, bound together by a network of communication and transportation. In Germany, large-scale enterprise had been developed only in chemicals, metals, and complex industrial machine-goods.[38] In these industries, cartels had been formed to control prices and ration markets. Whereas in the United States this practice was limited by antitrust laws, the German cartels could operate without fear of government intervention and without the threat of competition. The spirit of capitalism in the United States encouraged innovation and competition, and Weber saw this as his theme in the relation between Protestantism and modern enterprise.

Did large-scale enterprise require a cartel? Or could a capitalistic, market-oriented society develop large organizations and yet manage them in such a way as to promote the spirit of enterprise? Could any large organization, be it the church, government, business, or whatever, operate rationally and systematically?

BUREAUCRACY AS THEORY

While Weber was working on his book on economics and society, scientific management made its way across the Atlantic. Taylor's writings were translated, and the German version of scientific management became that of standardization and rationalization. Weber perceived the need to establish a rational basis for the organization and management of large-scale undertakings, whether political, ecclesiastical,

---

38. Alfred D. Chandler, Jr., "The Emergence of Managerial Capitalism," *Business History Review* 58 (Winter 1984), pp. 498–501.

industrial, or whatever. The problem was how any large organization might function more systematically. The answer, for Weber, was bureaucracy, which meant management by the office (German *Büro*) or position rather than by a person or "patrimonial." Bureaucracy was considered the ideal, which did not mean the most desirable, but meant the "pure form" of organization.[39] Combinations or alloys of various organizational arrangements would appear in practice, but Weber wanted to characterize one type for the purpose of theoretical analysis. The bureaucratic construct would serve as a normative model to ease the transition from small-scale entrepreneurial ("patrimonial") firms to large-scale professional management in larger organizations.

Weber's conceptualization of bureaucracy merits substantial consideration for naming him the founder of organization theory. Although other writings of Weber were translated earlier (Frank Knight's translation of Weber's *Economic History* in 1927 and Talcott Parsons's rendition of *The Protestant Ethic* in 1930), his work on bureaucracy was not rendered into English until 1947. However, Chester Barnard, who is discussed later, was influenced by Talcott Parsons and read Weber in the German. Weber's writings thus formed a partial foundation for Barnard's own analysis of the formal organization. Weber was the intellectual progenitor of the formal analysis of organizational structures. He was concerned with designing a blueprint structure of authority-activity relationships that would facilitate the attainment of the objectives of an organization.

KINDS OF AUTHORITY

Weber postulated three pure types of legitimate (i.e., socially acceptable) authority: (1) rational-legal authority, which rested on legality, or the "right of those elevated to authority ... to issue commands"; (2) traditional authority, which rested on a belief "in the sanctity of immemorial traditions and the legitimacy of the status of those exercising authority under them"; and (3) charismatic authority, which was based on "devotion to the specific and exceptional sanctity, heroism, or exemplary character of an individual person."[40] In the case of rational-legal authority, subordinates owed obedience to the legally established hierarchy, for example, a business, state office, military unit, or other organization. It was obedience to the authority of an established *position*, or rank. In traditional authority, obedience was owed to the *person* who occupied the traditionally sanctioned position of authority. In charismatic authority (*charisma*, from the early Christian concept of "the gift of grace"),

---

39. S. M. Miller, ed., *Max Weber* (New York: Thomas Y. Crowell, 1963), p. 10.

40. Max Weber, *The Theory of Social and Economic Organization,* trans. A. M. Henderson and Talcott Parsons, ed. Talcott Parsons (New York: Free Press, 1947), p. 328. In reality, Weber recognized that authority could be legitimated by a combination of these so-called pure types. In defining authority, Weber used "*Herrschaft* ('Autorität')" in *Wirtschaft und Gesellschaft*, Tübingen, 1922, p. 122. For a different translation of *Herrschaft* as "domination," see Richard M. Weiss, "Weber on Bureaucracy: Management Consultant or Political Theorist?" *Academy of Management Review* 8 (April 1983), p. 244.

the leader was obeyed by virtue of the follower's personal trust and belief in the leader's powers or revelations.

Some form of authority is the cornerstone of any organization. Without it, no organization can be guided toward an objective; authority brings order to chaos. Of the three pure types of authority, Weber thought that rational-legal must provide the basis for a bureaucracy, since it (1) provided a basis for continuity of administration; (2) was rational, that is, the member occupying the administrative office was chosen on the basis of competence to perform the duties; (3) provided the leader with a legal means for exercising authority; and (4) clearly defined and carefully delimited all authority to the functions necessary to accomplish the organization's task. In contrast, tradition as legitimate authority was less efficient, since the leaders were not chosen on the basis of competence and since the administrative unit would act to preserve traditions of the past. Likewise, charisma as authority was too emotional and irrational in the sense that it avoided rules and routine and depended on mystique and divine revelations.

THE ELEMENTS OF BUREAUCRACY

For Weber, like Taylor, management (administration) meant the exercise of control on the basis of knowledge. Both sought technical competence in leaders who would lead by virtue of fact and not whim, by ability and not favoritism. The essential elements of Weber's bureaucracy were:

1. The division of labor and authority and responsibility were clearly defined for each member and were legitimatized as official duties.
2. Offices or positions were organized in a hierarchy of authority resulting in a chain of command or the scalar principle.
3. All organizational members were selected on the basis of technical qualifications through formal examinations or by virtue of training or education.
4. Officials were appointed, not elected. (With the exception in some cases of the chief of the whole unit; for example, an elected public official.)
5. Administrative officials worked for fixed salaries and were career officials.
6. Administrative officials were not owners of the units they administered.
7. Administrators were subject to strict rules, discipline, and controls regarding the conduct of their official duties. These rules and controls were impersonal and uniformly applied in all cases.[41]

For Weber, bureaucracy was not rule-encumbered inefficiency as the term has come to connote in modern parlance:

> Experience tends universally to show that the purely bureaucratic type of administrative organization—that is, the monocratic variety

41. See Weber, *The Theory of Social and Economic Organization,* pp. 329–333.

of bureaucracy—is, from a purely technical point of view, capable of attaining the highest degree of efficiency and is in this sense formally the most rational known means of carrying out imperative control over human beings. It is superior to any other form in precision, in stability, in the stringency of its discipline, and in its reliability. It thus makes possible a particularly high degree of calculability of results for the heads of the organization and for those acting in relation to it. It is finally superior both in intensive efficiency and in the scope of its operations and is formally capable of application to all kinds of administrative tasks.[42]

Despite his apparent worship of the bureaucratic model, Weber had his doubts: "It is horrible to think that the world could one day be filled with nothing but those little cogs, little men clinging to little jobs and striving towards bigger ones.... This passion for bureaucracy ... is enough to drive one to despair."[43] Weber's goal was not perfection, but systematization—moving management practices and organizational design toward more logical ways of operating.

The one component of the German economy that had not succumbed to bureaucracy, according to Weber, was the capitalist-entrepreneur. These individuals had achieved "relative immunity" from bureaucracy while others in large-scale organizations had become subject to bureaucratic control. Although Weber's turgid prose did not define clearly why this happened, the reason may lie in the corporate life cycle. In its early stage, the entrepreneurial phase, an organization can be managed in a more personalized fashion; as the organization grows, perhaps through integration or diversification, authority and responsibility become more widely distributed, coordination is achieved by less personal devices, and the office tends to prevail over the person. Large-scale capitalistic organizations that were market driven but subject to government regulation needed stable, strict, intensive, and calculable management. This need gave bureaucracy a crucial role in society as the central element in any kind of large-scale organization.

From a historical perspective, Weber's writings reflected what he saw as a breakup of tradition-based society. The process of industrialization in Germany had led to a few dominant companies that served as cartels for a few industries. Germany stood at the crossroads between the old, family-based business system and the rise of large-scale enterprise. Weber's response to the breakup of tradition was to rationalize organizations to provide efficiency for a new capitalistic nation. In essence, Weber was the Adam Smith of Germany.[44] Whereas Adam Smith had struck a blow to destroy the mercantile policies that were retarding the development of capitalism in

---

42. *Ibid.*, p. 337.

43. Quoted in Reinhard Bendix, *Max Weber: An Intellectual Portrait* (Garden City, N.Y.: Doubleday, 1960), p. 464.

44. Miller, *Max Weber*, p. 6.

Great Britain, Weber's attack on tradition and the use of political control in the economy, which were to be replaced by administration by knowledge and technical competence, was a similar thrust to advance capitalism. Bureaucracy was conceived as a blueprint for efficiency, which would emphasize rules rather than people and competence rather than favoritism.

Weber's work on bureaucracy remained largely unrecognized in the United States until the 1940s and 1950s. Like Fayol, he had to wait until cultural conditions created the need to think in terms of theory. As organizations grew in size and complexity, the search for a theory of organizations led to Max Weber and his bureaucratic model.

SUMMARY

The emergence of management and organization theory took place in two forms: Fayol's contribution of the principles and elements of management and Weber's search for a blueprint of rationalized structural arrangements for the purpose of ensuring organizational efficiency. From different backgrounds and perspectives, both Fayol and Weber attempted to present schemes for coping with large-scale organizations. Henri Fayol stressed education for management rather than technical training, the importance of planning and organizing, and the ongoing phases of command, coordination, and control. Max Weber sought to avoid leadership and organization by tradition and charisma, to establish a rational-legal basis for authority, and to present orderly arrangements for the selection of personnel and the execution of activities. Both Weber and Fayol had history's misfortune of having to wait until others could give them their proper credit in the evolution of management thought.

CHAPTER

11

Scientific Management in Theory and Practice

W
hereas Taylor and other pioneers furnished the impetus for scientific management, several individuals helped bring the movement to maturity along a number of dimensions. First, there was an emerging recognition of the need to formalize the study of management in college curricula as well as to educate leaders in industry. Second, as scientific management found its way into practice in U.S. industry it sparked an international interest in Great Britain, continental Europe, the Soviet Union, and Japan. Finally, other disciplines began to feel the impact of scientific management, and these ideas spread beyond factory management to general management as expressed through organizational structure, policy, philosophy, and the emergence of large-scale enterprise.

THE STUDY AND PRACTICE OF SCIENTIFIC MANAGEMENT

The Wharton School of Finance and Economy, established at the University of Pennsylvania in 1881, marked the country's first successful undergraduate school of business. Not until seventeen years later (1898) did the University of Chicago and the University of California at Berkeley start the second and third schools of business in the United States. The Amos Tuck School of Administration and Finance at Dartmouth College, founded in 1900, was the first graduate school of business administration; the second graduate school of business was founded in 1908 at Harvard University. Despite Taylor's belief that people had to live management and learn through shop experience, the study of industrial management was becoming more formalized.

EDUCATION FOR INDUSTRIAL MANAGEMENT

The record of when management first became an academic subject is not clear. Towne's paper in 1886 and Taylor's "Piece Rate" paper in 1895 were landmarks for the ASME in terms of interest in the engineer as a person who economized on human efforts as well as on other factors of production. In October of 1895, John Richards (1834–1917) began a series of lectures on works administration before students at Stanford University. His ten lectures, ending in June 1896, were never published.[1] Since Richards was an engineer, it may be presumed that his audience consisted of engineering students. However, in his memoirs, Dexter Kimball (1865–1952), an engineering student at Stanford beginning in 1893 who received his degree in 1896, made no mention of Richards but credited Taylor's 1903 paper on shop management with inspiring his own course in works administration at Cornell University's Sibley College of Engineering.[2] Kimball's course, which began in the second term of the academic year 1904–1905 to teach "the economics of production" to engineering students, was patterned after Taylor's article and book on shop management. The course covered the application of scientific management to plant location, equipment policies, plant organization, coordination, control of production, and labor compensation. Kimball expanded the concept of scientific management in production and called for the scientific study of the distribution side of enterprise.[3]

The American Society of Mechanical Engineering (ASME), the forum for early papers on management such as those of Towne and Taylor, had an identity crisis: was its purpose to further mechanical engineering, or was it to provide an outlet for ideas about incentives, cost accounting, and other facets of shop management? The ASME refused to publish Taylor's *Principles of Scientific Management* in its transactions due to disagreements within the society about Taylor's work. As a result, Taylor had the book privately printed and distributed. By 1919, after Taylor's death, the ASME recognized industrial engineering as a legitimate subject for study and created a Management Division in 1920.[4] The goals of the Management Division were remarkably similar to Taylor's ideas; by 1922, this division was the largest in the ASME. Industrial engineering and industrial management became continuing threads in collegiate education as the work of Taylor, Gilbreth, Gantt, and others led to ergonomics and working smarter, not harder.

---

1. Richard J. Whiting, "John Richards—California Pioneer of Management Thought," *California Management Review* 6, no. 2 (Winter 1963), pp. 35–38.

2. Dexter S. Kimball, *I Remember* (New York: McGraw-Hill, 1953), p. 85.

3. Kimball's lectures were published in *Principles of Industrial Organization* (New York: McGraw-Hill, 1913).

4. Mikiyoshi Hirose, "The Attitude of the American Society of Mechanical Engineers Toward Management: Suggestions for a Revised Interpretation," *Kansai University Review of Economics and Business* 25 (September 1996), pp. 125–148.

At the graduate level, Harlow S. Person (1875–1955) of the Amos Tuck School at Dartmouth led the way; by 1910, the Dartmouth catalog listed a course in business management. As dean of the Tuck School, Person hosted the first scientific management conference in the United States.[5] Person had a broadening effect on the Taylor movement as president of the Taylor Society (successor to the Society to Promote the Science of Management). He extended the group's membership and its range of interests and took a broad view of industrial education. He tried to dissipate the prevailing notion that scientific management was merely the use of a stopwatch and methods analysis; in his view, educators should emphasize the philosophy of scientific management and focus on the creative study of leadership in industry.

Person also gave early recognition to the need to bring social scientists into the study of management. His thesis was that managers and workers were so closely entwined in everyday activities that they failed to see larger relationships; however, social scientists would be able to take a larger, more objective view of industrial evolution to chart a future course of action for research and practice.[6] One example of Person's ideas was his promotion of the relationship between industrial psychology and scientific management, which arose out of their common interest in improving human relations.

Clarence Bertrand Thompson (1882–1969) was "an educator, a missionary of the gospel" who taught at Harvard from 1908 to 1917 and was instrumental in inducing Taylor to give his Harvard lectures. Thompson compiled the most extensive bibliography of scientific management for that period, became a consultant (getting his start from Taylor), and did much to further the scientific management movement in both academia and industry.[7] As Nelson observed, scientific management gave credibility to the study of management among those who opposed business education as too vocational.[8]

Also among those contributing to early management education was Leon Pratt Alford (1877–1942). He was trained as an electrical engineer, worked in industry, became editor-in-chief of the influential journals *American Machinist, Industrial Engineering, Management Engineering,* and *Manufacturing Industries,* and pioneered

———

5. *Scientific Management,* addresses and discussions of the conference on Scientific Management, October 12–14, 1911 (Hanover, N.H.: Amos Tuck School of Administration and Finance, Dartmouth College, 1912).

6. H. S. Person, "The Manager, the Workman, and the Social Scientist," *Bulletin of the Taylor Society* 3 (February 1917), reprinted in Edward E. Hunt, ed., *Scientific Management since Taylor* (New York: McGraw-Hill, 1924), pp. 226–237.

7. Ronald G. Greenwood and Regina A. Greenwood, "C. Bertrand Thompson—Pioneer Management Bibliographer," *Academy of Management Proceedings,* R. L Taylor, M. J. O'Donnell, R. A. Zawacki, and D. D. Warwick, eds. (August 1976), pp. 3–6. See also C. B. Thompson, ed., *The Theory and Practice of Scientific Management* (Cambridge, Mass.: Harvard University Press, 1914).

8. Daniel Nelson, "Scientific Management and the Transformation of University Business Education," in Daniel Nelson, ed., *A Mental Revolution: Scientific Management since Taylor* (Columbus: Ohio State University Press, 1992), pp. 77–101.

the concept of management handbooks. His role in management education has not been generally acknowledged by management historians; nevertheless, his influence in the journals, on various professional committees, and through his books was substantial. Among Alford's early writings was an attempt to provide a correct interpretation of science in management. Writing with Alexander Hamilton Church, he deplored the term scientific management in that it was interpreted to mean that there was "a science rather than an art of management."[9]

The weakness of the Taylor approach, in Alford and Church's view, was that it superseded the art of leadership by substituting an "elaborate mechanism" or system. They did not mean that the mechanism was useless, but rather that it overlooked the dynamic possibilities of effective leadership. Alford thought that Taylor's so-called principles were too mechanical. To remedy this problem he (and Church) proposed three broad principles: (1) the systematic use of experience; (2) the economic control of effort; and (3) the promotion of personal effectiveness. The first emphasized both personal experiences of executives and scientific studies; the second was based on the subprinciples of division of labor, coordination, conservation (least effort expended to a given end), and remuneration; and the third stressed personal rewards, developing contented workers, and promoting the workers' physical and mental health. From these three broad, regulative principles, a truly scientific basis for the art of management could be discovered.

Alford's call for art plus science in management was a reflection of his admiration of Henry Laurence Gantt, about whom he prepared an excellent biography. In the style of Gantt, Alford pleaded for industrial engineers to become involved in leading the economy toward service to the community and better relations between employers and employees. Alford continued to stress this theme as a member of the prestigious American Engineering Council and contributed to the better known works of this group, such as the reports *The Elimination of Waste in Industry, The Twelve Hour Shift,* and *Safety and Production.* Parallel to his efforts on the council, Alford disseminated management knowledge through the device of management handbooks. The pioneering concept of the handbooks was to organize information on all facets of managing and operating business and industrial enterprises. Through the handbooks and his other publications L. P. Alford sought to develop both the art and science of management.[10]

---

9. Alexander H. Church and Leon P. Alford, "The Principles of Management," *American Machinist* 36, no. 22 (May 30, 1912), pp. 857–861. Reprinted in Harwood F. Merrill, ed., *Classics in Management* (New York: American Management Association, 1960), pp. 197–214.

10. Leon P. Alford, ed., *Management's Handbook* (New York: Ronald Press, 1924); and later, *Cost and Production Handbook* (New York: Ronald Press, 1934). See also L. P. Alford, *Laws of Management Applied to Manufacturing* (New York: Ronald Press, 1928), and *Principles of Industrial Management* (New York: Ronald Press, 1940).

THE INTERNATIONAL SCIENTIFIC MANAGEMENT MOVEMENT

Whereas the Industrial Revolution began in Great Britain and spread to the United States, the scientific management revolution began in the United States and spread abroad. As early as 1907, Taylor was in touch with the French scientist, Henri Le Chatelier (1850–1936), with regard to metal cutting, time study, and the introduction of scientific management in France. When Frederick and Louise Taylor visited Europe in 1912 and again in 1913, it was Le Chatelier who introduced Taylor to Louis Renault and the tire manufacturing Michelin brothers, Edouard and André. Before World War I, scientific management techniques began to be used by the Michelins, Renault, and in government-operated arsenals. Unfortunately for Taylor and for scientific management, the French experience was not a good one: the managers seized the techniques and forgot the mental revolution, hired untrained personnel to conduct time studies, clashed with labor, refused to delegate, and, in general, perverted what Taylor had described as scientific management.[11] After a strike at the Renault automobile plant, Taylor wrote Le Chatelier: "If a man [Renault] deliberately goes against the experience of men who know what they are talking about, and refuses to follow advice given in a kind but unmistakable way, it seems to me that he deserves to get into trouble."[12] Although the term *Taylorisme* was used to describe the practice of scientific management in France, in reality, the applications fell far short of the ideals.

Another Frenchman, Charles de Fréminville (1856–1936), learned of scientific management through Le Chatelier's translations of Taylor's writings. Fréminville became a second leading proponent and attempted to apply scientific management to the automobile manufacturer Panhard and Levassor, which, with Peugeot, was a pioneer in the industry. Unfortunately, French managers again resisted, or took what part of scientific management would appear to lead to a quick payout at little cost, and Panhard and Levassor became a declining force in the automobile industry in France. Fréminville did not lose his interest, however; he and Henri Le Chatelier helped form the Conference de l'Organisation Française in 1920 to advance the management movement in France.

Another branch of the management movement in France was due to the work of Henri Fayol, who formed a Center for Administrative Studies in 1917.[13] At the opening session of the Second International Management Congress in Brussels in 1925, Fayol announced that, according to the opinion of some, his ideas were not in competition or contrast with those of Frederick Taylor. Fréminville then proposed a merger

---

11. George G. Humphreys, *Taylorism in France, 1904–1920: The Impact of Scientific Management on Factory Relations and Society* (New York: Garland, 1986).

12. Cited in Daniel Nelson, *Frederick W. Taylor and the Rise of Scientific Management* (Madison: University of Wisconsin Press, 1980), p. 179.

13. John D. Breeze, "Henri Fayol's Centre for Administrative Studies," *Journal of Management History* 1 (1995), p. 43.

of Fayol's and Taylor's followers into a new association, Le Comité de l'Organisation Française, which served to bring together (for France) the pioneering contributions of Fayol and Taylor.[14]

International interest in scientific management continued to increase and widen its frontiers along separate, yet related, paths. The first International Congress on Scientific Management was held in Prague in 1924; among those attending were Harlow Person of the Taylor Society, and Lillian Gilbreth. An International Committee of Scientific Management (Le Comité International de l'Organisation Scientifique, known as CIOS), was formed to continue these meetings to exchange ideas about management. Subsequent meetings were held in Brussels (1925), Rome (1927), Paris (1929), Amsterdam (1932), London (1935), and Washington (1938). The 1941 meeting, to be held in Berlin, was cancelled and CIOS would not continue its work until after World War II.

Beginning in the 1920s, the Twentieth Century Fund, endowed by the Boston merchant Edward A. Filene (1860–1939), and the Rockefeller Foundation sought to promote improved management, particularly scientific management, in European industry which was rebuilding following World War I. The International Management Institute (IMI), a spin-off from the Geneva based International Labor Organization, was expected to enable exchange of research about better management practices. Paul Devinat was appointed as the first director of the IMI in 1927, but policy disagreements with the IMI's financial backers led to his dismissal.[15] He was succeeded in 1928 by Lt. Colonel Lyndall Urwick, who is discussed later, but the IMI continued to have problems with contending national employer groups, the threat of war with the rise of Fascism, and a subsequent worldwide economic depression that undercut its financial support. The IMI ceased its activities in January 1934.

The international management movement also received mixed acceptance and underwent various transformations in various countries. Authorities disagree on the British experience. According to Urwick and Brech, Taylorism was not well received. Taylor had engendered some bitterness with British manufacturers over patent rights to high-speed steel, and organized labor posed opposition so formidable that it made scientific management almost a negligible force.[16]

Whitson, however, found that British engineering journals referred to Taylor's work fairly frequently, and often positively.[17] The scientific management movement in Britain did not match the American experience, but the British journals agreed

---

14. Lyndall Urwick and E. F. L. Brech, *The Making of Scientific Management: Thirteen Pioneers*, vol. 1 (London: Sir Isaac Pitman and Sons, 1951), pp. 105–110.

15. Charles D. Wrege, Ronald G. Greenwood, and Sakae Hata, "The International Management Institute and Political Opposition to its Efforts in Europe, 1925–1934," *Business and Economic History* 16 (1987), pp. 249–265.

16. Urwick and Brech, *The Making of Scientific Management*, p. 111.

17. Kevin Whitson, "The Reception of Scientific Management by British Engineers, 1890–1914," *Business History Review* 71 (1997), pp. 207–229.

with Taylor that Britain needed a new type of management, but took a more conservative stance about how change would come about. Authorities agree that the chain-making firm of Hans Renold (1852–1943) was the first company to introduce scientific management as Taylor would have desired.[18] Renold met with Taylor in the United States on three occasions, and admired the installation of Taylor's ideas at the Link-Belt Company. Hans Renold and his son Charles were able to implement scientific management successfully, but their sterling example "did not appear to make scientific management any more widely accepted [in Great Britain]."[19]

In other countries, the international scientific management movement passed through various stages: first, propagandizing and translations by individuals such as Le Chatelier; second, adaptation by individual countries to meet their own needs; and finally, adjustment through various committees, conferences, and international organizations.[20] Different countries had different political and economic structures, which made it difficult to apply scientific management as Taylor would have advocated. Consequently, managers often grasped the mechanics of time study, incentive schemes, and so on, without applying the philosophy. Europe, having a long history of organized labor with an often radical nature, also encountered more resistance from unions than was encountered in the United States. Further, an anti-American sentiment led to a less than favorable reception before and during the war. The 1920s were marked, however, by a widespread recognition of the need for better management techniques. One researcher compared and contrasted U.S., British, French, German, and Italian management systems and found widespread acceptance of scientific management techniques.[21]

In Poland, Karol Adamiecki (1866–1933) developed a "harmonogram," which was a graphical device for simultaneously charting several complicated operations and thus enabling their harmonization. According to Mee, the harmonogram was similar to the idea of a Program Evaluation and Review Technique (PERT) network.[22] The harmonogram, developed in 1896, received some acceptance and use in Poland and Russia but Adamiecki's work was never translated into English. While Adamiecki's work languished, European interest in Gantt's charts was stimulated by the work of Wallace Clark, who popularized them and provided a basis for the European productivity movement.

—

18. Trevor Boyns, "Hans and Charles Renold: Entrepreneurs in the Introduction of Scientific Management Techniques in Britain," *Management Decision* 39 (2001), pp. 719–728.

19. E. F .L. Brech, *The Evolution of Modern Management*, vol. 2, *Productivity in Perspective, 1914–1974* (Bristol: Thoemmes Press, 2002), p. 30.

20. Paul Devinat, *Scientific Management in Europe* (Geneva: International Labor Office, 1927).

21. Dwight T. Farnham, *America vs. Europe in Industry* (New York: Ronald Press, 1921).

22. John Mee, "History of Management," *Advanced Management-Office Executive*, 1 (October 1962), pp. 28–29; see also Edward R. Marsh, "The Harmonogram of Karol Adamiecki," *Academy of Management Journal* 18, no. 2 (June 1975), pp. 358–364; and Lyndall F. Urwick, "Charles Adamiecki (1866–1933)," *Bulletin of the International Management Institute* 3 (January, 1929), pp. 102–103.

In the Soviet Union, Lenin advocated the use of scientific management to systematize industry after the 1917 revolution. In Lenin's view, scientific management was the most progressive means to achieve the socialist revolution. His rhetoric was intended to show the benefits to society if the workers controlled this latest means of production. Although numerous conferences were held, institutes established, and attempts made to implement the ideas of Taylor and the Gilbreths, few improvements were made because of a basic Bolshevik distrust of capitalistic methods and ideas.[23] Instead, the idea of the worker "hero" arose with Alexei Stakhanov, whose name became known nationally for his extraordinary performance in cutting coal loose from the mine face with a pneumatic drill. Stakhanov's efforts exceeded ordinary output and his work was hailed as an example for others.[24] Higher productivity for the Stakhanovites came not from job analysis and improved work methods, but from workplace competition to speed up output.

After Lenin's death, Stalin needed to advance the goal of national economic planning. To do so he needed help and hired one of Gantt's disciples, Walter N. Polakov (1879–1937), as a consultant. Born in the Soviet Union, Polakov became a U.S. citizen and worked with Gantt and Clark. In 1929, Stalin hired him to teach the Soviets how to plan and control performance in order to achieve the goals of the nation's five-year plans. Polakov's work was widely praised, and the Gantt chart concept was the only successful scientific management technique to be accepted in the USSR.[25]

After the Meiji Restoration of 1868, Japan began to move away from its feudal past and into the industrial period. Industrialization came slowly, however; in 1870, more than 80 percent of the population was employed in agriculture and less than 5 percent in manufacturing. Industry was dominated by family firms and entrepreneurs, employed few workers, was generally backward in production technology, and lacked knowledge of management methods. Japan needed to modernize and was in a period of transition from agriculture to industry; even by 1930, only 50 percent of the labor force was in manufacturing.[26]

The entrance into Japan of U.S. ideas on management appears to have been inspired by the visit of Yukinori Hoshino, director of Japan's Kajima Bank, to the United States in 1911. Hoshino encountered Taylor's writings and obtained permission to translate Taylor's *Principles of Scientific Management;* Taylor's work appeared in Japanese in 1912 or 1913. Landing in fertile soil, the seed of scientific

---

23. Daniel A. Wren and Arthur G. Bedeian, "The Taylorization of Lenin: Rhetoric or Reality?" *International Journal of Social Economics* 31 (2004), pp. 287–299.

24. Arthur G. Bedeian and Carl R. Phillips, "Scientific Management and Stakhanovism in the Soviet Union: A Historical Perspective," *International Journal of Social Economics* 17 (1990), pp. 28–35.

25. Daniel A. Wren, "Scientific Management in the U.S.S.R., with Particular Reference to the Contribution of Walter N. Polakov," *Academy of Management Review* 5 (January 1980), pp. 1–11.

26. Koji Taira, "Factory Legislation and Management Modernization during Japan's Industrialization, 1886–1916," *Business History Review* 44 (Spring 1970), pp. 84–109.

management grew rapidly and led to a managerial revolution, replacing the entrepreneur-dominated age. A leading teacher, author, and consultant was Yoichi Ueno (1883–1957), who authored a paper in 1912, "On the Efficiency," which described the work of Taylor, Frank Gilbreth, and C. B. Thompson. The ideas of scientific management entered the journals, the educational system, and the practice of management in Japan. Carl Barth visited Japan in 1924, and a chapter of the Taylor Society was formed in 1925. Ueno translated all of Taylor's writings, attended international conferences, and was the most articulate spokesperson for scientific management in Japan.[27]

In industry, the most advanced application of scientific management occurred at the Hyōgo Factory of the Kanegafuchi (Kanebō) Cotton Textile Company by its manager, Sanji Mutō.[28] Mutō had studied in the United States and saw no conflict between high wages and high profits. Like Taylor and Gantt, Mutō began paying more to attract better workers, to train the workers, and to improve factory supervision and organization. Mutō eventually became president of Kanebō and led it to a position as one of the leading textile firms in Japan. What Mutō and others of the scientific management persuasion perceived was that the improved well-being of the employees and a profitable company were in harmony rather than in conflict. To achieve harmony, the firm was a family in spirit and mutuality of interests. The link between high wages and high profits was productivity, which, in turn, was a function of technology, capital, and improved work methods.

The phenomenon that modern authors call Japanese-style management is not a recent creation but a product of the introduction of scientific management into Japan during the late Meiji period.[29] Under the influence of scholars such as Ueno and with the implementation of practitioners such as Mutō, scientific management provided the basis for the modernization of Japanese industry. In summary, scientific management was an international force in theory and in practice. Although variations occurred and perversions masqueraded as the real thing, the scientific management revolution began in the United States and facilitated the transition and modernization of industry in numerous countries.

SCIENTIFIC MANAGEMENT IN INDUSTRIAL PRACTICE

Concurrently with the spread of scientific management to other nations, U.S. industry experimented with the notions of systems and efficiency. Some companies, such as the Plimpton Press, Link-Belt, Clothcraft, and Tabor Manufacturing, were considered model installations. Henry P. Kendall (1878–1959), manager of the Plimpton

---

27. Ronald G. Greenwood, Regina A. Greenwood, and Robert H. Ross, "Yoichi Ueno: A Brief History of Japanese Management 1911 to World War II," in K. H. Chung, ed., *Academy of Management Proceedings* (San Diego, 1981), pp. 107–110.

28. Taira, "Factory Legislation," pp. 103–105.

29. William M. Tsutsui, *Manufacturing Ideology: Scientific Management in Modern Japan* (Princeton, N.J.: Princeton University Press, 1998).

Press of Norwood, Massachusetts, was an early promoter of scientific management in the printing industry. He thought that plants could become efficient by being systematized, but that a greater long-run effect could be achieved only if the philosophy of scientific management was fully accepted by all parties.[30] Plimpton Press also developed an advanced employment department, which centralized hiring, disciplining, and discharging. The employment manager, Jane C. Williams, credited scientific management with reducing labor turnover from 186 percent in 1912 to 13 percent in 1916.[31] James Mapes Dodge (1852–1915) pioneered the link-belt conveyor, which became the basis for later belt assembly line operations, and the Link-Belt Company (Philadelphia) was one of the major installations of the Taylor system.[32]

Wilfred Lewis, president of the Tabor Manufacturing Company (Philadelphia), a machine-tool producer, was an authority on gearing and a friend of metric reform. At Tabor, Taylor's system increased output 250 percent.[33] Horace King Hathaway (1878–1944) was general manager of the Tabor Company and assisted Taylor in the installation of his system. Hathaway advocated careful planning before installation, including an extensive program of educating the workers and supervisors as to the principles and purposes of the Taylor system. At the Clothcraft Company (Cleveland, Ohio), a manufacturer of men's suits, Richard A. Feiss and Mary Barnett Gilson recognized the merits of scientific management in the labor-intensive clothing industry. Feiss implemented time and motion study, bonuses for performance and attendance, and a planning department to smooth the flow of work, and employed an orthopedic surgeon to design chairs and tables for worker comfort, reduced fatigue, and efficiency. Gilson headed the Employment and Service Department (she disliked the phrase "welfare department") for employment testing and selection, proper placement, promotions for women to supervisory positions, and other advanced practices that made her that era's best known and most influential personnel manager.[34] At Clothcraft we see the ideas of Taylor in practice, combining the best of scientific management and personnel work, all in anticipation of the industrial relations movement (see Chapter 9) that joined collective bargaining and improved management practice.

---

30. Henry P. Kendall, "Unsystematized, Systematized, and Scientific Management," in Thompson, *The Theory and Practice of Scientific Management,* pp. 103–131.

31. Jane C. Williams, "The Reduction of Labor Turnover in the Plimpton Press," *The Annals of the American Academy of Political and Social Science* (hereinafter cited as *The Annals*) 71 (May 1917), pp. 71–81.

32. See George P. Torrence, *James Mapes Dodge* (New York: Newcomen Society of North America, 1950); and James M. Dodge, "A History of the Introduction of a System of Shop Management," in Thompson, *The Theory and Practice,* pp. 226–231.

33. Wilfred Lewis, "An Object Lesson in Efficiency," in Thompson, *The Theory and Practice,* pp. 232–241; see also H. K. Hathaway, "Wilfred Lewis," Bulletin of the Taylor Society 15 (February 1930), pp. 45–46.

34. David J. Goldberg, "Richard A. Feiss , Mary Barnett Gilson, and Scientific Management at Joseph and Feiss, 1909–1925," in Daniel Nelson, ed., *A Mental Revolution: Scientific Management Since Taylor* (Columbus: Ohio State University Press, 1992), pp. 40–57.

Thompson noted that an increase in the "stability of payroll" was one of the many benefits of scientific management in practice.[35] He was referring to employment stabilization through improved production planning, employee selection and placement, and training. Scientific management aimed at reducing waste, and one major contribution to increased costs was labor turnover. The first statistical analysis of labor turnover was by General Electric's Magnus Alexander, who studied GE's twelve factories in 1912.[36] He found that 42,571 employees were newly hired for 1912, amounting to an 82 percent rate of labor turnover. The cost of this turnover was estimated at $831,030, which included the cost of hiring, training, lower production by new employees in training, and breakage of tools, and so forth while new employees were learning their jobs. Joseph Willits, an instructor at the Wharton School of Finance and Commerce, followed Alexander's study by examining turnover in Philadelphia textile mills. He found the actual turnover ranged from 50 to 100 percent, and occasionally 500 percent.[37] Willits offered improved selection, placement, training practices, and wage incentives to bolster employee retention. In brief, Taylor's first-class worker and Münsterberg's search for the best possible worker for the best possible effect were means to reduce the cost of labor turnover and stabilize employment. Labor turnover carried a high cost, both for the employee and the employer, and scientific management sought to reduce that waste of resources.

THE HOXIE REPORT

The early position of organized labor vis-à-vis scientific management found its critical articulation in an investigation by the U.S. Commission on Industrial Relations. The chief investigator was Robert Franklin Hoxie (1866–1916), professor of political economy at the University of Chicago, and his assistants were Robert G. Valentine, an investigator and consultant in labor problems who was to represent management's viewpoint,[38] and John P. Frey, editor of the *International Molder's Journal,* representing labor. The purpose of the study was to investigate all systems

---

35. C. Bertrand Thompson, *The Taylor System of Scientific Management* (New York: A. W. Shaw, 1917), p. 27.

36. Magnus W. Alexander, "Hiring and Firing: Its Economic Waste and How to Avoid It," *The Annals* 65 (1916), pp. 128–144. I am indebted to Kyle Bruce's unpublished paper "Magnus Alexander, The Economists, and Labor Turnover," presentation for the Management History Division, Academy of Management, Seattle, Washington, 2003.

37. Joseph H. Willits, "The Labor Turn-Over and the Humanizing of Industry," *The Annals* 61 (1915), pp. 127–137. For turnover data for Ford Motor Company before the five-dollar-a-day minimum wage, see Boyd Fisher, "Methods of Reducing the Labor Turnover," *The Annals* 65 (1916), pp. 144–154.

38. Though calling himself a consultant to management on labor relations, Valentine had only brief experience in industry and that in banking. He taught English at the Massachusetts Institute of Technology and was at one time assistant commissioner of Indian Affairs. L. Urwick and E. F. L. Brech, *The Golden Book of Management* (London: Newman Neame, 1956), p. 3.

of shop management, including Taylor's, Gantt's, and Emerson's, and the investigators examined thirty shops employing scientific management and five shops that were not designated as scientifically managed during the period of January to April 1915.[39]

An early inkling of controversy occurred when Hoxie insisted on making no distinction between the theory and the practice of scientific management. To Hoxie, scientific management was what was practiced by any company if that firm called it "scientific"; to Taylor, scientific management ceased to exist if its principles and philosophy were violated in practice. Hoxie's distinction did not impress Taylor, and this undoubtedly led to his unfavorable reception of the report and the inclusion of a separate statement on his position in the appendix.[40]

The Hoxie report found a marked degree of diversity among the various shops studied. First, Hoxie found that practice violated the precepts of careful study and analysis prior to installation of any efficiency system. The efficiency experts who offered their services worked for the short run and did not have "the ability or the willingness to install scientific management in accordance with the Taylor formula and ideals."[41] Second, the concept of functional foremen found few adherents in practice. Some firms made the attempt but soon returned to the old-style, line type of organization. In a third area of inquiry, Hoxie found that little or no progress was being made with respect to the scientific selection of workers. "Labor heads," an early designation for employment or personnel managers, were poorly trained and of "doubtful experience and capacity."[42]

Instruction and training of workers was another area in which practice fell far short of theory. Learning proceeded by trial and error, specially trained instructors were scarce, and instruction more often than not focused on attaining the standard rather than on learning the job. Despite these faults, Hoxie concluded that training practices in scientific management shops were generally better than those that could be found elsewhere in industry. A fifth area of concern, and one of greater criticism, was the use of time study and task setting. Standards and incentive rates were often established after only a cursory inquiry and led to a variety of inaccuracies and injustices. In general, time-study personnel were poorly trained and inexperienced and often set rates based on management's desires and not on true scientific inquiry and observation. Incentive schemes also came under close scrutiny. Hoxie found no pure adoptions of the Taylor, Gantt, or Emerson plans. The Midvale differential piece-rate plan, used briefly by Taylor, was infrequently encountered, and most plans were modifications of the Gantt and Emerson plans.

---

39. Robert F. Hoxie, *Scientific Management and Labor* (New York: Appleton-Century-Crofts, 1915), p. 4.

40. *Ibid.*; app. II, pp. 140–149. Gantt, in app. III (pp. 150–151), and Emerson, in app. IV (pp. 152–168), also filed their positions regarding Taylor's claims. The three do not present a unified theory of the movement but do agree on the fundamental aims of scientific management.

41. *Ibid.*, p. 9.

42. *Ibid.*, p. 32.

On a broader plane, Hoxie tried to reconcile the opposing views of unions and Taylor regarding industrial democracy. Taylor maintained that scientific management was the essence of industrial democracy. Taylor's argument hinged upon harmony and the mutuality of interest between labor and management. Individuals were stimulated and rewarded on the basis of effort; discipline fell under scientifically derived laws and not under autocratic, driving management; and protests were to be handled by reliance upon scientific inquiry and mutual resolution. Scientific management, according to the union view, monopolized knowledge and power in the hands of management by denying the worker a voice in setting work standards and in determining wage rates and conditions of employment. It introduced a spirit of mutual suspicion among workers and destroyed the solidarity and cooperative spirit of the group by emphasizing the individual worker. It destroyed unions, the protection that unions gave workers, and in turn obviated the collective bargaining process. Hoxie concluded that industrial democracy could come only through the process of collective bargaining. He saw no other avenue, included no possibility for an educated, enlightened management, and seemed dedicated to the proposition that labor and management interests were inalterably opposed for all times and in all places. He brought no true bill against union leadership nor its membership for soldiering or resistance. On this count, his examination was less than equitable. Hoxie also blamed management for seeking shortcuts to efficiency, he faulted Taylor for trying to generalize his machine shop experience to all types and sizes of industries, and he denounced efficiency experts who were guilty of selling patent medicine panaceas to employers in dire financial straits and eager to improve performance.

Those who criticize are also open to criticism. What can be said of the research methodology of the Hoxie team? Professor Hoxie and his associates made numerous attempts to be fair to Taylor by noting that practice fell far short of theory. However, the predilections of Hoxie, Frey, and Valentine toward organized labor yielded a research bias that is inescapable. There is also evidence that the methodology of the research group was less than meticulous. Mary Barnett Gilson, employment manager at Clothcraft in Cleveland, one of the shops included in the study, wrote that Hoxie was "brilliant" but "prejudiced."[43] When Hoxie and Frey visited Clothcraft, they held a short interview with the president, Richard Feiss, and some of his managers, took some notes, but never visited the factory area itself. They promised to return to see the working conditions but never did. Gilson also wrote that Frey was especially antagonistic during the interview because Clothcraft had no union. If this encounter at Clothcraft was characteristic of the researchers' conduct at the other shops in the study, one must conclude that the Hoxie group was less than thorough. The investigation lasted only four months (January to April 1915) and could have been conducted only in a superficial manner. It is unfortunate that those who had the best opportunity to do a thorough empirical investigation of scientific management in its early days approached this chance with closed minds and hasty feet.

---

43. Mary B. Gilson, *What's Past is Prologue* (New York: Harper and Row, 1940), p. 93.

Nyland noted that the Hoxie report was "heavily skewed" toward organized labor's position and, as a consequence, "the Taylorists were charged publicly with a great many crimes, found innocent of none and guilty of many."[44] The pro-labor bias was evident in the selection of Robert Valentine to represent management. Taylor's objection, based on Valentine's lack of experience in business and familiarity with scientific management, was disregarded. Asked to give testimony before the commission, Valentine admitted his only experience with efficiency systems was "I have run into it on the slant in a number of places ... a half dozen cases." When asked if employees should participate if "any efficiency system" was introduced, he responded "I not only think the individual should participate, but I think he should participate as a part of a union."[45] Valentine was appointed to represent management, but he revealed his bias for unionism.

When John Frey reminisced for a Columbia University oral history project, he "admitted that when he and Hoxie came across evidence that did not support the claims of the AFL [American Federation of Labor], he reworked the data until it confirmed his preconceived ideas."[46] Frey also had unfavorable memories of Valentine, who "didn't care to come" to their meetings, and of Hoxie, who Frey viewed as one who knew little of practical matters and even less about work, workers, and industry.

John R. Commons (1862–1945), distinguished labor economist from the University of Wisconsin, who was a member of the Industrial Relations Commission, recalled two other events that shaped the commission's findings. Charles McCarthy, of the Wisconsin Legislative Library, and a supporter of Frederick Taylor, was appointed by Commons to lead the investigations. The commission's chair, Frank Walsh, soon found reasons to disagree with McCarthy and dismissed him from the commission. In the second instance, Commons recalled that Hoxie was "dropped by Walsh in the midst of his investigation of Scientific Management."[47] According to Commons, this explained why the Hoxie report was not included in the final report of the commission but was published later as a book. Hoxie's book was critically reviewed by a fellow economist who commented that "the effect of [Hoxie's] book as a whole will be to multiply misconceptions and misunderstandings with regard to the scientific management practice."[48] Hoxie and his colleagues missed a grand opportunity to evaluate the theory and practice of scientific management, and misled generations of scholars about its practice.

---

44. Chris Nyland, "Taylorism, John R. Commons and the Hoxie Report," *Journal of Economic Issues* 30 (1996), p. 1007.

45. *Industrial Relations. Final Report and Testimony Submitted to Congress by the Commission on Industrial Relations,* Volume 1 (Washington, D.C.: U.S. Government Printing Office, 1916), p. 853.

46. Frey, cited in Nyland, p. 1012.

47. John R. Commons, *Myself* (New York: Macmillan, 1934), pp. 176–177.

48. *Scientific Management and Labor,* by Robert Franklin Hoxie, reviewed by Charles W. Mixter, *American Economic Review* 6 (1916), p. 376.

THE THOMPSON AND NELSON STUDIES

Two other studies, one during the scientific management period and one more recently, provide more thorough analyses of the practice of scientific management. Harvard's C. Bertrand Thompson studied 172 "definitely known" applications of scientific management in eighty types of organizations; for example, municipal government, department stores, and publishing. Most (149) of the applications were in factories, and of these, the installation of scientific management had progressed far enough at 113 plants to permit an analysis by Thompson. Fifty-nine were judged complete successes; twenty were partially successful; and thirty-four were failures. Thompson attributed the failures to "the personality of the consulting engineers and … the personality of the managements."[49] Failures by consulting engineers were due largely to their "inexperience and incompetence," while managements' failures could be attributed to hasty installations, impatience with the initial slowness of results, dissension within the management group, and some factors completely outside the control of management (e.g., the business cycle). Never were any failures due to the workers themselves.

Thompson was aware of the Hoxie report and commented on the inclusion of plants that were not scientifically managed:

> If the system in the plant was developed by Mr. Taylor personally, or by any of his assistants or co-workers while associated with him, then the Taylor system may be held responsible for the results; otherwise not.

> When this qualification is kept in mind, an impartial investigator must admit that, from the viewpoint of the employer, the employee, or the public, the Taylor system is a demonstrated success.[50]

Nelson studied twenty-nine installations made by Taylor's closest followers and, although variations occurred, found a pattern of "general adherence to Taylor's ideas."[51] The two ideas of least applicability were the differential piece-rate (even Taylor moved to the Gantt plan) and the functional foremen. Nelson also noted a "strong positive correlation" between scientific management and industrial efficiency. Except for the heat-using industries (beverages, petroleum refining, chemicals, and primary metals), scientific management was "associated with growth, not stagnation."[52] Scientific management was used mostly in batch-assembly (job shop) and

---

49. C. Bertrand Thompson, *The Taylor System of Scientific Management* (New York: A. W. Shaw, 1917), p. 13.

50. *Ibid.*, p. 25.

51. Daniel Nelson, "Scientific Management, Systematic Management, and Labor, 1880–1915," *Business History Review* 48 (Winter 1974), p. 500.

52. Daniel Nelson, "Taylorism," *Proceedings of the International Colloquium on Taylorism* (Paris: Éditions la Découverte, 1984), pp. 55–57.

labor-intensive nonassembly operations. In more capital-intensive industries, however (such as in smelting primary metals), scientific management was less likely to be applied. In the automobile industry, scientific management was applied before the coming of Henry Ford's assembly line, but not afterward (in Chapter 12, we will examine the Ford production technology). Carl Barth and George Babcock were successful at the Franklin Motor Car Company, for example, but once the moving assembly line and mass-production techniques came to the auto industry, scientific management methods were less useful.[53]

Organized labor charged that scientific management "tends to eliminate skilled crafts...degrades the skilled worker...[and] displaces skilled workers and forces them into competition with the less skilled."[54] The Hoxie report agreed, concluding:

> Scientific management, fully and properly applied, inevitably tends to the constant breakdown of the established crafts and craftsmanship and the constant elimination of skill in the sense of narrowing craft knowledge and workmanship, except for the lower orders of workmen.[55]

The belief that skilled labor would be displaced by workplace improvements is as ancient as the Luddites who protested the introduction of water power to replace hand loom weavers. In the case of scientific management, however, it was not machinery but improved work processes that were protested by unions.

Later writers, such as David Montgomery and Harry Braverman, have perpetuated this "de-skilling" of the workers' tasks.[56] What is the evidence? If scientific management de-skilled jobs, we should expect a decline in craft workers and an increase in the number of unskilled laborers during this period. U.S. Bureau of the Census data indicate that the number of "craftsmen and kindred workers," excluding foreman, increased 72 percent from 1900 to 1920 (2,900,000 to 4,997,000) and 96 percent from 1900 to 1930 (2,900,000 to 5,695,000). The number of "operative and kindred workers" (semi-skilled) increased 77 percent (3,720,000 to 6,587,000) from 1900 to 1920 and 107 percent (3,720,000 to 7,691,000) from 1900 to 1930. The number of unskilled laborers, excluding farmers and miners, increased at a lesser pace: 35 percent (3,620,000 to 4,905,000) from 1900 to 1920, and forty-seven percent from 1900 to 1930.[57]

---

53. Charles B. Gordy, "Scientific Management in the Automobile Industry," Ph.D. dissertation (Ann Arbor: University of Michigan, 1929), pp. 5–7.

54. Hoxie, *Scientific Management and Labor*, p. 16.

55. *Ibid.*, p. 129.

56. David Montgomery, *The Fall of the House of Labor: The Workplace, the State and American Labor Activism, 1865–1925* (Cambridge, England: Cambridge University Press, 1987), pp. 214–256; Harry Braverman, *Labor and Monopoly Capitalism* (New York: Monthly Review Press, 1974), pp. 85–168.

57. *Historical Statistics of the United States: Colonial Times to 1970*, pt. I (Washington, D.C.: Bureau of the Census, 1975), pp. 139–142.

Eichar took a different tack, examining blue collar workers by skill level as a percentage of the total labor force. Craft workers were 10.5 percent of the labor force in 1900, 13 percent in 1920; semi-skilled operatives increased from 12.8 percent in 1900 to 15.6 percent in 1920; and unskilled nonfarm laborers decreased from 12.5 percent in 1900 to 11.6 percent in 1920.[58] Both in absolute numbers and as a percentage of the work force the number of skilled craft and semi-skilled operatives were increasing while the number of unskilled was increasing at a far slower pace. The claim that scientific management de-skilled labor is a myth that needs to be put to rest.

In summary, scientific management became an international movement, experiencing varying levels of acceptance and differing degrees of appropriate implementation. The first teaching of management began at the graduate and undergraduate levels in the form of workshop or industrial management. Despite misinterpretations, perversions, and erroneous charges, scientific management was generally associated with improvement in industrial practice.

Emerging General Management

Although scientific management thinking dominated the last part of the nineteenth century and the early part of the twentieth, there were some early indications of a broader concept of management. In large part, these ideas were founded in scientific management and were extensions of the need to systematize and rationalize organizational performance. It is important to remember that scientific management was a response to the growth of organizations and the need to examine and refine organizational practices. Scientific management inspired other disciplines, such as public administration, office management, marketing, and accounting; encouraged an interest in the theory and practice of organizational design; provided a basis for the study of business policy; and spawned a philosophy of management.

THE IMPACT OF SCIENTIFIC MANAGEMENT ON OTHER DISCIPLINES

Stimulated by scientific management, other disciplines began to reflect the search for efficiency through science. William H. Leffingwell applied the principles of scientific management to office management.[59] The University of Chicago's Leonard D. White picked up where Morris Cooke left off and made numerous contributions to public administration. White was the first to teach public administration in the classroom and also pioneered in personnel management for governmental offices.[60]

---

58. Douglas M. Eichar, *Occupation and Class Consciousness in America* (New York: Greenwood, 1989), p. 47.

59. William Henry Leffingwell, *Scientific Office Management* (Chicago: A. W. Shaw, 1917).

60. Leonard D. White, *Introduction to the Study of Public Administration* (New York: Macmillan Co., 1926); idem, *The City Manager* (Chicago: University of Chicago Press, 1927).

In marketing, Arch W. Shaw, Ralph Starr Butler, Louis D. H. Weld, Paul T. Cherington, and Paul D. Converse were pioneering scientific study.[61]

Accounting saw the development of standard costing in Emerson and Taylor's use of the railroad system of accounts. Through the combination of ideas of economy in engineering and accounting techniques, management was first exposed to contingencies in financial planning and control. A vexing problem for management has always been the relationships among the volume of production, fixed costs, variable costs, sales, and profits. An engineer, Henry Hess, developed a "crossover" chart in 1903, which showed these variables and their relationships.[62] The position on the graph where total costs equaled total revenues was the crossover point, that is, the point where losses turned to profits. Walter Rautenstrauch, a professor at Columbia University, coined the phrase "break-even point" in 1922 to describe this same phenomenon.[63] John H. Williams, an accountant, conceived the idea of a "flexible budget," also in 1922, showing how management could plan and control at various levels of output.[64] Taken together, these tools provided means for management to forecast, control, and account for unforeseen developments.

James O. McKinsey (1889–1937) also sought to expand upon traditional notions of accounting and pioneered in the development of budgets as planning and controlling aids. F. W. Taylor had deplored the traditional postmortem uses of accounting, and McKinsey furthered this notion by viewing accounting information as an aid to management rather than as an end in itself. For McKinsey, the budget was not a set of figures but a way of placing responsibility and measuring performance.[65] As a former professor at the University of Chicago and later as a senior partner of McKinsey and Co., McKinsey was also influential in the early days of the American Management Association. The AMA was founded in 1923 as sort of an adult extension university for practicing managers. Its objective was to broaden the study of management to encompass not only production and personnel but also to include sales, financial, and other facets of managerial responsibilities. In brief, education for management

---

61. For the extent of the influence of scientific management on these pioneers, see Joseph C. Seibert, "Marketing's Role in Scientific Management," in Robert L. Clewett, ed., *Marketing's Role in Scientific Management* (Chicago: American Marketing Association, 1957), pp. 1–3; Robert Bartels, *The Development of Marketing Thought* (Homewood, Ill.: Richard D. Irwin, 1962), and 2nd ed., published as *The History of Marketing Thought* (Columbus, Ohio: Grid, Inc., 1976); and Paul D. Converse, *The Beginnings of Marketing Thought in the United States* (Austin: Bureau of Business Research, University of Texas, 1959).

62. Henry Hess, "Manufacturing: Capital, Costs, Profits, and Dividends," *Engineering Magazine* 26 (December 1903), pp. 367–379.

63. Walter Rautenstrauch, "The Budget as a Means of Industrial Control," *Chemical Metallurgical Engineering* 27 (1922), pp. 411–416.

64. John Howell Williams, *The Flexible Budget* (New York: McGraw-Hill, 1934).

65. James O. McKinsey, *Budgeting* (New York: Ronald Press, 1922); *Organization* (New York: Ronald Press, 1922); *Budgetary Control* (New York: Ronald Press, 1922); and *Managerial Accounting* (Chicago: University of Chicago Press, 1924). See also: William B. Wolf, *Management and Consulting: An Introduction to James O. McKinsey* (Ithaca, N.Y.: Cornell University Press, 1978).

responsibilities was beginning to shift from that of production shop management toward a broader view that encompassed allied areas.

EARLY ORGANIZATIONAL THEORY

During this era, the study of organizations was oriented primarily toward the production shop and focused on designing a formal structure of authority-activity relationships. The early factory system, based on the division of labor, required the coordination of efforts, and the grouping of activities into departments satisfied that need. As previously indicated, the early business firms were typically family owned and managed and had but a few employees. Thus the textile firms, for example, had a limited hierarchy of authority and relied on personal supervision to coordinate efforts. The first large-scale enterprise in the United States (and the world) was the railroads, for which Daniel McCallum visualized the first known organization chart in the form of a tree. Almost half a century later Joseph Slater Lewis pioneered in the same task for British industry.[66] Emerson followed the military line-staff tradition, but Taylor sought modification through his functional foremen. Although Taylor's functional foreman concept did not become widely accepted, there was widespread recognition among others that new organizational forms were necessary.

In 1909, Russell Robb (1864–1927) gave a series of lectures on organization at the newly formed Harvard Business School, in which he attempted a compromise between the old military style and the new conditions of industry. Robb anticipated modern contingency theorists when he noted that "all organizations will differ somewhat from each other, because the objects, the results that are sought, and the way these results must be attained, are different … there is no 'royal road,' no formula that, once learned, may be applied in all cases with the assurance that the result will be perfect harmony, efficiency, and economy, and a sure path to the main purpose in view."[67] Thus the goals sought differed, as did the means (today we might say "strategy") to attain those goals, resulting in different organizational structures and no one way to organize. From this premise Robb developed his thesis that the objectives of business differed from those of the military and therefore the organizational emphasis had to differ. Much could be learned from the military framework of fixing responsibility and authority, clearly defining duties and channels of communication, and providing for order and discipline. However, the military stressed control and discipline as essential to its objectives to an extent not necessary in industry. The industrial organization, built on an extensive division of labor, needed to provide for coordination of efforts to a greater extent than did the military. Success in industry was not based on obedience, but on economy of effort; therefore, the industrial organization had to be different. More stress had to be placed on

---

66. Joseph Slater Lewis, *The Commercial Organization of Factories* (London: Spon Books, 1896).

67. Russell Robb, *Lectures on Organization* (privately printed, 1910), pp. 3, 14. Further insights into Robb's life and writings may be found in Edmund R. Gray and Hyler I. Bracey, "Russell Robb: Management Pioneer," *SAM Advanced Management Journal* 35 (April 1970), pp. 71–76.

worker and manager selection and training, processes had to be arranged for economy, and the manager had to be aware that a "great factor in organization is 'system,' the mechanism of the whole."[68]

Robb's lectures were truly remarkable for the times. He was heavily influenced by scientific management and the need for systematization, but he looked beyond that to see the organization as a whole. Although organizations differed, there were still general principles: "structure, lines of authority, responsibility, division of labor, system, discipline; accounting, records, and statistics; esprit de corps, cooperation, and team play."[69] As business organizations grew beyond the entrepreneurial stage where owners managed and managers owned, they discovered the need for line and staff, which was offered in different forms by Taylor and Emerson, and the need to see the organization as a whole, as Robb envisioned it. While these thoughts were developing, another set of ideas emerged that would lead to multidivisional organizations.

SCIENTIFIC MANAGEMENT AT DU PONT AND GENERAL MOTORS

No story is more fascinating to business historians than the growth of giant enterprise. Mingled into the development of two giants, Du Pont and General Motors, are the ideas of scientific management. One of Frederick Taylor's strongest suits lay in cost accounting and control techniques for manufacturing, and he installed such a system at the Steel Motor Company, which later found its way to the Du Pont Powder Company (see Chapter 7).

In 1902, Coleman, Pierre, and Alfred I. du Pont bought control of the Du Pont Powder Company from their cousins for $12 million in thirty-year notes—no cash—and subsequently molded this company into an industrial giant. The du Ponts, and especially Pierre as president, sought to broaden Taylor's cost concepts to include a measure of overall performance rather than just manufacturing efficiency. As early as 1903, the Du Pont Powder Company inaugurated "return on investment" as a measure of organizational performance, apparently the first use of this important managerial tool.[70] It is Pierre who is credited with implementing the financial, operational, and managerial techniques necessary to turn the Du Pont Company into an effective organization. Pierre learned from Taylor and Carnegie (who had learned McCallum's methods while working on the Pennsylvania Railroad).[71] One of Pierre du Pont's key people was Hamilton McFarland Barksdale, the firm's general manager, who stressed the human factor and was using psychological tests for

---

68. Robb, *Lectures on Organization*, p. 173.

69. *Ibid.*, p. 175.

70. H. Thomas Johnson, "Management Accounting in an Early Integrated Industry: E. I. Du Pont de Nemours Powder Company, 1903–1912," *Business History Review* 49 (Summer 1975), p. 189.

71. Alfred D. Chandler, Jr., and Stephen Salsbury, *Pierre S. du Pont and the Making of the Modern Corporation* (New York: Harper and Row, 1971), p. xxi.

personnel selection in 1910. He also pioneered in separating the line and staff functions, in developing uniform objectives and policies for the company, in the concept of decentralization of authority, and in the development of managerial talent.[72]

Another key figure was Barksdale's cousin, Donaldson Brown (1885–1965). Brown's contribution was to refine the concept of return on investment into a device for measuring and comparing the performance of various departments (rather than just measuring overall return on investment for the firm). Brown developed the formula $R = T \times P$, where R represented the rate of return on capital invested in each department, T stood for the rate of turnover of invested capital, and P for the percentage of profit on sales.[73] Brown also developed the famous Du Pont Chart System, which endures yet today, and used his return-on-investment (ROI) formula to portray the relative performance of various departments, to forecast, and to control.

The organizational legacy of Du Pont carried over to the emerging General Motors Corporation. William C. Durant conceived the idea of creating General Motors from an amalgam of motorcar and parts producers. The union was unwieldy, and General Motors was plucked from the brink of financial disaster by an infusion of du Pont money in 1920. Durant resigned, and Pierre came out of semiretirement to become president of General Motors. Pierre made at least two key personnel decisions: one was to bring Donaldson Brown to General Motors; the other was to handpick a successor to himself as president in 1923, Alfred P. Sloan, Jr. (1875–1966). Sloan created the concept of decentralized administration and operations, with centralized control and review. By decentralizing operations and centrally coordinating control, the separate parts of General Motors could work toward a common end. Establishment of this multidivisional ("M form") structure enabled organizational units to grow larger without the encumbrance of organizing by function.[74] The concept of decentralization into product divisions made use of Brown's ROI formula. Each division or unit, given a certain amount of resource investment, could then have its performance measured and controlled by judging the rate of return on investment. The result was a correlation between efforts expended and results obtained that enabled central management to judge and compare the effectiveness of each product division.

From Taylor, Pierre du Pont learned the necessity of a rational basis for organizational and managerial control. He used these techniques to build Du Pont, applied them to General Motors, and, through Sloan, used them to enable the overtaking of

---

72. Ernest Dale, *The Great Organizers* (New York: McGraw-Hill, 1960). See also Ernest Dale and Charles Meloy, "Hamilton McFarland Barksdale and the Du Pont Contributions to Scientific Management," *Business History Review* 36 (Summer 1962), pp. 127–152.

73. Donaldson Brown, *Some Reminiscences of an Industrialist* (privately printed, n.d.), pp. 26–28.

74. The General Motors story is a classic and is examined by, to name only a few: Alfred D. Chandler, Jr., ed., *Giant Enterprise* (New York: Harcourt Brace Jovanovich, 1964); Peter Drucker, *The Concept of the Corporation* (New York: John Day, 1946); and Alfred P. Sloan, Jr., *My Years with General Motors* (New York: Doubleday, 1963).

the Ford Motor Company. Pierre du Pont, Barksdale, Brown, and Sloan were the major figures in creating the concept as well as the reality of the modern corporation.

BUSINESS POLICY AND PHILOSOPHY

Although the notion of general management was beginning, it remained in the shadow of scientific management for some time. As the engineers lost interest in management and turned their attention to technical matters, the idea of collegiate schools of business began to spread rapidly. Economics, once called moral philosophy and later political economy, was the womb that nurtured the emerging business subjects. Thus Henry Towne's call for the "engineer as an economist" found fulfillment not in the ASME but in some of the schools of business whose rapid growth resulted in the formation of the Association of Collegiate Schools of Business (ACSB; the present-day American Assembly of Collegiate Schools of Business) in 1916. By 1925, the ACSB had thirty-eight members offering such courses as accounting, economics, finance, marketing, commercial law, transportation, statistics, physical environment, social control and ethics, production, personnel, and labor.[75]

Although education for business was growing rapidly in the first quarter of the twentieth century, the evidence indicates that the early curricula were oriented toward specialized business functions (for example, production, marketing, personnel, finance, accounting), and there was little evidence of integration from a general management viewpoint. The exception was Arch W. Shaw, a prominent Chicago business leader and editor and publisher of *System,* a leading periodical about improving managerial practices through systems and scientific management. In 1908, Shaw lectured at Northwestern University's new School of Commerce, and in 1910 he lectured at Harvard University's Graduate School of Business Administration. There he became familiar with the problem method of instruction, which had grown out of the case method of teaching law developed in the 1870s by Christopher Langdell of Harvard's School of Law. For the academic year 1911–1912, Shaw began a course in business policy at Harvard based on the problem, or case, method. The purpose of the course was "to deal with top management problems, and it aimed also at integrating subjects that the students had studied in their first year."[76] Shaw brought in business executives who described a problem confronting their organization at that time; the students were then required to discuss, analyze, and prepare reports, which were presented to the business leader at a subsequent meeting. Despite the pioneering work of Shaw, only two schools (Harvard and the University of Michigan) required the study of business policy in 1925, and not until 1959 did this subject become required in accredited schools of business as a capstone to integrate the business functions from the perspective of top management.

---

75. Leon C. Marshall, ed., *The Collegiate School of Business* (Chicago: University of Chicago Press, 1928), especially ch. 3.

76. Melvin T. Copeland, "The Genesis of the Case Method in Business Instruction," in M. P. McNair, ed., *The Case Method at the Harvard Business School* (New York: McGraw-Hill, 1954), p. 26.

More in the mainstream of management thought during the scientific management era was the work of Alexander Hamilton Church (1866–1936). Church began his career in Great Britain, became a consultant in cost accounting systems, and moved to the United States at the turn of the century. Tutored by Joseph Slater Lewis (1852–1901), one of Great Britain's management pioneers, Church sought a broader approach to the study of management than he saw in Taylor.[77] He became interested in the larger view of management after his work in the allocation of overhead costs, that is, those costs (such as management salaries) that were difficult to attribute to any one product. For Church, every industrial undertaking consisted of two elements: (1) the determinative element, which fixed the manufacturing and distribution policies of the firm; and (2) the administrative element, which took the policy as determined and gave it practical expression through buying, manufacturing, and selling.[78] Placed in the terminology of modern management, Church was describing *policy formulation* (the determinative element) and *implementation*.[79] In making these two elements operational, the manager used two fundamental "instruments": analysis, consisting of cost accounting, time and motion study, routing, machine layout, and planning; and synthesis, combining workers, functions, machines, and all activities effectively to achieve some useful result. In brief, managers analyzed to find better ways and then *coordinated* (synthesized) activities.

In Church's view, Taylor's ideas were analytical and formed a restricted view of the task of management. Management should be concerned with the total efficiency of the firm. In a manufacturing enterprise, management had five organic functions: *design*, which was essentially product design and production planning; *equipment*, choosing and installing the proper machinery; *control*, which specified duties and initiated and coordinated work; *comparison*, measuring and comparing the results attained with the standards of performance; and *operation*, which transformed the raw materials into the desired product.[80]

Although Church began with some ideas about general management, policy formulation, and implementation, his organic functions pulled him back to the manufacturing enterprise. Other organizations, according to Church, would have different organic functions. Church stopped short of the general management notions of Henri Fayol, but nevertheless broadened the views of Taylor and provided some early insights into policy formulation and implementation.

Scientific management also inspired an early philosophy of management. Taylor's philosophy was reflected in his "mental revolution," the fusing of labor and management's interests into a mutually rewarding whole. However, an Englishman,

---

77. Joseph A. Litterer, "Alexander Hamilton Church and the Development of Modern Management," *Business History Review* 35 (Summer 1961), p. 214.

78. Alexander H. Church, *The Science and Practice of Management* (New York: Engineering Magazine, 1914), pp. 1–2.

79. Mariann Jelinek, "Toward Systematic Management: Alexander Hamilton Church," *Business History Review* 54 (Spring 1980), p. 72.

80. Church, *Science and Practice of Management*, pp. 37–88.

Oliver Sheldon (1894–1951), was the first to lay claim to developing an explicit philosophy of management. Sheldon began and ended his business career with Rowntree & Company, Ltd., a British chocolate-manufacturing company headed by B. S. Rowntree (1871–1954). Sheldon was undoubtedly familiar with H. L. Gantt and his notion that business had a larger responsibility of service to society. Sheldon stated his own rationale for a philosophy: "we should devise a philosophy of management, a code of principles, scientifically determined and generally accepted, to act as a guide, by reason of its foundation upon ultimate things, for the daily practice of the profession."[81]

Adoption of isolated principles was not adequate to Sheldon's thesis; he sought a body of managers who would develop common motives, common ends, a common creed, and a common fund of knowledge. The basic premise of his philosophy, like that of Gantt, was service to the community:

> Industry exists to provide the commodities and services which are necessary for the good life of the community, in whatever volume they are required. These commodities and services must be furnished at the lowest prices compatible with an adequate standard of quality, and distributed in such a way as directly or indirectly to promote the highest ends of the community.[82]

This combination of the efficiency values of scientific management with the ethics of service to the community was the responsibility of each manager. Each manager must adopt three principles: (1) "the policies, conditions, and methods of industry shall conduce to communal well-being"; (2) "management shall endeavor to interpret the highest moral sanction of the community as a whole" in applying social justice to industrial practice; and (3) "management shall take the initiative…in raising the general ethical standard and conception of social justice."[83] In applying these principles, management must maintain industry on an economic basis and consider both human *and* technical efficiency. This duality of efficiency was based on scientific methods of work analysis and development of human potential to the greatest extent possible. In Sheldon's philosophy, the economic basis of service, the dual emphasis on human and technical efficiency, and the responsibility of management to provide social justice would all lead to a "science of industrial management" of benefit to all parties. Management, through the application of science in work and cognizant of its responsibility for justice, served by being both technically and humanly efficient.

---

81. Oliver Sheldon, *The Philosophy of Management* (London: Sir Isaac Pitman and Sons, 1923), p. 283.

82. *Ibid.*, p. 284.

83. *Ibid.*

Summary

Scientific management was a significant force in (1) the formal study of management; (2) the practice of management in the United States, Great Britain, continental Europe, Japan, and the Soviet Union; (3) preparation of the way for a broadening of the movement beyond shop management into other disciplines; (4) the study of organizations; and (5) the development of business policy and a philosophy of management. Taylor provided an impetus, but it was the efforts of many that led to the spreading influence of scientific management. In practice, scientific management did not always run true to its ideals: organized labor resisted it as a threat to its bargaining position; different countries adapted and sometimes perverted it by using it as a means to achieve national goals; and manufacturers often grasped the techniques and forgot the philosophy. Yet scientific management was not a failure. Growing out of the need to systematize business practices, it gave a voice to efficiency and rationality, purpose to practice, and content to theory. Its youth was robust, its maturity was fruitful, and it left behind intellectual children throughout the world who still write about, study, and practice its teachings. Scientific management reflected the spirit of its times and prepared the way for subsequent developments.

CHAPTER 12

Scientific Management in Retrospect

Scientific management must be understood within the context of its times by examining the forces that created it as an extension of systematic management and made it the spirit of that era. After Taylor's death, scientific management continued to evolve as individuals and ideas came forth in an ever-changing cultural environment. Interacting to form a giant web of currents and eddies of change, very substantial external forces shaped the emergence, course, and progress of the scientific management movement. In examining the cultural environment of scientific management, these economic, technological, social, and political forces are separated for expository purposes, although in reality they were interactive and mutually reinforcing. Within this framework, the whys and wherefores of Frederick W. Taylor and his intellectual heirs form a more coherent picture.

THE ECONOMIC ENVIRONMENT: FROM THE FARM TO THE FACTORY

In 1800, 90 percent of the U.S. population drew its sustenance from agriculture; by 1900, the proportion was 33 percent, and by 1929, 20 percent. The transformation from an agrarian to an industrial nation placed the United States at the world's helm in output of products and services, in wages, and in the standard of living of its citizens. The typical citizen who awakened on the morning of January 1, 1900, saw little change between the old and the new centuries. Yet the change was there, and the United States had moved into a new era. The accumulation of resources, though moving at varying speeds in various industries, was culminating in a new phase.

THE RATIONALIZATION OF RESOURCE UTILIZATION

Chandler noted that phase I (the resource accumulation phase of industrial growth) was complete in the United States by the beginning of World War I. Industrial growth in the latter part of the nineteenth century had created the giant enterprise, and in the first two decades of the twentieth century it was the task of the salaried managers to design and implement the appropriate managerial and organizational structures. The large corporation needed a formal structure of relationships between the firm's activities and personnel and also required a formalization of administrative procedures. Culmination of the resource accumulation phase meant that the typical corporation of the early twentieth century was faced with basically two problems: the need to reduce unit costs by improving production techniques and processes; and the need to facilitate planning, coordination, and appraisal of performance.[1]

This set the stage for phase II, the rationalization of resource utilization in industry. The work of Taylor and other scientific management writers was focused on meeting the industrial needs of the economic environment with respect to rationalizing resource utilization. The rational, scientific approach to problem solving was the foundation of scientific management. Time and motion study set standards, intended to reduce fatigue, and sought to eliminate wasted motions; it provided a logical approach to the design of work rather than using whimsical or rule-of-thumb methods. The "first-class man" and the scientific selection of personnel were attempts to provide a better match between people's abilities and job requirements. Piece-rate incentives sought to boost production and reduce per-unit labor costs while paying higher wages. The functional foremen were to bring specialized, expert advice and leadership; the separation of planning and doing was a concept designed to improve the planning of work; and the exception principle sought to focus managerial attention on critical performance problems. Even Taylor's philosophy of a mental revolution was an attempt to reduce friction and rationally bring together the interests of labor and management into a mutually rewarding whole. This mutuality of interests was in tune with the U.S. economic climate. A leading economist, Henry C. Carey (1793–1879), brought the optimism of Adam Smith to U.S. economic thought. Where David Ricardo, Karl Marx, and Thomas Malthus saw gloom and despair, Carey felt that the free development of a capitalistic society led to reconciliation and a harmony of interests.[2] Carey's reasoning antedated and may have influenced Taylor's mental revolution.

Those who came in Taylor's wake also followed the rationalization-of-resource-utilization theme. The Gilbreths sought economy of motion and waste reduction, and their systems books were detailed how-to-do-it procedures manuals. Gantt's

---

1. A. D. Chandler, Jr., *Strategy and Structure* (Cambridge, Mass.: MIT Press, 1962), pp. 386–390.

2. John Fred Bell, *A History of Economic Thought* (New York: Ronald Press, 1967), pp. 316–320.

work provided visual aids for scheduling, routing, dispatching, and controlling work. Carl Barth, Morris Cooke, and the others who espoused the gospel of efficiency all focused on basically this same problem of efficiency in production. Harrington Emerson, among others, wrote of efficiency through organization, a matter of some consequence to industrialists of that period. Stated succinctly, the economic milieu of the era created and accounted for the appeal of Taylor and scientific management. In summary, scientific management was a product of its environment in the sense that it grew out of the pressing needs of industry for efficiency. Resources were accumulated, phase I completed, and rationalization of resource utilization (phase II) became important.

MANAGEMENT AND THE WORKER

America was a very diverse nation during this period, in contrast with the ethnically homogenous industrial nations of Britain, France, Germany, Italy, and Japan. One exception was London, where 6 percent of its population in 1890 came from outside the British Isles. In contrast, however, immigrants or children of immigrants comprised 80 percent of New York's citizenry, 87 percent of Chicago's, and 84 percent of Milwaukee's and Detroit's. By 1900, there were more people of Italian ancestry in New York than in any Italian city except Rome; more of Polish descent in Chicago than in Warsaw; and by 1920 more Irish people had immigrated to the United States than the total remaining in Ireland at that time.[3] These individuals and families were responding to the message inscribed on the Statue of Liberty in New York harbor: "Give me your tired, your poor, your huddled masses yearning to breathe free ... I lift my lamp beside the golden door."[4]

In 1910, 48 percent of the workers in mining, 31.9 percent in manufacturing, and 26.3 percent in transportation were foreign born.[5] In 1913, Ford Motor's Highland Park (Michigan) plant had a work force of 71 percent foreign-born workers from twenty-two different national groups. Southern and eastern Europeans were the majority and included (in rank order from high to low percentages) Poles, Russians, Romanians, Italians and Sicilians, Austro-Hungarians, and Germans.[6] Few of these spoke English, making communication difficult for supervisors and coworkers. To lessen the problem, Ford Motor started an "English School" to find a common ground for diverse work group members to be able to communicate. The population and the workforce during this time was a heterogeneous one, perhaps with limited English

---

3. Thomas K. McCraw, "American Capitalism," in Thomas K. McCraw, ed., *Creating Modern Capitalism* (Cambridge, Mass.: Harvard University Press, 1997), p. 307.

4. Inscription by Emma Lazarus, November 2, 1883.

5. Sumner H. Slichter, "The Current Labor Policies of American Industries," *The Quarterly Journal of Economics* 3 (May 1929), p. 394.

6. Daniel A. Wren and Ronald G. Greenwood, *Management Innovators: The People and Ideas That Have Shaped Modern Business* (New York: Oxford University Press, 1998), p. 46.

skills, and with relatively little education. Recruiting, selecting, training, and monitoring the performance of these individuals presented a challenge to management. The nature of this workforce suggests why so much emphasis was placed on developing systems and procedures, standardizing tools and work methods, and the increased reliance on personnel departments as staff to assist managers.

Contrary to what might be expected in economic theory, this largely immigrant influx of labor did not drive down wages. As noted earlier, real wages (that is, purchasing power) doubled between 1865 and 1890; from 1890 to 1921, the annual compound increase in real wages was 1.6 percent, enabling another doubling. In addition to gaining in terms of real wages, the hours of labor were starting to decrease: in 1890 the average industrial work week was sixty hours; in 1910, fifty-five hours, and in 1920, fifty hours.[7] Life expectancy also increased during this period of industrial growth. For a male born in Massachusetts in 1855, the life expectancy was 38.7 years, and 40.9 years for a female. By 1929, a male's life expectancy had increased to 58.1 and a female's to 61.4 years.[8] Taylor's hope of a mental revolution, a mutuality of interests between labor and management, found new life in modern times as a mutual gains strategy:

> Taylor's claim that his system of management would benefit both worker and employer was accompanied by a call for the partners in production to work together to enhance the output of the firm. The pursuit of mutual benefits and cooperation as regards the enhancement of production amounts to a mutual-gains approach to industrial relations as the notion understood by analysts such as … Kochan and Osterman. That Taylor advanced a mutual-gains program is seldom recognized.…[9]

The scientific management era improved the condition of workers through higher real wages, increased longevity, and the opportunity to improve their skill levels. The "lamp beside the golden door" fulfilled its promises.

The new economics of mass production demanded an even sharper focus on the development of management. Large accumulations of resources were requisite to meet the demands of mass markets and mass distribution. As the industrial giants grew, the individuals who built the empires were passing from the helm and being replaced by a new breed of salaried managers. The personalized, informal structures of the family business yielded to the logic of size in industrial administration. No longer could owner-entrepreneurs depend on their own personal supervision. Technology demanded specialized knowledge, and staff departments were added to

---

7. Ross M. Robertson, *History of the American Economy,* 3rd ed. (New York: Harcourt Brace Jovanovich, 1973), pp. 379–380.

8. Edgar W. Martin, *The Standard of Living in 1860* (Chicago: Chicago University Press, 1942), p. 220.

9. Chris Nyland, "Taylorism and the Mutual-Gains Strategy," *Industrial Relations* 37 (October 1998), p. 521. See also Thomas A. Kochan and Paul Osterman, *The Mutual Gains Enterprise* (Boston: Harvard Business School Press, 1994).

handle personnel, engineering, production, purchasing, legal affairs, and other functional activities. Melman found that between 1899 and 1929 the percent of employees in management relative to those in production almost doubled (9.9 percent in 1899 to 18.5 percent in 1929); and between 1929 and 1947 the increase was from 18.5 percent to 22.2 percent. According to Melman, the only significant factor related to this growth of managerial vis-à-vis production employees was "the addition of new functions carried out by the [managerial] personnel ... [because of] the addition of specially designated persons or departments."[10] In short, this growth of staff specialists and other managers in the hierarchy reflected the need to perform the tasks required in the emerging large-scale enterprise of the twentieth century. The growth of a managerial hierarchy was necessary to plan, organize, lead, coordinate, and control the organizations' input-throughput-output system. The economics of mass production and mass distribution required a fund of managerial talent, and one familiar with the latest methods and the most current thinking in the management of organizations.

As previously indicated, scientific management was associated with growth and efficiency and was more likely to be used in labor- rather than capital-intensive industries. Improved work methods, reduced fatigue, accurate work standards, better personnel selection, incentive payment plans, and other scientific management techniques would have less impact in a capital-intensive industry where the most advanced technology leads to the greatest gains. One set of statistics indicates that manufacturing output per worker hour went from an index number of 21.2 in 1890 to 52.0 in 1929 (1958 = 100).[11] Another study, taking sort of a reverse view, found that the number of worker hours input per unit of output fell from an index number of 74 in 1919 to 42 in 1929 (1899 = 100), for a gain in efficiency of 43 percent.[12] Regardless of the approach, the result was still increased productivity. One historian attributed this increase in productivity during this period to "(1) the methods of mass production, (2) Taylorism, and (3) better and cheaper sources of power."[13]

President Calvin Coolidge, in a frequently misquoted speech, capsulized the era: "After all, the chief business of the American people is business. They are concerned with producing, buying, selling, investing, and prospering in the world ... wealth is a product of industry, ambition, character, and untiring effort.... So long as wealth

---

10. Seymour Melman, "The Rise of Administrative Overhead in the Manufacturing Industries of the United States, 1899–1947," *Oxford Economic Papers* 3 (January 1951), pp. 66–68, 91. Melman used the U.S. Census of Manufactures' definition of management as salaried employees (i.e., line and staff) and production as wage earners.

11. U.S. Dept. of Commerce, Bureau of the Census, *Historical Statistics of the United States: Colonial Times to 1970* (Washington, D.C.: U.S. Government Printing Office, 1975), pt. 1, p. 162.

12. Solomon Fabricant, *Labor Savings in American Industry: 1899–1939* (New York: National Bureau for Economic Research, 1945), pp. 43–46, 50.

13. George Soule, *Prosperity Decade: From War to Depression* (New York: Holt, Rinehart and Winston, 1947), pp. 127–128. Soule did not rank nor assign any weights to the influence of these three factors.

is made the means and not the end, we need not greatly fear it."[14] Economically, the United States came of age in this period. More complex organizational and hierarchical managerial structures were required to cope with the economics of mass production and mass distribution. Resource usage had to be rationalized, and scientific management was the conventional wisdom that could handle the task. It was an age of concern for economic efficiency.

TECHNOLOGY: OPENING NEW HORIZONS

In Chapter 6 we saw how developments in transportation and communication spurred the growth of enterprise. New firms and industries were forming and their growth and development led to a managerial hierarchy and for the need to improve the technologies of manufacturing and distributing their products. A survey of *Fortune* 500 companies in 1994 found that 247 of them had their beginnings during this period we are studying, roughly 1880 to 1929.[15] Although their original names might have been different, these were the start-ups for such modern firms as Eastman Kodak, Coca-Cola, Sears, General Electric, Pepsico, Goodyear, Ford Motor, General Motors, IBM, Boeing, Walt Disney, Delta Airlines, and so on. Many of these represented new industries, such as photographic film, automobiles, and aircraft.

New technologies enabled both old and new firms to compete more successfully. In steel, the Bessemer process would yield to the open hearth; in petroleum, developments in "cracking" oil molecules during refining enabled richer fuels for automobiles and aircraft. Orville Wright would never have flown at Kitty Hawk, North Carolina, in 1903 if the internal combustion engine had not been developed. Du Pont's research led to discoveries in synthetic materials, such as rayon. Charles F. Kettering removed the dangerous task of starting an internal combustion engine by a hand crank when he developed an electric self-starter for automobiles. Lee De Forest and Guglielmo Marconi pioneered the vacuum tube and wireless telephony, such as the radio. In some cases the improvements came by creating paths between the seas: the Suez Canal (1869) sped trade between Europe and Asia; the Panama Canal (1914) connected the Atlantic and Pacific Oceans. The developments of this time period were as astounding to our ancestors as those of today are to us.

Energy developments of the period also deserve mention. Coal was the primary source of energy for the steam-driven wheels of industry. Although coal continued to dominate, new discoveries of petroleum deposits were soon to reshape the energy base. Electrical energy also entered the scene. Although not invented in the usual sense, the principles of electricity were applied to generate a new power source for

---

14. Calvin Coolidge, "The Press under a Free Government," address before the American Society of Newspaper Editors, Washington, D.C., January 17, 1925; reprinted in Calvin Coolidge, *Foundations of the Republic: Speeches and Addresses* (New York: Charles Scribner's Sons, 1926), pp. 187–188.

15. Harris Corporation, "Founding Dates of the 1994 *Fortune* 500 U.S. Companies," *Business History Review* 70 (Spring 1996), pp. 77–84.

factory gears and home lights and appliances. Edison's central power plant in New York City was built in 1882. By 1920 one-third of the nation's industrial power came from electricity and half the urban homes had electricity. In the rural areas, 98 percent of the homes still relied on kerosene lamps and candles, but not for long.

The automobile was another technological advancement that brought about substantial economic and social change during this period. A four-cycle, internal combustion engine perfected by the German mechanic Nicholas August Otto was first shown at the Paris Exposition in 1869, patented in 1877, and soon became a part of a vehicle originally called the horseless carriage. The automobile gave people a new mobility, a freedom of movement that led to decentralization of the cities into suburban living and posed a threat to older, established forms of transportation. Automobile manufacturing began in small shops and experiments were made with electric (battery), steam, and internal combustion engines. In 1900, for example, the automobile industry produced 4,192 cars; of these, 1,681 were steam powered, 1,575 were electric, and 936 were gasoline powered. Previously, we saw how Carl Barth used scientific management to improve production at the Franklin Motor Car Company. In that case, and others, the parts were brought to an assembly platform where the automobile would be assembled. This process was labor intensive and relatively slow. Henry Ford, like other manufacturers, used this stationary assembly process, and Ford Motor historians have suggested that Ford's engineers "had doubtlessly caught some of Taylor's ideas...[and] kept in touch with the ideas of men like Taylor."[16] Nelson's study of the twenty-nine installations of scientific management from 1901 to 1917 by Taylor and his followers, however, does not include Ford Motor Company (but does include Barth's work at Franklin).[17] This suggests that Ford engineers may have been familiar with scientific management, but no work at Ford Motor Company was by Taylor, nor Gilbreth, nor Barth, nor anyone closely connected to scientific management. When interviewed by contemporaries, Henry Ford denied "any systematic theory or organization or administration, or any dependence on scientific management."[18] It would be difficult to make a connection between the practices at Ford Motor and scientific management.

The idea of bringing the chassis to the worker, not vice versa, was an idea that evolved slowly. The initial effort was the fly-wheel magneto, assembled as it moved on a conveyor by the workers. Previously, an employee did the entire assembly, averaging about twenty minutes per assembly, or thirty-five to forty magnetos in nine hours by one worker. After changeover to a moving belt, the assembly was divided into twenty-nine operations performed by twenty-nine workers spaced along the belt. The average assembly time dropped to thirteen minutes per magneto, then to seven minutes, and finally to five minutes.

---

16. Allan Nevins and Frank E. Hill, *Ford* (New York: Scribner's, 1954), p. 468, 474.

17. Daniel Nelson, "Scientific Management, Systematic Management, and Labor, 1880–1915," *Business History Review* 48 (Winter 1974), pp. 489–490.

18. Horace L. Arnold and Fay L. Faurote, *Ford Methods and Ford Shops* (New York: Engineering Magazine, 1915), p.20.

Ford was initially skeptical but the results were proof that the conveyor line worked. Next came the motor, and then the transmission, all with successful results. By 1913, three feeder lines (magneto, motor, transmission) could produce more subassemblies than the final assembly could tolerate. The solution was a motorized capstan that dragged a line of chassis along the floor, and parts were added as it flowed. Ford, Charles Sorenson, and their associates in the shop, W. C. Klann, Clarence W. Avery, James O'Connor, and P. E. Martin, created the moving assembly line for mass production.[19]

The results were impressive: in 1910 (pre-assembly line), 2,773 workers produced 18,664 autos (6.73 per worker); in 1914 (post-assembly line), 248,307 autos were produced by 12,880 workers (19.28 per worker). Prices were driven downward as productivity increased: in 1910 a fully equipped Model T touring car was priced at $950; in 1914, $490; and in 1916, $360; a Model T roadster was priced at $900 in 1910, $269 in 1924.

Scientific management was not applied on the assembly line at Ford. Jobs were timed to match the speed of the conveyor, and Frank Gilbreth complained about the poor job design (see Chapter 8). Scientific management and Henry Ford and his associates approached work design quite differently. For example, a film of Frank Gilbreth's work shows an employee trimming the edges of a bar of soap that was formed in a mold, polishing the soap, wrapping, and placing the soap bars in a box,[20] a very labor-intensive task that later manufacturers would seek to automate. Further, Taylor's pig-iron loading and shoveling studies would not have impressed Henry Ford. Ford's engineers developed conveyor belts for moving materials, such as sand and coal, and hoists for lifting heavy objects and relocating them. Scientific management focused on the work shop and labor-intensive activities; beyond this manufacturing stage, technology would use various power sources and machinery to replace the laborious monotonous tasks.

Henry Ford and his associates divided labor and standardized parts and transformed these old ideas into a logic of mass production on an assembly-line basis, which could be called the Second Industrial Revolution. Mass production yielded cost savings that in turn were passed on to the consumer via lower prices. Using lowered product prices to expand the market and the expanded market to achieve production savings, Ford personified Adam Smith's idea that the market was the only force limiting the division of labor. Ford's startling announcement in 1914 of a $5 a day minimum wage operated on two premises: that the best workers could be attracted and retained, and that workers needed the wherewithal to buy industry's output. Although Ford lost his domination of the automobile industry as consumer preferences changed and General Motors recognized that different product lines

---

19. Jay H. Heizer, "Determining Responsibility for Development of the Moving Assembly Line," *Journal of Management History* 4 (1998), pp. 94–103. See also David A. Hounshell, *From the American System to Mass Production, 1800–1932* (Baltimore: Johns Hopkins University Press, 1984), pp. 249–253.

20. *The Quest of the Best Way: The Original Films of Frank B. Gilbreth,* Harry W. Bass Business History Collection, University of Oklahoma.

would fit different market segments, his introduction of the logic of mass production had a lasting impact on U.S. thought.

Information technology in the spirit of Henry Poor's definition of information as "recorded communication" was also evolving. Partnerships and sole proprietorships could rely on informal communication, account books, and face-to-face exchanges to keep track of their business affairs. As the managerial hierarchy was extended with the growth of enterprise, this became more difficult and we see a revolution in the ways organizations gathered, recorded, and maintained information about business activities.[21] Decision making, coordination, and monitoring performance required more formally developed systems.

Christopher Latham Sholes' typewriter provided a means of communication in a more legible fashion than hand writing. Sholes also left us with the standard QWERTY keyboard when he de-engineered it to prevent speedy typing that often jammed the type face bars. In 1936, August Dvorak used time and motion study to rearrange the keyboard for greater efficiency. Alas, his innovative change met enduring resistance. Carbon paper was developed for copies made during typing; this was a lot less expensive than photocopying, which was accomplished with a camera and light-sensitive paper at a cost of ninety-eight cents per copy in 1911.[22] Vertical file cabinets facilitated arranging correspondence and records. The A. B. Dick Company bought the rights to Thomas Edison's "multiplying letters" device and turned it into a mimeograph machine that could print many copies from a typed stencil. Sir Isaac Pitman's method of taking "shorthand" notes enabled secretaries to take dictation and then polish it by typing. Pneumatic tubes were designed and installed in factories and retail stores to send money, receipts, and other papers from floor to floor and between departments. Long before Nike, the first "whoosh" was the sound of information transmitted via the pneumatic tube.

Another advancement was developing graphical means of displaying data. Gantt's chart and the Du Pont chart system were mentioned previously. Brinton collected and published numerous graphic methods for illustrating statistical facts.[23] He published two of Gantt's earliest charts; portrayed Hollerith's punched-card machine for recording, tabulating, and printing data; and criticized corporate annual reports for their poor job of informing shareholders. Brinton, and others such as Gantt, recognized the importance of information as firms grew beyond informal means of communicating. This revolution in information technology had an unintended effect: it shifted clerical work from males to females, and created office work as an alternative to the factory for females.[24]

---

21. For developments in the Illinois Central Railroad, Scoville Manufacturing Company, and Du Pont, see JoAnne Yates, *Control through Communication: The Rise of System in American Management* (Baltimore: Johns Hopkins University Press, 1989).

22. Yates, p. 54.

23. Willard C. Brinton, *Graphic Methods for Presenting Facts* (New York: Engineering Magazine, 1914).

24. Elyce J. Rotella, "The Transformation of the American Office: Changes in Employment and Technology," *Journal of Economic History* 41 (March 1981), pp. 51–57.

In brief, advancing technology was reshaping the nature of work by increasing number of skilled and semi-skilled workers, creating alternative career paths for females, substituting machinery and capital intensity for labor intensity, and providing improved means for material handling. The new horizons were at work and in transport by air and auto.

THE SOCIAL ENVIRONMENT: FROM ACHIEVEMENT TO AFFILIATION

Between the Civil War and 1900, Horatio Alger, Jr., wrote more than one hundred books for boys with such piquant titles as *Bound to Rise, Luck and Pluck, Sink or Swim,* and *Tom, the Bootblack.* At least twenty million copies were sold, and "Horatio Alger" became synonymous with a success story.[25] The typical plot involved a young but poor hero, beset by the unscrupulous on all sides, who worked his way to wealth by the virtues of diligence, honesty, perseverance, and thrift. Quite often he was befriended by a benevolent benefactor who recognized his latent talent for capital accumulation and aided him in the climb to the pinnacle of the financial world. The hero of Alger's books was a personification of McClelland's "high achiever" and Riesman's "inner-directed" individual, who had a personal gyroscope that enabled unerring progress on the path to success.[26] The hero exhibited the self-control, hard work, and frugality of the Protestant ethic and of Ben Franklin's Poor Richard. He learned in the school of hard knocks; no formal schooling could prepare him for success in business. Charles M. Schwab, a protégé of Andrew Carnegie, stated the case:

> If the college man thinks that his education gives him a higher social status, he is riding for a fall. Some college men ... have pride in their mental attainments that is almost arrogance. Employers find it difficult to control, guide, and train such men. Their spirit of superiority bars the path of progress.[27]

Elbert Hubbard sketched the traits of the worker desired by industry in "A Message to Garcia." In this story, Rowan was asked to carry a message from the president of the United States to the insurgent Cuban General Garcia during the

---

25. The life of Horatio Alger, Jr. (1832–1899), formed an interesting paradox to the type of novels he wrote. He wrote rags-to-riches success stories, yet he neither was born poor nor died rich. About fifteen million of the twenty million copies of his books were sold after his death. Frederick Lewis Allen, "Horatio Alger, Jr.," *The Saturday Review of Literature* 18 (September 17, 1938), pp. 3–17.

26. McClelland, in *The Achieving Society,* found that achievement increased regularly from 1800 to 1890, peaked, and declined thereafter. See also David Riesman, Nathan Glazer, and Reuel Denney, *The Lonely Crowd* (Garden City, N.Y.: Doubleday, 1950), pp. 29–32.

27. Charles M. Schwab, "The College Man in Business," in Alta G. Saunders, ed., *The Literature of Business,* rev. ed. (New York: Harper and Row, 1923), p. 5.

Spanish-American War.[28] Without questioning and whining, Rowan took the initiative and, operating on a minimum of guidance, got the message through. This display of the virtues of a self-starting, self-directed, highly motivated individual exemplified the business ideal—that of individual effort and initiative with a minimum of guidance from without.

Early scientific management theory was consonant with the social values of reward for individual effort and the classical virtues of the rational person directed by self-interest. Utilitarian economics, then in vogue, held that individuals rationally calculated what was to their own advantage based on the seeking of pleasure and the avoidance of pain. Workers, like all human beings, were motivated by their own self-interest. In the classical period of economics, this self-interest was largely the monetary reward that came from work, giving rise to the idea of the economic person. Before Taylor, management by incentives had failed largely because management had not cleared the obstacles to gain from the workers' paths and had indulged in rate cutting when earnings became too high. Taylor's conception of a management that facilitated worker effort by study and proper job design was supposed to open the door and free the workers' basic drive for economic rewards. Rate cutting was not in management's self-interest because it only served to force workers to return to their former habits of soldiering. The mental revolution between labor and management was the recognition of mutual self-interest. From management's vantage point, a rational system of work, proper incentives, no cutting of rates, and leadership by knowledge and not by drive would lead to lower costs and higher profits. For their part, workers would recognize that standards had been properly established by scientific study and that by following instructions and procedures they would be able to calculate rationally that they could best serve their own self-interest by following Taylor's system. In brief, the ideals of scientific management were compatible with the prevailing views of people's needs and aspirations.

THE COLLISION EFFECT

Cultural change, that third eternal inevitability, like death and taxes, is always difficult to pinpoint historically. But times were changing, and the milieu of scientific management slowly assumed new dimensions that affected the course of management thought. Two disparate yet strangely congenial forces were forming to mark a new era in U.S. cultural thought: the closing of the frontier and the Social Gospel and its successor, progressivism. The United States of the early twentieth century was in the turmoil of urbanization and industrialization. The noted historian Frederick Jackson Turner identified four forces that were reshaping U.S. economic, social, and political ideals: (1) the exhaustion of the supply of free land and the closing of the West; (2) the concentration of wealth and power in the hands of a few fundamental industries; (3) the political expansion by the United States into territories

---

28. Elbert Hubbard, "A Message to Garcia," in Saunders, *Literature of Business*, pp. 190–194.

beyond its own borders; and (4) the rise of populism.[29] The West in the United States typified the ideals of individualism, economic equality, freedom to rise on one's own initiative, and democracy. Whenever social conditions became too oppressive, capital pressed upon labor, or political restraints became too great, the West provided an avenue of escape. When the safety valve offered by the West closed, new institutional arrangements were necessary to attain the U.S. ideal of democracy for which the West had long provided.

William G. Scott built on Turner's thesis and called the culmination of these cultural forces the "period of collision" (see figure 12-1). The collision effect was characterized by conflict and resulted from forces that had drawn people into an inescapable proximity and interdependency. Unmitigated, the collision effect would have led eventually to social and psychological degeneration. However, Scott's thesis was that the decline of the "individualistic ethic" of the period of expansion was slowly being replaced by a "social ethic," which substituted human collaboration for human competition "with a prayer that a social philosophy would lead to industrial

---

FIGURE 12-1 **MANAGEMENT THOUGHT IN A CHANGING CULTURE**

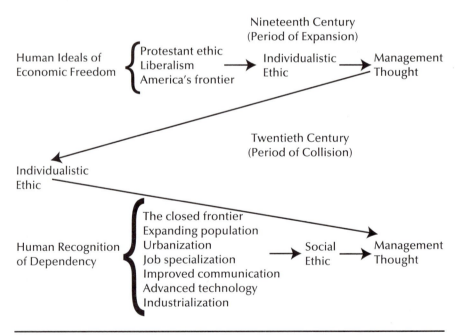

Adapted from William G. Scott, *The Ethic in Management Literature* (Atlanta: Georgia State College of Business Administration, 1959), p. 10.

---

29. Frederick Jackson Turner, *The Frontier in American History* (New York: Holt, Rinehart and Winston, 1921), pp. 244–247.

harmony."[30] Basic to this search were Taylor's notions of "harmony, not discord," "cooperation, not individualism," and the "mental revolution" on the part of both labor and management.

There were elements of both the individualistic and the social ethics in Taylor's philosophy. In Scott's analysis, the social ethic began with the group as a source of value and the individualistic ethic started with the person as the primary value. Taylor's "cooperation, not individualism" would suggest that he accepted the social ethic. However, people are neither purely individualistic, since they normally desire social intercourse, nor are they purely group-oriented, because of their own ego needs. Taylor's philosophy bridged the gap between the two ethics by stressing the mutuality of interests and collaboration at work (the social ethic) coupled with individually based economic incentives and the selection and development of each person to the highest extent possible (the individualistic ethic). Taylor was clearly in touch with the problems of the industrialized society of the period. Though not known nor regarded as a social philosopher, he perceived the industrial dilemma and proposed one means of alleviating the detrimental effects of the disharmonies of urbanization and industrialization.

THE SOCIAL GOSPEL

Emerging in the late nineteenth century as a counterpoint to social Darwinism, the Social Gospel shaped the field of personnel management, formed an antecedent for industrial sociology, and was a social precursor to the politics of progressivism. Whiting Williams imbibed the Social Gospel and used his shirtsleeve empiricism to study industrial conditions. The industrial betterment/welfare work movement stimulated the formation of employment departments and groups, such as the National Civic Federation, which sought remedies for industrial unrest.

To those of the Social Gospel persuasion, unions were instruments of social and economic reform, and such individuals as Robert G. Valentine envisioned the eventual replacement of trade unions by enlightened consumer unions in their evolution toward true industrial democracy.[31] The transition period was to be marked by a rapprochement between scientific management and organized labor based on efficiency and consent. Worker participation plans evolved; some involved union consent and cooperation, while others gave employees a voice and a choice through various types of employee representation plans. The industrial betterment/welfare movement was an uneven mixture of philanthropy, humanitarianism, and business acumen. Industrialists such as John H. Patterson of National Cash Register set the pattern for the industrial welfare movement.[32] Welfare schemes had the objectives of preventing

---

30. W. G. Scott, *The Social Ethic in Management Literature* (Atlanta: Georgia State College of Business Administration, 1959), p. 9.

31. R. G. Valentine, "Scientific Management and Organized Labor," *Bulletin of the Society to Promote the Science of Management* 1 (January 1915), pp. 3–9.

32. Samuel Crowther, *John H. Patterson: Pioneer in Industrial Welfare* (Garden City, N.Y.: Doubleday, 1923).

labor problems and improving performance by providing hospital clinics, lunchrooms, bathhouses, profit sharing, recreational facilities, and a host of other devices to woo worker loyalty. To this group, human happiness was a business asset, and it was the wise, profit-minded employer who nurtured worker loyalty to the firm through various employee welfare schemes. The efficiency engineers, especially Taylor, complemented the work of the betterment or welfare proponents by linking efficiency and morality. For Taylor, hard work led to morality and well-being; for the industrial betterment advocates, morality and well-being yielded hard work. This reciprocal work-welfare equation was the core of the romance between the progressives and scientific management. Societal uplift through efficiency was in vogue.

In retrospect it is clear that social forces were generating and sanctioning an efficiency craze during the Taylor era. A proliferation of popular and technical literature appeared on efficiency in the home, in education, in conservation of natural resources, in the church, and in industry. The noted psychologist H. H. Goddard thought that the efficiency of group endeavors was not a function so much of intelligence but of the proper assignment of workers to a grade of work that met their mental capacity.[33] This psychological notion of the "first-class man" reflected the grip of Taylor's ideas on the academic community. U.S. educational institutions, seeking reform and a broader base for their efforts, seized on Taylor's system and discovered the efficiency expert.[34] Conservationists, spurred by Presidents T. R. Roosevelt and William Howard Taft, also found comfort in the gospel of efficiency.[35] Feminists saw a saving grace in efficiency that would release women from the drudgery of housework and free them to assume an equal role in society. Reverend Billy Sunday recommended functional foremanship for the church so that each department could obtain expert advice and lasting results.[36]

This cultural fetish for efficiency was soon to wane. By the 1920s, a marked shift had occurred from the individualistic ideal of Horatio Alger. The gospel of production efficiency was dying as factories poured forth an abundance of goods. Prosperity reigned, and a new gospel of consumption emerged with a heavy stress on sales and selling all people on the importance of being middle class. Such individuals as Whiting Williams, Elton Mayo, and Mary Parker Follett were beginning to play down the emphasis on the individual and stress the importance of the group in

---

33. Henry Herbert Goddard, *Human Efficiency and Levels of Intelligence* (Princeton, N.J.: Princeton University Press, 1920).

34. See Raymond E. Callahan, *Education and the Cult of Efficiency* (Chicago: University of Chicago Press, 1962); and J. M. Rice, *Scientific Management and Education* (New York: Hinds, Noble and Eldredge, 1914).

35. Samuel P. Hays, *Conservation and the Gospel of Efficiency* (Cambridge, Mass.: Harvard University Press, 1959).

36. Samuel Haber, *Efficiency and Uplift: Scientific Management in the Progressive Era 1890–1920* (Chicago: University of Chicago Press, 1964), p. 63. See also Ernest J. Dennen, *The Sunday School under Scientific Management* (Milwaukee: Young Churchman, 1914); and Eugene M. Camp, *Christ's Economy: Scientific Management of Men and Things in Relation to God and His Cause* (New York: Seabury Society, 1916).

industry. The burgeoning discipline of personnel management emphasized industrial welfare, better worker selection, improved morale, and worker happiness as both social and business assets. Fictional critics of society were deploring the U.S. preoccupation with business. Sinclair Lewis's satire *Babbitt* came to symbolize the conforming mediocrity of the booster and joiner. The need for affiliation was rising, there was security in conformity, and people were becoming more conscious of social relations and less aspiring in maximizing individual gain. The frontier was closed, and new social values were replacing the Western ideal of rugged individualism. The seeds were sown for the social person.

THE POLITICAL ENVIRONMENT: FROM ONE ROOSEVELT TO ANOTHER

The task of government and political institutions throughout time has always revolved around balancing two basic themes: (1) the need to establish equity and order to protect one person from another, and (2) the need to limit governmental power to protect a person from the state. Political theorists, such as Machiavelli and Hobbes, saw a central role for the state over the individual; Rousseau and Locke sought a system of balances through which individuals could check the excess of governmental power. Constitutional or representative government, the philosophy of Locke and Rousseau made manifest in the United States, makes consent of the governed the proper source of all legislative authority. Pluralism is characteristic of a constitutional society, and it "seeks to diffuse power into many organizations and groupings and thus to prevent the development of imbalance of power and to assure the freedom of the individual from the tyranny of the one, the few, or the many."[37] The ballot box is the medium for making pluralism a reality. The United States of the late nineteenth century was seeking to perfect democracy, and dissatisfied groups and individuals were responding to the collision effect with an outpouring of legislation to change the relations between individuals and the state and between business and government. Founded on the premises of limited government, private property, freedom of economic opportunity, stress on individual initiative, and a government that should keep its hands off business, the United States encountered imbalances and imperfections between the ideals and practice of economic democracy.

SCIENTIFIC MANAGEMENT AND THE PROGRESSIVES

The political articulation of the Social Gospel was found in the Populist-Progressive movement that attempted to provide a broader base for democracy in order to mitigate the perils of the collision effect. It is a strange quirk of history that Taylor

---

37. Richard Eells and Clarence Walton, *Conceptual Foundations of Business* (Homewood, Ill.: Richard D. Irwin, 1961), p. 363.

would never have been considered progressive by modern critics, yet his work and philosophy eventually became embedded in Progressive thought. Progressivism had its roots in the populist movement of the 1870s and 1880s. Whereas populism was overwhelmingly rural and provincial, progressivism was urban, middle class, and nationwide.[38] Both were reform movements, and progressivism picked up where the populism of William Jennings Bryan left off. For both movements, the central problem was to restore equality of opportunity by removing the interventions of government that benefited large-scale capital and by replacing those interventions with ones that favored persons of little or no capital.[39] Populism waned because it was based on support from the declining segment of the population in the rural areas. Progressivism succeeded because it was concerned with labor, small business, and the urban population. The Progressives sought to enfranchise women, elect U.S. senators by direct popular vote, aid lower-income groups, establish a minimum wage, enact workers' compensation laws, encourage trade unions, and enact a federal income tax.

There was probably little in the Progressive platform that would have appealed to F. W. Taylor, but reform movements have a facility for making a union of odd couples. Scientific management caught the Progressives' eye at the Eastern rate hearings. Brandeis, a leading Progressive, helped coin the catchy title ("scientific management") that made efficiency synonymous with morality and social order. The public could be saved from a rate increase if efficiency was introduced and labor and management were denied unwarranted gains. Everyone would benefit from lower costs and higher wages if industrial leaders would accept Taylor's precepts. It was here that the Progressives' romance with scientific management began. The reformers did not wish to root out capitalism, but sought orderly change in the structure of industry vis-à-vis the public. Some reformers, like the Socialist Eugene Debs, wanted to replace the whole system. More moderate individuals, like Louis Brandeis, Herbert Croly, and Walter Lippman, thought that efficiency through science and leadership by professional experts would bring social order and harmony. Each envisioned a professionalization of business leadership that would remove management from the "cesspool of commercialism" and turn the manager into an "industrial statesman."[40] The appeal of scientific management was that it offered leadership by expertise and knowledge and hence would rise above class prejudice and rule by drive and whim. The high wages and low costs promised by efficiency systems would check the greed of the employer and the laziness of the employee. Finally, scientific management showed that the interests of the employer and the employee were identical and the wastes of class conflict were therefore unnecessary.[41]

---

38. Richard Hofstadter, *The Age of Reform* (New York: Vintage Books, 1955), p. 131.

39. Eric F. Goldman, *Rendezvous with Destiny* (New York: Vintage Books, 1952), p. 59.

40. Walter Lippman, *Drift and Mastery* (New York: Mitchell Kennerly, 1914), pp. 10–11. See also Louis Brandeis, *Business—A Profession* (Boston: Small, Baynard, 1914).

41. Haber, *Efficiency and Uplift*, pp. 58–59, 89–90.

BUSINESS AND THE PROGRESSIVES

The big change in the relations between government and business came in 1901 after the assassination of President McKinley and the succession of Theodore Roosevelt. At first, the new president gave business leaders and the financial interests no cause for alarm. His well-phrased first message to Congress did well to balance his own Progressive inclinations with a probusiness stance. Mr. Dooley, Peter Finley Dunne's fictional Irishman, aptly summarized President Roosevelt's position: "Th' trusts," says he, "are heejus monsthers built up be th' inlightened intherprise in th' men that have done so much to advance progress in our beloved counthry," he says. "On wan hand I wud stamp thim undher fut; on th' other hand not so fast."[42]

The honeymoon was brief. In 1902, President Roosevelt brought suit to dissolve the Northern Securities Company by invoking the Sherman Act. This direct blow at Northern Securities, a holding company set up by J. P. Morgan and Edward H. Harriman to control three major railroads, opened a new era in government-business relations. Known as a prime proponent of conservation of natural resources as well as a trustbuster, the first Roosevelt placed government in a new role as a regulator of business activity. Antitrust suits were filed against the Beef Trust (1905), the Standard Oil Company of New Jersey (1906), and the American Tobacco Company (1907); and new legislation regulated the railroads (Elkins Act, 1903, and Hepburn Act, 1906) and the telephone, telegraph, and wireless industries (Mann-Elkins Act, 1910). Other state and federal legislative enactments sought to limit hours of work and regulate female and child labor. The Clayton Act and the Federal Trade Commission Act (1914) strengthened the Sherman Act and made more explicit other discriminatory business practices. The Federal Reserve Act (1913) created a more elastic currency and weakened the hold of big New York City banks over cash and reserves.

To illustrate further the decline of laissez-faire economics, taxpayers lost their earlier reprieve with the passage of the Underwood-Simmons Tariff Act of 1913. The act provided for a 1 percent tax on personal incomes over $3,000, and a surtax was added progressively on incomes up to $20,000; the maximum rate was 7 percent on incomes in excess of $500,000. Taxpayers reported their income on Form 1040. The Supreme Court let this act stand; only the rates have changed. In retrospect, the political environment of the early scientific management era sought to bring a new balance between the power of business vis-à-vis the public. Though Taylor did not concern himself with the political environment to any large extent, his own battles with entrenched, resistant business leadership, for example that of Bethlehem Steel, indicate that he sought to replace management by privilege with management by science based on expertise. The mental revolution was to deemphasize the division of the surplus and stress production for lower prices and higher wages. The romance of Taylor and the Progressives had political as well as social ramifications. After the war, the United States witnessed the decline of the progressivism of Roosevelt and

---

42. Cited by Frederick Lewis Allen, *The Big Change* (New York: Harper and Row, 1952), p. 85.

Wilson and welcomed the return to normalcy of Warren Harding. The United States withdrew from the world arena of politics and turned inward to enjoy a decade of prosperity.

Summary of Part II

Figure 12-2 provides a visual summary of the emergence, growth, and evolution of the scientific management era. Scientific management was not an invention; it was a synthesis, a stage in evolving management thought. Charles Babbage could lay a valid claim to the formation of a rational, systematic approach to management, but it was Frederick W. Taylor who gave systematic management a voice.

Taylor was the deus ex machina who became the focal point for an idea. Scientific management was more than methods and time study; it was a much deeper philosophy of managing human and physical resources in a technologically advanced world where people had gained greater control over their environment than ever before. The Industrial Revolution had provided the impetus; Taylor provided the synthesis. As people gained greater power over the physical world, they sought to direct and guide the products of that greater prosperity to more rational ends. Taylor had an idea, a great idea, on how that might be done—by a mental revolution for all parties, founded on science and not whim, and leading to harmony and cooperation. Perhaps he was idealistic, even Utopian, but it would be wrong to criticize him for holding forth the promise of joining industrial harmony, individual betterment, and greater productivity.

Those who followed Taylor represented divergence from his orthodoxy. Some were major figures, leaving larger footprints in the sands of time, whereas others left merely tracings. But each in some way provided for industrial education, academic awareness of management, and improved productivity and service to society by industry. Two of Taylor's contemporaries, Fayol and Weber, were to achieve acclaim only in more modern times; but all those examined during this era reflected the imprint of Taylor's search for rationality in a world of large enterprise.

The historical question of whether the person makes the times or vice versa cannot be begged. Certainly it is a mutually reciprocating force, an action-reaction throughout history. Taylor and his followers were the products of an era that in economic terms sought a rationalization of resource utilization, in social terms sanctioned individual reward and effort, and in politic terms encouraged uplift through efficiency. In return, the individuals affected the times by giving voice to a movement toward material prosperity, industrial harmony to retard the collision effect, and making the United States into the world's economic and political leader. Scientific management was the child of its culture and in turn made its culture an adult of industrial, social, and political vigor.

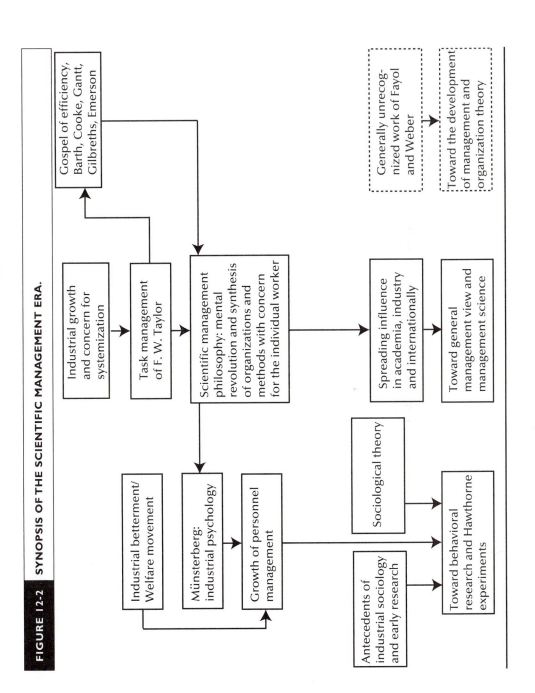

FIGURE 12-2   SYNOPSIS OF THE SCIENTIFIC MANAGEMENT ERA.

Gospel of efficiency, Barth, Cooke, Gantt, Gilbreths, Emerson

Industrial growth and concern for systemization

Task management of F. W. Taylor

Scientific management philosophy: mental revolution and synthesis of organizations and methods with concern for the individual worker

Generally unrecognized work of Fayol and Weber

Toward the development of management and organization theory

Spreading influence in academia, industry and internationally

Toward general management view and management science

Industrial betterment/Welfare movement

Münsterberg: industrial psychology

Growth of personnel management

Sociological theory

Antecedents of industrial sociology and early research

Toward behavioral research and Hawthorne experiments

The Social Person Era

Eras in management thought never begin and end neatly in any particular year. Instead there is a blending of movements and the themes are played in a shifting of major and minor keys. The notion of a social person era reflects more of an emerging philosophy than any settled criterion for managerial action. The social person was born late in the scientific management era but did not achieve any large degree of recognition until the 1930s. Part III examines first the Hawthorne research and Mayo's nascent philosophy, which gave academic credence to the human relations movement. The work of Mary Parker Follett and Chester Barnard is introduced to illustrate some unique notions of authority and organizational integration. Then evolving management thought is viewed in separate, parallel branches: the growth of widespread interest and research into industrial behavior; and the writings of a number of scholars who were slowly developing a top-management viewpoint of organizations. Part III concludes with a look at human relations in theory and practice and a discussion of the economic, social, and political environment of the social person.

CHAPTER 13

The Hawthorne Studies

No studies in the history of management have received so much publicity, been subjected to so many different interpretations, and been as widely praised and as thoroughly criticized as those conducted at the Hawthorne plant of Western Electric, the equipment supply arm of AT&T. Western Electric had a very advanced program in personnel relations and had employed Whiting Williams as a consultant. It was considered a progressive workplace, and "employee morale in the [Hawthorne] plant is high. Shop supervision and employee relations have been and are relatively good."[1] Under these circumstances, what could have happened to cause so much controversy and study?

THE STUDIES BEGIN

At first, the researchers tried to answer a very modest question: What was the effect of workplace illumination on worker productivity? Prior research had shown that improved lighting led to improved performance.[2] The spirit of further inquiry led the Council on Industrial Lighting, an element of the National Research Council of the National Academy of Science, to conduct a scientific study of the relation between factory illumination and employee performance. The group chosen to do the research was from the Massachusetts Institute of Technology and was headed by Dugald C. Jackson, a professor of electrical engineering. In the winter of 1924, the researchers observed existing lighting conditions and performance records in Western Electric's punch press, coil winding, and relay assembly departments to establish a baseline for the level of worker performance. The

1. George A. Pennock, "Test Studies in Industrial Research at Hawthorne," in Western Electric Company, *Research Studies in Employee Effectiveness and Industrial Relations* (1929), p. 1.

2. Charles D. Wrege, Michael Gill, and Jacqueline Mundy, "Who Were Elton Mayo's 'Many Hands'?" *Academy of Management Proceedings* (1981), pp. 116–120.

level of illumination was then varied in all groups with the result that "output bobbed up and down without direct relation to illumination."[3]

In the summer of 1925, the researchers selected two groups of coil-winding operators, equal in experience and performance, and designated one the variable group (that is, the level of lighting was to be varied), and one the control group (no changes in lighting were to be made). The groups were placed in different buildings, separate from the other workers. The outcome of this experiment was that output went up in both groups regardless of the level of illumination. Later, this experiment was repeated, and again efficiency was maintained even under conditions of insufficient lighting. In one instance, Homer Hibarger, a Western Electric employee and one of the researchers, studied two operators and gradually lowered the lighting down to the level of moonlight. Wanda Beilfus, one of these operators, recalled:

> Geri [Geraldine Sirchio]…was with me. We were taken to a small room. Mr. Hibarger was there with us, but it wasn't that bad. The lighting was a little darker but we could see what we were doing. They found out even with the bad lighting we did just as well.[4]

In April of 1927, the illumination tests were abandoned. Charles E. Snow, one of the experimenters and an instructor in electrical engineering at MIT, concluded in his report that illumination was not the answer to the research problem. There were too many variables, and Snow stated that the most important one could be "the psychology of the human individual." At this point, it would have been easy to drop the whole project. Fortunately, Homer Hibarger proposed to George Pennock, the assistant works manager, that the experiments should continue. Pennock agreed that supervision was a better explanation than lighting for the increase in productivity. With the approval of the works manager, Clarence Stoll, Hibarger designed and ran a series of experiments in the Relay Assembly Test Room.

THE RELAY ASSEMBLY TEST ROOM

The original participants were five relay assemblers (Adeline Bogotowicz, Irene Rybacki, Theresa Layman, Wanda Blazejak-Beilfus, and Anna Haug), one layout operator (Bea Stedry), and the observer-experimenter, Homer Hibarger. The number of assemblers was limited by the capability of the recording device, a printing telegraph tape that had only five channels and would punch a hole in the tape as a relay was completed and dropped down a chute. Frank Platenka, the relay assembly department supervisor, told Wanda Beilfus there were going to be "some studies"

---

3. From the report of C. E. Snow in the November 1927 issue of *Tech Engineering News,* reproduced on Reel 1, Box 1, Folder 9, of the microfilmed Records of the Industrial Relations Experiment Carried Out by the Western Electric Company at the Hawthorne Works, Hawthorne, Illinois.

4. Wanda Beilfus (née Blazejak), quoted in Alfred A. Bolton, "Relay Assembly Testroom Participants Remember: Hawthorne a Half Century Later," *International Journal of Public Administration* 17 (1994), p. 377.

Relay Assembly Test Room Participants, circa 1928: (L–R) Beatrice Stedry (layout operator), Anna Haug (operator #5), Wanda "Lottie" Beilfus (operator #4), Theresa Layman (operator #3), Geraldine Sirchio (operator #2), and Mary Volango (operator #1). Credit: Ronald G. Greenwood Collection, courtesy of Regina A. Greenwood.

and asked her to find some women "who would not be married soon" and who would like to work on a special room to be used for the studies.[5] The operators were invited to Pennock's office "where the plan and objectives of the study were explained ... [and] they readily consented to take part in the study."[6]

As the studies proceeded, changes were made and their impact on performance studied.[7] The assemblers were observed in their regular department for two weeks prior to moving to a special test room with their observer. After about six weeks, they were placed on an incentive plan that tied their pay to the performance of their small group rather than staying on the group payment plan that applied to all other assemblers. The subjects were told to work at a "comfortable pace" and that they would not suffer financially but had the chance to make more money than possible

---

5. *Ibid.*, p. 345.

6. C. E. Turner, "Test Room Studies in Employee Effectiveness," *American Journal of Public Health* 23 (June 1933), pp. 577–584.

7. Much of the following section is based on the seminal research of Charles D. Wrege, "Facts and Fallacies of Hawthorne: A Historical Study of the Origins, Procedures, and Results of the Hawthorne Illumination Tests and Their Influence on the Hawthorne Studies" (Ph.D. dissertation, New York University, 3 vols., 1961); and on Ronald G. Greenwood, Alfred A. Bolton, and Regina A. Greenwood, "Hawthorne a Half Century Later: Relay Assembly Participants Remember," *Journal of Management* 9 (Fall 1983), pp. 217–231.

under the group payment plan in the main department. Thus the experimenters reported that "we were able to easily convince the operators that any gains in output would be returned entirely to them and we were thus reasonably assured of their cooperation."[8]

During the first seven periods of the study (April 25, 1927, to January 21, 1928) various factors were changed to determine the effect, if any, on output. Two five-minute rest periods were introduced, followed by two ten-minute rests, then six five-minute rests, and later a lunch was provided in Western Electric's employee restaurant. During this time, output had bobbed up and down but the overall trend was upward. There was an emerging concern, however, about the behavior and production of Adeline Bogotowicz and Irene Rybacki. Hibarger had evidence that Bogotowicz was restricting output (she and Rybacki were consistently the lowest producers); and Theresa Layman, who sat the closest to Bogotowicz, said that Bogotowicz and Rybacki talked only to each other and refused to talk with others. Rybacki and Bogotowicz were dismissed from the test room and returned to the main relay assembly department. The reasons offered were "lack of cooperation and poor output" by employees who had a "talking problem."[9] An undated Hawthorne report, however, noted that Rybacki had been cooperative when the study began and became antagonistic only after her health declined. Medical tests disclosed that Irene was severely anemic: she received medical treatment and a two-week paid leave, and was able to recover her health and return to work in the main department.[10]

Bogotowicz and Rybacki's positions in the test room were assigned to Mary Volango and Geraldine Sirchio, two experienced relay assemblers. Output in period eight went up as soon as Sirchio and Volango arrived, exceeding any previous level by the original five assemblers. Sirchio became the group leader, and, although output would vary from one period to the next, the trend was upward, exceeding previous peak performances. Then, in period twelve, over a year after the experiments started, the rest periods were removed, the workday and workweek were returned to the original conditions, and operators once again had to furnish their own lunches. Total output went up as the workweek increased to five days (forty-eight hours), but hourly output declined. Rest periods were reinstated in period thirteen and weekly and hourly output reached an all-time high.

It was clear to Pennock, Hibarger, and others that something unusual was happening. Pennock visited his alma mater, MIT, in the winter of 1927 to seek professional advice. MIT's President Stratton recommended that Pennock seek out Clair E. Turner (1890–1974), a professor of biology and public health at MIT. Turner

---

8. Western Electric Company, "An Investigation of Rest Pauses, Working Conditions, and Industrial Efficiency," supplementary program report as of May 11, 1929, p. 144; also found on Reel 1, Box 1, Folder 6 of the microfilm records.

9. T. N. Whitehead, *The Industrial Worker* (New York: Arms Press, 1977), p. 117; and Fritz J. Roethlisberger and William J. Dickson, *Management and the Worker* (Cambridge, Mass.: Harvard University Press, 1939), p. 53.

10. "Explanation of Removal of Two Operators," no date, Hawthorne microfilm Reel 3, Box 5, Folder 2.

became a consultant in the relay test room and initiated the study of fatigue, health habits, and mental attitudes as potential explanations of the increasing output among the operators.[11] Turner was able to establish that reduced fatigue as a result of the rest periods was not the cause of the increased output. However, the rest periods gave the workers more opportunities for social interaction, and mental attitudes, more than anything else, explained the better performance. In order of importance, Turner attributed the rise in output to (1) the small group, (2) the type of supervision, (3) increased earnings, (4) the novelty of the experiment, and (5) the attention given to the test room operators by company officials and other investigators.[12]

Clair E. Turner, circa 1934. Courtesy of the MIT Museum.

Concerning the style of supervision, Pennock was the first to note the importance of supervisory style. Charles Snow, who was involved in the illumination experiment, was "relaxed and friendly," knew each operator well, and did not always adhere closely to company policy. His successor, Hibarger, also had a friendly, outgoing nature, as did Don Chipman, who replaced Hibarger in the relay test room. This different style of supervision was in dramatic contrast to that of the regular test-room supervisor, Frank Platenka. As one of the operators, Theresa Layman, explained, "we were more relaxed. We didn't see the boss [Platenka], didn't hear him ... he was mean. He died; I didn't even go to see him." Another operator, Wanda Beilfus added, "It [the test room] was just family, you know, real friendly."[13] Turner summed up the results: "[There was] a fundamental change in supervision ... no group chief ... but instead a 'friendly observer'.... Discipline was secured through leadership and understanding.... An esprit de corps grew up within the group."[14]

At this point, style of supervision and the formation of small groups to build esprit de corps were believed to explain the increases in productivity. One other factor, the wage incentive plan, was thought to contribute but had not yet been examined empirically. In the relay assembly test room, the payment plan paid each operator in a proportion close to the individual's effort, because an operator was paid on the output of six rather than one hundred or more operators. The average wage of the operators before going into the test room was $16 per week; in the test

11. C. E. Turner, *I Remember* (New York: Vantage Press, 1974); and Charles D. Wrege, "Solving Mayo's Mystery: The First Complete Account of the Origin of the Hawthorne Studies—The Forgotten Contributions of C. E. Snow and H. Hibarger," *Academy of Management Proceedings* (1976), pp. 12–16.

12. Turner, "Test Room Studies," p. 583.

13. Greenwood, Bolton, and Greenwood, "Hawthorne," pp. 222, 224.

14. Turner, "Test Room Studies," p. 579.

room, however, their average earnings ranged from $28 to $50 per week, a significant increase. Could this factor explain the increase in output?

To test this hypothesis, two new groups were formed: a second relay test assembly group and a group of mica splitters (Figure 13-1). Five experienced relay assemblers were selected to form the new group for study. They had been on a group incentive plan in the main department, and for the first nine weeks of the experiment they were placed on the small group incentive plan. Initially, total output went up, leveled off (for all but one worker whose output decreased), and then remained constant at the new higher level (112.6 percent over the base period of 100 percent). After returning to the original group incentive plan for a period of seven weeks, the second relay assembly group's performance dropped to 96.2 percent of the base of 100 percent before the experiment. The mica splitters had always been on an individual incentive system, and the only change in the experiment was to place a selected group in a special observation room. Rest periods and the length of the workday were varied, as they had been earlier, and changes in output were noted. The mica splitters were studied for fourteen months, and their average hourly output rose 15 percent.

Although output had gone up in both groups, except when the relay assemblers were returned to the large group incentive plan, Turner was hesitant to attribute the rise in output to the payment scheme: "[the] changed pay incentive may have been one factor in increasing output but it certainly was not the only factor."[15] An interim report of May 1929 summarized the results of these early experiments: output of the assemblers was up from 35 to 50 percent; fatigue reduction was not a factor in this increased output; payment in the small group "was a factor of the appreciable importance in increasing output"; and the workers were more "content" owing to the "pleasanter, freer, and happier working conditions" caused by the "considerate supervision."[16]

THE INTERVIEWING PROGRAM

During the illumination tests, C. E. Snow and Homer Hibarger began interviewing the workers using a list of formal questions, such as: How is your general health? Are you happy on the job? Are you influenced by any pressure from your working associates? Because these questions could be answered yes or no, they learned little in these directed interviews. Clearly, another approach was needed. To backtrack briefly, when George Pennock recruited Clair Turner from MIT to help explain the mysteries of the experiments, he crossed the Charles River to enlist the aid of Harvard professor George Elton Mayo (1880–1949).[17] Mayo was an Australian who had received his M.A. degree in logic and philosophy from the University of

---

15. *Ibid*, p. 582.

16. Western Electric Company, "Investigation," pp. 126–128.

17. George Pennock to Elton Mayo, March 15, 1928. Microfilm records Reel 7, Box 17, Folder 2.

| FIGURE 13-1 | **OVERVIEW OF THE HAWTHORNE STUDIES** |

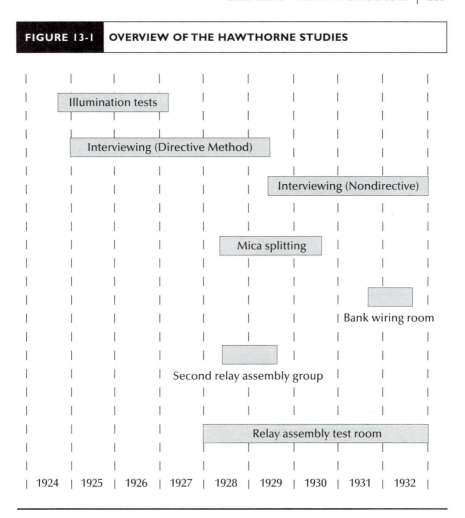

Based on Appendix A of Greenwood, Bolton, and Greenwood, "Hawthorne," pp. 229–230. One experiment involving a typewriting group has been omitted because no report was issued.

Adelaide in 1899. He had taught logic and philosophy at Queensland University and later studied medicine in Edinburgh.[18] While in Scotland, he became a research associate in the study of psychopathology; this experience served as a basis for his later development as an industrial researcher. Under a grant from the Laura

---

18. An excellent biography is Richard C. S. Trahair, *The Humanist Temper: The Life and Work of Elton Mayo* (New Brunswick, N.J.: Transaction Books, 1984).

Elton Mayo, circa 1945. Courtesy of the Harvard Business School Archives, Baker Library, Harvard Business School.

Spelman Rockefeller fund, Mayo emigrated to the United States, where he was associated with the Wharton School of Finance and Commerce of the University of Pennsylvania. In early research Mayo found that the problems of workers could not be explained by any one factor but had to be dealt with in what he called "the psychology of the total situation."[19] This was a Gestalt concept that formed the basis for his view of the organization as a social system. In his research, Mayo followed the conventional wisdom of the times and sought a relationship between working conditions and human performance in a textile mill near Philadelphia. By introducing rest periods, Mayo was able to reduce turnover from 250 to 5 percent and to improve efficiency. The work pauses, in Mayo's terms, reduced the "pessimistic reveries" of the workers, hence improving morale and productivity.

Mayo first visited the Hawthorne plant for two days in 1928, then for four days in 1929, and then began a deeper involvement in 1930. The 1929 visit, however, was critical for the interviewing program. Mayo felt that "a remarkable change of mental attitude in the group" was the key factor in explaining the Hawthorne mystery. In his opinion, the test room workers became a social unit, enjoyed the increased attention of the experimenters, and developed a sense of participation in the project. According to Mayo: "The most significant change that the Western Electric Company introduced into its 'test room' bore only a casual relation to the experimental changes. What the Company actually did for the group was to reconstruct entirely its whole industrial situation."[20]

To understand the workers' situation, Mayo felt that a conversational, or nondirective, approach to the interviews should be used. The basic premise of the interviewing program was that the new supervisory role was one of openness, concern, and willingness to listen. The observers had noted that the female workers were "apprehensive of authority" but that once the experimenter became more concerned with their needs, they lost their shyness and fear and talked more freely to company officials and observers. The workers developed a greater zest for work and formed new personal bonds of friendship, both on the job and in after-hours activities. Their improved morale seemed to be closely associated with the style of supervision and with greater

---

19. Elton Mayo, "The Basis of Industrial Psychology," *Bulletin of the Taylor Society* (December 1924), reprinted in Donald Del Mar and Rodger D. Collons, eds., *Classics in Scientific Management* (Tuscaloosa: University of Alabama Press, 1976), pp. 264–277. See also Elton Mayo, "The Irrational Factor in Human Behavior: The Night Mind in Industry," *Annals of the American Academy of Political and Social Science* 110 (November 1923), pp. 117–130.

20. Elton Mayo, *The Human Problems of an Industrial Civilization* (New York: Macmillan, 1933), p. 73.

productivity. This link between supervision, morale, and productivity became the foundation of the human relations movement.

Using the nondirective technique, the interviews allowed the workers to express their feelings more freely. The interviewer's job was to keep the workers talking, and the average length of the interviews went from thirty minutes to ninety minutes. After this modification, workers expressed the opinion in follow-up interviews that working conditions had improved (although they had not changed) and that wages were better (even though the wage scale was the same). In short, the opportunity to let off steam made the workers feel better about their situation even though it had not changed.

The complaints gathered in the interviews were thoroughly investigated and found generally to be irrelevant to the facts. This separation of fact and sentiment led the researchers to conclude that there were two levels of complaints, the *manifest,* or material, content versus the *latent,* or psychological, form of the complaint. For example, one interviewee was preoccupied with the noise, temperature, and fumes in his department. Further examination revealed that his latent concern was the fact that his brother had recently died of pneumonia and the worker feared that his own health might be impaired. In another case, complaints about a low piece rate were traced not to verification of this fact but to a worker's concern for medical bills arising from his wife's illness. In essence, "Certain complaints were no longer treated as facts in themselves but as *symptoms* or indicators of personal or social situations which needed to be explored."[21] From the researchers' viewpoint, workers' preoccupation with personal concerns inhibited their performance, a conclusion that Mayo had called "pessimistic reveries" in his early research. The outcome of the interviewing program was supervisory training in the need to listen and understand the personal problems of workers. The supervisors were trained to be interviewers, to listen rather than to talk, and "to exclude from their personal contacts with employees any moral admonition, advice, or emotion."[22]

Use of this nondirective interviewing technique enabled the supervisor to handle workers' personal problems more intelligently, to locate factors adversely affecting worker performance, and to remove the events or factors in the workers' social or physical environment that were having the adverse influence. The new supervisor was to be more people oriented, more concerned, less aloof, and skilled in handling social and personal situations. The product of this human-relations style of leadership was to be better morale, fewer pessimistic reveries, and improved output.

GROUP BEHAVIOR: THE BANK WIRING ROOM

Clair Turner wrote Mark Putnam in late 1930 that the mica splitting study was not yielding useful information and suggested that "we would do well to substitute a test

---

21. Roethlisberger and Dickson, *Management and the Worker,* p. 269. Italics added.

22. *Ibid.,* p. 323.

room study group of men" to gain additional information on what factors influence group output.[23] The Bank Wiring Department was chosen for a group to be studied. At this point, management's plans took a different turn because of objections by the department foreman, H. S. Wolff, and his fellow supervisors. They were concerned that the purpose was to increase output, as had happened in the relay assembly test room, and that this would reflect unfavorably upon the present supervisors and the current level of production. William Dickson summarized the sentiments of the supervisors:

> They felt that those girls [in the relay assembly test room] had been given special inducements in the form of a special gang rate, the ordinary production difficulties had been carefully eliminated, and that the operators had been petted and babied along from the start. "Of course," they said, "anybody could get production that way, only we [bank wiring supervisors] can't get away with things like that."[24]

To overcome supervisory resistance to the bank wiring room study, the researchers agreed to a number of changes: A group of workers would be segregated for study, but visitors would not be allowed; worker earnings would involve their output as a group, factored into the output of those remaining in the regular department; the supervisor would be the same, and the observer would be kept in the background rather than being "friendly and supportive" as Chipman and Hibarger had been with the relay assemblers; and workplace layout and procedures would remain constant. In brief, the only similarity to the relay test room would be placing the workers in a separate room.

A group of male operatives who assembled switches for central office switchboard equipment was chosen and isolated in an observation room. The bank wiring task involved three groups of workers whose work was highly interrelated: (1) the wirers who wired the terminals; (2) the solderers who solidified the connections; and (3) the inspectors who judged the quality of the work. In total, nine wirers, three solderers, and two inspectors were the objects of study. One of the first things noted by the researchers was that the workers had a clear-cut notion of what constituted a fair day's work and that this was lower than management's standard of output. If output exceeded that informal standard, the workers expected a cut in the wage rate or an increase in the "bogey" (i.e., management's standard) on which the incentive was based. The worker therefore faced two dangers: high output, which led to rate cuts or increased bogeys; and low output, which resulted in arousing the ire of the supervisor. Group sentiment prevailed on each worker not to exceed the informal output

---

23. C. E. Turner to M. L. Putnam, October 13, 1930, microfilm records Reel 7, Box 17, Folder 3. Although Turner planned these studies, the primary investigator was W. Lloyd Warner, a Harvard anthropologist.

24. W. J. Dickson, "Procedure in Establishing Bank Wiring Test Room," undated, but circa mid-July, 1931. Microfilm records Reel 3, Box 7, Folder 1, p. 3.

agreement and hence become a rate buster and not to injure his fellow workers by parasitically falling below the standard and becoming a rate chiseler. To enforce the group norm, the members engaged in some interesting intragroup disciplinary devices, such as sarcasm, ridicule, and "binging." Binging involved a rather firm blow on the upper arm of the person in disfavor and was used to enforce all violations of group norms. Avoiding bruises became a motivator, and workers engaged in numerous subterranean devices to maintain informal group membership. For example, on high-output days, a worker would hide a surplus and report only what conformed to the norm; later he would slow down and turn in the previous surplus units from his cache. Three facts neatly summarize the researchers' discoveries: (1) restriction of output was deliberate and set by the group regardless of management's notion of expected output; (2) workers smoothed out production reports to avoid the appearance of working too fast or too slowly; and (3) the group developed its own devices to bring recalcitrant members into line.

Discovery of the informal organization and the restriction of output surprised the Hawthorne researchers. Frederick W. Taylor was keenly aware of systematic soldiering and group pressures; Whiting Williams had recounted his own experiences of informal relationships and attitudes toward work; and Stanley Mathewson had made an extensive study of pressures leading to restriction of output.[25] Despite these early recognitions of group pressures, the researchers found it noteworthy that "attention had been called to the fact that social groups in shop departments were capable of exercising very strong control over the work behavior of individual members." Restriction of output was a new discovery to the researchers since they "had hitherto been unaware of its implications for management practice and employee satisfactions."[26] Knowledge builds on knowledge, and the failure of the researchers to glean from prior writings on informal group behavior is a fault, although it should not detract from the significance of their own research.

A second facet of the bank wiring room research was the assessment of interpersonal relations for the purpose of studying social structure, or group configuration. In this phase the Hawthorne group could lay claim to far more originality than was possible in its study of restriction of output. Analysis of social relations in the bank wiring room revealed two cliques, or informal groups, within the formal structure. The formal structure consisted of three work groups of three wirers each, one solderer serving each group, and inspection duties split between the two inspectors. In Figure 13-2 the circles indicate the presence of the two cliques, A and B, and the members of those sets. Wirer W2, shown with dotted lines, was not a member of clique A. Clique A was called the front group, and worked toward the front of the observation room, and clique B was the back group, because of its physical location.

25. Stanley B. Mathewson, *Restriction of Output Among Unorganized Workers* (New York: Viking Press, 1931). Literature related to restriction of output is reviewed in Roland E. Kidwell, Jr. and Nathan Bennett, "Employee Propensity to Withhold Effort: A Conceptual Model to Intersect Three Avenues of Research," *Academy of Management Review* 18 (1993), pp. 429–456.

26. Roethlisberger and Dickson, *Management and the Worker,* pp. 379–380.

| FIGURE 13-2 | INTERNAL ORGANIZATION OF GROUP
BANK WIRING OBSERVATION ROOM |

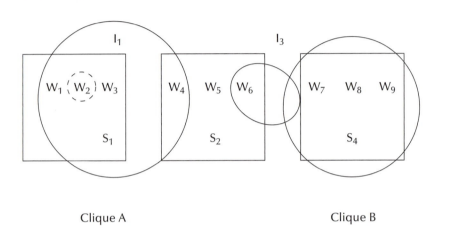

Clique A   Clique B

Reprinted with permission of the publishers from *Management and the Worker,* by F. J. Roethlisberger and William J. Dickson, p. 518, Cambridge, Massachusetts: Harvard University Press. Copyright © 1939, 1967, by the President and Fellows of Harvard College.

In analyzing these cliques, the researchers attempted to isolate the factors determining clique membership. Physical location (front and back) was one factor but did not govern; nor was occupation a determining factor, since clique A contained wirers, solderers, and an inspector. Members of the same clique engaged in intragroup activities, such as games (gambling, binging, etc.), trading jobs, and helping one another, even though these activities were against company policy. Each clique excluded members from the other clique in these particular activities, and clique A considered itself superior to clique B.

Wirers W2 and W5, solderer S2, and inspector I3 were isolates, who did not participate in clique activities and were excluded for various reasons: S2 had a speech impediment and did not contribute to social interaction; W2 was self-reliant and a nonconformist; W5 was ostracized from the group because he squealed to the supervisor about group activities that violated company policy. The inspector isolate (I3) was excluded because he took his inspection duties very seriously, whereas I1 often pointed out errors without formally charging them against the worker and acted more like one of the workers than did I3. In the final analysis, certain sentiments seemed to govern clique membership:

1. You should not turn out too much work. If you do, you are a rate buster.
2. You should not turn out too little work. If you do, you are a rate chiseler.

3. You should not tell a supervisor anything that will act to the detriment of an associate. If you do, you are a squealer.

4. You should not attempt to maintain social distance or act officious. If you are an inspector, for example, you should not act like one.[27]

What explained the variations in output between the relay assembly test room and the bank wiring room? In the former, the workers had increased productivity, but in the latter, restriction was the rule. Both groups were observed, but the role of the observer in each was different. In the relay assembly experiment, the observer took the workers into his confidence, asked for suggestions, and encouraged participation in decisions affecting their welfare. In the bank wiring room, however, the observer merely watched while the workers perpetuated the same informal schemes practiced in the past. The eventual explanation of the differences in output would add ammunition to the Hawthorne researchers' arsenal of arguments for new managerial skills. In explaining the cliques, additional vistas for social systems would be opened.

The researchers found that an informal group performed two functions for the workers: (1) it protected them from internal indiscretions of members, such as rate busting or chiseling; and (2) it protected them from the outside interference of management officials who would attempt to raise standards, cut rates, or stop their games. The group was an instrument for controlling the activities and sentiments of the workers. Analogous to the findings of the interview program, that in studying group behavior fact had to be separated from sentiment, the researchers began an exploration of the facts as perceived by the workers versus actual company practices as seen by the researchers. In regard to restriction of output, the researchers concluded that the fear of depression and layoff was not the sole reason for soldiering, since workers restricted output in both good and bad times. Restriction was actually detrimental to the workers, since it increased unit cost and could therefore induce management to make changes in rates, standards, or technology to offset the higher costs. Since the management of Western Electric had a long record of fair dealing with the workers, the researchers deemed the turning inward of the groups for protection nonlogical and a worker misconception of reality.

Having found that mismanagement or general economic conditions did not cause the informal groups to form, the researchers sought an explanation by viewing the bank wiring room as part of a larger social organization. Relations with extradepartmental personnel, such as efficiency experts and other technologists, were viewed as disturbing, since their actions could impinge on worker welfare. The technologists tended to follow a "logic of efficiency," which the workers perceived as an interference and a constraint on their activities. Further, supervisors (as a class) represented authority and the power to discipline the workers to ensure their conformity to management rules. Apprehensive of such authority, the workers resisted supervisory attempts to force their behavior into an efficiency mold. Again, the

---

27. *Ibid.*, p. 522.

researchers concluded that this was nonlogical behavior on the workers' part, but stressed that management must recognize this phenomenon and take into account sentiments along with the logic of efficiency. This position resulted in the admonition to management to view every organization as a social system. The logic of efficiency in the technical system failed because it omitted the sentiments and nonlogical components of the social system.

THE ORGANIZATION AS A SOCIAL SYSTEM

As seen earlier, Vilfredo Pareto's ideas were introduced to Mayo and others through the seminars of L. J. Henderson. Although Mayo was never a full-fledged Paretian, he did use some of Pareto's ideas. Closer to Paretian thinking, especially about the organization as a social system, was Fritz J. Roethlisberger (1898–1974). Roethlisberger received an A.B. degree from Columbia University in 1921 and a B.S. from the Massachusetts Institute of Technology in 1922. From 1922 to 1924 he was engaged in industrial practice as a chemical engineer; he then returned to Harvard in 1925 to pursue an M.A. degree. He later joined Harvard's industrial research department and soon became involved in the Hawthorne research.[28]

With William J. Dickson, chief of Hawthorne's employee relations research department, Roethlisberger prepared the most widely read version of the Hawthorne experiments, *Management and the Worker*. In this work the influence of Pareto is seen more definitely, especially the notion of the workplace as a social system. According to Roethlisberger and Dickson, the technical aspect of needs for efficiency and economic return should be viewed as interrelated with concern for the human aspect of every organization. The employees have physical needs, but they also have social needs. These needs arise from early social conditioning and persist through organizational life in relations with fellow workers and others in organizations. Events and objects in the physical work environment "cannot be treated as things in themselves. Instead they have to be interpreted as carriers of social value."[29] For example, a physical desk has no social significance; but if people who have desks are the ones who supervise others, then the desk becomes a status symbol and a carrier of social value. Other items, such as type of clothing, age, sex, seniority, and so on, can also take on social significance. The researchers concluded that since people are not motivated by facts and logic, sentiments about things of social value become very powerful considerations in dealing with personnel.

The existence of the formal organization with its rules, orders, and payment plans, coupled simultaneously with an informal organization with its bases of sentiments and human interactions, posed problems for management. The informal

28. F. J. Roethlisberger, *The Elusive Phenomena*, ed. George F. F. Lombard (Cambridge, Mass.: Harvard University Press, 1977). A special tribute to Roethlisberger appears in George F. F. Lombard, ed., *The Contributions of F. J. Roethlisberger to Management Theory and Practice* (Cambridge, Mass.: Harvard University Graduate School of Business, 1976).

29. Roethlisberger and Dickson, *Management and the Worker,* p. 557.

organization should not be viewed as bad but as a necessary, interdependent aspect of the formal organization. Viewing the organization as a social system enabled management to attack the conflict between the "logic of efficiency" demanded by the formal organization and the "logic of sentiments" of the informal organization.[30] The manager had to strive for an equilibrium between the technical organization and the human one by securing the economic goals while "maintaining the equilibrium of the social organization so that individuals through contributing services to this common purpose obtain personal satisfaction that makes them willing to cooperate."[31]

In short, the outcome of the Hawthorne research was a call for a different mix of managerial skills. These skills were those crucial to handling human situations: first, diagnostic skills in understanding human behavior, and second, interpersonal skills in counseling, motivating, leading, and communicating with workers. Technical skills alone were not enough to cope with the behavior discovered at the Hawthorne plant.

HUMAN RELATIONS, LEADERSHIP, AND MOTIVATION

What happened at Hawthorne and the interpretation of those results are part of an evolving story. For example, a phenomenon known as the Hawthorne effect has endured for many years as part of the research literature lore. One of the early explanations of increased output was the attention given to those participating in the experiment. The researchers removed the workers from the factory floor, placed them in special test rooms, and assumed many of the supervisory functions. This shift in control from the former line supervisor to the experimenters created a new social situation for the worker. The change in the quality of supervision was not different in its closeness, but in the special attention given the workers with regard to their sentiments and motives. This special attention resulted in the charge that the observers biased the experiment by their personal involvement, the so-called Hawthorne effect. The experimenters altered the previous managerial practices. Workers were advised and consulted about changes, their views were listened to sympathetically, and their physical and mental health became matters of great concern to the experimenters. As the research progressed, it became less a controlled experiment and more inclined toward creating a social situation in which workers felt free to air their problems and in which they established new interpersonal bonds with their coworkers and supervisors.

---

30. *Ibid.,* pp. 556–564. "Logic of sentiments" was a contradiction, since Roethlisberger and Dickson concluded that sentiments were nonlogical.

31. *Ibid.,* p. 569. The authors acknowledged their indebtedness to Chester Barnard (who is discussed later) for this distinction.

Was there a Hawthorne effect that biased the experiments? Did the rise in output occur because the workers were being observed? Theresa Layman, one of the relay assemblers, recalled, "No, we kept working. It didn't matter who watched us or who talked with us." Don Chipman, one of the observer experimenters, recalled, "I agree ... early in the study it had some bearing but ... that just wore off."[32] Clair Turner stated, "We at first thought that the novelty of test room conditions might be partly responsible for increased output but the continuing increase in production over a four-year period suggests it was not of great importance."[33] A survey of industrial/organizational and organizational behavior textbooks found a "development of mythical beliefs among students about the Hawthorne Studies ... [and] the Hawthorne Effect is probably an unfortunate tradition."[34] Although the Hawthorne effect is widely referenced, there is considerable doubt that being observed had any impact on worker performance.

HUMAN RELATIONS AND HUMAN COLLABORATION

As the economic depression that followed the stock market crash of October 1929 deepened, hours of work were reduced and the relay assembly test room experiments were finally abandoned. With the passage of time, Mayo changed his interpretation of what happened at Hawthorne.[35] As early as October 1931, Mayo began to emphasize the need for "effective collaboration" and a restoration of "social solidarity" in a changing world that left people without stability, purpose, or norms. When Mayo began to explain his social philosophy he gained a wider audience, while Clair Turner, who had been more involved in the experiments and had made a significant contribution, began to be less influential. Thus MIT's star waned, and Harvard's waxed. As Roethlisberger recalled, "Mayo was an adventurer in the realm of ideas... the [Hawthorne] data were not his; the results were not his; but the interpretations of what the results meant and the new questions and hypotheses that emerged from them were his."[36]

Mayo's education and experiences reveal the basis for his emerging interpretation of human behavior. For a short time Mayo studied medicine, and, though he never received a medical degree, he developed an interest in psychopathology, the scientific study of mental disorders. At that time, two individuals were in the vanguard of analyzing psychopathological thought, Pierre Janet of the French school and Sigmund Freud, the originator of psychoanalysis. Mayo claimed more affinity to

---

32. Greenwood, Bolton, and Greenwood, "Hawthorne," p. 223.

33. Turner, "Test Room Studies," p. 584.

34. Ryan Olson, Jessica Verley, Lindsey Santos, and Coresta Salas, "What We Teach Students about the Hawthorne Studies: A Review of Content within a Sample of Introductory I-O and OB Textbooks," *Industrial-Organizational Psychologist* 41 (January 2004), pp. 34–35.

35. Trahair, *Humanist Temper*, p. 254.

36. Roethlisberger, *Elusive Phenomena*, pp. 50–51.

Janet and wrote a scholarly work on his theories.[37] Janet was of the opinion that the primary mental disorder was obsession, or preoccupation with certain ideas to such an extent that the individual could not cope with them even though the individual knew such ideas to be irrational or untrue. The Freudians called this compulsion, and Mayo thought the work of Janet and that of Freud were complementary.[38] The essence of Mayo's obsession-compulsion interpretation was that individuals were incapacitated by their obsessions to such a degree that they were inflexible in their responses to life, including their personal, social, and industrial behavior. Obsessions, by reducing one's ability to adapt, had dysfunctional consequences for the worker and the supervisor.

Although Mayo never once concluded that any large number of the workers at Hawthorne were severe cases, he did think that the interviewing program had demonstrated that minimal levels of obsession (or preoccupation) existed in the sense that "conditions of work tended in some way to prevent rather than facilitate a satisfactory personal adaptation."[39] In Mayo's view, workers were unable to find satisfactory outlets for expressing personal problems and dissatisfactions in their work life. This blockage led to "pessimistic reveries" and preoccupations with personal problems at a latent level, which emerged on the manifest level as apprehension of authority, restriction of output, and a variety of other forms of behavior that reduced morale and output. To Mayo, industrial life caused a sense of personal futility, which led to social maladjustment and eventually to obsessive, irrational behavior.

> Human collaboration in work, in primitive and developed societies, has always depended for its perpetuation upon the evolution of a non-logical social code which regulates the relations between persons and their attitudes to one another. Insistence upon a merely economic logic of production… interferes with the development of such a code and consequently gives rise in the group to a sense of human defeat. This human defeat results in the formation of a social code at a lower level and in opposition to the economic logic. One of its symptoms is "restriction."[40]

From this psychopathological analysis of industrial life, Mayo and Roethlisberger formed the philosophical rationale for the human relations movement.[41] The goal was effective human collaboration; the means was the restoration of a social code to facilitate adjustment to industrial life.

---

37. Elton Mayo, *Some Notes on the Psychology of Pierre Janet* (Cambridge, Mass.: Harvard University Press, 1948).

38. Elton Mayo, *The Human Problems of an Industrial Civilization,* pp. 107–110.

39. *Ibid.,* p. 114.

40. *Ibid.,* pp. 120–121.

41. Roethlisberger also adopted the obsession-compulsion approach of Janet and Mayo. See F. J. Roethlisberger, "The Nature of the Obsessive Thinking," *Man-in-Organization: Essays of F. J. Roethlisberger* (Cambridge, Mass.: Belknap Press of Harvard University Press, 1968), pp. 1–19. This paper was written in June 1928 but was not published until 1968.

ANOMIE AND SOCIAL DISORGANIZATION

To develop his thesis for human collaboration, Mayo borrowed Émile Durkheim's term *anomie* (from the Greek word meaning "without norms") for his basic premise. In traditional societies people knew their place and their future and there was social solidarity. The domestic system, built around the family and kinship, gave people an identity in work as well as in their social life. The factory system and the process of industrialization destroyed this solidarity through the division of labor, increased social and physical mobility, and the growth of large-scale organizations in which the manner of dealing with interpersonal relations shifted from a personal, friendship base to one of an impersonal nature. The result was a normless, rootless mode of life in which individual identities were lost along with the social bonds that provided continuity and purpose to human existence. This anomie led to social disorganization in personal lives and in communities and effected a general overall sense of personal futility, defeat, and disillusionment. Social inventions to cope with industrial changes had not kept pace with technical inventions. This social lag was responsible for the widespread sense of futility and the resultant social disorganization. The rapid economic growth experienced by the United States both before and after the turn of the century had disturbed "communal integrity."

Mayo argued that the advance of a technically oriented society placed undue emphasis on engineering and yielded a technological interpretation of the meaning of work in the sense that achievement was based on the economic logic of efficiency. The social needs of individuals were pushed into the background, thereby reducing people's "capacity for collaboration in work."[42] Managerial emphasis on the logic of efficiency stifled the individual's desire for group approval, social satisfaction, and social purpose gained through communal life. Drawing from Pareto's notion of an elite, Mayo postulated that the administrative elite was technically oriented and that "in the important domain of human understanding and control we are ignorant of the facts and their nature."[43] The "new administrator" had to effectively restore opportunities for human collaboration in work and in life by recognizing people's need for social solidarity. Managers aided in accomplishing this goal by receiving training in the human and social aspects of industrial organization, developing listening and counseling skills, and recognizing and understanding the nonlogical side of the social code. The human problem, as Mayo perceived it, was that managers thought that the answers to industrial problems resided in technical efficiency, when in fact the problem was a social and human one.

DEVELOPING THE HUMAN RELATIONS LEADER

Elton Mayo had set the stage for the social person by seeking a new leadership, buttressed by social and human skills, that would overcome anomie and social

---

42. Mayo, *Human Problems*, p. 166.

43. *Ibid.*, p. 177.

disorganization. In its very essence Mayo's theory espoused the same goal as that of Taylor, collaboration and cooperation in industry. The means to this goal differed but the end that both anticipated was the recognition of a mutually beneficial relationship between the worker and management. Mayo felt that the world must rethink its concepts of authority by abandoning the notion of unitary authority from a central source, be it the government, the church, or the industrial leader. Drawing heavily from Chester Barnard, Mayo concluded that authority should be based on social skills in securing cooperation rather than on technical skill or expertise. The human-relations-oriented leader would be one who acted as an investigator of social sentiments to further collaborative efforts to achieve organizational goals. Since people spent so much time in a group, and since much of their satisfaction was the product of cooperative effort, management had to focus its efforts on the maintenance of group integrity and solidarity. The group became the universal solvent, and it was management's task to find the universal container.

The first-line supervisor as the primary point of contact between the worker and management played a particularly crucial and often conflicting role. In the bank wiring observation room, for example, the immediate supervisor did not push management's expectation that a wireman wire 7,312 terminals a day (the "bogey"), but accepted the average of 6,000–6,600 per day. The supervisor's dilemma was explained in an interim program report:

> In such circumstances the first line supervisor finds himself in a conflict situation. He can do either of two things: uphold the system of ideas common to management and attempt by driving or other methods to enforce them, or take the side of the workmen and conceal the true situation from his superiors. In the test room the Group Chief has seen fit to side with the workmen, and perhaps rightly. It is quite likely that by opposing them he would only aggravate the situation.[44]

The first-line supervisor was caught as Roethlisberger's "man-in-the-middle" and, in this instance, was not prepared to provide the necessary leadership. The problem for industrial leadership revolved around the premise that it was a rare supervisor who possessed technical and economic skills as well as human relations skills. The ability to meet the logic of efficiency was different from the ability to meet the nonlogic of worker sentiments. Supervisors tended to confuse fact with sentiment and, as the Hawthorne research group found in the interviewing program, assumed that what the workers told them was the way things really were. Communications and listening skills hence became an important part of the supervisor's tool kit.

---

44. Arthur C. Moore and William J. Dickson, "Report on Bank Wiring Test Group for the Period November 9, 1931 to March 18, 1932," March 21, 1932, microfilm records Reel 3, Box 7, Folder 3. See also Roethlisberger's often reprinted essay "The Foreman: Master and Victim of Double Talk," *Man-in-Organization,* pp. 35–58.

The answer to preparing leaders for the new human relations role was training at all levels to develop skills in understanding logical and nonlogical behavior, understanding of the sentiments of the worker through listening and communications skills, and developing the ability to maintain an equilibrium between the economic needs of the formal organization and the social needs of the informal organization. Equilibrium became the keynote of organizational effectiveness. Through the social structure, workers obtained the recognition, security, and satisfaction that made them willing to cooperate and contribute their services toward the attainment of the organization's objectives. Disequilibrium occurred when technical change was introduced too fast or when management was out of touch with worker sentiments. This was the new leadership, one that could distinguish fact from sentiment and one that balanced economic logic and the nonlogic of sentiment.

HUMAN RELATIONS AND MOTIVATION

How the human-relations-oriented leader motivated people became a controversial subject as the studies evolved and as we will see in Chapter 17. Early reports of the Hawthorne results gave some credence to the conclusion that changing to the small group incentive payment plan was one factor in explaining the increased output in the relay assembly test room. Mark Putnam, one of the Western Electric managers, told *Business Week* that pay was the number one concern expressed by employees during interviews in 1930.[45] When the operators were asked what they liked in the test room, one responded, "We made more money in the test room."[46] Wrege quoted from a November 12, 1930, memo to Mayo: "Economic and financial factors are of considerable importance in the Test Room. The employees are anxious for high earnings. The Test Room has apparently removed the doubt in the employees' minds that the company would permit them to make very high earnings."[47] The evidence regarding economic incentives and output at Hawthorne was available, but the published results took on a different interpretation.

There is evidence that the official accounts of Hawthorne assumed a meaning of their own owing to Mayo's influence. Mayo's writings, and his influence on those who wrote the official results, Roethlisberger and Dickson, presented a different interpretation of what happened at Hawthorne. An early indication of Mayo's influence is in a memo written by Roethlisberger in which he reported that there appeared to be a significant relationship between physiological factors and output. According to Roethlisberger, this made Mayo very happy because "it looked as if the organization of the girls in the test room was more conditioned by biological factors

45. "Human Factor in Production Subject of Unique Research," *Business Week,* January 21, 1931, p. 16.

46. Greenwood, Bolton, and Greenwood, "Hawthorne," p. 220.

47. Charles D. Wrege, "Review of 'The Hawthorne Myth Dies Hard,'" unpublished manuscript, August 1, 1979; quoted in Greenwood, Bolton, and Greenwood, "Hawthorne," p. 220.

rather than anything so naive as economic incentive. As this fits in with what Mayo has been saying for the last five years we were very pleased."[48]

In the official account, Roethlisberger and Dickson said that the "efficacy of the wage incentive was so dependent on its relation to other factors that it was impossible to consider it as in itself having an independent effect on the individual."[49] That is, pay for performance was only one factor that could not be addressed separately. As time went on, Roethlisberger mentioned other factors that explained human motivation:

> Whether or not a person is going to give his services whole-heartedly to a group depends, in good part, on the way he feels about his job, his fellow workers, and supervisors ... [a person wants] ... social recognition ... tangible evidence of our social importance ... the feeling of security that comes not so much from the amount of money we have in the bank as from being an accepted member of the group.[50]

Still later it appears that the notion of the economic person was discarded:

> Far from being the prime and sole mover of human activity in business, economic interest has run far behind in the list of incentives that make men willing to work ... man at work is a social creature as well as an "economic man." He has personal and social as well as economic needs. Work provides him with a way of life as well as a means of livelihood.... As we discarded the notion of "economic man," we began to question the concept of business organization as merely a logical organization of operations for the efficient production of goods.[51]

What was the human relationists' view of motivation? In the early evidence, the workers reported that they worked harder because "they made more money" or that pay was their "number one" concern. Clair Turner, however, felt that money was important, but not the only explanatory factor. As Roethlisberger and Mayo examined the data, the importance of financial incentives faded into the sunset. In brief, the Hawthorne studies have been subjected to so much manipulation and misinterpretation that the facts are clouded in myth and advocacy. Mayo wanted to

48. F. J. Roethlisberger to Emily Osborne, April 5, 1932, F. J. Roethlisberger Papers, Folder 1, Baker Library, Graduate School of Business Administration, Harvard University, Boston. Quoted in Richard Gillespie, *Manufacturing Knowledge: A History of the Hawthorne Experiments* (Cambridge, England: Cambridge University Press, 1991), p. 88.

49. Roethlisberger and Dickson, *Management and the Worker*, p. 160.

50. F. J. Roethlisberger, *Management and Morale* (Cambridge, Mass.: Harvard University Press, 1942), pp. 15, 24–25.

51. F. J. Roethlisberger, "A 'New Look' for Management," Worker Morale and Productivity, General Management Series, no. 141 (New York: American Management Association, 1948), pp. 12–13, 16.

promote social collaboration at work, not pay for performance, and it would require a later generation of scholars to indicate that the social person supplemented, but did not supplant, the economic one.

SUMMARY

Beginning as an inquiry into the relationship between workplace illumination and worker productivity, the studies at the Hawthorne plant of the Western Electric Company evolved into a series of attempts to explain the increased output, which was unrelated to lighting. Improved performance was not due to rest periods or refreshments, but was linked to the incentive payment scheme (in part) and the style of the supervisor, who was actually a part of the research group. This human relations style of thinking emphasized interpersonal relations, listening, communication, and sociohuman skills for the manager-leader. This human-relations-oriented person was expected to achieve equilibrium between the logic of efficiency and the nonlogic of worker sentiments. By separating fact from sentiment and by developing listening and human skills, the human-relations-oriented supervisor could overcome the dysfunctions of anomie and restore group solidarity and thereby satisfy both the social needs of humans and the economic needs of the organization.

CHAPTER
14

The Search for Organizational Integration

Interest in social behavior and social systems began before the research at Hawthorne but would require refinement before the concept of the social person could fully emerge. This chapter examines the lives and thoughts of two individuals who, though separated in time, made significant contributions to the development of ideas regarding the nature of authority, the necessity for coordination of effort, the resolution of conflict, and the design of organizations that would provide maximum opportunities for cooperative effort. One was a political philosopher turned business sage who never met a payroll in her life; the other, a utility executive whose hobbies were classical piano and the works of Johann Sebastian Bach. Together, they were integrators who provided insightful links between the eras of scientific management and the social person.

MARY PARKER FOLLETT: THE POLITICAL PHILOSOPHER

Born in Quincy, Massachusetts, in 1868, Mary Follett had a very difficult life. Her father, an alcoholic, died young; her mother was inclined to a social life rather than practical matters; and Mary had "a somber, lovely childhood."[1] A respectable inheritance from her maternal grandfather provided sustenance, but Mary Follett found intellectual uplift in reading and education. She attended Thayer Academy, a preparatory school for college bound students, and found a mentor in Anna Boynton Thompson, her history teacher. Thompson introduced Follett to the German Idealist school of philosophy, especially the works of Johann Fichte and Georg Hegel. Later Follett would tell a friend:

---

1. The definitive biography of Follett is Joan C. Tonn, *Mary P. Follett: Creating Democracy, Transforming Management* (New Haven, Conn.: Yale University Press, 2003). Urwick placed Follett's birth place in Boston, but Tonn's evidence indicates it was Quincy, Massachusetts (p. 13). See Lyndall F. Urwick, ed., *The Golden Book of Management* (London: Newman Neame, 1956), p. 134.

Mary P. Follett, circa 1928.
Ronald G. Greenwood Collection,
courtesy of Regina A. Greenwood.

One of these [business] men gave me in a nutshell the threads of a tangle he had with his employees. He wanted me to straighten it out. I answered him straight out of Fichte; he didn't know that of course, but I did, and it seemed to meet the case.[2]

After Thayer Academy, Follett continued her studies at the Annexe at Harvard (later named Radcliffe College) where she expanded her interests in philosophy and history to psychology, especially the emerging Gestalt movement, which led her to think in patterns or wholes. Anna Thompson encouraged her to interrupt her studies at the Annexe to study at Newnham College, Cambridge University in England where Follett's interests expanded into law, political science, and government. From these studies came *The Speaker of the House of Representatives,* a book that established her reputation as a political philosopher and scholar and drew her into the intellectual life of Boston.[3] Two years after publishing this book, Follett received her A.B. degree from the Annexe (Radcliffe College).

With academic opportunities limited at that time for females, she spent most of her early years working in various community service groups that sought to provide vocational guidance, education, recreation, and job placement activities for some of the less fortunate among Boston's youth. In these largely volunteer organizations, operating with little or no authority, she realized that there was a need to rethink previously held concepts of authority, organization, leadership, and conflict resolution. In observing and working with these groups, she gained firsthand experience in the dynamics of groups and the need for teamwork. Through her work in the Boston Placement Bureau she would gradually be drawn into work with business leaders and the Taylor Society in the period after Taylor's death. Chronologically, Follett belonged to the scientific management era; philosophically and intellectually, she was a member of the social person era. Her work served as a link between these two eras by generalizing from scientific management concepts and anticipating many of the conclusions of the social person period.

---

2. F. M. Stawell, "Mary Parker Follett," *Newnham College Roll Letter,* January 1935, p. 43; quoted in Elliot M. Fox and Lyndall F. Urwick, eds., *Dynamic Administration: The Collected Papers of Mary Parker Follett* (New York: Hippocrene Books, 1977), pp. xix–xx.

3. M. P. Follett, *The Speaker of the House of Representatives* (New York: Longmans, Green, 1896).

THE GROUP PRINCIPLE

Mary Follett's group principle evolved from her reading in philosophy, psychology, political science, and law. For one strand she drew from her understanding of Johann Fichte (1762–1814), about whom her mentor, Anna Thompson, had written a book.[4] Fichte espoused a nationalism in which the freedom of the individual had to be subordinated to the group. Fichte did not think that individuals had free will but thought that they were bound up in an interpersonal network to which all people were committed. Thus an individual's ego belonged to a wider world of egos, making the ego a social one, until all together swelled up into one "Great Ego," which was part of a common life among all people.[5]

Follett did not swallow Fichte's ideas entirely, but indicated the essence of the group principle was to bring out individual differences and integrate them into a unity. She quoted the early philosopher Heraclitus, who said, "Nature desires eagerly opposites and out of them it completes its harmony, not out of similars."[6] In Heraclitus the dialectic of thesis, antithesis, synthesis of Georg Hegel (1770–1831) found expression. Follett was not a pure Hegelian but felt he was misunderstood by those who interpreted his ideas to mean that the state was "above and beyond" the individual. Rather:

> When we say that there is the One which comes from the many, this does not mean that the One is above the many. The deepest truth of life is that the interrelating by which both are at the same time a-making is constant.[7]

This vague jargon of "interrelating" and "a-making" will form Follett's idea of circular response, as we shall see. These philosophical notions provided the foundation for Follett's book *The New State,* in which she challenged the prevailing political assumptions of her era. Follett's thesis was that "we find the true man only through group organization. The potentialities of the individual remain potentialities until they are released by group life. Man discovers his true nature, gains his true freedom only through the group."[8]

The group principle was to be the new psychology and was designed to renounce the old ideas that individuals thought, felt, and acted independently. Groups of people lived in association, not as a separate ego, and individuals were created by reciprocal

---

4. Anna Boynton Thompson, *The Unity of Fichte's Doctrine of Knowledge* (Boston: Ginn, 1895).

5. Henry D. Aiken, *The Age of Ideology* (New York: New American Library, 1956), pp. 54–60. Fichte was a disciple of Immanuel Kant and in his early years followed Kantian notions of rationalism and the absolutely inalienable rights of the individual. In his later years, Fichte broke with Kant, turned to nationalism and statism, and became part of the romantic revolt against reason.

6. Mary Parker Follett, *The New State: Group Organization the Solution of Popular Government* (London: Longmans, Green, 1918), p. 34.

7. *Ibid.,* p. 284.

8. *Ibid.,* p. 6.

social intercourse. This view demonstrated Follett's acceptance of Gestalt psychology and reflected Charles Horton Cooley's idea of the enlargement of the social self through association and the social looking glass. Using phrases such as "togetherness," "group thinking," and "the collective will," Follett sought a new society based on a group principle and not on individualism. The underlying rationale was not to destroy the individual but was based on her premise that only through the group could an individual find the "true self." Following the group principle, Follett concluded that a person's "true self is the group-self" and that "man can have no rights apart from society or independent of society or against society."[9] In opposing the notion that the purpose of government is to protect individual rights, she proposed a new concept of democracy: "Democracy then is a great spiritual force evolving itself from men, utilizing each, completing his incompleteness by weaving together all in the many membered community life which is the true theophany."[10]

For Follett, democracy was the development of a social consciousness, not individualism, and she felt that "the theory of government based on individual rights no longer has a place in modern political theory."[11] The new and true democracy was to build from small neighborhood groups to community groups, to state groups, to a national group, and eventually to an international group will. Without really coming to grips in this book with the problems of groups in conflict, she had faith that people could create a new "social consciousness" and live together peaceably in the "World State."[12] She demonstrated little confidence in ballot-box democracy, believing that it reflected crowd psychology and defined "right" by the sheer weight of numbers.

CONFLICT RESOLUTION

In *Creative Experience,* Follett developed the idea that through conference, discussion, and cooperation, people could evoke each other's latent ideas and make manifest their unity in the pursuit of common goals. Relying heavily on Gestalt psychology, which held that every psychological situation has a specific character apart from the absolute nature of the component parts, that is, the whole is a configuration greater than the sum of the parts, she felt that through group experiences individuals could reach a greater release of their own creative powers.[13] The goal of group effort was an integrative unity that transcended the parts. In essence, she began to answer the questions of group conflict that she had failed to examine in *The New State.* She hypothesized that any conflict of interests could be resolved in one of four ways: (1) voluntary submission of one side; (2) struggle and the victory

---

9. *Ibid.,* p. 137.

10. *Ibid.,* p. 161. Theophany is "the visible manifestation of God or a god."

11. *Ibid.,* p. 172.

12. *Ibid.,* pp. 359–360. Cf. Fichte's "Great Ego."

13. Mary Parker Follett, *Creative Experience* (London: Longmans, Green, 1924), ch. 5.

of one side over the other; (3) compromise; or (4) integration. The first and second methods were clearly unacceptable because they involved the use of force or power to dominate. Compromise was likewise futile because it postponed the issue and because the "truth does not lie 'between' the two sides."[14] Integration involved finding a solution that satisfied both sides without compromise and domination. In a later lecture she gave some examples of this concept of integration:

> Let us take some very simple illustration. In the Harvard Library one day, in one of the smaller rooms, someone wanted the window open, I wanted it shut. We opened the window in the next room, where no one was sitting. This was not a compromise because there was no curtailing of desire; we both got what we really wanted. For I did not want a closed room, I simply did not want the north wind to blow directly on me; likewise the other occupant did not want that particular window open, he merely wanted more air in the room.... Let us take another illustration. A Dairymen's Co-operative League almost went to pieces last year on the question of precedence in unloading cans at a creamery platform. The men who came down the hill (the creamery was on a downgrade) thought they should have precedence; the men who came up the hill thought they should unload first. The thinking of both sides in the controversy was thus confined within the walls of these two possibilities, and this prevented their even trying to find a way of settling the dispute which would avoid these alternatives. The solution was obviously to change the position of the platform so that both up-hillers and down-hillers could unload at the same time. But this solution was not found until they had asked the advice of a more or less professional integrator. When, however, it was pointed out to them, they were quite ready to accept it. Integration involves invention, and the clever thing is to recognize this, and not to let one's thinking stay within the boundaries of two alternatives which are mutually exclusive.[15]

Another illustration of an integrated solution was drawn from Henry Dennison's manufacturing firm:

> At a meeting of our [Dennison's] manufacturing committee recently the following question came up. Our paper had been six cents, and the competing firm reduced their price to five and three-quarters. We then cut to five and a half and they replied with a price and five and a quarter. The question before us then was whether or not we should

14. *Ibid.*, p. 156.

15. Henry C. Metcalf and Lyndall Urwick, eds., *Dynamic Administration: The Collected Papers of Mary Parker Follett* (New York: Harper and Row, 1940), pp. 32–33.

make a further reduction. Part were in favor; part, against. The solution came when something quite different was suggested: that we should stand for a higher quality of paper and make an appropriate price for it.[16]

Although Follett advocated integration, she recognized the obstacles. As one authority concluded:

> She ... insisted that although integration is not possible in every case, it is possible in more cases than we realize. And perhaps if it is not possible now, it will be later.... The important thing is to work for something better ... we need not be afraid of difference, but rather should welcome it as the opportunity for new social creation. She gave us a theory of human interaction that shows how the same factors that cause change also provide the means for solving the problems presented by change, a theory that tells us that the possibilities for the healthy resolution of conflict is part of the natural process of human intercourse.[17]

The search for integrative unity, for commonality of will, and for human cooperation earned Follett an international reputation as a political philosopher. *Creative Experience* was widely read by business leaders of the day, and Follett was drawn even more closely to the problems of industrial administration. In 1924, she lost her interest in political science because it "did not seem really to come to grips with our [present] problems"; she turned instead to business leaders because "there I found hope for the future. These men were not theorizing or dogmatizing [but] were thinking of what they had actually done and they were willing to try new ways."[18] She was asked to give a series of lectures in New York to a group of business executives under the auspices of the Bureau of Personnel Administration. It was from these lectures and subsequent work that she made the transition from a political to a business philosopher.

THE BUSINESS PHILOSOPHER

If management is viewed as a universal phenomenon, the processes that underlie political administration necessarily apply to business as well. The same problems of achieving unity of effort, defining authority and responsibility, achieving coordination and control, and developing effective leadership exist. It was toward the goal of

---

16. Follett, *Creative Experience*, p. 158.

17. Elliot M. Fox, "Mary Parker Follett: The Enduring Contribution," *Public Administration Review* 28 (November–December 1968), p. 528.

18. Lyndall F. Urwick, "Great Names in Management: Mary Parker Follett, 1868–1933" (speech, University of New South Wales, Australia, June 14, 1967), p. 3.

drawing this parallel that Mary Parker Follett turned her attention. First, from *Creative Experience* she developed further the ideas of "constructive conflict" and the integrative unity of business. Since domination and compromise led to further strife and futility, integration was paramount in all business activities. In dealing with labor, she deplored the notion of collective bargaining because it rested on the relative balance of power and inevitably ended in compromise. Bargaining meant that there were two sides to fight over, and both parties tended to lose sight of what they had in common. In taking sides, for example, prolabor or promanagement positions solidified and the parties failed to see the business as a "functional whole" for which they had joint responsibilities. This collective responsibility began at the departmental level where workers were to be given group responsibilities:

> When you have made your employees feel that they are in some sense partners in the business, they do not improve the quality of their work, save waste in time and material, because of the Golden Rule, but because their interests are the same as yours [the manager's].[19]

In Follett's view, this was not a reciprocal back-scratching arrangement, but a true feeling on the part of both labor and management that they served a common purpose. She suggested that in the past an artificial line had been drawn between those who managed and those who were managed. In reality, there was no line, and all members of the organization who accepted responsibility for work at any level contributed to the whole:

> Labor and capital can never be reconciled as long as labor persists in thinking that there is a capitalist point of view and capitalists that there is a labor point of view. There is not. These are imaginary wholes which must be broken up before capital and labor can co-operate.[20]

Douglas McGregor, who will be discussed soon, cited Follett in one of his early works, noting that collective bargaining was competitive and adversarial. Like Follett, McGregor advocated cooperation and building mutual understanding as a worthy goal.[21] Integration, the method she advocated, involved finding a solution that satisfied both sides without domination, surrender, or compromise. Follett's approach made both sides rethink the issues and their relationship since they were asked to share information openly, avoid win-lose quick fixes, be creative in examining the problem from different angles, and see the problem as "ours" and not "yours." Conflict, to be constructive, required respect, understanding, talking it through, and creating win-win solutions.

---

19. Metcalf and Urwick, *Dynamic Administration*, p. 82.

20. Follett, *Creative Experience*, pp. 167–168.

21. Irving Knickerbocker and Douglas McGregor, "Union-Management Cooperation: A Psychological Analysis," *Personnel* (1942), pp. 520–539.

Beyond the view of the firm as a unity, all should recognize the relation of the firm to its environment of creditors, stockholders, customers, competitors, suppliers, and the community. This larger view of the firm and its environment would enable an integrative unity of society and the economy. Integration then became an associative principle applicable to all levels of life.

AUTHORITY AND POWER

Integration as a principle of conduct would be less than fully effective unless people rethought their concepts of authority and power. In this second area Follett sought to develop "power-with" instead of "power-over," and "co-action" to replace consent and coercion. With both an order giver and an order taker, integration was difficult to achieve. The notions of boss and subordinate created barriers to recognizing the commonality of interests. To overcome this problem, Follett proposed to depersonalize orders and shift obedience to the "law of the situation": "One person should not give orders to another person, but both should agree to take their orders from the situation. If orders are simply part of the situation, the question of someone giving and someone receiving does not come up."[22]

The rationale for the law of the situation was based on scientific management in the sense that Taylor's functional management sought obedience to facts determined by study and not based on the will of one person. In a paper for the Taylor Society, Follett put it this way: "If, then, authority is derived from function, it has little to do with hierarchy of position as such.... We find authority with the head of a department, with an expert ... the dispatch clerk has more authority in dispatching work than the President ... authority should go with knowledge and experience...."[23]

By shifting authority to knowledge, personal confrontations could be avoided as each person felt the dictates of the situation and thereby acted with less friction in achieving an integrative unity. Follett admired this facet of scientific management, which divorced the person from the situation, because it was good psychology in dealing with subordinates. For her, the essence of good human relations was creating the feeling of working with someone rather than working under someone. In practice this became "power-with" versus "power-over" in her terms. Management should not exercise power over the worker, nor should the worker through unions exercise power over management. Jointly exercised power was "co-active," not coercive. Displaying a number of insights into the psychology of power, she rejected both the authoritarian's striving for power and Gandhi's noncooperation as insidious uses of power. Gandhi's concept of power through humility and nonviolence was still a desire for power-over. It was conflict, a search for bending the will of the British to his own movement. Integration and constructive conflict could not be found in any effort to dominate.

---

22. Metcalf and Urwick, *Dynamic Administration,* p. 59.

23. Mary Parker Follett, "The Illusion of Final Authority," *Bulletin of the Taylor Society* 2 (December 1926), p. 243.

In all forms of life, from interpersonal relations to the handling of international disputes, power-over had to be reduced and obedience had to be shifted to the law of the situation. The basis for such integration was what Follett called "circular response." By this she meant a process based on the opportunity for each party to influence the other; through open interaction, over a period of time, "power-with" could be obtained. For labor and management it would come through open disclosure of costs, prices, and market situations. Follett was a firm believer in the employee representation plans that were being developed in the 1920s. Under these plans, employees elected representatives to shop or work councils; these representatives then participated in decision making and gave the worker a voice in dealing with management. Follett found great promise in these plans because "management has seen that an enterprise can be more successfully run by securing the cooperation of the workers.... [further] the aim of employee representation ... should not be to share power, but to increase power...."[24] Employee representation should not be a struggle over who decided what and how the profits were to be divided, but a step toward attaining integration.

Follett thought that final authority was an illusion based on a false premise of power; authority accrued to the situation, not to the person or the position. Likewise, final responsibility was an illusion. Responsibility was inherent in the job or function performed and was cumulative in the sense that it was the sum of all individual and group responsibilities in a system of cross-relationships. At the individual level, a person was responsible for work, not to someone. At the departmental level, the responsibility for work was jointly shared by all those who contributed, with the manager merely interweaving the various individual and group responsibilities. The chief of the organization also had cumulative responsibility for interweaving interdepartmental work.

In this second area of analysis, Follett put forth some iconoclastic notions of authority and responsibility. Traditional notions of the military or other organizations that authority was power-over and that responsibility accrued to the source of final authority were rejected. Authority resided in the situation, not the person or position. Logically then, responsibility was inherent in the function performed and accumulated in interweaving functions. This was heady material for thought from this philosopher to the corporate manager.

THE TASK OF LEADERSHIP

Two facets of Follett's philosophy have been explored: the reduction of conflict through an integration of interests; and the necessary corollary of obeying the law of the situation. A third facet of her philosophy concerned building the underlying psychological processes necessary to achieve goals through coordinating and controlling effort. Follett's view of control reflected her Gestalt psychology of dealing

---

24. Metcalf and Urwick, *Dynamic Administration,* pp. 172, 181–182.

with the whole and the total situation to achieve unity. Control was impossible to achieve unless there was unity and cooperation among all elements, material and people, in a given situation. Any situation was out of control when interests were not reconciled. The basis for control resided in self-regulating, self-directing individuals and groups who recognized common interests and controlled their tasks to meet the objectives.

A manager controlled not single elements, but complex interrelationships; not persons, but situations; and the outcome was a productive configuration of a total situation. How was this configuration achieved? Follett called for a new philosophy of control that was "fact-control rather than man-control," and "correlated control" rather than "super-imposed control." Each situation generated its own control because the facts of the situation and the interweaving of the many groups in the situation were what determined appropriate behavior. Most situations were too complex for central control from the top to function effectively; therefore, controls were to be gathered, or correlated, at many points in the organizational structure. This interweaving and correlation was to be based on coordination, which Follett saw as:

1. Coordination as the reciprocal relating of all the factors in a situation
2. Coordination by direct contact of all the responsible people concerned
3. Coordination in the early stages
4. Coordination as a continuing process[25]

These were considered the "four fundamental principles of organization" and involved the conclusion that the organization *was* control, since the purpose of organizing and coordination was to ensure controlled performance; coordination achieved unity, and unity was control. For an illustration, Follett took the age-old conflict between the purchasing agent, who desired to reduce the cost of purchased materials, and the production manager, who maintained that better materials were needed with which to work. If they followed the principle of early and continuous coordination, each could see the reciprocal problems and would turn the search toward finding or developing a material that met both requirements. Goals and unity could be achieved for their particular departments, for the firm, and for the consumer or the community without either person making a sacrifice. This synthesis of interests was self-regulation through coordination to achieve integration.

For Follett, leadership would no longer be based on power but on the reciprocal influence of leader on follower and follower on leader in the context of the situation. The primary leadership task was defining the *purpose* of the organization; the leader "should make his co-workers see that it is not his purpose which is to be achieved, but a common purpose, born of the desires and the activities of the group.

---

25. Mary Parker Follett, "The Process of Control," in L. Gulick and L. Urwick, eds., *Papers on the Science of Administration* (New York: Institute of Public Administration, Columbia University, 1937), p. 161. One modern scholar believes that many modern control concepts are but reappearances of Follett's conceptualizations. See Lee D. Parker, "Control in Organizational Life: The Contribution of Mary Parker Follett," *Academy of Management Review* 9 (October 1984), p. 744.

The best leader does not ask people to serve him, but the common end. The best leader has not followers, but men and women working with him."[26] Further:

> The leader then is one...who can organize the experience of the group and thus get the full power of the group. The leader makes the team. This is pre-eminently the leadership quality—the ability to organize all the forces there are in an enterprise and make them serve a common purpose. Men with this ability create a group power rather than a personal power... When leadership rises to genius it has the power of transforming experience into power. And that is what experience is for, to be made into power. The great leader creates as well as directs power. Leader and followers are both following the invisible leader—the common purpose. The best executives put this common purpose clearly before their group.[27]

Company purposes were to be integrated with individual and group purposes, and this integration called for the highest caliber of executive leadership. These leaders did not depend on commands and obedience but on skills in coordinating, defining purposes, and in evoking responses to the law of the situation. Recognizing that mere exhortation would not achieve this new definition of leadership, Follett called for executive development aimed at relying more on science in making both physical and human decisions and creating a motive of service to the community. The combination of science and service would lead to a profession of management that enlisted knowledge for the service of others. To those who aspired to be managers, she advised:

> Men must prepare themselves as seriously for this profession as for any other. They must realize that they, as all professional men, are assuming grave responsibilities, that they are to take a creative part in one of the large functions of society, a part which, I believe, only trained and disciplined men can in the future hope to take with success.[28]

The notion of service was not to be substituted for the motive of profit but was to be integrated into a larger professional motive:

> We work for profit, for service, for our own development, for the love of creating something. At any one moment, indeed, most of us are not working directly or immediately for any of these things, but to put through the job in hand in the best possible manner.... To come back to the professions: can we not learn a lesson from them on this

---

26. Metcalf and Urwick, *Dynamic Administration,* p. 262.

27. Mary Parker Follett, *Freedom and Coordination: Lectures in Business Organization,* ed. L. Urwick (London: Management Publications Trust, 1949), pp. 52, 55.

28. *Ibid.,* p. 131.

very point? The professions have not given up the money motive. I do not care how often you see it stated that they have.... Professional men are eager enough for large incomes; but they have other motives as well, and they are often willing to sacrifice a good slice of income for the sake of these other things. We all want the richness of life in the terms of our deepest desire. We can purify and elevate our desires, we can add to them, but there is no individual or social progress in curtailment of desires.[29]

A FINAL NOTE

Seven decades after Mary Follett's death on December 18, 1933, the first full-scale biography of her was published and Tonn remarked "Although [her] name may be obscure, her ideas are not."[30] Lyndall Urwick brought Follett to the fore with the publication of her lectures at the London School of Economics (*Freedom and Coordination*); we saw Douglas McGregor's recognition of her call for integrating the interests of labor and management; in Chapter 15 we will see the influence Follett had on Eduard Lindeman; and Chester Barnard, to be discussed soon, praised her "great insights into the dynamic elements of organization."[31] When Rensis and Jane Likert sought new ways of resolving conflict, they turned to Follett's notion of integration, the law of the situation, and the consensus problem solving.[32] But time passed and many of her lessons were forgotten.

Are the elements of Follett's business philosophy the idyllic notions of a political philosopher? The naturalistic simplicity of people living and working together without the use of coercion and without the need to sacrifice themselves through compromise is certainly worthy of merit. Integration, moving to a broader plane for a solution, would call for much more creativity and imagination than are commonly witnessed in daily industrial, academic, political, and social life. Nevertheless, the goal is a deserving one and should be considered akin to Taylor's mental revolution and Mayo's call for human collaboration. Depersonalization of authority and obedience to the law of the situation would certainly sound the death knell for tyranny and autocracy. However, perceiving and defining the law of the situation would be most difficult in a world of constant competition.

Organizational control based on a perceived unity of purposes would make the world of the manager much more palatable. However, reward systems in practice often

---

29. *Ibid.*, p. 145.

30. Tonn, *Mary P. Follett*, p. 492.

31. Chester I. Barnard, *The Functions of the Executive* (Cambridge, Mass.: Harvard University Press, 1938), p. 122n.

32. Rensis Likert and Jane Gibson Likert, *New Ways of Managing Conflict* (New York: McGraw-Hill, 1976), especially ch. 8.

run counter to measuring the individual's contribution to total effort. A knowledgeable business leadership, dedicated to improving practices through science and service, is a recurrent plea throughout the evolution of management thought. As one of her colleagues recalled, "Mary Follett was a gentle person, not an impressive or aggressive spellbinder, but of all the pioneers she, more than others, approached management through human values, psychology and the laboratory of collaborative work experience. The significance and originality of her contribution cannot be overrated. Even today, she is the most modern management expert...."[33] Perhaps the ideals of Mary Follett can be attained, perhaps not. If not, it will be because too few heeded the pleas of this philosopher.

Chester I. Barnard as he entered Harvard University, 1906. Courtesy of William B. Wolf.

CHESTER BARNARD: THE ERUDITE EXECUTIVE

Chester Irving Barnard was a sociologist of organizations without portfolio. Born in Malden, Massachusetts, in 1886, he personified the Horatio Alger ideal of the farm boy who made good.[34] On a scholarship to Harvard, he supplemented his income by tuning pianos and running a small dance band. He studied economics at Harvard, completing the requirements in three years (1906–1909), but failed to receive a degree because he lacked a laboratory science. Even without a bachelor's degree, he did well enough to earn seven honorary doctorates for his lifelong labor in understanding the nature and purpose of organizations. Barnard joined the statistical department of the American Telephone and Telegraph system in 1909 and in 1927 became the president of New Jersey Bell. His unbounded enthusiasm for organizational work carried him into voluntary work in many other organizations: for example, he helped David Lilienthal establish the policies of the Atomic Energy Commission; he served the New Jersey Emergency Relief Administration, the New Jersey Reformatory, the United Service Organization (president for three years), the Rockefeller Foundation (president for four years); and was president of the Bach Society of New Jersey. Barnard was a self-made scholar who applied the theories of Vilfredo Pareto (whom he read in French), Kurt Lewin, and Max Weber (whom he read in German) and the philosophy of Alfred North Whitehead in the first in-depth

---

33. Luther Halsey Gulick, "Looking Backward to 1915" (paper presented at the Eastern Academy of Management, Hartford, Conn., May 13, 1977).

34. Biographical data and an excellent discussion of Barnard's ideas are found in William B. Wolf, *The Basic Barnard: An Introduction to Chester I. Barnard and His Theories of Organization and Management* (Ithaca: New York State School of Industrial and Labor Relations, 1974).

analysis of organizations as cooperative systems. By the time of his death in 1961, this Harvard dropout had earned a place in history as a management scholar.

THE NATURE OF COOPERATIVE SYSTEMS

Barnard's best known work, *The Functions of the Executive,* was an expansion of eight lectures given at the Lowell Institute in Boston in November and December of 1937. His explicit purpose for the lectures was to develop a theory of organizations and to stimulate others to examine the nature of cooperative systems. To Barnard, the search for universals in organizations had been obstructed by too much emphasis on the nature of the state and the church and their concomitant stress on the origin and nature of authority. He complained that most research focused on social unrest and reform and included "practically no reference to formal organization as the concrete social process by which social action is largely accomplished." Social failures throughout history were due to the failure to provide for human cooperation in formal organizations. Barnard said that the "formal organization is that kind of cooperation among men that is conscious, deliberate, and purposeful."[35]

By examining the formal organization, it was possible to provide for cooperation and to accomplish three basic goals: (1) to ensure the survival of an organization by the "maintenance of an *equilibrium* of complex character in a continuously fluctuating environment of physical, biological, and social materials, elements, and forces" within the organization; (2) to examine the external forces to which such adjustments must be made; and (3) to analyze the functions of executives at all levels in managing and controlling formal organizations.[36] Barnard's notion of including both internal equilibrium and external adjustment was an original view and brought criticism from those who adhered to the traditional view of intraorganizational analysis. Barnard rejected this traditional view of an organization having boundaries and comprising a definite number of members; he included investors, suppliers, customers, and others whose actions contributed to the firm even though they might not be considered members of the firm itself.[37]

Barnard's construction of a cooperative system began with the individual as a discrete being; however, he noted that humans did not function except in conjunction with other humans in an interacting social relationship. As individuals, people could choose whether or not they would enter into a specific cooperative system. They made this choice based on their purposes, desires, and impulses of the moment, or by considering whatever alternatives were available. These were motives, and the organization, through the executive function, modified individual actions and motives through influence and control. However, this modification did not always attain the goals

---

35. Barnard, *Functions of the Executive,* pp. 3–4.

36. *Ibid.,* p. 6. Italics added.

37. Barnard's rebuttal to his critics appeared in the *Harvard Business Review,* Spring 1940, and is reprinted in C. I. Barnard, *Organization and Management* (Cambridge, Mass.: Harvard University Press, 1948), pp. 111–113.

sought by the organization or by the person. The disparity between personal motives and organizational motives led Barnard to his effective-efficient dichotomy. A formal system of cooperation required an objective or purpose; and, if cooperation was successful, the goal was attained and the system was effective. The matter of efficiency was different; cooperative efficiency was the result of individual efficiencies, since cooperation was entered into only to satisfy "individual motives." Efficiency was the degree to which individual motives were satisfied, and only the individual could determine whether or not this condition was being met.[38]

Cooperation within formal organizations afforded possibilities for expanding the powers of the group beyond what the individual could accomplish alone, for example, moving a stone, producing an automobile, building a bridge, and so on. People cooperated in order to do what they could not do alone; and, when the purpose was attained, their efforts were effective. However, individuals also had personal motives, and the degree to which they continued to contribute to formal efforts was a function of the satisfaction or dissatisfaction they personally derived. If their motives were not satisfied, they withheld efforts or withdrew from the system, and from their point of view the system was inefficient. In the final analysis, "the only measure of the efficiency of a cooperative system is its capacity to survive"; by this Barnard meant its ability to continue to offer enough inducements to satisfy individual motives in the pursuit of group purposes.[39] Viewed in modern terms, the formal organization must renew its energy or acquire negative entropy by offering net satisfactions to contributing members. An inefficient organization could not be effective and therefore would not survive. For Barnard this was a universal principle of organizational theory and one recognized by the Hawthorne researchers and by most organizational theorists thereafter. This attempt to bridge the requirements of the formal organization with the needs of the sociohuman system was a landmark in management thought that stands to this day.

FORMAL ORGANIZATIONS: THEORY AND STRUCTURE

Barnard defined an organization as "a system of consciously coordinated activities or forces of two or more persons"[40] and used this definition to encompass all types of organizations, military, fraternal, religious, academic, business, or whatever. Variations existed in terms of the physical or social environment, the number and kinds of persons involved, or the bases on which persons contributed to the organization. The organization consisted of human beings whose activities were coordinated and therefore became a system. The system was to be treated "as a whole because each part is related to every other part included in it in a significant way."[41] Levels of systems

---

38. Barnard, *Functions of the Executive*, p. 44.

39. *Ibid.*, pp. 55–57.

40. *Ibid.*, p. 72.

41. *Ibid.*, p. 77.

existed, ranging from departments or subsystems in the firm to a conglomeration of many systems forming society as a whole. Regardless of the level of the system being analyzed, all contained three universal elements: (1) willingness to cooperate; (2) common purpose; and (3) communication.

An organization could not, by definition, exist without persons. In Barnard's terms, willingness to cooperate was indispensable, the first universal element of all organizations, and it meant "self-abnegation, the surrender of control of personal conduct, the depersonalization of personal actions."[42] People had to be willing to contribute to a system's objectives; but the intensity and timing of this willingness fluctuated, since it was based on the satisfaction or dissatisfaction experienced or anticipated by organizational members. The organization had to provide adequate inducements, both physical and social, to offset the sacrifices individuals made by forgoing alternative systems and participating in the existing one. For the individual, willingness was the joint effect of "personal desires and reluctances" to participate; for the organization, it was the joint effect of "objective inducements offered and burdens imposed."[43] The net result was subjective and largely individual; hence the need for organizations to be efficient in Barnard's terminology. Securing willingness to cooperate involved the "economy of incentives," which consisted of two parts: (1) offering objective incentives; and (2) changing subjective attitudes through persuasion. Objective incentives were material (money), nonmaterial (prestige, power, etc.), and associational (social compatibility, participation in decision making, etc.). Barnard evaded the question of which of these devices was more effective (or more efficient) by stressing the subjectivity of individual motives. Persuasion, or changing attitudes, was a subjective incentive method that sought by precept, example, and suggestion to condition the motives of individuals. It was not coercion, but inculcation of ideas designed to nurture cooperation. Appeals to loyalty, esprit de corps, belief in organizational purpose, and other abstractions fitted into this category.

Purpose, Barnard's second universal element, was a corollary to willingness to cooperate. Willingness could not be induced unless organizational members knew what efforts would be required of them and what satisfaction might accrue as a result of their cooperation. The executive had to inculcate members with the common purpose or objective of the organization. It was not necessarily what the purpose meant personally to the members, but what they perceived as its meaning to the organization as a whole. Organizational motives and personal motives differed, and individuals contributed not because their personal motives were the same as the organization's, but because they felt that personal satisfaction would come from accomplishing the purpose of the organization.

---

42. *Ibid.,* p. 84. Scott interpreted this (and other ideas of Barnard) as illustrating Barnard's advocacy of a managerial elite, which would concentrate organizational power and exercise undue control over people. For this interpretation of Barnard and the social commentary that accompanies it, see William G. Scott, *Chester I. Barnard and the Guardians of the Managerial State* (Lawrence: University Press of Kansas, 1992).

43. Barnard, *Functions of the Executive,* pp. 85–86.

The process by which these two universal elements became dynamic was through communication. All activity was based on communication, and Barnard developed some principles: (1) "channels of communication should be definitely known"; (2) "objective authority requires a definite formal channel of communication to every member of an organization," that is, everyone must report to or be subordinate to someone; and (3) "the line of communication must be as direct or short as possible" in order to speed communications and reduce distortions caused by transmission through many channels.[44] Barnard developed other principles, but these suffice to capture the essence of the stress he placed on communications, which might well have been expected considering his experience in the Bell system.

Identification of these three universal elements in the formal organization led Barnard to seek universals in the informal organization as well. He defined this informal organization as "the aggregate of the personal contacts and interactions and the associated groupings of people" that were not a part of nor governed by the formal organization.[45] Without structure, and often without conscious recognition of joint purpose, informal groupings arose out of job-related contacts and in turn established certain attitudes, customs, and norms. Informal organizations often created conditions leading to formal organizations and vice versa. Barnard found three functions served by the informal organization: (1) communication; (2) maintenance of cohesiveness in the formal organization by regulating willingness to serve; and (3) maintenance of feelings of personal integrity and self-respect. These functions appeared to be universal and made the informal organization an indispensable part of the formal organization. Informal activities served to make the organization more efficient and also facilitated effectiveness.

THE ACCEPTANCE THEORY OF AUTHORITY

One of Barnard's most unusual ideas was his theory of authority. He defined authority as "the character of a communication [order] in a formal organization by virtue of which it is *accepted* by a contributor to or 'member' of the organization as governing the action he contributes."[46] According to this definition, authority had two aspects: the personal, subjective acceptance of a communication as being authoritative, and the objective, formal character of the communication. In Barnard's theory, the source of authority did not reside in persons of authority, or those who gave the orders, but in the acceptance or nonacceptance of the authority by subordinates. If the subordinates disobeyed an order, they rejected the authority.

This notion was antithetical to all previous concepts of authority, which had been based on some hierarchy of rank or on the power of organizational position. Whereas Follett depersonalized authority and obeyed the law of the situation,

---

44. *Ibid.*, pp. 175–177.

45. *Ibid.*, p. 115.

46. *Ibid.*, p. 163.

Barnard retained the personal aspect but gave it a bottom-up interpretation. For Barnard, individuals needed to assent to authority and would do so if four conditions were met: (1) they understood the communicated order; (2) they believed that the order was consistent with the purpose of the organization at the time of their decision; (3) they believed that the order was compatible with their personal interests as a whole; and (4) they were mentally and physically able to comply with the order.

To explain how an organization could function on such a unique concept of authority, Barnard developed a "zone of indifference" for each individual within which orders were accepted without questioning authority. The zone of indifference might be narrow or wide, depending on the degree to which the inducements outweighed the burdens and sacrifices for the individual. If a subordinate thought the order ran counter to a personal moral code, for instance, then the advantages of staying employed had to be weighed against that personal value system. Not all cases were this clear-cut, and Barnard admitted to many borderline possibilities; however, the individual still had to balance the inducements versus the sacrifices to make the decision. In some organizations, the army for example, certain rules of the game were preestablished, and in those matters the zone of indifference would undoubtedly widen.

The objective aspect of authority was more closely akin to traditional ideas. It rested on the presumption that orders and communications were authoritative and had a "potentiality of assent" when they came from superior positions. In one case, the order might be accepted because authority was imputed to the superior regardless of personal abilities; this was formal authority, or the authority of position. In another instance, the order might be accepted because the subordinate had respect for and confidence in the individual's personal ability and not because of rank or position; Barnard called this the "authority of leadership."

When the authority of leadership was combined with the authority of position, the zone of indifference became exceedingly broad. Nevertheless, Barnard stressed that "the determination of authority remains with the individual."[47] In a free society, individuals always have the choice either to go along with the costs and benefits of directives or not. As long as labor is not conscripted, the acceptance theory is valid. What appears so striking in Barnard's theory is simply another way of stating that all organizations depend on leadership that can develop the capacity and willingness of members to cooperate.

THE FUNCTIONS OF THE EXECUTIVE

In Barnard's analysis, executives operated as interconnecting centers in a communications system and sought to secure the coordination essential to cooperative effort. Communication was a central value in all Barnard's writings, and undoubtedly his

---

47. *Ibid.*, pp. 173–174.

views were influenced by his own experience in the Bell system. To Barnard, executive work "is not of the organization, but the specialized work of maintaining the organization in operation…. The executive functions serve to maintain a system of cooperative effort. They are impersonal. The functions are not, as so frequently stated, to manage a group of persons."[48] To Barnard, the relation of the executive function to the organization was analogous to that of the brain and nervous system to the rest of the body: "It exists to maintain the bodily system by directing those actions which are necessary more effectively to adjust to the environment, but it can hardly be said to manage the body, a large part of whose functions are independent of it and upon which it in turn depends."[49]

Barnard postulated three executive functions: (1) to provide a system of communication; (2) to promote the securing of essential personal efforts; and (3) to formulate and define purpose. In providing for communication, the executive had to define organizational duties, clarify lines of authority and responsibility, and consider both formal and informal means of communication. Informal communication provided for organizational maintenance by allowing issues to be raised and discussed without forcing decisions and overloading executive positions. The second executive function was to bring people into a cooperative relationship and elicit their contributions to the organization. This was largely the task of recruiting and selecting those personnel who could best contribute and who would work together compatibly. It also included what Barnard called maintenance methods: (1) the maintenance of morale; (2) the maintenance of a scheme of inducements; and (3) the maintenance of schemes of deterrents, such as supervision, control, inspection, education, and training, which would ensure the viability of the cooperative system.

The third executive function, formulation of purpose and objectives, has already been examined in some depth. Slightly enlarging this function, Barnard included the functions of decision making and delegation. Delegation was a decision that involved both the ends sought and the means to those ends. The results were decisions about the placement of various responsibilities and authority within the cooperative system so that individuals would know how they contributed to the ends sought. Decision making had two facets: analysis, or the search for the "strategic factors" that would create the set or system of conditions necessary to accomplish the organization's purposes; and synthesis, or the recognition of the interrelationships between elements or parts that together made up the whole system.

Barnard credited John R. Commons for the idea of "strategic factors," those limiting factors that surround the decision making process. According to Barnard, "the strategic factor is, then, the center of the environment of the decision. It is the point at which choice applies. To *do* or not to do *this,* that is the question."[50] Like Fayol, Barnard saw the firm as a purposeful whole functioning in a changing environment.

---

48. *Ibid.,* pp. 215–216.

49. *Ibid.,* p. 217.

50. Barnard, *Functions of the Executive,* p. 202, p. 205.

Barnard's insights provided the foundation for the development of the business policy course at Harvard University and for the terminology of strategic management.[51]

Understanding the decision making process was another contribution of this experienced executive. In "mind in everyday affairs," an appendix to his *Functions of the Executive,* he noted there were two categories of mental processes, "logical" and "non-logical." Logical processes were "conscious thinking which could be expressed in words, or reasoning"; while non-logical processes were "not capable of being expressed in words or as reasoning, which are only made known by a judgment, decision, or action."[52] Non-logical processes were intuitive, or tacit knowledge, which could be correct even though the logic was not apparent. Like logical mental processes, non-logical conclusions could also be in error and Barnard concluded that "both kinds [of mental processes] together are much better than either alone if conditions permit."[53] Barnard's insights into intuitive knowledge furthered out understanding of how managers combine logical analysis and non-logical (intuitive) synthesis in decision making.

As a capstone to the executive functions, Barnard postulated an executive process, which was "the sensing of the organization as a whole and the total situation relevant to it."[54] This was the art of managing and the integration of the whole with respect to internal equilibrium and adjustment to external conditions. Working from the micro level to the macro, Barnard viewed all aspects of society as one large, cooperative system. Every organization had to secure personal and other services from its environment and could "survive only as it secures by exchange, transformation, and creation, a surplus of utilities in its own economy."[55] An organization, for example, had to produce both physical utilities and social utilities in order to survive.

The moving creative force in this organization was moral leadership. For Barnard this meant ethical behavior which was "governed by beliefs or feelings of what is right or wrong regardless of the personal interests..."[56] This included personal responsibility (an individual's character development); official responsibility (when acting "on behalf" of the firm or organization); and corporate responsibility (internal to the interests of stockholders, creditors, and employees, and external to

---

51. Dave McMahon and Jon C. Carr, "The Contributions of Chester Barnard to Strategic Management Theory," *Journal of Management History* 5 (1999), pp. 228–240; and Kenneth R. Andrews, "Introduction to the 30th Anniversary Edition" of Barnard's *Functions of the Executive* (Cambridge, Mass.: Harvard University Press, 1968), p. xix–xx.

52. Barnard, *Functions of the Executive,* p. 302. See also Milorad M. Novicevic, Thomas J. Hench, and Daniel A. Wren, "Playing by Ear ... in an Incessant Din of Reasons: Chester Barnard and the History of Intuition in Management Thought," *Management Decision* 40 (2002), pp. 992–1002.

53. Barnard, *Functions of the Executive,* p. 306.

54. *Ibid.,* p. 235.

55. *Ibid.,* p. 245.

56. Chester I. Barnard, *Elementary Conditions of Business Morals* (Berkeley, Calif.: Committee on the Barbara Weinstock Lectures, 1958), p. 10.

the community and society in general). Leaders had to hold some moral code, demonstrate a high capacity for responsibility, and be able to create a moral faculty in others. He observed that "the endurance of an organization depends upon the quality of leadership; and that quality derives from the breadth of the morality upon which it rests...A low morality will not sustain leadership long, its influence quickly vanishes."[57] *Historia magistra vitae est:* History is life's teacher. But too few pay attention to its lessons.

Chester Barnard was an erudite executive who drew on his own experiences and on sociological theory to build a theory of cooperative systems. As Fritz Roethlisberger recalled, "[Barnard was] the one and only executive in captivity who could not only run a successful organization but could also talk intelligently about what he was up to in the process."[58] Barnard also influenced Elton Mayo, who, in his later work, moved from his view of an organization as a biological organism to the view of an organization as a cooperative social system.[59] Barnard's influence extended the thinking of other Hawthorne researchers, particularly their notion of organizational equilibrium, and later influenced Herbert Simon and his ideas on organizational decision making. Barnard's effective-efficient dichotomy was an attempt to synthesize the ever-present conflict between the objectives and needs for economy of effort of the organization and the personal objectives and needs for satisfaction of the individual. His theory of authority, his call for moral leadership, and his identification of universal elements in both the formal and the informal organization were all significant contributions to evolving management thought.

Summary

Mary Parker Follett and Chester Barnard were bridges between eras. Follett ushered in a group view of humankind and Gestalt psychology while living and working in the scientific management era. Barnard put forth an analysis of the formal organization, yet introduced the role of the informal organization in achieving an equilibrium. Both operated more on a philosophical plane and sought to create a spirit of cooperation and collaboration. Both were concerned with individuals, not per se, but as they achieved being through cooperative group efforts. Both sought to reshape previous concepts of authority, both emphasized cooperation and unity, and both concluded that it was professional, moral leadership that would enhance the effectiveness of organizations and the well-being of people.

---

57. Barnard, *Functions of the Executive*, pp. 282–283.

58. F. J. Roethlisberger, *The Elusive Phenomena* (Cambridge, Mass.: Harvard University Press, 1977), p. 67. Roethlisberger also acknowledged his indebtedness to Barnard, who "greatly influenced my thinking about organizations."

59. Robert T. Keller, "The Harvard 'Pareto Circle' and the Historical Development of Organization Theory," *Journal of Management* 10 (1984), p. 199.

CHAPTER

15 People and Organizations

This and the next chapter examine two branches of developing management thought from about 1930 to the early 1950s. This chapter focuses on the growth and refinement of the human relations movement as it passed through micro and macro phases. The micro phase reflects a significant amount of empirical research that led to substantial modifications in previously held views about people in organizations. The macro phase is characterized by several individuals who built theoretical constructs of social systems analysis that were precursory steps for later developments in organization theory. The title of this chapter, "People and Organizations," indicates the human orientation of this branch of thought, with the structural aspects of organizations becoming a secondary subject of inquiry. Chapter 16, on the other hand, examines a parallel branch of thought in which organizations and organizational structures assume primary importance, while the human element receives relatively less emphasis.

PEOPLE AT WORK: THE MICRO VIEW

Although social scientists had started to probe human behavior in industry in the first three decades of the twentieth century, it was not until the 1930s and 1940s that the greatest outpouring of behavioral research occurred. Whereas the engineer appeared to dominate the scientific management movement, the human relations movement was interdisciplinary, drawing from the contributions of sociologists, psychologists, and anthropologists. A basic premise in their research into the social facet of human behavior was a Gestaltist notion that all organizational behavior involved some human multiplier effect. Each individual, highly variable and complex due to a unique genetic composition and family, social, and work experiences, became even more variable and complex when placed in interaction with other unique individuals. This multiplier effect meant that new means had to be devised to analyze, explain, predict, and guide human behavior.

DEVELOPING CONSTRUCTS FOR GROUP ANALYSIS

Interest in the study of groups appears to have been a product of the Social Gospel and its emphasis on industrial betterment. In 1921, the Federal Council of the Churches of Christ in America approved a national conference on the "meaning of Christianity for human relationships, with special attention to industry ... [and to] effectively stimulate group thinking."[1] This conference, later called The Inquiry, led to some seminal work in the study of groups. One of the leaders, sociologist Eduard Lindeman, worked with others to develop means to observe and categorize group interactions, measure participation, and classify the attitudes of various group members. Lindeman was a friend of Mary Follett, and there appears to have been some use of her notions of group conflict, integration, and power-with rather than power-over. Lindeman also coined the phrase "participant-observer" to describe the role of an observer planted inside a group to corroborate the findings of an outside observer.[2] Over a period of time, however, the role of the participant-observer changed from that of a plant, or stooge, to that of a legitimate researcher who wished to view the situation and its characters from inside, such as the role assumed by Whiting Williams in his travels. In 1933, financial difficulties resulted in the termination of The Inquiry and its pioneering work was forgotten.

The work of Jacob L. Moreno (1889–1974), an M.D. with a specialty in psychiatry, received wider acclaim. Moreno provided an analytical technique, sociometry, which had as its purpose "a process of classification, which is calculated to bring individuals together who are capable of harmonious interpersonal relationships and so create a social group which can function at the maximum efficiency and with a minimum of disruptive tendencies and processes."[3]

Moreno felt that the psychological activities of groups were not due to chance and that groups could be studied through the application of quantitative methods that probed the evolution and patterning of attitudes and interactions. For purposes of analysis, Moreno classified the basic attitudes people showed toward one another as attraction, repulsion, and indifference. In Moreno's sociometry, the members of the group to be studied were asked to indicate those with whom they would, and would not, like to associate. The resulting chart, called a sociogram, mapped the

---

1. Charles D. Wrege, Sakae Hata, and Ronald G. Greenwood, "Before Bales: Pioneer Studies in Analyzing Group Behavior: 1921–1930" (paper presented at the meetings of the Academy of Management, Boston, 1984), p. 2.

2. Eduard C. Lindeman, *Social Discovery: An Approach to the Study of Functional Groups* (New York: Republic, 1924).

3. Jacob L. Moreno, *Who Shall Survive?: A New Approach to Human Interrelations* (Washington, D.C.: Nervous and Mental Disease Publishing, 1934), p. 11.

pairings and rankings of the individuals' preferences for other individuals. These mutual preferences were considered dynamic, as members of the group changed and as problems facing the group changed. For example, in the New York Training School for Girls, where his basic sociometric research was conducted, Moreno found that different pairings appeared depending on whether the expressed choice was for a roommate or a workmate. This task-versus-friendship preference formed a foundation for important distinctions in further research. In industry, sociometric research has sought to combine work groups such that they would be superior in quality and quantity of work as well as conducive to higher morale for the participants.[4]

Psychodrama and sociodrama were also the contributions of J. L. Moreno, and together these ideas formed a basis for role-playing techniques and the analysis of interpersonal relations. Psychodrama consisted of placing a person or patient "on stage" to act out his or her deepest psychic problems with the aid of other "actors" and a therapist.[5] Because other actors were also in the situation, the person's manner of dealing with others was exposed in the role play. Once exposed, therapy could begin on whatever deviations in behavior were disclosed. Further, psychodrama was a cathartic experience, enabling individuals to release and relieve their innermost doubts, anxieties, and other disorders.

Sociodrama, an outgrowth of psychodrama, focused on the group as the method of analysis, whereas psychodrama focused on individual therapy. Sociodrama was based on the assumption that the contrived group was already organized by a set of previously held social and cultural roles. Catharsis and therapy were oriented toward understanding social and cultural roles, such as supervisor-worker, African-American-white, white-Asian, and so forth. Role reversal, or taking the role of the opposite social or cultural group—for example, a white supervisor playing the role of an African-American worker—could be used to broaden role flexibility and create an understanding of how the other person felt. In brief, it was group psychotherapy designed to reduce resentments, frustrations, and misunderstandings. Moreno's work would serve to supplement the counseling and interpersonal relations aspects of the human relations movement by providing methods for studying and changing a person's or group's behavior vis-à-vis other persons or groups. Psychology and psychoanalysis, both essentially concerned with the isolated individual, were inadequate for analyzing group behavior, which was the subject matter most frequently encountered in studying industrial behavior.

Another important construct for analyzing group behavior was that of group dynamics. Credit for originating this concept is generally given to Kurt Lewin (1890–1947), although there is evidence that Moreno substantially influenced

---

4. For example, see Raymond H. Van Zelst, "Sociometrically Selected Work Teams Increase Production," *Personnel* 5 (1952), pp. 175–185. See also Jacob L. Moreno, ed., *The Sociometry Reader* (New York: Free Press, 1960).

5. Jacob L. Moreno, *Psychodrama and Sociodrama* (Boston: Beacon Press, 1946), pp. 177–178.

Lewin's work.[6] Lewin studied at the University of Berlin under Max Wertheimer and Wolfgang Kohler, two of the founders of the Gestalt movement. Lewin's own notions were subsumed under the heading of field theory, which held that group behavior was an intricate set of symbolic interactions and forces that not only affected group structure but also modified individual behavior. A group was never at a steady state of equilibrium, but was in a continuous process of mutual adaptation that Lewin called "quasi-stationary equilibrium." An analogy might be that of a river flowing within its banks; it appears relatively stationary but there is nevertheless gradual movement and change.

Lewin saw behavior as a function of the person and the environment, or field. Using terms such as "life space," "space of free movement," and "field forces," that is, tensions emanating from group pressures on the individual, Lewin and his associates embarked on a series of investigations into resistance to change and the social climate of groups. For example, Lewin and his associates studied groups of ten- and eleven-year-old boys to determine how democratic or authoritarian behavior by the group's leaders affected the boys' behavior. They concluded that authoritarian behavior on the part of the leader impaired initiative and bred hostility and aggressiveness, while the leader behaviors they labeled democratic and laissez-faire were more effective in creating better morale and attitudes.[7] Unfortunately, history has left the incorrect interpretation that this was a study of leadership and its effect on productivity. In reality, one of the counselors (a group leader) interpreted *democratic* as meaning "let the boys do what they want to do." Rather than discard the observations of this group, Lewin designated this group counselor *laissez-faire* (literally, "to let do") and this notion has been erroneously passed down the years as a style of leadership when in fact it meant an absence of leadership.[8]

In research on changing family food habits during World War II, Lewin found that changes were more easily induced through group participation and discussion than through lectures and individual methods. This was a new idea about the introduction of change, the idea that change was facilitated when people felt that they had been involved in the decision to change rather than when they were simply told to change. Lewin viewed changing behavior as a three-step procedure: "unfreezing the present level, moving to the new level, and freezing group life on the new level. Since any level is determined by a force field, permanency implies that the new force

---

6. Barbara A. Wech, "The Lewin/Moreno Controversy," in D. R. Ray, ed., *Proceedings, Southern Management Association* (New Orleans, La.: 1996), pp. 421–423. See also Pitirim Sorokin, *Fads and Foibles in Modern Sociology* (Chicago: Henry Regnery, 1956), pp. 5–6 for the "Discoverer's [Columbus] complex."

7. Kurt Lewin, Ronald Lippitt, and Ralph K. White, "Patterns of Aggressive Behavior in Experimentally Created 'Social Climates,'" *Journal of Social Psychology* 10 (1939), pp. 271–299. For some applications to industrial leadership situations, see Kurt Lewin, *Resolving Social Conflicts* (New York: Harper and Row, 1948), pp. 125–141.

8. Recollections of Gertrud (Mrs. Kurt) Lewin, during discussion of the paper presented by Miriam Lewin Papanek, "Kurt Lewin and His Contributions to Modern Management Theory" (Boston: Academy of Management meetings, August 22, 1973).

field is made relatively secure."[9] Lewin's three-step procedure provided a foundation for future "action research" and organizational change and development techniques.

In 1945, Lewin founded the Research Center for Group Dynamics at the Massachusetts Institute of Technology; after his death, the center was moved to the University of Michigan in 1948 where Rensis Likert and others would further the study of subordinate participation in decision making and the use of the group to achieve changes in behavior. Another of Lewin's disciples, Dr. Leland P. Bradford, established at Bethel, Maine (1947), the first sensitivity training, or human relations, laboratory, called the National Training Laboratory. The essence of this sensitivity training was to achieve changes in behavior through "gut level" interactions that led to increased interpersonal awareness.

Briefly, Lindeman, Moreno, and Lewin brought a new focus to the group rather than the individual. Their work, reflecting Gestalt psychology, led to further studies of social change, social control, collective behavior, and, in general, the effects of the group on the individual. Research moved from the static state of the individual in isolation to the dynamic state of the individual in interaction with others.

THE GROWTH OF HUMAN RELATIONS RESEARCH AND TRAINING

The 1930s had witnessed the emergence of a more favorable political climate for organized labor in which explicit recognition of the role of the worker in industry was required. The passage of the National Labor Relations Act in 1935 (the Wagner Act) and the formation of the CIO brought a new emphasis to collective bargaining. Morris Cooke found a better environment for the rapprochement between labor and management that would ensure industrial peace through worker participation. Cooke and his labor leader coauthor Philip Murray called for management to get the workers involved by "tapping labor's brains" for ideas on how to achieve higher productivity.[10] The theme became that of industrial democracy, which was to mean in essence the application of human relations in the industrial setting in conjunction with organized labor.[11] Accordingly, a number of centers began to appear that would pave the way for the new industrial human relations. In 1943, an interdisciplinary group at the University of Chicago formed the Committee on Human Relations in Industry. Drawing its members from business (Burleigh Gardner), sociology (William Foote Whyte), and anthropology (W. Lloyd Warner), this committee was to characterize the new style of interdisciplinary behavioral research.

9. Kurt Lewin, "Group Decision and Social Change," in Theodore M. Newcomb and Eugene L. Hartley, eds., *Readings in Social Psychology* (New York: Henry Holt, 1947), p. 344.

10. Philip Murray and Morris L. Cooke, *Organized Labor and Production* (New York: Harper and Row, 1940), pp. 211–221.

11. For example, see Clinton S. Golden and Harold J. Ruttenberg, *The Dynamics of Industrial Democracy* (New York: Harper and Row, 1942).

Industrial relations centers also came into vogue. The first was the New York State School of Industrial and Labor Relations at Cornell (1945); others followed, such as the Yale Labor-Management Center and the Institute of Labor and Industrial Relations at the University of Illinois. In 1946, Rensis Likert, a psychologist and statistician, founded the Institute for Social Research at the University of Michigan. In 1947, a group of academicians, labor leaders, and others interested in advancing the state of knowledge in personnel and industrial relations formed the Industrial Relations Research Association.

Human relations training became popular during this period and was oriented toward overcoming barriers to communication and enhancing interpersonal skills. The pathway to opening hidden talents in leaders resided in group-oriented techniques, such as role playing, nondirective counseling, group discussion methods, and, eventually, sensitivity training. Carl Rogers, a clinical psychologist at the University of Chicago, refined the nondirective counseling techniques of the Harvard group.[12] The University of Michigan's Norman Maier (1900–1977) was one of the foremost advocates of "group-in-action" training techniques. For Maier, group decision making was:

A way of controlling through leadership rather than force.

A way of group discipline through social pressure.

Permitting the group to jell on the idea it thinks will best solve a problem.

Pooled thinking.

Cooperative problem solving.

A way of giving each person a chance to participate in things that concern him in his work situation.

A method that requires skill and a respect for other people.[13]

In role playing and cases, technically oriented supervisors were asked to take on new role dimensions, to consult the group, and to discuss various decision alternatives in order to develop human relations skills. Case problems for training in human relations skills were growing in use in industrial and business school education. Many of these cases were adaptable to role-playing situations or otherwise lent themselves to sharpening the students' perceptiveness of human behavior or to developing interpersonal ability. Training to secure teamwork and develop sensitive leaders led to a plethora of texts as managerial and employee education reached a new high in management history. The war had placed great emphasis on the need for trained managers; teamwork and group leadership notions were in vogue, and

12. Carl P. Rogers, *Counseling and Psychotherapy* (Boston: Houghton Mifflin, 1942).

13. Norman R. F. Maier, *Principles of Human Relations* (New York: John Wiley and Sons, 1952).

academic institutions sought to fill an industrial void that called for both productive and satisfied workers. Founded on the Mayoists' call for socially skilled supervisors, enhanced by the ideas and techniques of Moreno and Lewin, and carried out
in research centers and associations, human relations training reached its apogee in
the 1950s.

CHANGING ASSUMPTIONS ABOUT PEOPLE AT WORK

Whereas the scientific management movement was largely in the hands of engineers, the human relations era resided mainly in the hands of behavioral scientists.
Thence came a different perspective on the nature of motivation, the role of the
supervisor in eliciting human collaboration, and the importance of sentiments and
informal activities at work. Investigations in the post-Hawthorne era led to (1) a different interpretation of human motivation; (2) changing notions about the benefits
to be derived from the division of labor; and (3) obtaining greater employee commitment to organizational goals through participation in decision making.

PEOPLE AND MOTIVATION

One set of ideas about motivation is that human beings have certain needs that they
try to satisfy. Need theory is one of the oldest notions about motivation, but research
interest in the subject is fairly recent. In 1938, Henry Murray postulated twenty different needs that people attempt to satisfy.[14] Abraham H. Maslow (1908–1970) built
on Murray's work to form one of the most widely recognized theories of motivation.
Maslow proposed a theoretical hierarchy that identified at least five sets of these
needs: physiological, safety, love, esteem, and self-actualization. These basic needs
were related to one another and were arranged in a hierarchy of "prepotency" (i.e.,
urgency of the drive). The most basic drives were physiological; when these needs
were satisfied, prepotency diminished and the next higher need emerged to dominate behavior. Once a need was gratified, it no longer motivated behavior. In
Maslow's theory, people moved up the ladder of needs as each level was satisfied,
and they could move in a reverse direction if fulfillment of a lower-order need was
threatened or removed. Humans acted as if they were unfilled cups, and all needs
were really never fully gratified. The top rung of the hierarchy was self-actualization,
a phrase that Maslow attributed to Kurt Goldstein, a well-known "holistic" psychologist. While Goldstein saw self-actualization as the fundamental motive from which
sprang all other motives, Maslow took it in a more limited fashion as emerging only
after the other needs were satisfied: "A musician must make music, an artist must

---

14. Henry A. Murray, *Explorations in Personality* (New York: Oxford University Press, 1938). In addition
to inspiring Maslow, Murray also developed the Thematic Apperception Test (TAT), which provided the
basis for the work of John Atkinson and David McClelland on the need for achievement.

paint…What a man *can* be, he must be…to become or more and more what one is, to become everything that one is capable of becoming."[15] Self-actualization varied greatly among individuals, such as being an ideal parent, being an athlete, inventing, creating, or whatever it took to reach one's potential.

The two most widely accepted views of psychology in the mid-1900s were behaviorism and psychoanalysis. As Maslow moved along in his career, he became disenchanted with the behaviorist view of stimulus and conditioned responses. The dominant thinker in psychoanalysis was Sigmund Freud, but there Maslow saw an emphasis on the study of neurotics, or worse. Maslow saw shortcomings in basing psychology on the emotionally disturbed or on infra-human creatures. Maslow proposed that psychology should be a study of the whole person, those values and choices that people make that can be good, honorable, creative, heroic, and so on, and not limiting the field to the evil and ugly, but expanding our human understanding. Maslow's "humanistic psychology" was a revolt against behaviorism and psychoanalysis, creating what became known as the Third Force in psychology. The Third Force gathered momentum as other prominent psychologists agreed that previous thinking had omitted the majority of people, those who were well-adjusted and leading productive, rewarding lives.

Far less well-known than his hierarchy of needs, Maslow's later years brought a richness of insights into the motives of leaders/managers in business organizations. In the summer of 1962, Maslow became a visiting fellow at Non-Linear Systems, in Del Mar, California, at the request of Andrew Kay, the firm's president. This was Maslow's first contact with industry, and he kept journals that summer and later published these in book form as *Eupsychian Management. Eupsychian* was a neologism, a new word, and meant "healthward" or "moving toward psychological health." Coupled with "management," the phrase meant management by competent, mentally healthy, self-actualizing individuals. Maslow felt that one way to improve the mental health of all people would be to begin at the workplace and its management since most people were employed. For example: "The best managers under the American research conditions seem to be psychologically healthier people than the poorer managers in the same researchers. This is easily enough supported by the data from [Rensis] Likert.…"[16]

While Maslow focused on the evolutionary, dynamic qualities of human needs, human relations thinking emphasized the social, belonging needs. Accordingly, the new focus of motivational efforts was to be on the social aspects of the workplace and on the group. Adhering to the Mayo thesis that industry must promote collaboration and social solidarity, individual incentive plans began to receive less prominence while group plans received more. One such plan was the Scanlon plan, named

---

15. A. H. Maslow, "A Theory of Human Motivation," *Psychological Review* 50 (1943), p. 380. See Kurt Goldstein, *The Organism: A Holistic Approach to Biology, Derived from Pathological Data in Man* (New York: American Book, 1939).

16. Abraham H. Maslow, *Eupsychian Management: A Journal* (Homewood, IL: Richard D. Irwin, 1965), p. 75.

after Joseph N. Scanlon (1899–1956), a steelworker, later union official, and eventually a professor at the Massachusetts Institute of Technology.[17] Scanlon's ideas were first implemented at the Adamson Company, a maker of steel storage tanks, and then at the La Pointe Steel Company, a marginal producer that was on the brink of bankruptcy in 1938. Scanlon, in consultation with steelworker officials, worked out a union-management productivity plan that provided for worker bonuses for tangible savings in labor costs. The plan succeeded in saving La Pointe from bankruptcy and spread to other firms. The heart of the Scanlon plan was in a suggestion plan and production committees that sought methods and means to reduce labor costs. There were no individual awards for suggestions, and the first principle of the whole plan was group oriented. Cooperation and collaboration were stressed over competition, and everyone benefited from the suggestions of any one individual. Rewards were plantwide or companywide, encouraging union-management cooperation to reduce costs and share benefits. The traditional suggestion system rewarded the individual, but under Scanlon's notion the group was rewarded.

The Scanlon plan had great appeal to labor because it could save jobs in failing firms, such as La Pointe, and because it explicitly required union participation in the production committees that sought to solve pressing problems. According to Scanlon, such participation was not to create a feeling of belonging or a sense of participation, but was management's explicit recognition of a definite role for the worker and union representatives in suggesting improvements. It was not profit sharing because it did not establish any fixed percentage of profits, nor was it based on profits made available to employees. The Scanlon plan was and is unique in these many respects: (1) a group reward for suggestions; (2) joint committees for discussion and proposing laborsaving techniques; and (3) workers' sharing in reduced costs, not increased profits per se.

Although the Scanlon plan typified the industrial human relations approach to motivation, individual incentives did not pass entirely from the industrial scene. James F. Lincoln (1883–1965) pleaded for and gave experience-based confirmation of appeals to the individual in his *Incentive Management*. Lincoln thought that people were giving up freedom for security, that they were relying on someone else (the government) to assume the responsibility for this security, and that pride in work, self-reliance and other time-tested virtues were declining. The proper answer to this decline, in Lincoln's view, was to return to the "intelligent selfishness" of individual ambition. People were not primarily motivated by money, nor by security, but by recognition for their skill. Lincoln's plan sought to develop employees to their highest ability and then to reward them with a bonus for their contributions to the success of the company. This bonus was over and above the workers' other wages and fringe benefits, which were comparable to those of other manufacturers in Lincoln's Cleveland area. At Lincoln Electric there was no history of work stoppages, labor turnover was almost nonexistent, individual productivity was five times as great as

---

17. Frederick G. Lesieur, ed., *The Scanlon Plan: A Frontier in Labor-Management Cooperation* (Cambridge, Mass.: MIT Press; New York: John Wiley and Sons, 1958).

James F. Lincoln, circa 1951. Courtesy of the Lincoln Electric Company.

that for all manufacturing, dividends per share were constantly rising, product prices were steadily declining, and worker bonuses remained high.[18] The individual incentive plan at Lincoln Electric is still in effect and is as successful as ever. Individuals are responsible for product quality and quantity of output, self-management (in the current vernacular, "empowerment") is practiced, and rewards and recognition are high.[19] Individual incentives à la Lincoln Electric were a minority case, however, and motivational research and advice during this era emphasized factors other than economic ones and stressed the group as the focal point for managerial stimulation.

JOB ENLARGEMENT

In 1776, Adam Smith warned that division of labor could lead to an adverse impact on workers despite its economic advantages. Almost 175 years later some pioneering social scientists and innovative companies began to take Smith's admonition seriously. In 1944, at its Endicott (New York) plant, the International Business Machines Corporation began to combine the jobs of two or more machine operators into one job. IBM called this job enlargement and found that this practice led to higher product quality, less idle time for workers and machines, and "enriched the job" for workers by introducing variety and responsibility.[20]

Walker and Guest found that assembly line workers rebelled against the anonymity of their work even though they declared themselves satisfied with their rate of pay and job security.[21] Having met these more basic needs, the workers sought to avoid the mechanical pacing of the conveyor belt and the repetitiveness of work. Discouraged about their inability to influence the quality of their work, and

18. James F. Lincoln, *Incentive Management: A New Approach to Human Relationships in Industry and Business* (Cleveland, Ohio: Lincoln Electric Co., 1951), pp. 251–289.

19. Virginia P. Dawson, *Lincoln Electric: A History* (Cleveland, Ohio: History Enterprises, Inc. 1999). Although the incentive payment plan has undergone minor changes, the rewards remained high until an economic downturn in 2002–2003. For example, in 1998, a $74 million bonus pool was shared by 3,259 eligible employees, an average of $22,706 plus regular salary and benefits for each employee; however, in 2003 the bonus averaged $10,800 per worker.

20. Charles R. Walker, "The Problem of the Repetitive Job," *Harvard Business Review* 28 (May 1950), pp. 54–58.

21. Charles R. Walker and Robert H. Guest, "The Man on the Assembly Line," *Harvard Business Review* 30 (May–June 1952), pp. 71–83.

unable to fully engage in social interaction because of mechanical pacing of the line, workers were dissatisfied with their jobs. As a result of the pioneering efforts of Walker and Guest, job enlargement and job rotation assumed a new focus in studies of industrial behavior. Job enlargement served to relieve monotony, enhance skill levels, and increase the workers' feeling of commitment to the total product.

PARTICIPATION IN MANAGEMENT

A third area of changing assumptions may be broadly viewed as a "power-equalization" thesis. This was an exhortation to play down the importance of the organizational hierarchy and to give a greater voice to subordinates through participation. Operating on the premise that worker participation would yield a greater commitment to organizational goals and would also further individual and group satisfaction, researchers sought to design work arrangements to permit the involvement of subordinates in decision making. James C. Worthy (1910–1998), drawing on his experiences in the Sears, Roebuck organization, argued for "flatter," less complex organizational structures that would maximize administrative decentralization and thereby lead to improved subordinate attitudes, encourage individual responsibility and initiative, and provide outlets for individual self-expression and creativity.[22] Sears, Roebuck also collaborated with the University of Chicago's Committee on Human Relations in a comprehensive study of employee morale and the influence of the organizational structure on employee relations. Worthy's analysis of "tall" versus "flat" structures, their impact on employee behavior, and the influence of the attitudes and assumptions of executives about people on the organizational structure provided a landmark in management thought, adding to knowledge of the relationship between managerial assumptions and the practice of management.[23]

William B. Given, Jr. (1886–1968), and Charles P. McCormick (1876–1970) were two industrialists who sought to apply the human relations philosophy to their organizations. Using the catchphrase "bottom up management," Given sought to develop and apply a philosophy of participation that essayed "to release the thinking and encourage the initiative of all those down from the bottom up."[24] The notion involved widespread delegation of responsibility and authority, considerable managerial freedom in decision making, a free interchange of ideas at all levels, and the corollary acceptance of the fact that managers grow by having the freedom to fail. Recognizing that a "push from the top" was occasionally needed, Given tried to confine top-down management to setting policy, clarifying goals, and providing training programs for subordinates who needed them.

---

22. James C. Worthy, "Organizational Structure and Employee Morale," *American Sociological Review* 15 (April 1950), pp. 169–179.

23. James C. Worthy, *Brushes with History: Recollection of a Many Favored Life* (privately printed, 1998), pp. 84–101.

24. W. B. Given, Jr., *Bottom Up Management* (New York: Harper and Row, 1949), pp. 3–4.

McCormick's plan of participation became a model for developing junior executive boards in three score or more companies by 1938. The McCormick Multiple Management Plan used participation as a training and motivational method in the early Depression years with the selection of seventeen promising younger managers from various departments to form a junior board of directors. The board was given free access to financial and other company records, encouraged to elect its own officers, and told that "every recommendation they made for the advancement of the business would have the serious consideration of the company."[25] The junior board met with the senior board once a month and at that time submitted its suggestions, which were generally accepted and acted on to a greater extent than McCormick himself had expected. In fact, McCormick attributed company success during the lean Depression years to the efforts of the junior board. One example involved the redesign of the traditional bottle for extracts, which McCormick expected his older executives to wish to retain. The junior board conducted a market investigation, took homemakers' ideas into account, and came up with a new design that was immediately accepted by the senior board and the marketplace.

The junior board evidenced additional successes, such as seeking out other capable young people and sponsoring them as protégés for further development. This early identification of management talent led to better appraisal methods, and the junior board members graduated to the senior board at an average rate of one person per year. Success with the junior board led to the creation of two others, the sales and factory boards, which operated essentially as the junior board for the sales and production departments. In brief, the entire system of boards included a number of advantages: (1) it opened communication channels for the junior managers; (2) it involved these young executives in decision making; (3) it provided a means for identifying and developing executives; (4) it relieved senior board members of a great deal of detailed planning and research; and (5) it provided for interlocking arrangements between various departments to coordinate and follow through on company activities. The McCormick plan as participation in action realized the ideals of Follett's integration and Barnard's effectiveness and efficiency.

In brief, participation in decision making received greater and greater acclaim during this period of management history. Participation was viewed as democracy in action, opening communication channels, diffusing authority, and motivating people to give a greater commitment of themselves to organizational goals.[26] Participative management was a challenge to hierarchical, unilateral authority and sought to bring group forces into play.

---

25. McCormick, *Multiple Management* (New York: Harper and Row, 1938), pp. viii, 5. McCormick's sequel, *The Power of People* (New York: Harper and Row, 1949), indicated further success and international acceptance in nearly four hundred companies.

26. See Gordon W. Allport, "The Psychology of Participation," *The Psychology Review* 53 (May 1945), pp. 119–127.

LEADERSHIP: COMBINING PEOPLE AND PRODUCTION

Kurt Lewin's experiences as a German Jew who fled Nazi Germany undoubtedly influenced his thinking about democratic and authoritarian leaders and their influence on the social climate of groups. Lewin's work exemplified the rise of proparticipation and anti-authoritarian literature during this period. Others of this genre were T. W. Adorno and his associates, who made a significant impact on leadership literature in 1950 with *The Authoritarian Personality*.[27] This behemoth of a volume, influenced by Nazism and fascism, tried to relate personality structure to leadership, followership, morals, prejudices, and politics. The F scale (Fascist Scale), developed as a part of the book, became an instrument for analyzing leadership styles as well as followers' preferences for leaders.

Empirical research, however, was beginning to challenge the idea that one leadership style was good and another was bad. As early as 1945, the Institute for Social Research at the University of Michigan under the direction of Rensis Likert (1903–1981) began a series of empirical studies in a variety of organizations in order to determine what kinds of organizational structures and what principles and methods of leadership resulted in the highest productivity, the least absenteeism, the lowest turnover, and the greatest job satisfaction. Over a period of years, this research led to the identification of two different leadership orientations: (1) an employee orientation, in which the supervisor stressed interpersonal relationships on the job; and (2) a production orientation, in which the supervisor focused on producing and was more concerned with the technical aspects of the job.[28] The Michigan studies found that an employee orientation, coupled with relatively general, rather than close, supervision, led to superior productivity, greater group cohesiveness, higher morale, less worker anxiety, and lower worker turnover. The supervisor obtained higher productivity by building a team spirit, showing concern for the worker, and shifting from a close, production-oriented style to a looser, employee-centered, supportive style.

Contemporaneous with the Michigan studies, the Ohio State University Bureau of Business Research began a series of investigations that would result in the development of a situational approach to leadership. Professors Ralph M. Stogdill (1904–1978) and Carroll L. Shartle formed the core of the research efforts but were aided by numerous others in analyzing leaders and their interaction with the group. Relying heavily on sociometric techniques, the researchers explored members' perceptions of the organization, status, measures of group performance, characteristics of groups, and effective leader behavior in various group situations.[29] The Ohio State

---

27. T. W. Adorno, Else Frenkel-Brunswick, D. J. Levinson, and R. M. Sanford, *The Authoritarian Personality* (New York: Harper and Row, 1950).

28. The bulk of this research and the findings may be found in Rensis Likert, *New Patterns of Management* (New York: McGraw-Hill, 1961).

29. The extent of this research is quite large; for only a sample see Ralph M. Stogdill and Carroll L. Shartle, *Methods in the Study of Administrative Leadership* (Columbus: Ohio State University, Bureau of Business Research Monograph no. 80, 1955); and R. M. Stogdill, *Leadership and Structures of Personal Interaction*, Monograph no. 84, 1956. A symposium honoring Stogdill was edited by David D. Van Fleet for the *Journal of Management* 5 (Fall 1979), pp. 125–165.

findings put forth a two-dimensional view of leadership: an initiating structure dimension in which the leader acted to further the work objectives of the group, and a consideration dimension in which the emphasis was on the needs of the followers and on interpersonal relationships.

Even though the Michigan and Ohio State studies used different terms, each developed a two-by-two matrix of leader behaviors. One dimension was a production-oriented, initiating structure (task-oriented) axis; and another was an employee-oriented, consideration (interpersonal relations–oriented) axis. The two dimensions did not appear to be mutually exclusive; that is, a leader could combine a high initiating structure with high consideration, or a high initiating structure with low consideration, and so on. The advances in understanding leadership were in viewing every leadership situation as one of interaction between the leader and the group. Instead of a single style that led to the best results, there were more dimensions in every situation.

In brief, the micro facet of people and organizations may be characterized as the generation and extension of significant research into industrial behavior. The emphasis was on people in the group, on social motivation, on redesigning organizational tasks to yield greater worker satisfaction, on participation in decision making, and on leadership as a way of combining people and production.

People at Work: The Macro View

On the macro side, research was building into some essential notions of human behavior from a larger viewpoint. There were a number of attempts to conceptualize and theorize about what was being discovered about people at work, and the results were precursory steps to later developments in organizational theory.

THE SEARCH FOR FUSION

One of the earliest and most perceptive studies of the interaction of the social system with the technical-work system was a study of restaurants by William Foote Whyte (1914–2000). A key concept in his analysis was that of status, or the relative prestige of a job in the jobholder's eyes or in the regard of others. The restaurant was characterized by many levels of job status, ranging from the low status of those who bused tables and washed dishes to the relatively high status of cooks. Whyte found that the flow of work of taking customer orders, preparing the food, and serving the food posed a number of human relations problems. Cooks, typically male, held a higher set of culturally derived status distinctions; on the other hand, food servers, usually female, were considered lower status and were typically in the position of initiating work for the cooks by placing the customers' orders to be filled. Since those who initiated work for others were traditionally held to be in a higher status (supervisors initiate work for subordinates), conflicts were inevitable when a lower-status person initiated work for a higher-status one. The conflict was mediated by placing orders on spindles and using high counters so that the initiation of work was depersonalized. In this way the cook could remove and prepare the order under the pretext that it had come not from a lower-status person but from the spindle.[30]

Whyte, an advocate of "participatory action research," developed other nuances of status on the job, such as differentiations among cooks who prepared different types of dishes, but his main argument focused on the use of knowledge of social science to improve performance as well as human relations by (1) understanding the nature and functioning of the social system, and (2) developing teamwork through incentives that fostered collaboration rather than conflict. In brief, Whyte's work was a contribution to the analysis of the interaction of the work system with the social system in an effort to reduce the interpersonal frictions that arose when these two systems met.

Another significant step in developing a macro view was an empirical investigation of a New England telephone company by E. Wight Bakke (1903–1971), then director of Yale University's Labor-Management Center.[31] Bakke sought to determine how the company and the union were bound together in an intricate social system. He found five major elements of "bonds of organization": (1) the functional specifications or the organization's definitions of jobs and departmental relations; (2) the status-system bond, which placed people in a vertical hierarchy of authority and deference with respect to direction; (3) a communication system, which accomplished the transmission of essential information; (4) the reward and penalty system, which provided incentives and controls in order to achieve organizational objectives; and (5) the organization charter bond, which included all those elements that contributed to giving the organization a "character" or a quality of entity. Through analysis of these bonds, Bakke sought to provide an understanding of the interaction between the formal system of relationships and the informal one. Bakke concluded that all five bonds could be analyzed to demonstrate that the formal and informal systems interacted to influence human behavior and that any initiation of change would affect both sides of the equation.

In later work, Bakke attempted to classify the process by which the two systems, formal and informal, could be brought into conjunction. The elements of this fusion process were the "socializing process," by which the organization determined people's position in the organization and the function they performed, and the "personalizing process," which was the workers' determination of the standing they wanted to obtain in the organization and the conduct they expected of themselves. Fusion occurred when formal position and informal standing interacted to define the members' status and when formal function and informal conduct interacted to

---

30. W. F. Whyte, *Human Relations in the Restaurant Industry* (New York: McGraw-Hill, 1948), pp. 69–76. See also Elias H. Porter, "The Parable of the Spindle," *Harvard Business Review* 40 (May–June 1962), pp. 58–66. The spindle was an ideal application of M. P. Follett's ideas; it depersonalized authority and required all to obey the "law of the situation."

31. E. Wight Bakke, *Bonds of Organization: An Appraisal of Corporate Human Relations* (New York: Harper and Row, 1950).

determine the members' role.[32] Bakke was not giving answers to specific human relations problems, but was proposing a conceptual diagnostic tool for organizational analysis. In perspective, it was a building block for the later analysis of sociotechnical systems.

The Tavistock Institute (London) was also responsible for a number of studies concerning the factory both as a social system and as a part of the broader social community. Elliott Jaques (1917–2003) conducted an extensive case study of the Glacier Metal Company based on Lewin's field theory and examined industrial changes as they moved through work groups into the larger community.[33] Such longitudinal research into the ongoing firm was rare, and the results indicated the general theme of studying organizations as interacting sociotechnical systems. Although the Tavistock studies largely reaffirmed the theories of Barnard, they did provide empirical data for studying and coping with social adaptation to technological and organizational changes.

Technological change disrupts the social system, a factor that should be considered in any initiation of change by management. A classic instance was the introduction of new technology in the British coal industry following World War II.[34] The new technology required a breakup of small work groups with high cohesiveness and the substitution of specialized, larger groups working in shifts. The logic of efficiency, that is, the economic benefits of the new long wall method of mining coal, resulted in severe emotional disturbances for the workers, low productivity, and an increasing sense of anomie. The object lesson in this case was that the imperatives of efficiency disrupted the social organization to such an extent that all the hoped-for advantages of the new system could not come about. Technological changes cannot be effective unless there are corresponding provisions to redesign the system of social relationships.

NEW TOOLS FOR MACRO ANALYSIS

Nobel laureate Herbert A. Simon (1916–2001) of Carnegie Mellon University opened another facet of organizational analysis with *Administrative Behavior,* which was greatly influenced by the writings of Chester Barnard. For Simon, management was decision making and he substituted "administrative man" for "economic man" of classical economic theory. Predating Alfred Chandler's *Visible Hand* of the managerial hierarchy, Simon's "administrative man" was the allocation of resources by internal firm decision making rather than the market of classical economic theory. Where Barnard said executives had "limited choices," Simon wrote of limits that

---

32. E. W. Bakke, *The Fusion Process* (New Haven, Conn.: Labor and Management Center, Yale University, 1953); and E. W. Bakke, *Organization and the Individual* (New Haven, Conn.: Labor and Management Center, Yale University, 1952), pp. 14–18.

33. Elliott Jaques, *The Changing Culture of a Factory* (London: Tavistock, 1951).

34. E. L. Trist and K. W. Bamforth, "Some Social and Technical Consequences of the Longwall Method of Coal-Getting," *Human Relations* 4 (1951), pp. 6–38.

"bound the area of rationality" and "the environment that bounds the area of rationality of the person making the decision."[35] Forty years later, he would call this "bounded rationality."[36] He postulated that individuals were limited in their ability to grasp the present and anticipate the future and that these limits to rationality made it difficult to achieve maximizing decisions. "Good enough," or "satisficing," decisions were the result. All administrative activity was group activity; an organization took some decision-making autonomy from the individual and substituted for it an organizational decision-making process. To Simon, this was necessary, since it was impossible for any single, isolated individual to reach any high degree of objective rationality. Decision making then became the result of the participation of many groups in the organization, rather than residing in the scalar chain, and the effect was a "composite" decision.[37] This latter notion appears to be closely related to Mary Parker Follett's interweaving of individual and group decisions into a "cumulative" responsibility. Throughout his work, Simon reflected primarily the influence of Barnard, especially on authority, inducements, and communications, and to a lesser degree the ideas of Follett. For instance, where Barnard wrote of "strategic factors," Simon indicated that these factors and choices "determine behavior over some stretch of time may be called a strategy."[38]

Simon sought a science of decision making from the standpoint of the psychology of human choice and logic. This led to his disagreement with Chester Barnard about nonlogical decision making (see Chapter 14). As he matured professionally, Simon conceded, or perhaps accommodated, Barnard's nonlogical, intuitive thought processes: "[Intuition] is simply the product of stored knowledge and the problem solving by recognition it permits. Intuition, judgment, [and] creativity are basically expressions of capabilities for recognition and response based upon experience and knowledge."[39] Or, one scholar put it: "Thinking is not sandwiched between activities; rather it exists in the form of circumspection present when activities are executed."[40] Intuition, then, is parallel rather than serial processing of information.

With James March (1928–), Simon wrote the influential *Organizations*.[41] March and Simon's theme was that to study organizations, one had to study the complex network of decisional processes that were all directed toward influencing human choices and behavior within the firm. By studying the distribution and allocation of decision-making functions, it would be possible to comprehend the

35. Herbert A. Simon, *Administrative Behavior* (New York: Macmillan, 1945), pp. 41, 243–244.

36. Simon, *Administrative Behavior,* 4th ed. (1997), p. 20.

37. Simon, *Administrative Behavior* (1945), p. 221. Simon says that the term was suggested to him by Chester Barnard. In retrospect, the notion sounds more like Follett than Barnard.

38. Simon, *Administrative Behavior* (1945), p. 67.

39. Simon, *Administrative Behavior,* 4th ed. (1997), pp. 128–129.

40. Karl Weick, "Managerial Thought in the Context of Action," in S. Srivastva, ed., *The Executive Mind* (San Francisco: Jossey-Bass, 1983), p. 223.

41. James G. March and Herbert A. Simon (with the collaboration of Harold Guetzkow), *Organizations* (New York: John Wiley and Sons, 1958).

influences on human behavior, the human choices with respect to organizational inducements, and the establishment of an effective and meaningful equilibrium between the freedoms afforded the individuals to make the decision on the job and the necessity for the organization to impose restrictions on the individual's freedom. Simon's *Administrative Behavior* and Simon and March's *Organizations* were insightful links between Chester Barnard and later refinements in organizational theory.

L. J. Henderson's work on Vilfredo Pareto formed the foundation for another step forward in the analysis of social systems by Harvard's George C. Homans. Homans attended Henderson's seminar on Pareto and coauthored a scholarly work on Pareto that formed the basis for the development of his own view of sociotechnical systems in *The Human Group*.[42] Homans divided the total social system of a group into an external system and an internal system. The external social system was composed of forces or environmental factors, such as policies, job descriptions, work flow, and so forth, outside the group. The internal social system consisted of elements within the life of the group that could influence the external system. Conversely, the external system impinged on the internal system, resulting in an interaction between the formal and informal organizations. Further, Homans categorized various dimensions of group behavior that interacted and could be found in both the internal and the external system: (1) activities, what was formally required of members or behavior that informally emerged; (2) interactions, any transaction between any two or more group members that could be either organizationally prescribed or informally originated; and (3) sentiments, an intangible, elusive concept that had to be inferred from observing behavior. Although the Homans model was exceedingly broad and some of its dimensions elusive, it provided a building block for further developments in organization theory.

Talcott Parsons, another of the Pareto Circle, also played a role in this emerging field of social systems analysis. Parsons received his doctorate from Heidelberg, wrote his dissertation on Max Weber, and introduced Chester Barnard to Weber's bureaucracy. In an early work, Parsons drew together the ideas of Weber, Pareto, Alfred Marshall, and Durkheim and developed a "voluntaristic theory of social action."[43] His ideas influenced Barnard's search for a theory of "cooperative systems," and Parsons provided further work in social systems analysis. In brief, a number of individuals paved the way for organization theory and a view of the organization as a sociotechnical system.

---

42. The results of Henderson's seminar may be found in George C. Homans and Charles P. Curtis, Jr., *An Introduction to Pareto: His Sociology* (New York: Alfred A. Knopf, 1934); the later work was George C. Homans, *The Human Group* (New York: Harcourt Brace Jovanovich, 1950); see also George C. Homans, *Coming to My Senses: The Autobiography of a Sociologist* (New Brunswick, N.J.: Transaction Books, 1984).

43. Talcott Parsons, *The Structure of Social Action* (New York: McGraw-Hill, 1937); and Talcott Parsons, *The Social System* (New York: Free Press, 1951).

Summary

The people and organizations facet of evolving management thought was presented in two phases: (1) the micro level of inquiry into sociometry, group dynamics, participation in decision making, leadership, and the motivational appeals to group members; and (2) the macro search for analytical tools and conceptual models to explain the interactions of the formal and informal aspects of organizations.

The human relationists and their behavioral descendants were to bring about a substantial number of amendments to previously held concepts of management. Among them were (1) an increasing emphasis on the social, group-belonging needs of people; (2) the desire to enlarge jobs to dispel the discouraging side effects of over-specialization of labor; (3) a marked decline in the emphasis on the hierarchy of authority and a call for bottom up, participative management; (4) an increasing recognition of the informal side of the organization and the role of worker sentiments and informal activities; and (5) the development of means to study the interaction of the formal and informal organizations.

The group was the process, the social person the product. Management was exhorted to turn its attention to the social side of behavior, to get people involved, and to thereby couple worker satisfaction and higher productivity.

16 Organizations and People

Contemporaneous with the developments at Western Electric, the writings of Chester Barnard, and the empirical work in human relations, another stream of management thought focused on the structure and design of organizations and the nature of management in the firm. People were not entirely omitted from the equation but were placed in a relatively subordinate role to other concerns. This chapter, covering the period from the advent of the Great Depression to 1951, shows an evolution through three phases: (1) interest in and concern for organizational structure, authority, coordination, span of control, and other issues relevant to organizational design; (2) an increasing concern for a top-management viewpoint that preceded renewed interest in the work of Henri Fayol; and (3) antecedents to later thinking about the nature of the firm and the role of management.

ORGANIZATIONS: STRUCTURE AND DESIGN

The impact of the economic holocaust of 1929 on management thought has never been fully examined. Whereas Chapter 18 attempts such an examination, the focus here is on one set of theorems, the use of organizational design, to alleviate human want and misery. The Mayoist school put forth another set, one of group solidarity and human collaboration. The authors examined here felt that efficient design and operation of organizations was another possible alternative for industry.

JAMES D. MOONEY: THE AFFABLE IRISHMAN

During the cold, dark days of the Depression, the exhortation *Onward Industry!* reflected the premise that through organizational efficiency, the lot of humankind could be improved. *Onward Industry!*, the joint effort of a General Motors executive, James D. Mooney (1884–1957), and a historian-turned-executive, Alan C. Reiley (1869–1947), was an attempt "to expose the *principles of organization*, as they reveal themselves in various forms of human group movement, and to help industry to protect its own growth through a greater knowledge and use of these principles."[1] Although both men were credited as authors, it later became evident that Mooney was responsible for the organizational aspect of the book and Reiley assumed a lesser role and contributed primarily to the historical analysis of organizations. James Mooney was president of the General Motors Export Corporation and traveled over the world as a goodwill ambassador and negotiator for the General Motors Corporation. Described as "affable" and an "experienced diplomat," Mooney completed high school through correspondence, received a degree in mining engineering from the Case Institute in 1908, joined General Motors in 1920, and rose through the organization to head its Export Corporation.[2] Mooney was selected by President Roosevelt as his personal, secret emissary to Hitler when there were attempts to stop the war in 1939 and 1940 before the United States became involved. Failing in this, Mooney was given a special GM assignment to convert the company to defense production. He left GM in 1942 to head the U.S. Navy Bureau of Aeronautics and after the war became president and chairman of the board of Willys Overland Motors.

In *Onward Industry!* Mooney and Reiley set out to develop principles of organizational efficiency that would meet the industrial objectives of "profit through service," which they viewed as an obligation to contribute to "the alleviation of human want and misery."[3] Productive efficiency, though necessary, was not enough to ensure the goal of industrial service. The entire organization, both production and distribution, had to be efficient in terms of providing for organized group effort toward organizational aims and purposes. For Mooney and Reiley, the efficient organization was based on formalism, "the efficient coordination of all relationships."[4] There is no evidence that either Mooney or Reiley had ever heard of Max Weber, but the purposes and methods of these two sets of organizational theorists were more similar than dissimilar. Mooney and Reiley defined what they meant by organization: "Organization is the form of every human association for the attainment of a common purpose."[5] To clarify the role of management in organizations, they made this distinction:

---

1. James D. Mooney and Alan C. Reiley, *Onward Industry!: The Principles of Organization and Their Significance to Modern Industry* (New York: Harper and Row, 1931), p. xiii. This book was revised by Mooney and Reiley in 1939 and retitled *The Principles of Organization*. Mooney revised the book again in 1947. References that follow distinguish between *Onward Industry!* and the revised edition where appropriate.

2. Personal insights into Mooney are from [W. Jerome Arnold], "Drawing the Rules from History," *Milestones of Management*, vol. 1 (repr. McGraw-Hill, New York, 1965), pp. 10–11.

3. Mooney and Reiley, *Onward Industry!*, p. xiii.

4. *Ibid.*, p. xv.

5. *Ibid.*, p. 10.

> Management is the vital spark which actuates, directs, and controls the plans and procedure of organization. With management enters the personal factor, without which no body could be a living being with any direction toward a given purpose. The relation of management to organization is analogous to the relation of the psychic complex to the physical body. Our bodies are simply the means and the instrument through which the psychic force moves toward the attainment of its aims and desires.[6]

Using the body-mind analogy for organization and management, Mooney and Reiley formulated their principles of organization. The first principle was that of coordination, which meant "the orderly arrangement of group effort, to provide unity of action in the pursuit of a common purpose."[7] Coordination was a broad principle that contained all the other principles of organization. Coordination had its foundation in authority, or "the supreme coordinating power." This did not mean autocracy, but the source of responsibility for direction. Authority was a right that inhered legitimately in the organization, as opposed to power, which was an individual possession. In government, for example, authority represented de jure governments, while power represented de facto governments. Since coordination implied an aim or objective, every member of the organization had to understand this common purpose, and Mooney and Reiley called this *doctrine,* or the "definition of the objective." Doctrine was similar to the religious concept of creed, but for industry it meant the attainment of "surplus through service," which was the objective of business. The greater the members' understanding of the organization's doctrine, the greater the degree of teamwork and the accomplishment of objectives.

Another principle was the *scalar principle,* which meant that there was a hierarchy of degrees of authority and corresponding responsibility in every organization. The scalar principle had its foundation in leadership, which "represents authority." The essence of this idea was that leaders were designated through the process of delegation, which conferred authority on a subordinate by a superior. Delegation always meant the conferring of authority, whether authority over people or authority for task performance. Conversely, authority always carried with it responsibility for accomplishing what was authorized.

The *functional principle* was the "distinction between different kinds of duties." Every organization had functional differentiation in the sense that people performed different kinds of duties, such as production, sales, accounting, security, and so on. This principle of functional differentiation could be seen in the division of labor, which, as indicated in earlier discussion, created a need for coordination. Another example of functional differentiation was the distinction between line and

---

6. *Ibid.,* p. 13.

7. J. D. Mooney, *The Principles of Organization,* rev. ed. (New York: Harper and Row, 1947), p. 5. The substance of Mooney's revision and the original *Onward Industry!* differ only slightly, the revision being more concise and definitive.

staff. According to Mooney and Reiley, there should never be any confusion about line and staff because line represented "the authority of man; … Staff, the authority of ideas."[8] Line commanded, staff advised, and they envisioned no potential conflict in line-staff relations as long as this dichotomy was kept in mind.

Following their section on the principles of organization, Mooney and Reiley examined the history of organizations to demonstrate these principles in operation. They examined Greece, Rome, and other ancient civilizations and rulers to show the scalar and other principles. Though largely a description of governments and the military, the Catholic Church came in for some close scrutiny by the two Irish Catholics. The principle of coordination found its authority in God, who delegated it to the pope as the supreme coordinating authority. The scalar principle operated from the pope, through the cardinals (who were often both line and staff), to the bishops and priests in the delegation of authority. In the development of staff, the church operated on a *compulsory staff service* concept. Under this rule, a superior had to consult the elder monks even on minor matters. On matters of major importance, everyone had to be consulted. This concept did not abridge the line authority but compelled the superior to consult everyone before rendering a decision. The superior could not refuse to listen. In industry, the compulsory staff principle would not protect the manager from errors in judgment, but it would serve to allay errors of knowledge.

In retrospect, Mooney and Reiley's principles resembled Weber's bureaucratic hierarchy, his rational-legal notion of authority, and his requirement for specifically defined duties and responsibilities. Mooney and Reiley made no reference to Weber, and, since Weber's work had not been translated into English at this time, it must be assumed that they independently developed their format for efficiency through the proper organizational structure. The perspective that Mooney and Reiley brought to their writing was that of mass-production industry. Their study of governments, armies, and the Catholic Church undoubtedly reinforced their conclusions that large-scale organizations required formalism in design. Hierarchical structures, departmentation, the use of staff, the importance of objectives in promoting teamwork, and the need for coordination all were found to be appropriate to their view of organization. The human element was not missing entirely, but was relegated to a secondary role. For organization theory, Mooney and Reiley's principles became a building block for a formalistic view of organizations.

TEXTS, TEACHERS, AND TRENDS

A number of individuals continued the industrial engineering type of texts for management education and reflected more of a shop management view of organizations. Some were unique in their approach, but for the most part they continued to stress production layout, scheduling, materials handling, organizing the shop,

---

8. *Ibid.*, p. 34.

production control, and other largely technique-oriented subjects. One unique approach was that of Henry Dennison (1877–1952), who had been a pioneer in the installation of the Taylor system in his own firm. The title of Dennison's book, *Organization Engineering,* was misleading, for it advocated a design of organizational structure that was diametrically opposed to Mooney and Reiley's approach. Dennison began with the idea that organizational engineering was "making a success of group life" and built the organizational structure from groups of people who, under capable leadership, resolved their frictions and unified their motives in a single direction. Instead of designing the structure and tasks first, Dennison would find like-minded people, group them, and develop the total organizational structure last. In this sense, Dennison actually anticipated by a decade or more the behavioralists who advocated sociometrically selected work teams or other mutual-choice devices to group workers by compatibility.

Dennison's view of motivation was also unique:

> Four general groups of tendencies which may actuate a member of any organization are: (1) regard for his own family's welfare and standing; (2) liking for the work itself; (3) regard for one or more members of the organization and for their good opinion, and pleasure in working with them; and (4) respect and regard for the main purposes of the organization…. Only when impelled by the four combined can all of man's power be brought into steady and permanent play.[9]

Dennison advocated modifying jobs so that they would provide greater satisfaction. He did not develop any notion of job enlargement but was on the fringe of later behavioral theory, which sought to make work satisfying. He recognized informal groups and their influence on restriction of output and proposed nonfinancial incentives that, when properly mixed with economic incentives, built loyalty. Principles of organization were not to be "sacred in and of themselves," and the final organizational structure should be flexible to strengthen group performance, not to ossify it. Authority and responsibility should be clearly defined; a sound organizational structure furthered organizational efficiency if it was flexible enough to meet changing group and organizational needs, that is, if it promoted "success of group life." Dennison also recognized limits to and variations in the number of persons to whom the executive could give attention. The span of control, in his view, "seldom runs beyond six to twelve people."[10]

Dennison was a progressive employer, initiating advanced ideas of profit sharing, low interest loans for employees to purchase homes, employee representation plans, unemployment insurance to stabilize employees' incomes, and one of the early (1913) personnel departments.[11] Dennison quoted Mary Follett on coordination and

---

9. Henry S. Dennison, *Organization Engineering* (New York: McGraw-Hill, 1931), pp. 63–64.

10. *Ibid.,* pp. 137–138.

11. W. Jack Duncan, "Henry Sturgis Dennison," in Morgen Witzel, ed., *Biographical Dictionary of Management,* vol. 1, pp. 233–236.

the law of the situation and this appears to have influenced his view of the labor-management relationship.[12] The labor and institutional economist, John R. Commons, quoted Dennison: "We never give an order, we sell the idea to those who must carry it out."[13] This has the flavor of Follett's thinking, and Commons used this as an example of "a managerial transaction" in Dennison's firm of negotiating with labor in an exchange relationship.

Other contributions during the 1930s were more production oriented. C. Canby Balderston and his associates defined management as "the art and science of organizing, preparing, and directing human effort applied to control the forces and to utilize the materials of nature for the benefit of man."[14] They said that all managers, regardless of the type of enterprise, were concerned with four basic elements: "men, money, machines, and material." They proceeded to analyze product design, physical facilities and equipment, power, heat, light, ventilation, inventory control, production control, and other shop-oriented subjects. Organization was treated within a formal framework in the Mooney and Reiley style, and personnel management, an emerging area of consideration during the era, was one of the few subjects to appear outside shop-management boundaries.

On the academic front, some were sensing a need for a synthesis in management education. Professors E. H. Anderson of the University of Alabama and G. T. Schwenning of the University of North Carolina perceived the fragmentary nature of management literature and made a contribution by attempting to "appraise and synthesize" the work of others.[15] Though few new ideas were introduced, their synthesis and extensive bibliography provide a valuable research insight into this era. Anderson and Schwenning did note, however, the appearance of Coubrough's 1930 translation of Henri Fayol's work, although they did not give it more than passing mention.

In 1936, Charles L. Jamison of the University of Michigan and William N. Mitchell of Chicago invited a group of management teachers to the University of Chicago's Quadrangle Club for the purpose of discussing the formation of a society to advance the philosophy of management.[16] Enough interest was evoked for Wharton's Balderston to invite the group to Philadelphia for another conference in

---

12. Dennison, *Organization Engineering,* pp. 100, 166.

13. John R. Commons, *Institutional Economics: Its Place in Political Economy* (New York: Macmillan, 1934), p. 67. For the Commons-Dennison connection, see Kyle Bruce, "Activist Management: The Institutional Economics of Henry S. Dennison" (doctoral dissertation, University of Wollongong, New South Wales, Australia, 1997), pp. 285–286.

14. C. Canby Balderston, Victor S. Karabasz, and Robert P. Brecht, *Management of an Enterprise* (New York: Prentice-Hall, 1935), p. 5.

15. E. H. Anderson and G. T. Schwenning, *The Science of Production Organization* (New York: John Wiley and Sons, 1938).

16. Preston P. LeBreton, "A Brief History of the Academy of Management," appendix in Paul M. Dauten, Jr., ed., *Current Issues and Emerging Concepts in Management* (Boston: Houghton Mifflin, 1962), pp. 329–332.

1937. R. C. Davis of Ohio State wrote the constitution in 1940–1941, officers were elected, and the Academy of Management began formal operations in 1941. The objectives of the academy were stated as follows:

> The Academy is founded to foster the search for truth and the general advancement of learning through free discussion and research in the field of management. The interest of the Academy lies in the theory and practice of management ... as it relates to the work of planning, organizing, and controlling the execution of business projects. It is also concerned with activities having to do with the forming, directing, and coordinating of departments and groups which are characteristic of administrative management....
>
> The general objectives of the Academy shall be therefore to foster: (a) A philosophy of management that will make possible an accomplishment of the economic and social objectives of an industrial society with increasing economy and effectiveness. The public's interest must be paramount in any such philosophy, but adequate consideration must be given to the legitimate interests of Capital and Labor. (b) Greater understanding by Executive leadership of the requirements for a sound application of the scientific method to the solution of managerial problems, based on such a philosophy. (c) Wider acquaintance and closer co-operation among such persons as are interested in the development of a philosophy and science of management.[17]

Academy membership was primarily restricted to professors, although a few businesspeople could be selected. The outbreak of World War II and consequent travel restrictions held academy activities dormant until 1947, when annual meetings were resumed. Jamison, as founder, presided from 1936 to 1940; Brecht was president from 1941 to 1947, and Davis became president in 1948. The academy reflected the increased awareness of the necessity of teaching management and of bringing together diverse ideas into a search for management theory.

Another trend indicated an increasing awareness of the relationship of industry to society as a whole. In 1928, Arthur G. Anderson of the University of Illinois had published *Industrial Engineering and Factory Management*.[18] This first edition took the works administration-industrial engineering approach typical of that era. In 1942, Merten J. Mandeville (University of Illinois) and John M. Anderson (Minneapolis Honeywell, Inc.) became coauthors with A. G. Anderson and introduced a larger view of the management function that stressed the need

---

17. *Ibid.*, p. 330. See also Charles D. Wrege, "The Inception, Early Struggles, and Growth of the Academy of Management," in Daniel A. Wren and John A. Pearce II, eds., *Papers Dedicated to the Development of Modern Management* (Chicago, Ill.: Academy of Management, 1986), pp. 78–88.

18. A. G. Anderson, *Industrial Engineering and Factory Management* (New York: Ronald Press, 1928).

for management to relate effectively to its public. In the authors' view, management had to assume its social responsibility and promote both economic and social progress through productive and distributive efficiency as well as through emphasis on "the human side" of the company.[19] Discussing relations with customers, stockholders, the public at large, and employees, the authors showed an awareness of other stakeholders in management. Although a large portion of the book was devoted to traditional production subjects, it did reflect an increasing concern for a larger view of the role of management.

BUILDING BLOCKS FOR ADMINISTRATIVE THEORY

In 1937, Gulick and Urwick assembled a series of papers that reflected a variety of ideas about management. Included were essays by Mooney, Dennison, Henderson, Whitehead, Mayo, Follett, Graicunas (discussed shortly), and the editors themselves. The publication comprised the first U.S. rendition of Henri Fayol's work, including Urwick's comparison of Fayol with Mooney, and an early account of the Hawthorne research.[20] Luther Gulick (1892–1993) was director of the Institute of Public Administration at Columbia University and had served as a member of President Roosevelt's Committee on Administrative Management, which attempted, without much success, to reform and reorganize the federal bureaucracy.[21] Gulick credited Fayol as describing managerial work and then amplified it with POSDCORB—Gulick's view of the functions of the manager. The initials represented the following activities:

> Planning, that is working out in broad outline the things that need to be done and the methods for doing them to accomplish the purpose set for the enterprise;
>
> Organizing, that is the establishment of the formal structure of authority through which work subdivisions are arranged, defined, and coordinated for the defined objective;
>
> Staffing, that is the whole personnel function of bringing in and training the staff and maintaining favorable conditions of work;
>
> Directing, that is the continuous task of making decisions and embodying them in specific and general orders and instructions and serving as the leader of the enterprise;

———

19. A. G. Anderson, Merten J. Mandeville, and John M. Anderson, *Industrial Management,* rev. ed. (New York: Ronald Press, 1942), p. 3.

20. Luther Gulick and Lyndall Urwick, eds., *Papers on the Science of Administration* (New York: Institute of Public Administration, Columbia University, 1937).

21. *Report of the President's Committee on Administrative Management* (Washington, D.C.: U.S. Government Printing Office, 1935). This report called for restructuring of governmental agencies and offices to eliminate overlapping duties and provide for more effective measures of executive responsibility.

Co-ordination, that is the all important duty of interrelating the various parts of the work;

Reporting, that is keeping those to whom the executive is responsible informed as to what is going on, which thus includes keeping himself and his subordinates informed through records, research, and inspection;

Budgeting, with all that goes with budgeting in the form of fiscal planning, accounting, and control.[22]

Gulick visualized management as a universal activity, but his description of the managerial function was applied primarily to governmental administration. Gulick also developed a theory of departmentation and expanded on Aristotle's questions of two thousand years before concerning whether to group activities by subjects or by persons (see Chapter 2). Gulick began with the premise that the major purpose of organization was coordination. He then formulated a "principle of homogeneity," which required the grouping of similar activities under one head; otherwise friction and inefficiency would result. In grouping activities by this principle, Gulick noted four primary methods: (1) purpose, or function performed, such as "furnishing water, controlling crime or conducting education"; (2) the process used, such as "engineering, medicine ... stenography, statistics, accounting"; (3) persons or things dealt with or served, such as "immigrants, veterans, Indians"; and (4) the place where the service is rendered.[23]

In Gulick's scheme, these would be major groupings, or primary levels of departmentation, and any one could be chosen depending on which best served the organization's objectives. For example, if the primary level was grouped by place (i.e., geographically), the secondary level might be grouped by purpose, process, clientele, or even again by place. The same would be true for the third level and so on. Any decision about how to group activities had to follow the principle of homogeneity, ensure coordination, and maintain flexibility as the organization grew or as its objectives changed.

Lt. Colonel Lyndall Fownes Urwick (1891–1984), coeditor with Gulick of the *Papers on the Science of Administration,* distinguished himself by his efforts to develop a general theory of organization and management. Educated at Oxford, he served honorably in Great Britain's army and government in World Wars I and II, was organizing secretary of Rowntree and Company Cocoa Works (1920–1928), was elected and served as director of the International Management Institute in Geneva (1928–1933), and was chairman of Urwick, Orr and Partners, Ltd., management consultants, until his retirement. Influenced to a great degree by B. S. Rowntree and Oliver Sheldon, Urwick wrote on a wide range of subjects: in collaboration with

22. Luther Gulick, "Notes on the Theory of Organization," in Gulick and Urwick, *Papers on the Science of Administration,* p. 13.

23. *Ibid.,* p. 15, pp. 21–31.

E. F. L. Brech on biographical sketches of pioneers in scientific management, with Henry Metcalf on Mary Follett's papers, with Gulick, and on his own on various aspects of organizations.

Although his writings spanned many decades, his work in the late 1920s and 1930s was heavily oriented toward developing principles of organization. He identified eight principles applicable to all organizations: (1) the "principle of the objective," that all organizations should be an expression of a purpose; (2) the "principle of correspondence," that authority and responsibility must be coequal; (3) the "principle of responsibility," that responsibility of higher authorities for work of subordinates is absolute; (4) the scalar principle; (5) the "principle of the span of control," concluding that no superior can supervise directly the work of more than five or six subordinates whose work interlocks; (6) the "principle of specialization," or limiting one's work to a single function; (7) a coordination principle; and (8) the "principle of definition," or a clear prescription of every duty.[24]

THE SPAN OF CONTROL

While Gulick and Urwick were building organization and management theory, V. A. Graicunas was furnishing a mathematical interpretation of the span of control. Graicunas (1898–1947), an American of Lithuanian descent, was a noted international consultant in industrial administration. After a career in consulting, he served in the United States Army Air Corps during World War II. In the Soviet Union on a business trip in 1947, Graicunas was arrested by the secret police and subsequently died somewhere in the labor camps.[25] Graicunas's ideas on the span of control were largely influenced by Lyndall Urwick, who, in turn, followed the theme of the British general Sir Ian Hamilton: "As to whether the groups [of subordinates] are three, four, five, or six, it is useful to bear in mind a by-law: the smaller the responsibility of the group member, the larger may be the number of the group—and vice versa ... the nearer we approach the supreme head of the whole organization, the more we work towards groups of six."[26]

Graicunas observed that industrial managers were hampered by trying to supervise too many subordinates; this situation was due, in part, to their desire "to enhance their prestige and influence" by adding sections and departments to their

24. See L. Urwick, "Principles of Direction and Control," in John Lee, ed., *A Dictionary of Industrial Administration* (London: Sir Isaac Pitman and Sons, 1928); L. Urwick, *Management of Tomorrow* (London: Nisbet, 1933), in which he developed a "pure theory of organization"; and L. Urwick, *Scientific Principles of Organization* (New York: American Management Association, 1938). For the contributions of Urwick and others in the development of management in Great Britain, see E. F. L. Brech, *The Evolution of Modern Management*, 5 vols. (Bristol, England: Thoemmes Press, 2002).

25. An interesting account of Graicunas's life, career, and demise may be found in Arthur G. Bedeian, "Vytautas Andrius Graicunas: A Biographical Note," *Academy of Management Journal* 17, no. 2 (June 1974), pp. 347–349.

26. Ian Hamilton, *The Soul and Body of an Army* (London: Arnold Publishing House, 1921), p. 229.

responsibilities. Such ego bolstering could be deadly from the standpoint of delays, lack of coordination, and confusion from trying to control too many subordinates. Graicunas indicated two factors to support his argument for a narrow or limited span of control: the psychological principle of "span of attention," which stated that the human brain could cope with only so many variables at any one time; and his own development of "cross relationships" and "direct group relationships" in addition to "direct single relationships." On this second point, Graicunas described these relationships this way:

> In almost every case the superior measures the burden of his responsibility for the number of direct single relationships between himself and those he supervises. But in addition there are direct group relationships and cross relationships. Thus, if Tom supervises two persons, Dick and Harry, he can speak to them as a pair.... Further what Dick thinks of Harry and what Harry thinks of Dick constitute two cross relationships which Tom must keep in mind in arranging any work over which they must collaborate in his absence.... Thus, even in this extremely simple unit of organization, Tom must hold four to six relationships within his span of attention.[27]

With the addition of these different sets of relationships, Graicunas postulated that when the number of direct single relationships increased arithmetically with the addition of one subordinate, the corresponding increase in the number of direct group and cross-relationships caused the total number of relationships to increase in exponential proportion. Where n represented the number of persons supervised, Graicunas' formula demonstrated this growth:

n	1	2	3	4	5	6	7	8	9	10	11	12
Total	1	6	18	44	100	222	490	1,080	2,376	5,210	11,374	24,708

The significance of this geometric growth was that increasing n from 4 to 5 increased working capacity 20 percent, whereas the possible number of relationships increased from 44 to 100, or 127 percent. Hence, Graicunas argued that the span of control should be limited to a "maximum of five and most probably, only four."

Exceptions to this decision rule were permissible in the case of routine work at lower organizational levels where workers worked relatively independently of others, where they had little or no contact with others, and where supervisory responsibilities were less complex and therefore allowed a wider span of control. However, at upper levels, where responsibility was greater and often overlapped, the span should be less. Graicunas also noted that "it is not possible to assign comparable weights to these different varieties of relationship," suggesting that he was aware that not all interaction possibilities were operative at all times. If some interactions were not

---

27. V. A. Graicunas, "Relationship in Organization," in Gulick and Urwick, *Papers on the Science of Administration,* p. 184.

required, for example, if Dick's work did not interlock with Harry's or if the job was routine, then the number of relationships would be less and the span might be wider. Graicunas's formula represented maximum possible relationships, not what might actually be operative at one given point in time.

TOWARD A TOP-MANAGEMENT VIEWPOINT

A second facet of this era involved developments that shifted management thought from a shop-management, production orientation to a larger view of the activity of management. The design of organizational structures and the search for organizational principles were still subjects for discussion; however, organizations per se were beginning to take a back seat to the study of management as a prelude to the rediscovery of Henri Fayol. Finally, we will examine issues about the separation of ownership and control and the nature of the business firm.

RALPH C. DAVIS: *PATER FAMILIAE ET MAGISTER*

Ralph Currier Davis (1894–1986) received his mechanical engineering degree in 1916 from Cornell, where he studied under the pioneering Dexter Kimball.[28] After becoming a registered industrial engineer he went to work on the staff of the Winchester Repeating Arms Company, where, as he put it, "I quickly discovered that I knew practically nothing about management."[29] His experiences were soon enriched by observing Carl Barth, Dwight Merrick, and members of the staff of A. Hamilton Church's consulting firm, who were all on assignment at Winchester. In 1923, Davis was invited to Ohio State University to establish a department of management in the College of Commerce and Administration. His first book was in the traditional, shop-level, "operative management" orientation. Davis stated that the fundamental functions and principles of factory management were universal in their application and that a sound organization was essential:

> In developing the organization, consideration should be given to (1) the fundamental functions to be performed and their relation to one another, (2) the proper division of responsibility, (3) the definite location of responsibility, (4) the proper functioning of the system, (5) the flexibility of the organization, (6) provision for future growth, (7) personal characteristics and abilities, (8) the creation of an ideal, and (9) the quality of the leadership.[30]

---

28. Biographical information is based on personal correspondence from Ralph C. Davis, May 18, 1969, and on John F. Mee, "*Pater Familiae et Magister*" [Father of family and teacher], *Academy of Management Journal* 8 (March 1965), pp. 14–23.

29. Ralph C. Davis, personal communication, May 18, 1969.

30. Ralph C. Davis, *The Principles of Factory Organization and Management* (New York: Harper and Row, 1928), p. 41.

In 1927, Davis was asked by General Motors to set up a department of management in the General Motors Institute at Flint, Michigan. It was at General Motors from 1927 to 1930 that he was exposed to the philosophies and principles of Donaldson Brown and Alfred P. Sloan, Jr., and from that time on he began to formulate his administrative approach, as opposed to his previous operative, or shop-level approach, to management. Davis's viewpoint was further reshaped by his acquisition (in 1930 or 1931) of Coubrough's translation of Henri Fayol's *Industrial and General Administration*. In 1934, this melding of ideas led Davis to develop his "organic functions" of management—planning, organizing, and controlling.[31] R. C. Davis's life and work illustrate the ecology of evolving management thought over a span of more than four decades. His 1928 work was largely a shop-level, operative-oriented approach to management; in 1934, he developed the organic functions of planning, organizing, and controlling; and in 1940, he developed the management process further, but still devoted a large portion of his book to production-shop subjects. His notions of management theory and practice were clearly in transition when he published *The Fundamentals of Top Management* in 1951. In this effort, he moved almost entirely to an administrative management viewpoint.

In *Fundamentals of Top Management*, Davis defined management as "the function of executive leadership" and stressed the need for professional managers who had a sound philosophy of management with respect to leadership and the relations between business and the community. Since the business organization was largely an economic institution, its objectives were "any values that the business organization is required or expected to acquire, create, preserve, or distribute."[32] Organizational objectives were constrained by community ideals or commonly held standards of business conduct. Executive leadership was a motivating force that stimulated and directed the members of the organization toward the satisfactory achievement of its objectives.

In developing the management process, Davis viewed his organic functions as universally applicable to all types of enterprises. Planning was the "specification of the factors, forces, effects and relationships that enter into and are required for the solution of a business problem" and provided "a basis for economical and effective action in the achievement of business objectives."[33] Planning was mental work of a creative nature that facilitated understanding and accomplishment of the organization's mission. Organizing involved "bringing functions, physical factors, and personnel into proper relationships with one another" and was based on authority, which was "the right to plan, organize, and control the organization's activities."[34] This represented the traditional formal view of authority as the right to decide, which Davis found ultimately legitimated in organized society. For example, society

---

31. Ralph C. Davis, *The Principles of Business Organization and Operation* (Columbus, Ohio: H. L. Hedrick, 1935), pp. 12–13.

32. Ralph C. Davis, *The Fundamentals of Top Management* (New York: Harper and Row, 1951), p. 10.

33. *Ibid.*, p. 43.

34. *Ibid.*, p. 281.

upholds the right of private property; individuals exercise this right through stock ownership in a company and delegate the management of their property to the board of directors, who in turn delegate authority down through the scalar chain.

Davis defined control as "the function of constraining and regulating activities that enter into the accomplishment of an objective."[35] Davis identified eight control functions: routine planning, scheduling, preparation, dispatching, direction, supervision, comparison, and corrective action. In this scheme, he made a useful distinction by indicating the importance of *timing* in phases of control. For instance, routine planning, which provided information for the execution of plans, was a phase of control. On the other hand, creative planning involved advance planning of a general nature and was part of the organization's total planning function. The phases of control were (1) *preliminary* control, which included routine planning, scheduling, preparation, and dispatching; (2) *concurrent* control, or direction, supervision, comparison; and (3) *corrective action.* Preliminary control tried to design in advance constraints and regulations that would ensure proper execution of the plan; on the other hand, concurrent control operated while performance was in progress. Corrective action completed the control cycle and began the preliminary phase again by identifying deviations and by replanning or taking other actions to prevent recurrence of deviations. Although many of his predecessors had written of control, Davis presented a much more insightful and comprehensive view of this function.

In comparing Davis and Fayol, it is possible to see that despite their similarities, they were both unique. Both stressed the universality of management, recognized the necessity and importance of teaching management, and held to a formalized view of management. Fayol's process added command and coordination to planning, organizing, and controlling. Davis did not include command, but included it under the more descriptive label of "executive leadership," which permeated all other functions. Likewise, Davis treated coordination as operating throughout his organic functions and not separate, as regarded by Fayol. On the other hand, Fayol developed staffing as a subfunction of organizing, but Davis paid relatively less attention to the personnel function.

HARRY HOPF: TOWARD THE OPTIMUM

During this era another individual began with the precepts of Frederick Taylor and concluded with a broader conception of the role of top management. Harry Arthur Hopf (1882–1949) was a penniless immigrant to the United States who became a widely respected consultant, author, and executive.[36] Hopf began his career as a clerk

---

35. *Ibid.*, p. 663.

36. See Homer J. Hagedorn, "White Collar Management: Harry Arthur Hopf and the Rationalization of Business" (Ph.D. dissertation, Harvard University, Cambridge, Mass., 1955); more readily available is Edmund R. Gray and Richard J. Vahl, "Harry Hopf: Management's Unheralded Giant," *The Southern Journal of Business* 6 (April 1971), pp. 69–78.

in the office of a life insurance company and became acquainted with the ideas of Taylor, which were then in vogue. Hopf applied the principles of scientific management to office work and became more interested in efficiency and the scientific approach to work. He did studies of compensation methods for office workers and wondered why so little attention had been paid to the compensation of executives. In his studies of the problem, he was critical of the typical executive payment plans, such as profit sharing, stock options, and deferred payments. Hopf felt that these plans did not adequately tie payment to performance, which was a conclusion Taylor had reached about worker compensation some years before. The conventional answer of Hopf's era was that executives did a different kind of work, which was intangible and not subject to measurement. Not satisfied with that position, Hopf proposed principles and standards for measuring executive work in a manner that would link performance with pay.[37] Hopf believed that all managers should be judged (and should be rewarded) by the results they obtained.

In designing the organizational structure, Hopf adopted the architectural notion that form follows function; thus structure had to follow the objectives to be sought. Otherwise, "[if] form dominates over function in organizational structure, we are bound to discover conditions of fixity and rigidity which exercise a baneful influence over accomplishment [of the objectives]."[38] In this analogy, Hopf anticipated the dictum that "structure follows strategy," which became a guiding rule for organizational theory and business policy in the modern era.

Hopf wrote of many other ideas concerning the job of the manager: the span of control, policies, coordination, and executive control, to name a few. None of these were as far-reaching, however, as his concept of "optimology." It was this idea that would take Hopf beyond Taylor's shop management to view the firm as a whole. Hopf defined the optimum as "that state of development of a business enterprise which tends to perpetuate an equilibrium between the factors of size, cost, and human capacity and thus to promote in the highest degree regular realization of the business objectives."[39] Hopf felt that business firms usually reversed the order of priority in fulfilling their societal role: the typical firm sought to maximize earnings and thereby serve society, while Hopf argued that the organization should serve society and thereby maximize earnings. He also felt that the goal of corporate growth was a *faux ami:* growth as a goal more often than not sacrificed one part to the whole, benefiting one party at the expense of another. Instead, the optimum would balance all factors and could be achieved by a scientific approach based on measurement. Hopf's most significant contribution was the notion that the scientific approach could be applied to the organization as a whole. In brief, Hopf's ideas had evolved from the application of scientific management to the office to a view of

---

37. Harry Arthur Hopf, *Papers on Management,* 2 vols. (Easton, Pa.: Hive, 1973), vol. 1, pp. 267–286; vol. 2, pp. 140–157, 169–174, 231–245.

38. *Ibid.,* p. 247.

39. *Ibid.,* p. 91.

the total enterprise. Harry Hopf provided another step forward toward the top-management viewpoint.

ANALYZING TOP MANAGEMENT

The depression of the 1930s quelled economic activity, but World War II mobilized vast productive capabilities, and the postwar period found U.S. enterprise trying to cope with the problems of managing operations on a larger scale than ever before. Top management faced greater responsibilities in determining common ends toward which efforts must be directed, in maintaining the coordination of functions, in relating growing and emerging activities brought about by new products, processes, and markets, and in harmonizing, measuring, and controlling the results of these efforts. It was toward these new responsibilities of top management that scholars turned their attention. For example, Sune Carlson conducted an empirical study of executive communications and concluded that they occupied a major portion of the manager's time.[40]

Searching for corporate excellence is not a new idea. One study during this period examined the top management of thirty-one blue-chip companies for the purpose of compiling the state of the management art with respect to long-range planning and objectives, organization, staffing, and controlling. The authors found that only about half their sample prepared detailed plans for periods up to a year in advance and that very few companies developed fully integrated systems of plans for the firm as a whole or developed long-range objectives. The authors stated that "one of [the] greatest needs observed during the course of this study is for more adequate planning and clarification of future objectives, both near-term and long-range." The authors traced this failing to inadequate organizational arrangements in which jurisdictions, responsibilities, and relationships were ill-defined, staff departments were poorly conceived and coordinated, and committees, the bane of all organizational work, were poorly designed and used for the wrong tasks. In staffing, "many companies" left provisions for the development and succession of key management personnel "largely to providence."[41] Control practices brought little solace; only one-half of the companies studied used budgets as a means of planning and, subsequently, for measuring "over-all results of efforts."

Jackson Martindell also sought to find criteria for successful top-management. Martindell was a securities analyst who had been very successful in his investment counseling firm in the 1920s. When the stock market crashed and the Great Depression followed, Martindell looked back on the investment criteria he had used

---

40. Sune Carlson, *Executive Behavior* (Stockholm: Strombergs, 1951).

41. Paul E. Holden, Lounsbury S. Fish, and Hubert L. Smith, *Top Management Organization and Control* (Stanford, Calif.: Stanford University Press, 1941), pp. 4–8. In a later follow-up study of fifteen leading corporations, many improvements in managerial practices were noted, especially with respect to long-range planning, executive development, and management information systems. See Paul E. Holden, Carlton A. Pederson, and Gayton E. Germane, *Top Management* (New York: McGraw-Hill, 1968).

to see if any had correctly predicted which firms were better able to weather the Depression. He found one answer, "the quality of the management."[42] From that point in time, Martindell began a search for the factors that led to excellently managed companies. The result was a management audit that established criteria for the purposes of evaluating management practices. His criteria included (1) the economic function of a company; (2) its organizational structure; (3) the health of its earnings growth; (4) its practices with regard to fairness to stockholders; (5) its research and development practices; (6) its fiscal policies; (7) the value contributed by the board of directors; (8) the company's productive efficiency; (9) its sales organization; and (10) the executive abilities of the company. The method of evaluation consisted of allocating points for performance ratings in each of the ten areas, summing these points for an overall evaluation, and then comparing the excellence of any particular company with the score obtained from companies in similar industries.[43] Although Martindell's American Institute of Management published its last (eleventh) edition of the *Manual of Excellent Managements* in 1970, this approach was significant in that it sought to establish means for evaluating and comparing overall company practices from a top-management viewpoint.

OWNERSHIP AND CONTROL

At the outset of the Depression in the 1930s, Adolf Berle, a lawyer, and Gardiner Means, an economist, criticized the top management of large enterprise for losing sight of whose interests they served, the shareholders. Citing Adam Smith's warning about those who managed "other peoples' money" (Chapter 2), Berle and Means observed that the concentration of capital and power in large corporations far exceeded anything that Smith could envision. Smith, according to Berle and Means, preferred that ownership and control be combined; resulting in joint-risk in decision making. Rather, Berle and Means found that managers and directors of large corporations rarely held any appreciable share of stock in the company they managed. Managers and directors were "economic autocrats" who formed "a controlling group [that] may hold the power to divert profit into their pockets."[44] Shareholders had little control over the selection of managers and directors, having surrendered control to top management. While Berle and Means offered no clear solution to this separation of ownership and control, they revived Adam Smith's earlier concerns and prepared the way for later work in agency theory.

Berle and Means' concern found further expression in Stanford University's Robert A. Gordon, who presented a broader study of 155 large corporations in which

---

42. Lloyd K. Marquis, "A Comprehensive Framework for Analyzing the Management of a Business Enterprise," in Charles J. Kennedy, ed., *Papers of the Sixteenth Business History Conference* (Lincoln: University of Nebraska, 1969), pp. 38–48.

43. Jackson Martindell, *The Scientific Appraisal of Management* (New York: Harper and Row, 1950).

44. Adolf A. Berle, Jr. and Gardiner C. Means, *The Modern Corporation and Private Property* (New York: Macmillan, 1932, pp. 124, 333.

he focused on the direction and coordination of big business in the United States. Noting the separation of ownership and management of the large corporation and that many U.S. industries were dominated by one or a few large firms, Gordon stressed the need for professionalization of management. The era of the entrepreneurial motive of profit from managing one's own investment had passed, and the new era was one dominated by salaried managers hired by the board of directors. The result was a lessening of the profit motive in corporations, leading to inflexibility and bureaucracy in decision making. Gordon saw dangers in this increased insulation of the decision makers from ownership, especially with respect to the establishment of a self-perpetuating oligarchy of an executive group that placed its own interests above the interests of stockholders and others whose welfare was involved. Gordon's answer to this corporate leadership dilemma was dynamic, professional executives who were responsive to the needs of the groups served by the organization.[45]

INVISIBLE AND VISIBLE HANDS

Earlier we saw economists Jean Baptiste Say, Edward Atkinson, and Alfred and Mary Marshall describing management as a fourth factor of production requiring special, more rare abilities to manage a business firm. The earnings of management were different from rent to property owners, and wages to labor, and interest to capital. While these economists recognized management as important in allocating resources within the firm, other economists focused on what occurred in the external market, largely ignoring what happened between the purchase of the factors of production and the sale of the goods and services produced. Two separate yet compatible developments in the 1930s would have a substantial impact on organization and management theory, but would only later be rediscovered by modern writers.

John R. Commons (1868–1945), noted labor economist and founder of institutional economics, noted that *transactions* were the smallest unit of analysis in the transfer of property rights. Transactions were not the exchange of commodities, but transfers of ownership that must be negotiated "before labor can produce, or consumers can consume, or commodities by physically delivered to other persons."[46] These were three types of ownership transfers: "bargaining," "managerial," and "rationing." Bargaining transactions were derived from a market of willing buyers and sellers who negotiated the transfer not of commodities but of ownership rights. Managerial transactions were derived from a superior-subordinate relationship, such as employer-employee, where authority was used to direct the work to be done. Managerial transactions resembled bargaining ones because labor was free to negotiate. Quoting Dennison, Commons concluded that managing was not giving orders but gaining the cooperation of those who carried out the orders (recall Barnard's

---

45. Robert A. Gordon, *Business Leadership in the Large Corporation* (Washington, D.C.: Brookings Institution, 1945).

46. John R. Commons, *Institutional Economics: Its Place in Political Economy* (New York: Macmillan, 1934), p. 58.

notion of acceptance). Rationing transactions came from a "collective superior," such as governmental laws regarding wages and hours of work.[47] For Commons, economics must be understood as the underlying legal and institutional relations that evolved over time, and consisted of the ownership and transfer of rights. Some transactions occurred outside the firm, but those within the firm could not be dismissed by economists as *ceteris paribus* (other things being equal). Commons' ideas remained relatively dormant until later writers discovered the power of his ideas.

English born and educated Ronald H. Coase (1910–) approached the question from a different perspective. He was introduced to the "invisible hand" of Adam Smith at the London School of Economics, but a trip to the United States to study the vertical and horizontal integration of firms led to new questions: if the market is so efficient, why do we have business firms? Age twenty-one and still an undergraduate student, he drafted "The Nature of the Firm," later published (1937), becoming a classic contribution to understanding the workings of the business firm vis-à-vis the market. He asked:

> ... in view of the fact this it is usually argued that co-ordination will be done by the price mechanism, why is such organization necessary? ... Outside the firm, price movements direct production, which is co-ordinated through a series of exchange transactions on the market. Within a firm, these market transactions are eliminated and in place of the complicated market structure with exchange transactions is substituted the entrepreneur co-ordinator, who directs production. It is clear that these are alternative methods of co-ordinating production.[48]

Coase saw there was a "cost" to using the market mechanism that might be reduced if a firm could coordinate these market transactions. With few exceptions, such as Alfred Marshall, economists engaged in "blackboard economics" that failed to explain the firm as a central agent in employing and monitoring activities at a lower cost than market forces.[49] The young Coase did not pursue this subject in more depth until later. In accepting the Nobel Prize for Economics in 1991, he commented, "it is a strange experience to be praised in my eighties for work I did in my twenties." Later we will see how Coase's ideas re-entered organization and management theory as a way of explaining the business firm as the visible hand and typically superior to the invisible hand of the market.

---

47. *Ibid.*, pp. 59–74. See also Andrew H. Van de Ven, "The Institutional Theory of John R. Commons: A Review and Commentary," *Academy of Management Review* 18 (1993) pp. 139–152.

48. R. H. Coase, "The Nature of the Firm," *Economica*, n.s., 4 (1937), p. 388.

49. In addition to Marshall, Coase mentioned John Bates Clark, Frank Knight, and Dennis H. Robertson, but not J. B. Say.

Summary

Whereas the Mayoists sought greater productivity and satisfaction based on building social solidarity and collaboration, the individuals examined in this chapter were more concerned with the proper structuring of activities and relationships in order to reach essentially the same ends. These formalists postulated that people worked better when they knew what was expected of them and that they would be more satisfied and productive under those conditions. Hence, these formalists stressed organizational structure and design as a means to both employee satisfaction and organizational productivity. Their efforts were characterized by a search for principles of organization and eventually by the quest for broader principles of management. Mooney and Reiley extricated rules of organization from history to increase organizational efficiency and thereby alleviate "human want and misery"; Henry Dennison built his structure from compatible work groups aimed toward flexible overall structures that would make work more satisfying; and Gulick, Urwick, Graicunas and others also tended toward formalizing relationships to reduce confusion and foster certainty and predictability.

While this stress on organizational structure and on management of production operations persisted for much of the period, Ralph C. Davis personified the shift in management thinking from the operative to the top-management viewpoint with his organic functions. Gulick and Urwick brought Henri Fayol to the fore, and Urwick in turn attempted to synthesize management theory. Hopf applied the scientific approach to the study of the firm as a whole, and others displayed an increasing awareness of large-scale managerial problems in the separation of ownership and control, creating governance issues. Finally, the roots of transaction cost economics were discussed in the writings of Coase and Commons.

17 Human Relations in Concept and Practice

W hat began as a study of workplace illumination and its effect on worker productivity at the Hawthorne plant of Western Electric was another step toward understanding human behavior in organizations. This chapter (1) examines and reviews the impact of human relations thinking on academia, industry, and organized labor; and (2) provides a critical review of the assumptions, methods, and results of the Hawthorne experiments and other research.

THE IMPACT OF HUMAN RELATIONS ON TEACHING AND PRACTICE

The roots of concern for people in organizations may be traced historically to the humanists of the Renaissance who called for the overthrow of monolithic church authority, the participation and enlightenment of the citizenry, the breakup of rigid social structures, and the rediscovery of the human being as a unit of study. Throughout the preceding pages, varying views and assumptions about people vis-à-vis the organization have been presented. Robert Owen admonished the factory owners to pay as much attention to their "vital machines," their workers, as to their physical machines. Taylor was concerned with individual development and provided the roots for the empirical investigation of human behavior when he wrote: "There is another type of scientific investigation which should receive special attention, namely, the accurate study of the motives which influence men."[1] The industrial psychology of Hugo Münsterberg was the response to this call for better understanding of people at work. Earlier, the antecedents of

---

1. Frederick W. Taylor, *The Principles of Scientific Management* (New York: Harper and Row, 1911), p. 119.

industrial sociology were traced to the Social Gospel and the contributions of Whiting Williams. Williams extended the meaning of personnel/employee relations to include human relations and suggested that attention to people should be an organization-wide function rather than the province of personnel managers alone. By improving human relations within the organization, all parties—workers, managers, and the public—would benefit: "The coming together of factory management and factory man for the development of both will do more than humanize and justify this factory age."[2] From these varied beginnings, human relations would spread and dominate an era in management thought.

EXTENDING AND APPLYING HUMAN RELATIONS

After the Hawthorne studies, human relations began to take on more of an "interpersonal relations" flavor, but it still dealt with the same issues of improving labor-management relations. While it has been traditional to connect the human relations movement to the researchers from Harvard, the fact is that there were numerous branches of this tree of knowledge, reflecting the interest of many people and institutions. There was the Chicago group that formed the Committee on Human Relations in Industry, consisting of individuals such as Burleigh Gardner, William Foote Whyte, W. Lloyd Warner, David G. Moore, and others.[3] Also at Chicago was Carl Rogers, who furthered nondirective counseling. The Chicago group focused on field research methods, such as Whyte's study of restaurants, and studied numerous organizations, including Sears, Roebuck, where James Worthy came under the influence of this branch of thinking. Although the Chicago group disbanded in 1948, its intellectual offspring took human relations methods and ideas to numerous other places.

In London, the Tavistock Institute used many of Lewin's ideas to study the Glacier Metal Company and the coal mining study by Trist and Bamforth. From the Tavistock branch of human relations came more of an emphasis on longitudinal and sociotechnical systems research. At Harvard the approach was more clinical and oriented toward the case study. Chester Barnard was closer to this Harvard group; he influenced their thinking and vice versa. A fourth branch stemmed from Lewin and flowed to the University of Michigan after Lewin's death. Here Lewin's Center for Group Dynamics became part of the Institute for Social Research, headed by Rensis Likert. Survey research was the forte of this branch and their research led them into many organizations, such as Prudential Life Insurance, Detroit Edison, the Baltimore and Ohio Railroad, and the International Harvester Company.

---

2. Whiting Williams, *Human Relations in Industry* (Washington, D.C.: U.S. Department of Labor, 1918), pp. 9–10.

3. David G. Moore, "The Committee in Human Relations in Industry at the University of Chicago," in K. H. Chung, ed., *Proceedings of the Academy of Management* (New York, August 1982), pp. 117–121.

Although all the individuals and research studies mentioned here have been discussed in greater depth in the preceding chapters, it is important to recognize that the human relations idea and movement had manifold proponents. Like scientific management, human relations was an idea whose time had come to ripen and bear the fruit from the seeds planted much earlier and nurtured in many places. As seen, human relations was also in practice in the restaurant industry, at Givens' American Brakeshoe Company, and at McCormick's spice and extract firm. The Scanlon plan, too, was influenced by the notions of teamwork and participation.

Although the human relations movement was fostered by numerous individuals and groups and the idea existed long before Elton Mayo entered the Hawthorne plant, the literature traditionally emphasizes the Harvard contribution. Why has it been traditional to find the roots of human relations in the Hawthorne studies rather than in earlier work? As seen in Chapter 9, there appears to be an academic distaste or disregard for anything that is found by nonacademicians. Keller noted the influence of institutional academic prestige on the acceptance of a theory.[4] O'Connor has suggested that Hawthorne represented a sociopolitical gambit by the Harvard Business School to establish its legitimacy in academia and industry.[5] Further, the relatively young social sciences were striving to become scientific and rigorous. The prestige of established scholars from Harvard and MIT provided a legitimate cornerstone for the study of human relations.

ORGANIZED LABOR AND HUMAN RELATIONS

Although human relations gained academic credibility and found its way into industrial practice, Mayo and his colleagues were placed under fire for a promanagement, antilabor bias. According to the critics, it was not the worker but management that the Mayoists sought to save. For example, Mary Barnett Gilson noted: "In all the more than six hundred pages describing the Western Electric experiments…no reference is made to organized labor except a short statement, unindexed, that it was so seldom mentioned by any workers that it was not considered sufficiently important to discuss.…"[6] Although it is true that the Mayoists made no reference to the role of organized labor, it would be unfair to conclude that this constituted an antilabor bias. Until 1935, the dominant labor organizations were the American Federation of Labor, which consisted of skilled workers, and the brotherhoods that represented various groups of railroad employees. As will be seen in Chapter 18, the passage of the National Labor Relations (Wagner) Act in 1935 provided the legislative basis for a

---

4. Robert T. Keller, "The Harvard 'Pareto Circle' and the Historical Development of Organization Theory," *Journal of Management* 10 (Summer 1984), p. 193.

5. Ellen S. O'Connor, "The Politics of Management Thought: A Case Study of the Harvard Business School and the Human Relations School," *Academy of Management Review* 24 (1999), pp. 117–131.

6. Mary B. Gilson, "Review of Management and the Worker," *American Journal of Sociology* (July 1940), p. 101.

spurt in union membership from a turn-of-the-decade three and a half million to almost nine million union members by 1939.

Since the Hawthorne studies were concluded in 1932, before organized labor made its great strides, it should not be surprising to find little mention of unions in the writings of Mayo and his colleagues. The Mayoists did not draw any distinction between union-management relations and human relations, thus suggesting that in both union and nonunion places of employment there was a need for human-relations-oriented supervisors to fill the workers' needs for security, recognition, and the expression of grievances.

Despite the erroneous conclusion that the Mayoists were antiunion, human relations thought entered a revisionist period in the 1950s with an emphasis on industrial human relations. Just as Robert Valentine and Morris Cooke tried to bring about a rapprochement between scientific management and organized labor, the post-Mayo revisionists quickly put unions into the human relations picture. Industrial sociologists devoted more and more space to organized labor and examined industry as an institution of groups of social classes, workers, supervisors, managers, and so on, who operated in a larger societal complex.[7]

A basic assumption that appeared to prevail in this approach to industrial human relations was that there was natural conflict between labor and management with respect to dividing the surplus created by an advanced technological society. This perception of increased industrial conflict was not a figment of someone's imagination. A comparison of work stoppages and their causes for the period 1920–1929 with the decade of the 1930s evidences dramatic differences. The 1920s, characterized by employee representation plans and union-management coopera-tion, showed a steady decline in work stoppages, while in the 1930s this trend was reversed. Of a total of 14,256 work stoppages during the 1920s, 51 percent were over wages and hours of work and 21 percent were the result of union organizing drives. From 1930 to 1934, the stoppages caused by union organizing attempts increased to 34 percent, but wages and hours still accounted for 51 percent. For the rest of the 1930s, however, and following the passage of the Wagner Act in 1935, a reversal occurred: of the 14,290 stoppages from 1935 to 1939, 31 percent concerned wages and hours, and 53 percent were due to union organizing efforts.[8] To the industrial human relationists, the answer to industrial conflict resided not in human relations training per se but in overcoming the conflicting interests and ideologies of manage-ment and the worker, usually meaning the organized worker. Industrial harmony

---

7. Examples of this way of thinking may be found in Eugene V. Schneider, *Industrial Sociology* (New York: McGraw-Hill, 1957); and Delbert C. Miller and William H. Form, *Industrial Sociology* (New York: Harper and Row, 1951). A historical perspective is provided by Bruce E. Kaufman, *The Rise and Decline of the Field of Industrial Relations in the United States* (Ithaca, N.Y.: ILR Press, Cornell University, 1993), ch. 5.

8. U.S. Department of Commerce, Bureau of the Census, *Historical Statistics of the United States: Colonial Times to 1970* (Washington, D.C.: U.S. Government Printing Office, 1974), pt. 1, p. 179.

would come through collective bargaining and from professional industrial-relations specialists.

In addition to bringing unions into the fold, the human relations texts of the 1940s and early 1950s typically postulated that the feelings of people were more important than the logics of organizational charts, rules, and directives. Human relations was based on intangibles, not on hard, scientific investigation, and there were no final answers, that is, nothing positive or fixed in solutions to human problems. In general, the early texts emphasized feelings, sentiments, and collaboration.[9] They were heuristic rather than specific or systematic, that is, the texts encouraged others to investigate and discover for themselves rather than prescribing techniques. In brief, human relations ideas led to a revisionist movement that took organized labor into consideration. The Hawthorne findings were not antiunion, but reflected the low influence of organized labor during the period of the studies. Whether organized or not, it was the worker who was the center of attention for management's understanding and application of human relations skills.

HAWTHORNE REVISITED

No studies in the evolution of management thought have attracted as much attention as those at the Hawthorne plant of Western Electric. The Hawthorne research did not inspire any investigating commission, congressional inquiry, or any confrontations such as occurred at the Watertown Arsenal. Nevertheless, critics have had their day regarding the assumptions, methods, and results of the Hawthorne experiments. Henry Landsberger furnished an extensive list of critical reviews of *Management and the Worker* up to 1958 and put forth a defense of that work. Landsberger identified four separate areas of criticism: (1) the Mayoists' view of society as one characterized by anomie, social disorganization, and conflict; (2) their acceptance of management's views of the worker and management's "willingness to manipulate workers for management's ends"; (3) their failure to recognize other alternatives for accommodating industrial conflict, such as collective bargaining; and (4) their specific failure to take unions into account as a method of building social solidarity.[10] Since Landsberger's work, more evidence and controversy has led to numerous revisitations of the Hawthorne experiments. The following discussion will update the critical evaluations of human relations in concept and practice by reviewing (1) the assumptions about an industrial civilization and (2) the research methods and the interpretation of the results.

---

9. Schuyler D. Hoslett, ed., *Human Factors in Management* (New York: Harper and Row, 1946), preface; and Burleigh B. Gardner and David G. Moore, *Human Relations in Industry* (Homewood, Ill.: Richard D. Irwin, 1955).

10. Henry A. Landsberger, *Hawthorne Revisited*, Cornell Studies in Industrial and Labor Relations, vol. 9 (Ithaca, N.Y.: Cornell University, 1958), pp. 29–30.

THE PREMISES OF AN INDUSTRIAL CIVILIZATION

Mayo and Roethlisberger both began with a view of industrial society characterized by anomie. People, bound up in their obsessive-compulsive pessimistic reveries, needed identification with others and constructive outlets for their latent fears and frustrations. Industrial civilization, though making giant strides in technological progress, had created a cultural lag by diminishing the importance of collaborative social skills. The Mayoists' response was to build from small group structures to a view of people in a larger social system. Some have questioned these assumptions about the nature of industrial society and the Mayoist view of social systems. For example, Bell charged that the Mayoists considered themselves social engineers, who managed not people, but a social system in an effort to "adjust" the worker so that the human equation fitted the industrial equation. According to Bell, to think that contented workers were productive workers was to equate human behavior with "cow sociology," that is, the notion that contented cows give more milk. Counseling at Hawthorne, for which Bell used the colorful phrase "ambulatory confessors," was to be the new method of controlling humans. When employees exposed their inner-most doubts and fears, they were more susceptible to managerial manipulation. The socially skilled supervisor could move from the use of authority to coerce humans to psychological persuasion for worker "manipulation as a means of exercising dominion."[11] Another facet of Bell's criticism was that the human relations style of supervision was to replace thinking about improving work itself. The social person, relieved of pessimistic reveries by the catharsis of counseling, would feel better and forget all other problems. Bell recalled a folktale to make this point:

> A peasant complains to his priest that his little hut is horribly over-crowded. The priest advises him to move his cow into the house, the next week to take in his sheep, and the next week his horse. The peas-ant now complains even more bitterly about his lot. Then the priest advises him to let out the cow, the next week the sheep, and the next week the horse. At the end the peasant gratefully thanks the priest for lightening his burdensome life.[12]

Another attack on premises came from those who maintained that the Mayoists presented a naive view of societal conflict. According to these critics, the Mayoists assumed that a commonality of interests could be found between labor and man-agement when in fact society was much more complex in terms of conflict between classes and interest groups. Some tensions and conflict were inevitable in every human situation and some were even necessary. The goal should not be to eliminate conflict and tension but to provide healthy outlets for resolution.[13] The Mayoists'

---

11. Daniel Bell, *Work and Its Discontents: The Cult of Efficiency in America* (Boston: Beacon Press, 1956), pp. 25–28.

12. *Ibid.*, p. 26.

13. Landsberger, *Hawthorne Revisited*, pp. 30–35.

notion of a conflict-free state of equilibrium was a worthy goal, but too idealistic for the critics. The Mayoists, like the Taylorists, found faddists and perversions of their original intentions. The human relations cult that followed the original conception of a person as a social being often concluded that the goal of their efforts was to keep everyone happy in a conflict-free state of equilibrium with resultant worker-management marital bliss. When bliss was attained, higher productivity was the corollary. As Fox put it:

> Among the guilty are the "human relationists" with an inadequate concept of human relations, who mistakenly preach participation, permissiveness, and democracy for all, and those employers who confuse popularity with managerial effectiveness and misinterpret the Golden Rule in dealing with their subordinates.... Many mistakenly regard it [human relations] as an "end" toward which the organization shall endeavor rather than as what it should be—a "means" for achieving the organization's primary service objectives.[14]

According to Fox, the regard for human relations as an end rather than a means misled the manager to think that a conflict-free state and worker contentment would automatically lead to company success when in fact the company might fail. Human relations could not be substituted for well-defined goals, policies, high standards of performance, and other managerial functions necessary for attainment of organizational goals.

Or, as McNair saw it, the executive needed more than listening and human relations skills to be effective in accomplishing organizational goals. In teaching human relations as a separate skill, McNair saw the dangers of compartmentalizing knowledge when it should be an integral part of all managerial development, whether in marketing, management, or whatever. In essence, McNair concluded, "It is not that the human relations concept is wrong; it is simply that we have blown it up too big and have placed too much emphasis on teaching human relations as such at the collegiate and early graduate level.... Let's treat people like people, but let's not make a big production of it."[15]

Knowles also called for a better mix of managerial skills but one that would avoid the evangelism and mysticism that so often characterized human relations training. Evangelism represented a thesis that only human relations could "save Western Civilization from impending doom."[16] The doom theme was an old one, having its

---

14. William M. Fox, "When Human Relations May Succeed and the Company Fail," *California Management Review* 8 (Spring 1966), reprinted in Max S. Wortman and Fred Luthans, eds., *Emerging Concepts in Management* (New York: Macmillan, 1969), p. 184.

15. Malcolm P. McNair, "Thinking Ahead: What Price Human Relations?" *Harvard Business Review* 35 (March–April 1957), pp. 15–23.

16. William H. Knowles, "Human Relations in Industry: Research and Concepts," *California Management Review* 1 (Fall 1958); reprinted in S. G. Huneryager and I. L. Heckman, eds., *Human Relations in Management,* 2nd ed. (Cincinnati, Ohio: South-Western Publishing Co., 1967), p. 52.

roots in the revulsion of the romantic philosophers at the perceived ravages of the Industrial Revolution. For social philosophers such as Durkheim and Mayo, advancing technology and the specialization of labor destroyed social cohesiveness and yielded a loss of pride in work for humankind. Increased interpersonal competition and concern for material things destroyed primary groups, caused status anxiety, and created obsessive-compulsive reactions. The answer to impending doom was an evangelical zeal by the human relationists to play down material acquisitiveness, rebuild primary groups, and teach people to love other people once more. The world could be saved by a sense of belonging, and people could once more find themselves by losing themselves in some larger entity. This mystical overtone, reflecting the Gestalt psychology of the totality, attributed to groups wisdom that could not be found in individuals. It was not the logic of efficiency but the illogic of sentiments that would save people from the brink. The moral uplift of scientific management had been efficiency; for the human relationists, it was belonging and solidarity.

In brief, the challenges to the basic premises of the Mayoists were that they (1) accepted a premise that the worker could be manipulated to fit into the industrial equation; (2) assumed that cooperation and collaboration were natural and desirable and thus overlooked more complex issues in societal conflict; and (3) confused means and ends in assuming that the goal of contentment and happiness would lead to harmonious equilibrium and organizational success.

THE RESEARCH METHODS AND RESULTS

The modern management researcher is much more sophisticated in statistics and research methodology than those who started the Hawthorne experiments in 1924, than people like George Pennock who kept the project alive, and than those who followed to interpret and disseminate the findings. Industrial research is full of cracks and crevices and the researcher is pinioned between the need for the controlled experiments of a laboratory and the empirical reality of ongoing activity. Seen in this light, the Hawthorne researchers were vulnerable to those critics who challenged their methods and findings. One vexing issue, seen in Chapter 13, dealt with financial incentives. A number of critics have challenged the Hawthorne findings on this question of motivation. Sykes contended that human relations advocates believed that money did not motivate when in fact the Hawthorne evidence led to just the opposite conclusion.[17]

Carey also concluded that it was completely erroneous for the researchers to decide that wages were not a variable and chastised the researchers for their claims of "friendly supervision."[18] First, the researchers selected "cooperative" workers who

---

17. A. J. M. Sykes, "Economic Interest and the Hawthorne Researchers," *Human Relations* 18 (August 1965), p. 253.

18. Alex Carey, "The Hawthorne Studies: A Radical Criticism," *American Sociological Review* 32 (June 1967), p. 410.

were willing to participate in the project. Second, two workers from the original group began causing some problems and "were removed for a lack of cooperation, which would have otherwise necessitated greatly increased disciplinary measures."[19] After reviewing production records, Carey concluded that output did not increase until the two workers were dismissed and two "more cooperative" workers were added to the original group. Was this friendly supervision or the use of negative sanctions to increase output? In summary, Carey maintained that the Hawthorne experiments were really consistent with the view of economic incentives and the use of a firm hand in discipline in order to get higher output.

Franke and Kaul also doubted the Hawthorne results. Using multiple regression analysis, they claimed that "three variables—managerial discipline, the economic adversity of the depression, and time set aside for rest" explained most (over 90 percent) of the variance in the quantity of output.[20] Thus Franke and Kaul concluded that it was not supervisory style, nor financial incentives, but the use of discipline, the economic milieu, and relief from fatigue that led to increased productivity.

In rebuttal, Schlaifer alleged that Franke and Kaul had used the wrong statistical methods, that "managerial discipline" was not harsh because it involved merely sending two operators back to their original department, and that the wrong dates were used to measure the impact of the depression. Schlaifer then built his own statistical interpretation to show that the passage of time alone was sufficient to explain the increased productivity, which, according to Schlaifer, was "in all respects consistent with the conclusions reached by the original researchers."[21] Toelle confirmed Schlaifer's findings and added another criticism of Franke and Kaul—that they treated (statistically) the relay assembly group as one group when in fact it was two: the first group of five included the two who were later removed; the second group comprised the original three plus the two replacements. If the groups were split and a stepwise regression model applied, the passage of time alone accounted for over 91 percent of the total variance in output.[22]

Undoubtedly, the last analysis of the Hawthorne experiments has not yet been heard. What did happen at Hawthorne? What can twenty-twenty hindsight tell about the methods and conclusions of the researchers? First, there is doubt that the human relationists neglected the economic motives. True, there were statements that could be interpreted as a rejection of the economic person. For example, Sykes quoted Roethlisberger and Dickson as concluding that "none of the

---

19. T. N. Whitehead, *The Industrial Worker,* vol. 1 (Cambridge, Mass.: Harvard University Press, 1938), p. 118. In *The Human Problems of an Industrial Civilization,* Mayo said they "dropped out" (p. 56); cf. Carey, p. 411.

20. Richard H. Franke and James D. Kaul, "The Hawthorne Experiments: First Statistical Interpretation," *American Sociological Review* 43 (October 1978), p. 636.

21. Robert Schlaifer, "The Relay Assembly Test Room: An Alternative Statistical Interpretation," *American Sociological Review* 45 (December 1980), p. 1005.

22. Richard Toelle, "Research Notes Concerning Franke and Kaul's Interpretation of the Hawthorne Experiments" (unpublished paper, University of Oklahoma, Norman, 1982).

results ... [substantiated] the theory that the worker is primarily motivated by economic interest." Sykes did not quote the rest of that paragraph: "The evidence indicated that the efficacy of a wage incentive is so dependent on its relation to other factors that it is impossible to separate it out as a thing in itself having an independent effect."[23] Thus financial incentives should not be excluded from an explanation of increased output, but should be viewed as part of a larger, more complex situation. As Shepard commented, Roethlisberger and Dickson saw monetary incentives as "carriers of social value" rather than as absolute explanations of employee behavior and motivation.[24] In short, the social person supplemented, but did not supplant, the economic person.

Second, the "passage of time" interpretation suggests that trust is an important factor in building human relationships and that it took a period of time for trust to develop. The interviews with the surviving relay group members and their observer-supervisor, Don Chipman, indicated that this trust and friendly atmosphere did develop during the studies. In situations where the trust relationship did not develop, such as in the bank wiring room, productivity did not increase.

Finally, there is the "science versus advocacy" problem.[25] It is difficult, if not impossible, for researchers to exclude personal values from their research. Thus Mayo, who had already formed conclusions about obsessive-compulsive behavior and pessimistic reveries, found Hawthorne to be a clinical example of these industrial problems. In his view, socially skilled managers, counseling, and other appropriate leader behaviors would overcome the human problems of industry, relieve anomie, provide catharsis, and fulfill people's needs to be important and recognized. If these conclusions went beyond the data from the experiments, it was Mayo speaking as an advocate, not as a scientist. Gillespie claims that the Hawthorne findings were "manufactured" by Mayo and his colleagues because "in Mayo's hands, the Hawthorne experiments provided the experimental data on which he could base his political and social theory."[26] If Mayo and his colleagues became advocates it was easy for others to follow, to perceive selectively, to tinge the intent of human relations with the flavor of a cult.

In Roethlisberger's memoirs he noted that the Hawthorne findings "have been so often restated and misstated that it [*Management and the Worker*] has a life of its own ... human relations was first and foremost an *investigatory and diagnostic tool*. It was not a model of what an organization should be; it was a conceptual scheme for

---

23. Roethlisberger and Dickson, *Management and the Worker* (Cambridge, Mass.: Harvard University Press, 1939), pp. 575–576; a similar statement appears on p. 185.

24. Jon M. Shepard, "On Alex Carey's Radical Criticism of the Hawthorne Studies," *Academy of Management Journal* 14 (March 1971), pp. 23–32.

25. Lyle Yorks and David A. Whitsett, "Hawthorne, Topeka, and the Issue of Science versus Advocacy in Organizational Behavior," *Academy of Management Review* 10 (January 1985), pp. 21–30.

26. Richard Gillespie, *Manufacturing Knowledge: A History of the Hawthorne Experiments* (New York: Cambridge University Press, 1991), p. 181.

finding out what the relations in a *particular organization at a particular place and time* were, not what they should be."[27] If Roethlisberger's plea sounds familiar, it should, because it reflects the theory-practice gap that plagues the field of management. Anxious to get results or to appear up-to-date, practitioners often grasp the straws of expediency or pick and choose the facts that are palatable. In a similar fashion, theorists fall into the advocacy trap and promote interpretations that fit their preconceptions. Hawthorne, like scientific management, will be revisited frequently in this continued attempt to disclose the past to better understand the present.

Summary

The Hawthorne studies were an important step in advancing the idea of improving human relations in all types of organizations. Human relations was not new, but rather a revival of humanist thinking that carried the prestige of Harvard and MIT into the classroom and the practice of management. Although Elton Mayo's name is closely connected with Hawthorne and the promotion of human relations, he was but one person in a cast of many who kept the experiments going. If George Pennock, Clair Turner, and others had faltered, Mayo's efforts would have been for naught. After 1931, Mayo became more of an advocate and less of a scientist, and the Hawthorne experiments achieved a life of their own in Mayo's social philosophy for an industrial civilization. As the facts became clouded with ideologies, it became easier and easier to misperceive, misquote, and misinterpret what really happened at Hawthorne. In retrospect, certain conclusions stand out: (1) human relations was intended as a tool for understanding organizational behavior rather than as an end in itself; (2) trust was crucial in building the interpersonal relationships that provided for melding the interests of management and the worker; (3) financial incentives had to be included in seeking productivity gains, but these incentives could not explain the entire situation; and (4) care should be exercised to avoid going beyond or selectively perceiving the facts in order to promote some prior preferences. The task is not easy, and this is undoubtedly only the beginning of understanding the chain of events that followed the original illumination experiments.

---

27. F. J. Roethlisberger, *The Elusive Phenomena*, ed. George F. F. Lombard (Boston: Division of Research, Graduate School of Business Administration, Harvard University, 1977), pp. 305, 311. The italics are Roethlisberger's.

CHAPTER 18

The Social Person Era in Retrospect

The ideas of individuals in the context of their times form an interesting topic for historical discussion. Within its cultural context, scientific management as the gospel of efficiency found its basis in the economic necessities of large-scale corporate organizations, in the social sanction of individual achievement and the moral uplift of efficiency, and in political concern for national productivity and the conservation of resources. What can be said of the era from the advent of the Hawthorne experiments to the early 1950s? It has been postulated that management thought forms a more coherent picture when viewed in its changing cultural milieu of economic, technological, social, and political forces. Management is both a process in and a product of its environment. The era of the social person was an age of individual hopes dashed on the reefs of economic misfortune, of social collisions and maladies, and of political shifts heralding a transformation in traditional relationships. Though treated independently here, these cultural facets interacted to form the cultural milieu of the social person.

THE ECONOMIC ENVIRONMENT: FROM DEPRESSION TO PROSPERITY

The great crash of 1929 found the winter of its discontent in earlier days. The 1920s were prosperous, characterized by price stability, a doubling of industrial productivity, and a 55 percent rise in the real income of individuals.[1] Industrial efficiency and mass-production technology held costs down and increased the purchasing power of the dollar. But the end of this decade of prosperity came on October 29, 1929,

---

1. David N. Alloway, *Economic History of the United States* (New York: Monarch Press, 1966), p. 29.

known in U.S. economic history as Black Tuesday. On that day, the stock market crashed and wiped out $14 billion of stock values. By November 13, 1929, the stock values lost totaled $30 billion, and for more than a decade afterward life in the United States was substantially changed by that crash and the Great Depression. In 1929, 48 million persons were employed and only about 1.5 million (3.2 percent) persons were unemployed. Using Bureau of Labor Statistics data, unemployment rose, peaking at 12,830,000 unemployed (24.9 percent) in 1933. The number of unemployed dropped below 8 million only once thereafter in that decade—in 1937, when the number was 7,700,000 (14.3 percent).[2] Using "Darby corrected" figures, that is, following today's practice of counting government (federal and state) relief workers as employed, the late 1930s unemployment rates decline, suggesting that contracyclical work projects provided relief from unemployment. Darby-corrected unemployment rates in 1937 and 1940, for example, are more than 5 percent lower than the rates reported by the Bureau of Labor Statistics.[3] Despite federal and state attempts to create jobs, businesses failed, incomes dropped, homes were lost, family savings were wiped out, and, worst of all, national morale was at an all-time low. Gone was the optimism of prosperity and promise; the old guideposts apparently had failed, as "rags to riches" became the midnight pumpkin. Recovery from the economic morass was painfully slow, but from the social and psychological view-point, it was even slower. Feeling inept in adjusting to economic deprivation, people turned to the government for relief.

ATTEMPTS AT ECONOMIC RECOVERY

In November 1929, President Herbert Hoover asked for labor-management cooperation in reducing the hours of work per worker per week rather than laying off workers. This work sharing plan would reduce a worker's total weekly wages, but it was judged to be better than no work at all. To provide an example of how the hardship should be shared, Daniel Willard, president of the Baltimore and Ohio Railroad, reduced his own salary from $150,000 to $60,000 per year when the railroads were requesting a 10 percent wage reduction from the railway unions.[4]

In the early days of the Depression, labor and management responded positively to work sharing, and the workers had a better cushion against the decline. The cushion had been built out of the progressive labor policies of management during the 1920s; employer-sponsored thrift plans, for instance, gave the workers some savings to fall back on, and more workers than ever before owned their homes because

---

2. U.S. Department of Commerce, Bureau of the Census, *Historical Statistics of the United States: Colonial Times to 1970* (Washington, D.C.: U.S. Govt. Printing Office, 1974), pt. 1, p. 135.

3. Michael R. Darby, "Three-and-a-Half Million U.S. Employees Have Been Mislaid: Or, an Explanation of Unemployment, 1934–1941," *Journal of Political Economy* 84 (1976), pp. 1–16.

4. John N. Ingham, *Biographical Dictionary of American Business Leaders*, 4 vols. (Westport, Conn.: Greenwood, 1983), pp. 1632–1634.

they had been able to save for this investment. Employee stock ownership plans had been a mixed blessing: as stock prices soared in the late 1920s, some employees had sold their stock and entered into the general orgy of stock-market speculation only to regret this decision later; other employees had kept their stocks and had seen them plummet in 1929, also with regret. Intended to give the workers a share in the company, these plans proved that some modifications would have to be made in the future to protect these stocks from severe ups and downs. There was also a change in attitude about women working outside the home. From economic necessity, women were entering the labor force to try to bolster family income. Finally, evidence of the most dramatic difference between previous depressions and this one was that the workers used their automobiles to look for work. Rather than walking or hitchhiking from one employment line to another, the workers took their flivver. As the humorist Will Rogers noted: "We are the first nation in the history of the world to go to the poor house in an automobile."[5]

The new political regime of Franklin Roosevelt promised freedom from fear, from want, and from the other anxieties that bound the United States. Hoover had tried the Reconstruction Finance Corporation in 1932 as a scheme to pump government funds into private business enterprise. Roosevelt went much further with the New Economics of John Maynard Keynes. Keynesian economics was a challenge to the Protestant ethic dogma of thrift; Keynes held that savings withheld from consumption could lead to dislocation and underutilization of economic resources. Therefore, the federal government should intervene and prime the pump to stimulate consumption and provide for economic recovery. This strategy was designed to destroy the financial control of Wall Street, to link government assistance with industrial capitalism, to aid agriculture and small business in the Progressive tradition, and to increase benefits to the workers who formed the chief electorate.

Although Keynesians held that economic stimulation through government spending contributed to recovery, Friedman's supporters maintained that proper monetary action by the Federal Reserve could have prevented contraction of the money supply and allayed the Depression. Heilbroner concluded that World War II was the factor that really pulled the United States from its economic doldrums, not government pump priming.[6] Economists may fuss and fume about proper remedial actions, but in reality what might have been is a matter for other historians. The fact for management was that the government did become increasingly involved in economic life; though capitalism was preserved, with ownership and management remaining in the hands of private individuals, control and policy guidelines became

---

5. Will Rogers, in a radio broadcast, October 29, 1931. Cited in Richard M. Ketchum, *Will Rogers: His Life and Times* (New York: McGraw-Hill, 1973), p. 229.

6. Milton Friedman and Anna J. Schwartz, *The Great Contraction: 1929–1933* (Princeton, N.J.: Princeton University Press, 1965); and Robert Heilbroner, *The Making of Economic Society* (Englewood Cliffs, N.J.: Prentice-Hall, 1962), p. 167. Although "Darby corrected" data indicate that federal and state projects lessened unemployment, a substantial decline in percentage of unemployed is not apparent until the onset of World War II. See Darby, p. 8.

more and more lodged in the hands of the dominant political party. The new concept of the corporation tied it more closely than ever before to the public interest with concomitant calls for economic statesmanship on the part of business leaders and for public regulation of corporate concentrations of power.

THE GRASS ROOTS AND BOTTOM-UP MOVEMENT

Economically it was to be the age of the farmer, the worker, the small-business owner, the unemployed, the hungry, and all others who were the waifs of economic misfortune. Somehow it was Wall Street and Big Business who were alleged to be the primary contributors to the ills of the economy. Economic policy was to come from the grass roots up to counterbalance the concentration of power in Big Business. People were concerned that there was an economic elite and sought to democratize industry, reduce power differentials, and restore the influence of those at the base of the pyramid. Boulding warned of the moral dilemma caused by the conflict between the industrial aristocracy of a hierarchy of authority and the democratic ideal of equality.[7] Following Berle and Means, James Burnham predicted that owners would delegate business operations to professional managers who would take over the firm for their own selfish interests, dooming egalitarianism.[8] Burnham continued the long line of those who doubted the motives of those who managed other people's money.

For management scholars, this movement found its expression in bottom-up management, multiple management, and participative leadership. The Mayoists saw the root of economic problems in social problems. For them, people's anomie was made manifest in pessimistic reveries, in obsessive-compulsive behavior, in the turning inward of groups to protect themselves from management, and in the expressed needs of the workers to find social satisfaction on the job. Once social solidarity was restored, primary groups rebuilt, communications channels opened, and social and psychological needs fulfilled, people could turn their efforts to being more productive. Follett would certainly support this thesis in her call for depersonalizing authority, for integration, and for enlightened leadership. Barnard indicated that an organization had to be efficient in terms of satisfying individual and group needs in order to be effective in meeting organizational goals. Cooperation was a reciprocal process for both management and the worker. From the people and organizations point of view, industrial problems were to be solved by democratizing the workplace and thereby improving human relationships within the organization.

ORGANIZATION AS THE ANSWER

Whereas concern for organizational structures to rationalize resource utilization dominated the first three decades of the twentieth century, industrial attention in

---

7. Kenneth E. Boulding, *The Organizational Revolution: A Study of the Ethics of Economic Organization* (New York: Harper and Row, 1953).

8. James Burnham, *The Managerial Revolution* (New York: John Day, 1941).

the 1930s was focused primarily on survival. For Mooney and Reiley, Gulick, Urwick, and others of the organizational bent, the solution resided in the proper, orderly arrangement of formal relationships. People, preferring order and certainty, would function better within a well-structured system, and management could better ensure economic survival through the practice of sound organizational principles. In their cultural context, those who focused on people and those who focused on the organization were attempting to cope with the massive social and industrial dislocations presented by the Depression.

Whereas the Depression delayed industrial growth, mobilization for the war effort created both technological and managerial advancements. Vast productive resources had been gathered, training within industry had created a deeper pool of employee talent, consumer products had been rationed, worker earnings were high, and the postwar era found the United States with a pent-up demand for products and services. With demand outrunning productive ability, the United States did not experience the anticipated postwar business slumps. The war had created new products, new technologies, new markets, and a more highly skilled, broader-based labor force. Management thought was in transition in this era, shifting from a production orientation to a top-management viewpoint that called for a changed executive role in balancing and coping with larger-scale enterprises and markets. Managers sought a broader, more flexible conceptual framework, a process of action on which they could build for a more dynamic interplay of inputs and outputs. The work of R. C. Davis was cited previously to show this transition in thought; Henri Fayol was awaiting rediscovery, and others were writing with more emphasis on top management.

The postwar period promised a new era of prosperity, expansion, and diversification. The regained prosperity and the further growth of industry were to create a new focus in evolving management thought.

SEEDS OF CHANGE: THE NEW TECHNOLOGIES

Writing in gloomy times, Joseph Schumpeter was pessimistic about the future of capitalism. Schumpeter saw the door to economic development in innovation and the entrepreneur. Economic development, according to Schumpeter, came from new products, new methods of production, new markets, using new raw materials, or a reorganization of a sector of the economy. Innovation "incessantly revolutionizes the economic structure *from within,* incessantly destroying the old one, incessantly creating a new [economic structure]."[9] "Creative Destruction," as he called this process, sometimes occurred in rushes with intervening quiet periods, but nevertheless was incessant. Contrary to John Maynard Keynes, who advocated stimulating

---

9. Joseph A. Schumpeter, *Capitalism, Socialism, and Democracy* (New York: Harper and Brothers, 1942), p. 83. Italics are Schumpeter's. See also Tim Kiessling, "Entrepreneurship and Innovation: Austrian School of Economics to Schumpeter to Drucker to Now," *Journal of Applied Management and Entrepreneurship* 9 (2004), pp. 80–92.

the demand side of the economic equation, Schumpeter favored the supply side to create the new technological forces for development. Schumpeter would have been less pessimistic if he had observed the new technologies, which were emerging in the late 1920s until the mid-1930s.

In transportation, automobiles were miraculous inventions, but were limited in their scope of travel by the lack of paved roads. Enabling legislation in 1926 provided for a "national" highway, Route 66, which began on the shores of Lake Michigan in Chicago, sloped westward across Illinois and Missouri, crossed the great plains and deserts of the southwest, and culminated on the shores of the Pacific Ocean at Santa Monica, California. All two thousand miles were paved by 1938, beginning the construction of a truly national highway system.

Only forty years since Orville Wright's inaugural machine powered flight, test pilot Chuck Yeager broke the sound barrier in a jet powered test plane, the X-1, at the speed of 640 miles per hour. Charles Lindbergh soloed the Atlantic Ocean in 1927; Igor Sikorsky perfected the first helicopter in 1943; German rockets were built for World War II but became useful in later years for exploring space and launching communication satellites; and radar was invented for air defense, then became vital for air traffic control, and, in the kitchen, for microwave ovens. Travel was expedited by the emergence of aircraft manufacturers such as Boeing, Lockheed, and McDonnell Douglas, who supplied new airlines such as Delta, American, Pan American, and others. Piston-driven craft, then jet-powered ones, essentially removed long distance passenger travel from the railroads.

In communication and entertainment, the radio was becoming a household staple. The first Rose Bowl football game was broadcast in 1927; by 1930, twelve million homes had a radio. RCA provided the first glimpse of television at the 1939 World's Fair in New York City; fifteen years later, one-half of the American homes wired for electricity had television sets; and someday, it was hoped, Ed Sullivan could be seen in color. Ampex invented the first video tape recorder, a three-quarter inch band of ribbon to preserve television images; and reel to reel magnetic tape recorders could preserve voices and music. General Electric invented the first practical device for recording sound on film in 1926 for the movies, a growing industry. True to Schumpeter's notion, however, Western Electric made technological advances to replace GE as the leading provider of sound recording and reproducing equipment.

Alan Turing knew of Charles Babbage's calculating engines and turned this knowledge to developing a special purpose computer that broke the German signal code during World War II. This was only the beginning of a revival of interest in computing machinery. Remington-Rand, IBM, Minneapolis-Honeywell, RCA and others began making monster computers. The ENIAC, for example, had eighteen thousand vacuum tubes, weighed thirty tons, performed five thousand calculations per second, and required an air-conditioned room to avoid meltdowns. If anyone had suggested in 1950 that a computer could be held on one's lap, that person would have been considered daft. The miracle that transformed the computer industry was Bell Lab's transistor, invented in 1947, that would make vacuum tubes a relic, only to be replaced by later technological advances.

Another advance in the office was dry-copying, developed in 1937 by Chester Carlson, whose request for financing the venture was spurned by Western Union and IBM. It would be a decade before the Haloid Company took over in the company that became Xerox. Some medical advances during this period from the mid-1920s to the 1950s were noteworthy: Jonas Salk developed the first polio vaccine; the World Health Organization announced that smallpox had been eradicated; and Alexander Fleming's serendipitous discovery of penicillin touched off research in antibiotics. Even further in the future, Rosalind Franklin and Maurice Wilkins' X-ray of the deoxyribonucleic acid (DNA) helix became relevant when James Watson and Francis Crick realized it had to be a double helix and a clue in understanding the building blocks of life.

We must not neglect the role the public sector, both state and federal, played in projects that provided employment and public works. One federal project, the atomic bomb, was the original weapon of mass destruction, but there remained hope for peaceable uses for atomic energy. The 1930s provided a building boom that no decade has surpassed: dams for hydroelectric power, irrigation, and recreation, such as the Hoover, Bonneville, Grand Coulee, and Shasta Dams; and bridges, such as the George Washington Bridge, the Golden Gate Bridge, the San Francisco–Oakland spans, and the Huey P. Long Bridge over the Mississippi River at New Orleans.

The Tennessee Valley Authority (TVA) dams along the Tennessee River provided electricity for economic expansion and household use. Morris Cooke headed the Rural Electrification Authority, which brought electricity to non-urban dwellers. As electrical supplies increased, the home appliance industry blossomed: electric vacuum sweepers, food freezers, refrigerators, stoves, washing machines, clothes dryers, and a continuing host of domestic servants.

War and depression did not quell innovations and inventions. There was a lag as these products and services came into fruition in a booming post-war economy. Automobile production resumed after the war, gas was no longer rationed, and the new roads and bridges could carry the consumers to a revived marketplace.

The Social Environment: The Social Ethic and the Organization Man

The economic temper of the times most certainly shaped the social values that came to dominate the period under analysis. Attitudes and aspirations are the founts of human strength, and the crushing economic burden for many was a violation of the previously held precepts of abundance and success for everyone. The 1920s had brought Madison Avenue to Peoria and Dubuque, and U.S. productivity and sales ability presaged more than a car in every garage and a chicken in every pot. What happened to social relationships and the assumptions that guided people's behavior in the troubled 1930s? Broadly viewed, two fairly distinct paths were reshaping social values: (1) a decline of the tenets of the Protestant ethic and the rise of a social ethic; and (2) a decline in the level of esteem given the business leader.

SHIFTING SOCIAL VALUES

The Lynds, in their famous study of the typical U.S. city of the late 1920s, found a split in values between the working-class person and the white-collar employee. For the worker, economic motives appeared to be primary: "This dominance of the dollar appears in the apparently growing tendency among younger working class men to swap a problematic future for immediate 'big money.'"[10] While the workers measured social status by financial status and tended to hold to the traditional virtues of individualism, including a declining interest in belonging to organized labor, the business leaders represented a different outlook. The Lynds noted a decline in individualism among business leaders and a rapidly increasing conformity and need to belong. In their follow-up study, conducted during the Depression, the Lynds found that "the insecurity during the depression has brought with it greater insistence upon conformity and a sharpening of latent issues."[11] Workers were turning to unions for collective action, and business leaders combined to maintain the open shop; these "latent issues" sharpened class distinctions and engendered social bitterness. The economic catastrophe had brought about a shift in social values for the worker as well as for the manager.

After the crash, of what value were the time-tested Protestant ethic virtues of thrift and hard work? Apparently nearly everyone had been affected in some way, the loss of a job here, a savings account there, or a friend who had lost everything in the stock market. The new consciousness was that the disaster had struck the virtuous as well as the prodigal, the tycoon as well as the tyro, and the energetic as well as the feckless. People found their own fortunes intertwined with those of others in a pattern not subject to reason or justice.

> As time went on: ... there was a continuing disposition among Americans young and old to look with a cynical eye upon the old Horatio Alger formula for success; to be dubious about taking chances for ambition's sake; to look with a favorable eye upon a safe if unadventurous job, social insurance plans, pension plans.... They had learned from bitter experience to crave security.[12]

This craving for security, this turning inward of people to others who shared the same tribulations, marked that generation as well as its children, and even perhaps another generation or more. Perhaps people have a natural reaction to form groups when faced with threatening circumstances—when these circumstances assume a major cultural impact, such as a depression, then people become more and more

---

10. Robert S. Lynd and Helen M. Lynd, *Middletown: A Study in Contemporary American Culture* (New York: Harcourt Brace Jovanovich, 1929), p. 81.

11. Robert S. Lynd and Helen M. Lynd, *Middletown in Transition: A Study in Cultural Conflicts* (New York: Harcourt Brace Jovanovich, 1937), p. 427.

12. Frederick Lewis Allen, *The Big Change* (New York: Harper and Row, 1952), p. 132.

group beings. The presence of others must offer some psychological sense of relief under threatening or frustrating conditions. Erich Fromm also noted this desire of people to escape the loneliness of standing alone. In Fascist Germany, to escape this loneliness, people turned to an authoritarian regime that made their decisions for them and gave them a sense of identity, however evil it might have been. According to Fromm, this need to belong also pervaded U.S. industrial life, and an individual more frequently than not was willing to give up self to conform to the group. Whereas the Reformation and the Industrial Revolution drove people from the security of medieval life, enabling them to find freedom in the spiritual, political, and economic spheres of life, industrialization created new threats to these newfound freedoms.[13] People felt alone in the individualism of capitalism and the Protestant ethic and needed something larger than themselves—God, the Nation, the Company, the Union, or whatever—with which to identify and in which to lose the self.

The conditions of the troubled 1930s must have compounded this desire for group affiliation as a source of strength. McClelland found in his studies that the need for achievement increased in the United States from 1800 to 1890 but decreased regularly after that date. The trade-off between the need for achievement and the need for affiliation took a dramatic shift between 1925 and 1950. In 1925, the need for affiliation was primarily a familial concern; by 1950, affiliation had become an alternative for economic achievement. By that time, people were showing more concern for affiliation and less concern for achievement.[14]

David Riesman and his associates furnished additional evidence for this era by noting the shift from the inner-directed to the other-directed person. The inner-directed person represented the era of laissez-faire capitalism and the Protestant ethic and emphasized self-direction and control. The other-directed person was characterized by high social mobility and by emphasis on consumption rather than production and on getting along and being accepted by others as the magic key to accomplishment. Riesman called the Taylor period "job-minded" and the other-directed person of the Mayoist era "people-minded."[15]

For Riesman, the shift from "invisible hand to glad hand" actually began about 1900. Up until that time, laissez-faire and the utilitarian philosophy of individualism had been the dominant force. After 1900, the closing of the frontier and restrictions on immigration began to bring less confidence in self-interest and more confidence in "groupism." The inner-directed person persisted for a period after 1900 but individuals began to feel more lonely in the crowd. People had to live where they were and were unable to move to a new frontier and use the West as a safety valve. Most of the pressing problems of production began to disappear, and the

---

13. Erich Fromm, *Escape from Freedom* (New York: Holt, Rinehart and Winston, 1941), pp. 7–10.

14. David C. McClelland, *The Achieving Society* (New York: Van Nostrand Reinhold, 1961), pp. 166–167; David C. McClelland, "Business Drive and National Achievement," *Harvard Business Review* 40, no. 4 (July–August, 1962), p. 110.

15. David Riesman, Nathan Glazer, and Reuel Denney, *The Lonely Crowd* (New Haven, Conn.: Yale University Press, 1950), pp. 19–40, 151.

problems of consumption became more apparent. Inner-directed individuals had to cope with a niggardly material environment; the new problems that arose following relative conquest of a hostile material environment were problems with people. Entrepreneurs could deal face-to-face with most of their employees—they knew them, their problems, their likes and dislikes. Growth made industry less personal, replacing the personal style of the entrepreneur with the bureaucratic style of the administrator. The personal touch of leadership was gone, only to be replaced with the directives from the technically trained specialists required by an advanced industrial nation. Social competence, influencing others, began to assume a new importance, and technical skills were played down.

Individual loneliness in the organizational crowd led to the rise of groupism and the social person. Progressive education began fitting the child to the group in the socialization process, and the parental socialization function was replaced by peer socialization. Small groups became the panacea for individual adjustment to the loneliness of industrialization. Getting along and being accepted was the magic key to accomplishment. People were judged by what others thought of them, not what they thought of themselves. The psychological gyroscope of the inner-directed person began to waver and needed the helping North Star of others.

THE CONFUSION OF SOULS

Industrialization had not made people less religious, but they found they could more easily segment their lives into religious and nonreligious duties. When God smiled on the division of labor, thrift, and success, people found comfort in combining secular drives with spiritual grace. For one authority, the Depression caused a "confusion of souls" and a crisis for the Protestant ethic.[16] Self-help had failed and the notion of the self-made person was rejected as the guarantee of economic order. Charity became a public rather than a private concern, and the power for the individual of the Protestant gospel of success fell into disfavor. Out of this confusion of souls and the debris of laissez-faire, the moral order needed to take on new dimensions. On the one hand there was the "mind cure" approach offered by Norman Vincent Peale in *The Power of Positive Thinking;* on the other hand, the "getting along" cure of Dale Carnegie. Peale advised seeking the inner power of Christianity to cope with stress and crises. This turning inward helped people escape their loneliness and malaise by drawing on the greater power of God.

Dale Carnegie established the personal magnetism ethic in 1936 with *How to Win Friends and Influence People.*[17] This book, replete with how-tos of human relations,

---

16. Donald Meyer, *The Positive Thinkers: A Study of the American Quest for Health, Wealth and Personal Power from Mary Baker Eddy to Norman Vincent Peale* (Garden City, N.Y.: Doubleday, 1965), pp. 233–237.

17. Dale Carnegie, *How to Win Friends and Influence People* (New York: Simon and Schuster, 1936). Dale Carnegie was founder and president of the Dale Carnegie Institute of Effective Speaking and Human Relations.

advised that the path to success resided in (1) making others feel important through a sincere appreciation of their efforts; (2) making a good first impression; (3) winning people to one's way of thinking by letting others do the talking and being sympathetic, with the caveat, "never tell a man he is wrong"; and (4) changing people by praising good traits and giving the offender the opportunity to save face. Although *Management and the Worker* had not been published at that time, the Carnegie formula bore a striking resemblance to the rules the Hawthorne researchers laid down for the counselors in the interviewing program. For Carnegie, the way to success was through winning the cooperation of others.

These positive thinkers stressed two ways out of the confusion of souls: drawing on the inward power of faith and drawing personal strength by winning the cooperation of others through personal magnetism. The social ethic of the times played down achievement by individual striving because the Protestant ethic had run its course. This new ethic was others-oriented, with moral uplift coming not from efficiency but from getting along with others. For the most part, the social person was conceived, born, and nurtured in these trying times. People sought belonging in the group, solace in association, and fulfillment in affiliation.

THE SOCIAL ETHIC

A second facet of this attempt to understand the era of the social person must come through an analysis of the changing societal views toward the business leader. The business leader represented in fiction may or may not be a barometer of social esteem. Kavesh warned that the fictional business executive is generally portrayed in an unrealistic manner because of the writer's need to dramatize in contrasts and gain sympathy for characters.[18] Although it would be impossible to hold the business leader to blame for the Depression era's hard times, it was evident that the executive became through fictional writings the symbol of society's ills. The 1920s had canonized the business executive as hero and symbol of prosperity and the good life; when times turned turbulent, was it not fair to heap the blame on the "bankster" who robbed people of their homes and savings? Although such charges were not entirely just, the business leader as portrayed in fiction undoubtedly became a convenient focal point for public wrath.

Scott noted that the novels of the 1930s and 1940s were of disillusionment with individualism. Individualism became futile, and the novelists shifted the keynote to pleas for "humanitarianism and collectivism in the form of proletarian fiction."[19] The hero vanished to be replaced by a "they" who did things without reason and

---

18. Robert A. Kavesh, *Businessmen in Fiction* (Hanover, N.H.: Amos Tuck School of Business Administration, 1955), p. 11. An exception that he noted, however, was Cameron Hawley's *Executive Suite.*

19. William G. Scott, *The Social Ethic in Management Literature* (Atlanta: Bureau of Business and Economic Research, Georgia State College of Business Administration, 1959), p. 47.

were beyond the control of mere mortals. "They" represented power, machines, and forces, not individual managers who could be held responsible. The corporation was a monster of oppression in which people and their lives were ground down piece by piece. Representative of this type of fiction were John Steinbeck's *Grapes of Wrath* and Nathaniel West's *A Cool Million.* For Steinbeck, it was not individuals but "they" who gave the migrants a hard time. West's Alger-type hero was caught between the contending forces of international bankers and world revolutionists, who slowly but surely destroyed his spirit of individualism and quest for free enterprise.

As the 1940s and 1950s unfolded, the manager completed the shift from the hero image by becoming more and more of an organization person. In conformity there was security, and the manager became a hero not because of "great or daring deeds, but because he tolerates grinding mediocrity and conformity."[20] In Marquand's *The Point of No Return,* Pawel's *From the Dark Tower,* and Sloan Wilson's *The Man in the Gray Flannel Suit,* the emphasis was on conformity and the futility of rebelling against the organization as a system. In Scott's thesis, novelists portrayed the shift from the individualistic ethic to the social ethic in management literature. The reference point in the social ethic was the group and the collective nature of people, a need for collaboration and social solidarity. This occurred not only in fiction, but also in the technical literature of Follett, the Mayoists, and others who were playing down the individual and reinforcing the group or collective nature of people.

The social ethic in fiction underscored conformity and depersonalization of the individual into a "they" and portrayed the corporation as a monster machine. In technical literature, the ideas of teamwork, participation, group decision making, small rather than large groups, committee management, the interweaving of responsibilities, and democratic leadership were abundant. Scott's striking parallel between the fictional and technical writers of the social person era is food for thought. Taken together with the low esteem of the business leader as symbol of the corporate monster, it was understandable that the Mayoists and others strove to remodel organizations from the bottom up in order to meet people's needs.

As the Mayoists sought to reform the organization through the group, the organizational engineers sought to reform the group through the organization. In their view, *Onward Industry!* was a rallying cry for coordinating and focusing group efforts, not to subdue individuals, but to release their potential. Principles were not only organizational rules, but also guides for human conduct toward a purpose. Mooney, Gulick, and others knew of people's need to belong and sought to fulfill that need through organizational definition. To these writers, it was through structure and not catharsis that people could release their potential.

Some critics held business people and industrialization responsible for the ills of modern civilization. Intellectuals maintained an uneasy truce with industrial life by idealizing agriculture and denigrating business. Jeffersonian and Jacksonian

---

20. *Ibid.,* p. 50.

democracy were examples of the praise of an agricultural, small-unit, family-owned, ideal base of society. To be big was to be bad, and to live in the city was a sign of decline. Why did intellectuals idealize agriculture and sully business? Kavesh perceptively noted that "the growth of cities is the history of business: the big businessman is the symbol of the city, and the city became the symbol of degradation."[21]

Baritz suggested that Mayo was one of those who was committed to an "Agrarian Golden Age":

> "[Mayo] believed that there was a mystical but direct relationship between farming and truth.... An industrial society, by definition, could not be virtuous, for as men lost sight of the soil they lost sight of nature; and in so doing, they lost sight of the meaning of life and fell victim to the glossy gadgetry of modern industrialism. For Mayo, then, the problem of the modern factory was clear; how to make possible the re-creation of Agrarian Virtue, Agrarian Loyalty, and the Agrarian Sense of Community in the twentieth century's world of skyscrapers and subways, of smoke and steam?[22]

For Mayo, the answer was to rebuild social solidarity and collaboration through the small group. Once the communal integrity of agrarian life was reestablished, people could cope with the evils of the city, the deskilling of work, and the anomic depersonalization of factory routine. Perhaps the Australian Mayo was caught up in the American Jeffersonian-Jacksonian democratic tradition. He was certainly influenced by Durkheim, who saw evils in industrial life much as Robert Owen had seen them in the early nineteenth century. While Durkheim admonished people to love one another unselfishly and Owen tried to build communal centers, Mayo accepted the parameters of industrialization and tried to rebuild people's interpersonal relations within that framework. The gloom of the Depression, World War II, and the threat of the atomic bomb would certainly cause Mayo to harken back to an Agrarian Golden Age in which people could find solace in small groups.

THE POLITICAL ENVIRONMENT: FROM FDR TO EISENHOWER

While the economic cycle went from prosperity to depression and the social environment reflected increasing needs for affiliation, the political cycle saw an increasing role for government in individual and business affairs. No other period in U.S. history has seen a political administration begin in such dire times, endure for such a long period, and cope with as many adversities as the tenure of Franklin Delano Roosevelt. Roosevelt, scion of a patrician family, cousin of former president

---

21. Kavesh, *Businessmen in Fiction*, p. 6.

22. Loren Baritz, *The Servants of Power* (New York: John Wiley and Sons, 1960), p. 111.

Theodore Roosevelt, and paralyzed from the waist down by polio, brought charisma to the people in the depths of their despair. In his acceptance speech for the Democratic nomination he said, "I pledge you, I pledge myself, to a New Deal for the American people." This became the slogan of the policies of the Roosevelt administration, which promised to reshuffle the old cards of society.

THE NEW DEAL

FDR saw as his first task restoring confidence to a stricken nation. The first hundred days (March 9 to June 16, 1933), in which a special session of Congress passed a multitude of bills enabling emergency legislation and giving Roosevelt tremendous political and economic powers, served as a landmark of the lengths to which he went. With his keynote phrase, "The only thing we have to fear is fear itself," Roosevelt hoped to instill in the people feelings of confidence and hope. In those first hundred days, legislation created such agencies as the Agricultural Adjustment Administration (AAA), Civilian Conservation Corps (CCC), Securities and Exchange Commission (SEC), Tennessee Valley Authority (TVA), the Home Owners Loan Corporation (HOLC), the Federal Relief Act, the Railway Reorganization Act, the Federal Deposit Insurance Corporation (FDIC), and the National Industrial Recovery Act (NIRA). The day of alphabet-soup government had been created.

Whereas some viewed the New Deal as "creeping socialism" and prophesied the end of capitalism, others saw the reforms as a necessary adjustment of capitalism while the motor was running in order to save free enterprise. Private enterprise endured, but in the process a lot of socialism did creep in. The restacking of the social, political, and economic order was to bring an activist role for government. Hands-off as a policy was defunct, and the role of government increased in an effort to shift the balance of power as people perceived it from the financiers of Wall Street to the farmers and organized labor. One of FDR's brain trusters, Rexford Tugwell, wrote that the idyllic days of business doing what it willed were gone and that the new leadership of industry must recognize unions, democratize industry by encouraging participation, and keep in mind the "greatest good for the greatest number."[23] Tugwell felt that industry had failed to provide security for the working class and that government had to fill this vacuum. The response to this craving for security was made manifest in a number of pioneering legislative acts: the Social Security Act of 1935 sought to provide for old-age assistance; the Fair Labor Standards Act of 1938 established a guaranteed minimum hourly wage of twenty-five cents and a maximum work week of forty-four hours for certain workers; and the Railroad Unemployment Insurance Act of 1938 was the first national unemployment protection. These and other acts marked the shift from Adam Smith's "invisible hand" to Riesman's "glad hand," from private to public charity, and from the Protestant ethic to the social ethic.

---

23. Rexford Guy Tugwell, *The Industrial Discipline* (New York: Columbia University Press, 1933), p. 158.

AUGMENTING THE POSITION OF LABOR

During the Roosevelt era, the role of federal power in relations between government and business achieved a dimension that even the Progressives had not envisioned. Of all the changes in the balance of power, none had a more immediate significance for management thought than the position of organized labor. The 1930s were witness to the first real successes at organizing workers on a national scale by industry rather than by craft. Previous attempts to organize workers regardless of their skills had met with limited success—the National Labor Union of William Sylvis and the Noble Order of the Knights of Labor, led by Terence V. Powderly, had been colossal failures in the nineteenth century. The American Federation of Labor (AFL), a federation of craft workers formed in 1886, and numerous railroad brotherhoods, beginning as early as 1863, had demonstrated that unions could be successful when the workers held common skills. There had been some successful industrial unions, such as those of the garment workers, milliners, and mine workers, but their memberships were typically small vis-à-vis the craft workers. For example, almost 60 percent of the union members in 1929 were in the building trades (919,000), which were predominantly AFL; and in transportation (892,000 members), mostly in the rail brotherhoods. The largest noncraft unions were in mining (271,000 members) and garments and millinery (218,000).[24]

The political climate of the 1930s created the opportunity for industrial unionism to flourish. The first significant piece of legislation, the Federal Anti-Injunction Act of 1932, more commonly known as the Norris-LaGuardia Act, was passed during the Hoover administration. This act, for all practical purposes, completely divested federal courts of injunctive powers in cases growing out of a labor dispute. In 1933, Congress passed the National Industrial Recovery Act, the first in a series of New Deal enactments designed to lift the nation out of the Depression. Section 7a of the NIRA, in similar but stronger language than that of the Norris-LaGuardia Act, specifically guaranteed that "employees shall have the right to organize and bargain collectively through representatives of their own choosing … free from interference, restraint, or coercion of employers."

When the NIRA was declared unconstitutional by the U.S. Supreme Court in 1935 *(United States v. A.L.A. Schechter Poultry Corporation)*, Congress quickly replaced it with a law that was even more pleasing to organized labor. The National Labor Relations Act, more commonly known as the Wagner Act, was far more definitive in what it expected of collective bargaining than was the NIRA. The Wagner Act guaranteed employees "the right to self-organization, to form, join, or assist labor organization, to bargain collectively through representatives of their own choosing, and to engage in concerted activities for the purpose of collective bargaining." In addition, it placed specific restrictions on what management could do by specifying five unfair management practices. To implement these provisions, the act established a National Labor Relations Board (NLRB) that was granted the

---

24. U.S. Dept. of Commerce, Bureau of the Census: *Historical Statistics of the United States*, pt. 1, p. 178.

authority not only to issue cease-and-desist orders against employers violating the restrictions, but also to determine appropriate bargaining units and to conduct representation elections.

The NLRB was also instrumental in destroying employee representation plans such as the one described earlier of the Dennison Manufacturing Company. Organized labor bitterly opposed such plans, seeing them as "company unions" that hindered their organizing efforts. In 1938, the United States Supreme Court ruled that these plans were employer dominated and in violation of the National Labor Relations Act *(NLRB v. Pennsylvania Greyhound Lines)*. Thus ended one era in labor-management relations, while yet another began.[25]

The passage of the Wagner Act marked a critical turning point in labor-management relations. John L. Lewis, president of the United Mine Workers, led the fight for industrial unionism within the AFL. Rebuffed, Lewis formed the Committee for Industrial Organization (known after 1938 as the Congress of Industrial Organizations), whose purpose was to bring workers into unions regardless of occupation or skill level. The newly founded CIO enjoyed almost instant success and was able to claim nearly 4 million members by 1937. While the CIO prospered, the AFL did too—almost doubling its membership from 2,126,000 in 1933 to 4,000,000 in 1939. With the legal climate created by the New Deal legislation, total union membership spurted from a turn-of-the-decade 3.5 million (6.8 percent of the total labor force) to almost 9 million (15.8 percent) by 1939.[26]

In retrospect, it is clear that labor gained substantial power during the 1930s through legislation. The New Deal labor policy was part of a power-equalization drive. This new role for the worker fitted into the calls for teamwork, cooperation, and democratization of the workplace through worker participation. During the war, all shoulders were turned to the wheels of industry and differences were temporarily laid aside. Employment regulation, such as through the War Labor Board, prevailed and in general enhanced the power of labor. After the war, numerous strikes led to the public opinion that labor had too much power and resulted in the passage of the Labor-Management Relations Act (Taft-Hartley Act) in 1947. Although this act did bring about some redress in the balance of power, the employer was no longer able to pursue unilateral actions with respect to labor policies. In general, the whole environment of management had changed, not just with respect to labor, but also in all relations with government.

The political environment brought a new focus for management thought. The manager had a new set of variables with which to contend, new relationships to be managed, and a revised set of assumptions with respect to the balance of power. After World War II, the search for general management theory would emerge as a solution to the complexities of managing in the modern era.

---

25. An excellent analysis is C. Ray Gullett and Edmund R. Gray, "The Impact of Employee Representation Plans Upon the Development of Management Worker Relations in the United States," *Marquette Business Review* 20 (Fall 1976), pp. 85–101.

26. U.S. Dept. of Commerce, Bureau of the Census: *Historical Statistics of the United States*, pt. 1, p. 178.

Summary of Part III

Figure 18-1 depicts the developments in the era of the social person. Scientific management was the dominant theme in the 1920s, but sociologists and social psychologists introduced the ideas of behavioralism in management before the advent of the Hawthorne studies. Mary Follett, though chronologically belonging to the scientific management era, served as an intellectual bridge to the emerging group approach to management's problems. The Hawthorne studies brought the human relations movement to the forefront and led to the theme of the social person. The heirs of Taylor and scientific management found new dimensions in organizations and in the job of the manager in coping with the new Zeitgeist of this era.

The Hawthorne research, beginning before but enduring through the early days of the Depression, brought about a shift in emphasis, including (1) an increased concern for people rather than production; (2) exhortations to play down the rigidity of organizational structures in order to increase the fulfillment of people's needs; (3) a view of financial incentives as but one part of a motivational picture; and (4) more concern for the illogic of sentiments rather than the logic of efficiency. The human relations movement and the research that followed reflected several basic themes that were products of the cultural environment: (1) calls for social, human skills rather than technical skills; (2) emphasis on rebuilding people's sense of belonging through groups and social solidarity in order to overcome the confusion of souls; and (3) concern for equalizing power through unions, through participative leadership, and by fusing the formal organization with the social system of the factory.

The post-Hawthorne research assumed two separate yet congenial approaches. The micro researchers established constructs for studying people in groups, postulated a hierarchy of human needs, and viewed leadership as a group-interactive-situational phenomenon. Along the macro branch, W. F. Whyte, George Homans, and E. W. Bakke sought to understand and bring about an integration of the formal system with the informal system of sentiments, activities, and interactions. These paths would lead to organizational behavior and to organization theory in the modern era.

Chronologically parallel to these developments in the human relations movement, the descendants of scientific management offered different types of solutions to the vexing problems of the Depression. Largely shop-management oriented at the beginning, as in the case of R. C. Davis, this branch of management thought also began to assume new dimensions. On the one hand, organizational constructs were offered as one way out of the cultural impasse. Mooney and Reiley urged *Onward Industry!* and Chester Barnard presented a sociological study of the formal organization and attempted to synthesize the formalists and the human relationists with his efficiency-effectiveness dichotomy. Alongside the organizational approach to management's problems, the elements of a top-level management viewpoint began to appear in the work of R. C. Davis, the translation of Fayol's process in the "Papers on Administration," and the efforts of Lyndall Urwick to synthesize principles of management.

FIGURE 18-1   **SYNOPSIS OF THE SOCIAL PERSON ERA**

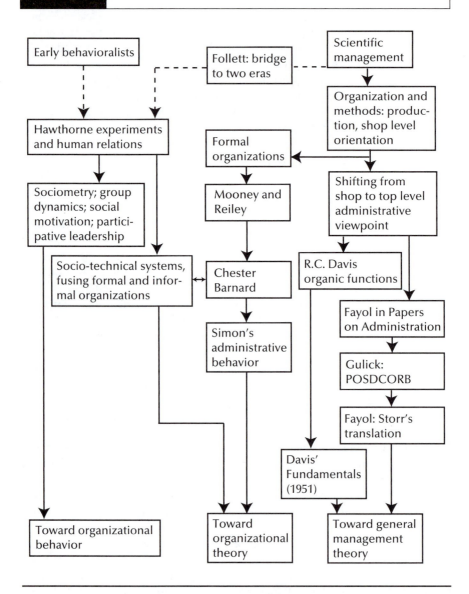

Culturally, management thought was shaped by stressful times. The Great Depression, which began in 1929, was an economic, social, political, and psychological watershed. The United States was changing as the Depression brought new interpretations of the role of government in economics and in schemes to establish social floors and hedges against social maladies, such as unemployment. No longer would the virtues of self-help, thrift, and hard work be seen as the keys to success. If you were down, the government helped you up; if you lost your savings in a bank failure, the government would reimburse you; if you had saved nothing for retirement, the government would provide a pension, and so on through a host of social measures to take some of the sting out of life. Further economic growth was retarded by the Depression, and the postwar boom created a need for a top-level managerial viewpoint. The Protestant ethic and the need for achievement, though they did not disappear, declined in significance as people tried to find their identity and raison d'être through affiliation and getting along with others. People, not production, were the main concern of the manager. Politically, an increased role for government and the growth, power, and legal protection afforded organized labor introduced new variables to be considered in managerial decision making. It was out of this age of confusion, trauma, and diversity that the modern era in management thought was about to begin.

The Modern Era

Nestled between the knowns of yesterday and the unknowns of tomorrow, the present is the twilight of history. It is difficult to put more recent developments in perspective; some years from now we will be able to look on this era with the aid of historical analysis, see the course of progress after it has evolved, and be better able to place this era in a clearer perspective. It is not possible to examine the full extent of modern management writings, for they are too diverse and too extensive for an in-depth analysis. Instead, it must suffice to sketch the broad outlines of evolving management thought and try to perceive major trends, shifts, and influences in the modern era.

Modern management thought is a product of past developments in four broad areas: general management theory and the study of managerial activities as extensions of the work of Henri Fayol; behavioral developments, which arose out of humanist, human relations, and other people-oriented approaches; evolving notions of the structure of organizations; and advances in quantitative and/or scientific problem-solving approaches as typified by Aristotle, Babbage, scientific management pioneers, and their heirs. In these four areas there is commonality as well as diversity. Each seeks to provide a better understanding of management, its purpose, functions, and scope; to facilitate better organizational performance and understanding of people; to balance the needs of the individual and of the organization as each seeks its objectives; and to relate the organization to its economic, technological, social, and political environment. Yet the means used by these areas of management to attain their common ends differ. This part first analyzes the search for integration in management theory for teaching, research, and practice. Next, it focuses on the organizational behavioralists and theorists to illustrate the search for harmony between the formal requirements of the organization and the informal dimensions of people in organizations. Management science and information systems are depicted as attempts to quantify variables in management decision making and to bring order from chaos through systematization and information technology. Finally, we will examine the renewed interest in business ethics, corporate social responsibility, and management thought in cross-cultural, global arena. It is in this modern era that management thought experiences its adolescence of diversity and seeks the professional posture of maturity.

CHAPTER

19

Management Theory and Practice

Chapter 16 described an increased concern for general management theory and postulated that this was necessitated by the further growth of organizations after World War II, the proliferation of staff specialists, increased government regulation, the spurt in the growth of unions, the need to apply the advanced technologies developed during World War II, and a greater awareness of relating management tasks to their more complex environment. If any one factor had to be chosen to explain the concern for a general theory, it would be the need for more broadly educated managers who could improve performance within the firm and understand the firm in its environmental setting. In this period, management scholars turned from a shop-level management orientation to general management theory.

THE RENAISSANCE OF GENERAL MANAGEMENT

It is easy to forget just how ancient the practice of management is. Only within the last century did people begin to reflect systematically on their experiences and observations in an attempt to sort out and identify those managerial practices that seemed to work better than others. These better practices were called principles but more closely resembled guides to managerial thought and action than scientific fact. The impetus for codifying these sound practices (principles) into a theory was the desire to transmit knowledge more coherently to those who aspired to become management practitioners. Those who tried first to describe management were primarily practitioners. The names of Owen, McCallum, Taylor, Gantt, Fayol, and Barnard are suggestive of these practitioners who tried to distill their experiences and observations for the use of others.

Henri Fayol was the first to propose a general theory of management. He defined theory as "a collection of principles, rules, methods, and procedures tried and checked by general experience."[1] Theory attempts to bring together what is known in a discipline, to explain the relationship between these knowns, and to predict likely outcomes given certain causes and relationships. Fayol's theory consisted of two parts: (1) the elements, which described what managers did—plan, organize, command, coordinate, and control; and (2) the principles, which were lighthouses, or guides, to how to manage. The purpose of theory, in Fayol's view, was to provide a body of knowledge that could be taught, since managerial ability was crucial to organizational success. Fayol also noted, "There is nothing rigid or absolute in management affairs," so no theory is expected to endure for all time. As the history of management thought shows, new knowledge reshapes previously held theories. Principles and theories emerge, are tested, prove useful or not; the course of management thought is traced in this crucible of experience.

FAYOL'S INTELLECTUAL HEIRS

As seen earlier, Fayol's work received belated recognition. In the post–World War II environment, Constance Storrs's translation of Fayol's book was a timely contribution that touched off a renewal of interest in general management. The first effort in the modern period was that of William H. Newman (1909–2002) of Columbia University. In 1948, Newman copyrighted materials as "Principles of Management," which was later published as *Administrative Action: The Technique of Organization and Management.*[2] Newman defined administration as "the guidance, leadership, and control of the efforts of a group of individuals toward some common goal" and developed a logical process of administration as a separate intellectual activity. The elements in Newman's process were planning, organizing, assembling resources, directing, and controlling. For Newman, planning involved recognizing the need for action; investigating and analyzing; proposing action; and making a decision. The outcome of planning was the development of three broad groups of plans: (1) goals or objectives, which defined purposes of organizational effort and made integrated planning easier; (2) single-use plans, which established a course of action to "fit a specific situation and are 'used up' when the goal is reached"; and (3) standing plans, which endured over time and were changed only as the occasion warranted.

Although Newman's elements were closely akin to Fayol's, they did have some unique features: (1) the distinction between the types of plans; (2) the "assembling resources" element; and (3) the treatment of coordination under directing rather

---

1. Henri Fayol, *General and Industrial Management,* trans. Constance Storrs (London: Sir Isaac Pitman and Sons, 1949), p. 15.

2. William H. Newman, *Administrative Action: The Technique of Organization and Management* (Englewood Cliffs, N.J.: Prentice-Hall, 1951).

than as a separate activity. Beyond this early contribution, Newman also noted the importance of objectives in shaping the character of an organization. He felt that the basic objectives of the firm should define its place or niche in the industry, define its social philosophy as a business "citizen," and serve to establish the general managerial philosophy of the company.[3] Newman's experiences with James O. McKinsey and his approach to managing and consulting provided the framework for *Business Policies and Management,* published in 1940. Newman recalled, "This was the first textbook on business policy ever published (Richard D. Irwin did not start publishing collections of Harvard cases until after World War II)."[4] This text evolved through ten editions, the last one simply titled "Strategy," and Newman's work bridged the years from general management as "policy" to general management as "strategy."

George Terry (1909–1979) was the first to call his book *Principles of Management.* Terry defined management as "the activity which plans, organizes, and controls the operations of the basic elements of men, materials, machines, methods, money, and markets, providing direction and coordination, and giving leadership to human efforts, so as to achieve the sought objectives of the enterprise."[5] Terry's elements included planning, organizing, directing, coordinating, controlling, and leading human efforts. Later, Terry combined the functions of directing and leading human efforts into an "actuating" function and stopped treating coordinating as a separate function. Terry defined a principle as "a fundamental statement providing a guide to action," and his principles, like Fayol's, were lighthouses to knowledge and not laws in a scientific sense.

In 1954, the Department of the Air Force prepared and distributed for training and operational purposes Air Force Manual 25-1, *The Management Process.*[6] This manual established five functions of management: planning, organizing, coordinating, directing, and controlling. Objectives, or missions in the military sense, were stressed a great deal as the foundation stone of all managerial activity. This governmental interest in the process was significant for two reasons: it signaled a further interest in the study of management as a separate activity; and it recognized the activity of management beyond the previous emphasis on the study of management in the business concern.

Harold Koontz (1908–1984) and Cyril O'Donnell (1900–1976) of the University of California at Los Angeles defined management as "the function of

---

3. William H. Newman, "Basic Objectives Which Shape the Character of a Company," *Journal of Business of the University of Chicago* 26 (October 1953), pp. 211–223.

4. William H. Newman, "The Takeoff," in Arthur G. Bedeian, ed., *Management Laureates: A Collection of Autobiographical Essays,* vol. 2 (Greenwich, Conn.: JAI Press, 1993), p. 381.

5. George R. Terry, *Principles of Management* (Homewood, Ill.: Richard D. Irwin, 1953), p. 3.

6. *The Management Process,* Air Force Manual 25-1 (Washington, D.C.: U.S. Government Printing Office, 1954).

getting things done through others."[7] They furthered Fayol's ideas and sought to provide a conceptual framework for the orderly presentation of the principles of management. According to Koontz and O'Donnell, managers were known by the work they performed, which was planning, organizing, staffing, directing, and controlling. These authors pointed out that, although some authorities maintained that these functions were exercised in the sequence given, in practice managers actually used all five simultaneously. They stressed that each of these functions contributed to organizational coordination. However, coordination was not a separate function itself but was the result of effective utilization of the five basic managerial functions. Koontz and O'Donnell offered a number of principles: in organizing, for example, "the principle of parity of authority and responsibility" and "the principle of unity of command"; in planning, "the principle of strategic factors"; and so on. The Koontz and O'Donnell text became an enduring, integral part of the search for a systematic body of management knowledge.

Fayol's heirs built on the elements and principles and saw the job of the manager as a cycle or process of functions. They attempted to identify management as a distinct intellectual activity and sought a generally accepted body of knowledge that could be distilled into principles and hence lead to a general theory of management. The applicability of planning, organizing, and controlling achieved the greatest agreement. Fayol's *diriger,* directing, was the term used by some; for others, supervising, leading, actuating, or whatever. Staffing, which Fayol had subsumed under organizing, achieved some recognition as a separate function either explicitly for human resources or more generally under the heading of assembling resources. Coordination began and endured as a separate managerial function until 1954; afterward, it became an integral part of the entire process. As Fayol's heirs were advancing general management theory, studies of business education would lead to some changed ideas about what managers needed to know.

MANAGEMENT EDUCATION: CHALLENGES AND RESPONSES

In 1959, two reports on business education appeared that would have a significant impact on management education. Unlike Morris Cooke's study for the Carnegie Fund in 1910, these reports were taken more seriously by educators. The Ford Foundation commissioned and financed a study by Robert A. Gordon of the University of California at Berkeley and James E. Howell of Stanford University. The Carnegie Corporation sponsored a study by Frank C. Pierson of Swarthmore College.[8]

---

7. Harold Koontz and Cyril O'Donnell, *Principles of Management: An Analysis of Managerial Functions* (New York: McGraw-Hill, 1955), pp. v, 3.

8. Robert A. Gordon and James E. Howell, *Higher Education for Business* (New York: Columbia University Press, 1959); and Frank C. Pierson, *The Education of American Businessmen: A Study of University-College Programs in Business Administration* (New York: McGraw-Hill, 1959).

Although the authors of the two reports exchanged information, they reached their conclusions independently; both reports were sharp indictments of the state of business education in the United States. Both reports noted that schools of business administration were in a state of turmoil in trying to define just what should be taught and how it should be done. By adhering to outworn precepts of education, the business schools were not preparing competent, imaginative, flexible managers for an ever-changing environment. Schools overemphasized vocationalism, which is training for specific jobs, rather than preparing broadly educated individuals for maximum future growth in a business career.

The path to preparing managers for the future resided in changing the content of the business school curriculum. More stress needed to be placed on a general education, especially in the humanities and the liberal arts; on expansion of requirements in mathematics; and on extended study in the behavioral and social sciences. For management education in particular, Gordon and Howell noted at least four different aspects of the field of organization and management: (1) managerial problem solving through the scientific method and quantitative analysis; (2) organization theory; (3) management principles; and (4) human relations.[9] Each played a part in the study of management, and the authors recommended some integration of these ideas into a sequence of courses that would better prepare future leaders rather than leave them with a fragmented picture of the tasks of management.

To achieve this integration, Gordon and Howell recommended that business policy become a capstone course to pull together the various functions of business and provide the general management overview of the firm. The call for more mathematics and behavioral sciences led to an influx of more specialists from nonbusiness backgrounds into the business schools. The impact of these changes is examined in later chapters. What follows here is a look at how the Gordon and Howell report inspired the "management theory jungle."

THE MANAGEMENT THEORY JUNGLE

Although the Gordon and Howell report noted the diversity of approaches to the study of management, it was Harold Koontz who delineated the differences and applied the catchy label "management theory jungle."[10] Koontz noted six main groups, or schools, of management thought: the *management process school* "perceives management as a process of getting things done through and with people operating in organized groups." Often called the traditional or universalist approach, this school was originated by Henri Fayol and sought to identify and analyze the functions of the manager in order to form a bridge between management theory and practice. The

---

9. Gordon and Howell, *Higher Education for Business*, pp. 179–182.

10. Based on Harold Koontz, "The Management Theory Jungle," *Journal of the Academy of Management* 4 (December 1961), pp. 182–186.

empirical school identified management as the "study of experience" and used case analyses or Ernest Dale's "comparative approach" (in *The Great Organizers*) as vehicles for teaching and drawing generalizations about management. The basic premise of this school was that examining the successes and failures of managers would further the understanding of effective management techniques.

The *human behavior school,* variously called the human relations, leadership, or behavioral sciences approach, studied management as interpersonal relations, since management was getting things done through people. This school used psychology and social psychology to concentrate on the people part of management. The *social system school* saw management as a system of cultural interrelationships in which various groups interacted and cooperated. The founder of this approach was Chester Barnard, and its adherents drew heavily from sociological theory. The *decision theory school* concentrated on analyzing and understanding who made decisions and how, as well as the entire process of selecting a course of action from various alternatives. Economic theory, and especially the theory of consumer choice, represented the intellectual foundations of this approach to management. The *mathematical school* viewed management as a "system of mathematical models and processes." This approach included the contributions of operations researchers, operations analysts, and management scientists who thought that management or decision making could be "expressed in terms of mathematical symbols and relationships."

Koontz conceded that each school had something to offer to management theory but suggested that the student of management *should not confuse content with tools.* For instance, the field of human behavior should not be judged the equivalent of the field of management, nor should a focus on decision making or mathematics be considered as encompassing the entire area of analysis. Preferably, each of these areas would provide insights and methods to aid managers in performing their tasks, and hence were tools and not schools. The causes of confusion and the "jungle warfare" between the various approaches were many: (1) "the semantics jungle" of varying uses and meanings of such terms as *organization, leadership, management, decision making,* and so on; (2) problems in defining management as a body of knowledge, since the term was used under such varying circumstances and in a variety of situations; (3) the misunderstanding of principles through trying to disprove an entire framework of principles when one principle was violated in practice; and (4) the "inability or unwillingness of management theorists to understand each other" caused by professional walls of jargon between disciplines and personal and professional desires to protect one's own idea or cult. Koontz was hopeful that the jungle could be disentangled if these problems could be resolved.

In the hope of resolution, a symposium of distinguished teachers and practitioners of management met at the University of California at Los Angeles in 1962. The objective of the seminar was to convene a group of "eminent scholars with diverse research and analytical approaches to management, as well as perceptive and experienced practitioners of the managerial art from business, education, and government."[11] After much discussion and debate, Wilfred Brown capsulized much of the conference sentiment when he said, "Frankly, gentlemen, I have not been able to follow much of what's been said in the discussions."[12] As Koontz concluded, "Semantic confusion was evident throughout the discussions."[13] The UCLA symposium was indicative of the incoherent state of management theory. Perhaps the seminar topic should have been subtitled "Is Anybody Listening?" Academicians could understand only those from their own specialty, and practitioners could not understand academicians and vice versa.[14]

Some individuals remained optimistic that a general theory could be developed. William Frederick reflected this optimism in 1963 when he said: "Within perhaps five years—certainly not more than ten years hence—a general theory of management will be evolved, stated, and generally accepted in management circles."[15] Others, such as George Odiorne, posited that management situations were too complex for precise principles and propositions that would yield a sound theory. According to Odiorne: "The successful manager is too busy succeeding (existing) to spend much time on theories which would explain his success … this doesn't mean that principles aren't there [but that they] … haven't yet been uncovered nor described."[16] Thus managers had to decide and act, moving from one situation to another. Managers were action oriented, not reflective, and pragmatic, not theoretical, and the numerous and different managerial situations defied theorizing.

In brief, the pros and cons of various authors only illustrated what Koontz had said in the beginning—that a theory thicket existed. As the search continued, other ways of describing the job of the manager were offered.

OTHER VIEWS OF MANAGERIAL WORK

It was Henri Fayol who began to reflect systematically on his experiences and observations in an attempt to sort out and identify what managers did and what managerial practices seemed to work better than others. Although Fayol's ideas provided the

---

11. Harold Koontz, ed., *Toward a Unified Theory of Management* (New York: McGraw-Hill, 1964), p. xi.

12. *Ibid,* p. 231. Brown was president of the Glacier Metal Co., Ltd., where a number of organizational systems studies were made.

13. *Ibid,* p. 238.

14. For an historical view of this problem, see Arthur G. Bedeian, "A Historical Review of Efforts in the Area of Management Semantics," *Academy of Management Journal* 17 (March 1974), pp. 101–114.

15. William C. Frederick, "The Next Development in Management Science: A General Theory," *Journal of the Academy of Management* 6 (September 1963), p. 212.

16. George S. Odiorne, "The Management Theory Jungle and the Existential Manager," *Academy of Management Journal* 9 (June 1966), p. 115.

conceptual basis for teaching management, other researchers used different methods to study the nature of managerial work. Henry Mintzberg observed five chief executives, studied their mail, and reported that their activities were sporadic, short-term copings rather than deliberative, analytical, and logical as Fayol had suggested. Rather than engaging in the traditional functions (Fayol's elements), Mintzberg concluded that managers performed ten roles that could be described under three general categories: (1) interpersonal, (2) informational, and (3) decisional. The interpersonal role arose from the manager's formal authority and occurred when a manager dealt with others as a *figurehead, leader,* or *liaison.* The informational role involved the manager's receiving, storing, and sending information as a *monitor, disseminator,* or *spokesperson.* The decisional role involved making decisions about organizational activities as an *entrepreneur, disturbance handler, resource allocator,* or *negotiator.*[17] Although the notion of managers performing certain roles had an intuitive appeal, other investigations into Mintzberg's conclusions have not always been supportive of this approach. His findings were based on only five chief executives and there is no reason to believe that this group represented typical managers. Further, the roles were based on observed behavior without asking the purpose of that activity.[18] Finally, there was no apparent connection between time spent in those roles and the effectiveness of task performance.[19]

Rosemary Stewart offered another view of the manager's job by examining: (1) demands—what had to be done in the job; (2) constraints—internal and external limits on what could be done; and (3) choices—areas in which different managers could do the job in different ways.[20] Using staffing as an example, the manager must find and select well-qualified people to perform the work (demands); constraints are placed on managers by company wage scales, the available supply of labor, general economic conditions, and laws with respect to employment practices; and a choice must be made about the person to select within the given constraints. Stewart's research was useful for understanding how managers allocated their time, and these findings added to current knowledge of managerial work.

John Kotter's study of general managers found that (1) successful managers could be very different in terms of personal characteristics and behaviors; (2) general managers thought of themselves as generalists, yet each had a very strong specialty that fitted the job demands; and (3) each had a detailed knowledge of the business and a network of relationships with other people in that business. Kotter

---

17. Henry Mintzberg, *The Nature of Managerial Work* (New York: Harper and Row, 1973).

18. Stephen J. Carroll and Dennis J. Gillen, "Are the Classical Management Functions Useful in Describing Managerial Work?" *Academy of Management Review* 12 (January 1987), pp. 38–51. See also Neil H. Snyder and Thomas L. Wheelen, "Managerial Roles: Mintzberg and the Management Process Theorists," in K. Chung, ed., *Academy of Management Proceedings* (San Diego, 1981), pp. 249–253.

19. Mark J. Martinko and William L. Gardner, "Beyond Structured Observation: Methodological Issues and New Directions," *Academy of Management Review* 10 (1988), pp. 676–695.

20. Rosemary Stewart, "A Model for Understanding Managerial Jobs and Behavior," *Academy of Management Review* 7 (January 1982), pp. 7–13.

concluded that "management at the [general manager] level looks far more like an art than a science [although] there are many regularities."[21] Kotter used the term *demands* to describe these regularities in the work of the fifteen general managers he observed in terms of setting goals, policies, and strategies; balancing the allocation of scarce resources; identifying problems and getting them under control; getting information and cooperation from others; motivating, controlling, appraising performance, and handling conflict; and, overall, "getting things done (implementation) through a large and diverse group of people."[22] The activities that Kotter identified as demands and regularities bear a remarkable resemblance to the traditional management functions of planning, coordinating, staffing, controlling, and so forth. Kotter identified the differences in responsibilities and relationships that caused the job demands to vary, such as organizational size, age, performance level, culture, and product or market diversity; however, although these irregular forces influenced the demands, they did not eliminate them. Kotter concluded that managers developed agendas, sets of loosely connected plans, events, and tasks necessary to accomplish organizational objectives.

Luthans, Hodgetts, and Rosenkrantz used trained observers to record the behavior and activities of forty-four managers from different hierarchical levels in different kinds of organizations. The Delphi technique was used to reduce these unstructured observations to twelve general categories of managerial activity. These twelve categories, each with behavioral descriptors, were collapsed further into four: routine communication, traditional management (planning, organizing, coordinating, supervising, etc.), networking (interacting with outsiders and "socializing/ politicking"), and human resource management (staffing, motivating, etc.).[23] A variety of subsequent studies sought to determine how managers allocated their activities among these categories. In one study of 248 managers the authors found that the managers distributed 32 percent of their activities to traditional management, 29 percent to routine communication, 20 percent to human resource management, and 19 percent to networking. When the behavior descriptors were cast into Fayol's terminology, the results were highly supportive of the traditional functions of management. Planning, controlling, coordinating, and organizing fitted the Fayolian framework; human resource management was a modern label for staffing, motivating, and performance evaluation; and routine communication activities fitted well into Fayol's command (directing/leading) and coordination functions. Although networking was not part of Fayol's ideas, he did include contacts with others outside the organization as part of the manager's job.[24]

---

21. John P. Kotter, *The General Managers* (New York: Free Press, 1982), p. 9.

22. *Ibid.*, p. 21.

23. Fred Luthans, Richard M. Hodgetts, and Stuart A. Rosenkrantz, *Real Managers* (Cambridge, Mass.: Ballinger, 1988), pp. 10–11.

24. Daniel A. Wren, "The Nature of Managerial Work: A Comparison of Real Managers and Traditional Management," *Journal of Managerial Issues* 4 (Spring 1992), pp. 17–30.

In brief, the labels used for describing managerial work were relatively new, but the underlying activities of what managers did were supportive of Fayol's earlier work. As Carroll and Gillen concluded, the traditional elements "still represent the most useful way of conceptualizing the manager's job, especially for management education ... [because these elements] provide clear and discrete methods of classifying the thousands of activities that managers carry out and the techniques they use in terms of the functions they perform for the achievement of organizational goals."[25] Fells concluded that Fayol "stands the test of time" and Lamond compared Fayol and Mintzberg, concluding that Fayol's ideas are compatible with the roles approach to understanding managerial work.[26] After years of investigation, Rosemary Stewart concluded that "His [Fayol's] five-fold classification has been used, with minor modifications, to the present day."[27] To improve management teaching and research, it is necessary to beware of new labels for previously recognized activities and to connect observed behavior with what is to be achieved by that action.

Although other studies of managerial work differ in research methodology or terminology, they are related ways of examining the same activity—that is, what managers do. To illustrate: in planning, managers receive, store, monitor, and disseminate information; they also make decisions about strategy and allocation of resources and initiate planned changes. In organizing, managers act as liaisons, establish relationships between people and activities, and make decisions about the placement and utilization of resources. The staffing job involves hiring, training, and appraising performance as well as negotiating with labor unions. In leading, managers use their authority to accomplish goals; information and communication are two important parts of this job. Controlling is based on information about performance, decisions are made about corrective action, and coordination is essential. Stewart's work helped in understanding why some research finds managers doing similar activities (because of demands or constraints), while other studies find differences in managerial activity (choices). Kotter's agenda helped explain why observations of managers in action reveal behaviors that do not appear to fit some neat categories of planning and organizing—there are regularities in managerial work in terms of accomplishing goals.

Indeed, Fayol's ideas have a remarkable longevity as a basic framework for understanding the manager's job. In brief, what often appears to be disagreement about the manager's job may in fact be only superficial and semantic. Although no

———
25. Carroll and Gillen, "Classical Management Functions," p. 48.

26. Michael J. Fells, "Fayol Stands the Test of Time," *Journal of Management History* 6 (2000), pp. 345–360; David A. Lamond, "Henry Mintzberg vs. Henri Fayol: Of Lighthouses, Cubists, and the Emperor's New Clothes," *Journal of Applied Management and Entrepreneurship* 8 (2003), pp. 5–23; and David A. Lamond, "A Matter of Style: Reconciling Henry and Henri." *Management Decision/Journal of Management History* 42 (2004), pp. 330–356.

27. Rosemary Stewart, *The Reality of Management*, 3rd ed. (Boston: Butterworth-Heineman, 1999), p. 4.

general theory of management has emerged, research has enriched our understanding and has served to confirm that Fayol's ideas continue to be fundamentally sound. Although it is necessary to continue to build on Fayol's ideas to fit changing markets, technologies, and people, his work was seminal and enduring. Of course the task of writing history is never done, for each day brings fresh ideas, new evidence, and variant ways of examining the tasks of the manager. It is difficult for modern scholars, so steeped in their own daily activities and so influenced by the current press of today's ideas, to sit back and put them in perspective. The zoom lens of history often leaves the near present slightly out of focus.

THE SEARCH FOR EXCELLENCE

Thomas Peters and Robert Waterman, who were more closely associated with management consulting and practice, challenged the academic theories, elevated the art of management over the technique and tool approach, and identified eight attributes of corporate excellence: (1) a bias for action rather than contemplation; (2) a closeness to customer needs in products and services; (3) the encouragement of autonomy and loose rather than close supervision; (4) an attitude toward employees that encouraged productivity and avoided a "we" versus "they" feeling; (5) a close touch with people in a technique called "management by walking (or wandering) around"; (6) a "sticking to knitting" by staying close to the business competencies, thus avoiding unrelated ventures; (7) a simple organizational structure and a lean staff; and (8) a control system that had simultaneous loose-tight properties of keeping on target but without stifling innovation.[28]

U.S. business leaders responded to the Peters and Waterman book in legions, making it a best-seller. The book gave U.S. business managers a positive target, not an inferiority complex. Academicians, however, were not so enthralled. Carroll, for example, criticized Peters and Waterman's conceptual foundations and research methods as narrow, inadequate, and poorly developed.[29] Others suggested that "excellence" was too narrowly defined; that samples from *Fortune* 500 firms revealed other firms that outperformed the so-called well-managed ones; and that some of the excellence principles were contradictory (for example, was it possible to stick to the firm's "knitting" and still be innovative and entrepreneurial?).[30] The criticisms

---

28. Thomas J. Peters and Robert H. Waterman, Jr., *In Search of Excellence* (New York: Harper and Row, 1982). Within a decade Tom Peters had recanted his yellow brick road to success: see Thomas J. Peters, *Liberation Management* (New York: Knopf, 1992). *Caveat lector.*

29. Daniel T. Carroll, "A Disappointing Search for Excellence," *Harvard Business Review* 61 (November–December 1983), pp. 78–88.

30. See Michael A. Hitt and R. Duane Ireland, "Peters and Waterman Revisited: The Unended Quest for Excellence," *Academy of Management Executive* 1 (May 1987), pp. 91–98; and Kenneth E. Aupperle, William Acar, and David E. Booth, "An Empirical Critique of *In Search of Excellence:* How Excellent Are the Excellent Companies?" *Journal of Management* 12 (1986), pp. 499–512.

acknowledged, however, that the excellence principles could be useful for improved practice but were not a magic formula for instant organizational success.

The quest for excellence in management practice is not new, as seen earlier in the work of Jackson Martindell of the American Institute of Management and Paul Holden and his Stanford colleagues. None of this pioneering work was acknowledged by Peters and Waterman, who relied solely on financial measures of success. If history provides a lesson in this case, it is that no one factor guarantees organizational success; that excellence is a composite of many things—sound strategies, action-oriented plans, clearly defined work relationships, sound leadership, motivated people, and balanced, flexible controls, to name a few of these important factors. No one technique or set of techniques will ensure successful performance; no one measure stands alone.

MANAGEMENT EDUCATION: ANOTHER LOOK

As practitioners questioned academic relevance, academicians created new approaches to management. Harold Koontz revisited the management theory jungle and found that it had expanded from six to eleven approaches. The operational school (a new name for the management process school) continued to study the managerial functions but had spawned two new schools, managerial roles and the contingency, or situational, approach. The empirical school remained, although its case-study approach had been influenced by the role and situational approaches. The human behavior school had led to two new approaches: interpersonal behavior and group behavior. The social system approach had undergone the most proliferation, multiplying into the sociotechnical systems, cooperative social systems, and systems approaches. The decision theory and mathematical schools had remained the same, except for adding management science to the mathematical branch. Koontz noted, "the management theory jungle is still with us.... Perhaps the most effective way [out of the jungle] would be for leading managers to take a more active role in narrowing the widening gap ... between professional practice and our college and university business [schools]."[31] Koontz also chastised his fellow academicians for failing to make their research more relevant to practice:

> I see too many academics forgetting what I think our job is in management, and that is to organize available knowledge; develop new knowledge, of course, but organize it in such a way that it can be useful to practicing managers to underpin management. I am surprised as I watch the literature, that some people are discovering what we've

---

31. A discussion of each of these schools and a comparison of 1961 and 1980 views are presented in Harold Koontz, "The Management Theory Jungle Revisited," *Academy of Management Review* 5 (April 1980), pp. 175–187.

known for years. For example, some things like this: that technology affects management organization. I found that out when I was in the airline industry a few years ago and I never thought it was anything very surprising. Another, that the actual managing depends on the situation.... I thought, my gosh, there must be something new there. Only to find, after spending a lot of time reading, that there wasn't anything, and I don't know any practicing manager who doesn't manage in light of the situation. I think we have to agree that management theory and science should underpin practice, otherwise why develop it?[32]

According to some observers, the business schools were prime contributors to the gulf between theory and practice. For instance, some felt that the Gordon and Howell and Pierson reports had led to unintended consequences, such as a proliferation of quantitative and behavioral science courses, the hiring of mathematicians, sociologists, psychologists, and others who had no training or background in business, and a multiplication of specialized journals that appealed to and could be read only by other academicians. As a result, academicians focused on research that "would fail any reasonable test of applicability or relevance to consequential management problems or policy issues ... [and] ignore[d] any utility to managers or business organizations."[33] Others blamed the organization of business education into disciplines, the tradition of academic freedom, and the academic reward system (publish or perish) for the intransigence of professors with respect to relevance in business education.[34]

So the American Assembly of Collegiate Schools of Business (currently the AACSB International) sponsored a three-year comprehensive study of management education that surveyed practitioners and academics. The authors of the report, Lyman Porter and Lawrence McKibbin, commented that faculty members required breadth in order to integrate problem finding and problem solving across various business functions. Yet many professors lacked relevant work experience and were too narrowly educated to "appreciate the complexities and subtleties of business."[35] Porter and McKibbin recommended that management educators should pay more attention to external factors, especially developments in international business; develop more ability to integrate across business functions; emphasize

---

32. Quoted by Ronald G. Greenwood in "Harold Koontz: A Reminiscence" (presented at the meetings of the Academy of Management, Boston, August 14, 1984).

33. Jack N. Behrman and Richard I. Levin, "Are Business Schools Doing Their Job?" *Harvard Business Review* 62 (January–February 1984), p. 141.

34. Ben M. Oviatt and Warren D. Miller, "Irrelevance, Intransigence, and Business Professors." *Academy of Management Executive* 3 (1989), pp. 304–312.

35. Lyman Porter and Lawrence E. McKibbin, *Management Education and Development: Drift or Thrust into the 21st Century?* (New York: McGraw-Hill, 1988), p. 132.

interpersonal and communication skills more; and develop Ph.D.'s who would have analytical sophistication as well as "the sharpened and broadened perspective of real world work experience."[36] Although there is an apparent gap between academic theory and management practice, and although some academicians do write for other academics, the blame must be shared. Managers still tend to look for quick fixes—seven or eight simple steps to solve all their problems—and leap from fad to fad.[37] One who has contributed to practice as well as being read by academicians is Peter Drucker.

DRUCKER: THE GURU OF MANAGEMENT PRACTICE

Peter F. Drucker (1909–) achieved prominence through his writings and consulting; his contributions have been primarily to the world of management practice. Largely influenced by the economist Joseph Schumpeter, a fellow Austrian, Drucker viewed society and business as in a constant state of creation, growth, stagnation, and decline. Abandonment of stagnating or declining ventures was also innovative, according to Drucker, because it freed up resources for another innovative step. What kept the organization from failing was its ability to perform an entrepreneurial task of innovating—finding a new or better product, creating new customers or uses for old or new products, and making, pricing, or distributing the product or service in a more competitive way.

We will see Drucker's view on business strategy later in this chapter, but he stressed the need to define key areas for setting objectives and evaluating results. These were market standing (measured against the market potential); innovation (in products and services, or in improving how these products and services were made or delivered); productivity (a yardstick as a target for "constant improvement"); physical and financial resources (defining needs, planning, and acquiring); profitability (for rate of return on investment); manager performance and development (managing by objectives and self control); worker performance and attitude (employee relations); and public responsibility (participating "responsibly in society").[38] In setting objectives, the firm had to ask the "right questions": What is our business? Who is the customer? What does the customer buy? What is value to the customer? What will our business be? And what should it be?[39] For Drucker, 90

---

36. *Ibid.,* p. 327.

37. Recommended reading for the fashion of writing about fads: Eric Abrahamson, "Management Fashion," *Academy of Management Review* 21 (1996), pp. 254–285; Paula Phillips Carson, Patricia A. Lanier, Kerry David Carson, and Brandi N. Guidry, "Clearing a Path through the Management Fashion Jungle: Some Preliminary Trailblazing," *Academy of Management Journal* 43 (2000), pp. 1143–1158; and Jane Whitney Gibson and Dana V. Tesone, "Management Fads: Emergence, Evolution, and Implications for Managers," *Academy of Management Executive* 15 (2001), pp. 122–133.

38. Peter F. Drucker, *The Practice of Management* (New York: Harper and Row, 1954), pp. 63–84.

39. *Ibid.,* pp. 49–61.

percent of managerial work was generic, working with and through people to lead in such a manner that each individual is enabled to use his or her strengths and knowledge productively. The remaining 10 percent varied according to the mission, culture, history, and vocabulary of any specific type of organization, profit seeking as well as not for profit.[40]

Peter F. Drucker, 1985. Ronald G. Greenwood Collection, courtesy of Regina A. Greenwood.

Although many had written about the need for organizational objectives, Drucker was the first to publish the concept and coin the phrase "management by objectives" (MBO). According to Drucker, "A manager's job should be based on a task to be performed in order to attain the company's objectives.... [T]he manager should be directed and controlled by the objectives of performance rather than by his boss."[41] Management by objectives was to replace management by drive, and control was to be self-control rather than control from above. Knowing the objectives of the unit and those of the enterprise, managers could direct their own activities:

> The only principle that can do this is management by objectives and self-control.... It substitutes for control from outside the stricter, more exacting and more effective control from the inside. It motivates the manager to action not because somebody tells him to do something ... but because the objective needs of his task demand it.[42]

Although Drucker got the credit for MBO, it was a General Electric Company executive, Harold Smiddy (1900–1978), who practiced the concept. Drucker was a friend of Smiddy and a consultant to GE; what Drucker did was conceptualize the label and write about it for a general audience. Drucker, with a show of intellectual modesty, maintained that MBO was not new, having been practiced earlier at GE by Smiddy, at GM by Alfred Sloan, and at Du Pont by Pierre du Pont and Donaldson Brown. Although this was an accurate analysis, Ronald Greenwood concluded, "it took Drucker to put it all together, think through the underlying philosophy, and then explain and advocate it in a form others could use."[43]

---

40. Peter F. Drucker, *Management Challenges for the 21st Century* (New York: Harper Business, 1999).

41. Drucker, *The Practice of Management*, p. 137.

42. *Ibid.*

43. Ronald G. Greenwood, "Management by Objectives: As Developed by Peter Drucker, Assisted by Harold Smiddy," *Academy of Management Review* 6 (April 1981), p. 230.

George Odiorne, a student of Drucker and the first person to write a full-scale book on MBO, said, "[Drucker] has been a voice of sanity in graduate schools. Faculty members are still busy running mathematical models and measuring the distance between managers' eyeballs but Drucker has always focused on what managers actually do, the practice of management."[44] Drucker's emphasis on practice underscores the perceived gap between academic research and the practice of management. Porter and McKibbin observed that "key managers and executives pay little or no attention to [business school] research or its findings."[45] Drucker agreed:

> Specialization is becoming an obstacle to the acquisition of knowledge and an even greater barrier to making it effective. Academia defines knowledge as what gets printed. But surely this is not knowledge; it is raw data. Knowledge is information that changes something or somebody—either by becoming grounds for action, or by making an individual (or an institution) capable of different and more effective action.... Who or what is to blame for the obscurantism of the learned is beside the point. What matters is that the learning of the academic specialist is rapidly ceasing to be "knowledge." It is at best "erudition" and at its more common worst mere "data."[46]

As Zahra noted, Drucker's work is "grounded in management practice, [and] has also been able to communicate his ideas well to academics and leading executives."[47] Perhaps Drucker's work will help us leaven academic rigor and make it more managerially relevant; if not, knowledge will remain data and the theory-practice gap will continue.

FROM BUSINESS POLICY TO STRATEGIC MANAGEMENT

Management is an activity found in all organizations, for profit and not for profit, and seeks the optimum use of human and other resources in pursuit of objectives. Emphasis in this part of management theory and practice will be on the business firm, especially on the task of top management in integrating the functions of the firm into a coherent whole. In the late nineteenth century, Henry Towne asked engineers to think like economists; here the issue is to get economists to think like

---

44. George Odiorne, quoted in Randall Poe, "A Walk and Talk with Peter Drucker," *Across the Board* (February 1983), p. 32.

45. Porter and McKibbin, *Management Education*, p. 170.

46. Peter F. Drucker, *The New Realities* (New York: Harper and Row, 1989), pp. 251–252.

47. Shaker A. Zahra, "Introduction: Peter F. Drucker's *The Practice of Management*," *Academy of Management Executive* 17 (2003), p. 8.

managers. This will involve recognizing once more the role of management in the firm, the notion of transaction costs, and issues within the firm such as governance and agency theory. Then we will see how early ideas of business policy evolved into strategic management. Strategic management is not the entire task of top management, but complements general management theory by helping us understand the process of management through formulating plans and policies that must be implemented by organizing, staffing, directing/monitoring, coordinating, and controlling.

MARKETS AND HIERARCHIES

In previous chapters we have examined, in the writings of Say, Marshall, and Atkinson, views of management as a factor of production, able to provide a competitive advantage and to make a difference in performance of the firm. Chapter 16 introduced John R. Commons indicating a transaction as a basic unit of economic analysis, and Ronald Coase asking why the business firm exists. I find it surprising that we are still asking two-hundred-year-old questions about the economies to be gained by the efficient and thoughtful management of a business enterprise. Nevertheless, Coase's 1937 article marked the reemergence of this question, although his theory of the firm was occluded by Keynesian economics for many years. In his Nobel Laureate (1991) address, Coase commented on Adam Smith's example of barter being difficult because a match had to be found between the person who wanted to trade and the other person who had what the first party wanted as well as wanting what the first party had to offer.[48] Money reduced the difficulties of this transaction by exchange proceeding from a common denominator. In a similar fashion, "the operation of a market costs something and by forming an organization and allowing some authority... to direct the resources, certain marketing costs are saved."[49] The firm was an alternative method of coordinating market factors and could, up to certain limits, be more efficient than the market. Coase did not try to explain why some firms were better at organizing and coordinating than others, but concluded that his point was to indicate the "dynamic factors" of a "moving equilibrium" influenced by how managers arrange the firm's factors of production. When we discuss strategic management, we will see how Coase opened the door for others to question why some firms were more competitive than others.

It would be a considerable length of time, however, before others pried open the "black box" of economics.[50] While engaged in theorizing and mathematical model

---

48. Ronald H. Coase, "Prize Lecture [1991]," *Nobel Lectures, Economics,* 1991–1995 (Singapore: World Publishing, 2003).

49. R. H. Coase, "The Nature of the Firm," *Economica,* n.s., 4 (1937), pp. 386–405.

50. Kyle Bruce, "Economists' Evolving Conceptualism of Management: Opening the 'Black Box,'" in Gerard Griffin, ed., *Management Theory and Practice: Moving to a New Era* (South Yarra, Australia: Macmillan, 1998), pp. 15–36.

building, many economists focused on the market for factors of production and the market for the sale of products to the neglect of the throughput within the firm. Oliver Williamson (1932–) inherited a great intellectual base for the development of his contributions. In his doctoral dissertation at the Carnegie Institute of Technology (today's Carnegie-Mellon University) he studied with Herbert Simon (who learned much from Chester Barnard) and Richard Cyert and James March of the so-called "Carnegie School" of decision making. Williamson's dissertation concerned managerial discretion in decision making, and he found that this exercise of discretionary authority often undermined the efficiency of the firm in contrast to the assumptions of classical economic theory.[51] Continuing his work, he found other flaws in classical economic theory, especially the neglect of the internal operations of the firm. By 1973, he was referring to the work of Coase and offered his initial statement of markets and hierarchies.[52]

Williamson referred to this view of the firm as the "new institutional economics" in contrast with previous work by institutionalists such as Commons. From history, Williamson saw the move from markets to "nonmarkets" based on two assumptions: one, bounded rationality; and two, opportunism, which was the "effort to realize individual gains through a lack of candor or honesty in transactions."[53] Williamson's bounded rationality evolved from Barnard's limits to "the power of choice" that was transformed in stages by Simon to factors that "bound the area of rationality" to "bounded rationality."[54] Firms were more efficient than markets because of the internalization of the costs of market transactions (Coase) and monitoring mechanisms existed to thwart (hopefully) opportunism. Williamson's interests in opportunism followed Barnard's "theory of opportunism" to a limited degree, and would be deemed by Williamson as "self-interest seeking with guile" which was present in everyone since "even the less opportunistic have their price."[55] Williamson's extensions of the work of Coase and others created widespread interest in transaction-cost economics. The "visible hand" of Alfred Chandler would be found more efficient, in most cases, than the "invisible hand" of Adam Smith because of the actions of the managerial hierarchy.

---

51. Oliver E. Williamson, "Managerial Discretion and Business Behavior," *American Economic Review* 53 (1963), pp. 1032–1057.

52. Oliver E. Williamson, "Markets and Hierarchies: Some Elementary Considerations," *American Economic Review* 63 (1973), pp. 316–325; and O. E. Williamson, *Markets and Hierarchies: Analysis and Antitrust Implication: A Study in the Economics of Internal Organization* (New York: Free Press, 1975).

53. Oliver E. Williamson, "Markets and Hierarchies," *American Economic Review* (1973), p. 317.

54. Chester I. Barnard, *The Functions of the Executive* (Cambridge, Mass.: Harvard University Press, 1938), p. 14; Simon, *Administrative Behavior* (1945), pp. 39–41, 243–244. In the preface to the 1957 edition, Simon used "bounded rationality."

55. Oliver E. Williamson, "Transaction-Cost Economics: The Governance of Contractual Relations," *Journal of Law and Economics* 22 (1979), p. 234.

GOVERNANCE AND AGENCY ISSUES

Assuming that the managerial hierarchy of a firm is more efficient, in most cases, than the market, then the actions of those who guide the conduct of the enterprise becomes a critical issue. In a corporation, the shareholders elect a group, the board of directors, who, in turn, are expected to employ others as managers to oversee day-to-day operations. In theory and legally, the board and these senior managers are *agents* of the shareholders and are expected to maximize the wealth of these investors. In practice, this is not always the case, raising the vital question of corporate governance.

We have discussed Adam Smith's concern about the intentions of those who managed "other peoples' money"; but John Stuart Mill was not concerned, believing that the "zeal" of hired managers could be aligned by pecuniary incentives with the interests of the shareholders. Others, such as Berle and Means, Burnham, and Robert Gordon expressed concerns about the separation of ownership and control, and the possibility of senior management becoming a self-perpetuating oligarchy. Peter Drucker advocated an outside board, that is, persons who had never served as full-time managers of the firm; and Myles Mace found that boards of directors were selected by the president of the firm, did what they were told, rarely evaluated the performance of president, and typically did not ask discerning questions.[56]

Michael Jensen has been a perennial critic of internal control systems as inadequate to the purposes of efficiency and value for the firm and its stakeholders. Except for external crises, Jensen judges boards as failures if they have allegiance to the president, if the board culture favors consensus and frowns on dissent, if presidents set the agendas and fail to fully disclose vital information, and if the possibility of legal liability leads board members to minimize risks and cover their backsides.[57]

The question of corporate governance is a broad one, touching issues such as executive compensation, the size and inside/outside "mix" of a board, risk-taking and innovation, executive selection and development, and strategic leadership, to touch a few of the vital components of effective governance. In addition, a related issue is whose interests are being served.

Experienced executives Chester Barnard and Henri Fayol were apparently well acquainted with opportunistic behavior among employees, managers and workers alike. Barnard wrote of "self-abnegation" and willingness to cooperate; Fayol made the subordination of individual interest to the general interest one of his principles. In both instances, they were urging individuals to contribute their efforts to the enterprise rather than seeking personal gain. In neither case does this suggest self-sacrifice, but recognition of divergent interests. Agency theory, which may or may

---

56. Drucker, *The Practice of Management,* ch. 14; and Myles Mace, *Directors: Myth and Reality* (Boston: Harvard University, Graduate School of Business Administration, 1971), pp. 205–206.

57. Michael C. Jensen, "The Modern Industrial Revolution, Exit, and the Failure of Internal Control Systems," *Journal of Finance* 48 (1993), pp. 831–880.

not be a theory, addresses opportunistic behavior, or, as we saw Williamson define it, "self-interest seeking with guile." A staunch believer in agency theory would affirm that everyone, even the less opportunistic, has his or her price. This places a negative spin on what we would like to believe about our fellow human creatures, but too often we are shocked to find the price is but a few pieces of coin.

Since persons are expected to act opportunistically (except, of course, ourselves), the exercise of prudence in interpersonal and contractual relations is advised. Trust is elusive if we expect others to lie, cheat, shirk, and so on to take advantage of the situation. Means must be designed to reduce the occurrence of opportunistic behavior such as pay for performance, careful selection procedures, performance evaluation, close monitoring of behavior at work, or other methods of tying the motives of individuals to the firm's goals. If errors are made in preventing opportunistic behavior, post hoc actions such as audits, random inspections, and information systems that provide some measure of effort are implemented. Hammurabi was no fool when he passed a law some 3,000 years ago requiring receipts.

Governance and agency issues are intertwined with other management topics: organizing, human resource management, motivation, ethics, strategic leadership, interpersonal relations, communication and information systems, and control techniques, to touch the main connections. Historically, governance and agency are evergreen issues; the stuff for morality dramas, for seeking exemplars of virtue, and to paraphrase Shakespeare's Hamlet, to catch the conscience that lies within.

MANAGEMENT AS AN INTEGRATING AND INNOVATING TASK

The preceding pages have provided glimpses of business policy and strategy as they evolved to provide a general management view of organizations. Wren positioned Henri Fayol as a strategist in his actions to revive Comambault as it was headed for bankruptcy.[58] Fayol stated:

> The responsibility of general management is to conduct the enterprise toward its objective by making optimum use of available resources. It [general management] is the executive authority, it draws up the plan of action, selects personnel, determines performance, ensures and controls the execution of all activities.[59]

In Britain, Alexander Hamilton Church wrote of the determination of policy and its implementation in the functions of the firm. A more recent executive's description of his job rhymes with Church: "You might ask, 'OK, you are a business

---

58. Daniel A. Wren, "Henri Fayol as Strategist: A Nineteenth Century Corporate Turnaround," *Management Decision* 39 (2001), pp. 475–487.

59. Fayol, *General and Industrial Management* (1949), pp. 60–61.

person, what is it that you have to do?' I am of the school that says we have to do two things: we decide what to do, and we try to make it happen."[60] In the early twentieth century, Arch Shaw (1876–1962) pioneered the study of business policy at Northwestern University and Harvard University as a course intended to integrate the business functions from the general management viewpoint. Individuals such as Edmund Learned and Roland Christensen were among those who followed in Shaw's path with Harvard's tradition of teaching by the case method.[61] Chester Barnard wrote of "strategic factors" and executive functions from his experience; and William Newman, author and co-author of a long-lived policy text and cases, traced his roots to James O. McKinsey (1889–1937), founder of the consulting firm of that name and an advocate of budgets and planning and controlling aids. Newman focused on the role of objectives and policy as defining the character of the firm, its philosophy, and its role in society.[62]

Peter Drucker, well known for his interest in general management, established the basic conceptual framework for the business policy/strategy in 1954:

> The important decision, the decisions that really matter, are strategic. They involve either finding out what the situation is, or changing it, either finding out what the resources are or what they should be…. Anyone who is a manager has to make such strategic decisions, and the higher his level in the management hierarchy, the more of them he must make.
>
> Among these are all decisions on business objectives and on the means to achieve them…. The important and difficult job is never to find out the right answer, it is to find the right question.[63]

Drucker's ideas would inspire others. One possible influence appeared in the Gordon and Howell report, which proposed business policy as a capstone course to bring together the knowledge acquired in the various business functional areas. Another seminal work was Alfred Chandler's study of the influence of strategy on the organizational structure of the firm. "Structure follows strategy" would become an enduring part of the literature.[64] As the study of policy and strategy evolved, it was

---

60. John A. Reed, "Citigroup's John Reed and Stanford's James March on Management Research and Practice," Anne S. Huff, ed., *Academy of Management Executive* 14 (2000), p. 57. Reed was CEO of Citigroup.

61. Edmund P. Learned, "Reflections on Leadership, Teaching, and Problem Solving Groups," in Arthur G. Bedeian, ed., *Management Laureates*, vol. 2 (Greenwich, Conn.: JAI Press, 1993), pp. 149–175.

62. William H. Newman, "The Takeoff," in Arthur G. Bedeian, ed., *Management Laureates*, vol. 2 (Greenwich, Conn.: JAI Press, 1993), pp. 375–397.

63. Drucker, *Practice of Management*, pp. 352–353.

64. Alfred D. Chandler, Jr., *Strategy and Structure* (Cambridge, Mass.: MIT Press, 1962).

rechristened many times. George Steiner, based on his experiences at Lockheed Aircraft, entitled his 1963 book *Managerial Long Range Planning* to describe the study of the role of management in preparing for the future.[65] Long range planning seemed an inadequate phrase for describing the task of the general manager and the necessity of a broader view of the firm. General management was more than planning and involved integrating the parts into a whole.

H. Igor Ansoff (1918–2002) was employed by the Rand Corporation, and one of his projects involved the vulnerability of the U.S. Air Force's Strategic Air Command (SAC) to attack from the USSR. After assisting in developing a strategy to cope with that possibility, which, incidentally, was never implemented, Ansoff joined the Corporate Planning Department of Lockheed Aircraft. Ansoff assisted in long range planning and examining opportunities for Lockheed to diversify from the erratic defense industry business. In a later role in academia, Ansoff encountered the ideas of Peter Drucker and Alfred Chandler, and formulated his notion of corporate strategy, which involved formulating objectives and strategy based on an analysis of opportunities in the environment.[66] The transition from business policy was apparent and Dan Schendel and Charles Hofer renamed the field strategic management in 1979, calling for a "new" view of business policy and planning.[67] Thus policy was replaced (largely) by strategy, which originally was only a part of planning, which, in turn, was only part of management.

STRATEGY AND VIEWS OF THE FIRM

The format of combining industry notes with cases in the texts developed at Harvard for business policy was in recognition of a need to place the strategy of a firm in its competitive environment. Michael Porter, a Harvard doctoral student, studied both in the business school and the economics department and recalled it as a "surreal experience" to find that both academic units were discussing industries in the study of business policy and industrial organization (I/O) economics. In Harvard's economics department, Edward Mason and Joe Bain had studied industry structure, the conduct of buyers and sellers, barriers to competition, and how these factors could impact performance and profitability.[68] "On the business school

---

65. George Steiner, "My Roads to Management Theory and Practice," in Arthur G. Bedeian, ed., *Management Laureates*, vol. 3 (Greenwich, Conn.: JAI Press, 1993), pp. 113–143.

66. H. Igor Ansoff, "A Profile in Intellectual Growth," in Arthur G. Bedeian, ed., *Management Laureates*, vol. 3 (Greenwich, Conn.: JAI Press, 1993), pp. 1–39; see also H. Igor Ansoff, *Corporate Strategy* (New York: McGraw-Hill, 1965).

67. Dan E. Schendel and Charles W. Hofer, *Strategic Management: A New View of Business Policy and Planning* (Boston: Little, Brown, 1979).

68. Edward S. Mason, "Price and Production Policies of Large-Scale Enterprise," *American Economic Review* 29 (1939), pp. 61–74; Joe S. Bain, *Barriers to New Competition* (Cambridge, Mass.: Harvard University Press, 1956); and Richard E. Caves, *American Industry: Structure, Conduct, Performance* (Englewood Cliffs, N.J.: Prentice-Hall, 1967).

side of the [Charles] river, *ceteris paribus* [Latin for 'other things the same'] assumptions don't work. Managers must consider everything. I [Porter] concluded that we needed frameworks rather than models."[69]

The result was a frame-breaking set of ideas that would dominate the strategic management field for nearly a decade. Porter's position was that profitability of the firm was a function of "five forces" of industry structure: threat of entry of new competitors, the bargaining power of suppliers, the threat of product substitutes, the bargaining power of buyers, and rivalry among existing competitors. Barriers to entry and the stage of the industry's life cycle were other industry characteristics that shaped the ability of a firm to compete effectively. The external factors in the industry structure shaped how firms could seek to create and sustain a competitive edge. Firms must consider its "value chain," that is, how activities were organized and linked to produce, deliver, and support products for the ultimate user. Porter suggested "generic" strategies: low cost, product differentiation, or a focus option that cut across these two where perhaps cost was less of a factor or where both cost and differentiation had to be considered.[70] Porter made a significant impact on strategic management and changed its direction from case study to industry studies regarding structure, conduct, and performance.

The next path to finding ideas about strategic management received belated recognition. While Coase had asked why the firm exists, the next step was to ask why firms differ. The American-born and -educated British economist Edith Penrose (1914–1996) observed that "It is the heterogeneity, and not the homogeneity, of the productive services available or potentially available from its resources that give each firm its unique character."[71] The key words were "heterogeneity" and "resources," and Penrose was pushing economic thinking out of its "black box" by reintroducing the role of management:

> A firm is more than an administrative unit; it is also a collection of productive resources the disposal of which between uses and over time is determined by administrative decision ... management tries to make the best use of the resources available ... [and] a firm is essentially a pool of resources the utilization of which is organized in an administrative framework.[72]

---

69. Nicholas Argyres and Anita M. McGahan, "An Interview with Michael Porter," *Academy of Management Executive* 16 (2002), p. 43.

70. Michael E. Porter, *Competitive Strategy: Techniques for Analyzing Industries and Competitors* (New York: Free Press, 1980); Michael E. Porter, *Competitive Advantage: Creating and Sustaining Superior Performance* (New York: Free Press, 1985).

71. Edith Tilton Penrose, *The Theory of the Growth of the Firm* (New York: John Wiley and Sons, 1959), p. 75.

72. *Ibid.*, p. 24, 5, 149.

Penrose noted that a firm's resources were "inherited," that is, left over from prior decisions about location, special purpose equipment, the pool of managerial talent, and "indivisible" resources, all of which posed potential limits to decisions about the future direction of the firm. "Knowledge" was also inherited as it resided in the experience, education, and intuition of the firm's human resource. She used "entrepreneurs" to describe persons within the firm who could provide changes in knowledge about products, markets, technology, administrative processes, and opportunities. Rather than being closed to change, the firm could grow by "changes in the knowledge possessed."[73] Penrose's ideas would lie fallow for some years, but she had offered seminal ideas on two subsequent views of the firm.

In the 1960s, the Harvard business policy group began using SWOT analysis in the classroom. An acronym for "strengths" and "weaknesses" (within the firm) and "opportunities" and "threats" (outside the firm), SWOT was promoted by a conference held at Harvard to spread this concept in practice and academia.[74] Harvard's Kenneth Andrews credited Howard Stevenson's doctoral thesis at Harvard as "making the first formal study of management practice in defining corporate strengths and weaknesses as part of the strategic planning process."[75] Andrews added "distinctive competence" from Philip Selznik's definition as the organizational "character…[that] reflects the general orientation of personnel, the flexibility of the organizational forms, and the nature of the institutional environment to which the organization is committed."[76] SWOT became a neat framework for case study and discussion that incorporated specifics about the firm and information about the industry setting. For learning and teaching, the bottom line was to match strengths and distinctive competencies to opportunities while minimizing weaknesses and threats.

After a quarter of a century of neglect, Penrose's ideas found a home in an article by Wernerfelt in which he proposed a resource-based view (RBV) of the firm. This RBV was an extension of Andrews, Caves, and Porter's I/O economics and strategy by proposing that a firm's resources could be thought of as strengths and weaknesses. Tied to Porter's five forces framework, Wernerfelt proposed that "*what a firm wants is to create a situation where its own resource position directly or indirectly makes it more difficult for others to catch up.*"[77] One example is being a "first mover"

---

73. *Ibid.*, pp. 76–80.

74. Pankaj Ghemawat, "Competition and Business Strategy in Historical Perspective," *Business History Review* 76 (2002), pp. 41–42.

75. Kenneth R. Andrews, *The Concept of Corporate Strategy* (Homewood, Ill.: Dow-Jones Irwin, 1971), p. 90. See also Howard H. Stevenson, *Defining Corporate Strengths and Weaknesses* (doctoral thesis, Harvard Business School, 1969).

76. Philip Selznick, *Leadership in Administration* (Evanston, Ill.: Row, Peterson, 1957), p. 42, 50–51.

77. Birger Wernerfelt, "A Resource-Based View of the Firm," *Strategic Management Journal* 5 (1984), p. 173. Italics are in the original.

in an industry. Mergers and acquisitions, according to Wernerfelt, provided the opportunity to acquire or sell bundles of resources. Built on Harvard's policy group perspective, Penrose's work enabled the firm to think in terms of resources rather than products.

In retrospect, Wernerfelt admitted that the resource-based view did not gain credence until some years later in the work of Prahalad and Hamel and their paper on the "core competencies" of the firm.[78] For these authors, the previously used notion of the strategic business unit (SBU) focused on products rather than on the core competencies that drove current success and, in the long run, spawned new products. Rumelt had noted bundles of connected and unique resources earlier, but core competencies had a more stimulating effect.[79] Barney made competencies more specific as means to gaining a competitive advantage by suggesting the firm's resources should be rare, valuable, not easily imitated, and nonsubstitutable.[80]

In addition to stimulating numerous articles and books about the resource-based view of the firm, Penrose spawned another—the knowledge-based view: "There is no reason to assume that the new knowledge and services will be useful only in the firm's existing products; on the contrary, they may ... provide a foundation which will give the firm an advantage in some entirely new area."[81] She cites Joseph Schumpeter on numerous occasions regarding the role of innovation through discovery. Rather than being bound and rigid by existing knowledge, the firm also has the ability to extend its capabilities through learning. Others have built on Penrose's idea and recognize the firm as a potential storehouse of knowledge.[82] At this writing, it is difficult to reach conclusions about the potency of the knowledge based view (KBV) of the firm. For instance, how do organizations learn? Perhaps this is a property of individuals who operate at the organizational interface with customers, scientists, financiers, labor leaders, community representatives, or at conferences where communities of practice share experience. In the year before her death, Penrose said "history matters"; where we go from here depends on the cumulative growth of knowledge from the past through the present in understanding the goal-directed firm for the future.[83]

---

78. Birger Wernerfelt, "A Resource-Based View of the Firm: Ten Years After," *Strategic Management Journal* 16 (1995), p. 171; and C. K. Prahalad and Gary Hamel, "The Core Competence of the Corporation," *Harvard Business Review* 68 (May–June 1990), pp. 79–91.

79. Richard Rumelt, "Toward a Strategic Theory of the Firm," in R. B. Lamb, ed., *Competitive Strategic Management,* (Englewood Cliffs, NJ: Prentice Hall, 1984), pp. 556–570.

80. Jay B. Barney, "Firm Resources and Sustained Competitive Advantage, *Journal of Management* 17 (1991), pp. 771–792.

81. Penrose, *Theory of the Growth of the Firm,* p. 115.

82. Bruce Kogut and Udo Zander, "Knowledge of the Firm, Combinative Capabilities, and the Replication of Technology," *Organization Science* 3 (1992) pp. 383–397.

83. Penrose, foreword to *Theory of the Growth of the Firm* (3rd ed., 1995), p. xiii.

STRATEGIC LEADERSHIP AND EVOLUTIONARY DYNAMICS

Robert Hoskisson and his colleagues have studied the swinging pendulum of strategic management theory.[84] From case studies, to I/O economics and industry studies, and to resource and knowledge-based theories of the firm, there has been an ebb and flow from specific to more encompassing theories about the firm in its quest for a competitive advantage. While we can skim only a portion of a rich literature, certain nagging questions continue: what roles does the general manager play in defining purpose, securing cooperation, coordinating efforts, anticipating change, and making the best possible use of the firm's resources? Once core competencies are defined and a strategy is selected, how long can these capabilities persist and sustain the firm's prosperity? Can an organization learn and change in the appropriate manner? Does the firm's past, its inheritances, lead to rigidities that narrow its discretionary scope? It has been said that history matters and management makes a difference. Those are our next topics.

In observing business practice, reading the literature of ongoing economic activity, or studying business policy/strategy cases, it is not apparent that business firms' actions can be explained by economic theories of maximizing or optimizing profits. Nelson and Winter have offered a view of "evolutionary economics" based on the writings of individuals such as Penrose and Schumpeter emphasizing the ability of the firm to generate and gain competitive advantages over time through innovation.[85] A firm's inherited resources, even though they may be valuable, non-substitutable, and so on, may not sustain these rare capabilities over the long term. Core competencies may evaporate as new technologies emerge—for instance, the decline of Baldwin Locomotive and its advantages in steam power, which were eclipsed by General Motor's diesel-fueled locomotives. The firm's resources, both human and physical, are specific and not easily deployed to other uses, thus limiting the choices the firm has for growth. Child emphasized the role of managerial discretion in making strategic choices, but these too would be bounded by the previous paths chosen and decisions taken.[86]

The theory of evolutionary economics suggests that a firm must develop dynamic capabilities that will enable it to transform itself as competitive conditions change. This transformation comes through invention or innovation, discovering the new or finding and developing new and better ways of doing business in the Schumpeterian tradition. Transaction-cost economics, according to Lazonick, fails because it does not account for innovation and the means necessary for the enterprise to change.

---

84. Robert E. Hoskisson, Michael A. Hitt, William P. Wan, and Daphne Yiu, "Theory and Research in Strategic Management: Swings of a Pendulum," *Journal of Management* 25 (1999), pp. 417–456.

85. Richard R. Nelson and Sidney G. Winter, *An Evolutionary Theory of Economic Change* (Cambridge, Mass.: Harvard University Press, 1982).

86. John Child, "Organisational Structure, Environment and Performance: The Role of Strategic Choice," *Sociology* 6 (1972), pp. 1–22.

Transaction costs may explain why a firm is often superior to the market in allocating resources, but it does not provide for confronting change and adjusting to meet evolving circumstances.

In contrast to transaction-cost economics, Lazonick proposes organizational learning to "unbound" rationality and to provide organizational incentives to overcome "opportunism."[87] This places him in line with the work of Penrose and Alfred Chandler. For Chandler, "learned skills and knowledge [are] company-specific and industry-specific."[88] These skills came from capabilities learned while exploiting economies of scale and capabilities developed from exploiting economies of scope. Penrose also emphasized learning, with the human resources playing a critical role in innovation. Similar to Chandler and Penrose, the dynamic capabilities position is

> ...the firm's ability to integrate, build, and reconfigure internal and external competencies to address rapidly changing environments. Dynamic capabilities thus reflect an organization's ability to achieve new and innovative forms of competitive advantage, given path dependencies and market positions.[89]

The evolutionary/dynamic capabilities theories place responsibility for change and learning squarely on the firm and its human resources. Management can make a difference and particularly in the ability of its general managers to implement incentives, policies, and actions necessary to achieve change through learning.[90] The general management task has been labeled "strategic leadership" to distinguish the work of chief executives, directors, and other top level executives from leadership activities of lower-level managers. Examining what top managers do is not a recent topic: Fayol and Barnard were chief executive officers and are part of our intellectual heritage; Newman, Stewart, Kotter, Mintzberg, Drucker and others have been keen observers of executives in action. Indeed, we may have a better understanding of top management than we have of lower levels of the hierarchy. The word *strategy* comes from the Greek verb *stratego*, meaning "to plan the destruction of one's enemies through effective use of resources."[91] Thus, from the military analogy of a general who led an army and made the necessary plans to accomplish the goal of defeating

---

87. William Lazonick, "Innovative Enterprise and Historical Transformation," *Enterprise and Society* 3 (2002), pp. 13–16.

88. Alfred D. Chandler, Jr., "Organizational Capabilities and the Economic History of the Industrial Enterprise," *Journal of Economic Perspectives* 6 (1992), pp. 79–100.

89. David J. Teece, Gary Pisano, and Amy Shuen, "Dynamic Capabilities and Strategic Management," *Strategic Management Journal* 18 (1997), p. 524.

90. For example, Richard Langlois and Nicolai Foss, "Capabilities and Governance: The Rebirth of Production in the Theory of Economic Organization," *Kyklos* 52 (1999), pp. 201–218.

91. Jeffrey Bracker, "The Historical Development of the Strategic Management Concept," *Academy of Management Review* 5 (1980), pp. 219–224.

an enemy, it was not a far leap to the executive who developed objectives and the plans (strategic and operational) to compete effectively in the marketplace.

Similar to Rosemary Stewart's findings regarding managerial "choices," Hambrick and Finkelstein offered "managerial discretion" to refer to the latitude of action allowed the chief executive.[92] This discretionary authority may be wide or narrow, and research continues to probe this topic. That the organization is a "reflection of its top managers" indicates the ability of the chief executive and the top management group to establish the firm's character.[93] The historian is reminded in this case of Chester Barnard's observation that the moral tone of an organization starts at the top. In this concept of strategic leadership is found the bridge to general management theory, to the legacy of Fayol, Barnard, and others who have studied the tasks of top level managers. *Strategos,* the art of generalship, is found in business chief executives "who must also have a strategy—a central, integrated, externally oriented concept of how the business will achieve its objectives."[94] From our understanding of dynamic capabilities, this generalship must achieve present objectives and set the stage for the learning that leads to innovation and renewal.

Viewed from the historian's position, strategic management is part of general management theory and has the potential to add to an understanding of people and organizations. Implementation is often shortchanged in the strategy literature, and the art of business policy is often estranged from the search for science in strategy. Wisdom and experience cannot be taught, but management theory provides the foundation for the practice of its application in cases, simulations, and other devices.

The factor that makes management different from other business functions, such as marketing, production, accounting, finance, and information systems, is that management pulls these functions together and aligns the firm as a whole with its economic, technological, social, and political environment. Strategic management is but one part of this model and must recognize its integrative, capstone role and how it relates to the body of management thought.

SUMMARY

The reawakening of general management theory occurred as organizations grew and diversified and with the need for more broadly educated general managers. Fayol's heirs took his elements and formed them into the management process approach.

92. Donald C. Hambrick and Sydney Finkelstein, "Managerial Discretion: A Bridge Between Polar Views of Organizations," in Larry L. Cummings and Barry M. Staw, eds., *Research in Organizational Behavior* (Greenwich, Conn.: JAI Press, 1987), pp. 369–406.

93. Donald C. Hambrick and Phyllis A. Mason, "Upper Echelons: The Organization as a Reflection of its Top Managers," *Academy of Management Review* 9 (1984), pp. 193–206.

94. Albert A. Cannella, Jr., "Upper Echelons: Donald Hambrick on Executives and Strategy," *Academy of Management Executive* 15 (2001), p. 49.

Studies of business education led to a reformulation of curricula, identified the diversity that Koontz turned into the jungle, and brought non-business-trained specialists into the business schools. In the practice of management, managers looked to practices found in "excellent" organizations, but this did not provide the quick fix expected nor did excellence prove so easy to measure and implement. Koontz revisited the jungle and found more schools, more diversity, in management. The Porter and McKibbin report updated the state of management education and criticized the drift that academia was experiencing. Drucker, too, emphasized the need to improve the practice of management and condemned the often sterile research output of the academics. Fayol "stood the test of time" and his general management theory provided a framework for the transition to business policy and strategic management.

In accord with general management we saw the need for economists to think like managers and a resurgence of interest in industrial/organizational economics. The firm was deemed a better allocator of resources than the market, but the visible hand of the managerial hierarchy posed governance and agency issues. With the view of the firm, however, attention was turned to general management as an integrating activity in business policy as it evolved to strategic management. The literature on this subject is vast, but strategy in the grand manner has its critics. Quinn, for example, argued that real-world managers developed strategies "incrementally, as a series of ... somewhat fragmented decisions."[95] One of the greatest military strategists of all times, Von Moltke, agreed: "No plan of operations can look with any certainty beyond the first meeting with the ... enemy [because one cannot control] the independent will of the opposing commander."[96] Mintzberg sees strategies "emerging" rather than leaping into full bloom in the mind of the strategist.[97] When the Academy of Management's membership was examined, the business policy/strategy folk clustered with those in the organization and management theory group.[98] This connection suggests a compatibility between general management theory and strategic leadership as firms are led to invent and innovate in a dynamic fashion to survive.

---

95. James Brian Quinn, *Strategies for Change: Logical Incrementalism* (Homewood, IL: Richard D. Irwin, 1980), p. 204.

96. Von Moltke, quoted in Jeffrey Record, "The Fortunes of War," *Harper's,* April 1980, p. 19.

97. Henry Mintzberg, *The Rise and Fall of Strategic Planning* (New York: Free Press, 1994), pp. 24–27.

98. Jone Pearce, "President's Message: A Bifurcated Academy?" *Academy of Management News* 34 (March, 2003), p. 1.

CHAPTER

20

Organizational Behavior and Theory

P art III detailed the development of management thought along two lines: (1) the micro analysis of human behavior in motivation, group dynamics, and leadership; and (2) the macro search for the fusion of the social and technical systems. This chapter examines these micro and macro approaches as they evolved into modern views of people vis-à-vis the organization. Modern management makes more sense when viewed in the light of its foundations; the search for a harmony of people and organizations undertaken by the modern behavioralists actually began many years earlier. These efforts were directed at a just adaptation of human needs and aspirations to the requirements and goals of the organization. "Harmony" means agreement between the parts of a design or composition that gives a pleasing unity of effect, whether it is in music, art, or organizational life. This chapter probes the modern quest to resolve the conflict between the logic of efficiency and the logic of sentiments, the search to meet human needs while fulfilling the objectives of the organization.

PEOPLE AND ORGANIZATIONS

Until the 1960s, those trained in the behavioral sciences, such as psychologists, sociologists, and anthropologists, had little impact on general management theory. True, there had been Münsterberg, Whiting Williams, Mayo, Lewin, and others, but their ideas remained in the shadow of the intellectual off-spring of Fayol and Taylor. The Gordon and Howell report in 1959 on business education, however, was to change that posture with a clarion call for more behavioral science studies in business school curricula: "Of all the subjects which he might undertake formally, none is more appropriate for the businessman-to-be than human behavior.... The very nature of the firm and of the manager's role in the firm suggests that every person anticipating a responsible position in a modern business enterprise needs a substantial amount of knowledge about human behavior."[1] The behavioral sciences were seen as one way in which more powerful analytical and conceptual tools could be put to use in handling the problems of human behavior.

The behavioral scientists were trained differently in research methods, drew on a different body of literature, often had little experience in business practice, but gradually they found business schools receptive to their ideas and methods. By the turn of the millennium, Miner noted that almost one-half (47 percent) of those individuals in Bedeian's laureate series came from psychology, and another 32 percent came from other disciplines outside the business school.[2] The laureates were selected by Bedeian as "the management discipline's most distinguished" and influential scholars.[3] The Academy of Management, the leading international association of teachers and researchers in management, also demonstrated a split between those whose professional interests clustered around organizational behavior and those whose interests clustered around business policy and strategy.[4] Organization and management theory was a bridge between these two groups, but it was clear that those from the behavioral sciences brought substantial influence to management teaching and research in the years following the Gordon and Howell report.

HUMAN RELATIONS AND ORGANIZATIONAL BEHAVIOR

Nowhere was the evolution in human relations thought more evident than in the work of Arizona State University professor Keith Davis (1918–2002), "Mr. Human Relations." In 1957, Davis defined human relations as "the integration of people into a work situation in a way that motivates them to work together productively, cooperatively, and with economic, psychological, and social satisfaction."[5] This marked the beginning of a modern view of human relations that was more empirically rigorous in understanding organizational behavior and philosophically broader in understanding people's interactions in a more complex network of societal forces.

---

1. Robert Gordon and James Howell, *Higher Education for Business* (New York: Columbia University Press, 1959), p. 166.

2. John B. Miner, *Organizational Behavior: Foundations, Theories, and Analyses* (New York: Oxford University Press, 2002), p. 84, 834. Miner's analysis was based on the first five volumes of A. G. Bedeian's *Management Laureates*. Adding Bedeian's sixth volume (2002) would not have altered Miner's findings.

3. Arthur G. Bedeian, ed., *Management Laureates: A Collection of Autobiographical Essays*, vol. 1 (Greenwich, CT: JAI Press, 1992), p. vii.

4. Jone Pearce, "President's Message: A Bifurcated Academy?" *The Academy of Management News* 34 (2003), pp. 1–2.

5. Keith Davis, *Human Relations in Business* (New York: McGraw-Hill, 1957), p. 4.

Davis held that modern human relations really had two facets: one was concerned with understanding, describing, and identifying causes and effects of human behavior through empirical investigation; the other facet was the application of this knowledge to operational situations. The first could be termed *organizational behavior,* and the second facet was *human relations.* The facets were complementary in that one investigated and explained, while the other was a way of thinking about people at work and applying behavioral insights to operating situations. The modern human relations of Keith Davis added economic and psychological facets to the social nature of people. He brought unions into the equation, added a broader consideration of societal forces, and moved human relations from its "feelings" base toward the search for the empiricism of organizational behavior.

Chris Argyris (1923–) proposed a "personality versus organization" hypothesis, or the "immaturity-maturity" theory of human behavior, based on humanist ideas.[6] Argyris thought that some basic trends existed in the personality growth of healthy, mature individuals. From infancy to adulthood, there was a tendency for the healthy personality to develop along a continuum from immaturity to maturity by moving from being passive to being active, from dependence to independence, from a lack of awareness of self to awareness and control over self, and so on. An individual's degree of self-actualization could be determined by plotting his or her position on the immaturity-maturity continuum. According to Argyris, four basic properties of the formal organization kept individuals immature and mediated against self-actualization: specialization of labor required individuals to use only a few of their abilities; the chain of command made individuals dependent on and passive toward their leader; the unity-of-direction principle meant that the path toward the goal was directed and controlled by the leader; and, finally, the span-of-control principle encouraged closer control, which presupposed the immaturity of the subordinates.

Using these organizational principles, Argyris built his case for the incongruency between the needs of the healthy personality and the requirements of the formal organization. Faced with the demands of the organization, individuals might seek more autonomy, daydream, become aggressive, become apathetic, create and formalize informal groups, restrict output, and so on through a host of defensive reactions. Management, faced with the reactions of the workers, might respond by using more autocratic and directive leadership, tightening organizational controls, or turning to human relations. To Argyris, managers adopted pseudohuman relations in many cases in order to sugarcoat the work situation rather than trying to remove the causes of employee discontent. Through Argyris's numerous books and articles, his proposals for designing organizations to reduce incongruency and achieve harmony between individuals and the organization can be traced. Like E. Wight Bakke, his erstwhile colleague at Yale University, Argyris has sought to integrate the individual and the organization.

---

6. Chris Argyris, *Personality and Organization: The Conflict between the System and the Individual* (New York: Harper and Row, 1957), p. 50.

Another important influence on Argyris was William F. Whyte, one of his professors in his doctoral program at Cornell University. We saw Whyte earlier as an advocate of "participatory action research," which became "action science" for Argyris and his long-time collaborator, Donald Schon (1930–1997). The duo of Argyris and Schon pioneered the idea of organizational learning, which grew out of Argyris' early work on personality and organization. The question was, Why do individuals (and groups) develop defensive reasons to interfere with organizational change? The answer, according to Argyris and Schon, echoed Lewin and resided in "unfreezing" and altering the defensive reasoning of individuals and to encourage productive reasoning that led to "double-loop" learning, that is, to learn by doing and to make corrections as needed based on the information fed back from that action.[7] Their work on organizational learning influenced Ikujiro Nonaka and Hirotaka Takeuchi's view of the knowledge-based view of the firm and the popular writings of Peter Senge.[8]

THEORIES X AND Y

Douglas McGregor (1906–1964) taught psychology at the Massachusetts Institute of Technology and served that institution, except for six years as president of Antioch College (1948–1954), until his death. As president of Antioch College, McGregor found that the precepts of the human relations model were inadequate for coping with the rigors and realities of organizational life.

> It took the direct experience of becoming a line executive ... to teach me what no amount of observation of other people could have taught. I believed, for example, that a leader could operate successfully as a kind of advisor to his organization. I thought I could avoid being a "boss." Unconsciously, I suspect, I hoped to duck the unpleasant necessity of making difficult decisions, of taking the responsibility for one course of action among many uncertain alternatives, of making mistakes and taking the consequences. I thought that maybe I could operate so that everyone would like me—that "good human relations" would eliminate all discord and disagreement.
>
> I couldn't have been more wrong. It took a couple of years, but I finally began to realize that a leader cannot avoid the exercise of authority any

7. Chris Argyris and Donald A. Schon, *Organizational Learning: A Theory of Action Perspective* (Reading, Mass.: Addison-Wesley, 1978). See also Chris Argyris, *On Organizational Learning* (Cambridge, Mass.: Blackwell, 1994 and 1999).

8. Peter Senge, *The Fifth Discipline: The Art and Practice of the Learning Organization* (New York: Doubleday, 1990); and Ikujiro Nonaka and Hirotaka Takeuchi, *The Knowledge Creating Company: How Japanese Companies Create the Dynamics of Innovation* (New York: Oxford University Press, 1995).

more than he can avoid responsibility for what happens to his organization.[9]

Douglas McGregor, 1959. Courtesy of the MIT Museum.

As early as 1953, McGregor began to formulate the ideas that would change his conception of management: "A manager who believes that people in general are lazy, untrustworthy, and antagonistic toward him will make very different decisions [from] a manager who regards people generally as cooperative and friendly."[10] In *The Human Side of Enterprise,* McGregor expanded the idea that managerial assumptions about human nature and human behavior were all-important in determining managers' styles of operating. Based on their assumptions about human nature, managers could organize, lead, control, and motivate people in different ways. The first set of assumptions he examined was Theory X, which was to represent the "traditional view of direction and control." Theory X assumptions were:

1. The average human being has an inherent dislike of work and will avoid it if he can....

2. Because of this human characteristic of dislike of work, most people must be coerced, controlled, directed, threatened with punishment to get them to put forth adequate effort toward the achievement of organizational objectives....

3. The average human being prefers to be directed, wishes to avoid responsibility, has relatively little ambition, wants security above all.[11]

McGregor thought that these X assumptions were the ones prevailing in modern industrial practice. While he did note a shift from hard X (presumably scientific management) to soft X (human relations), McGregor maintained that no fundamental shift in assumptions or managerial philosophies had occurred. McGregor's Theory Y was put forth as a "modest beginning for new theory with respect to the management of human resources." The assumptions of Theory Y were:

---

9. Douglas McGregor, "On Leadership," in John Desmond Glover and Ralph M. Hower, eds., *The Administrator: Cases on Human Relations in Business,* 4th ed. (Homewood, Ill.: Richard D. Irwin, 1963), p. 719.

10. *Causes of Industrial Peace under Collective Bargaining* (Washington, D.C.: National Planning Association, 1953), p. 72. This work presents cases of successful labor-management cooperation. Case number 4, "Dewey and Almy Chemical," was coauthored by McGregor and his MIT colleague Joseph Scanlon.

11. Douglas McGregor, *The Human Side of Enterprise* (New York: McGraw-Hill, 1960), pp. 33–34.

1. The expenditure of physical and mental effort in work is as natural as play or rest. The average human being does not inherently dislike work.

2. External control and the threat of punishment are not the only means for bringing about effort toward organizational objectives. Man will exercise self-direction and self-control in the service of objectives to which he is committed.

3. Commitment to objectives is a function of the rewards associated with their achievement. The most significant of such rewards, such as the satisfaction of ego and self-actualization needs, can be direct products of effort directed toward organizational objectives.

4. The average human being learns, under proper conditions, not only to accept but to seek responsibility. Avoidance of responsibility, lack of ambition, and emphasis on security are generally consequences of experience, not inherent human characteristics.

5. The capacity to exercise a relatively high degree of imagination, ingenuity, and creativity in the solution of organizational problems is widely, not narrowly, distributed in the population.

6. Under the conditions of modern industrial life, the intellectual potentialities of the average human being are only partially utilized.[12]

Using Mary Follett's terms, with a slight twist of Argyris, McGregor called Theory Y "the integration of individual and organizational goals" and held that it led to the "creation of conditions such that the members of the organization can achieve their own goals best by directing their efforts toward the success of the enterprise."[13] Managers who accepted the Y image of human nature would not structure, control, or closely supervise the work environment. Instead, they would attempt to aid the maturation of subordinates by giving them wider latitude in their work, encouraging creativity, using less external control, encouraging self-control, and motivating through the satisfaction that came from the challenge of work itself. The use of the authority of external control by management would be replaced by getting people committed to organizational goals because they perceived that this was the best way to achieve their own goals. A perfect integration was not possible, but McGregor hoped that an adoption of Y assumptions by managers would improve existing industrial practice.

Unfortunately, many have misinterpreted McGregor, claiming that X and Y represent opposite beliefs, but he is quite clear when he says that the "cosmologies do not lie on a continuous scale. They are qualitatively different ... *not* polar opposites; they do not lie at extremes of a scale. They are simply *different* cosmologies ... [they]

---

12. *Ibid.*, pp. 47–48.

13. *Ibid.*, p. 49.

are not managerial strategies: They are underlying beliefs about the nature of man that *influence* managers to adopt one strategy rather than another."[14]

McGregor served as a bridge from the old view of human relations to the new organizational humanism. It was McGregor's fundamental belief that harmony could be achieved, not by being hard or soft, but by changing assumptions about people and believing that they could be trusted, could exercise self-motivation and control, and had the capacity to integrate their own personal goals with those of the formal organization. To McGregor, how people were treated was largely a self-fulfilling prophecy; if managers assumed that people were lazy and treated them as if they were, then they would be lazy. On the other hand, if managers assumed that people desired challenging work and exploited this premise by increasing individual discretion, workers would in fact respond by seeking more and more responsibility.

In short, Theories X and Y were sets of assumptions about human nature and represented a twentieth-century reemergence of the ideas of earlier philosophers such as Robert Owen and Jean Jacques Rousseau. Owen's "new harmony" would rebuild society to fit humanity's basic goodness. Rousseau, a French philosopher of the eighteenth century, felt that people were basically good but that their nurturing institutions (family, school, etc.) made them bad. Assumptions about human nature guide our thoughts, but no one set of assumptions is going to cover all the people all the time.

PERSONNEL/HUMAN RESOURCES MANAGEMENT AND INDUSTRIAL RELATIONS

The importance of people as necessary contributors to the accomplishment of organizational objectives is not a new idea. Traditional economic theory identified land, labor, and capital as factors of production, and Robert Owen referred to his employees as "vital [i.e., living] machines." The preceding pages traced the evolution of the staffing job of the manager as recruiting, selecting, training, developing, compensating, appraising, and performing other tasks with respect to providing for the attraction, placement, reward, and retention of employees. It was customary for some period of time for this job to be done by the direct supervisor, the line manager, and this process placed a great deal of authority in the supervisor's role. Frederick Taylor replaced this practice with functional foremen, which evolved in the use of specialists to advise line managers in the employment task. For Fayol, staffing was part of the organizing job of the manager. From these beginnings personnel management gradually evolved as a standard label for this task of advising managers about recruitment, selection, and so forth. Performance of the personnel function was

---

14. Douglas McGregor, *The Professional Manager,* ed. Caroline McGregor and Warren G. Bennis (New York: McGraw-Hill, 1967), pp. 79–80.

enhanced with the contributions of individuals, such as Hugo Münsterberg (personnel testing); disciplines, such as labor economics (for understanding labor market factors as they affected the supply of employees and prevailing wage rates); and industrial relations (for promoting better union-management relations).

Personnel management borrowed from many disciplines but did not always receive the acclaim and status that those in the field thought it deserved. In their report, Gordon and Howell made some very disparaging remarks: "Next to the course in production, perhaps more educational sins have been committed in the name of personnel management than in any other required course in the business curriculum. Personnel management is a field which has had a particularly small base of significant generalization with which to work (beyond what is important in the area of human relations), and, partly for this reason, it is an area which has not been held in high regard in the better schools."[15] As seen, one outcome of the Gordon and Howell report was to bring more behavioral scientists into U.S. business schools. These individuals could bring their research skills and training to personnel management, and, with the growth of industrial relations and labor-management research centers, personnel management could begin to build a firmer theoretical base.

The labor economist, John R. Commons, appears to have been the first to use the phrase "human resource" as among other factors of production. Edward Wight Bakke, a member of the Yale Labor-Management Center, repeated the notion that all managers managed resources, including the human one, but that more emphasis had to be placed on the human resource to elevate its importance to be commensurate with the other resources of money, materials, and so forth. The central concern of the human resources function was not "personal happiness" but "productive work," and humans had to be integrated into the total task of every organization. Human resources work was the responsibility of all managers, not just those in personnel or labor relations departments.[16] A substantial period of time would pass before managing the human resource became every manager's job.

Wendell French appears to have been the first author to add "human resources" as a subtitle to a personnel management text.[17] This did not create a title wave of changes in textbooks or course names, but it was a beginning. Human resource management carried a certain dignity with it that proposed to establish personnel management as a more legitimate field with a more rigorous basis for understanding the forces influencing decisions about employees. Beginning in the 1960s and accelerating thereafter, a series of laws about hiring practices, employment tests,

---

15. Robert Gordon and James E. Howell, *Higher Education for Business* (New York: Columbia University Press, 1959), p. 189.

16. E. Wight Bakke, *The Human Resources Function* (New Haven, Conn.: Yale Labor-Management Center, 1958).

17. Wendell French, *The Personnel Management Process: Human Resources Administration* (Boston: Houghton Mifflin, 1964).

compensation, pension plans, safety and health, and other facets of the staffing job of the manager made the role of the personnel specialist more important.

In the early 1900s, economists, such as Commons and others discussed in Chapter 9, were concerned with personnel activities and spearheaded the industrial relations movement. Numerous centers and institutes were established for teaching and research in industrial relations, but these centers were distanced both from economics and management. Kaufman asserts, "It is common today to view the field of personnel/human resource management ... as distinct and largely unrelated to the discipline of economics and the field of industrial relations."[18]

George Strauss and Thomas Kochan are two notable exceptions to the drift of personnel/human resources management from industrial relations. In graduate studies and his early career, Strauss was influenced by individuals such as Douglas McGregor, Paul Samuelson, John Dunlop, and others who provided a broad base of knowledge in economics, human relations, and industrial relations.[19] During his career, Strauss saw the transition from human relations to organizational behavior but never abandoned his belief that unions and sound labor-management relations were based on employee participation in decision making. He was a cofounder of the Organizational Behavior Teaching Society (1973) and, in collaboration with Leonard Sayles, produced an abundant body of literature that spanned personnel management, industrial relations, and organizational behavior.[20]

Thomas Kochan came out of a long line of the "Wisconsin School" of labor relations scholars, such as Richard Ely, John R. Commons, Selig Perlman, and others. Similar to Strauss, Kochan saw human resources management and industrial relations as complementary: industrial relations added public policy and labor market forces in the firm's environment to intrafirm issues such as selection. Unions were legitimate and valuable components of a democratic society, enabling labor, management, and public policy to forge an agenda for mutual progress and prosperity. Reflecting Frederick Taylor's mental revolution and Mary Follett's integration, it was possible to have a "mutual gains enterprise" that promoted productivity through labor and managerial cooperation to remove barriers to efficiency and to work toward satisfaction of their mutual goals.[21]

In the resource-based, knowledge-based, and dynamic evolutionary theories of the firm, the human resource is crucial to gaining a competitive edge. The history of

---

18. Bruce E. Kaufman, "The Role of Economics and Industrial Relations in the Development of the Field of Personnel/Human Resource Management," *Management Decision* 40 (2002), p. 962.

19. George Strauss, "Present at the Beginning: Some Personal Notes on OB's Early Days and Later," in Arthur G. Bedeian, ed., *Management Laureates*, vol. 3 (Greenwich, Conn.: Jai Press, 1993), pp. 145–190.

20. For examples: George Strauss and Leonard R. Sayles, *Personnel: The Human Problems of Management* (Englewood Cliffs, N.J.: Prentice-Hall, 1960); and Leonard R. Sayles and George Strauss, *Human Behavior in Organizations* (Englewood Cliffs, N.J.: Prentice-Hall, 1966).

21. Thomas A. Kochan and Paul Osterman, *The Mutual Gains Enterprise: Forging a Winning Partnership Among Labor, Management, and Government* (Boston, Mass.: Harvard Business School Press, 1994).

personnel/human resource management illustrates the need to look to industrial relations, industrial/organizational psychology, and economics for better practices and to practitioners for how well theory meets their needs. One recent review noted that the field has become a research-driven rather than practice-driven study, resulting in a "scientist/practitioner gap" in which practicing managers fail to find useful implications from academic research.[22] Human resource management has the potential to draw from multiple disciplines to discover what is of practical, if not always statistical, significance.

WORK DESIGN

How tasks should be performed is a subject of long-standing interest as well as a variety of ideas. The division of labor is an ancient practice, but as early as 1776, Adam Smith observed that this practice could be overdone and have dysfunctional effects. Taylor, Frank Gilbreth, and other scientific management pioneers studied workers' movements and their tools and work methods with the hope of finding a better way to work in order to reduce fatigue and increase efficiency while rewarding the worker for improved performance. Allan Mogensen started the work simplification movement in the hope that people could learn to work smarter, not harder. Charles Walker and Robert Guest provided job enlargement to lengthen the work cycle in order to overcome job monotony. This brief history of work design indicates a long-standing assumption that management has a responsibility to make jobs more meaningful as well as to improve performance.

In the modern era, Frederick Herzberg (1923–2000) and his associates began research to discover the importance of attitudes toward work and the experiences, both good and bad, that workers reported. An important influence on Herzberg's life and research was John Flanagan, a psychologist who worked with the U.S. Air Force in developing methods for crew selection. Herzberg worked in this program and there learned Flanagan's "critical incidents" research technique, a way of questioning that helped isolate the behaviors of promising candidates from less promising ones.

Recalling Flanagan's critical incident method, Herzberg asked workers to respond to this question: "Think of a time when you felt exceptionally good or exceptionally bad about your job, either your present job or any other job you have had.... Tell me what happened."[23] From the responses to this question and a series of follow-up questions, Herzberg set out to discover the kinds of things that made people either happy and satisfied on their jobs or unhappy and dissatisfied. From people's responses he was able to isolate two different kinds of needs that appeared to be independent. When people reported unhappiness and job dissatisfaction, they

---

22. Gerald R. Ferriss, Wayne A. Hochwarter, M. Ronald Buckley, Gloria Harnell-Cook, and Dwight D. Frink, "Human Resources Management: Some New Directions," *Journal of Management* 25 (1999), p. 407.

23. Frederick Herzberg, Bernard Mausner, and Barbara B. Snyderman, *The Motivation to Work* (New York: John Wiley and Sons, 1959), app. I, p. 141.

attributed those feelings to their job environment, or the *job context*. When people reported happiness or satisfaction, they attributed the feelings to work itself or to the job *content*.

Herzberg called the factors identified in the job context "hygiene" factors, "for they act in a manner analogous to the principles of medical hygiene. Hygiene operates to remove health hazards from the environment of man. It is not curative: it is, rather, a preventive."[24] The hygiene factors included supervision, interpersonal relations, physical working conditions, salaries, company policies and administrative practices, benefits, and job security. When these factors deteriorated below what the worker considered an acceptable level, job dissatisfaction was the result. When the job context was considered optimal by the worker, dissatisfaction was removed; this did not lead to positive attitudes, however, but to some sort of a neutral state of neither satisfaction nor dissatisfaction.

The factors that led to positive attitudes, satisfaction, and motivation were called the "motivators," or things in the job content. The motivators were such factors as achievement, recognition for accomplishment, challenging work, increased job responsibility, and opportunities for growth and development. If present, these factors led to higher motivation. In this sense, Herzberg was saying that traditional assumptions of motivation about wage incentives, improving interpersonal relations, and establishing proper working conditions did not lead to higher motivation. They removed dissatisfaction and acted to prevent problems, but once these traditional motivators were optimal, they did not lead to positive motivation. According to Herzberg, management should recognize that hygiene was necessary, but that once it had neutralized dissatisfaction, it did not lead to positive results. Only the motivators led people to superior performance.

In rebuttal to those who claimed success for wage incentive plans such as that at Lincoln Electric, Herzberg said that money in this case was actually a direct reward for recognition, achievement, and responsibility. It was not wage increases in an across-the-board manner (which would be a hygiene factor), but added earnings as a reward for growth, achievement, and responsibility. For Herzberg, "hygiene is not enough"; the motivation to work had to come from job enrichment, opportunities for growth, and supervisors who were aware of the need for recognition and achievement and gave employees chances for self-actualization.

Herzberg's motivation-hygiene theory has received both support and criticism. Critics have observed that when asked to do so, people take the credit when things go well, attributing satisfaction to events they can control in the job content area. They place the blame for dissatisfaction not on themselves, but on the job context—the work environment. The conclusion, then, is that Herzberg's way of asking his questions led to his results. Further, if correct, Herzberg's theory would have found that highly satisfied people were highly motivated and high producers. The evidence so far has not found a positive relationship between worker satisfaction and productivity. Satisfied workers are not always the best producers, nor are

---

24. *Ibid.*, p. 113.

dissatisfied workers the worst producers. To illustrate, one worker may respond to the challenge of job enrichment while another may prefer to be told what to do. Work is a means for some people, not an end.

Credence for Herzberg's ideas was found in an early extension of his work by Hackman and Lawler and later by Hackman and Oldham.[25] These scholars were concerned with how to identify and change, if possible, specific job characteristics for employees. The key job characteristics examined were task identity, task significance, skill variety, autonomy, and knowledge of results (feedback). If these characteristics could be enhanced, for example by increasing the variety of skills used or by providing information about how well a person was performing, then the employee would experience more "meaningfulness" on the job. Hackman and Oldham added a situational flavor by suggesting that the degree of success of this approach depended on the individual's "growth-need strength." If a person already felt sufficiently challenged and experienced the job as meaningful, growth-need strength would be low and further efforts to improve the job would be less effective. Some individuals seek more challenge, others do not; further, some jobs can be made more meaningful, others cannot. Job characteristics theory provided a way to provide a closer match between the nature of the job and employee needs.

The nature of working has changed since these theories were developed. A job may no longer be a career and many employment arrangements have changed by outsourcing work, using temporary employees, dual-career couples, electronic commuting, postretirement careers, and individuals needing to retool their skills/abilities at different career stages. Working is central to living and another generation of study is needed as jobs and careers change.

MOTIVATION

Human motivation has been problematic since the first hominid wondered why his or her fellow hominids did what they did. The ancient Greek philosophy of hedonism postulated that people sought pleasure and avoided pain, opening the door to behavior modification. The utilitarian movement of early economists believed that humans tried to calculate what actions would bring the most utility with the least cost, opening the way for expectancy theory. Chapter 9 described how a mid-nineteenth-century branch of economics, plutology, was able to deduce the existence of a hierarchy of human needs that changed once lower-order needs were satisfied. Abraham Maslow rediscovered this notion in the twentieth century and, along with David McClelland and John Atkinson, explained motivation in terms of needs, the "what" portion of motivation.

Perhaps it was the shortcomings of human need theories that caused later motivation theories to change their tack. It was not the fact that need theories were

---

25. J. Richard Hackman and Greg R. Oldham, *Work Redesign* (Reading, Mass.: Addison-Wesley, 1980). Miner notes that job characteristics theory emerged originally as the work of Hackman and Edward E. Lawler III. Miner, *Organizational Behavior,* p. 173.

completely refuted and discarded; rather, it was their incompleteness, unpre-dictability, and uncertainty. The response was to try to understand the *how* of motivation rather than the *what;* that is, how the motivational process worked. The focus of these how theories was understanding how human motivation might be triggered, what gave it direction, what kept it going, and how it might be extin-guished if the behavior was inappropriate.

One of these, expectancy theory, was developed by Victor H. Vroom and based on early psychological theories, such as Kurt Lewin's "force field" notion.[26] The premise of expectancy theory was that motivation was a process of making choices between behaviors and that people pursued the behaviors that they hoped would lead to pleasurable outcomes. According to expectancy theory, motivation was a product of valence, the value of the particular reward to the individual, and expectancy, the individual's perception of whether or not a given pattern of behav-ior was likely to lead to the satisfaction of his or her needs. Valences could be posi-tive (something highly desired) or negative (something to be avoided) and could vary in strength of the drive. Lyman Porter and Edward Lawler extended expectancy theory by adding a feedback loop from performance to the future expectancy of effort being rewarded, thus strengthening subsequent performance.[27] In subsequent publications, Lawler continued the theme of relating compensation to organiza-tional development and effectiveness.

Expectancy theory helped explain the choosing process involved in motivation. Motivation to perform was an interaction between the goals sought, the value placed on these goals, and the worker's expectation that a certain path would lead to those goals. Expectancy theory is a complex notion, however, and leaves numerous ques-tions unanswered, such as: do individuals seek to maximize their rewards, or do they "satisfice?" Do the valences remain stable over time, and if not, how much of a change must occur before a person's behavior changes?

Although equity theory is not new, only recently have management scholars paid much attention to it. Whiting Williams, an industrial executive who quit his job to find out "what's on the worker's mind," put forth what was most likely the first equity theory of wages. Williams argued that pay was relative from the worker's point of view; that is, what was important was not the absolute pay a person received but the amount relative to what others received. Not until the 1960s did scholars begin to formulate the bases of equity theory. Although there were slight differences between the ideas of Eliot Jaques and those of John Stacy Adams, the primary pro-ponents of this theory, the essential rationale was that pay was a matter of distribu-tive justice and social comparison.[28] A person's perception of salary was based on at

——
26. Victor H. Vroom, *Work and Motivation* (New York: John Wiley and Sons, 1964).

27. Lyman W. Porter and Edward E. Lawler, *Management Attitudes and Performance* (Homewood, IL: Richard D. Irwin, 1968).

28. Eliot Jaques, *Equitable Payment* (New York: John Wiley and Sons, 1961); and J. Stacy Adams, "Toward an Understanding of Inequity," *Journal of Abnormal and Social Psychology* 67 (1963), pp. 422–436.

Edwin A. Locke, 2004. Courtesy of Edwin A. Locke.

least two ratios: (1) the person's pay relative to the pay of others; and (2) the person's "inputs" (that is, effort expended, education, skill level, training, experience) relative to the person's "outcomes" (salary). In the first case, the comparison was that of the person's pay relative to what others were getting. In the second, the comparison was that of how hard the person worked, how long the person had trained, and so on, relative to the pay received for the work. For example, a worker might be dissatisfied with his or her salary if the worker perceived that another person doing the same job was paid more; hence the cries of "equal pay for equal work" from those who feel discrimination in terms of salary. The source of dissatisfaction may not necessarily be the absolute amount of salary but the salary in relation to others and in relation to inputs and outcomes.

So far equity theory has focused on pay, although this does not preclude future research on other rewards or recognitions that are seen by a worker as relative. Certain questions remain unanswered, such as: how do people select those they consider their cohorts and how accurate is the information on which the comparisons are based? Equity theory contributed to notions of why people might be dissatisfied, but contributed less to an understanding of how they might be motivated.

After being in eclipse, money returned to credibility as a motivational factor. To illustrate, in an extensive survey of field and experimental studies of motivation, Edwin Locke, Gary Latham, and their associates examined four widely used techniques and their impacts on employee productivity. Monetary incentives showed the greatest median increase, followed by goal setting, while job enrichment and participation lagged behind.[29] Locke and his associates did not conclude that money was the only motivator, but emphasized the "instrumentality" of money; that is, money as a medium of exchange that allowed individuals to choose how they wished to satisfy their needs.

Goal-setting theory, with its roots in Frederick Taylor's task management, Frank Gilbreth's "three position plan" of promotion, Peter Drucker's MBO, and Cecil Mace's pioneering studies, also gained a renewed vigor in the modern era.

---

29. Edwin A. Locke, Dena B. Feren, Vickie M. McCaleb, Karyll N. Shaw, and Anne T. Denny, "The Relative Effectiveness of Four Methods of Motivating Employee Performance," in K. D. Duncan, M. M. Gruneberg, and D. Wallis, eds., *Changes in Working Life* (Chichester, England: John Wiley and Sons, 1980), pp. 363–388.

Contemporary credence for goal setting was provided by Edwin Locke, who credited his mentor, Thomas Ryan, as a cocreator of this notion. Goal setting consisted of "purposefully directed action" in the process of developing and setting specific work goals or targets for employees to accomplish.[30] The more specific the goal, the better: "produce one hundred units that will pass the quality inspection" rather than "do the best you can today." Further, difficult goals were better than easy ones—the goal should challenge (but not exceed) the individuals' abilities rather than ask the employees to spread a four-hour job over an eight-hour day. Employees also needed to be able to keep track of their performance by receiving regular feedback about results. Without knowledge of results, employees could not gauge the relationship between their performance and the expected performance. Incentives (both financial and nonfinancial) were also necessary to reward the meeting of the goals. Goal setting as a motivational force appeared to work equally well whether goals were assigned by management or with group participation. The assignment of goals by management worked best with people already internally motivated to do the job, such as those persons with a high need for achievement or high self-efficacy. When subordinates were familiar and at ease with participative techniques and when their need for achievement was lower, participative goal setting was more likely to be effective. Acceptance of goals depended on a number of factors, including the extent to which employees trusted management, the fairness and difficulty of the goals, and the perceived legitimacy of management's demands.

Goal-setting theory was found to be compatible with expectancy theory and social learning theory with respect to self-efficacy; for example, people with high self-efficacy chose more difficult goals, and positive performance feedback enhanced self-efficacy, creating a new cycle of high performance. Further, goal setting promoted more self-regulation of performance as individuals learned what the appropriate level of performance was. Thirty-five years of empirical tests of Locke and Latham's goal setting theory have been successful, and it has been of more value to practicing managers than most theories proposed to date.[31] More importantly, they provided an integration of behavioral science methods and findings with the practical world of the manager as it relates to general management theory. Understandable, useful research has long been the desire of practitioners, and goal setting theory has filled this longstanding void. Theory and research are not ends in and of themselves. The goal of research is to advance teaching and practice, and teaching and practice are the crucibles in which the mettle of theory and research is tested.

---

30. Edwin A. Locke and Gary P. Latham, *A Theory of Goal Setting and Task Performance* (Englewood Cliffs, N.J.: Prentice Hall, 1990); and Gary P. Latham and Edwin A. Locke, "Self-Regulation through Goal Setting," *Organizational Behavior and Human Decision Processes* 50 (1991), pp. 212–247.

31. Edwin A. Locke and Gary P. Latham, "Building a Practically Useful Theory of Goal Setting and Task Motivation: A 35-Year Odyssey," *American Psychologist* 57 (September 2002), pp. 705–717. See also Miner, *Organizational Behavior*, pp. 247–248.

LEADERSHIP

Leadership fits into general management theory because it focuses on the attainment of organizational goals by working with and through people and other resources. Various terms have been used to describe this function, such as directing, leading, actuating, and supervising, and various views of how to become a leader or what a leader does have also evolved. The earliest leadership notions were dominated by trait theory, meaning that leaders could be characterized as having different traits from nonleaders. Technical ability, intelligence, energy, initiative, honesty, and other personal qualities joined the tribal remnants of the idea that those in charge were taller, stronger, wiser, better warriors, or whatever. As these lists grew longer, and as more and more exceptions were found, the search for other explanations of leadership began. The second stage in the evolution of leadership notions sought to identify the behaviors that could be connected to those who were the leaders. Early behavioral research, such as that of Kurt Lewin, placed leadership styles on a continuum ranging from authoritarian to democratic. This clustering of leader-behavior modes reflected the idea that the authoritarian used formal authority, was production oriented, and operated unilaterally in making decisions. The democratic or participative leader, on the other hand, used formal authority sparingly, was employee centered, and involved subordinates in the decision-making process.

Participative leadership, espoused by human relationists and organizational humanists, followed the theme of power equalization, a movement to reduce the power and status differentials between the superior and the subordinate. The goal was to play down the organizational hierarchy of authority, give the worker a greater voice in decisions, encourage creativity, and overcome apathy by getting people involved and committed to organizational goals. In modern parlance, "empowerment" is used to describe this phenomenon; it is very likely that Chris Argyris, Douglas McGregor, and Rensis Likert would be very comfortable with this more recent terminology.

Rensis Likert (1903–1981), as one example of the foremost proponents of participative management, was trained as a psychologist and developed the widely used Likert Scale for the measurement of attitudes and values in conducting organizational research. Likert spent most of his life studying leadership in organizations and thought that of all the tasks of management, leading the human component was the central and most important one because all else depended on how it was done. He identified four types of leader behavior: "exploitive authoritative," System 1; "benevolent authoritative," System 2; "consultative," System 3; and "participative group," System 4.[32] Likert's System 4 management involved three basic concepts: (1) the principle of supportive relationships; (2) the use of group decision making and group methods of supervision; and (3) setting high performance goals for the organization. The principle of supportive relationships meant that the leader had to

---

32. Rensis Likert, *The Human Organization: Its Management and Value* (New York: McGraw-Hill, 1967), p. 4, *passim*.

ensure that each member viewed the experience as supportive and one that built and maintained a sense of personal worth and importance. The second concept involved group decision making and an overlapping group form of structure with each work group linked to the rest of the organization by means of persons who were members of more than one group (called "link pins"). The third concept was high perform-ance goals. Superiors in System 4 organizations would have high performance aspi-rations, as would every work group member. Employees were involved in setting the high-level goals required for the satisfaction of their own needs.

In his last book, Likert proposed System 5, "an even more sophisticated, com-plex, and effective system" that would emerge as the social sciences advanced.[33] Although he never lived to advance System 5 thinking, his wife and others contin-ued his work. In System 5, an organization's hierarchy of authority would be replaced with a reciprocal system of participation and influence. In case of conflict, groups would work together through overlapping memberships ("link pins") until a consensus could be reached. The organizational chart would look like a fishnet rather than a pyramid, as multiple linkages occurred between work units and departments. Authority would depend on the interpersonal skills of creative leaders who had the ability to get others committed and working toward organizational goals. Employees would be called "associates" (there would be no organizational titles for persons), and leadership would be a "shared sense of purpose" and a "one-ness" feeling in the organization. If these ideas sound familiar, they should, because Likert was a great admirer of Mary Parker Follett.[34] It is apparent that Likert's ini-tial formulations of System 5 owe a bow of gratitude to her.

As ideas about leadership continued to evolve, there was dissatisfaction with prescribing any one way to lead, such as the participative style. Instead, the focus shifted to contingency, or situational leadership. Gary Yukl identified at least nine different situational theories and described and critiqued them.[35] The purpose here is to see these notions as a stage in the evolution of management thought rather than to try to repeat what Yukl has done so well. Fred Fiedler pioneered the idea that a number of leader behavior styles might be effective or ineffective depending on important elements of the situation.[36] In his research, Fiedler identified leadership style by the use of the LPC (least preferred coworker) scale. High LPC persons were concerned about interpersonal relations, felt a need for the approval of their associ-ates, and were less distant in describing themselves and others. Low LPC persons

33. Rensis Likert and Jane Gibson Likert, *New Ways of Managing Conflict* (New York: McGraw-Hill, 1976), p. 41.

34. Jane Gibson Likert, "The Likert Legacy: System 5 and New Organizational Forms for the Future" (paper presented at the Academy of Management meeting, Boston, August 13, 1984). See also Jane Gibson Likert and Charles T. Araki, "Managing without a Boss: System 5," *Leadership and Organizational Development Journal* 3 (1986), pp. 17–20.

35. Gary Yukl, "Managerial Leadership: A Review of Theory and Research," *Journal of Management* 15 (1989), pp. 251–289.

36. Fred E. Fiedler, *A Theory of Leadership Effectiveness* (New York: McGraw-Hill, 1967).

were relatively independent of others, were less concerned with feelings, and were willing to reject a person who could not complete an assigned task. In essence, the high LPC leader was "consideration oriented," and the low LPC leader was "task oriented" in terms of the Ohio State studies.

Fiedler also identified three major factors in the leadership situation: (1) "leader-member relations," or the degree to which a group trusted, liked, or was willing to follow the leader; (2) the "task structure," or the degree to which the task was ill- or well-defined; and (3) "position power," or the formal authority as distinct from the personal power of the leader. Depending on whether the situation was very favorable or very unfavorable, Fiedler concluded that (1) task-oriented (low LPC) leaders tended to perform best in group situations that were either very favorable or very unfavorable to the leader, and (2) relationship-oriented (high LPC) leaders tended to perform best in situations that were intermediate in favorableness.

Following Fiedler, other contingency views emerged such as House and Dessler's path-goal theory and Vroom and Yetton's decision process theory.[37] These numerous situational theories sought to define in more precise terms upon what conditions the appropriate leadership style would be—in effect, to provide the "if" and "then" of situations. For this stage of evolving theories of leadership, there was no one best way to lead and the question was how the leader should behave under what situations.

As situational theories proliferated, with minute differences and with limited empirical evidence to confirm those theories, the literature appeared to recycle history by placing more emphasis on leader personality and leader traits. Charisma returned to leadership theory after resting for a number of years in the ideas of Max Weber (see Chapter 10). Charismatic leaders got things done by virtue of their ability to attract followers to their cause. Followers would trust, share the vision of, often attribute mystical powers to, and offer blind obedience to their leader. As a leadership theory, charisma combined leader traits, followers, and situational variables. In House's theory, charismatic leaders seemed to emerge under certain conditions, had personal qualities that distinguished them from others, and were able to manage the impression they made on others in order to build and maintain their followers' confidence and trust.[38] For Bass, charisma was but one part of becoming a transformational leader (see below) by inspiring followers through setting high expectations, focusing efforts, and expressing important goals in influential ways.[39] It is not always clear in charismatic theories what would happen if the leader's intents were not socially desirable; for instance, some historical figures (Adolf Hitler comes to

37. Robert House and Gary Dessler, "The Path-Goal Theory of Leadership: Some Post Hoc and A Priori Tests," in J. G. Hunt and L. L. Larson, eds., *Contingency Approaches to Leadership* (Carbondale: Southern Illinois University Press, 1974), pp. 29–55; and Victor H. Vroom and Philip W. Yetton, *Leadership and Decision Making* (Pittsburgh, Pa.: University of Pittsburgh Press, 1973).

38. Robert J. House, "A 1976 Theory of Charismatic Leadership," in J. G. Hunt and L. C. Larson, eds., *Leadership: The Cutting Edge* (Carbondale: Southern Illinois University Press, 1977), pp. 189–207.

39. Bernard M. Bass, *Leadership and Performance Beyond Expectations* (New York: Free Press, 1985).

mind) have demonstrated this personal magnetism and led others in blind obedience but toward evil ends. Further, it is important to recall Max Weber's conclusion that charisma was an unstable situation and that after the charismatic leader departed there could be chaos.

James MacGregor Burns coined the terms *transactional* and *transformational* to describe the types of political leaders he studied, but other leadership literature found them useful.[40] Transformational leadership theories also reflected personality traits, with the exception that these leaders appeared to be more willing to share power with ("empower") their followers. These leaders also seemed to emerge at particular times, such as when an organization declined and revitalization and a renewed vision was needed. Transformational leaders are often described as those who bring a vision of the major changes needed in the organization's structure, culture, market, or whatever. This distant vision will succeed, however, only if the leader can transform the high-powered vision of the future into localized implementation in the present.

Leadership theory presents the possibility of déjà vu to the historian. Traits such as drive, energy, initiative, honesty/integrity, self-confidence, adaptability, and others have been suggested by modern authors in a manner reminiscent of Henri Fayol (although supported by a richer research base).[41] Jerry Hunt's early "stratified systems theory" has "core notions of (a) increasing organizational complexity as leaders move up in the organization, and (b) a concurrent of increased required amount of leader cognitive complexity at higher organizational levels."[42] Fayol identified "intelligence and mental vigor" as becoming more important further up the hierarchical chain; "mental vigor" was defined as the ability to "deal simultaneously with many varied manifold subjects." Has the winding path of leadership theory come back to the starting point?

Leader-member exchange theory (originally "vertical dyad linkage theory") suggests that, over time, leaders classify their followers as in-group or out-group members and treat the former more favorably. In exchange, these in-group members resemble informed assistants and are motivated, sometimes by participative decision making, to put forth more effort that enhances the job of the leader.[43] The exchange is reciprocal, at least for in-group followers, as the leader distributes resources (perhaps rewards) for those who give the extra effort. The quality of the exchange is associated with performance outcomes, and to some extent, with career

---

40. James M. Burns, *Leadership* (New York: Harper and Row, 1978).

41. Edwin A. Locke, *The Essence of Leadership* (New York: Lexington Books, 1991). See also Henri Fayol, *General and Industrial Management* (1949), pp. 7, 76–77.

42. James G. Hunt, *Leadership: A New Synthesis* (Newbury Park, Calif.: Sage, 1991), p. 268. See also Fayol, op. cit., pp. 76–77.

43. George B. Graen and Mary Uhl-Bien, "Relationship-based Approach to Leadership: Development of Leader-Member Exchange (LMX) Theory of Leadership over 25 Years: Applying a Multi-level Multi-domain Perspective," *Leadership Quarterly* 6 (1995), pp. 219–247.

development. George Graen, the pioneer of this theory, has been careful to empha-size that in-group and out-group categories are based on task and not friendship rela-tionships.[44] Otherwise, there could be legal issues, as in employment discrimination, or interpersonal ones, such as playing favorites. Leader-member exchange theory has enriched previous relationships-based research, such as improved interpersonal relations at Hawthorne, and has furthered our understanding of intraorganiza-tional connections.

Leadership theory has been dominated by micro analyses, such as leader-member relations, and devoid of a broader understanding of organizational and cultural settings. For example, relatively little attention is paid in leadership studies to moral leadership as advocated by Burns and Barnard. One exception is Bass, who points out that Adolf Hitler was a transformational leader, but with very negative consequences.[45] Hunt notes a direction of promise in the study of strategic leader-ship, that is, the leadership *of* in contrast to leadership *in* organization.[46] Another promising avenue is the cross-cultural study of leadership. Project GLOBE repre-sents an ambitious program to discover differences in cultural values between coun-tries that influence leader-follower behavior and relations.[47] The past is full of different theories, reevaluations of theories, and mixed results as theories are tested.

Despite the mountains of literature on leadership, very little is conclusive. Ralph Stogdill (1904–1978), a prominent researcher on leadership, reviewed some 3,000 studies in 1974 and concluded: "Four decades of research on leadership have pro-duced a bewildering mass of findings.... The endless accumulation of empirical data has not produced an integrated understanding of leadership."[48] The latest hand-book of leadership has over 1,100 pages, and a recent reviewer of the leadership lit-erature concluded: "[after] over 5,000 studies ... the confused state of the field can be attributed in large part to the sheer volume of publications, the disparity of approaches, the proliferation of confusing terms, the narrow focus of most researchers, the high percentage of irrelevant or trivial studies, and the absence of an integrating conceptual framework."[49]

For far too long "leaders" have been described in contrast to "managers." It is time to combine leader and manager into "managerial leadership" rather than dif-ferentiating the two. Evidence has been provided that adding managerial activities

---

44. Miner, *Organizational Behavior*, pp. 344–351.

45. Bass, *Leadership and Performance*, p. 20.

46. James G. Hunt, "Leadership Déjà Vu All Over Again," *Leadership Quarterly* 11 (2000), pp. 435–458.

47. Mansour Javidan and Robert J. House, "Cultural Acumen for the Global Manager: Lessons from Project GLOBE," *Organizational Dynamics* 29 (2001), pp. 289–306.

48. Ralph M. Stogdill, *Handbook of Leadership: A Survey of Theory and Research* (New York: Free Press, 1974), p. xvii.

49. Gary A. Yukl, *Leadership in Organizations*, 2nd ed. (Englewood Cliffs, N.J.: Prentice Hall, 1989), pp. 267–268. See also Bernard M. Bass, *Bass & Stogdill's Handbook of Leadership*, 3rd ed. (New York: Free Press, 1990).

to leader behaviors increased the ability to understand employee satisfaction, commitment, and performance.[50] Stafford Beer said, "A man who excels in drive and leadership but is not skilled in the three intellectual functions of management (policy making, decision making, and control) may be compared to a man on a unicycle— the unicyclist gives a virtuoso display over the short term, but a delivery boy on a tricycle will make steadier progress and carry a more useful load."[51]

ORGANIZATIONS AND PEOPLE

In contrast to the organizational behavioralists who looked to leadership, motivation, and group processes within the organization, organizational theorists assumed more of a total organization or macro point of view of goals, structure, and the processes necessary to accomplish organizational goals. Early organizations, such as the Roman Catholic Church, the military, and the government, were faced with the problems of integrating human efforts to achieve expected results. They did not face the rigors of market competition, and organizational structures were designed to keep humans within the boundaries of administrative desire. In ancient Greece, Aristotle wrote of centralized and decentralized authority, division of labor, and departmentation. Daniel McCallum gave the organizational structure of the Erie Railroad the appearance of a tree and developed ideas about authority, accountability, and communication. Frederick Taylor recognized the need for expert advice with his functional foreman; and Harrington Emerson improved this scheme with a line-staff concept of organizations. In Germany, Siemens introduced the idea of product divisions, an "M-form" structure, prior to its use in the United States.[52] In the United States, Du Pont organized around products in a multidivisional structure and carried this idea over into the General Motors Corporation. Henri Fayol identified organizing as an element of management, placing organizational theory squarely in the conceptual framework of general management theory. Max Weber, a contemporary of Taylor and Fayol whose works were translated into English much later, described bureaucracy as an ideal form of organizations based on rational-legal authority. In Chapter 16 we saw the early search for "principles" of organizations and the writers who looked at the inner workings of the organization. Others were interested in socio-technical systems and Barnard wrote of decision making and the formal and informal organizations, thus making a lasting impact on the Hawthorne studies and Herbert Simon. With James March, Simon saw organizations

---

50. Avis L. Johnson and Fred Luthans, "The Relationship between Leadership and Management: An Empirical Assessment," *Journal of Managerial Issues* 2 (Spring 1990), pp. 13–25.

51. Stafford Beer, quoted in Jack Young, "From the Editor," *Academy of Management Executive* 5 (May 1991), p. 5.

52. Alfred D. Chandler, Jr., *Scale and Scope: The Dynamics of Industrial Capitalism* (Cambridge, Mass.: Harvard University Press, 1990), pp. 469–471, p. 544.

as a complex network of decision processes (see Chapter 15). From Barnard onward, the study of organizations took a new tack.

ORGANIZATIONS AS OPEN SYSTEMS

Although Chester Barnard broke with the conventional wisdom of intraorganizational analysis and viewed organizations as open systems that included investors, suppliers, customers, and others, it was not until the 1960s that systems theory made an impact on management thought. Ludwig von Bertalanffy (1901–1972), a biologist, noted the "openness" of all systems, that is, an organism was both affected by and affected its environment.[53] "Organism" has the same Greek and Latin roots as "organization" in that both deal with the function, structure, and relationship of parts to a whole. It became appropriate, then, to think in terms of an organization as an open system, taking its inputs from the environment, processing these as throughputs, resulting in outputs which are returned to the environment. Organization-environment interactions became crucial to understanding organizational design.

As open systems, organizations faced an environment that might be placid and benevolent, or turbulent and harsh. Economic, social, political, and technological changes could come rapidly or slowly, and some organizational arrangements might be better able to cope with the changing environment than others. Could it be that there was no one way to structure the organization, that design was influenced by environmental factors and could vary depending on technology?

Joan Woodward classified organizations by the complexity of the technology used in producing goods and found that it influenced the organizational structure. Her classification, ranging from less complex (1) to more advanced (3), consisted of (1) unit and small-batch production systems that produced made-to-order and customized products to meet consumers' needs; (2) large-batch and mass production, which involved a fairly standardized or uniform product with but few variations in its final appearance; and (3) long-run continuous-process production, which involved a standard product manufactured by moving through a predictable series of steps. Woodward's organizations in classifications 1 and 3 delegated more authority, were more permissive in leading people, and had more loosely organized work groups; so the more successful firms exhibited more organizational flexibility. Successful organizations in classification 2 tended to use the line-staff type of organization, exercised closer supervision over personnel, used more elaborate control techniques, and relied more on formal, written communications.[54] The answer to "it depends on …" in organizational design, according to Woodward, would be technology.

---

53. Ludwig von Bertalanffy, "General Systems Theory: A New Approach to the Unity of Science," *Human Biology* 23 (December 1951), pp. 302–361.

54. Joan Woodward, *Industrial Organization: Theory and Practice* (London: Oxford University Press, 1965).

The "Aston Group," so-called because of varying teams of researchers at the University of Aston, Birmingham, England, under the primary leadership of Derek Pugh, examined technology from a broader perspective. These studies focused on how the flow of work was coordinated, operations technology, and the like, but they did not support Woodward's contention that technology was a determining factor. Rather, it seemed the size of the firm influenced the degree of formality, with larger firms being more specialized.[55] Subsequent research, however, found that neither Woodward's technological determinism nor the Aston group's work could be supported.[56] Technology might play a role, but it did not answer the "if…then" contingency view of organizing.

Another approach to organizational design was suggested by a number of researchers, notably Paul Lawrence and Jay Lorsch.[57] They took the position that structure depended on environmental factors: (1) the rate of change in environmental conditions; (2) the certainty of information available; and (3) the time span of feedback of results on decisions made or action taken. Lawrence and Lorsch found that the more successful firms were those that adjusted to their relevant environments. Firms that faced a more stable, more certain environment were more formal and centralized. Firms that faced more unstable, less certain environments were more flexible and decentralized. In both cases, success was due to organizational design consonant with the environment. The work of these authors and others led to a proliferation of research on the contingency approach to organizational design. The results of these studies, however, failed to provide clear support for either approach. Technology was not an overriding factor in determining structure, nor did environmental factors provide clear guides to organizational design.[58]

Another area of interest concerned the possibility that organizational age or size influenced an organization's structure. This notion extended the idea of a product life cycle to that of an organizational life cycle. Products appeared to go through the stages of introduction, growth, maturity, and decline. Of course, some products died young, while some products did not decline but were revitalized through new markets, "new and improved" versions, or other tactics devised to prevent the product's demise. Could it be that organizations also went through these stages of start-up, growth, maturity, and decline? The numerous models developed typically described the life cycle in terms of stages, such as birth, growth, and so on, with each stage leading to a point at which adjustments had to be made before another stage could

---

55. From a vast literature, see Derek S. Pugh, David J. Hickson, and Diana Pheysey, "Operations Technology and Organization Structure: An Empirical Reappraisal," *Administrative Science Quarterly* 14 (1969), pp. 378–397.

56. Miner, *Organizational Behavior,* p. 465, 470, 525.

57. Paul R. Lawrence and Jay W. Lorsch, *Organization and Environment* (Homewood, Ill: Richard D. Irwin, 1969).

58. Paul R. Lawrence and Jay W. Lorsch , "Review of Organization and Environment: Managing Differentiation and Integration," *Journal of Management* 17 (1991), pp. 491–493.

be entered.[59] For instance, moving from a starting point to a growth stage could mean that the entrepreneur had to go public to raise capital, add more employees, expand production, and so on to meet the demands placed on the firm by its growth. If unsuccessful in making the necessary adjustment, the resulting crisis could mean the failure of the enterprise. Some firms expired young, others persisted, but all were vulnerable to failure at any stage of the life cycle. From the various studies of the organizational life cycle, no clear-cut, best way of organizing emerged. Creativity and innovation were necessary to successful start-up ventures, flexibility was needed for growth, stability and formality for maturity, and, in the stage of decline, where flexibility was most needed, senescence too often prevailed.

Neither technology, nor environment, nor stage of the life cycle provided any best way of organizing. Although this outcome appeared discouraging, perhaps internal processes could provide answers.

BEHAVIORAL THEORIES OF THE FIRM

A turn from structure to internal processes was the theme of authors such as Richard Cyert and James March, Daniel Katz and Robert Kahn, and Karl Weick.[60] Cyert, an economist, and March, a psychologist, emphasized internal competition for scarce resources, interest groups forming coalitions, conflict resolution, organizational learning, and, among other concepts, the adaptive processes of decision making and performance feedback. Psychologists Katz and Kahn emphasized organizational roles, role conflict and ambiguity, the organization as an open input-output system, and circumstances when the hierarchy was preferable to participative styles. Weick, another psychologist, emphasized the organizing process rather than the organizational product and suggested that actions precede goals (goals are retrospective), that individual behaviors are interlocking, and so on.

All but one of those mentioned above was a psychologist by education, so it should not be surprising that their view of organization theory emphasizes internal processes and resembles the micro approach of organizational behavior. Another group of theorists, all but one educated as a sociologist, viewed organizations as a product of macro environmental forces. These behavioralists were Jeffrey Pfeffer and Gerald Salancik, Michael Hannan and John Freeman, and John Meyer and Richard Scott.[61] Pfeffer (the

59. Larry E. Greiner, "Evolution and Growth as Organizations Grow," *Harvard Business Review* 50 (July–August 1972), pp. 37–46; and Gordon L. Lippitt and Warren H. Schmidt, "Crises in a Developing Organization," *Harvard Business Review* 45 (November–December 1967), pp. 102–112.

60. Primary works: Richard M. Cyert and James G. March, *A Behavioral Theory of the Firm* (Englewood Cliffs, N.J.: Prentice-Hall, 1963); Daniel Katz and Robert Kahn, *The Social Psychology of Organizations* (New York: John Wiley and Sons, 1966); and Karl E. Weick, *The Social Psychology of Organizing* (Reading, Mass.: Addison-Wesley, 1969).

61. Primary works: Jeffrey Pfeffer and Gerald R. Salancik, *The External Control of Organizations: A Resource Dependence Perspective* (New York: Harper and Row, 1978); Michael T. Hannan and John Freeman, *Organizational Ecology* (Cambridge, Mass.: Harvard University Press, 1989); and John W. Meyer and W. Richard Scott, *Organizational Environments: Ritual and Rationality* (Beverly Hills, Calif.: Sage, 1983).

only nonsociologist) and Salancik present a resource dependent theory that postulates organizations require support from their external environment and can only survive to the extent that this support is forthcoming. Managers form coalitions to gather support in an open system of external relationships in which there are constraints that create either a munificent or scarce resource situation. Hannan and Freeman's organizational ecology theory offers the idea that organizational survival is a process of adaptation and success, or fail to adapt and exit. The authors recognized the Darwinian nature of their theory, but have used it to study organizational populations such as labor unions and newspapers for population entries, adaptation and mortality. The neoinstitutional theory of Meyer and Scott (and others) holds that organizational environments are shaped by societal expectations that provide legitimacy to the organization's existence. By conforming to cultural rules, such as custom or law, formal organizations are able to take on the prevailing view of society.

In the space and time permitted, the presentation of these internally and externally focused behavioral theories does not do justice to the mega-ocean of literature and the theorists extant. There are variations, refinements, added authors, and numerous critiques of these notions. The purpose has been to show how theories of organization have evolved from examining formal structures to contingency notions to emphasizing internal processes to recognizing external forces. At this point, however, we need to examine reactions to this proliferation of theories.

THE PARADIGM WARS

"Paradigm" comes from the Latin and Greek words meaning to show an example, model or pattern. As such, a paradigm is normative, informing and showing us what is a reasonable way to view situations and events, or, as in this case, an organization. Van de Ven notes a "buzzing, blooming, confusing world" of organization and management theories resulting in "a tower of babbling and fragmented explanations" of differing paradigms.[62] He is not perturbed by this, although these paradigms may be confusing and lacking empirical support, but sees this as a healthy sign of the pursuit of knowledge.

Others are not so sure: Donaldson sees this theory thicket as "fragmented...[of] an anti-management quality...[and] long on assertion and short on empirical evidence."[63] Pfeffer attributes this paradigm proliferation to "journal editors and reviewers [who] seem to seek novelty, and there are great rewards for coining a new term ... for formulating 'new concepts' but not for studying or rejecting concepts that are already invented."[64] Miner analyzed seventy-three theories, finding no

---

62. Andrew H. Van de Ven, "The Buzzing, Blooming, Confusing World of Organization and Management Theory: A View from Lake Wobegon University," *Journal of Management Inquiry* 8 (1999), p. 119.

63. Lex Donaldson, *American Anti-Management Theories of Organization: A Critique of Paradigm Proliferation* (Cambridge, England: Cambridge University Press, 1995), p. xi.

64. Jeffrey Pfeffer, "Barriers to the Advance of Organizational Science: Paradigm Development as a Dependent Variable," *Academy of Management Review* 18 (1993), p. 612.

organization theory high in "estimated scientific validity" and "estimated usefulness in application."[65] The judges of Miner's theories were past presidents of the Academy of Management and past editors and editorial reviewers from academy's research and theory journals, that is, knowledgeable academics. How these theories would have fared if practicing managers were surveyed would be interesting. In short, scholarly impulses have created a plethora of theories and an abundance of proponents and critics. Outside the halls of academe, what was happening?

STRATEGY AND STRUCTURE

"Structure follows strategy" was the thesis of Alfred Chandler, a business historian, who selected four companies from some fifty or so examples of decentralization using the multidivisional organization as their strategies unfolded in the 1920s. While he built from cases, other early organization theorists were practicing executives such as Chester Barnard and Henri Fayol. Fayol, for example, observed that an organization's structure had to be consistent with the "objectives, resources, and requirements" of the firm (see Chapter 10). Barnard's influence has been long-lasting, from shaping the Hawthorne studies to Oliver Williamson and transaction cost economics. Despite the experience of practicing managers (which, incidentally, is also "empirical"), academics spin theories with little, or no, reference to their work.

The need for economies of scale drove organizations in the late nineteenth and much of the twentieth centuries. Organizations integrated vertically to optimize their input-throughput-output operations, and they integrated horizontally to expand the scope of their distribution or production functions. The growth of a managerial hierarchy, a proliferation of staff specialists, and multidivisional structures made sense under those circumstances as Chandler observed. Examining the U.S. economy since the 1960s, a period of increasing paradigm spinning, we can see changing strategies and structures. The 1960s and early 1970s were characterized by two dominant forces: one political and one economic. Business prosperity, willing lenders, and a stock market boom encouraged firms to expand; politically, however, strict enforcement of antitrust regulations discouraged horizontal integration (acquiring firms within its industry). Firms responded with a flurry of mergers and acquisitions to diversify outside their industry.

By the late 1960s, Textron, for example, "sold zippers, pens, snowmobiles, eyeglass frames, silverware, golf carts, machine tools, helicopters, rocket engines, ball bearings, and gas meters."[66] ITT (International Telephone and Telegraph) had 150

---

65. John B. Miner, The Rated Importance, Scientific Validity, and Practical Usefulness of Organizational Behavior Theories: A Quantitative Review," *Academy of Management Learning and Education* 2 (2003), pp. 258–259.

66. Wyatt Wells, *American Capitalism, 1945–2000: Continuity and Change from Mass Production to the Information Society* (Chicago, Ill.: Ivan R. Dee, 2003), p. 64.

separate divisions, each a profit center. RCA (Radio Corporation of America) produced consumer electronics, owned a broadcasting company (NBC), printed books, wove carpets, sold frozen food, leased automobiles, and built a line of computers to compete with IBM. These mergers and acquisitions led firms into unrelated fields, that is, unrelated to their primary line of business. A line-staff structure could not accommodate such diversity, so the multidivisional (M-form) structure was used to follow the strategy of unrelated product diversification.

To manage these firms, called conglomerates, the acquiring or takeover company must do a better job than the previous management—which did not always happen. These "higher levels of diversification [made] it increasingly difficult for corporate executives to use strategic controls. Their span of control is greater and, therefore, the volume of information received is increased and becomes overwhelming."[67] To cope, top management turned to financial controls, such as return on investment (ROI) and overemphasized short-term performance measures to the neglect of long-range innovation to gain technological superiority. The rate of growth of U.S. productivity had peaked near 4 percent in 1973 (the year of an international oil embargo) but then declined to about 1.5 percent per annum for the period 1973–1979. Operating costs increased, squeezing profitability and stock prices of conglomerates declined as lower earnings were reported. Consequently, a period of divestment or leveraged buyouts shrank the former conglomerates, moving them closer to the products and businesses they knew best. When the Reagan and Clinton administrations in the 1980s and 1990s eased up on antitrust enforcement and moved to deregulate the economy, subsequent mergers and acquisitions were horizontal integrations such as the oil industry, banking, aluminum, and the railroads.

What lessons does history offer for understanding firm survivability over the long term? One study indicates that 39 percent (193) of the *Fortune* 500 of 1994 were over one hundred years old. Almost one-half (247) were founded between 1880 and 1920—a period characterized by increasing mass production; mass marketing; revolutions in transportation and communication; and incidentally, systematic/scientific management. These 247 companies "were often the first in their industries to make the necessary investments and create the corporate organizations essential to exploit the new technologies and markets."[68] In the last half of the twentieth century, industrial growth was fueled by science and its handmaiden, technology, in pharmaceuticals, petrochemistry, aerospace, and firms employing integrated circuitry. Some 16 percent of *Fortune*'s 500 were founded in the last half of the twentieth century.

---

67. Michael A. Hitt, Robert E. Hoskisson, and Jeffrey S. Harrison, "Strategic Competitiveness in the 1990s: Challenges and Opportunities for U.S. Executives," *Academy of Management Executive* 5 (1991), pp. 7–22.

68. [Harris Corporation], "Founding Dates of the 1994 *Fortune* 500 U.S. Companies," *Business History Review* 70 (1996), p. 70.

This evidence does not prove that standing among the largest five hundred companies in 1994 was due to longevity. Rather, the implication is that the firms that grew and survived were able to take advantage of changing technologies and markets, design the appropriate corporate structures to seize the opportunities offered by these developments, and foster staying power by adapting to changes over the long term. Organization theory debates will continue, but without reflecting successful practices they will be devoid of usefulness.

Summary

The influx of the behavioral scientists into business schools had a significant impact on management thought. The behavioral scientists brought different perspectives, research tools, and ideas to reshape human relations into organizational behavior. A philosophy of organizational humanism had mental health overtones, called for redesigning organizations to promote individual maturity, and posited that the assumptions a manager made about people determined the managerial style. Job design sought to provide for greater employee involvement, and goal-setting theory provided a means of rewarding to promote self-efficacy. Personnel management evolved into human resource management, and some connections with industrial relations were suggested. Leadership theories cycled from traits through contingency notions and back to leader styles and leader-member relations in transformational, charismatic, transactional, and leader-member exchange theories.

Organizational theory evolved from examining structure, hierarchy of authority, span of control, departmentation, and related ideas to possibilities of external determinants, such as technology or environment. Theories proffered by psychologists and sociologists differed—the former emphasizing internal processes, the latter external ones that shaped the organizational structure. Finally, it was suggested that better theory can be built by examining successful practices in firms over the long term.

CHAPTER 21

Science and Systems in Management

Numbers have always held a fascination for humankind; people have ascribed magical powers to some numbers, malignancy to others, and throughout history have used numbers to account for flocks of sheep as well as to reach for the stars. Having no intrinsic value in themselves, numbers have become symbols of the quest for knowledge because they lend a preciseness and orderliness to our environment. In observing nature, it was also noted that there was a natural rhythm of all seasons, of the solar system, and of life and death in all things. Our inquisitiveness led us to explore, to attempt to explain the inexplicable, and to search for a great force that binds the complexities observed in nature into some rational order of events. People have sought to bring order from chaos by searching for interrelationships between observed events and activities. Although we are curious and seek variety in life, we also have a need for closure, a need to bring our observations into some unity of perception. Humans are basically orderly, rational beings who desire to control their environment insofar as that is possible.

The preceding pages have described numerous attempts to rationalize and systematize the workplace and to measure and control organizational operations. Management's need for information to monitor performance and keep in touch with external events is also ancient. In earlier chapters we saw how new technologies, such as the telegraph, enabled managers to have a systematic means of gathering, recording, and using information to make decisions. This chapter carries on from those deep roots to trace developments in the modern era.

THE QUEST FOR SCIENCE IN MANAGEMENT

The scientific method denotes a rational approach to problem solving through a statement of hypothesis, accumulation of data, identification of alternatives, and testing, verification, and selection of a path of action based on facts. In his break with the mystics who held that reality was unknowable, Aristotle established the foundations for the scientific method. After Greece and Rome fell, reason yielded to the Age of Faith during the Middle Ages, only to reemerge in the Renaissance and the Age of Reason. It was during this time that the foundations for modern mathematics and science were established. Rene Descartes (1596–1650) thought the world operated mechanistically and prescribed the use of mathematics to describe its movements. Isaac Newton (1642–1727) developed calculus and laws of motion and gravitation, furthering Descartes' conception of the world as a giant machine. Others also saw an orderly universe. Mathematics was the building block for bringing the parts together into one grand formula. The rediscovery of Aristotle during this time and the renewed interest in mathematics and in science led to the vast technological changes in humankind's environment that became known as the Industrial Revolution.

Charles Babbage, and to some extent Andrew Ure, applied a scientific approach to the solution of the problems of the burgeoning factory system. Industrialization demanded order and predictability, and the engineers were well equipped to cope with the scientific study and systematization of work. Scientific management and the work of Taylor, Barth, Gantt, the Gilbreths, Emerson, and others constituted the Age of Reason in twentieth-century management thought. In the 1930s, scientific management declined in emphasis as society had to cope with problems beyond the production of goods. World War II and the renewed growth of large-scale enterprise, however, created a new environment for management. In the modern era, new ideas were formed to add to the tradition of Aristotle, Descartes, Babbage, and scientific management.

OPERATIONS RESEARCH

World War I gave widespread recognition and acceptance to the notion of science in management. Governmental and industrial organizations seized on the precepts of scientific management in order to cope with the mass assemblages of resources required to carry on the war. For more than three decades the ideas of Gantt, Taylor, and other scientific management thinkers were carried forward as "industrial administration" or "production management." This approach was, more often than not, a view of how to improve the production function as part of the firm's throughput rather than as a vital ingredient of the general management of the firm. Outside events, however, soon led to added dimensions for production management.

World War II brought about a union of managers, government officials, and scientists in an attempt to bring order and rationality to the global logistics of war. The British formed the first operations research teams of various specialists in an effort to bring their knowledge to bear on the problems of radar systems, antiaircraft gunnery, antisubmarine warfare, the bombing of Germany, and civilian defense matters.[1] One of the best-known groups was under the direction of Professor P. M. S. Blackett (1897–1974), physicist, Nobel Prize winner, and codeveloper of radar. Blackett's team, called "Blackett's circus," included three physiologists, two mathematical physicists, one astrophysicist, one Army officer, one surveyor, one general physicist, and two mathematicians. It was in groups such as this one that various specialists were brought together under one tent to solve the complex problems of the war and defense efforts.

Operations research was conceived as the application of scientific knowledge and methods to the study of complex problems with the stated purpose of deriving a quantitative basis for the decisions that would accomplish an organization's objectives. While the British formed the first operations research groups, U.S. industrial organizations and private consulting firms also began to recognize that the methods of operations research were applicable to problems of a nonmilitary nature. Arthur D. Little, Inc., a private consulting firm, was one of the first to seek industrial uses for operations research. The Operations Research Society of America was founded in 1952 and began publishing a journal, *Operations Research*. In 1953, The Institute of Management Science (TIMS) stated its objectives as "to identify, extend, and unify scientific knowledge that contributes to the understanding of the practice of management" and began publishing the journal *Management Science*.

The application of operations research techniques came very naturally to production management, an area with structured kinds of problems and decisions for which decision rules could be rationally devised. There were problems with stocking the proper level of inventories, scheduling and controlling production, manufacturing in economical batches, controlling quality, and acquiring capital, as well as a host of other physical resource problems. The similarities between operations research and scientific management were striking. For his metal-cutting experiments, Frederick Taylor brought together a team of researchers that included a mathematician (Carl Barth), a metallurgist (Maunsell White), an engineer (Henry Gantt), and others to assist him in the solution of various problems. Further, Taylor, Gilbreth, and others spoke of the "one best way" as the objective of their scientific analysis. The modern management scientist has merely put the quest more euphemistically: "The approach of optimality analysis is to take various alternatives into account and to ask which of these possible sets of decisions will come closest to meeting the businessman's objectives, i.e., which decisions will be best or optimal."[2] The difference between the "one best way" and an "optimal" decision is moot. The old school and the new have both sought through the scientific method to rationally evaluate alternatives in an effort to find the best possible decision. In Taylor's

---

1. Joseph F. McClosky, "The Beginnings of Operations Research: 1934–1941," *Operations Research* 35 (1987), pp. 143–152.

2. William J. Baumol, *Economic Theory and Operations Analysis* (Englewood Cliffs, N.J.: Prentice-Hall, 1961), p. 4.

time, people had confidence that science could lead to a perfect society; today, because people are less confident in such a scheme, "optimal" sounds better than the "one best way."

Another striking similarity was that the modern researchers, like their predecessors, sought to apply the scientific method in the analysis of human behavior. The Institute of Management Science formed an interest group, the College on Management Psychology, "to investigate the processes of work and managing work by applying psychology, psychiatry, and the behavioral sciences in order to enhance our understanding of management." Hugo Münsterberg could not have stated the case more clearly. Modern behavioral scientists frequently viewed management science as a continuation of a mechanistic view of people and considered the behavioral and quantitative approaches mutually exclusive. However, it was not the wheel that was humankind's great invention, but the axle; it is important to search for how these areas complement one another and how they might be brought together in some grand scheme.

Modern management science, inverted from scientific management, was not so much the search for a science of management as a striving for the use of science *in* management. In this endeavor the tools of mathematics and science were enlisted to help solve the age-old management problem of the optimum allocation of scarce resources toward a given goal.

PRODUCTION MANAGEMENT IN TRANSITION

The Gordon and Howell report had few kind words for production management (in 1959): "Production management courses are often the repository for some of the most inappropriate and intellectually stultifying materials to be found in the business curriculum... many faculty members have little respect for such courses ... and students complained more strongly to us about the pointlessness of the production requirement than of any other."[3] Gordon and Howell were also particularly critical of the state of business education with respect to mathematics. The typical business school curriculum, preparing students for leadership in a computerized space age, had few, if any, requirements for mathematics. The modern era saw a reversal of this state of affairs, and business schools began to require more and more statistics and mathematics of their students. The burgeoning appearance of quantitative methods in curricula brought a proliferation of new management specialties and eventually an enrichment in the semantic problems of the management theory jungle.

For many, the language of the management scientist resembled the mumbo jumbo of the witch doctor. There was the ritual of model building, the symbols manipulated during the ceremony, and the awe-inspiring incantation of magical

---

3. Robert A. Gordon and James E. Howell, *Higher Education for Business* (New York: Columbia University Press, 1959), p. 190. In a footnote, Gordon and Howell stated that statistics courses received a greater number of complaints questioning the relevance of requiring the statistics course.

phrases. To the uninitiated, the rite inspired awe, fear, and reverence for the mathematical elite. Hence, there should be little wonder that the quantitative specialists had such an impact on traditional management theory. A new genre of production management textbooks emerged, heavily influenced by operations research techniques. The outcome for management education was to move beyond the idea of factory/industrial/production management into an era that blended the old and the new into "production/operations management."

The new language of production/operations management was heavily oriented toward statistics and mathematics. At its base was the scientific method of problem solving; the body was composed of specific techniques for quantifying variables and relationships; and its apex was the notion of a model representing the variables and their relationships for the purposes of prediction and control. Such techniques as statistics, linear programming, waiting line or queuing theory, game theory, decision trees, the transportation method, Monte Carlo methods, and simulation devices were part and parcel of the new language. Statistics and probability theory aided in sampling for quality control and other uses; linear programming and its special techniques facilitated the choice of a desirable course of action given certain constraints; and queuing theory helped balance the costs and the services of a machine or other service facility. Competitive strategies could be best understood by drawing upon game theory; capital acquisitions could be simulated through computers and the use of probability theory; and quantitative models could be built and manipulated to test the impact of changes on one or more of the variables or the model as a whole.

Along with presenting the analytical techniques, serious attempts were made to bring the operations research tools into a conceptual framework. The "decision theorists" sought to combine the economic concepts of utility and choice with the more modern quantitative tools. One early landmark attempt was that of David Miller and Martin Starr, who stressed the executive's decision making role in optimizing corporate goals and placed less emphasis on the techniques.[4] These more sophisticated decision-making tools reshaped notions of educating managers through changes in business school curricula and also created a new variety of specialists with whom the manager had to communicate. The ideas of Henri Fayol, who had found the use of higher mathematics of no value in his managerial experience, probably would be severely shaken by today's business school.

Henry Gantt would also be surprised to find what the new quantitative methods meant to his ideas. Gantt, under pressure to handle complex industrial military interactions in World War I, had devised a graphic method of scheduling and controlling activities. In 1956–57, the DuPont Company developed a computerized arrow diagram or network method for planning and controlling, which became known as the Critical Path Method (CPM). This method used only one

---

4. David W. Miller and Martin K. Starr, *Executive Decisions and Operations Research* (Englewood Cliffs, N.J.: Prentice-Hall, 1960). See also David W. Miller and Martin K. Starr, *The Structure of Human Decisions* (Englewood Cliffs, N.J.: Prentice-Hall, 1967).

time estimate and included only activities (arrows). In 1957–58, in managing the development of the Polaris missile, the United States Navy encountered many of the same problems in project scheduling and evaluation as it had in Gantt's day with shipbuilding. Together with the consulting help of Booz, Allen, and Hamilton, Inc., and the Lockheed Missile System Division (the prime contractor), the U.S. Navy devised the Program Evaluation and Review Technique (PERT). This technique used statistical probability theory to furnish three time estimates (pessimistic, most probable, and optimistic) and added "events" (circles) to the graphing of activities.

Taken together, the PERT and CPM techniques served to plan a network of activities, their relationships, and their interaction along a path to a given completion date. They graphed paths for the flow of activities, provided events as checkpoints, and focused managerial attention on a critical path or paths in an effort to keep the total project on course. Although these techniques are much more complex than this brief description implies, they are really little more than the Gantt chart concept enlarged and enriched by many years of advancing management and statistical knowledge.

In brief, the earlier notions of production management were reshaped by operations researchers, statisticians, and decision theorists. The application of the scientific method and the use of mathematics in some types of managerial problems could provide better information for decision makers. While more advanced techniques enhanced the academic credibility of production/operations management, some began to wonder whether these tools were placing too much emphasis on problem solving and not enough on problem finding. It would take a competitive challenge from abroad to move production/operations management into another stage of development.

OLD LESSONS RELEARNED

The importance of product quality is not new; in early craft guilds, for example, it was the practice to place a mark on the product (hallmark) so that customers could connect quality with the maker of the item. The manufacture of interchangeable parts increased the need to produce to close tolerances, making measurement and inspection necessary. Andrew Carnegie considered quality the bedrock of the success of his enterprise: "even in these days of fiercest competition, when everything would seem to be a matter of price, there lies still at the root of business success the much more important factor of quality.... After that, and a long way after, comes cost."[5] In his 1903 paper before the American Society of Mechanical Engineers, Frederick Taylor designated one of the functional foreman to be the first to be brought into contact with the worker and added that the inspection system must be in place and understood "before any steps are taken toward stimulating the men to a larger

---

5. Andrew Carnegie, *Autobiography of Andrew Carnegie* (Boston: Houghton Mifflin, 1920), pp. 122–123.

output; otherwise an increase in quantity will probably be accompanied by a falling off of quality."[6] In the period following World War II, however, production management began to take a back seat to human relations, the financial management of corporate portfolios, and unrelated product diversification.

Hayes and Abernathy charged that U.S. industry had forgotten how to compete, produce efficiently, keep prices down, and maintain product quality.[7] As the global competitive challenge arose, especially from Japan, and U.S. productivity lagged, production management became once more a glamour stock. In contrast to the industrial engineering, shop-management approach of earlier years, the call was for improving product quality and placing production in the corporate strategy, general management mainstream. The challenge was whether the United States could relearn the lessons about quality, efficiency, and productivity that it had been teaching the rest of the world since the scientific management period.

After World War II, as part of U.S. efforts to rebuild the Japanese economy that the war had just finished destroying, a series of events occurred that would make Japan an industrial phoenix. The Japanese productivity "miracle" was based on ideas introduced into Japan in the period immediately following World War ll. During the U.S. occupation, U.S. engineers were given the task of helping Japanese industry recover. Two engineers, Charles Protzman and Homer Sarasohn, started a series of seminars on policy, organization, operations, production controls, quality controls, and U.S. production management methods for Japanese managers. Although Protzman worked for the Hawthorne Plant of Western Electric, he felt that the Japanese needed production skills rather than human relations skills.[8]

At Western Electric, Walter A. Shewhart (1891–1967) began working on industrial quality control problems in the early 1920s with the goal of replacing the phrase "as alike as two peas in a pod" with "as alike as two telephones." Shewhart took samples of the work done and applied statistical analysis to identify variations in performance. He devised a control chart to define the acceptable limits of random variation in any worker's task so that any output outside those limits could be detected and studied as to what caused the unacceptable variation. To illustrate his point, Shewhart used different colored chips drawn from a bowl to show that there were always differences in the number of one color of chips drawn by one person compared with the number drawn by any other person. Thus, there was always some random variation in industrial production over which the worker had no control. But over numerous trials, there would be some limits to this random variation. It

6. Frederick W. Taylor, *Shop Management* (New York: Harper and Row, 1911), p. 144.

7. Robert H. Hayes and William J. Abernathy, "Managing Our Way to Economic Decline," *Harvard Business Review* 58 (July–August 1980), pp. 67–77.

8. Based on the research of Kenneth Hopper as reported in Rebecca R. Tsurumi, "American Origins of Japanese Productivity: The Hawthorne Experiment Rejected," *Pacific Basic Quarterly* (Spring–Summer 1982), pp. 14–15. See also Robert C. Wood, "A Lesson Learned and a Lesson Forgotten," *Forbes* (February 6, 1989), pp. 70–78, for Sarasohn's recollections of those events.

W. Edwards Deming. Courtesy of The W. Edwards Deming Institute®.

was what happened outside these limits that could be examined for corrective action. Shewhart pioneered statistical quality control, but it would be one of his followers who would revive the idea of product quality in the post–World War II period.[9]

William Edwards Deming (1900–1993), educated as a mathematical physicist, applied Shewhart's ideas of sampling for statistical quality control in the U.S. Department of Agriculture and later as an employee of the U.S. Census Bureau. His reputation as an expert on statistical sampling led to his employment during World War II to teach engineers and technicians how to use these techniques in the production of war materials. In 1947 he went to Japan to help prepare for a 1951 census of that country. Deming was pleased when Kenichi Koyanagi, managing director of the Union of Japanese Scientists and Engineers (JUSE), invited him in 1950 to present some lectures on statistical quality control. Koyanagi and his colleagues had continued their study of U.S. manufacturing methods after Sarasohn and Protzman returned to the United States and had read Walter Shewhart's classic *Economic Control of Quality of Manufactured Product* and Shewhart's lectures, edited by Deming, on statistical quality control.[10]

Deming began his seminars in Japan in 1950 and for three decades he lectured and consulted in Japan. As a result of an NBC television program in 1980, entitled "If Japan Can ...Why Can't We?," American audiences finally became aware of Deming, but they did not find a smiling face. Deming was critical of U.S. management, perhaps because he had been ignored for so long, but more likely because U.S. firms were losing market share to other, more quality oriented and more productive competitors. He blamed U.S. management: "The wealth of a nation depends on its people, management, and government, more than its natural resources. The problem is where to find good management. It would be a mistake to export American management to a friendly country."[11]

Deming identified seven deadly diseases that caused U.S. industry to go into decline.

---

9. Joe Stauffer, "SQC before Deming: The Works of Walter Shewhart," *The Journal of Applied Management and Entrepreneurship* 8 (October 2003), pp. 86–94.

10. Walter A. Shewhart, *Economic Control of Quality of Manufactured Product* (New York: Van Nostrand, 1931).

11. W. Edwards Deming, *Out of the Crisis* (Cambridge: Massachusetts Institute of Technology, Center for Advanced Engineering Study, 1986), p. 6.

1. Lack of constancy of purpose toward improvement of products and services
2. An emphasis on short-term profits
3. Merit rating or other evaluation of individual performance
4. Job hopping by managers
5. Managing by the numbers without considering figures that are unknown or unknowable
6. Excessive medical costs (peculiar to the United States)
7. The litigious nature of the U.S. citizenry, causing excessive costs of liability that increased as lawyers worked on contingency fee

Deming attributed 95 percent of all errors to the systems under which people worked, not the people themselves. Quality management began at the top of the organization, not with the employee. The goal was the reduction of variation through continuous improvement (*Kaizen*), discovering what was out of control as a result of special causes. For a decade and a half before his death, Deming berated American managers for their faults, stimulating a new interest in quality management.[12]

Another significant person in the early quality movement was Joseph M. Juran (1904–). Juran worked at Western Electric, and like Deming was inoculated with the statistical quality control ideas of Walter Shewhart whose influence was throughout the Bell system at this time. Juran questioned, however, that quality was solely a matter of statistics and traced the beginning of a separate quality inspection responsibility to the writings of Frederick W. Taylor. After World War II, Juran became an independent consultant on quality control, but, like Deming, found a waning interest among U.S. manufacturers. He assembled and edited a weighty handbook on quality control that became a standard reference tool on the subject and also led JUSE to invite him to Japan in 1954. Japanese managers and workers struggled trying to understand Deming's ideas on statistical quality control until Juran came and established quality control as a job for everyone. His approach asked the firm to identify and work on the most critical problems first, which he called the "vital few," before moving on to resolve the "trivial many" problems. Juran called this the "Pareto Principle," although he later admitted that this was an improper attribution to Vilfredo Pareto, a late nineteenth and early twentieth century economist.[13] Regardless, the Pareto effect has been passed down as an eighty-twenty rule: for example, 80 percent of the quality problems are caused by 20 percent

---

12. A valuable resource on Deming is Peter B. Petersen, "Library of Congress Archives: Additional Information about W. Edwards Deming (1900–1993) Now Available," *Journal of Management History* 3 (1997), pp. 98–119.

13. Pareto quantified a nonuniform distribution of wealth in society but did not apply this to other phenomena. A U.S.-born statistician, Max Otto Lorenz, developed a "Lorenz Curve" to display the deviation of an individual's income from a perfect equality of wealth. In statistical quality control terms and in Juran's thinking, this was the deviation of a sample from the standard.

of the manufacturing operations. By focusing on Juran's "vital few" operations first, a large number of problems could be resolved before management turned to the "trivial many."

Juran's three-part system was aimed at improving quality year after year. Firms began by setting goals, organizing into teams to work on these projects, and working with Juran and his staff through each project. This approach blended statistical analysis with traditional managerial actions of planning, organizing, and controlling. Clients admired Juran's methodical, company-wide approach and the improved results as the vital few and the trivial many problems were solved.

The Japanese also pioneered the idea of forming small problem-solving groups of workers, supervisors, and specialists for the purpose of developing better ways of doing a job with higher quality. These groups, known as quality circles, enabled an industrial renaissance in Japan. As they became more competitive, their products threatened and, in some cases, surpassed, U.S. products in the marketplace. As concern for quality grew, numerous others also began to write and consult about how the United States and other nations could catch up with Japan. Space does not permit a lengthy discussion of this stream of literature, so thumbnail sketches must suffice. Armand V. Feigenbaum began his career at General Electric and coined the phrase "total quality control" in the 1950s. This was a forerunner of GE's well-known "six sigma" quality program. Philip Crosby started with the Crosley Corporation but worked for other firms, consulted, and concentrated on attaining "zero defects" in manufacturing. In addition to these, numerous Japanese authorities became well known: Genichi Taguchi of Nippon Telephone and Telegraph; Taiichi Ohno and Shigeo Shingo, who were inspired by Frederick Taylor's writings to instill quality control at Toyota; and Ichiro Ueno, son of Yoichi Ueno, who promoted scientific management in Japan. The list of contributions to the quality control movement could easily get out of control, given the confines of this historical perspective. Buzzwords may abound (e.g., "total quality management"), but the important lesson of history is that we often lose sight of very basic practices and common-sense ideas, such as making quality products and meeting customer needs, when distracted by the Lorelei songs of fancy fads.

Quality was one facet of the changing character of production/operations management. The idea that manufacturing needed to become part of a firm's strategy took longer to emerge. Gordon and Howell's characterization of production management as "intellectually stultifying" did little to promote interest in viewing manufacturing as a competitive weapon. Wickham Skinner's pioneering work indicated the need to incorporate manufacturing strategy into corporate strategy and to look beyond efficiency and production at the lowest cost to seek competitive costs, and it suggested the possibility that sound manufacturing strategy could yield a competitive advantage.[14] In product design, efficient processing technologies, and quality control, the production function could promote corporate goals.

---

14. Wickham Skinner, "Manufacturing—Missing Link in Corporate Strategy," *Harvard Business Review* 47 (May–June 1969), pp. 136–145.

Richard Schonberger urged the view that the functions of the firm (e.g., marketing, engineering, and manufacturing) should be integrated so as to be linked in a continuous "chain of customers."[15] Every department had a customer, a user of that department's output, and human and physical resources should be organized around the flow of products or services provided. For instance, product design employees would work with process engineers, accountants, market researchers, and others in a collaborative team rather than passing a proposed new product from one department to another. The notion resembles (to this historian) Henri Fayol's "gangplank," which was intended to provide for horizontal communication and coordination across functional boundaries. The lesson to be relearned is that a commonality of goals requires recognition of this common purpose and, in turn, there must be a willingness to break down functional barriers to provide for cooperative effort.

In terms of production techniques, advances were made in production and inventory planning and control. As computer technology developed to handle the masses of data involved, Americans created Materials Requirements Planning (MRP) to provide the parts for products as they were needed for assembly; Japan's Taiichi Ohno, however, went one step further with a "just-in-time" system which was more exacting than MRP in terms of timing the arrival of materials. In 1980, Ohno, creator of Toyota's assembly system, was asked how he got his idea for the just-in-time method of handling inventories. Ohno's response was that it came from reading about Henry Ford's experiences.[16] Ford, but primarily Ernest Kanzler, one of his managers, developed the idea of reducing his inventory "float" by carefully planning and coordinating the input of raw materials in the factory.[17] Raw materials could be acquired and transformed into automobiles that would be on dealers' lots in fourteen instead of twenty-eight days. The savings in inventory carrying costs were substantial. Toyota's assembly line, designed by Ohno, *pulled* the parts to be assembled in the quantity and at the time they were needed.

Production, a vital function of the firm, underwent substantial changes with the addition of quantitative techniques developed in operations research, and improved information handling technologies reshaped planning and controlling, especially in inventory management. While the means differed, the goals of increased productivity and reduced waste continued.

---

15. Richard J. Schonberger, *Building a Chain of Customers: Linking Business Functions to Create the World Class Company* (New York: Free Press, 1990).

16. Taiichi Ohno, quoted by Norman Bodek in Henry Ford (in collaboration with Samuel Crowther), *Today and Tomorrow* (1926, repr. Cambridge, Mass.: Productivity Press, 1988), p. vii.

17. Peter B. Petersen, "The Misplaced Origin of Just-in-Time Production Methods," *Management Decision* 40 (2002), pp. 82–88.

Systems and Information

Throughout history people have observed orderliness in nature. They saw an ecological balance in plant and animal life; noted that the planets and stars operated predictably enough and made gods of stars and used them to chart their own life forecasts; and followed a rhythm in the coming and going of seasons to plant and harvest their crops. Primitive people built their life activities around rituals that were a part of this natural order; such ceremonies gave them the security of order and predictability. For example, the Egyptians depended on the orderliness of nature in the rise and fall of the Nile in order to transport the materials for the construction of the pyramids.

As people designed their organizations, they sought once more the orderliness in their operations that they observed in nature. Under the domestic system, entrepreneurs operated their various undertakings as a system built on the receipt of orders for products, the putting-out of work, and the return of the completed product. Early factory managers sought systematic management that would arrange the workplace, secure the proper flow of materials, and facilitate the performance of human effort in order to achieve some predictable result. Behavioralists spoke of social systems, studied work places as sociotechnical systems, and noted the need for equilibrium both within the organization and with elements outside the organization. In these notions of systems there are a number of common characteristics: (1) a goal or purpose for the organization, some reason for its existence, whether tombs for the pharaohs, industrial products, governmental services, or social satisfaction; (2) some presumed inflow or input of materials, equipment, and human effort into the organization; (3) something done in the organization to transform these inputs into some useful product or service to meet the goals of the organization; and (4) a need to measure, control, and acquire the necessary information about performance to see whether plans were being carried out. There was a search to study the parts, to understand their interrelationships, and to arrange them to lead to the desired outcome.

GENERAL SYSTEMS THEORY

Although notions of systems existed before, the major distinction between the modern era and prior eras was in the way of thinking, or the philosophy of the systems approach. Again there are deep roots in prior thought. In the early twentieth century psychologists and sociologists began the organismic or Gestalt approach in theories of behavior, representing a break with the previous mechanistic or fundamental unit method analysis.

Ludwig von Bertalanffy (1901–1972), a biologist, is credited with coining the phrase "general systems theory." Bertalanffy thought that it was possible to develop a systemic, theoretical framework for describing relationships in the real world and that similarities among different disciplines could enable a general systems model to be developed. Bertalanffy's objective was to search for parallelisms in disciplines that would give rise to a general theoretical framework. Bertalanffy noted certain characteristics similar in all sciences: (1) the study of a whole, or organism; (2) the tendency of organisms to strive for a steady state or equilibrium; and (3) the "openness" of all systems, that is, an organism affects and is affected by its environment.[18] Bertalanffy's influence on management and organizational theory was described earlier.

Bertalanffy's efforts were the beginning piece in a jigsaw puzzle on which others began to build. Norbert Wiener (1894–1964) adopted the word "cybernetics" from the Greek *kubernētēs* meaning pilot or person at the helm.[19] The study of cybernetics showed that all systems could be designed to control themselves through a communications loop, which fed information back to the organism, thus allowing it to adjust to its environment. This information feedback meant that an organization could "learn" and adapt for future situations. General systems theory provided a theoretical and philosophical framework for recognizing the openness of systems for developing information feedback to adapt and maintain a relatively steady state. From Wiener, cybernetics stressed that information feedback was essential to this adjustment. Organizations needed information; from systems theory came the notions that they could, with some technological help, provide a means for communication and control.

FROM THE COMPUTER AGE TO THE INFORMATION AGE

Engineers such as Henry R. Towne, Frederick W. Taylor, and others who wished to perform their mathematical calculations used a slide rule, an early seventeenth-century development. Another seventeenth-century mathematician, Blaise Pascal, invented the mechanical adding machine. Charles Babbage's dream went beyond Pascal's to a mechanical device that could be programmed to solve all sorts of problems. The analytical engine was not built during Babbage's time because manufacturing technology was not advanced enough to build the parts to the necessary precision; besides, where could it be plugged in?

Another step in computer development was made by the British mathematician Alan Turing. In 1938, as the armies of Hitler's Germany threatened Europe, the British intelligence services became concerned with a new German message-encoding

18. Ludwig von Bertalanffy, "General Systems Theory: A New Approach to the Unity of Science," *Human Biology* 23 (December 1951), pp. 302–361.

19. Norbert Wiener, *Cybernetics* (Cambridge, Mass.: MIT Press, 1948).

machine called Enigma. If the code could be broken, British intelligence could intercept and use the German messages to anticipate Hitler's moves. Cryptology (the devising and breaking of coded messages) was a complicated process, and the Enigma machine had defied all traditional cryptanalysis. Turing, among others, was employed by the British to break the Enigma system. Since almost all codes depend upon the substitution of numbers for letters in various ways, and since a huge number of combinations are possible, only a machine that could process masses of numbers could hope to break the code. Turing led the effort and developed an electrical machine, essentially a computer, to handle these calculations.[20]

Along a parallel path, Herman Hollerith developed a punch card and sorter to aid the United States Census Bureau. He left the bureau and formed the Tabulating Machine Company (1903) which, after a period of time, became the International Business Machines Corporation. During the period 1937–1944, Howard Aiken designed and built an electromechanical computing machine, called the Mark I, for IBM. In Chapter 18 we saw Eckert and Mauchly's development of the gigantic ENIAC. The Eckert-Mauchly patents for ENIAC, however, were disputed in a lawsuit. John V. Atanasoff had built an electronic digital computer for Iowa State University in the 1930s. Neither Atanasoff nor Iowa State filed for a patent, but the court upheld Atanasoff's creation and stopped the royalty payments to Sperry-Rand, the holder of the Mauchly-Eckert patents.[21]

After more than a century from Charles Babbage's conception to Atanasoff's reality, the computer evolved rapidly in technological capability and in applications. The first computers were monster mainframes; expert observers thought that only a few computers would be necessary to handle the U.S. census, scientific calculations, and maybe even accounting, payroll, and inventory problems. "Electronic data processing" was the common phrase for computers, emphasizing their ability to handle masses of transactions and calculations. Computer capabilities were enhanced, however, by an advancing technology that moved from vacuum tubes, to transistors, to miniaturized chips that could store more data and perform more calculations. These microprocessors triggered a host of changes in both hardware (equipment) and software (operating systems). Originally called "microcomputers," an early, if not the first, was the Altair 8800, powered by an Intel-made chip. By 1977, some 72 percent of the microcomputer market was held by three firms: Apple, Commodore, and Tandy. Only two years earlier, Bill Gates and Paul Allen founded Microsoft. In 1980, International Business Machines (IBM) decided to enter the market, and the microcomputer began its evolution to personal computers and eventually to laptops.

---

20. Andrew Hodges, *Alan Turing: The Enigma* (New York: Simon and Schuster, 1983), especially pp. 166–170, 181–195.

21. "After Almost Half a Century, the Father of the Computer Gets a Celebration," *The Chronicle of Higher Education* 27, no. 8 (October 19, 1983), p. 17; and Clark R. Mollenhoff, *Atanasoff: Forgotten Father of the Computer* (Ames: Iowa State University Press, 1988).

Silicon chips and new data compression technologies, such as fiber optics, would have a dramatic impact on the telecommunications industry, collapsing former giants while elevating innovative newcomers. Satellites would enable wireless messages across geographic boundaries; and the Internet, founded by the Department of Defense in 1960, would be privatized and provide a worldwide network for messages. This new technology would influence the way we managed.

Technology is the handmaiden of management theory and practice. Advancing computer technology provided the *means* to advance the managerial tasks of planning, measuring, evaluating, and controlling organizational performance. From her study of organizational communications in the age before computers, JoAnne Yates concluded that "technologies were adopted, not necessarily when they were invented, but when a shift or advance in managerial theory led managers to see an application for them…. The technology alone was not enough—the vision to use it in new ways was needed as well."[22] This conclusion appears to apply as well to computer technology in recent years as electronic data processing was transformed into management information systems; that is, computers became more than number crunchers, and evolved toward providing information for management throughout an organization. The computer age was a time of data processing; but as technology advanced, an information age became possible. Data could be distributed through networks, interactive systems could be designed for users to access databases as decision support systems, and groups could work together to make decisions.

Information has always been necessary for managerial decision making; the Egyptian scribes who recorded their employer's inventory with a stylus on a clay tablet were the forerunners of the modern information specialists. As transactions and interactions became more complex, information was needed for internal uses as well as for reporting to external constituents and regulatory agencies. As information-providing capabilities advanced, managers found new uses for computing machines in performing their tasks. Chandler observed that business firms need to develop competitive strengths in technical, functional, and managerial capabilities.[23] Technical capabilities develop by learning from new and existing knowledge from engineering and science. These may be firm or industry specific, but involve gathering knowledge from basic and applied research to develop or improve existing products or processes. In short, technical capabilities are the "R" in R and D (research and development) and connect the firm to our earlier discussion of innovation and dynamic capabilities for the firm. For information systems, technical capabilities involve finding and applying the appropriate computer hardware and software that will position the firm in a stronger competitive position.

———

22. JoAnne Yates, *Control through Communications: The Rise of System in American Management* (Baltimore: Johns Hopkins University Press, 1989), pp. 274–275.

23. Alfred D. Chandler, Jr., *Inventing the Electronic Century: The Epic Story of the Consumer Electronics and the Computer Industries* (New York: Free Press, 2001), pp. 2–5.

Functional capabilities are those activities the firm must have to acquire, transform, and market its product. One of these would be the "D" of R and D, which is the capability to bring an innovation to the marketplace in a timely fashion with the desired level of quality and price. Production, marketing, distribution, and human resource capabilities must be developed to attain the desired volume of output and sales. Information systems are important in all functional areas: finding, developing, and rewarding the right people; planning and tracking production; maintaining contact with suppliers and customers; and engaging in electronic commerce (e-commerce) if that is appropriate or can be used to supplement traditional marketing channels.

Managerial capabilities determine strategy, formulate plans, design appropriate organizational arrangements, coordinate work flow through the value chain, and monitor performance. Huber has indicated the importance of "computer-assisted decision-making technologies (e.g., expert systems, decision support systems, on-line management information systems, and external information retrieval systems)" in the management process.[24] These management activities are familiar ones—the electronic age has provided assistance for acquiring, storing, retrieving, and distributing information to be used in making decisions. Earlier, we saw Daniel McCallum design an information system for the Erie Railroad, using the telegraph to dispatch trains, monitor their movement, gather information on costs and revenues, and use this information for decision making. A twenty-first-century "McCallum" would do similar things with computer assistance.

SUMMARY

This chapter has described the search for order through science and systems in management. Operations research was viewed as a modernized version of early scientific approaches to problem solving and of management's search to improve its ability to explain, predict, and control events. Operations research modified traditional production management into a broader view of production/operations management, based on more advanced statistical and mathematical techniques. For a period of time, however, interest in production quality was eclipsed by conglomerate portfolios, behavioral scientists, and market diversification. As others learned America's lessons about how to produce quality goods more efficiently, they outstripped U.S industrial productivity gains. U.S management relearned some old lessons, but the battle continues.

Another part of this search for order and system arose out of the development of micro circuitry and more powerful computers. Evolving from scientific data handling to swifter methods of gathering and using information, computer hardware

---

24. George P. Huber, "A Theory of the Effects of Advanced Information Technologies on Organizational Design, Intelligence, and Decision Making," *Academy of Management Review* 15 (1990), p. 47.

and software provided managers with aids to decision making. Information systems for management carried the potential to enhance technical, functional, and managerial capabilities in seeking a competitive edge.

22 Obligations and Opportunities

I n the late nineteenth century, a revolution in transportation and communication broke down local and regional barriers to commerce and created a national economy in the United States. The twentieth century saw more marvels: jet-propelled aircraft for intercontinental travel; spacecraft for travel to earth's satellite, the moon; and communication via space-based satellites that could provide wondrous services for geological mapping, weather tracking, and message transmitting. This newest revolution would break down national barriers, expose the most closeted societies to notions from others, and create opportunities for trade, travel, and ideas.

Management thought is both a process in and a product of its changing environment. Managers operate and make decisions in an open system of economic, social, political, and technological forces of change. Management thought is influenced by these changing forces, yet all is built on the past. From a historical perspective, this chapter examines the evolving expectations and obligations concerning business ethics and the relationship between business and society. It also examines opportunities in the global marketplace and how competing cross-culturally has influenced business decisions.

INDIVIDUALS AND ORGANIZATIONS: RELATING TO EVOLVING EXPECTATIONS

Machiavelli once said that "there is nothing more difficult to carry out nor more doubtful of success, nor more dangerous to handle, than to initiate a new order of things. For the reformer has enemies in all those who profit by the older order, and only lukewarm defenders in all those who would profit by the new order."[1] Change can come from within an individual or organization, but it is far more likely to come from without. The economic environment can bring new opportunities as well as added competitive pressures; technology can change how we live and earn our living; the political environment may create freedom as well as limits to individual and organizational discretion; and the social environment in an open system can place more, or different, expectations on appropriate conduct. This social environment is discussed first, although it must be kept in mind that the social thread is but one part of the whole cloth.

ETHICS

The subject of ethics is one of human moral conduct, good or bad, and has occupied the thinking of theologians and philosophers since time immemorial. Ethics are the moral "oughts" that sustain a civilized society. Business transactions, so deeply embedded in trust and confidence in one's fellow human beings, have been an integral part of the search for guidelines to moral conduct beyond the question of legal boundaries. What price to charge for a product was one issue in medieval trade. Saint Thomas Aquinas stated that it should be the current market price but that, in instances of emergency or collusion, public authorities had the right to intervene and impose a fair price.[2] Sellers had a right to recover their costs, prices could vary because of supply and demand, but fraud and coercion were prohibited. Chapter 2 examined how the expansion of trade promoted the need for business ethics and how Friar Johannes Nider (1468) argued that business contracts for gain or profit could be spiritually acceptable as well as temporally legal.

Theologians and philosophers dominated ethical thinking for an extended time, but the founder of the world's first collegiate business school, Joseph Wharton, proposed that the curriculum of instruction

> should be made as to inculcate and impress upon the students ... the immorality and practical inexpediency of seeking to acquire wealth by winning it from another rather than earning it through some sort of service to one's fellowmen ... [and] the necessity of punishing by legal penalties and by social exclusion those persons who commit frauds, betray trusts, or steal public funds.[3]

Wharton set the moral and ethical standards high, posing a challenge to future business schools and educators to transmit this in the classroom in the hope it

---

1. Nicolo Machiavelli, *The Prince*, trans. Luigi Ricci (New York: New American Library, 1952), pp. 49–50.

2. Raymond de Roover, "The Concept of Just Price: Theory and Economic Policy," *Journal of Economic History* 18 (December 1958), especially pp. 420–423.

3. Joseph Wharton to the Trustees, quoted in Stephen A. Sass, *The Pragmatic Imagination: A History of the Wharton School, 1881–1981* (Philadelphia: University of Pennsylvania Press, 1982), p. 38.

would be attained in practice—a mark that would be reached with varying degrees of success. The Social Gospel led to individual betterment, or employee welfare, departments; ill-advised business practices accelerated the passage of legislation; and economic booms and busts encouraged political intervention to smooth these recurring events. Human relations influences convinced Robert W. Johnson of the Johnson and Johnson Company of the need for "service capitalism" by "rendering good service in return for its right to operate." He explained:

> I do not mean that a successful business must give up the idea of earn-ing profits, nor is it compelled to promote public welfare at the expense of its owners or stockholders ... however, business must meet the needs and desires of human beings, whether they work for it, purchase its products, or live in the same community....[4]

Johnson and Johnson's credo, first stated in 1948, became a statement of corpo-rate beliefs that evolved as times changed and provided moral guides to be used in decision making as the company faced some very perilous situations. The corporate credo provided a means to align the interests of management with others as well as serving as a guide to moral conduct.

Previously we saw that agency theory involves the relationship between a prin-cipal, for example, a business owner, and an agent, for example, an employee of that business. The notion of an agency relationship is not new (Hammurabi's Code spec-ified the need for a merchant's agent to keep records and provide receipts), but inter-est in the topic was revived as the owners of the business, the stockholders, became separated from the management of the firm by their agents, the managers. Chapter 5 showed how nineteenth-century courts provided narrow interpretations of corpo-rate charters and viewed managers as trustees of the shareholders. In the cases out-lined, the courts intervened to align the interests of the principals with their agents. Still later, the separation of owners and managers became more pronounced and the courts have been less restrictive, leading to more ethical dilemmas as principal and agent interests come into conflict. For instance, shareholders may want higher divi-dends, whereas managers prefer to reward themselves with higher bonuses. These and other ethical issues beg for some credo, a statement of belief about how to align the interests of the parties and prescribe the moral oughts of the decision makers.

When John Shad donated $23 million to the Harvard Graduate School of Business Administration for the teaching of business ethics, he commented on the decline of ethical values in the United States:

> The erosion of ethical attitudes in America since the end of World War II can be attributed to the dispersion of families, rising divorce rates, the Vietnam War, and "permissive" and "me" generations, the drug

---

4. Robert Wood Johnson, *Robert Johnson Talks It Over* (New Brunswick, N.J.: Johnson and Johnson, 1949), p. 168. The original corporate credo is on pp. 173–174.

culture, the affluent society and, most important, the substitution of television for the family, church, and school as the principal purveyor of social mores.[5]

Further, he believed that business schools had a responsibility.

It is not enough for these schools to certify that their graduates have mastered the fundamentals of their profession. The schools must hone their ability to certify that their graduates have the character and integrity to use the knowledge gained for the benefit—rather than the abuse—of society.[6]

True, business schools have an opportunity to elevate business morality by developing courses and cases to permeate the curriculum and increase awareness of ethical problems as well as what might be appropriate ways of handling these situations. Less evident in Shad's comments is the responsibility of parents, schools, churches, and communities to inculcate moral dos and don'ts from the cradle onward. The expression "how the twig is bent, so grows the tree" may be trite, but it is true. Business schools and those who employ their graduates have a responsibility for developing ethics but sometimes inherit a progeny shaped by earlier influences, making the probability of a substantial change much less.

An early reaction to business malpractices has been legislation: such as the Interstate Commerce Act or the Sherman Anti-Trust Act. Competition from other modes of travel was more effective than legislation in limiting the strengths of the railroads; and the Clayton Anti-Trust Act (1914) closed loopholes in the Sherman Act. The Securities and Exchange Commission was established in 1934 to implement the Securities Act of 1933 and the Securities Exchange Act of 1934 to regulate securities markets: for example, full financial disclosure and independent audits of financial statements, prohibitions on "insider trading," and so forth. Violations of these laws were rampant at the turn of the twenty-first century and independent auditors had conflicts of interest (e.g., Arthur Andersen), top management individuals used the corporate treasury as their personal piggy bank (e.g., Adelphia), and certain firms manipulated accounting records to conceal indebtedness (e.g., Enron) and to overstate earnings (e.g., WorldCom). So, another law, the Sarbanes-Oxley Act of 2002, was passed to create a board to oversee public auditing firms, create new disclosure requirements, provide for stronger criminal penalties for fraud, and legislate other means to protect investors and others. Will the new act prevent future unsavory corporate and individual practices? History should teach us to be dubious about legislating to prevent unethical and illegal behavior.

---

5. John S. R. Shad, quoted in Gerald E. Cavanagh, *American Business Values,* 3rd ed. (Englewood Cliffs, N.J.: Prentice Hall, 1990), p. 209.

6. *Ibid.*

Virtuous conduct is seldom newsworthy. Illegal and unethical practices splatter mistrust over all, regardless of their deeds. Machiavelli's statement about the difficulty of change is correct: ethical behavior can be produced only by a cooperative venture among all those formative influences on people before they reach positions of influence. Others, such as elected public officials, religious leaders, and educators have been known to engage in unethical behavior; thus the problem is not confined to business. Arguably, business ethics may not be able to rise above the ethics of society in general. This situation does not release managers from responsibility, but suggests that change must originate from and be implemented by multiple sources.

BUSINESS AND SOCIETY

The line between ethics and the social responsibility of business is not always clear. Johnson and Johnson's credo defined how its employees ought to behave and recognized a broader community in which it played a role. Ethics typically refers to the moral conduct of individuals, whereas social responsibility usually addresses the expectations that society has about a business firm. Ethics appears to be a broader notion, applying to expectations of personal behavior throughout life, whereas the obligations of business firms appear to be more variable and changing as social values and legal obligations change.

Persons in business are known throughout history for their patronage and preservation of cultural heritage in literature, music, and art. Merchants as well as church officials, for instance, provided the means for artists, sculptors, and writers to become the glorifiers of the Renaissance. Business leaders, such as Robert Owen and Francis Cabot Lowell and his Waltham Associates, provided a view of the obligations of firms as the Industrial Revolution made an impact on society. Andrew Carnegie made a great deal of money and gave it all away because he believed that the acquisition of wealth imposed a duty

> to set an example of modest, unostentatious living, shunning display or extravagance; to provide moderately for the legitimate wants of those dependent upon him; and, after doing so, to consider all surplus revenues which come to him simply as trust funds, which he is called upon to administer, and strictly bound as a matter of duty to administer in the manner which, in his judgment, is best calculated to produce the most beneficial results for the community—the man of wealth thus becoming the mere trustee and agent for his poorer brethren.[7]

Nineteenth-century court rulings placed corporations in a straitjacket, insisting that management was a trustee of the shareholder and could not do as it wished with

---

7. Andrew Carnegie, *The Gospel of Wealth and Other Timely Essays* (New York: Century Co., 1901), p. 15.

corporate assets. Carnegie, like other business leaders of that time, engaged in individual philanthropy, as the courts did not intervene in private charity.

The legal precedents that raised doubts about whether or not a corporation
could give away a portion of its profits to non-business-related endeavors were not
resolved until the twentieth century. In the United States, a historic revision of the
Federal Revenue Act in 1935 included a "5 percent" clause, which permitted corporations to deduct up to that amount from net income for contributions to eleemosy-
nary institutions. Another landmark arose in 1953 with *A. P. Smith Manufacturing
Company v. Barlow et al.* (13 N.J. 145). The company had donated $1,500 to Princeton
University for general educational purposes. Some stockholders sued, claiming that
this action was outside the powers granted by the charter of incorporation. The New
Jersey Supreme Court ruled for the company, reasoning that business support of
higher education was in the best interest of a free-enterprise society. The case was
not appealed, and the precedent for corporate involvement in social activities had
been established.

In his study of social responsibility for the 1900–1960 period Morrell Heald wrote:

> American businessmen fully shared the social concerns and preoccu-
> pations of their fellow citizens. Although they have often been
> depicted—indeed, caricatured—as single-minded pursuers of profit,
> the facts are quite otherwise.... Like others, they were frequently trou-
> bled by the conditions they saw; and, also like others, they numbered
> in their ranks men who contributed both of their ideas and their
> resources to redress social imbalance and disorganization.[8]

Donna Wood's study of the forces behind the passage of the Meat Inspection
Act (1906) and the Pure Food and Drug Act (1906) found that business leaders were
proactive, desirous of laws to protect themselves as well as consumers. Passage of
these laws has often been attributed to Upton Sinclair's dyspepsia-inducing book
The Jungle, but the facts do not support this conclusion. Individuals such as Henry
J. Heinz, Frederick Pabst, Edward R. Squibb, and others from the food processing,
pharmaceutical, brewing, baking, and distilling industries collaborated to support
this legislation.[9] These regulations protected the honest producer from the adulterer
and were in the interest of business as well as being desirable public policy. This brief
historical summary should provide the perspective that business firms and individuals have typically demonstrated a concern for and made contributions toward the
betterment of the society in which they lived, although these socially conscious
efforts have been generally unpublicized.

---

8. Morrell Heald, *The Social Responsibilities of Business: Company and Community 1900–1960* (Cleveland,
Ohio: Case Western Reserve University Press, 1970), p. 1.

9. Donna J. Wood, "The Strategic Use of Public Policy: Business Support for the1906 Food and Drug Act,"
Business History Review 59 (Autumn 1985), pp. 403–432.

The modern era of concern for the appropriate relationship between business and society appears to have been spearheaded by Howard Bowen. He defined social responsibility as "the obligations of businessmen to pursue those policies, to make those decisions, or to follow those lines of action which are desirable in terms of the objectives and values of our society."[10] Synonymous with this concept are the phrases "public responsibility," "social obligations," and "business morality." Bowen's book was sponsored by the Federal Council of the Churches of Christ in America and focused on the ethics and human values in economic life as part of a larger society. Although Bowen sought to promote a more thoughtful attitude of business people regarding their societal obligations, he recognized that business alone could not solve the problems of economic life: "Such an assumption would be unwise and dangerous not only for society … but also for businesses themselves. They cannot be saddled with responsibilities which they cannot hope to discharge effectively."[11] Drawing this fine distinction between what business could do and should do sparked a debate that continues today.

Keith Davis recalled that Bowen's book "crystallized" his thinking about social issues in management. "If you mess it up, you clean it up," a lesson from Davis's childhood, led him to the conclusion that since business influenced society, it had to accept the social obligations that followed.[12] In a widely cited article, Davis stated the pros and cons of social responsibility for business. Arguments in favor of social responsibility included that social responsibility served the long-run interest of business; that social responsibility improved the public image of business and increased its legitimacy in society; that with social responsibility, government regulation could be avoided; and that business had the resources and expertise to apply to social problems. Arguments against business acceptance of social responsibility included that as a trustee of the stockholders, management should optimize their return; that social involvement was costly and diluted the primary economic purpose of the firm; and that business should not be given responsibilities for which it was neither equipped to perform nor could be held accountable.[13] On balance, Davis favored social involvement on the part of business, but acknowledged Bowen's caveat that certain things should not be expected of business but should be left to others who were better able to carry out those responsibilities.

---

10. Howard R. Bowen, *Social Responsibilities of the Businessman* (New York: Harper and Brothers, 1953), p. 6.

11. *Ibid*, p. 7.

12. Keith Davis, "A Journey through Management in Transition," in Arthur G. Bedeian, ed., *Management Laureates: A Collection of Autobiographical Essays*, vol. 1 (Greenwich, Conn.: JAI Press, 1992), p. 285. See also Keith Davis and Robert L. Blomstrom, *Business and Its Environment* (New York: McGraw-Hill, 1966).

13. Keith Davis, "The Case for and against Business Assumptions of Social Responsibilities," *Academy of Management Journal* 16 (June 1973), pp. 312–322.

The idea that business had stakeholders became part of the domain of social responsibility. The term *stakeholder* was offered as a means of justifying the various constituencies of business who had to be considered in making decisions. Earlier writers, such as Henry L. Gantt and Chester Barnard, observed that a business firm was a part of a much larger system of investors, suppliers, employees, customers, and so on, and that the actions of these groups influenced the firm even though they did not appear on an organizational chart. Thus, whereas in the traditional view management served the stockholders, in the emerging view management had obligations toward others, its stakeholders.

R. Edward Freeman noted that the word *stakeholder* entered the literature in 1963, originated by the Stanford Research Institute and defined as "those groups without whose support the organization would cease to exist."[14] Igor Ansoff, a corporate planner at Lockheed Aircraft, and his colleagues at the Stanford Research Institute intended to convey the idea that corporate objectives could not be accomplished if these stakeholder groups did not provide the necessary support. When Ansoff furthered his study of corporate strategy, however, he distinguished between "objectives" and "responsibilities":

> The firm has both (a) "economic" objectives aimed at optimizing the efficiency of its total resource conversion process and (b) "social" or noneconomic objectives.... In most firms the economic objectives exert the primary influence on the firm's behavior and form the main body of explicit goals used by management for guidance and control of the firm ... [while] the social objectives exert a modifying and constraining influence on management behavior.[15]

The purpose of the firm was to maximize the long-term return on its assets; secondary responsibilities could not be met unless the economic objectives had been achieved. Ansoff acknowledged the earlier view of Peter Drucker that management must put economic considerations first and could justify its existence only through the economic results it produced:

> [M]anagement has failed if it fails to produce economic results. It has failed if it has not supplied goods and services desired by the consumer at a price the consumer is willing to pay. It has failed if it does not improve or at least maintain the wealth producing capacity of the economic resources entrusted to it.[16]

Drucker recognized that there could be noneconomic consequences of managerial decisions, such as improved community well-being, but that these were

---

14. R. Edward Freeman, *Strategic Management: A Stakeholder Approach* (Boston: Pitman, 1984), p. 31.

15. H. Igor Ansoff, *Corporate Strategy* (New York: McGraw-Hill, 1965), pp. 37–38.

16. Peter F. Drucker, *The Practice of Management* (New York: Harper and Row, 1954), p. 8.

by-products made possible only by an emphasis on economic performance. The consensus of Drucker and Ansoff was that economic results took priority and that social or noneconomic objectives could be pursued only if the primary objectives had been attained.

Although the stakeholder concept proved useful in understanding the firm in a changing economic, social, and political environment, issues remained with respect to determining who would be the primary claimants and who would be secondary. Could economic objectives override consumer safety? or a corporate gift to education? or the closure of an uneconomical plant that would contribute to the decline of a community or region? Archie Carroll helped clarify these issues by describing four categories of responsibilities: economic, legal, ethical, and discretionary (later labeled philanthropic). These were "not mutually exclusive, nor ... intended to portray a continuum with economic concerns on one end and social concerns on the other.... They are neither cumulative nor additive ... [but] are simply to remind us that motives or actions can be categorized as primarily one or another of these four kinds."[17] Economic responsibilities were primary, since the business organization was the fundamental producer and seller of products and services. Legal responsibilities were those regulations and rules created by political institutions to legitimize and govern business activities. Ethical responsibilities were expectations of how a firm should conduct its business beyond what the law required. Philanthropic responsibilities were voluntary choices. The intent of this conceptual scheme was to show that corporate responsiveness was not an either-or proposition, that is, profits to the exclusion of other categories, but that each domain could interact and overlap.[18]

From a historical point of view, ethics and social responsibility vary by time and by place and are both influenced by the cultural values of that place at that time. Unanswered is the question about who defines what is ethical or socially responsible behavior. The consumer? The producer? Special interest groups? The individual? Or are these socially desirable modes of conduct ingrained in the home, the church, or the school? While searching for an answer, it behooves everyone, as an individual and as a member of an organization, to exercise good common sense, be prudent, and use that uniquely human capacity to reason about the likely consequences of a certain action.

Management Opportunities in a Global Arena

The history of trade among nations is more ancient than the recording of those transactions. Coins, clay tablets, and the walls of ancient forts tell the story of people

---

17. Archie B. Carroll, "A Three-Dimensional Conceptual Model of Corporate Performance," *Academy of Management Review* 4 (October 1979), pp. 499–500.

18. See Mark Schwartz and Archie B. Carroll, "Corporate Social Responsibility: A Three Domain Approach," *Business Ethics Quarterly* 13 (2003), pp. 503–530.

engaged in economic transactions and weave the threads of civilization to bind as well as to put people of differing cultures in a competitive stance.[19] The idea of the globalization of business is not new, and this section will briefly trace the beginnings and examine the challenges and opportunities that face management.

THE GLOBALIZATION OF BUSINESS

Trade among nations has, more often than not, been initiated and carried out as a political strategy. This conclusion does not preclude those voyages motivated by curiosity or the desire for a more varied menu or assortment of products, but the main driving force behind the great discoveries of unknown lands and peoples was provided by the kings, queens, and potentates of various nations. National treasuries held the finances that could set upon the uncharted waters the ships and explorers who would venture forth to discover new trade routes, find novel products, build empires, and strengthen the homeland in its standard of living and its political clout. The practice of mercantilism used politics to subsidize local business, tariffs to keep out products from alien lands, colonies to ensure a steady supply of raw materials, and a strong navy to keep the lanes of commerce free from pirates and interlopers.

Mercantilism was not a particularly successful economic policy: inefficient industries were kept alive, consumers had less from which to choose, colonists were bound in economic servitude, and strong defense forces had to be maintained to protect a nation's economic privileges. Adam Smith intended to sweep away mercantilism, to show that national wealth depended on trade rather than on the balance of power, and on free markets rather than on the care and feeding of uneconomical enterprise. David Ricardo, an early nineteenth-century economist, suggested that free trade provided the best of all possible worlds because all nations would concentrate on what they could best produce. What was needed was not a national economic policy, such as mercantilism, but rather a market exchange system that allowed each nation to find its comparative advantage among other trading nations.

Technology has always been an important factor in the advancement of trade. Early trade routes hugged the shoreline because of fragile ships and poor navigational aids. Stronger masts, larger sails, and the mastery of celestial navigational techniques broadened trade horizons. Steam-powered ships, the telegraph, and transoceanic cables improved communication and reduced travel time. Faster ships, aircraft, and the wireless radio presaged the coming of jet travel and global communication by sky-based and orbiting satellites. Transportation and communication revolutions pushed back the frontier for trade, enabling the local markets of yesteryears to become the electronic commerce and global markets of today.

---

19. Miriam Beard, *A History of Business,* 2 vols. (Ann Arbor: University of Michigan Press, 1938); and Karl Moore and David Lewis, *Foundations of Corporate Empire: Is History Repeating Itself?* (London: Prentice Hall, 2000).

The notion of multinational enterprise has undergone an evolution with changing technologies and market opportunities. In Renaissance Florence, for example, the Medici family became the international financiers and bankers for the Roman Catholic church. To evade the church admonition about lending money for interest (usury), the Medicis developed a bill of exchange in which currencies of different cities or states changed hands at differing rates of exchange, with the difference being, in effect, interest on the money that changed hands. Later, the British, Dutch, Portuguese, and other mercantilistic nations created trading companies to carry out transactions in other lands—for example, the Dutch East India Company, the East India Company, and the Hudson Bay Company.

As colonialism and mercantilism faded, trade among nations continued to thrive even though transportation was by sail or steam on the sea, by railroads on land, and by barges on the canals and rivers. In its early economic development, the United States was a debtor nation, depending on capital from abroad. The J. & W. Seligman Company, one of the first U.S. investment banking houses, had branches in London, Paris, and Frankfurt in addition to its New York headquarters. The Seligmans and representatives of other emerging U.S. banking houses went abroad to sell the securities necessary to provide the capital for the growing U.S. industrial system. Mira Wilkins observed that as late as 1914 the United States was still a debtor nation, borrowing more from abroad than it invested.[20] The United States was a lively trader in the Pacific (some eighty U.S. firms had branches in China alone), South America, Africa, continental Europe, and Great Britain, but it still imported capital to fuel the fires of financing the growth of its own industry.

The tire and rubber industry provides an example of evolving multinational enterprise in the twentieth century. Natural rubber was an imported raw material for the United States, Great Britain, Germany, France, Italy, and other nations. At one stage, these nations integrated backward by starting plantations in favorable climates to cultivate the rubber tree, while other nations had to buy from rubber-producing nations. The tire-manufacturing nations (primarily those mentioned earlier) provided for their home markets as well as distributing and selling abroad. As markets expanded, it became economical to establish tire-manufacturing plants in other countries: for example, Great Britain's Dunlop went to Canada, where U.S. tire makers also competed; and France's Michelin opened factories in the United States and Italy in 1907. U.S. Rubber, Goodyear, Goodrich, and other companies built factories and sales organizations in Canada, France, and other countries in Western Europe. Michael French stated that "the overall expansion of multinational investment was primarily a response to protectionism."[21] As an illustration, Michelin and Dunlop built plants in the United States to avoid exclusion from that expanding market, while at the same time U.S. firms built factories and sales outlets in France for the same reason.

20. Mira Wilkins, *The Emergence of Multinational Enterprise: American Business Abroad from the Colonial Era to 1914* (Cambridge, Mass.: Harvard University Press, 1970), pp. 201–207.

21. Michael J. French, *The U.S. Tire Industry: A History* (Boston, Mass.: Twayne, 1991), p. 127.

Michael French's explanations of the growth in the tire industry are essentially parallel to Mira Wilkins's findings regarding stages of development for sewing machines, agricultural equipment, and mining, petroleum, and other products in the historical development of multinational enterprise.[22] As firms of various nations expand to other nations to avoid tariffs, exploit growing markets, move closer to raw materials, or for whatever reason, there appear to be comparable stages of development across nations and time.

What some authors refer to as the new global competition is, in historical perspective, an extension of the past. The modern era is, however, more intense in terms of improvements in communication and transportation that enable global exchanges of products, services, and information in a speedier fashion. If anyone had suggested in the 1960s that the U.S. automobile, electronics, tire, and other industries were in danger of losing market share to competitors from other nations, the idea would have appeared ridiculous. Seemingly safe in their market enclaves, once-dominant firms were beset by imports from nations that had cheaper labor, had found a better way to produce, or could deliver improved quality at a better price. This global rivalry has led to "outsourcing" jobs, that is, finding ways to lower costs and/or gain outside expertise by putting out work to other nations. For history, it is the recurring problem of free trade versus protectionism, of opening product and factor markets or protecting indigenous special interest groups. The ultimate resolutions of the past have been, more often than not, a matter of national policy.

This more recent wave of globalization has also touched off numerous attempts at trade alliances, some successful, some still formative. The North America Free Trade Agreement (commonly known as NAFTA), the European Union, and the Asia-Pacific Economic Cooperation agreement represent attempts to break down trade barriers among nations. Is this David Ricardo's law of comparative advantage coming to fruition? Will these alliances foster a new mercantilism, favoring a nation's partners but excluding free trade among all nations? Vernon warns of the tensions between national and regional trade agreements and the promise and the issues that face multinational enterprises in a world of nation-states.[23] Neomercantilism would be dangerous as a national or regional trade policy, for it could represent protectionism raised to a new level. This book focuses on history and the lessons it offers: what happens from here on depends on what lessons are learned.

MANAGING ACROSS CULTURES

As firms become more global in their outlook and operations, they find themselves working with diverse cultures. Speedier transportation and communication affects

---

22. Mira Wilkins, *The Maturing of Multinational Enterprise: American Business Abroad from 1914 to 1970* (Cambridge, Mass.: Harvard University Press, 1974).

23. Raymond Vernon, *In the Hurricane's Eye: The Troubled Prospects of Multinational Enterprises* (Cambridge, Mass.: Harvard University Press, 1998).

the way management must think and act as it transcends national borders. Culture is a slippery concept, but for convenience's sake, the term here will be used to mean a set of beliefs held in common by a group of people about economic, social, and political forms of behavior. How people believe and behave is a product of their heritage as well as the present influences in their lives. Culture exists on numerous levels, in a religious group, an ethnic group, a region, or a nation, for example. These different levels confound, rather than simplify, the problems encountered in addressing the issue of managing across cultures.

In addition, it is difficult to find complete uniformity even across a group or regional culture; members of a group with a common ethnic culture might differ in political beliefs, or economic status, or whatever. At a national level, some cultures may be more homogeneous than others: the Japanese culture is an example of relative homogeneity; the United States is a melting pot of religions, ethnic groups, and other diverse components that create heterogeneity. The reunification of Germany had to overcome a great deal of diversity between the East and the West even though these geographical regions were separated a mere half-century ago.

Management theories, typically developed "by Americans for Americans," face their most serious challenge as cross-cultural studies are made. Bernard Bass summarized an extensive literature on leadership in different countries and cultures.[24] He found a clustering of values that had an impact on leader-follower relations, such as traditionalism versus modernity; collectivism versus individualism; and so on. For example, the importance of the collective group over the individual in Japan, China, and Korea reflected a long-standing heritage of loyalty to one's family, which was transferred to the firm in more recent history. The United States, on the other hand, represented a greater degree of emphasis on the individual, an emphasis that appeared in an "Anglo" cluster of countries as contrasted with Far Eastern culture. Project GLOBE has continued the cross-cultural leadership question, seeking to determine which leadership attributes and behaviors are endorsed widely and which appear to be culturally contingent.[25]

Bill England and his colleagues probed the meaning of work in different countries. They found a clear differentiation between people who defined work as something they had to do or were forced to do and those who viewed work positively and as an activity that produced something of value for society. For the former group, work had a low central value in life; these individuals placed more emphasis on the physical and economic conditions of work. The latter group placed a high centrality value on work and saw it as more of an avenue for self-expression. Of the countries studied, Japan had high work centrality; Yugoslavia (before its breakup) and Israel had moderately high work centrality; the United States and Belgium had average

---

24. Bernard M. Bass, *Bass and Stogdill's Handbook of Leadership*, 3rd ed. (New York: Free Press, 1990), pp. 760–803.

25. Principal investigators for Project GLOBE are Robert J. House and Paul J. Hanges. To date, different editors have compiled three volumes of results in *Advances in Global Leadership* (Greenwich, Conn.: JAI Press, 1999, 2001, and 2003).

work centrality; the Netherlands and Germany had moderately low centrality; and Great Britain had the lowest centrality.[26] Although there were some differences by age, sex, and education, these attitudes toward working were clearly differentiated by the value attached to work as an activity. Overall, interesting work ranked number one, followed in order of importance by good pay, good interpersonal relations, job security, autonomy, and the opportunity to learn new things.

The literature on managing across cultures has had its Big Bang and forms a constantly expanding universe of studies. In addition to the aforementioned summaries on leadership and the meaning of working are studies on human resource management, organizational behavior, information and technology transfer, strategic management, and business-government relations. There are enduring questions, such as, How much do cultures vary? How does this variance influence, for example, human resource management practices? Is this variance converging, diverging, or stable in terms of culturally held attitudes and beliefs when one country moves further along in becoming industrialized? If there is variance across cultures and, at best, a clustering of similarities among some cultures, does this mean that management theories and practices are culture bound? Geert Hofstede maintained that U.S. management theories are culturally constrained because management is different in every country. Hofstede characterized these cultural differences in terms of the following dimensions: power distance, defined as the degree of inequality among individuals considered by that culture as normal; individualism versus collectivism; masculinity ("tough values," such as assertiveness) versus femininity ("tender values"); uncertainty avoidance; and long-term versus short-term orientation.[27] Hofstede presented the United States as below average on uncertainty avoidance (i.e., more willing to take risks), while Japan was high on this dimension; Japan was high on masculinity, the Netherlands, low; France showed greater power distance (less equality) and somewhat more femininity; Asian countries appeared to be more oriented toward the long term, Americans less so. Other comparisons could be drawn, but Hofstede's research is far from complete. Indeed, in drawing sweeping comparisons such as these, extreme care should be used to avoid the danger of national stereotyping and thereby reinforcing previously held beliefs.

Ethics, corporate social responsibility, and laws further complicate the issue of competing across national borders. The U.S. Foreign Corrupt Practices Act of 1977 (amended in 1988) forbade publicly traded U.S. companies from making illicit payments to officials of foreign governments or to foreign political parties, their officials, or intermediaries. The law has been applied rarely and also criticized for handicapping U.S. firms when competing in other countries. Should U.S. standards of legal

---

26. MOW International Research Team, *The Meaning of Working* (New York: Academic Press, 1987), especially pp. 84, 244–245.

27. Geert Hofstede, *Culture's Consequences: Comparing Values, Behavior, Institutions, and Organizations Across Nations* (Thousand Oaks, Calif.: Sage, 2001); Hofstede's pioneering work was a cross-cultural study of IBM, *Culture's Consequences: International Differences in Work-Related Values* (Thousand Oaks, Calif.: Sage, 1980).

business practice be applied to other nations? Similarly, should U.S. ethics apply abroad; or do we do whatever is ethically acceptable in a particular nation? This is a sticky issue and history provides no clear answer. Donaldson characterizes the issue as a continuum from "cultural relativism" (do whatever local customs, traditions, and ethics permit) to "ethical imperialism" (one set of standards everywhere).[28] The search for universally applicable standards has not yielded absolutes, but has revealed a diversity of belief systems. An extensive survey by Enderle found a general belief that "good business and good ethics go hand in hand" but different nations and regions faced particular types of problems. The most common ethical issues mentioned were corruption (defined as the "misuse of power for private benefits"), the need for integrity in business and political leadership, and for greater corporate responsiveness to stakeholders and making more companies accountable.[29]

Choosing to enter the global market involves more than an understanding of cultural and ethical issues. Firms must ask if their core competencies/strengths are appropriate to the opportunities in a particular market; will foreign investment be welcomed; can a transfer of technology benefit all; does the political system provide safeguards for employees and intellectual and physical property; is the economic system conducive to private, market-driven enterprise; is the rivalry in the intended market currently too formidable; and the list could continue. Overall, the question is a strategic one: will competing abroad serve the long-run best interests of our stakeholders? Technologies in communication and transportation make global trading more attractive, but age-old questions of economics, politics, and social values persist.

SUMMARY

This chapter has been about obligations to behave in a legally, ethically, and socially responsible manner and opportunities to compete globally across different cultures. Management thought evolves and arrives at a different, but not always a better, place. This chapter has used history as a framework to enrich an understanding of the present human condition. Ethics, codes of moral conduct, have long been of concern in history, but people still struggle to make the right decisions as individuals and this struggle is confounded as they come under the influence of others in organizations. Social responsibility, the moral conduct of business in its environment, has also undergone changes over time. Managers were previously held to be trustees of the shareholders, but their role became more complicated with the introduction of the notion of stakeholders. Economic performance is necessary for

---

28. Thomas Donaldson, "Values in Tension: Ethics Away From Home," *Harvard Business Review* 74 (September–October 1996), pp. 48–62.

29. Georges Enderle, "A Worldwide Survey of Business Ethics in the 1990s," *Journal of Business Ethics* 16 (1997), pp. 1475–1483.

survival of the firm; compliance with legal bounds must exist; but beyond that the firm can choose how to be responsive to the needs of its social environment.

The ancient practice of trade among nations was reviewed. The world is now a closer community because of advancements in transportation and communication. Global markets bring new opportunities, yet jingoism threatens the prospects of more open markets. Although people may have gained knowledge of those of other nations, it is often without a greater understanding of them. Stereotypes of individuals and of nations must be avoided if progress is to follow.

CHAPTER

23   Epilogue

Within the practices of the past there are the lessons of history for tomorrow; there is a flow of events and ideas that link yesterday, today, and tomorrow in a continuous stream. We occupy but one point in this stream of time: we can see the distant past with a fairly high degree of clarity, but as we approach the present, our perspective becomes less clear. New ideas, subtle shifts in themes, and emerging environmental events will influence evolving management thought.

Throughout this study, management has been viewed as an activity essential to all organized efforts. Management finds its basis in the economic allocation and utilization of human and physical resources in order to attain organizational objectives. Management is more than an economic activity, however; it is a conceptual task that must mold resources into a proper alignment with the economic, technological, social, and political facets of its environment. Management thought is the mirror reflection of managerial activity. Management thought brings form to function and philosophy to practice.

Fairly definite trends, forces, and philosophies have emerged in this conceptual analysis of evolving management thought. Management is both a product of and a process in its environment. Internally, management thought has passed through phases of differing emphases on the human and on the organizational and methods facets of the problems encountered in guiding goal-directed systems. Externally, management thought has been affected by evolving technology, by shifting assumptions about the nature of people, and by the dynamics of economic, social, and political values.

Figure 23-1 is a somewhat sketchy summary of the broad swath that has been cut through this study of management. The modern era has seen a proliferation of approaches to management thought and advancing technologies that expanded the environment of management. The search continues for both better theory and improved

FIGURE 23-1 **SYNOPSIS OF THE MODERN ERA**

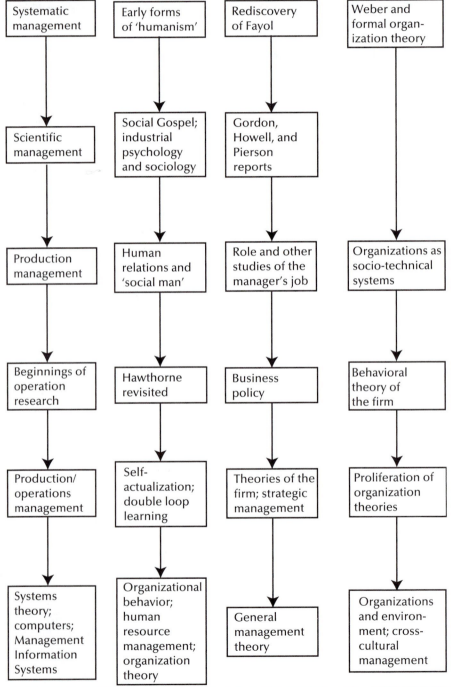

practice in management. It is this search that makes the study of management a most worthy intellectual and practical exercise. Management is one of the most dynamic of all disciplines; as technology, institutions, and people change, ideas of management evolve to cope with humanity's oldest problem—the allocation and utilization of scarce resources to meet the manifold desires of society. Today is not like yesterday, nor will tomorrow be like today; yet today is a synergism of all our yesterdays, and tomorrow will be the same. There are many lessons in history for management scholars, and the most important one is the study of the past as prologue.

Name Index

Subject Index